We Are the American People

Our Nation's History Through Its Documents, Volume II

William D. Young
Maple Woods Community College

Greg Sanford
Lyle Gibson
Penn Valley Community College

KENDALL/HUNT PUBLISHING COMPANY
4050 Westmark Drive   Dubuque, Iowa 52002

Contents

Preface

Almost every college history instructor has heard one of the following from students: "Why should I study history, it is so boring" or "History is just about old dead people that I don't have anything in common with." The students reflect the comment made in Jane Austen's novel *Northanger Abbey* that they read history only a little because "…it tells me little that does not either vex or weary me. The quarrels of popes and kings, with wars and pestilences, and in every page; the men all so good for nothing, and hardly any women at all." Historians today write accurately, with the intent to present a story that both informs and entertains. But to reach out to students, to take their minds beyond entertainment, to the realm of critical thinking that is necessary for good citizens in a democracy, requires more than clear prose.

Based on our combined sixty-plus years of teaching experience, we created *We Are the American People: Our Nation's History Through Its Documents* to supplement the usual text and lectures in a United States history survey course. The survey course, in fact any good United States history course, should provide insights and basic background on our historic past, encourage further exploration by students, and promote critical thinking. Too often the survey fails to accomplish any of these goals, because instructors are forced to use a panoramic approach. Forced to sprint across hundreds of years in two, sixteen-week courses professors paint a picture of our past with broad strokes, seldom having time for detailed work.

As attempts to remedy this, instructors assign student book critiques, create special in-class projects and group discussions, and use handouts of articles or primary documents. We believe that using primary documents is one of the best ways to do this: it's even essential. We also believe that this new primary documents reader provides an excellent way to incorporate documents into your classes.

First, this is an exciting collection of documents, which will make history classes come alive. We want this collection to let you smell the gunpowder from battles, hear the laughter of children, listen to the cries of workers, and feel the frustrations of people from all classes. Americans who face anxiety over moving can identify with the stories of traveling west into unknown areas; those arguing over critical decisions at work can identify with the intensive debates over using the atomic bomb. These documents personalize American history. They help students connect with the past as they discover that earlier Americans had worries, hopes and dreams similar to their own. This is part of learning to "think historically." History is more than just retelling the past in a chronological fashion. Students, just as historians do, must put themselves in the mindset and time of earlier Americans, understand their crisis and conflicts, and how they handled the challenges of their time. At the same time this means learning to separate fact from opinion, determine the reliability of past accounts, and understand how the events and people of our nation's past influence us today.

Second, we wanted to give instructors one of the widest possible ranges of documents. In our own classes we have often thought, "I wish I could use several readers. Then I could have the students read all the documents I wanted." To address this issue we have included materials from the entire spectrum of social and political history, from a diverse variety of people, from different ethnic groups, classes, races, regions and nationalities. "Old chestnuts" like Winthrop's sermon on the *Arabella* are here, as well as women's diaries, political speeches, first-hand accounts of slavery and business promotions.

Third, college accreditation is now tied closely to assessment of student learning. This volume specifically addresses the issues of critical thinking that so many colleges and universities, like the Metropolitan Community Colleges where we teach, identify as a learning priority. MCC has employed several standardized instruments like the Watson Glaser *Appraisal of Critical Thinking,* the Cornell *X Critical Thinking Test,* and the *Collegiate Assessment of Academic Proficiency* to evaluate the critical thinking skills of their students. The authors have also used some of these reader materials in embedded assessments to refine their understanding of students' critical thinking abilities. The presentation of materials in these volumes and the formulation of questions about the readings represent a response to student needs identified by these studies.

Further, they are using the texts to monitor their students' progress with critical thinking in general and to assess their inference skills in particular.

Fourth, this book will help students recognize issues from past points of view and learn to understand the past on its own terms. Doing these things help students think critically. We believe students learn the best, and learn to think critically, when they read specific historical content, examining the materials from the living past. This does not mean believing blindly anything put in print in texts placed before them, but questioning where and how historians reach their conclusions. Part of the critical thinking process requires students to confront the issues, themes and cultural debates from the past that often continue to this very day. These themes should be considered in every United States history course, since we have debated their meanings even before becoming independent.

Work and economic issues are a good example. How should work be rewarded, and who should determine the division of goods and services? Should everyone be rewarded equally for similar work? Does the value of goods derive from the labor producing them? How important is labor? Is there an absolute conflict between labor and capital? Does technology always improve the lives of citizens, whether they are housewives, farmers, or industrial workers? Is there true equality of opportunity in the nation, or has there been at any time? Why is this concept so important in our national history?

Human needs are important as well. What role do families, organizations, and communities play in United States history? Are they all part of what Americans define as the "good life"? Do men and women have the same needs, enjoy the same opportunities and rewards, or share the same experiences in our history? What do different groups of immigrants, ethnic and religious minorities, or anyone else have to do to belong in approved society? How do we determine what is more important, individual greed and accomplishment or the welfare and health of the entire community? How do we define community in the United States? Who gets to create and monitor these definitions and peoples behavior?

What is the relationship between individuals, citizenship, and the state? What are the origins of our government, why was it formed and who formed it? Where does the government derive its power to rule? What rights do citizens have, and how do we know this? Do all Americans enjoy these same rights throughout time, and if not, why not? What is the relationship between liberty and order, between natural rights and property rights in United States history? If the government is supposed to provide order and justice for citizens, does this mean the same for everyone in society? (i.e. slaves, women, white males, religious minorities, workers, students and the poor.) When, and on what grounds should the people challenge the authority of the government? What is the importance of security in national history, and how should this issue be defined? What is the proper role of the government in creating and preserving all types of security?

What does all of this mean to me? How am I affected by America's past, by government actions and individual accomplishments, by both virtuous citizens and evildoers? How does the past explain the United States today? How do political and business leaders misuse and abuse history for their own purposes? What is my own "sense of history"; how do I create my own perspective of the past? Where do my personal views and experiences intersect with the public history that academics teach? When I evaluate historical events, do I interpret them based on my gender, my class, my race or ethnicity?

To the Instructor

How often do students tell you that history is their worst or least favorite subject, that back in high school the coach taught it by reading out of the book while drinking coffee, or that they were taught to prepare for standardized state exams? We hear that from freshmen, who describe high school history as nothing more than memorizing names, dates and treaties. As historians we know that is learning trivia, not real history. College history classes examine why and how events happened, how they affected the nation and its people, rather than simply repeating what happened. History is learning how to put information in proper perspective, to use documents and historic accounts to understand the past.

Each chapter of this reader is organized around an issue or event in United States history. Unlike some readers we chose not to focus simply on problems in our past. For example, Chapter 5 examines the struggle to ratify the Constitution, focusing on the arguments and tactics used by both sides. Students learn that not everyone embraced the document, and that its ratification was not a sure thing. Chapter 7 examines the impact of the market economy on local communities, on workers, and on American society. We create a balance sheet of positive and negative impacts for students to consider. Chapter 16 considers the reality of urban life in the late Nineteenth and early Twentieth centuries. Cities might have meant opportunities for millions, but also meant unsafe living and working conditions, costing people their lives. In chapter 21 we take a closer look at the Cold War. Different views of the Marshall Plan, of Truman's firing of General MacArthur, and of McCarthyism force students to realize there is often not one simple answer or truth to the past.

Every chapter begins with an introduction to the topic, providing historical background and introducing the historical arguments over the issue. This is followed by clues on how to consider the evidence in the readings. Each document has its own introduction, with additional background on the material, the writer/speaker, and additional questions to help students focus on key issues.

At the end of each chapter is a worksheet, with a series of questions requiring students to apply the information in the documents. History students must learn to apply their own insights to questions, utilize data to support arguments, and compare materials in the reader to determine historical accuracy. This means cultivating critical thinking skills through open-ended questions requiring students to synthesize the documents before them with other knowledge and personal opinions. These worksheets are perforated so students may complete them and turn them in as assignments.

We included many different types of evidence in this book. Instructors who want a variety of materials will find presidential addresses, Congressional debates and hearings, personal diaries, formal speeches, musical lyrics, folk tales, advertisements, court cases, memoirs, personal letters, oral interviews, newspaper accounts, and wartime propaganda. You will hear from religious and secular leaders, from the rich and the poor, from slaveowners and slaves, from our friends and our enemies, from land-hungry whites and Native Americans, from men and women, from business and labor, from those who favor a strong government and those who oppose it, from Yankees and Confederates. Some of the documents are important classics, such as John Winthrop's sermon on the *Arabella*, the Declaration of Independence, Ida B. Wells's anti-lynching articles, and Roosevelt's "Day of Infamy" speech. Other selections have not been included in readers before, and should be a refreshing look at new material. We made sure the documents vary in length as well. Sometimes small snippets suffice, but other times instructors want (and students need) complete documents to understand the author's intent. Because the documents often assume conflicting positions, students are forced to think like historians. Our nation's past is full of conflict: our ancestors did not agree on everything, so students can try to understand what they disagreed on and why. Common assumptions and popular myths that students grew up with are challenged as well. For example, while we take the Constitution for granted today, its passage was not a sure thing, nor was support for the new government anywhere unanimous.

This reader and its contents may be used in a variety of ways. These documents can be the basis for classroom discussion and group projects. The authors write specific questions for their examinations and require students to use the documents to answer the questions. Instructors can compare materials in different chapters, to trace the development of attitudes across time. For example, does the obligation of all citizens to the health and well being of their community demonstrated in Chapter 2 continue throughout the rest of Volume I? Are there similarities in the attitudes expressed before the American Revolution in Chapter 4 and during the Civil War in Chapter 12? Do the conservative concerns in Chapter 18 on the 1920s resemble conservative concerns in Chapter 21 on the 1950s? If you want other suggestions feel free to contact the authors. We have suggestions for additional documents to use as well.

To the Student

What do you do in class when you need information, or do not understand something? You usually raise your hand and ask a question. Critical thinking is about asking questions, about not accepting statements and information blindly, but to question and evaluate what is presented. That is what historians do when they look at documents; they ask questions for the document to answer. You already do this too. Your class syllabus is a document. It contains key information about your course, insights into your instructors thinking and values, and his expectations for you and the timing of the current semester. Ten instructors may teach the same course, and every syllabus will be different. The course is the same, but uses different ideas on how and what to teach. Learning to read any historical document is like reading your syllabus. It is important to ask the right questions and reach the correct conclusions, even in the face of conflicting arguments. What types of questions should you ask about each document? Consider the following:

- Who wrote the document? This means the name of the person and their position, because their experiences and position in life affect the point-of-view expressed in the document. A slave and his owner will obviously view slavery differently, as will a factory owner and his employees. So consider what social status, specific group, religion, or gender influences the information in the document. Everyone is molded by their past experiences, their relationships with others, their occupation, and their class status. Also important to your understanding is the background information on the period covered in the module, information gained from your textbook and instructor. This will help you know how reliable a source the author of the document is, and how biased their opinions might be.

- Who is the intended audience? Every document has a specific audience, and determining who the audience is also lets you understand the document better. Was this intended as a private letter between friends, with no holds or secrets between them? Was it private and personal, as in a diary? Was the document intended for public consumption, such as an editorial, letter to the editor, speech, autobiography, or pamphlet? What story are they trying to tell? Sometimes the audience influences how the story is told. The writer includes certain details to inflame the audience, or leaves out bits of information he/she assumes the audience already knows. Knowing who the audience is helps you understand why the document was written, and also helps explain the form the document took, i.e. poem, diary etc. Was it intended to help win an election, or perhaps arouse the population into righteous indignation? Would all people accept or respond to the arguments the same way as the intended audience?

- You also need to go beyond the facts you can observe from the document if you are going to think critically like a historian; you must learn to distinguish between fact and opinion. Assuming the document intended to sway an audience at the other end, can you believe the information presented? Is the letter, diary etc. believable? Can you accept the claims of slaveowners that slavery is the best life for African Americans? Can you accept the claims of Joseph McCarthy that over 200 communists are working in the State Department in 1950? Has the document been altered from its original form, so you are reading an altered version?

- What does the document tell you about American society at that time period? Documents reveal the way their authors think about politics, class structure, immigration and other issues. Does the choice of words reveal certain attitudes or biases? Are there covert messages being spread with the overt ones? Do you think the attitudes expressed in the document, or the lifestyle described, reflect the views and lives of everyone in American society at that time? Is the author really an eyewitness to the events he/she describe? Always keep in mind that many events are linked together.

- What do these documents mean to you, a United States history student in the Twenty-first Century? What do these documents tell you about whom we are as a nation today, where our values and ideas come from? How much have we changed? What events from the past directly affect you today? Using the skills you honed comparing arguments in the chapters, can you dissect political arguments and advertisements today?

Finally, remember that this is your book, and it is speaking to you. Write in the book. Take possession of the pages and the documents included. As you question the documents, the author's ideas, or the editor's introductions, write the questions in the margins so you don't forget them. As you come across key ideas in the book, note them in the margin, so you can easily refer back to them when answering the worksheet questions, or reference them for tests and discussions. Always be sure to ask yourself, how and why I reached my own conclusions. That too is part of "thinking historically."

Acknowledgements

An enormous amount of time and labor went into preparing this reader. The authors wish to thank the following people, without whom we never could have completed the book.

William D. Young: I must begin by thanking my wife Michelle and sons, Benjamin and Michael. Once again they served as sounding boards for ideas, read documents as I acquired them, and waited patiently as I took over the work space in two rooms. Michelle has supported me through five such projects now, and is the steadiest support in my life. At Maple Woods Community College librarian Patricia M. Eklund pursued documents for me from across the country, with a smile on her face (and I suspect a song in her heart.) The chairman of the Social Sciences division, Paul Long, provided as much support and encouragement as anyone can. Our discussions about historical thinking v. philosophical ideas while team teaching the honors program were a great help. He is the ultimate example of academic peer and good friend. Steve Jansen, a.k.a. "Mr. History" in Lawrence, Kansas, helped me hunt down certain documents on the 1850s and 1860s. As a lifetime advocate of using documents to teach students, as well as the model for combining enthusiasm for local history with professional standards, his comments were always appreciated. My co-authors are special people, friends and scholars. Greg and I have known each other for almost thirty years. His dedication to teaching, knowledge of technology and philosophy, and deep-seated cynicism are greatly appreciated. Lyle willingly joined us on the project, despite this being his first year in the district. At times he must have felt we threw him into the deep end of the pool, but his scholarship and teaching enthusiasm are evident in the book. I could not ask for better co-authors, academic peers, or friends.

Greg Sanford: Completing a volume like this gives a person the chance to reflect upon and appreciate the special people who inhabit their world. Let me begin by thanking my wife Amy who is my inspiration. Without her insights and patient support, this work would not have been completed. I would also like to thank Bill Young for envisioning this project, giving me the opportunity to work on it, and counseling me about how to do this sort of thing. Lyle Gibson has my deepest appreciation as a great co-worker, colleague, and sounding board. We are both privileged to work with a Chair who has created an environment that nurtures special projects. I would like to thank Karen Curls as well for taking a personal interest in the work, listening to my concerns, and providing sage advice throughout the project. I owe a special debt of gratitude to Terry Davin who helped launch this project through his concern for knowing what it is students actually learn. Our discussions about assessment and work on it are some of the reasons for this volume. A special thanks to Charles VanMiddlesworth for his constant designing, enjoying and conducting assessment.

Lyle Gibson: This work entailed the assistance, encouragement, and patience of a formidable number of people, and it would be impossible for me to thank all of them, but I do wish to express my gratitude to some of them. First I would like to thank my wife Cynthia. She has been at my side for eight years, inspiring me to reach greater heights. Next I would like to thank my two children, Camron James and Cynae Elizabeth. Everything that I do, I do it all for you. I also want to thank Bill Young and Greg Sanford for inviting me to participate in this project. Our time spent completing this work has been educational—thank you both for your votes of confidence. Special thanks go to Karen Curls, chair of the Social Sciences Division at Penn Valley Community College, Dorether M. Welch and Cebra Sims; your words of encouragement and guidance helped me to mature professionally. More important, I thank my parents Urel and Elizabeth Gibson for believing in me—you are the best parents in the world. Special gratitude goes to Mary Burtzloff, archivist at the national Archives and Records Administration, Kansas City, Missouri, for providing me with primary documents that aided my research in this project.

All of us want to thank our students, without whom this project would not be possible. They stimulate us, frustrate us, and ask the darndest questions, which in turn inspire us. They also help us learn what works in the classroom. We also thank our editor, Eric Klosterman of Kendall Hunt for his interest in, and perseverance in pushing this work through to its conclusion. His unceasing reminders that we had to finish the book to really enjoy using it helped us along. Special thanks to Angela Puls of Kendall Hunt for her assistance in finishing both volumes. We never imagined anyone could have such patience and understanding as deadlines passed us by.

We may be reached at:

Professor William D. Young
Social Science Division
Maple Woods Community College
2601 N.E. Barry Road
Kansas City, MO 64156
William.Young@kcmetro.edu

Professor Greg Sanford and Professor Lyle Gibson
Social Science Division
Penn Valley Community College
3201 Southwest Trafficway
Kansas City, MO 64111
Greg.Sanford@kcmetro.edu
Lyle.Gibson@kcmetro.edu

Old South, New South: Reconstruction and Beyond

Few events in United States history are commemorated as much as the Civil War. A trip to Gettysburg or any other battle site reveals statues dedicated to fallen heroes, paid for by friends, relatives, and grateful state governments. During the war itself the American people celebrated heroes marching valiantly off to war, fighting and dying for their ideals. During the horrible conflict, both governments used those ideals to rally the civilian population as well, urging them to make sacrifices as great as the troops at the front. This is the heroic stuff that unifies a nation during wartime, and makes people remember the Civil War and raise monuments to fallen heroes. But where are the monuments to Reconstruction, to the people and leaders who struggled to rebuild the nation and justify the great sacrifices of the late war? Where are the fallen heroes and hard-fought successes of Reconstruction? The fighting was over in 1865. The last Southern armies surrendered and troops from both sides returned home. The Old South was destroyed and four million slaves were free. But what comes next? After the guns fall silent, how do you reunite the nation? Few people agreed in 1865 on the answers to these questions, and historians have disagreed about Reconstruction ever since.

The end of the Civil War in 1865 left three questions to be answered about the South. First, what was going to happen to all of the "traitors," those men who fought in Southern armies or served in the government? Second, what would be the fate of the Southern states? Would they be treated as conquered provinces, or as colonies, or would they be restored to their pre-war status as equals to all Northern states? Third, what will happen to the four million former slaves? What do they receive besides freedom, and what responsibility does the national government have for the people it set free? Attempting to answer these questions during the next 12 years, the national government passed civil rights acts, amended the Constitution three times, and set up agencies such as the Freedman's Bureau. Northerners and Southerners, Republicans and Democrats disagreed over what actions to take, over the proper use of the United States army to act as a national constabulary in the South, and over forcing social change through legislation. Should Southern society be restructured now, collapsing the plantations and making every freedman a landowner, or should free market capitalism direct the economic future of the South? In the end, the South was treated quite mildly compared to the losers in other attempted revolutions. In most western nations the losers would face massive executions, land seizures, and permanent loss of wealth and privileges. Despite myths about Reconstruction, the South was handled with kid gloves.

The last days of the war and the early years of Reconstruction were filled with misery and uncertainty. Eva Jones complained from Georgia that poverty was widespread. Losing slaves meant losing property, and she complained that Yankees and former slaves stole all the food before they left the area. Confederate veterans across the South complained about shortages of beans, corn, and meat. For former slaves, emancipation was both bewildering and dangerous. Some owners took out their frustrations and vengeance for defeat by whipping and killing former slaves. The system that had regulated the freedmen's lives vanished without training them how to survive. Many wandered about in search of family members sold before the war.

Bloody vengeance was not visited upon the traitors/Southern patriots who fought in the Civil War. Despite Union soldiers singing "We'll Hang Jeff Davis from a Sour Apple Tree" as they marched south, he did not die. He went to jail for two years, and came out as a martyr. Robert E. Lee and other military leaders, who had sworn an oath to defend the United States when they were in the antebellum Army, were never tried for treason, nor were they even arrested. If you could not prosecute Robert E. Lee, then the lesser soldiers were safe. The promise of safety, which General Grant included in the surrender terms, made sure of that. Former congressmen and federal judges who had also violated their oaths were safe as well. The only rebel tried and executed was Henry Wirz, Commandant of Andersonville Prison. He was tried for war crimes, not treason.

The popular myth of Reconstruction claimed that Radical Republicans plotted to rule the South through Northern carpetbaggers (criminals) and former slaves, plundering everything of value and terrorizing innocent White Southerners. The former states did go through a formal process to regain their equal status in the American political system. To protect their ownership rights to the land, Southern landowners were forced to swear a loyalty oath to the Union. Radical Republicans were never in charge of the Northern government, and moderate Republicans held off formal action until violent acts and continued signs of treason forced their hand. George Templeton Strong, a conservative New Yorker who never really trusted President Lincoln or the Republican Party, symbolized the moderates and conservatives who gradually accepted harsher treatment of the South. Strong's diary and daily newspapers reported planters who refused to accept the reality of defeat and shot their former slaves for refusing to work. He noted in horror the White mob that killed 48 people in Memphis, most of them families of Black soldiers. Outrage increased with the New Orleans riots, where Whites killed 37 White and Black Unionists. The creation of Black Codes, enforced by Southern militias still wearing confederate grey uniforms, was the final insult.

The Reconstruction Acts of 1867 set up a process for federal control and law enforcement in the South, partial disenfranchisement of former Confederates, and assistance to the freedmen until the conquered states proved their loyalty. The Habeas Corpus Act of 1867 facilitated state citizens' transferring their cases from biased state courts to federal courts. New state constitutions had to ensure Black suffrage and "equal justice." State governments were required to pass the 14th and 15th Amendments, renouncing both secession and the Confederacy's wartime debts, and eliminating the Black Codes restricting the rights of freedmen. During the years that Reconstruction governments controlled Southern states, they increased democracy by opening up most state offices for election, building schools for Blacks and for Whites, stimulating industry, and diversifying the Southern economy. Despite later Southern claims, these governments were controlled by White leaders, who were no more corrupt than the Southern "Redeemer" governments that replaced them, and actually improved the Southern standard of living.

What of the freedmen? Former Confederate General Robert V. Richardson reflected the popular view when he declared, "The emancipated slaves own nothing, because nothing but freedom has been given to them." In the wake of emancipation, many former slaves fled the plantations for towns and cities, where "freedom was free-er." Others took steps (after locating missing family members) to legalize earlier marriages and living arrangements, and by 1870 most Black Southerners were living in traditional two-parent homes. African Americans had their own agenda, which called for political power and economic independence. This meant the right to vote and hold office, and the opportunity to hold land. If not land, they needed the opportunity to earn a decent wage at skilled labor. The former slaves realized, as did their former masters, that the right to vote is easily removed without economic independence. The freedmen collected money and built both churches and schools. The Civil Rights Act of 1866, and the 14th and 15th Amendments, helped achieve the goal of political rights, but economic successes were far fewer. Years after the war ended, many African-American veterans and their dependents were still waiting for the federal government to pay overdue pay and bounties.

Prejudice and resentment fueled continued Southern White resistance to Reconstruction. Anger and bigotry saw insults to White honor with each liberty granted African Americans. Tax increases, used to build schools and fuel economic development, made any corruption in the "carpetbagger" governments seem to be too much. Using a variety of illegal methods, Whites disenfranchised Black voters, segregated public facilities, partially re-enslaved freedmen on the farms and former plantations, and used massive violence to keep them in their "place." By 1877, Southern Whites proclaimed the South was redeemed (meaning they regained control of the state governments); for the rest of the century they systematically eliminated the political and social advances that African Americans had achieved because of the Civil War. Share-cropping and crop-liens, intimidation by the night-riding Ku Klux Klan and other White Leagues, and lynching of any

African American seeking equality led many to question what about the South was actually reconstructed by the beginning of the twentieth century.

Considering the Evidence in the Readings

The documents in this chapter provide first-hand accounts of the South during Reconstruction. As you learn what happened and how people were treated, consider what actions the federal government needs to take to protect the rights of all its citizens. This is what these reports and first-hand testimony are all about: giving the government information so it can act as needed. Be sure to trace the evolution of the South from the end of the war to the twentieth century, and consider how much the region did or did not change.

Document 13.1 An Anonymous Journalist Describes the South in 1866

More than two hundred writers visited the South in the first 15 years after the Civil War. Most worked for Northern newspapers and journals, and were assigned to investigate Southern conditions and report back to their readers. This meant primarily observing the lives of the freedmen and checking on the loyalty of the former Confederates. Some writers hoped for a quick reconciliation between sections, while others expected treason to still be rampant. Whitelaw Reid, who made three separate trips South in 1865 and 1866, reported that former Confederate soldiers accepted the outcome of the war, but civilians who never fought were filled with hatred. He and Sidney Andrews filed reports of White women murdering their former servants, of women teaching their children to hate the North, and of reporters threatened with violence. The following report is from the *Atlantic Monthly* of February 1866. How does the author describe Southern attitudes? Have they accepted the outcome of the war, or the supremacy of the national government? What is the attitude toward the former slaves or Northern soldiers and officials? What action does this writer recommend?

I spent the months of September, October, and November, 1865, in the States of North Carolina, South Carolina, and Georgia. I travelled over more than half the stage and railway routes therein, visited a considerable number of towns and cities in each State, attended the so-called reconstruction conventions at Raleigh, Columbia, and Milledgeville, and had much conversation with many individuals of nearly all classes.

I was generally treated with civility, and occasionally with courteous cordiality. I judge, from the stories told me by various persons, that my reception was, on the whole, something better than that accorded to the majority of Northern men travelling in that section. Yet at one town in South Carolina, when I sought accommodations for two or three days at a boarding-house, I was asked by the woman in charge, "Are you a Yankee or a Southerner?" and when I answered, "Oh, a Yankee, of course," she responded, "No Yankee stops in this house!" and turned her back upon

me and walked off. In another town in the same State I learned that I was the first Yankee who had been allowed to stop at the hotel since the close of the war. In one of the principal towns of Western Carolina, the landlord of the hotel said to a customer, while he was settling his bill, that he would be glad to have him say a good word for the house to any of his friends; "but," added he, "you may tell all d—d Yankees I can git 'long jest as well, if they keep clar' o me"; and when I asked if the Yankees were poor pay, or made him extra trouble, he answered, "I don't want 'em 'round. I ha'n't got no use for 'em nohow." In another town in the same State, a landlord said to me, when I paid my two-days' bill, that "no d—d Yankee" could have a bed in his house. In Georgia, I several times heard the people of my hotel expressing the hope that the passenger-train wouldn't bring any Yankees; and I have good reason for believing that I was quite often compelled to pay an extra price for accommodations because I was known to be from the

---

From *Atlantic Monthly*, February 1866.

North. In one town, several of us, passengers by an evening train, were solicited to go to a certain hotel; but the clerk declined to give me a room, when he learned that I was from Massachusetts, though I secured one after a time through the favor of a travelling acquaintance, who sharply rebuked the landlord.

It cannot be said that freedom of speech has been fully secured in either of these three States. Personally, I have very little cause of complaint, for my role was rather that of a listener than of a talker; but I met many persons who kindly cautioned me, that at such and such places, and in such and such company, it would be advisable to refrain from conversation on certain topics. Among the better class of people, resident in the cities and large towns, I found a fair degree of liberality of sentiment and courtesy of speech; but in travelling off the main railway-lines, and among the average of the population, any man of Northern opinions must use much circumspection of language; while in many counties of South Carolina and Georgia, the life of an avowed Northern radical would hardly be worth a straw but for the presence of the military. In Barnwell and Anderson districts, South Carolina, official records show the murder of over a dozen Union men in the months of August and September; and at Atlanta, a man told me, with a quiet chuckle, that in Carroll County, Georgia, there were "four d—d Yankees shot in the month of October." Any Union man, travelling in either of these two States, must expect to hear many very insulting words; and any Northern man is sure to find his principles despised, his people contemned, and himself subjected to much disagreeable contumely. There is everywhere extreme sensitiveness concerning the negro and his relations; and I neither found nor learned of any village, town, or city in which it would be safe for a man to express freely what are here, in the North, called very moderate views on that subject. Of course the war has not taught its full lesson, till even Mr. Wendell Phillips can go into Georgia and proclaim "The South Victorious."

I often had occasion to notice, both in Georgia and the Carolinas, the wide and pitiful difference between the residents of the cities and large towns and the residents of the country. There is no homogeneity, but everywhere a rigid spirit of caste. The longings of South Carolina are essentially monarchical rather than republican; even the common people have become so debauched in loyalty, that very many of them would readily accept the creation of orders of nobility. In Georgia there is something less of this spirit; but the upper classes continually assert their right to rule, and the middle and lower classes have no ability to free themselves. The whole structure of society is full of separating walls; and it will sadden the heart of any Northern man, who travels in either of these three States, to see how poor, and meagre, and narrow a thing life is to all the country people. Even with the best class of townsfolk it lacks very much of the depth and breadth and fruitfulness of our Northern life, while with these others it is hardly less materialistic than that of their own mules and horses.

Thus, Charleston has much intelligence, and considerable genuine culture; but go twenty miles away, and you are in the land of the barbarians. So, Raleigh is a city in which there is love of beauty, and interest in education; but the common people of the county are at least forty years behind the same class of people in Vermont. Moreover, in Macon are many fine residences, and the city may boast of its gentility and its respect for the nourishing elegancies of life; but a dozen miles out are large neighborhoods not yet half-civilized. The contrast between the inhabitants of the cities and those of the country is hardly less striking than that between the various classes constituting the body of the common people. Going from one county to another is frequently going into a foreign country. Travel continually brings novelty, but with that always came pain. Till all these hateful walls of caste are thrown down, we can have neither intelligent love of liberty, decent respect for justice, nor enlightened devotion to the idea of national unity. "Do men gather grapes of thorns, or figs of thistles?"

It has been the purpose of the ruling class, apparently, to build new barriers between themselves and the common people, rather than tear away any of those already existing. I think no one can understand the actual condition of the mass of whites in Georgia and the Carolinas, except by some daily contact with them. The injustice done to three fourths of them was hardly less than that done to all the blacks. There were two kinds of slavery, and negro slavery was only the more wicked and debasing than white slavery. Nine of every ten white men in South Carolina had almost as little to do with even State affairs as the negroes had. Men talk of plans of reconstruction;— that is the best plan which proposes to do most for the common people. Till civilization has been carried down into the homes and hearts of all classes, we shall have neither regard for humanity nor respect for the rights of the citizen. In many sections of all these States human life is quite as cheap as animal life. What a mental and moral condition does this indicate! Any plan of reconstruction is wrong that does not assure toleration of opinion, and the elevation of the common people to the consciousness that ours is a republican form of government. Whether they are technically in the Union or out of the Union, it is the national duty to deal with these States in such a manner as will most surely exalt the lower and middle classes of their inhabitants. The nation must teach them a knowledge of their own rights, while it also teaches them respect for its rights and the rights of man as man.

Stopping for two or three days in some back county, I was always seeming to have drifted away from the world which held Illinois and Ohio and Massachusetts. The difficulty in keeping connection with our civilization did not so much lie in the fact that the whole structure of daily life is unlike ours, nor in the other fact that I was forced to hear the Union and all loyal men reviled, as in the greater fact that the people are utterly without knowledge. There is everywhere a lack of intellectual activity. Schools, books, newspapers,—why, one may almost say there are none outside the cities and towns. The situation is horrible enough, when the full force of this fact is comprehended; yet there is a still lower deep,—there is small desire, even feeble longing, for schools and books and newspapers. The chief end of man seems to have been "to own a nigger." In the important town of Charlotte, North Carolina, I found a white man who owned the comfortable house in which he lived, who had a wife and three half-grown children, and yet had never taken a newspaper in his life. He thought they were handy for wrapping purposes, but he couldn't see why anybody wanted to bother with the reading of them. He knew some folks spent money for them, but he also knew a many houses where none had ever been seen. In that State I found several persons—whites, and not of the "clay-eater" class, either—who never had been inside a schoolhouse, and who didn't mean to 'low their children to go inside one. In the upper part of South Carolina, I stopped one night at the house of a moderately well-to-do farmer who never had owned any book but a Testament, and that was given to him. When I expressed some surprise at this fact, he assured me that he was as well off as some other people thereabouts. Between Augusta and Milledgeville I rode in a stage-coach in which were two delegates of the Georgia Convention. When I said that I hoped the day would soon come in which school-houses would be as numerous in Georgia as in Massachusetts, one of them answered: "Well, I hope it'll never come,—popular education is all a d—d humbug in my judgment"; whereunto the other responded, "That's my opinion, too." These are exceptional cases, I am

aware, but they truly index the situation of thousands of persons. It is this general ignorance, and this general indifference to knowledge, that make a Southern trip such wearisome work. You can touch the masses with few of the appeals by which we move our own people. There is very little aspiration for larger life; and, more than that, there is almost no opportunity for its attainment. That education is the stairway to a nobler existence is a fact which they either fail to comprehend or to which they are wholly indifferent.

Where there is such a spirit of caste, where the ruling class has a personal interest in fostering prejudice, where the masses are in such an inert condition, where ignorance so generally prevails, where there is so little ambition for improvement, where life is so hard and material in its tone, it is not strange to find much hatred and contempt. Ignorance is generally cruel, and frequently brutal. The political leaders of this people have apparently indoctrinated them with the notion that they are superior to any other class in the country. Hence there is usually very little effort to conceal the prevalent scorn of the Yankee,—this term being applied to the citizen of any Northern State. Any plan of reconstruction, is wrong that tends to leave these old leaders in power. A few of them give fruitful evidence of a change of heart,—by some means save these for the sore and troubled future; but for the others, the men who not only brought on the war, but ruined the mental and moral force of their people before unfurling the banner of rebellion,—for these there should never any more be place or countenance among honest and humane and patriotic people. When the nation gives them life, and a chance for its continuance, it shows all the magnanimity that humanity in such case can afford.

In North Carolina there is a great deal of something that calls itself Unionism; but I know nothing more like the apples of Sodom than most of this North Carolina Unionism. It is a cheat, a Will-o-the-wisp; and any man who trusts it will meet with overthrow. Its quality is shown in a hundred ways. An old farmer came into Raleigh to sell a little corn. I had some talk with him. He claimed that he had been a Union man from the beginning of the war, but he refused to take "greenback money" for his corn. In a town in the western part of the State I found a merchant who prided himself on the fact that he had always prophesied the downfall of the so-called Confederacy and had always desired the success of the Union arms; yet when I asked him why he did not vote in the election for delegates to the Convention, he answered, sneeringly,—"I shall not vote till you take away the military." The State Convention declared by a vote of ninety-four to nineteen that the Secession ordinance had always been null and void; and then faced squarely about, and, before the Presidential instructions were received, impliedly declared, by a vote of fifty-seven to fifty-three, in favor of paying the war debt incurred in supporting that ordinance! This action on these two point exactly exemplifies the quality of North Carolina Unionism. There may be in the seed of loyalty, but woe to him who mistakes the germ for the ripened fruit! In all sections of the State I found abundant hatred of some leading or local Secessionist; but how full of promise for the new era of national life is the Unionism which rests only on this foundation?

In South Carolina there is very little pretence of loyalty. I believe I found less than fifty men who admitted any love for the Union. There is everywhere a passionate devotion to the State, and the common sentiment holds that man guilty of treason who prefers the United States to South Carolina. There is no occasion to wonder at the admiration of the people for Wade Hampton, for he is the very exemplar of their spirit,—of their proud and narrow and domineering spirit. "It is our duty," he says, in his letter of last November, "it is our duty to support the President of the United States so long as he manifests a disposition to restore all our rights as a sovereign State."

That sentence will forever stand as a model of cool arrogance, and yet it is in full accord with the spirit of the South-Carolinians. He continues:—"Above all, let us stand by our State,—all the sacred ties that bind us to her are intensified by her suffering and desolation. . . . It only remains for me, in bidding you farewell, to say, that, whenever the State needs my services, she has only to command, and I shall obey." The war has taught this people only that the physical force of the nation cannot be resisted. They will be obedient to the letter of the law, perhaps, but the whole current of their lives flows in direct antagonism to its spirit.

In Georgia there is something worse than sham Unionism or cold acquiescence in the issue of battle; it is the universally prevalent doctrine of the supremacy of the State. Even in South Carolina a few men stood up against the storm, and now claim credit for faith in dark days. In Georgia that man is hopelessly dead who doubted or faltered. The common sense of all classes pushes the necessity of allegiance to the State into the domain of morals as well as into that of politics; and he who did not "go with the State" in the Rebellion is held to have committed the unpardonable sin. At Macon I met a man who was one of the leading Unionists in the winter of 1860–1861. He told me how he suffered then for his hostility to Secession, and yet he added,—"I should have considered myself forever disgraced, if I hadn't heartily gone with the State, when she decided to fight." And Ben Hill, than whom there are but few more influential men in the State, advises the people after this fashion,— "I would vote for no man who could take the Congressional test-oath, because it is the highest evidence of infidelity to the people of the State." I believe it is the concurrent testimony of all careful travellers in Georgia, that there is everywhere only cold toleration for the idea of national sovereignty, very little hope for the future of the State as a member of the Federal Union, and scarcely any pride in the strength and glory and renown of the United States of America.

Much is said of the hypocrisy of the South. I found but little of it anywhere. The North-Carolinian calls himself a Unionist, but he makes no special pretence of love for the Union. He desires many favors, but he asks them generally on the ground that he hated the Secessionists.

He expects the nation to recognize rare virtue in that hatred, and hopes it may win for his State the restoration of her political rights; but he wears his mask of nationality so lightly that there is no difficulty in removing it. The South-Carolinian demands only something less than he did in the days before the war, but he offers no pleas of Unionism as a guaranty for the future. He rests his case on the assumption that he has fully acquiesced in the results of the war, and he honestly believes that he has so acquiesced. His confidence in South Carolina is so supreme that he fails to see how much the conflict meant. He walks by such light as he has, and cannot yet believe that Destiny has decreed his State a secondary place in the Union. The Georgian began by believing that rebellion in the interest of Slavery was honorable, and the result of the war has not changed his opinion. He is anxious for readmission to fellowship with New York and Pennsylvania and Connecticut, but he supports his application by no claim of community of interest with other States. His spirit is hard and uncompromising; he demands rights, but does not ask favors; and he is confident that Georgia is fully as important to the United States as they are to Georgia.

Complaint is made that the Southern people have recently elected military men to most of their local State offices. We do ourselves a wrong in making this complaint. I found it almost everywhere true in Georgia and the Carolinas the best citizens of to-day are the Confederate soldiers of yesterday. Of course, in many individual cases they are bitter and malignant; but in general the good of the Union, no less than the hope of the South, lies in the bearing of the men who were privates and minor officers in the armies of Lee and Johnston. It may not be pleasant to us to recognize this fact; but I am confident that we shall make sure progress toward securing domestic tranquillity and the general welfare, just in proportion as we act upon it. It should be kept in mind that comparatively few of those who won renown on the field were promoters of rebellion or secession. The original malcontents,—ah! where are they? Some of them at least are beyond interference in earthly affairs; others are in hopeless poverty and chilling neglect; others are struggling to mount once more the wave of popular favor. A few of these last have been successful,—to see that no more of them are so is a national duty. I count it an omen of good, when I find that one who bore himself gallantly as a soldier has received preferment. We cannot afford to quarrel on this ground; for, though their courage was for our wounding, their valor was the valor of Americans. The really bad feature of the situation with respect to the relations of these States to the General Government is, that there is not only very little loyalty in their people, but a great deal of stubborn antagonism, and some deliberate defiance. Further war in the field I do not deem among the possibilities. Be the leaders never so bloodthirsty, the common people have had enough of fighting. The bastard Unionism of North Carolina, the haughty and self-complacent State pride of South Carolina, the arrogant dogmatism and insolent assumption of Georgia,—how shall we build nationality on such foundations? That is the true plan of reconstruction which makes haste very slowly. It does not comport with the character of our Government to exact pledges of any State which are not exacted of all. The one sole needful condition is, that each State establish a republican form of government, whereby all civil rights at least shall be assured in their fullest extent to every citizen. The Union is no Union, unless there is equality of privileges among the States. When Georgia and the Carolinas establish this republican form of government, they will have brought themselves into harmony with the national will, and may justly demand readmission to their former political relations in the Union. Each State has some citizens, who, wiser than the great majority, comprehend the meaning of Southern defeat with praiseworthy insight. Seeing only individuals of this small class, a traveller might honestly conclude that the States were ready for self-government. Let not the nation commit the terrible mistake of acting on this conclusion. These men are the little leaven in the gross body politic of Southern communities. It is no time for passion or bitterness, and it does not become our manhood to do anything for revenge. Let us have peace and kindly feeling; yet, that our peace may be no sham or shallow affair, it is painfully essential that we keep these States awhile within national control, in order to aid the few wise and just men therein who are fighting the great fight with stubborn prejudice and hide-bound custom. Any plan of reconstruction is wrong which accepts forced submission as genuine loyalty, or even as cheerful acquiescence in the national desire and purpose.

Before the war, we heard continually of the love of the master for his slave, and the love of the slave for his master. There was also much talk to the effect that the negro lived in the midst of pleasant surroundings, and had no desire to change his situation. It was asserted that he delighted in a state of dependence, and throve on the universal favor of the whites. Some of this language we conjectured might be extravagant; but to the single fact that there was universal goodwill between the two classes every Southern white person bore evidence.

So, too, in my late visit to Georgia and the Carolinas, they generally seemed anxious to convince me that the blacks had behaved well during the war,—had kept at their old tasks, had labored cheerfully and faithfully, had shown no disposition to lawlessness, and had rarely been guilty of acts of violence, even in sections where there were many women and children, and but few white men.

Yet I found everywhere now the most direct antagonism between the two classes. The whites charge generally that the negro is idle, and at the bottom of all local disturbances, and credit him with most of the vices and very few of the virtues of humanity. The negroes charge that the whites are revengeful, and intend to cheat the laboring class at every opportunity, and credit them with neither good purposes nor kindly hearts. This present and positive hostility of each class to the other is a fact that will sorely perplex any Northern man travelling in either of these States. One would say, that, if there had formerly been such pleasant relations between them, there ought now to be mutual sympathy and forbearance, instead of mutual distrust and antagonism. One would say, too, that self-interest, the common interest of capital and labor, ought to keep them in harmony; while the fact is, that this very interest appears to put them in an attitude of partial defiance toward each other. I believe the most charitable traveller must come to the conclusion, that the professed love of the whites for the blacks was mostly a monstrous sham or a downright false pretence. For myself, I judge that it was nothing less than an arrogant humbug.

The negro is no model of virtue or manliness. He loves idleness, he has little conception of right and wrong, and he is improvident to the last degree of childishness. He is a creature,—as some of our own people will do well to keep carefully in mind,—he is a creature just forcibly removed from slavery. The havoc of war has filled his heart with confused longings, and his ears with confused sounds of rights and privileges: it must be the nation's duty, for it cannot be left wholly to his late master, to help him to a clear understanding of these rights and privileges, and also to lay upon him a knowledge of his responsibilities. He is anxious to learn, and is very tractable in respect to minor matters; but we shall need almost infinite patience with him, for he comes very slowly to moral comprehensions.

Going into the States where I went,—and perhaps the fact is true also of the other Southern States,—going into Georgia and the Carolinas, and not keeping in mind the facts of yesterday, any man would almost be justified in concluding that the end and purpose in respect to this poor negro was his extermination. It is proclaimed everywhere that he will not work, that he cannot take care of himself, that he is a nuisance to society, that he lives by stealing, and that he is sure to die in a few months; and, truth to tell, the great body of the people, though one must not say intentionally, are doing all they can to make these assertions true. If it is not said that any considerable number wantonly abuse and outrage him, it must be said that they manifest a barbarous indifference to his fate, which just as surely drives him on to destruction as open cruelty would.

There are some men and a few women—and perhaps the number of these is greater than we of the North generally suppose—who really desire that the negro should now have his full rights as a human being. With the same proportion of this class of persons in a community of Northern constitution, it might be justly concluded that the whole community would soon join or acquiesce in the effort to secure for him at least a fair share of those rights. Unfortunately, however, in these Southern communities the opinion of such persons cannot have such weight as it would in ours. The spirit of caste, of which I have already spoken, is an element figuring largely against them in any contest involving principle,—an element

of whose practical workings we here know very little. The walls between individuals and classes are so high and broad, that the men and women who recognize the negro's rights and privileges as a freeman are almost as far from the masses as we of the North are. Moreover, that any opinion savors of the "Yankee"— in other words, is new to the South—is a fact that even prevents its consideration by the great body of the people. Their inherent antagonism to everything from the North—an antagonism fostered and cunningly cultivated for half a century by the politicians in the interest of Slavery,—is something that no traveller can photograph, that no Northern man can understand, till he sees it with his own eyes, hears it with his own ears, and feels it by his own consciousness. That the full freedom of the negroes would be acknowledged at once is something we had no warrant for expecting. The old masters grant them nothing, except at the requirement of the nation,—as a military and political necessity; and any plan of reconstruction is wrong which proposes at once or in the immediate future to substitute free-will for this necessity.

Three-fourths of the people assume that the negro will not labor, except on compulsion; and the whole struggle between the whites on the one hand and the blacks on the other hand is a struggle for and against compulsion. The negro insists, very blindly perhaps, that he shall be free to come and go as he pleases; the white insists that he shall come and go only at the pleasure of his employer. The whites seem wholly unable to comprehend that freedom for the negro means the same thing as freedom for them. They readily enough admit that the Government has made him free, but appear to believe that they still have the right to exercise over him the old control. It is partly their misfortune, and not wholly their fault, that they cannot understand the national intent, as expressed in the Emancipation Proclamation and the Constitutional Amendment. I did not anywhere find a man who could see that laws should be applicable to all persons alike; and hence even the best men hold that each State must have a negro code. They acknowledge the overthrow of the special servitude of man to man, but seek through these codes to establish the general servitude of man to the commonwealth. I had much talk with intelligent gentlemen in various sections, and particularly with such as I met during the conventions at Columbia and Milledgeville, upon this subject, and found such a state of feeling as warrants little hope that the present generation of negroes will see the day in which their race shall be amenable only to such laws as apply to the whites.

I think the freedmen divide themselves into four classes: one fourth recognizing, very clearly, the necessity of work, and going about it with cheerful diligence and wise forethought; one fourth comprehending that there must be labor, but needing considerable encouragement to follow it steadily; one fourth preferring idleness, but not specially averse to doing some job-work about the towns and cities; and one fourth avoiding labor as much as possible, and living by voluntary charity, persistent begging, or systematic pilfering. It is true, that thousands of the aggregate body of this people appear to have hoped, and perhaps believed, that freedom meant idleness; true too, that thousands are drifting about the country or loafing about the centres of population in a state of vagabondage. Yet of the hundreds with whom I talked, I found less than a score who seemed beyond hope of reformation. It is a cruel slander to say that the race will not work, except on compulsion. I made much inquiry, wherever I went, of great numbers of planters and other employers, and found but a very few cases in which it appeared that they had refused to labor reasonably well, when fairly treated and justly paid. Grudgingly admitted to any of the natural rights of man, despised alike by Unionists and Secessionists, wantonly outraged by many and meanly cheated by more of the old planters, receiving a hundred cuffs for one helping hand and a thousand curses for one kindly word,—they bear themselves toward their former masters very much as white men and women would under the same circumstances. True, by such deportment they unquestionably harm themselves; but consider of how little value life is from their stand-point. They grope in the darkness of this transition period, and rarely find any sure stay for the weary arm and the fainting heart. Their souls are filled with a great, but vague longing for freedom; they battle blindly with fate and circumstance for the unseen and uncomprehended, and seem to find every man's hand raised against them. What wonder that they fill the land with restlessness!

However unfavorable this exhibit of the negroes in respect to labor may appear, it is quite as good as can be made for the whites. I everywhere found a condition of affairs in this regard that astounded me. Idleness, not occupation, seemed the normal state. It is the boast of men and women alike, that they have never done an hour's work. The public mind is thoroughly debauched, and the general conscience is lifeless as the grave. I met hundreds of hale and vigorous young men who unblushingly owned to me that they had not earned a penny since the war closed. Nine tenths of the people must be taught that labor is even not debasing. It was pitiful enough to find so much idleness, but it was more pitiful to observe that it was likely to continue indefinitely. The war will not have borne proper fruit, if our peace does not speedily bring respect for labor, as well as respect for man. When we have secured one of these things, we shall have gone far toward securing the other; and when we have secured both, then indeed shall we have noble cause for glorying in our country,—true warrant for exulting that our flag floats over no slave.

Meantime, while we patiently and helpfully wait for the day in which "All men's good shall Be each man's rule, and Universal Peace Lie like a shaft of light across the land, " there are at least five things for the nation to do: make haste slowly in the work of reconstruction; temper justice with mercy, but see to it that justice is not overborne; keep military control of these lately rebellious States, till they guaranty a republican form of government; scrutinize carefully the personal fitness of the men chosen therefrom as representatives in the Congress of the United States; and sustain therein some agency that shall stand between the whites and the blacks, and aid each class in coming to a proper understanding of its privileges and responsibilities.

Document 13.2 Reports from the Joint Committee on Reconstruction, June 20, 1866

In December 1865, Republicans in Congress voted to create a joint committee of fifteen (nine representatives and six senators) to create national reconstruction policy. Dominated by moderate members of the Republican Party, this committee held hearings and solicited testimony from Freedman's Bureau agents, traveling correspondents, military commanders, and Southern Unionists about growing hostility and violence in the South, violence aimed at undoing the results of the war. Based on the evidence presented, the committee determined that new laws were required to protect Blacks, insure the loyalty of the South, and help the freedmen become productive citizens. The committee also looked into the recent elections in the South, where avowed disunionists and former Confederate leaders were elected to seats in Congress.

To many moderates, Southern behavior suggested that they had not learned any lesson, and that the 360,000 Northern deaths were for nothing. At a time when Blacks were denied chances to vote in the South, and the Southern states had not yet renounced secession, were these elections valid? What justifications or evidence indicate the need for further federal controls and regulation of the South? What steps are suggested by the speakers and the committee?

A claim for the immediate admission of senators and representatives from the socalled Confederate States has been urged, which seems to your committee not to be founded either in reason or in law, and which cannot be passed without comment. Stated in a few words, it amounts to this: That inasmuch as the lately insurgent States had no legal right to separate themselves from the Union, they still retain their positions as States, and consequently the people thereof have a right to immediate representation in Congress without the imposition of any conditions whatever. . . . It has even been contended that until such admission all legislation affecting their interests is, if not unconstitutional, at least unjustifiable and oppressive.

It is believed by your Committee that these propositions are not only wholly untenable, but, if admitted would tend to the destruction of the government.

It must not be forgotten that the people of these States, without justification or excuse, rose in insurrection against the United States. They deliberately abolished their State governments so far as the same connected them politically with the Union. . . . They opened hostilities and levied war against the government. They continued this war for four years with the most determined and malignant spirit. . . . Whether legally and constitutionally or not, they did, in fact, withdraw from the Union and made themselves subjects of another government of their own creation. And they only yielded when they were compelled by utter exhaustion to lay down their arms . . . expressing no regret, except that they had no longer the power to continue the desperate struggle.

It cannot, we think, be denied by any one, having tolerable acquaintance with public law, that the war thus waged was a civil war of the greatest magnitude. The people waging it were necessarily subject to all the rule which, by the law of nations, control a contest of that character, and to all the legitimate consequences following it. One of those consequences was that, within the limits prescribed by humanity, the conquered rebels were at the mercy of the con-

querors. That a government thus outraged had a most perfect right to exact indemnity for the injuries done, and security against the recurrence of such outrages in the future, would seem too clear for dispute.

Your committee came to the consideration of the subject referred to them with the most anxious desire to ascertain what was the condition of the people of the States recently in insurrection, and what, if anything, was necessary to be done before restoring them to the full enjoyment of all their original privileges. It was undeniable that the war into which they had plunged the country had materially changed their relations to the people of the loyal States. Slavery had been abolished by constitutional amendment. A large proportion of the population had become, instead of mere chattels, free men and citizens. Through all the past struggle these had remained true and loyal, and had, in large numbers, fought on the side of the Union. It was impossible to abandon them, without securing them their rights as free men and citizens. . . . Hence it became important to inquire what could be done to secure their rights, civil and political. It was evident to your committee that adequate security could only be found in appropriate constitutional provisions. By an original provision of the Constitution, representation is based on the whole number of free persons in each State, and three-fifths of all other persons. When all become free, representation for all necessarily follows. As a consequence the inevitable effect of the rebellion would be to increase the political power of the insurrectionary States, whenever they should be allowed to resume their position as States of the Union. . . . It did not seem just or proper that all the political advantages derived from their becoming free should be confined to their former masters, who had fought against the Union, and withheld from themselves, who had always been loyal. . . . Doubts were entertained whether Congress had power, even under the amended Constitution, to prescribe the qualifications of voters in a State, or could act directly on the subject. It was

Report from Joint Committee on Reconstruction, June 20, 1866.

doubtful . . . whether the States would consent to surrender a power they had always exercised, and to which they were attached. As the best if not the only method of surmounting the difficulty, and as eminently just and proper in itself, your committee came to the conclusion that political power should be possessed in all the States exactly in proportion as the right of suffrage should be granted, without distinction of color or race. This it was thought would leave the whole question with the people of each State, holding out to all the advantage of increased political power as an inducement to allow all to participate in its exercise. Such a provision would be in its nature gentle and persuasive, and would lead, it was hoped, at no distant day, to an equal participation of all, without distinction, in all the rights and privileges of citizenship, thus affording a full and adequate protection to all classes of citizens, since all would have, through the ballot-box, the power of self-protection. . . .

With such evidence before them, it is the opinion of your committee

I.   That the States lately in rebellion were, at the close of the war, disorganized communities, without civil government, and without constitutions or other forms, by virtue of which political relations could legally exist between them and the federal government.

II.   That Congress cannot be expected to recognize as valid the election of representatives from disorganized communities, which, from the very nature of the case, were unable to present their claim to representation under those established and recognized rules, the observance of which has been hitherto required.

III.   That Congress would not be justified in admitting such communities to a participation in the government of the country without first providing such constitutional or other guarantees as will tend to secure the civil rights of all citizens of the republic; a just equality of representation; protection against claims founded in rebellion and crime; a temporary restoration of the right of suffrage to those who had not actively participated in the efforts to destroy the Union and overthrow the government, and the exclusion from positions of public trust of, at least, a portion of those whose crimes have proved them to be enemies to the Union, and unworthy of public confidence.

Document 13.3 The Louisiana Black Code, 1865

One action that particularly disturbed Northerners was the passage of "Black Codes" by the Southern legislatures during 1865 and 1866. These codes regulated Black behavior and restricted their rights, segregated public facilities, prohibited interracial marriage, and excluded Blacks from juries—all actions similar to some Northern laws. The overall goal was to keep the former slaves "in their place" and insure they remained a cooperative agricultural labor force, but the Codes essentially reinvented slavery. Blacks would be declared vagrants if they could not produce evidence of employment every year, and then were hired out to planters to pay off the court-imposed fines. Black workers were not allowed to leave plantations without permission of their employer. White courts could decide if underaged Blacks had adequate parental support; then apprentice the young freedmen to their former masters for an undetermined length of time. Consider the sections of the Louisiana Black Code in the following reading. This was one of the milder codes among Southern states. What basic rights are Blacks denied? Is this an attempt to overturn the results of the Civil War? Why would Northern voters and Congressmen see the laws as such, and how would they react after the losses in the Civil War?

Sec. 1. *Be it ordained by the police jury of the parish of St. Landry,* That no negro shall be allowed to pass within the limits of said parish without special permit in writing from his employer. Whoever shall violate this provision shall pay a fine of two dollars and fifty cents, or in default thereof shall be forced to work four days on the public road, or suffer corporeal punishment as provided hereinafter. . . .

Sec. 3. . . . No negro shall be permitted to rent or keep a house within said parish. Any negro violating this provision shall be immediately ejected and compelled to find an employer; and any person who shall rent, or give the use of any house to any negro, in violation of this section, shall pay a fine of five dollars for each offence.

Sec. 4. . . . Every negro is required to be in the regular service of some white person, or former owner, who shall be held responsible for the conduct of said negro. But said employer or former owner may permit said negro to hire his own time by special permission in writing, which permission shall not extend over seven days at any one time. . . .

Sec. 5. . . . No public meeting or congregations of negroes shall be allowed within said parish after sunset; but such public meetings and congregations may be held between the hours of sunrise and sunset, by the special permission in writing of the captain of patrol, within whose beat such meetings shall take place. . . .

Sec. 6. . . . No negro shall be permitted to preach, exhort, or otherwise declaim to congregations of colored people, without a special permission in writing from the president of the police jury. . . .

Sec. 7. . . . No negro who is not in the military service shall be allowed to carry fire-arms, or any kind of weapons, within the parish, without the special written permission of his employers, approved and endorsed by the nearest and most convenient chief of patrol. . . .

Sec. 8. . . . No negro shall sell, barter, or exchange any articles of merchandise or traffic within said parish without the special written permission of his employer, specifying the article of sale, barter or traffic. . . .

Sec. 9. . . . Any negro found drunk within the said parish shall pay a fine of five dollars, or in default thereof work five days on the public road, or suffer corporeal punishment as hereinafter provided.

Sec. 11. . . . It shall be the duty of every citizen to act as a police officer for the detection of offences and the apprehension of offenders, who shall be immediately handed over to the proper captain or chief of patrol.

Document 13.4 African American Citizens Petition the United States Government 1865

The former slaves realized that they had their freedom, but without federal protection they would not have much else. Vengeful Southern whites could deny them (or take violently from them) food, shelter, and almost every basic right. After finding their lost/sold family members, they needed a way to support them that was free from extortion. Gathering in conventions across the South, African Americans discussed the best way to protect their new freedoms, and many sent petitions to Congress. Most petitions declared the loyalty of the freedmen, reminded the government of their service in the Union army, and described the conditions they faced. The following is a petition from a convention held in Alexandria, Virginia from August 2 to August 5, 1865. What do they warn the national government about? Why do they need protection and aid? What actions do they recommend the national government take? How do their claims and issues compare with the issues raised in the Declaration of Independence in Chapter 4?

We, the undersigned members of a Convention of colored citizens of the State of Virginia, would respectfully represent that, although we have been held as slaves, and denied all recognition as a constituent of your nationality for almost the entire period of the duration of your Government, and that by *your permission* we have been denied either home or country, and deprived of the dearest rights of human nature: yet when you and our immediate oppressors met in deadly conflict upon the field of battle the one to destroy and the other to save your Government and nationality, *we*, with scarce an exception, in our inmost souls espoused your cause, and watched, and prayed, and waited, and labored for your success.

When the contest waxed long, and the result hung doubtfully, you appealed to us for help, and how well we answered is written in the rosters of the two hundred thousand colored troops now enrolled in

Louisiana Black Code, 1865.
Petition from a Convention of Loyal African American Citizens, 1865.

your service; and as to our undying devotion to your cause, let the uniform acclamation of escaped prisoners, *"whenever we saw a black face we felt sure of a friend,"* answer.

Well, the war is over, the rebellion is "put down," and we are *declared* free! Four fifths of our enemies are paroled or amnestied, and the other fifth are being pardoned, and the President has, in his efforts at the reconstruction of the civil government of the States, late in rebellion, left us entirely at the mercy of these subjugated but unconverted rebels, in *everything* save the privilege of bringing us, our wives and little ones, to the auction block. . . . We *know* these men—know them *well*—and we assure you that, with the majority of them, loyalty is only "**lip deep**," and that their professions of loyalty are used as a cover to the cherished design of getting restored to their former relations with the Federal Government, and then, by all sorts of "unfriendly legislation," to render the freedom you have given us more intolerable than the slavery they intended for us.

We warn you in time that our only safety is in keeping them under Governors of the *military persuasion* until you have so amended the Federal Constitution that it will prohibit the States from making any distinction between citizens on account of race or color. In one word, the only salvation for us besides the power of the Government, is in the *possession of the ballot*. Give us this, and we will protect ourselves. . . . But, it is said we are ignorant. Admit it. Yet who denies we *know* a traitor from a loyal man, a gentleman from a rowdy, a friend from an enemy? The twelve thousand colored votes of the State of New York sent Governor Seymour home and Reuben E. Fenton to Albany. Did not they know who to vote for? . . . All we ask is an *equal chance* with the white traitors varnished and japanned with the oath of amnesty. Can you deny us this and still keep faith with us?

We are *"sheep in the midst of wolves,"* and nothing but the military arm of the Government prevents us and all the truly loyal white men from being driven from the land of our birth. Do not then, we beseech you, give to one of these "wayward sisters" the rights they abandoned and forfeited when they rebelled until you have secured our rights by the aforementioned amendment to the Constitution.

Trusting that you will not be deaf to the appeal herein made, nor unmindful of the warnings which the malignity of the rebels are constantly giving you, and that you will rise to the height of being just for the sake of justice, we remain yours for our flag, our country and humanity.

Document 13.5 The *Atlanta News* Calls for the Use of Brute Force to Maintain White Control

Southern Whites resisted Congressional Reconstruction with violence. Violence was epidemic in the South from the late 1860s onward, but by the early 1870s Whites made open appeals to use force. Conservative newspapers, politicians, and ministers all claimed this was the only way to "redeem" the South from Northern and African-American control. The options were "a White man's government or military rule," and they claimed this was a revolution of principle, not a matter of politics. Independent voters who would not follow racial appeals were considered race traitors, spawns of corruption and worse than Blacks. Besides brute force, other methods of intimidation discouraged Black voters and ostracized Whites cooperating with Republican rule, including loss of jobs, shared land, and other livelihoods. Rifle clubs were formed to attack Reconstruction supporters, and the Ku Klux Klan and White Leagues stepped up open attacks on Blacks. These groups proclaimed their goals to be the restoration of honest, White, Christian governments; but many wore their old grey uniforms as they attacked opposition voters. The following is the editorial appeal of a major newspaper, the *Atlanta News*, for increased violence in the cause of redeeming the South. What specific actions does the writer approve or advocate? What justifications does he offer for such extreme measures?

From *Atlanta News*, 1870.

Let there be White Leagues formed in every town, village and hamlet of the South, and let us organize for the great struggle which seems inevitable. If the October elections which are to be held at the North are favorable to the radicals, the time will have arrived for us to prepare for the very worst. The radicalism of the republican party must be met by the radicalism of white men. We have no war to make against the United States Government, but against the republican party our hate must be unquenchable, our war interminable and merciless. Fast fleeting away is the day of wordy protests and idle appeals to the magnanimity of the republican party. By brute force they are endeavoring to force us into acquiescence to their hideous programme. We have submitted long enough to indignities, and it is time to meet brute-force with brute-force. Every Southern State should swarm with White Leagues, and we should stand ready to act the moment Grant signs the civil-rights bill. It will not do to wait till radicalism has fettered us to the car of social equality before we make

an effort to resist it. The signing of the bill will be a declaration of war against the southern whites. It is our duty to ourselves, it is our duty to our children, it is our duty to the white race whose prowess subdued the wilderness of this continent, whose civilization filled it with cities and towns and villages, whose mind gave it power and grandeur, and whose labor imparted to it prosperity, and whose love made peace and happiness dwell within its homes, to take the gage of battle the moment it is thrown down. If the white democrats of the North are men, they will not stand idly by and see us borne down by northern radicals and half-barbarous negroes. But no matter what they may do, it is time for us to organize. We have been temporizing long enough. Let northern radicals understand that military supervision of southern elections and the civil-rights bill mean war, that war means bloodshed, and that we are terribly in earnest, and even they, fanatical as they are, may retrace their steps before it is too late.

Document 13.6 Personal Accounts of Ku Klux Klan Attacks

The oldest and best known of all the Southern White supremacist organizations is the Ku Klux Klan (KKK). Originally organized to insure a steady labor supply on postwar plantations, the KKK moved on to other goals. Its night-riding, white-hooded members enforced a code of behavior, "visiting" freed African Americans who acted or spoke "improperly" to Whites. The Klan was determined to maintain White supremacy at all costs. By the 1870s their primary goal was terrorizing Black Republican voters in the South, allowing White Southern Democrats to regain control of the states and end Reconstruction. This terrorist organization utilized whippings, shootings, and psychological terror, and murdered hundreds of voters and elected state officials. Following are three accounts of Klan activity. Note that the KKK attacked field hands, women, and even members of state legislatures. African Americans who owned or rented land were often targets, because they had an independence that threatened White power. What do the following accounts have in common? What response is needed by the federal government to combat these terrorist attacks?

Elias Hill is a remarkable character. He is crippled in both legs and arms, which are shriveled by rheumatism; he cannot walk; cannot help himself, has to be fed and cared for personally by others; was in early life a slave, whose freedom was purchased, his father buying his mother and getting Elias along with her, as a burden of which his master was glad to be rid. Stricken at seven years old with disease, he never was afterward able to walk, and he presents the appearance of a dwarf with the limbs of a child, the body of

a man, and a finely developed intellectual head. He learned his letters and to read by calling the school children into the cabin as they passed, and also learned to write. He became a Baptist preacher, and after the war engaged in teaching colored children, and conducted the business correspondence of many of his colored neighbors. He is a man of blameless character, of unusual intelligence, speaks good English, and we put the story of his wrongs in his own language:

Personal Accouts of Ku Klux Klan Attacks, 1870.

"On the night of the 5th of last May, after I had heard a great deal of what they had done in that neighborhood, they [the Ku Klux Klan] came. It was between 12 and 1 o'clock at night when I was awakened and heard the dogs barking, and something walking, very much like horses. . . . At last they came to my brother's door, which is in the same yard, and broke open the door and attacked his wife, and I heard her screaming and mourning. . . . At last I heard them have her in the yard. She was crying and the Ku-Klux were whipping her to make her tell where I lived. . . . Some one then hit my door. It flew open. One ran in the house, and stopping about the middle of the house, which is a small cabin, he turned around, as it seemed to me as I lay there awake, and said, 'Who's here?' Then I knew they would take me, and I answered, 'I am here.' He shouted for joy, as it seemed, 'Here he is! Here he is! We have found him!' and he threw the bedclothes off of me and caught me by one arm, while another man took me by the other and they carried me into the yard between the houses. . . . The first thing they asked me was, 'Who did the burning? Who burned our houses?' —gin-houses, dwelling-houses and such. Some had been burned in the neighborhood. I told them it was not me; I could not burn houses; it was unreasonable to ask me. Then they hit me with their fists, and said I did it, I ordered it. They went on asking me didn't I tell the black men to ravish all the white women. No, I answered them. They struck me again with their fists on my breast, and then they went on. . . .

"They pointed pistols at me all around my head once or twice, as if they were going to shoot me, telling me they were going to kill me; wasn't I ready to die, and willing to die" Didn't I preach? That they came to kill me—all the time pointing pistols at me. . . . One said 'G-d d—n it, hush!' He had a horse-whip, and he told me to pull up my shirt, and he hit me. He told me at every lick, 'Hold up your shirt.' I made a moan every time he cut with the horsewhip. I reckon he struck me eight cuts right on the hip bone; it was almost the only place he could hit my body, my legs are so short—all my limbs drawn up and withered away with pain. . . . They all had disguises on. I then thought they would not kill me. One of them then took a strap, and buckled it around my neck and said, 'Let's take him to the river and drown him . . .'

"They said 'Look here! Will you put a card in the paper next week like June Moore and Sol Hill?' They had been prevailed on to put a card in the paper to renounce all republicanism and never vote. I said, 'If I had the money to pay the expense, I could.' They said I could borrow, and gave me another lick. They

asked me, 'Will you quit preaching?' I told them I did not know. I said that to save my life. They said I must stop the republican paper that was coming to Clay Hill. It has been only a few weeks since it stopped. The republican paper was then coming to me from Charleston. It came to my name. They said I must stop it, quit preaching, and put a card in the newspaper renouncing republicanism, and they would not kill me; but if I did not they would come back the next week and kill me."

Harriet Hernandez

Q: Did the Ku-Klux ever come to your house at any time?
A: Yes, sir; twice.
Q: Go on to the second time. . . .
A: They came in; I was lying in bed. Says he, "Come out here, sir; Come out here, sir!" They took me out of bed; they would not let me get out, but they took me up in their arms and toted me out— me and my daughter Lucy. He struck me on the forehead with a pistol, and here is the scar above my eye now. Says he, "Damn you, fall!" I fell. Says he, "Damn you, get up!" I got up. Says he, "Damn you, get over this fence!" And he kicked me over when I went to get over; and then he went to a brush pile, and they laid us right down there, both together. They laid us down twenty yards apart, I reckon. They had dragged and beat us along. They struck me right on the top of my head, and I thought they had killed me; and I said, "Lord o' mercy, don't, don't kill my child!" He gave me a lick on the head, and it liked to have killed me; I saw stars. He threw my arm over my head so I could not do anything with it for three weeks, and there are great knots on my wrist now.
Q: What did they say this was for?
A: They said, "You can tell your husband that when we see him we are going to kill him."
Q: Did they say why they wanted to kill him?
A: They said, "He voted the radical ticket, didn't he?" I said, "Yes, that very way."
Q: When did your husband get back after this whipping? He was not at home, was he?
A: He was lying out; he couldn't stay at home, bless your soul! . . .
Q: Has he been afraid for any length of time?
A: He has been afraid ever since last October. He has been lying out. He has not laid in the house ten nights since October.
Q: Is that the situation of the colored people down there to any extent?

Chapter 13   **15**

A: That is the way they all have to do—men and women both.

Q: What are they afraid of?

A: Of being killed or whipped to death.

Q: What has made them afraid?

A: Because men that voted radical tickets they took the spite out on the women when they could get at them.

Q: How many colored people have been whipped in that neighborhood?

A: It is all of them, mighty near.

Testimony of Abram Colby (1872)

On the 29th of October 1869, they broke my door open, took me out of bed, took me to the woods and whipped me three hours or more and left me for dead. They said to me, "Do you think you will ever vote another damned radical ticket?" I said, "I will not tell you a lie." I supposed they would kill me anyhow. I said, "If there was an election tomorrow, I would vote the radical ticket." They set in and whipped me a thousand licks more, with sticks and straps that had buckles on the ends of them.

Q: What is the character of those men who were engaged in whipping you?

A: Some are first-class men in our town. One is a lawyer, one a doctor, and some are farmers. They had their pistols and they took me in my night-clothes and carried me from home. They hit me five thousand blows. I told President Grant the same that I tell you now. They told me to take off my shirt. I said, "I never do that for any man." My drawers fell down about my feet and they took hold of them and tripped me up. Then they pulled my shirt up over my head. They said I had voted for Grant and had carried the Negroes against them. About two days before they whipped me they offered me $5,000 to go with them and said they would pay me $2500 in cash if I would let another man go to the legislature in my place. I told them that I would not do it if they would give me all the county was worth.

The worst thing about the whole matter was this. My mother, wife and daughter were in the room when they came. My little daughter begged them not to carry me away They drew up a gun and actually frightened her to death. She never got over it until she died. That was the part that grieves me the most.

Q: How long before you recovered from the effects of this treatment?

A: I have never got over it yet. They broke something inside of me. I cannot do any work now, though I always made my living before in the barber-shop, hauling wood, &c.

Q: You spoke about being elected to the next legislature?

A: Yes, sir, but they run me off during the election. They swore they would kill me if I staid. The Saturday night before the election I went to church. When I got home they just peppered the house with shot and bullets.

Q: Did you make a general canvas there last fall?

A: No, sir. I was not allowed to. No man can make a free speech in my county. I do not believe it can be done anywhere in Georgia.

Q: You say no man can do it?

A: I mean no Republican, either white or colored.

Document 13.7 General Alfred Terry Testifies about Race Relations in Georgia

General Alfred Terry filed this official report to the Secretary of War in 1869. Many army officers advocated harsh treatment of the South, and were removed from their commands by President Johnson for voicing their opinions. By contrast, General Terry was a moderate in his views, but was increasingly concerned with the growing violence and threat to the freedmen. In this official report he discusses the deteriorating state of race relations, the increased intolerance and attacks by groups such as the KKK, and the overall attitude of the Southern people. What does he propose as a government response? What justifications does Terry give for the use of force by the national government?

I have delayed making the report thus called for until the present time, in order that I might become acquainted with the condition of affairs in Georgia before expressing any opinion in regard to them. Now I have reluctantly come to the conclusion that the situation here demands the interposition of the national government, in order that life and property may be protected, freedom of speech and political action secured, and the rights and liberties of the freedmen maintained. This opinion is based upon complaints made to me, the reports of officers detailed to investigate alleged outrages, and upon the statements of many persons of respectability and high position from different parts of the State, in whose representations I must repose confidence; some of whom have given me information only under the pledge of secrecy, the state of affairs in their section being such that they feared the extreme of personal violence should it become known that they had been in communication with me.

In many parts of the State there is practically no government. The worst of crimes are committed, and no attempt is made to punish those who commit them. Murders have been and are frequent; the abuse in various ways of the blacks is too common to excite notice. There can be no doubt of the existence of numerous insurrectionary organizations known as "Ku-Klux Klans," who, shielded by their disguise, by the secrecy of their movements, and by the terror which they inspire, perpetrate crime with impunity. There is great reason to believe that in some cases local magistrates are in sympathy with the members of these organizations. In many places they are overawed by them and dare not attempt to punish them. To punish such offenders by civil proceedings would be a difficult task, even were magistrates in all cases disposed and had they the courage to do their duty, for the same influences which govern them equally affect juries and witnesses. A conversation which I have had with a wealthy planter, a gentleman of intelligence and education, and a political opponent of the present national administration, will illustrate this difficulty. While deploring the lamentable condition of affairs in the county in which he lives, he frankly admitted to me that, were the most worthless vagabond in the county to be charged with a crime against the person of a republican or a negro, neither he nor any other person of property within the county would dare to refuse to give bail for the offender, nor

would they dare to testify against him, whatever might be their knowledge of his guilt.

That very many of the crimes which have been committed have no political bearing I believe; that some of them were prompted by political animosity, and that most of the numerous outrages upon freedmen result from hostility to the race induced by their enfranchisement, I think cannot be controverted.

The same difficulties which beset the prosecution of criminals are encountered by negroes who seek redress for civil injuries in the local courts. Magistrates dare not do their duty toward them, and instances are not wanting where it has even been beyond the power of a magistrate to protect a negro plaintiff from violence in his own presence while engaged in the trial of his case. I desire it to be understood that in speaking of magistrates I in no degree refer to the judges of the superior courts; they are gentlemen of high character. I have every confidence that they will do their duty fearlessly and impartially, but it is to be observed that even they cannot control grand and petty juries; they cannot compel the former to indict, nor the latter to render unprejudiced verdicts.

The executive of the State would gladly interpose to give to all citizens the protection which is their right, but under the constitution and laws he has power neither to act directly in bringing offenders to justice nor to compel subordinate officers to do their duty. I do not suppose that the great majority of the people of the State, of either race, approve of the commission of these crimes. I believe that not only would they gladly see good order restored, peace and quiet maintained, and the law vindicated; but would lend their aid to secure these ends were they not controlled by their fears. Governed, however, by their apprehensions, and having no confidence that the civil authorities will afford them protection, in many counties they suffer these evils to exist without an effort to abate them, and meekly submit to the rule of the disorderly and criminal minority.

While I have been in command of the department I have endeavored to take no action which could not be justified by the letter of the law, even if Georgia should be held to be restored to its original relations to the general government. I have confined myself to giving support to the civil authorities and

---

Official Report to the Secretary of War, 1869.

moving detachments of troops into some of the disturbed counties, where their presence would exert a good influence, and where they would be ready to act if properly called upon. I think that some good has in this way been accomplished, but the great evil has by no means been reached. As a department commander I can do no more; for whatever may be the status of Georgia, and whatever may be the powers which an officer assigned to command the third district created by the reconstruction acts would possess, it is only an officer so assigned who could exercise them; they are not vested in me by my assignment to the command of this department. Where, therefore, the civil authorities are in sympathy with or are overawed by those who commit crime, it is manifest that I am powerless. In this connection I respectfully call the special attention of the General commanding the army to the reports in regard to the attempt made in Warren County to secure the arrest and punishment of persons charged with crime, which are this day forwarded. It appears to me that the national honor is pledged to the protection of the loyalists and the freedmen of the South. I am well aware that the protection of persons and property is not ordinarily one of the functions of the national government, but when it is remembered that hostility to the supporters of the government is but a manifestation of hostility to the government itself, and that the prevailing prejudice against the blacks results from their emancipation—the act of the government—it would seem that such protection cannot be denied them if it be within the power of the government to give it. I know of no way in which such protection can be given in Georgia except by the exercise of the powers conferred on military commanders by the reconstruction acts.

Document 13.8 Black Lives during Reconstruction

Not all freedmen were attacked, and life consisted of more than dodging White bullets. During the 1930s the New Deal's Federal Writers' Project sent interviewers out to collect first-hand biographies of the survivors of slavery and Reconstruction. Between 1936 and 1938, interviewers in 17 states recorded the memories of thousands of former slaves. These materials left a record of daily life that went beyond contemporary newspaper accounts. In the two accounts that follow, what do the participants remember most about life? Is the Klan ever too far from their minds? How does the fear of violence compare with fear of discipline during slave days? How does freedom compare with slavery?

Mingo White

Interviewed at Burleson, Alabama
Interviewed by Levi D. Shelby, Jr.
Age when interviewed: 85–90

De day dat we got news dat we was free, Mr. White called us niggers to the house. He said: "You are all free, just as free as I am. Now go and get yourself somewhere to stick your heads."

Just as soon as he say dat, my mammy hollered out: "Dat's 'nough for a yearlin'." She struck out across de field to Mr Lee Osborn's to get a place for me and her to stay. He paid us seventy-five cents a day, fifty cents to her and two bits for me. He gave us our dinner along with de wages. After de crop was gathered for that year, me and my mammy cut and hauled wood for Mr. Osborn. Us left Mr. Osborn dat fall and went to Mr. John Rawlins. Us made a sharecrop with him. Us'd pick two rows of cotton and he'd pick two rows. Us'd pull two rows of corn and he'd pull two rows of corn. He furnished us with rations and a place to stay. Us'd sell our cotton and open corn and pay Mr. John Rawlins for feedin' us. Den we moved with Mr. Hugh Nelson and made a sharecrop with him. We kept movin' and makin' sharecrops till us saved up 'nough money to rent us a place and make a crop for ourselves.

Us did right well at dis until de Ku Klux got so bad, us had to move back with Mr. Nelson for protection. De mens that took us in was Union men. Dey lived here in the South but dey taken us part in de

From *New Deal's Federal Writers' Project*.

slave business. De Ku Klux threat to whip Mr. Nelson, 'cause he took up for de niggers. Heap of nights we would hear of de Ku Klux comin' and leave home. Sometimes us was scared not to go and scared to go away from home.

One day I borrowed a gun from Ed Davis to go squirrel huntin'. When I taken de gun back I didn't unload it like I always been doin'. Dat night de Ku Klux called on Ed to whip him. When dey told him to open de door, he heard one of 'em say, "Shoot him time he gets de door open." "Well," he says to 'em, "Wait till I can light de lamp." Den he got de gun what I had left loaded, got down on his knee and stuck it through a log and pulld de trigger. He hit Newt Dobbs in de stomach and kilt him.

He couldn't stay round Burleson any more, so he come to Mr. Nelson and got 'nough money to get to Pine Bluff, Arkansas. The Ku Klux got bad sure 'nough den and went to killin' niggers and white folks, too.

Charles Davenport

Interviewed at Natchez, Mississippi
Interviewed by Edith Wyatt Moore
Age at interview: About 100

Like all de fool niggers o' dat time I was right smart bit by de freedom bug for awhile. It sounded powerful nice to be told: "You don't have to chop cotton no more. You can throw dat hoe down and go fishin' whensoever de notion strikes you. And you can roam 'round at night and court gals just as late as you please. Ain't no marster gwine to, say to you, 'Charlie, you's got to be back when de clock strikes nine.'"

I was fool 'nough to believe all dat kind o' stuff. But to tell de honest truth, most o' us didn't know ourselfs no better off. Freedom meant us could leave where us'd been born and bred, but it meant, too, dat us had to scratch for us ownselfs. Dem what left de old plantation seemed so all fired glad to get back dat I made up my mind to stay put. I stayed right with my white folks as long as I could.

My white folks talked plain to me. Dey say real sadlike, "Charlie, you's been a dependence, but now you can go if you is so desirous. But if you wants to stay with us you can sharecrop. Dey's a house for you and wood to keep you warm and a mule to work. We ain't got much cash, but dey's de land and you can count on havin' plenty o' victuals. Do just as you please."

When I looked at my marster and knowed he needed me, I pleased to stay. My marster never forced me to do nary thing about it.

Lord! Lord! I knows about de Kloo Kluxes. I knows a-plenty. Dey was sure 'nough devils a-walkin' de earth a-seekin' what dey could devour. Dey larruped de hide off de uppity niggers an' drove de white trash back where dey belonged.

Us niggers didn't have no secret meetin's. All us had was church meetin's in arbors out in de woods. De preachers would exhort us dat us was de chillen o' Israel in de wilderness an' de Lord done sent us to take dis land o' milk and honey. But how us gwine-a take land what's already been took?

I sure ain't never heard about no plantations bein' divided up, neither. I heard a lot o' yaller niggers spoutin' off how dey was gwine-a take over de white folks' land for back wages. Dem bucks just took all dey wages out in talk. 'Cause I ain't never seen no land divided up yet.

In dem days nobody but niggers and "shawl-strap" folks voted. Quality folks didn't have nothin' to do with such truck. If dey hada wanted to de Yankees wouldn'ta let 'em. My old marster didn't vote and if anybody knowed what was what he did. Sense didn't count in dem days. It was powerful ticklish times and I let votin' alone. . . . [O]ne night a bunch o' uppity niggers went to a entertainment in Memorial Hall. Dey dressed deyselfs fit to kill and walked down de aisle and took seats in de very front. But just about time dey got good set down, de curtain dropped and de white folks rose up without a-sayin' a word. Dey marched out de buildin' with dey chins up and left dem niggers a-sittin' in a empty hall.

Dat's de way it happen every time a nigger tried to get too uppity. Dat night after de breakin' up o' dat entertainment, de Kloo Kluxes rode through de land. I heard dey grabbed every nigger what walked down dat aisle, but I ain't heard yet what dey done with 'em.

Document 13.9 Black Land Ownership and Sharecropping in the Postwar South

For most former slaves, freedom meant owning and farming their own land, but this rarely happened in the postwar South. The legendary promises of "forty acres and a mule" for the former slaves never became a reality. Approximately 80 percent of former slaves ended up as sharecroppers on land owned by Whites, sometimes by their former masters. On the plus side, this arrangement provided them more autonomy than slavery did because they worked the land without a slave driver, and they could keep their wives out of the fields if they chose. However, it also bound them to the land and guaranteed perpetual poverty. The property owner provided the land, seed, livestock, and farm implements, as well as credit to live on before harvest. The cropper provided the labor and received half of the crop in return, but then had to pay off his debts—if he ever could. This system also kept the South producing cotton, the closest thing to ready cash they had, even as over-production wore out the soil. The following are accounts of freed African Americans discussing their attempts to make a living through honest labor. What are they able to accomplish? Do they reach any sort of financial independence through their hard work? What obstacles stand in their way?

Henry Blake

After freedom, we worked on shares a while. Then, we rented. When we worked on shares, we couldn't make nothing—just over-alls, and something to eat. Half went to the white man, and you would destroy your half, if you weren't careful. A man that didn't know how to count would always lose. He might lose anyhow. The white folks didn't give no itemized statements. No, you just had to owe so much. No matter how good account you kept, you had to go by their account, and—now, brother, I'm telling you the truth about this—it's been that way for a long time. You had to take the white man's words and notes on everything. Anything you wanted you could get, if you were a good hand. If you didn't make no money, that's all right; they would advance you more. But you better not try to leave and get caught. They'd keep you in debt. They were sharp. Christmas come, you could take up twenty dollars in somethin' to eat and much as you wanted in whiskey. You could buy a gallon of whiskey—anything that kept you a slave. Because he was always right and you were always wrong, if there was a difference. If there was an argument, he would get mad and there would be a shooting take place.

Emanuel Fortune

They will not sell our people any land. They have no disposition to do so. They will sell a lot now and then in a town, but nothing of any importance.

Q: What could you get a pretty good farm for—how much an acre?

A: Generally from $10 to $15 an acre. Very poor people cannot afford that

Q: You can get it if you have the money?

A: They will not sell it in small quantities. I would have bought forty acres if the man would have sold me less than a whole tract. They hold it in that way so that colored people cannot buy it. The lands we cultivate generally are swamp or lowlands.

Q: Is there not plenty of other land to buy?

A: Not that is worth anything. I do not know of any Government land that will raise cotton.

Henry M. Turner

Q: You say that colored men employed in the country have not been able to get anything for their labor. Why is that?

A: During the year there is very little money paid to them and if they want to obtain provisions or

From *New Deal's Federal Writers' Project.*

clothing they are given an order on some store. At the end of the year these little bills are collected and however small a quantity of things have been taken, almost always the colored man is brought into debt. That is alleged as a reason why they should be bound to stay with their employers and work out what they say they owe them.

Q: A sort of practical peonage?

A: Yes, sir. Whenever there is fear that the laborer will go to work with someone else the following year, he is apt to come out $25 to $30 in debt and his employer calls upon him to work it out.

There was a bill introduced the other day to make it a penal offense for a laborer to break his contract. For instance, a white man writes out a contract. He reads the contract to the black man and, of course, reads just what he pleases. When the black man takes it to somebody else and gets him to read it, it reads quite differently. Among other things there is a provision in the contract that he must not go to any political gathering or meeting. If he does, he will lose $5 for every day that he is absent, and yet he is to receive only $50 or $75 a year. Every day that he is sick, a dollar or a dollar and a half is to be deducted. The man may want to quit and work for some person else who will pay him better wages.

Q: The effect of the legislation would be to render the laborer practically a slave during the period of his contract?

A: Or else he would be liable to punishment by imprisonment. There is no doubt that they will pass some kind of law to that effect.

Q: With a view to harmonize the relations of labor and capital?

A: Yes, sir, that is the phrase.

Document 13.10 A Texas Shares Contract

Sharecropping contracts usually spelled out clearly what the obligations of both parties were, but greater detail was given to the local sharecropper's duties, including what crops must be produced, number of hours to work each day, extra work required beyond normal, and how debts are to be repaid. Some freedmen worked for wages instead of a share of the crops. The following shares contract provides a typical division of obligations and rewards. What obligations does each side assume? What are the penalties for failing to meet your obligations?

Said _____ of the first part furthermore agrees to furnish the said Freedmen of the second part with good and sufficient quarters, _____ wholesome food, fuel, and such medical treatment as can be rendered by the person superintending the place. Said *J C Mitchell* of the 1st part in consideration of the faithful discharge of the duties assumed by the parties of the second part, does hereby agree to furnish *the freedmen* the necessary tools and implements for the cultivation of the land, and allow said Freedmen *one third* interest in the crops raised on said *plantation* by their labor. It is also mutually agreed that ten hours shall constitute a day's work, and if any labor in excess of ten hours per day is rendered it shall be paid for as extra labor. Said parties of the second part do furthermore agree to do all necessary work on Sundays or at night when it is for the protection of plantation or crops against destruction by storms, floods, fire or frost, provided always that such service shall be paid for as extra labor; extra labor to be paid for at the rate of one day's labor and one-half rations extra for each six hours work. Provided that our employer failing to comply with any part of this agreement, this contract shall be annulled; also provided, that should any of the parties of the second part leave said *plantation* without proper authority, or engage elsewhere, or neglect or refuse to work as herein agreed, they or any part of them so offending shall be liable to be discharged and forfeit all wages due up to that time.

Also Provided, that this Contract shall constitute the first lien upon all crops raised by the labor of said parties of the Second part.

Said J C Mitchell shall have power to make such rules and regulations necessary to the management of the plantation as are not inconsistent with the term of this contract; all lost time to [be] deducted from the one third interest in crop to the freedmen.

Document 13.11 Lynching in the South

After Reconstruction, Southern Whites steadily eroded the rights that Blacks had acquired after the war. Jim Crow laws regulated association between Whites and Blacks, enforced segregation, and restricted Black job opportunities. A strict code of social etiquette was also in place, and Blacks were expected to behave deferentially around Whites at all time. This behavior included removing hats, addressing them as Mister or Ma'am, and bowing—behavior reminiscent of slavery's heyday. To enforce these laws and rules, two types of justice system were in place in the South: formal court systems and lynch mobs. Between 1889 and 1918, there were 2,522 African Americans lynched, 50 of them women. They were hacked to death, burned alive, or hanged. Some form of torture usually preceded death. While Whites claimed that lynching occurred for sexual offenses, most took place because Blacks attempted to vote, argued with a White man, or became economically successful. Following are two examinations of lynching. The first is a report from the *Crisis*, of the lynching of Samuel Petty in Leland, Mississippi in 1914. The second is an article written by Mary Church Terrell of Washington D.C., criticizing the practice. What do the two accounts have in common? Why did lynchings take place, according to White Americans? What are the real causes according to these accounts? Is this law and order, or just racism run amuck?

The news spread like wildfire and in twenty minutes the entire white population was armed and headed for the cabin which was situated about a half mile from the depot, which is in the center of the town. I looked in every direction and could see men and mere boys, some not over 12 years old, carrying rifles, shotguns, pistols and, in fact, every imaginable thing that would shoot. They were acting as though there was an entire army of Negroes to be taken. The man who had killed the officer submitted to arrest by the mob, which by this time numbered about 400. Placing a rope around his neck he was led to the center of the town and in the presence of women and children they proceeded to hold a conference as to the kind of death that should be meted out to him. Some yelled to hang him; some to burn him alive. It was decided in a few minutes. Willing hands brought a large dry goods box, place it in the center of the street, in it was straw on which was poured a tub of oil; then the man was lifted with a rope around his neck and placed in this box head down, and then another tub of oil was poured over him. A man from the crowd deliberately lit a match and set fire to the living man. While in this position the flames shot up at great height. The crowd began to yell as the flames shot upward. In an instant the poor creature managed to lift himself out of the box, a mass of flames. He was fighting the flames with his hands in an effort to shield his face and eyes, and in this condition attempted to run. The crowd allowed him to run to the length of the rope, which was held by willing hands, until he reached a distance of about twenty feet; then a yell went up from the crowd to shoot. In an instant there were several hundred shots and the creature fell in his tracks. The crowd deliberately walked up to the prostrate form and shot the remainder of their guns into his lifeless body. With the flames still leaping into the air, he was pulled back into the fire that was now roaring with boxes and oil brought out of the different stores by men and boys. Every time they would throw on more oil and boxes the crowd would yell as though they were at a bull fight. Standing about fifty or seventy-five feet from the scene I could actually smell the flesh of the poor man as it was being burned. Not a voice was raised in the defense of the man. No one attempted to hide their identity. I looked into the faces of men whom I knew to be officers of the town lending a willing hand in the burning of this man. No wonder the coroner who held the inquest returned a verdict that the Negro came to his death "at the hands of an enraged mob unknown to the jury," because to get a jury in that town they had to get some who participated in the burning. I can never feel toward the white man as I have felt after seeing what I have attempted to describe. After burning the body into ashes the burned bones and ashes were buried in the edge of

From *Crisis*, 1914.

the street in front of a colored barber shop. May God forbid that any other living man will ever see a sight as I witnessed; this is the third Negro who has been killed in this vicinity in the last three weeks. The man burned was named Sam Pettie [sic], known by everybody to be quiet and inoffensive. I write this hoping you may get enough out of what I have tried to describe to tell your great number of readers what we are up against. To mention my name in connection with this would be equivalent to committing suicide.

Mary Church Terrell

Hanging, shooting and burning black men, women and children in the United States have become so common that such occurrences create but little sensation and evoke but slight comment now. . . . In the discussion of this subject, four mistakes are commonly made.

In the first place, it is a great mistake to suppose that rape is the real cause of lynching in the South.

Beginning with the Ku Klux Klan, the negro has been constantly subjected to some form of organized violence ever since he became free. It is easy to prove that rape is simply the pretext and not the cause of lynching. Statistics show that, out of every 100 negroes who are lynched, from 75–85 are not even accused of this crime, and many who are accused of it are innocent. . . .

In the second place, it is a mistake to suppose that the negro's desire for social equality sustains any relation whatsoever to the crime of rape. . . . It is safe to assert that, among the negroes who have been guilty of ravishing white women, not one had been taught that he was the equal of white people or had ever heard of social equality. . . . Negroes who have been educated in Northern institutions of learning with white men and women, and who for that reason might have learned the meaning of social equality and have acquired a taste for the same, neither assault white women nor commit other crimes, as a rule. . . . Strange as it may appear, illiterate negroes, who are the only ones contributing largely to the criminal class, are coddled and caressed by the South. To the educated, cultivated members of the race, they are held up as a bright and shining examples of what a really good negro should be. The dictionary is searched in vain by Southern gentlemen and gentlewomen for words sufficiently ornate and strong to express their admiration for a dear old "mammy" or a faithful old "uncle," who can neither read nor write, and who assure their white friends

they would not if they could. On the other hand, no language is sufficiently caustic, bitter and severe, to express the disgust, hatred and scorn which Southern gentlemen feel for what is called the "New Issue," which, being interpreted, means negroes who aspire to knowledge and culture, and who have acquired a taste for the highest and best things in life. At the door of this "New Issue, " the sins and shortcomings of the whole race are laid. This "New Issue" is beyond hope of redemption, we are told, because somebody, nobody knows who, has taught it to believe in social equality, something, nobody knows what. The alledged fear of social equality has always been used by the South to explain its unchristian treatment of the negro and to excuse its many crimes. . . . In the North, which is the only section that accords the negro the scrap of social equality enjoyed by him in the United States, he is rarely accused of rape. The only form of social equality ever attempted between the two races, and practised to any considerable extent, is that which was originated by the white masters of slave women, and which has been perpetuated by them and their descendants even unto the present day. . . . There is no more connection between social equality and lynching today than there was between social equality and slavery before the war, or than there is between social equality and the convict-lease system, or any other form of oppression to which the negro has uniformly been subjected in the South.

The third error on the subject of lynching consists of the widely circulated statement that the moral sensibilities of the best negroes in the United States are so stunted and dull, and the standard of morality among even the leaders of the race is so low, that they do not appreciate the enormity and heinousness of rape. . . . Only those who are densely ignorant of the standards and sentiments of the best negroes, or who wish willfully to misrepresent and maliciously slander a race already resting under burdens greater than it can bear, would accuse its thousands of reputable men and women of sympathizing with rapists, either black or white, or of condoning their crime. . . .

What, then is the cause of lynching? At the last analysis, it will be discovered that there are just two causes of lynching. In the first place, it is due to race hatred, the hatred of a stronger people toward a weaker who were once held as slaves. In the second place, it is due to the lawlessness so prevalent in the section where nine-tenths of the lynchings occur. . . .

Lynching is the aftermath of slavery. The white men who shoot negroes to death and flay them alive, and the white women who apply flaming torches to their oil-soaked bodies today, are the sons and daughters of women who had but little, if any, compassion on the race when it was enslaved. The men who lynch negroes today are, as a rule, the children of women who sat by their firesides happy and proud in the possession and affection of their own children, while they looked with unpitying eye and adamantine heart upon the anguish of slave mothers whose children had been sold away, when not overtaken by a sadder fate . . . It is impossible to comprehend the cause of the ferocity and barbarity which attend the average lynching-bee, without taking into account the brutalizing effect of slavery upon the people of the section where most of the lynchings occur. . . . It is too much to expect, perhaps, that the children of women who for generations looked upon the hardships and the degradation or their sisters of a darker hue with few if any protests, should have mercy and compassion upon the children of that oppressed race now. But what a tremendous influence for law and order, and what a mighty foe to mob violence Southern white women might be, if they would arise in the purity and power of their womanhood to implore their fathers, husbands and sons no longer to stain their hands with the black man's blood! . . . Whenever Southern white people discuss lynching, they are prone to slander the whole negro race. Not long ago, a Southern writer of great repute declared without qualification or reservation that "the crime of rape is well-nigh wholly confined to the negro race," and insisted that "negroes furnish most of the ravishers. " These assertions are as unjust to the negro as they are unfounded in fact. According to statistics recently published, only one colored male in 100,000 over five years of age was accused of assault upon a white woman in the South in 1902, whereas one male out of every 20,000 over five years of age was charged with rape in Chicago during the same year. If these figures prove anything at all, they show that the men and boys in Chicago are many times more addicted to rape than are the negroes in the South. . . .

But even if the negro's morals were as loose and as lax as some claim them to be, and if his belief in the virtue of women were as slight as we are told, the South has nobody to blame but itself . . . Men do not gather grapes of thorns nor figs of thistles. Throughout their entire period of bondage, colored women were debauched by their masters. From the day they were liberated to the present time, prepossessing young colored girls have been considered the rightful prey of white gentlemen in the South, and they have been protected neither by public sentiment nor by law. In the South, the negro's home is not considered sacred by the superior race. White men are neither punished for invading it, not lynched for violating colored women and girls. . . .

How can lynching be extirpated in the United States? . . . Lynching can never be suppressed in the South, until the masses of ignorant white people in that section are educated and lifted to a higher moral plane. . . . Lynching cannot be suppressed in the South, until all classes of white people who dwell there . . . respect the rights of other human beings, no matter what may be the color of their skin . . . and learn a holy reverence for the law. . . .

Until there is a renaissance or popular belief in the principles of liberty and equality upon which this government was founded, lynching, the Convict-Lease System, the Disfranchisement Acts, the Jim Crow Car Laws, unjust discriminations in the professions and trades and similar atrocities will continue to dishearten and degrade the negro, and stain the fair name of the United States. For there can be no doubt that the greatest obstacle in the way of extirpating lynching is the general attitude of the public mind toward this unspeakable crime. The whole country seems tired of hearing about the black man's woes. The wrongs of the Irish, or the Armenians, of the Romanian and Russian Jews, or the exiles of Russia and of every other oppressed people upon the face of the globe, can arouse the sympathy and fire the indignation of the American public, while they seem to be all but indifferent to the murderous assaults upon the negroes in the South.

Document 13.12 Booker T. Washington: The Atlanta Compromise

What is the best way for African Americans to get ahead? Should they behave in a certain way to please Whites? Should they only train for, or pursue, certain jobs, so they do not challenge White status? Should they seek higher education, or just vocational training? These themes are prominent in the famous speech made by Booker T. Washington in 1895. Washington was born a slave in 1856, earned a living, and paid for his education through a series of menial jobs. His whole life was dedicated to hard work. A guiding force behind the Tuskegee Institute in Alabama, Washington argued that Blacks should learn basic skills to provide for themselves, and thus earn the respect of Whites. In his Atlanta speech, what does he say Blacks should do? What should they not push for, as that might offend Whites? How do you think Southern Whites responded to this speech? Is this a surrender of the rights promised in the 14th and 15th Amendments, and won by the blood shed in the Civil War? Why do you think many prominent African-American leaders, such as W.E.B. DuBois, opposed Washington's views?

Mr. President and Gentlemen of the Board of Directors and Citizens:

One-third of the population of the South is of the Negro race. No enterprise seeking the material, civil, or moral welfare of this section can disregard this element of our population and reach the highest success. I but convey to you, Mr. President and Directors, the sentiment of the masses of my race when I say that in no way have the value and manhood of the American Negro been more fittingly and generously recognized than by the managers of this magnificent Exposition at every stage of its progress. It is a recognition that will do more to cement the friendship of the two races than any occurrence since the dawn of our freedom.

Not only this, but the opportunity here afforded will awaken among us a new era of industrial progress. Ignorant and inexperienced, it is not strange that in the first years of our new life we began at the top instead of at the bottom; that a seat in Congress or the state legislature was more sought than real estate or industrial skill; that the political convention or stump speaking had more attractions than starting a dairy farm or truck garden.

A ship lost at sea for many days suddenly sighted a friendly vessel. From the mast of the unfortunate vessel was seen a signal, "Water, water; we die of thirst!" The answer from the friendly vessel at once came back, "Cast down your bucket where you are." A second time the signal, "Water, water; send us water!" ran up from the distressed vessel, and was answered, "Cast down your bucket where you are." And a third and fourth signal for water was answered, "Cast down your bucket where you are." The captain of the distressed vessel, at last heeding the injunction, cast down his bucket, and it came up full of fresh, sparkling water from the mouth of the Amazon River. To those of my race who depend on bettering their condition in a foreign land or who underesti-

mate the importance of cultivating friendly relations with the Southern white man, who is their next-door neighbor, I would say: "Cast down your bucket where you are"—cast it down in making friends in every manly way of the people of all races by whom we are surrounded.

Cast it down in agriculture, mechanics, in commerce, in domestic service, and in the professions. And in this connection it is well to bear in mind that whatever other sins the South may be called to bear, when it comes to business, pure and simple, it is in the South that the Negro is given a man's chance in the commercial world, and in nothing is this Exposition more eloquent than in emphasizing this chance. Our greatest danger is that in the great leap from slavery to freedom we may overlook the fact that the masses of us are to live by the productions of our hands, and fail to keep in mind that we shall prosper in proportion as we learn to dignify and glorify common labour, and put brains and skill into the common occupations of life; shall prosper in proportion as we learn to draw the line between the superficial and the substantial, the ornamental gewgaws of life and the useful. No race can prosper till it learns that there is as much dignity in tilling a field as in writing a poem. It is at the bottom of life we must begin, and not at the top. Nor should we permit our grievances to overshadow our opportunities.

To those of the white race who look to the incoming of those of foreign birth and strange tongue and habits for the prosperity of the South, were I permitted I would repeat what I say to my own race, "Cast down your bucket where you are." Cast it down among the eight millions of Negroes whose habits you know, whose fidelity and love you have tested in days when to have proved treacherous meant the ruin of your firesides. Cast down your bucket among these people who have, without strikes and labour wars, tilled your fields, cleared your

---

Booker T. Washington, 1895.

forests, builded your railroads and cities, and brought forth treasures from the bowels of the earth, and helped make possible this magnificent representation of the progress of the South. Casting down your bucket among my people, helping and encouraging them as you are doing on these grounds, and to education of head, hand, and heart, you will find that they will buy your surplus land, make blossom the waste places in your fields, and run your factories. While doing this, you can be sure in the future, as in the past, that you and your families will be surrounded by the most patient, faithful, law-abiding, and unresentful people that the world has seen. As we have proved our loyalty to you in the past, in nursing your children, watching by the sick-bed of your mothers and fathers, and often following them with tear-dimmed eyes to their graves, so in the future, in our humble way, we shall stand by you with a devotion that no foreigner can approach, ready to lay down our lives, if need be, in defense of yours, interlacing our industrial, commercial, civil, and religious life with yours in a way that shall make the interests of both races one. In all things that are purely social we can be as separate as the fingers, yet one as the hand in all things essential to mutual progress.

There is no defense or security for any of us except in the highest intelligence and development of all. If anywhere there are efforts tending to curtail the fullest growth of the Negro, let these efforts be turned into stimulating, encouraging, and making him the most useful and intelligent citizen. Effort or means so invested will pay a thousand per cent interest. These efforts will be twice blessed—blessing him that gives and him that takes. There is no escape through law of man or God from the inevitable:

The laws of changeless justice bind Oppressor with oppressed;

And close as sin and suffering joined We march to fate abreast.

Nearly sixteen millions of hands will aid you in pulling the load upward, or they will pull against you the load downward. We shall constitute one-third and more of the ignorance and crime of the South, or one-third [of] its intelligence and progress; we shall contribute one-third to the business and industrial prosperity of the South, or we shall prove a veritable body of death, stagnating, depressing, retarding every effort to advance the body politic.

Gentlemen of the Exposition, as we present to you our humble effort at an exhibition of our progress, you must not expect overmuch. Starting thirty years ago with ownership here and there in a few quilts and pumpkins and chickens (gathered from miscellaneous sources), remember the path that has led from these to the inventions and production of agricultural implements, buggies, steam-engines, newspapers, books, statuary, carving, paintings, the management of drug stores and banks, has not been trodden without contact with thorns and thistles. While we take pride in what we exhibit as a result of our independent efforts, we do not for a moment forget that our part in this exhibition would fall far short of your expectations but for the constant help that has come to our educational life, not only from the Southern states, but especially from Northern philanthropists, who have made their gifts a constant stream of blessing and encouragement.

The wisest among my race understand that the agitation of questions of social equality is the extremest folly, and that progress in the enjoyment of all the privileges that will come to us must be the result of severe and constant struggle rather than of artificial forcing. No race that has anything to contribute to the markets of the world is long in any degree ostracized. It is important and right that all privileges of the law be ours, but it is vastly more important that we be prepared for the exercise of these privileges. The opportunity to earn a dollar in a factory just now is worth infinitely more than the opportunity to spend a dollar in an opera-house.

In conclusion, may I repeat that nothing in thirty years has given us more hope and encouragement, and drawn us so near to you of the white race, as this opportunity offered by the Exposition; and here bending, as it were, over the altar that represents the results of the struggles of your race and mine, both starting practically empty-handed three decades ago, I pledge that in your effort to work out the great and intricate problem which God has laid at the doors of the South, you shall have at all times the patient, sympathetic help of my race; only let this be constantly in mind, that, while from representations in these buildings of the product of field, of forest, of mine, of factory, letters, and art, much good will come, yet far above and beyond material benefits will be that higher good, that, let us pray God, will come, in a blotting out of sectional differences and racial animosities and suspicions, in a determination to administer absolute justice, in a willing obedience among all classes to the mandates of law. This, coupled with our material prosperity, will bring into our beloved South a new heaven and a new earth.

Chapter 13 Worksheet and Questions

1. Use specific examples from the documents in Chapter 13 to prove that most Southerners never accepted losing the Civil War, or warmed to the idea that African Americans had rights. Demonstrate whether their attitudes improved, or that racism decreased, at any time during Reconstruction or afterwards.

_____

_____

_____

_____

_____

_____

_____

_____

2. After traveling through the un-reconstructed South and consulting with both freedmen and government officials, present a case for strict Reconstruction laws and the need for federal troops in the South to enforce them. What laws and actions are necessary to protect Southern Blacks and White Republicans, and why are they needed? Have conditions improved any by the beginning of the twentieth century?

_____

_____

_____

_____

_____

_____

_____

_____

3. According to the freedmen, what rights and opportunities are necessary to give real meaning to their new status as citizens? Why were these rights so important? Why did African Americans believe land ownership was just as important as political rights? Describe the life of the sharecropper. How is this relationship with their former owners an improvement over slavery, and how is it just the same?

_____

_____

_____

_____

_____

_____

_____

_____

4. There has just been a lynching in your rural Mississippi town. Justify this from a White point of view, not only the recent event but also how lynching is a White public ritual aimed at keeping Blacks "in their place." Then, as a Black resident in the same community, explain the reality of lynching. What are the real causes of lynching? Why do Whites lie about the causes of the violence?

_____

_____

_____

_____

_____

_____

_____

_____

Chapter 14

Native Americans and the West

In 1890, Superintendent of the Census Robert P. Porter announced that the days of a western frontier had come to an end. With settlements stretching from Missouri to California, he noted, there, "can hardly be said to be a frontier line." On December 29th of that year, elements of the 7th Cavalry engaged and killed nearly 250 Sioux men, women, and children at Wounded Knee, South Dakota. Subsequently, the Sioux surrendered, ending their armed resistance to western expansion. The two dates mark the conclusion of a series of events started over 25 years earlier when the 7th Cavalry under Colonel George Armstrong Custer attacked a Sioux and Cheyenne camp at Little Big Horn, Montana. The allied tribes killed Custer and over 200 cavalrymen. Between the Little Big Horn and Wounded Knee, settlement transformed the West.

What people had once called the Great American Desert became a crucial part of the Second Industrial Revolution then taking place in the eastern United States. The West became the primary source for food and raw materials for eastern cities and a market for finished products produced there. The construction of railroad systems joined the two regions of the country, transferring materials in both directions. The process even changed the ecology of the West from one of prairie grass and buffalo herds (technically bison) to cereals, grains, hay, cattle, and sheep. The human population changed as well. Americans rushed onto the Great Plains, building cities, mines, farms, and ranches. The Sioux, like other Native Americans, resisted settlement and strove to preserve their culture. The steady incursion by Whites into lands promised by treaties to the Sioux led to violent resistance in the 1860s. By 1890, however, settlement had proceeded, the frontier had closed, and the Sioux had lost their tribal lands.

In terms of historical time, the Sioux themselves were relatively new to the Great Plains. They called themselves the Dakota, Lakota, or Nakota, meaning "allies" in the three tribal dialects. Linguistic differences were reflected in the geographic divisions of Santee, Teton, and Yankton Sioux. Further, each of the branches consisted of different tribes. For example, the Teton included the Oglala, Brulé, Hunkpapa, Miniconjou, Blackfoot, Sans Arc, and Two Kettle tribes. In the 1600s the Sioux resided primarily in Northern Minnesota and Canada. During the 1700s, they acquired horses and guns through trade with the French and British. They also came into conflict with tribes who were forced west by colonial and later American expansion. In response, the Teton and Yankton Sioux moved onto the plains west and southwest of Minnesota. There they adopted a nomadic way of life based primarily upon the buffalo, which provided skins for tipis, blankets and clothing, meat for food, bones for tools and ornaments, sinew for rope, and chips for fires. As they expanded, the Sioux displaced the Cheyenne, Kiowa, Omaha, and other tribes. According to Lewis and Clark in 1803, the Sioux controlled the territory along the Missouri River as far north as Yellowstone. During the early 1800s, they pushed further into the Dakotas and occupied land as far south as the Platte River in Nebraska. Population growth accompanied geographical expansion, rising from about 5,000 in 1800 to 25,000 at mid-century. As the Civil War ended in 1865, the Sioux were the most powerful tribe on the plains.

Following the war, Americans began to settle the western territories. Railroads led the way. The completion of the Union Pacific Railroad between Omaha and Sacramento connected the eastern states and California on the Pacific Ocean. Four other transcontinental lines followed. The Atchison, Topeka, and Santa Fe ran from Kansas through Colorado and on to San Francisco. The Southern Pacific connected New

Orleans through the southernmost states to Los Angeles. The Great Northern and the Northern Pacific ran parallel courses from Duluth and Minneapolis through North Dakota and Montana to Seattle and Portland.

While originally intended to link two distant parts of the nation, the roads also promoted development in and settlement of the western states. To encourage railroad construction, the government had granted over 130 million acres of land, representing 13 percent of the west. The companies in turn marketed the land to prospective American and European settlers. At the same time, in order to attract and serve new customers in cities, farms, and mines, the railroads constructed 72,000 miles of track tying western settlements into the national rail network and industries of the East. Further they systematized operations by adopting standardized track gauge, establishing regular schedules and time zones, and adding specialized cars to move people, steers, crops, and natural resources.

Farmers, ranchers, and miners followed. Like the railroads, the federal government offered land to induce settlement. The Homestead Act of 1862 granted 160 acres of land free to anyone who occupied and worked it for five years. Land offices received over 700,000 applications. Similarly, the Desert Lands Act of 1877, the Timber Culture Act of 1878, and the Timber and Stone Act of 1878 offered free land to farmers, ranchers, and miners. The Mining Act of 1872 alone transferred 3.2 million acres of federal land into private hands. Farmers took advantage of government and railroad offers. Between 1860 and 1900, over 3.5 million persons moved west.

Ranchers, too, set up operations. Far fewer in numbers, they occupied vast stretches of land. The J.A. Ranch alone laid claim to over one million acres. Similarly, 15 to 25 ranchers organized the Wyoming Stock Growers Association, which reportedly oversaw the use of most grazing land in Wyoming and Colorado. Farmers, ranchers, and miners all found the West to be incredibly productive. In terms of agriculture, the West raised over half of the nation's cattle and sheep, one third of its corn, and three fourths of its wheat. At the same time, miners extracted a wealth of resources as well. After initial gold strikes, corporations purchased mining claims and expanded their operations into other minerals, like silver, copper, zinc, and lead. Railroads carried the products of the West to markets in the growing industrial cities of the East and Midwest, and returned with the goods manufactured there.

The establishment of railroads, farms, ranches, and mines changed the ecology of the West. Cattle, sheep, corn, and wheat replaced buffalo herds and prairie grass. Buffalo were the first casualty. Prior to the Civil War an estimated 13 million animals roamed the prairie in two large herds. Initially hunters moved onto the plains to satisfy demand for buffalo coats and capes. Another market opened when engineers and mechanics interested in belts for power transmission from steam engines to factory machinery discovered that the cheap and plentiful leather made from buffalo pelts served their purposes quite well. Buffalo hunting began in earnest. As railroads moved west, companies discovered that sports hunters enjoyed killing the beasts from the relative comfort of the train cars. Further, Army officers promoted the slaughter as a method of subduing the Plains tribes. General Phil Sheridan observed, "Kill the buffalo, and you kill the Indians." By 1890 perhaps 1,000 buffalo remained alive. At the same time, farmers settling on the plains turned the prairie grass with their new John Deere steel plows and replaced it with domesticated cereals, grains, and grasses. Settlement would also change human populations on the Great Plains.

As the farmers, ranchers, and miners migrated west they constantly encroached upon lands that the United States had promised to Native Americans in perpetuity or as long as the streams run. Complaints from settlers and pressure from their political supporters in Congress constrained presidents and the Department of Interior to seek a new accord with the tribes, demanding that the Native Americans renegotiate treaties to accommodate settlement. Frequently Native Americans resisted violently. In the case of the Sioux, sporadic warfare continued for almost 30 years. Almost invariably, the United States prevailed and tribes were moved onto new and smaller reservations situated at some distance from White settlement. Even when Natives successfully defended their land, expansion proceeded, eliciting another round of complaints, threats, violence, and demands that Native Americans agree to new treaties. The case of the Sioux is representative of all western tribes.

Relations between the Sioux and the U.S. government were first defined by the Treaty of Traverse des Sioux and the Treaty of Mendota, 1851. The agreements recognized Yankton and Teton Sioux rights to land in the Dakotas and surrounding territory. The Santee branch occupied a reservation situated along the Minnesota River, approximately 20 miles wide and 150 miles long. By 1858, the White population had increased to the point where the territory applied for and became a state. Federal officials then proceeded to invite the Santee Chief, Little Crow, to Washington D.C. to negotiate a new treaty. In the agreement, the Santee ceded the upper half of their reservation in return for a $1.5 million trust fund and government promises to feed, house, and educate the tribe, as well as to teach them the practice of farming. Over the next two years, the U.S. failed to honor any of its commitments. Forests were felled to build townships and clear farm land, while wild game became scarce. The Santee rebelled in 1862, attacking farms, villages, and trading posts. When Little Crow defeated a small army of volunteers, the state called upon President Lincoln for help. He responded by dispatching General John Pope with orders to organize two regiments. After six weeks of fighting, the Sioux surrendered. Subsequently, the government punished the Santee. It prosecuted and hanged 38 of them for murder and rape, the largest execution in the nation's history. The United States also took possession of all reservation lands, and expelled over 1,300 into Nebraska and the Dakota Territory.

The discovery of gold in western Montana precipitated conflict with the Teton Sioux four years later. In the Great Sioux War (1866-1868), the tribe successfully resisted expansion by miners, settlers, and the U.S. Army into the Powder River, land promised to the Sioux in the 1851 treaties. John Bozeman and John Jacobs started the war when they marked a wagon route, the Bozeman Trail, to the goldfields. The Tetons responded by attacking travelers and turning back wagons as they started up the trail. Settlers demanded protection from the government, which sent troops to construct three forts in the Powder River territory along the wagon route. Sioux war parties continued to harass the troops. In one pitched battle, 1,800 Teton, Cheyenne, and Arapaho killed all 80 men under the command of Captain William J. Fetterman.

After two years, lack of success on the battlefield and the perceived determination of the Sioux and their allies forced the government to sue for peace. In the Fort Laramie Treaty, the United States agreed to close the Bozeman Trail and withdraw from the three forts. The pact also divided into two parts the territory held by the Sioux under the 1851 treaty. One, a reservation, was "set apart for the absolute and undisturbed use and occupation of the Indians," where "no persons, except (U.S. government officials would) ... ever be permitted to pass over, settle upon, or reside." A second area became known as "unceded" land. The Sioux did not explicitly own the area and promised they would not build permanent settlements on it, but they did retain the right to hunt, "so long as the buffalo may range thereon." They also agreed to permit the construction of railroads through the land, and pledged not to attack White settlers or travelers. Overall, the Sioux succeeded in defending their rights, and a short period of relative peace followed.

Agitation to open the Black Hills for mining and settlement provoked another war. For the Sioux, the hills were sacred, and their possession had been guaranteed by two treaties. Whites, however, especially those living in the eastern part of South Dakota, were convinced that the area held gold. As early as 1861, they asked the federal government for an official geological survey to settle the question. For the next 13 years, the Army and the Department of the Interior refused, while attempting to stop prospectors from entering and working the territory. In 1874, rumors about the discovery of gold attracted even larger numbers of miners to the area and caught the attention of railroads. Violent confrontations between the Sioux and settlers became more common as Whites explored the Black Hills and Sioux retaliated by attacking settlements outside of them. To establish order, General Phillip Sheridan assigned Colonel George Armstrong Custer the tasks of investigating the possibility of placing a fort in the area and determining once and for all whether there was gold. The Civil War veteran reported affirmatively on both issues. While the fort was not built, thousands of miners moved onto the Sioux reservation to seek their fortune. Unable to prevent or control the migration, the Department of Interior in 1875 asked Sioux leaders to come to Washington D.C. to negotiate another treaty. The chiefs declined the offer. Relinquishing the Black Hills was not something they would consider.

Department officials proceeded to order the Sioux onto their reservation. That is, they commanded Sioux in the "unceded" territory to move to the reservations defined in the Fort Laramie Treaty. The Sioux questioned the government's authority to take such an action, and refused to obey. To force compliance, the

War Department authorized General Sheridan to go to war with the Sioux. From the outset, Sheridan and his officers lacked two important pieces of information. First, they did not know where they would find the tribe. More importantly, they were unaware of the fact that the Cheyenne had joined the Sioux, under the leadership of the war chief Crazy Horse and medicine man Sitting Bull. Consequently the U.S. faced a far larger force than anticipated. (Estimates of the number range from 5,000 to 12,000.)

In a very loosely coordinated plan, Sheridan sent out three columns of troops that would converge and trap the tribe somewhere in the vicinity of the Rosebud Creek and Yellowstone River. General George Crook with 1,000 men approached from the south. Leading another 1,000 men, General Alfred Terry moved from the east and Colonel John Gibbon, under Terry's command, came from the west with 450 men. Crooks force first encountered the Sioux on June 17, 1876. After an inconclusive engagement, Crook retreated to await reinforcements and the Sioux returned to their encampment near the Little Big Horn River. Terry's column found the tribe's trail and the General surmised the location of their camp. He proceeded to plan a two-pronged attack in which he and Custer would lead simultaneous attacks from the north and south. Terry then sent Custer and the 7th Cavalry to locate the Sioux and prepare for the assault.

Scouts found the Sioux encampment and were astounded by its size. In exaggerated accounts, some reported that it stretched for 12 miles along the river. The scouts informed the colonel of the camp's size and the potential number of warriors. Custer decided to act anyway, dismissing the intelligence and disobeying orders to wait for Terry's forces. On June 25, 1876, after considering the possibility of a pre-dawn attack, he opted instead to strike immediately and divided his command so as to approach the Sioux from three different directions. In this, the Battle of the Little Big Horn, Custer proceeded to engage a force of 2,500 to 5,000 warriors (estimates vary widely) with slightly more than 500 troops divided into three separate units. Major Marcus Reno's force of 175 men arrived at the encampment first. After an initial surprise, the Sioux repelled the attack. They then pursued the troopers and drove them across a river and up onto a bluff. Both sides took heavy casualties. As the battle progressed, Captain Frederick Benteen's force of 120 also retreated and joined Reno's on the bluff overlooking the river. Custer's unit, 210 men, had reached the camp just as Reno was forced to retreat. Cheyenne and Sioux cavalry stopped his advance and forced him back. Sioux commanded by Crazy Horse then succeeded in encircling Custer and his troops. In less than an hour, all 210 were slain. Attacks against Reno and Benteen continued until the next morning when the columns led by Terry and Gibbon arrived. Over the course of the battle, they suffered casualties of about 47 dead and 37 wounded. The Little Big Horn represented the worst loss in U.S. military history.

The victory was short-lived, followed by reprisals against the Sioux and ultimately their surrender. After having dealt the cavalry such a devastating defeat, the Sioux and Cheyenne expected them to withdraw to forts for the winter. Consequently the tribes disbanded and left the encampment in small groups. However, after giving his troops a month to recover, Sheridan ordered them to undertake a winter campaign against the Sioux. For the next year, Crook's and Terry's forces chased, harassed, and defeated the bands of Sioux. Their tactics changed from direct assaults on villages to attacks conducted only after protracted artillery bombardments. Crazy Horse's village fell on January 8, 1877. The last large group, led by Lame Bear, submitted in May. By the following summer, most of the Sioux had been forced back to the reservations. Crazy Horse himself surrendered in September 1877, after which he was bayoneted to death for resisting arrest. Sitting Bull, who had moved to Canada with a small band, surrendered in 1881.

While the army pursued the Sioux, Congress enacted the first of a series of laws fundamentally changing U.S. treaties with the tribe. To punish the Sioux for Little Big Horn, Congress stripped the tribe of the Black Hills and Powder River country, opening both to settlement. Furthermore, they confiscated the rest of the "unceded" areas surveyed in the Fort Laramie Treaty and restricted the Sioux to a now much diminished reservation in South Dakota. Ten years later, again responding to the calls for land by settlers, Congress passed the Sioux Act, which transferred over half of that reservation to the government and established five small reservations at Pine Ridge, Rosebud, Lower Brule, Cheyenne River, and Standing Rock. Effectively, the law made the Sioux wards of the state, dependent upon the government for the needs of life. It was also designed to complement legislation passed a year earlier intended to assimilate Native Americans.

The Dawes Severalty Act or General Allotment Act of 1887 established a plan whereby Congress envisaged replacing the communal ties of tribal culture with values more suited to life as farmers and businessmen. The legislation gave the executive branch the authority to distribute 160 acres of farm land or 320 acres of grazing land from the reservation to individual families. Smaller parcels of 80 acres could be given to single adults and orphans. The government promised to teach the practice of farming to ease the transition. Furthermore, it would hold the land for 25 years and so prevent sales to unscrupulous land speculators. However, all land left unclaimed on the reservations would be opened for White settlement. Congress hoped the result would be a generation of Native American farmers, ranchers, and entrepreneurs fully integrated into the national economic system. At the same time, they opened more of the Sioux reservation lands for settlement. Where Native Americans held 138 million acres of land when the Act passed, at its repeal the figure had dropped to 48 million.

The Dawes Act failed to assimilate the natives of the Great Plains. In fact, two years after its passage, a new religion found a wide audience among western tribes. In January 1889, a Paiute prophet named Wovoka claimed to have a vision in which all of the Native Americans living and dead would return to earth in the youth of life. With them would come the buffalo and wild game. A natural disaster would then destroy all Whites, allowing the Native Americans to enjoy the life they once knew. Wovoka announced that a messiah was present on earth, and predicted that these events would come to pass in the near future. However, to make the vision real, Native Americans would have to live peacefully with each other and with the Whites. They would also have to perform a dance every six weeks. In what became known as the Ghost Dance, participants formed a circle around a sacred object, danced counter-clockwise, and sang songs. The ceremony lasted for hours, sometimes days. Wovoka had given instructions that a feast should accompany the dance, but some refused food and drink to collapse and experience visions. Several plains tribe adopted the message and rituals. By 1890 they reached the Sioux through contacts with the Shoshone and Arapaho. Further, a small group led by Good Thunder had investigated the Ghost Dance and returned seeking followers among the Sioux.

Historians debate whether or not the Sioux changed Wovoka's message. Some argue that they did not observe his strictures about keeping peace with the Whites. Furthermore, they point to the Ghost Dance shirts, white cloth with feathers and designs, which were worn by dancers in every tribe. However, only among the Sioux did the belief arise that the shirts would protect a person from bullets. Others argue that the Sioux accepted the prophet's message but took defensive measures against the possibility of an attack by Whites.

They had reason to be concerned. Relations with the Department of Interior deteriorated in 1890. As the Sioux debated over the dance, the government prepared to distribute reservation land to settlers under provisions of the Dawes and Sioux Acts. Furthermore, for two years the government failed to deliver funds promised to the tribe while it drastically cut their food allocations. During that time, crops failed and three epidemics visited the Sioux. In these circumstances, many, especially the young men who believed in Wovoka and followed the Ghost Dance, counseled resistance.

If the Sioux were of different minds about the Prophet and whether or not to resist the Department of Interior, Indian agents were convinced that the Ghost Dance activities represented a threat. They reported the "craze," and Wovoka's vision of the imminent annihilation of Whites, to the Department, and demanded the protection of U.S. troops. Officials in Washington again responded, sending 5,000 men under General Nelson Miles to the Rosebud and Pine Ridge Reservations. The army included elements of the 7th Cavalry, Custer's former command. Expecting an attack, the Ghost Dancers found protection in a highland surrounded by cliffs, which became known as the Stronghold.

The arrival of troops also set the Indian Police at the Standing Rock Reservation into action. They had heard rumors that Sitting Bull had converted to the Ghost Dance vision and was preparing to lead the Sioux in another rebellion. When they attempted to arrest him, one of his supporters, a Ghost Dancer, opened fire. In the exchange that followed, Sitting Bull was killed, along with several others on both sides. The medicine man's adherents decided to go to the Cheyenne River Reservation, where they met another band, led by Big Foot. The Chief had once believed Wovoka's prophecy, but had begun to doubt that it would actually happen. He proposed taking the two bands, totaling 120 men and 230 women and children, to Rosebud

Reservation and meeting with the Army about the situation. Informed of Big Foot's movements, General Miles assumed they were hostile in intent. He sent troops from the 7th Cavalry under Major Samuel Whitside to intercept them. On December 28, 1890, they did so. They found Big Foot in a wagon flying a white flag, deathly ill with pneumonia. Whitside ordered his troops to provide the Sioux with rations and Big Foot with medicine, and to accompany the two bands to Wounded Knee.

Colonel James Forsyth arrived with reinforcements, bringing the cavalry total to 500 men, and assumed command. He brought four small pieces of artillery, Hotchkiss guns, which were positioned around the Sioux camp. Forsyth then ordered his troops into the village to disarm the Sioux. They met little resistance, although one Ghost Dancer urged the group to resist. However, a deaf warrior named Black Coyote refused to give up his rifle. When soldiers tried to take it from him, the gun discharged, killing an officer. Fighting between the Sioux and soldiers broke out at close quarters. When they separated, Forsyth bombarded the camp with artillery while troops surrounded the village, cut off escape routes, and sent rifle fire into it. The shooting continued for an hour, directed at men, women, and children indiscriminately. When it ended, between 150 and 300 Sioux lay dead and approximately 50 wounded. The soldiers suffered 25 deaths and 39 wounded.

Wounded Knee ended armed resistance by the Sioux. The government continued to move them onto farms and ranches, while distributing the remaining land to settlers. By 1890 the frontier was closed. An unbroken line of settlement–farms, ranches, and mines–stretched from the Missouri River to California, and railroads linked the wealth of food and ore to the laborers and factories of the eastern industrial cities.

Considering the Evidence in the Readings

The documents in this chapter focus on two violent conflicts that took place between the Sioux and U.S. troops. They provide the Sioux accounts of battles of the Little Bighorn and Wounded Knee. They also examine the Native American understanding of the Ghost Dance in the events leading to Wounded Knee. One document by the Commissioner of Indian Affairs provides the official U.S. Government understanding of why the massacre that followed took place. As you read these documents, look for similarities and differences in the accounts. Try to piece together the pieces of evidence to gain an overall understanding of how the conflicts proceeded and why they took place. Finally, both battles have been called massacres. What do we mean by that term and were they, in fact, massacres?

Document 14.1 A Sioux Woman's Account of the Battle of Little Big Horn

This document gives a Sioux Woman's account of the Battle. Focus on how the battle started and how it developed. Was it a massacre? You might want to look at the Chapter Introduction for an overview of the battle. This eyewitness account describes the movements of Reno's column as well as Custer's.

Account given to Walter S. Campbell in 1931

I was born seventy-seven winters ago, near Grand River, [in present-day] South Dakota. My father, Slo-

han, was the bravest man among our people. Fifty-five years ago we packed our tents and went with other Indians to Peji-slawakpa (Greasy Grass). We were then living on the Standing Rock Indian Reservation. I belonged to Sitting Bull's band. They were great fighters. We called ourselves Hunkpapa. This

---

means confederated bands. When I was still a young girl (about seventeen) I accompanied a Sioux war party which made war against the Crow Indians in Montana. My father went to war 70 times. He was wounded nearly a dozen times.

But I am going to tell you of the greatest battle. This was a fight against Pehin-hanska (General Custer). I was several miles from the Hunkpapa when I saw a cloud of dust rise beyond a ridge of bluffs in the east. The morning was hot and sultry. Several of us Indian girls were digging wild turnips. I was then 23 years old. We girls looked towards the camp and saw a warrior ride swiftly, shouting that the soldiers were only a few miles away and that the women and children including old men should run for the hills in an opposite direction.

I dropped the pointed ash stick which I had used in digging turnips and ran towards my tipi. I saw my father running towards the horses. When I got to my tent, mother told me that news was brought to her that my brother had been killed by the soldiers. My brother had gone early that morning in search for a horse that strayed from our herd. In a few moments we saw soldiers on horseback on a bluff just across the Greasy Grass (Little Big Horn) River. I knew that there would be a battle because I saw warriors getting their horses and tomahawks.

I heard Hawkman shout, Ho-ka-he! Ho-ka-he! (Charge.) The soldiers began firing into our camp. Then they ceased firing. I saw my father preparing to go to battle. I sang a death song for my brother who had been killed.

My heart was bad. Revenge! Revenge! For my brother's death. I thought of the death of my young brother, One Hawk. Brown Eagle, my brother's companion on that morning, had escaped and gave the alarm to the camp that the soldiers were coming. I ran to a nearby thicket and got my black horse. I painted my face with crimson and unbraided my black hair. I was mourning. I was a woman, but I was not afraid.

By this time the soldiers (Reno's men) were forming a battle line in the bottom about a half mile away. In another moment I heard a terrific volley of carbines. The bullets shattered the tipi poles. Women and children were running away from the gunfire. In the tumult I heard old men and women singing death songs for their warriors who were now ready to attack the soldiers. The chanting of death songs made me brave, although I was a woman. I saw a warrior adjusting his quiver and grasping his tomahawk. He started running towards his horse when he suddenly

recoiled and dropped dead. He was killed near his tipi.

Warriors were given orders by Hawkman to mount their horses and follow the fringe of a forest and wait until commands were given to charge. The soldiers kept on firing. Some women were also killed. Horses and dogs too! The camp was in great commotion.

Father led my black horse up to me and I mounted. We galloped towards the soldiers. Other warriors joined in with us. When we were nearing the fringe of the woods, an order was given by Hawkman to charge. Ho-ka-he! Ho-ka-he! Charge! Charge! The warriors were now near the soldiers. The troopers were all on foot. They shot straight, because I saw our leader killed as he rode with his warriors.

The charge was so stubborn that the soldiers ran to their horses and, mounting them, rode swiftly towards the river. The Greasy Grass river was very deep. Their horses had to swim to get across. Some of the warriors rode into the water and tomahawked the soldiers. In the charge the Indians rode among the troopers and with tomahawks unhorsed several of them. The soldiers were very excited. Some of them shot into the air. The Indians chased the soldiers across the river and up over a bluff.

Then the warriors returned to the bottom where the first battle took place. We heard a commotion far down the valley. The warriors rode in a column of fives. They sang a victory song. Someone said that another body of soldiers were attacking the lower end of the village. I heard afterwards that the soldiers were under the command of Long Hair (Custer). With my father and other youthful warriors I rode in that direction.

We crossed the Greasy Grass below a beaver dam (the water is not so deep there) and came upon many horses. One soldier was holding the reins of eight or ten horses. An Indian waved his blanket and scared all the horses. They got away from the men (troopers). On the ridge just north of us I saw blue-clad men running up a ravine, firing as they ran.

The dust created from the stampeding horses and powder smoke made everything dark and black. Flashes from carbines could be seen. The valley was dense with powder smoke. I never heard such whooping and shouting. "There was never a better day to die," shouted Red Horse. In the battle I heard cries from troopers, but could not understand what they were saying. I do not speak English.

Long Hair's troopers were trapped in an enclosure. There were Indians everywhere. The Cheyennes attacked the soldiers from the north and Crow King from the South. The Sioux Indians encircled the troopers. Not one got away! The Sioux used tomahawks. It was not a massacre, but [a] hotly contested battle between two armed forces. Very few soldiers were mutilated, as oft has been said by the whites. Not a single soldier was burned at the stake. Sioux Indians do not torture their victims.

After the battle the Indians took all the equipment and horses belonging to the soldiers. The brave men who came to punish us that morning were defeated; but in the end, the Indians lost. We saw the body of Long Hair. Of course, we did not know who the soldiers were until an interpreter told us that the men came from Fort Lincoln, then [in] Dakota Territory. On the saddle blankets were the cross saber insignia and the letter seven.

The victorious warriors returned to the camp, as did the women and children who could see the battle from where they took refuge. Over sixty Indians were killed, and they were also brought back to the camp for scaffold burial. The Indians did not stage a victory dance that night. They were mourning for their own dead. . . .

Document 14.2 A Sioux Man's Account of the Battle of Little Big Horn

This document provides another eyewitness account of the battle. Focus on how the battle started and how it developed. What does he add to the Sioux woman's account about Reno's and Custer's actions? Was the battle a massacre? How did it end? Again, you might want to refer to the Chapter Introduction for an overview of the battle.

I was in Sitting Bull's camp on [Little] Big Horn River, One Horn Band Hinkowoji [Minneconjou] Tepee. They were called that because they planted their gardens near the river. Itazipco (Without Bow, or Sans Arc) was another band. Ogalala was the Red Cloud band. Another band, Schiyeio, means Cheyenne. They were a different tribe, not Lakota. They were friends of Lakota.

Pili (Gall) had another band. All the different bands camped together. There were many other chiefs with their bands, Four Horn and Two Moon and many others. Whenever the chiefs held a council, they went to Sitting Bull's camp because he was a good medicine man.

Lakota and Cheyennes had gone to this camp to look after their buffalo and so young men and women could get acquainted. White men had driven our buffalo away from Lakota land. So we went where buffalo were to take care of them and keep white men away.

I was a strong young man 22 years old. On the day of the fight I was sitting in my tepee combing my hair. I don't know what time it was. About this time maybe (2:00 P.M.). Lakota had no watches in those days. I had just been out and picketed my horses and was back in my tepee. I saw a man named Fat Bear come running into camp, and he said soldiers were coming on the other side of the river and had killed a boy named Deeds, who went out to picket a horse. Then I came out of my tepee and saw soldiers running their horses toward our camp on same side of the river. We could hear lots of shooting. I went to [the] tepee of my uncle, Sitting Bull, and said I was going to go take part in the battle. He said, "Go ahead, they have already fired."

I had a rifle and plenty of shells, but I took that off and gave it to Sitting Bull, and he gave me a shield. Then I took the shield and my tomahawk and got on my horse and rode up to where the soldiers were attacking us. They were firing pretty heavy. They were all down near the river in the timber. Lakota were riding around fast and shooting at them. I rode up to some Lakota and said, "Let's all charge at once." I raised my tomahawk and said, "Wakon-tanka, help me so I do not sin but fight my battle." I started to charge. There were five Lakota riding behind me. We charged for some soldiers that were still fighting, and they ran to where their horses were in the timber. Then the soldiers all started for the river. I turned my horse and started that way too, and there was a man

From *Lakota and Cheyenne: Indian Views of the Great Sioux War*, 1876-1877, edited by Jerome A. Green. Copyright © 1994 by the University of Oklahoma Press. Reprinted by permission.

named Mato Wasbte (Pretty Bear) right behind me, and he and his horse were shot down. I followed the soldiers. They were running for the river. I killed two with my tomahawk. Then the soldiers got across the river. I came back to where Pretty Bear was and got him up on my horse. He was wounded and covered with blood. I started my horse toward the river where the soldiers were, trying to get across.

Then I let Pretty Bear get off my horse, and I went across the river after the soldiers. I killed one more of them with my tomahawk.

Then I saw four soldiers ahead of me running up the hill. I was just about to charge them when someone rode along beside me and said, "You better not go any farther. You are wounded." That was Sitting Bull. I was not wounded, but I was all covered with blood that got on me when I had Pretty Bear on my horse. So I did what Sitting Bull told me. Then Sitting Bull rode back, but I went on. Another Lakota went after these four soldiers. He had a rifle and shot one of them off his horse. One of the soldiers kept shooting back but without hitting us. The man that was with me was a Lakota, but I did not know who he was. Now the soldiers were getting together up on the hill, and we could see the other soldiers coming with the pack mules a long way off.

Then I went back across the river and rode down it a way; then I rode with the man who was shooting at the four soldiers, and we crossed the river again just east of Sitting Bull's camp. We saw a bunch of horsemen up on a hill to the north, and they were Lakotas. We rode up to them and I told them I had killed a lot of soldiers and showed them my tomahawk. Then I said I was going up and help kill Custer's soldiers, but Sitting Bull told me not to go so I didn't go but we rode up where we could see the Lakotas and Cheyennes killing Custer's men. The had been shooting heavy, but the Indians charged them straight from the west and then some rode around them shooting, and the Indians were knocking them off their horses and killing them with tomahawks and clubs. THEY WERE ALL KILLED. There were a lot of Sioux killed. The others were picking them up on their horses and taking them back to camp.

Then we had a war dance all night, and in the morning we heard that the soldiers with the pack mules were up on the hill, and the Sioux started up after them. I went with Sitting Bull and volunteered to go help kill these soldiers, but Sitting Bull said no. So we watched the fight from a hill. I didn't have my rifle with me then, just my tomahawk. The Sioux surrounded them and they fought that way all day. The soldiers had ditches dug all around the hill. Then along towards sundown the Sioux broke camp and went to the mountains.

The Sioux did not take any prisoners that I know of. I didn't see any. I don't know how many Indians there were, but it was a very big band. Many bands together. The Indians had rifles with little short cartridges. I didn't use mine.

After the fight we all stayed in the Big Horn Mountains about ten days. After that they broke camp and went north following along the Tongue River. Then we went to the Little Missouri, and we found a place where there must have been some soldiers, for we found a lot of sacks of yellow corn piled up. Then some of the bands went one way and some went another. One little band went to Slim Buttes, and they were all killed by soldiers.

I was with Sitting Bull all the time we were in camp on the [Little] Big Horn and saw him during the battle. He was telling his men what to do. The first I knew of any soldiers was when they killed the boy who went to picket his horse across the river from Sitting Bull's camp. Before we broke camp that night, we saw the walking soldiers coming from down the river, but my uncle said, "We won't fight them. We have killed enough. We will go...."

Document 14.3 An Indian Scout's Account of the Battle of Little Big Horn

This document provides another eyewitness account of the battle. This source rode with Major Reno during the battle and so relates the story of the battle from the other side. Focus on his understanding of what Custer should have done, or what they expected to happen because of Custer's orders. Is his account of the battle similar to the two Sioux accounts? How did the battle start and develop? How did it end? Was it a massacre? Again, you might want to refer to the Chapter Introduction for an overview of the battle.

Reno Charge and Retreat— into the Night

General [Lieutenant Colonel] Custer, with his Seventh Cavalry, a pack train carrying fifteen days' rations and extra cartridges, his own scouts, and six Crow scouts under John Bruyer [Mitch Bouer], from Gibbon's command, left the mouth of the Rosebud about noon, June 22d. My brother and I rode with an old friend of ours. Frank [Fred] Girard [Gerard], a man who had once been captured by Crazy Horse's band of Sioux, and had lived with them so long that he had acquired no little of their ways, and their religion.

On the third day, we struck the trail of the hostiles, the one that Reno had found several days before. And what a trail it was; a trail all of three hundred yards wide, and deeply worn by travois, and lodge-pole ends. We went into camp close to the trail, and, cooking our supper, we scouts counciled together about the outlook. All agreed that at least fifteen hundred lodges of the enemy had made that broad trail. Said [the Arikara scout] Bloody Knife: "My friends, this big trail proves what we heard, that the Ogalalla, Minneconjou, Sans Arc, and Teton Sioux have left their agencies to join Sitting Bull and Crazy Horse; but I am sure that even this trail does not account for all that have left their agencies. There surely are other trails of them; and trails, too, of Cheyennes and Arapahoes."

"Many Yanktonnais and Assiniboin have answered Sitting Bull's call for help, and joined him," said Frank Girard.

"Yes. They too," Bloody Knife continued. "It is as I have told Long Hair: this gathering of the enemy tribes is too many for us. But he will not believe me. He is bound to lead us against them. They are not far away; just over this ridge, they are all encamped and waiting for us. Crazy Horse and Sitting Bull are not men-without-sense; they have their scouts out, and some of them surely have their eyes upon us. Well, to-morrow we are going to have a big fight, a losing fight. Myself, I know what is to happen to me; my sacred helper has given me warning that I am not to see the set of to-morrow's sun."

Sad words, those. They chilled us. I saw [scout] Charlie Reynolds nod agreement to them, and was chilled again when he said in a low voice: "I feel as he does: tomorrow will be the end for me, too. Any one who wants my little outfit of stuff—pointing to his war

sack—"can have it right now." He opened it, began passing out tobacco; a sewing-kit; several shirts and so on. Many refused the presents; those who accepted them did so with evident reluctance.

We had little appetite for our coffee and hardtack, and the meat that we were broiling. While we were eating, word was passed from mess to mess to put out the fires. That was quickly done, and soon afterward, Lieutenant [Charles A.] Varnum, who was in charge of the scouts, came over and said that it was General Custer's plan to attempt a surprise attack upon the camp of the enemy. The command was to rest until about midnight, and then again take the trail; some of us scouts, meantime, were to push on ahead and try to locate the camp.

Said Bloody Knife: "We cannot surprise the enemy! They are not crazy; without doubt their scouts have watched every move that we have made."

"Well, Bloody Knife, that is probably true, but we must try to surprise them, must we not?"

"Yes, o' course. We try." he replied.

"Very well. We will go out in three parties: Bryer, you take two of your Crows and go forward on the right of the trail. Bloody Knife, you take the left of the trail, with two of your Rees. You Jackson boys, and you, Reynolds, come with me on the trail," ordered Varnum.

We saddled our horses, mounted, and struck out all together. We kept together for all of a mile, and then Bruyer and the Crows and Bloody knife and the Rees branched off and left us to follow the trail. We moved on cautiously, often stopping to listen for the barking of camp dogs in answer to the howling of the wolves, and to look for the red gleam of sparks from some sick one's lodge-fire. So we went on and on through the night, getting no sight or sound of the enemy. At dawn, the command overtook us, and Lieutenant Varnum reported to General Custer. There we rested and had some breakfast.

While we were eating, several of the packers rode swiftly up through the command to General Custer, and we soon learned that they had lost a box of hardtack off one of the mules, and, on going back, had found some Indians around it, stuffing the contents into their clothing. None could now doubt that the enemy had all along kept watch of our advance. With a grim laugh, Charlie Reynolds said to me: "I knew well enough that they had scouts ahead of us, but I

From *Battles and Skirmishes of the Great Sioux War*, 1876-1877, edited by Jerome A. Green. Copyright © 1993 by the University of Oklahoma Press. Reprinted by permission.

didn't think that others would be trailing along to pick up stuff dropped by our careless packers."

Convinced at last that we could not possibly surprise the enemy, General Custer ordered a quick advance, with the scouts and himself in the lead. We had not gone far when Bloody Knife and his two Rees joined us, and reported that on the other side of the ridge they had found the day-old trail of many more of the enemy going toward the valley of the Little Bighorn.

On we went over the divide. We soon met John I'Bruyer and his two Crows. They were excited, and Bruyer said to Custer: "General, we have discovered the camp, down there on the Little Horn. It is a big one! Too big for you to tackle! Why, there are thousands and thousands of Sioux and Cheyennes down there."

For a moment the general stared at him, angrily, I thought, and then sternly replied: "I shall attack them! If you are afraid, Bruyer—"

"I guess I can go wherever you do," Bruyer quickly answered; and at that, the general turned back to the command, we following him. He had the bugler sound the officers' call, and the command rested while they got together, and Custer gave his orders for the attack upon the camp.

None of the scouts had been far in the lead, and they all came in. Rees and Crows and whites and Robert and I, we were a gathering of solemn faces. Speaking in English, and the sign language, too, so that all would understand Bruyer described the enemy camp. It was, he said, all of three miles long, and made up of hundreds and hundreds of lodges.

Above it and below and west of it were thousands and thousands of horses that were being close-herded. With his few riders, Long Hair had decided to attack the camp, and we were going to have a terrible fight; we should all take courage, fight hard, make our every shot a killer. He finished, and none spoke. But after a minute or two, Bloody Knife looked up and signed to Sun: "I shall not see you go down behind the mountains to-night." And at that I almost choked. I felt that he knew that his end was near, that there was no escaping it. I turned and looked the other way. I thought that my own end was near. I felt very sad.

The officers' council did not last long, and, when it ended, Lieutenant Varnum came hurrying to us scouts and said that the command was going to split up to make the attack on the camp, and that we were to go with Major Reno's column, down the trail of the hostiles that we had been following from the Rosebud. We were soon in the saddle and headed down a narrow valley toward the river.

Bruyer told us that the big camp of the enemy was well below the foot of the narrow valley and on the other side of the Little Bighorn. We crossed the river, turned straight down the valley, went down it for more than a mile, and saw some of the enemy retreating before our advance. A grove of timber in a bend below prevented our seeing their camp. As we neared the timber, we heard a single shot fired beyond it, and then the Indians began firing at us. We then went on, and, passing the timber, saw a great camp, and a horde of riders coming up from it to attack us. We all turned into the timber then, and got our horses into an old timber and brush dry channel of the river.

Within two minutes from the time that we left our horses, and climbed up the bank from them, we had a line of defense in the brush and out across toward the west bluff of the valley. Then came the rush of the enemy, all of five hundred well-mounted riders in all their war finery, eager to get at us. Their shots, their war-cries, the thunder of their horses' feet were deafening.

It was the intention of the enemy to charge straight through the center of our line, but, by the time they had come within fifty yards, we had shot so many of them that they swung out and went streaming past the other end of our line, lying low upon their horses and firing rapidly. The dust that their swift charge raised—the ground was very dry—almost choked us: it drifted upon us like a thick fog, and obscured the sun.

As the enemy were coming straight at our line, Robert, at my side in the brush, exclaimed, "Look! That one on the big white horse! He's Black Elk!"

So he was Black Elk, our enemy of the Round Butte and Fort Buford. We both fired at him, our shots apparently missing, but, just as he with the others was swerving off to flank us, he suddenly pitched head first from his horse, and Robert shouted to me: "I got him!"

Several hundred of the enemy went thundering past that outer end of our line, and, swinging in, began attack upon our rear; others were starting to cut us off from the river, and more and more arrivals from the camp swarmed in front of us. I thought that we were about to meet our end right there, every one of us. Then an officer ordered us in to our horses. By the time we got to them, we were entirely surrounded. As we mounted, a man right beside me fell dead out of his saddle. I saw Bloody Knife, Reynolds, and Girard all getting upon their horses. I saw Major Reno, hatless, a handkerchief tied around his head, getting up on his plunging horse. Waving his six-shooter, he shouted something that I couldn't hear, and led swiftly off, up out of the depression that we were in. We all swarmed after him, and headed back up the way that we had come, our intention being to recross the river and get up onto the bluffs, where we could make a stand. By this time hundreds more of the enemy had come up from the camp, and all together they swarmed in on us and a hand-to-hand fight with them began.

I saw numbers of our men dropping from their horses, saw horses falling, heard their awful neighs of fright and pain. Close ahead of me, Bloody Knife, and then Charlie Reynolds, went down, right there met the fate that they had foretold.

A big heavy-set Indian brushed up against me, tried to pull me out of the saddle, and I shot him. Then, right in front, a soldier's horse was shot from under him, and as I came up, he grasped my right stirrup and ran beside me. I had to check my horse so that he could keep up, and so began to lag behind. Numbers of Indians were passing on both sides of us, eager to get at the main body of the retreat. At last one of the passing Indians made a close shot at the soldier and killed him, and, as I gave my horse loose rein, Frank Girard came up on my left, and we rode on side by side. Ahead, there was now a solid body of Indians between us and the retreating, hard-pressed soldiers, and Girard shouted to me: "We can't go through them! Let's turn back!"

Indians were still coming on from the direction of the camp, and, as we wheeled off to the left, and then went quartering back toward the timber, several of them shot at us, but we finally got into thick, high brush, dismounted and tied our horses. Just then we saw some one coming toward us, and were about to fire at him when we discovered that he was Lieutenant [Charles C.] De Rudio. He told us that his horse had run away from him. As we stood there, listening to the heavy firing up on the river, we were joined by [Private] Thomas O'Neil, of Company G, also horseless.

Lieutenant De Rudio asked that Girard and I put our horses farther back in the brush, and then all four look for a hiding-place. We did that, and were soon lying in a small, round, sandy depression surrounded by brush, about twenty yards from the open flat, up which a few Indians were still hurrying from the camp below. We lay each of us facing a different direction.

The sound of the fighting up the river seemed to be farther and farther from us. We learned later that, after we were cut off from the retreat, the enemy, at least a thousand of them against Reno's one hundred, drove the troops down a steep bank into the river and began following them across it. On the other side was a very high, steep bank, and some of the troops man-

aged to get up onto it and check the Indians until the remaining troops got up, when they all went to the top of the main bluffs and there made a stand, and were there joined by [Captain Frederick W.] Benteen and his three companies, and then by [Captain Thomas B.] MacDougall and the pack train. They then went north along the bluffs, to try to find General Custer's column and join it, but were driven back to the point from which they started.

Great numbers of the enemy now went down the flat in front of us, riding fast, and we heard heavy firing away down the valley and knew that they were fighting Custer there. The sun beat down upon us, and we began to suffer from heat and thirst. Women from the camp came up on horseback, on foot, and leading travois-horses, and began carrying off their dead and wounded, and stripping our dead of their clothing, and slashing their bodies. That was a tough sight. Said O'Neil: "That's the way they will cut us up if they get us."

"But does it matter what happens to our bodies after we die! The point is, we mustn't die!" Girard exclaimed.

As the day wore on, we suffered terribly from want of water. We seldom spoke to one another; just watched and suffered.

When night came, we decided to try to make our way to the remains of our column, several miles up the river, and on the bluffs on the opposite side. Girard and I were to ride our horses, the others walking close at our side. Then, if we were discovered, De Rudio and O'Neil were to drop down flat upon the ground, and we were to ride away, drawing the enemy after us.

We were no sooner out of the brush than we began to pass the bodies of the men and horses that had been killed along the line of Reno's retreat. The men had all been stripped of their clothing, and were so badly cut up that, try as I would, I could not force myself to see if my brother were one of the slain.

We went on to the river, coming to a halt at the edge of a bank dropping straight down to the water; on the other side, a high, black, very steep bank faced us. Close under us the current was swift but noiseless, and we doubted that it was fordable. O'Neil jumped in to ascertain the depth, went in almost to his neck and would have been carried downstream had he not seized some overhanging brush and drawn himself to footing closer in. He filled his hat with water and passed it up to De Rudio, who handed it to me. I drank every drop it contained and wanted more. After the hat had been filled and passed up again and again, De Rudio got down into the stream to test its current and depth, and soon agreed with O'Neil that it was too swift and deep for us to ford. We went on up the shore, looking for a place to cross.

Back of us, down the valley, the enemy had built many fires in the open, and were singing, dancing, and counting their *coups* around them. Ahead of us was black darkness, heavy silence. As we went on, our hearts became more and more heavy; we feared that all of the troops had been killed.

We came to a place where the river was rippling and murmuring, as water does over a shallow stony bed, and De Rudio urged that we attempt to ford it there. I saw Girard, close beside me, take his watch out—it was a valuable gold watch—hold it aloft; and then, in Sioux, he murmured: "Oh Powerful One, Day Maker! And you, people of the depths, this I sacrifice to you. Help us, I pray you, to cross safely here!" And with that, he tossed out the watch. We heard it splash into the water. "What were you saying—what was that splash?" De Rudio asked.

"Take hold of my horse's tail, I will lead in," Girard replied. In we went, slowly, feeling our way. Nowhere across was the water up to our horses' knees! When we reached the other shore I bit my lips hard to keep from laughing; all for nothing had been Girard's sacrifice to his gods.

Here on the other shore was high grass and thick brush. We went quartering up through it, and realized eventually that we were on an island. We found ourselves facing the main channel of the river. As no shots had been fired on the opposite bluffs since nightfall, we now believed that the remnant of Reno's troops had been killed up there, and, after some talk, decided to go up where we had crossed the river after separating from Custer and Benteen, and take the back trail for Powder River.

Girard led off up the island, with De Rudio at his side, and I followed with O'Neil on the left of my horse. We had not gone more than two hundred yards, when, from a clump of brush not far ahead, a deep voice demanded in Sioux: "Who are you!"

The sudden challenge almost stunned me. I saw De Rudio and O'Neil drop down into the waist-high grass, heard Girard reply, as he checked up his horse: "Just us few."

"And where are you going?"

"Out here a way," Girard calmly answered as he turned and rode back past me, saying: "Quick! We must draw them after us!"

We rode swiftly down the island for several hundred yards, saw that we were not pursued, and stopped, then heard a few shots up where we had left De Rudio and O'Neil, and a moment later heard the splashing of horses crossing the west channel of the river, and then the thudding of their feet as they went swiftly down the flat toward the enemy camp.

"Those Indians were pickets! Reno's outfit has not been wiped out; it is still on the bluffs on the other side," I said.

"Right you are!" Girard replied.

We knew that our friends had fired the shots and frightened that group of pickets so badly that they had left the island. We did not dare return to them, lest we should reveal their hiding-place to others of the enemy; all up and down the valley the brush might be full of them. We were ourselves in great danger, crashing through the brush with our horses, and decided that, if we were ever to rejoin the troops, we should have to do it on foot. We tied our horses in a dense growth of willows, left the island, and went on up the valley. Below, the Indians were still dancing and singing victory songs around their open fires.

A little way above the head of the island, we came to a very wide reach of the river that looked as though it was fordable, and decided to try it. As we were taking off our shoes and socks and trousers, I whispered to Girard: "If you had your watch now to sacrifice it"

"I have given it; I have faith that we shall cross," he answered.

We waded in, each carrying a stick with which we prodded ahead for quicksand or sudden drop of the bottom. On the other side we ran up into the brush, put on our clothes, and, with rifles cocked and ready, started on. Moving cautiously, we began climbing a steep brush and timber slope. We had reached a height from which, looking down the valley, we could see the many dancing fires of the enemy, when I stepped upon a dry stick that broke with a loud snap.

Close above us, a Sioux said: "Spotted Elk, did you hear that?"

"Yes, Maybe a deer," came the reply, up off to our left.

"I am thirsty; let us go down to the river," said another picket, above on the right, and at that, Girard and I turned and went leaping down the slope. I stumbled and fell over a log and crashed into a clump of rose-brush.

Below me, still another picket cried out. "What is the trouble up there?"

"Something running; sounds like a bear," one off to my left replied.

As I sat up, I could no longer hear Girard, and did not know whether he had stopped or gone back to the river. There were Sioux below me, above me, probably others scattered all along the slopes running up to the bluffs. The one who had said that he was thirsty said, "Any one going to the river with me?"

None replied. I heard him go down the slope; after a time, go back up it. Then all was silent. Weakened by lack of sleep and food, I began to *doze* as I sat there in the brush, surrounded though I was by the enemy. My head would nod. I would lean over more and more until about to lose my balance, then straiten up with a jerk. After a time I realized that I had slept, for I felt refreshed. I opened my eyes and saw that day was coming. All was still quiet there on the slope and down in the valley. Then, in the half-light of the coming day, a number of shots were fired below. This aroused the pickets surrounding me. One of them cried out: "There are still a few soldiers alive down there!"

"Yes. But probably those shots ended them," said another.

"Let us go down and see," one to my left proposed.

"You know that Gall told us to stay up here until he comes to make the big attack," said another.

"Well, anyhow, we can go down to our horses, and be ready to join him when he comes with his many," still another proposed.

"Yes, yes. Let us do that," the others agreed, and I heard them coming down on each side of me. I crouched still lower in my little brush corral. One of them passed within fifteen feet of me, the tail of his war bonnet fluttering behind him. As they went, a few more shots were fired, down in the valley. I may as well explain right here what was taking place down there:

When Girard and I left De Rudio and O'Neil, they remained on the island. In the dim light of dawn, they saw a large number of riders going up the valley, made out that one of them was wearing buckskin clothes, were sure that they recognized him, and De Rudio shouted: "Tom Custer! Wait!"

The answer to that was forty or fifty shots that struck all around the two, strangely enough, not one of them taking effect. They ran, dodging this way and that way around the thick clump of brush, and finally, coming to a big jam of driftwood and brush, they dropped down in it, and none came to look for them there.

This was because, just at that time, heavy firing broke out on top of the bluffs, and the party that was searching for them hurried to cross the river and join in the daylight attack upon Reno's position. The hillside pickets who had gone down past me came hurrying up on their horses and passed on each side of my brush patch as they went on to get into the fight. The firing on the day before had been terrible, but this was far heavier. I concluded that Reno and Custer and Benteen had got their troops together, and were doing the best that they could against three thousand Sioux and Cheyennes. I did not have the slightest hope that they would last an hour, so great were the odds against them.

After a time, the firing slackened, died out, and I said to myself: "That settles it; the last ones of the troops have been killed." But soon the shooting broke out again, and I knew that it wasn't the end for them. Then, as the day wore on, and I knew by the sound of the firing that successive attacks upon the troops were being repulsed, I felt that they might hold their position until General Terry, with General Gibbon and his troops, could come to aid them. This was June 26th, the day that they were due to arrive here.

The day wore on. Now and then straggling riders passed up and down near my hiding-place. Late in the afternoon, I heard a commotion below, and, at some risk of discovery, I stood up to see what it was about: a multitude of people, countless bands of horses, were going up the valley. The women and children and old men were moving camp while their warriors continued to fight up on the bluffs. I could hear, more clearly than the firing above, the shrill voices of the women as they sang. They were happy, they were singing victory songs, but still the fighting was going on. I could not understand that. Where was victory for them when the fight was not ended? I worried about it. I got up again, and looked down into the valley: there were more people, more horses in the long broad column going up the valley, than I had ever seen together. I said to myself "Now I understand. Their warriors are so many that they know that they will wipe out the troops. They sing of the sure victory that their fighters are winning." I sank down in my hiding-place with heavy heart.

From that time I saw no more riders on the slope where I lay, and when, at nightfall, the firing entirely ceased, I decided that the last of the troops had been wiped out, and the victorious warriors had passed above me as they went to join their moving camp. Of the three men who had been with me the night before, I believed that De Rudio and O'Neil were dead, and that Girard was probably already on his way back to the Yellowstone. I decided to strike out for there, too. It would be useless for me to go out where the troops had made their last stand; I could not bury the dead, there would be no wounded for the to aid: Sioux and Cheyennes never left any wounded enemies on the field. Well, first I must have some water. I got up, stretched my numb legs, and started for the river.

Document 14.4 A Sioux Account of the Battle of Wounded Knee

This document provides several eyewitness accounts of the Battle at Wounded Knee. All four are Sioux who survived the action. Focus on their explanation of why the battle took place, especially the role of the Ghost Dance. Also, pay attention to how the battle was fought. The army used very different tactics since the time of the Little Big Horn. Was this a massacre?

The Indian Story of Wounded Knee

Turning hawk, Pine Ridge (Mr Coot, interpreter). Mr Commissioner, my purpose to-day is to tell you what I know of the condition of affairs at the agency where I live. A certain falsehood came to our agency from the west which had the effect of a fire upon the Indians, and when this certain fire came upon our people those who had farsightedness and could see into the matter made up their minds to stand up against it and fight it. The reason we took this hostile attitude to this fire was because we believed that you yourself would not be in favor of this particular mischief-making thing; but just as we expected, the people in authority did not like this thing and we were quietly told that we must give up or have nothing to do with this certain movement. Though this is the advice from our good friends in the east, there were, of course, many silly young men who were longing to become identified with the movement, although they knew that there was nothing absolutely bad, nor did they know there was anything absolutely good, in connection with the movement.

In the course of time we heard that the soldiers were moving toward the scene of trouble. After awhile some of the soldiers finally reached our place and we heard that a number of them also reached our friends at Rosebud. Of course, when a large body of soldiers is moving toward a certain direction they inspire a more or less amount of awe, and it is natural that the women and children who see this large moving mass are made afraid of it and be put in a condition to make them run away. At first we thought that Pine Ridge and Rosebud were the only two agencies where soldiers were sent, but we heard that the other agencies fared likewise. We heard and saw that about half our friends at Rosebud agency, from fear at seeing the soldiers, began the move of running away from their agency toward ours (Pine Ridge), and when they had gotten inside of our reservation they there learned that right ahead of them at our agency was another large crowd of soldiers, and while the soldiers were there, there was constantly a great deal of false rumor flying back and forth. The special rumor I have in mind is the threat that the soldiers had come there to disarm the Indians entirely and to take away all their horses from them. That was the oft-repeated story.

So constantly repeated was this story that our friends from Rosebud, instead of going to Pine Ridge, the place of their destination, veered off and went to some other direction toward the "Bad Lands." We did not know definitely how many, but understood there were 300 lodges of them, about 1,700 people. Eagle Pipe, Turning Bear, High Hawk, Short Bull, Lance, No Flesh, Pine Bird, Crow Dog, Two Strike, and White Horse were the leaders.

Well, the people after veering off in this way, many of them who believe in peace and order at our agency, were very anxious that some influence should be brought upon these people. In addition to our love of peace we remembered that many of these people were related to us by blood. So we sent out peace commissioners to the people who were thus running away from their agency.

I understood at the time that they were simply going away from fear because of so many soldiers. So constant was the word of these good men from Pine Ridge agency that finally they succeeded in getting away half of the party from Rosebud, from the place where they took refuge, and finally were brought to the agency at Pine Ridge. Young-Man-Afraid-of-his-Horses, Little Wound, Fast Thunder,

---

From the *Report of the Commissioner of Indian Affairs for 1891*, volume 1, pages 179-181. Extracts from verbatim stenographic report of council held by delegations of Sioux with Commissioner of Indian Affairs, at Washington, February 11, 1831.

Louis Shangreau, John Grass, Jack Red Cloud, and myself were some of these peacemakers.

The remnant of the party from Rosebud not taken to the agency finally reached the wilds of the Bad Lands. Seeing that we had succeeded so well, once more we sent to the same party in the Bad Lands and succeeded in bringing these very Indians out of the depths of the Bad Lands and were being brought toward the agency. When we were about a day's journey from our agency we heard that a certain party of Indians (Big Foot's band) from the Cheyenne River agency was coming toward Pine Ridge in flight.

Captain Sword. Those who actually went off of the Cheyenne River agency probably number 303, and there were a few from the Standing Rock reserve with them, but as to their number I do not know. There were a number of Ogallalas, old men and several school boys, coming back with that very same party, and one of the very seriously wounded boys was a member of the Ogallala boarding school at Pine Ridge agency. He was not on the warpath, but was simply returning home to his agency and to his school after a summer visit to relatives on the Cheyenne river.

Turning Hawk. When we heard that these people were coming toward our agency we also heard this. These people were coming toward Pine Ridge agency, and when they were almost on the agency they were met by the soldiers and surrounded and finally taken to the Wounded Knee creek, and there at a given time their guns were demanded. When they had delivered them up, the men were separated from their families, from their tipis, and taken to a certain spot. When the guns were thus taken and the men thus separated, there was a crazy man, *a young man of very bad influence and in fact a nobody, among that bunch of Indians fired his gun,* and of course the firing of a gun must have been the breaking of a military rule of some sort, because immediately the soldiers returned fire and indiscriminate killing followed.

Spotted Horse. This man shot an officer in the army; the first shot killed this officer. I was a voluntary scout at that encounter and I saw exactly what was done, and that was what I noticed; that the first shot killed an officer. As soon as this shot was fired the Indians immediately began drawing their knives, and they were exhorted from all sides to desist, but this was not obeyed. Consequently the firing began immediately on the part of the soldiers.

Turning Hawk. All the men who were in a bunch were killed right there, and those who escaped that first fire got into the ravine, and as they went along up the ravine for a long distance they were pursued on both sides by the soldiers and shot down, as the dead bodies allowed afterwards. The women were standing off at a different place from where the men were stationed, and when the firing began, those of the men who escaped the first onslaught went in one direction up the ravine, and then the women, who were bunched together at another place, went entirely in a different direction through an open field, and the women fared the same fate as the men who went up the deep ravine.

American Horse. The men were separated, as has already been said, from the women, and they were surrounded by the soldiers. Then came next the village of the Indians and that was entirely surrounded by the soldiers also. When the firing began, of course the people who were standing immediately around the young man who fired the first shot were killed right together, and then they turned their guns, Hotchkiss guns, etc., upon the women who were in the lodges standing there under a flag of truce, and of course as soon as they were fired upon they fled, the men fleeing in one direction and the women running in two different directions. So that there were three general directions in which they took flight.

There was a women with an infant in her arms who was killed as she almost touched the flag of truce and the women and children, of course were strewn all along the circular village until they were dispatched. Right near the flag of truce a mother was shot down with her infant; the child not knowing that its mother was dead was still nursing, and that especially was a very sad sight. The women as they were fleeing with their babes were killed together, shot right through and the women who were very heavy with child were also killed. All the Indians fled in these three directions, and after most all of them had been killed a cry was made that all those who were not killed or wounded should come forth and. they would be safe. Little boys who were not wounded came out of their places of refuge, and as soon as they came in sight a number of soldiers surrounded them and butchered them there.

Of course we all feel very sad about this affair. I stood very loyal to the government all through those troublesome days, and believing so much in the government and being so loyal to it, my disappointment was very strong, and I have come to Washington with a very great blame on my heart. Of course it would have been all right if only the men were killed; we would feel almost grateful for it. But the fact of the killing of the women, and more especially the killing of the young boys and girls who are to go to make up the future strength of the Indian people, is the saddest part of the whole affair and we feel it very sorely.

I was not there at the time before the burial of the bodies, but I did go there with some of the police and the Indian doctor and a great many of the people, men from the agency, and we went through the battlefield and saw where the bodies were from the track of the blood.

Turning Hawk. I had just reached the point where I said that the women were killed. We heard, besides the killing of the men, of the onslaught also made upon the women and children, and they were treated as roughly and indiscriminately as the men and boys were.

Of course this affair brought a great deal of distress upon all the people, but especially upon the minds of those who stood loyal to the government and who did all that they were able to do in the matter of bringing about peace. They especially have suffered much distress and are very much hurt at heart. These peacemakers continued on in their good work, but there were a great many fickle young men who were ready to be moved by the change in the events there, and consequently, in spite of the great fire that was brought; upon all, they were ready to assume any hostile attitude. These young men got themselves in readiness and went in the direction of the scene of battle so they might be of service there. They got there and finally exchanged shots with the soldiers. This party of young men was made up from Rosebud, Ogallala (Pine Ridge), and members of any other agencies that happened to be there at the time. While this was going on in the neighborhood of Wounded Knee—the Indians and soldiers exchanging shots—the agency, our home, was also fired into by the Indians. Matters went on in this strain until the evening came on, and then the Indians went off down by White Clay creek. When the agency was fired upon by the Indians from the hillside, of course the shots were returned by the Indian police who were guarding the agency buildings.

Although fighting seemed to have been in the air, yet those who believed in peace were still constant at their work. Young-Man-Afraid-of-his-Horses, who had been on a visit to some other agency in the north or North West, returned, and immediately went out to the people living about White Clay creek, on the border of the Bad Lands, and brought his people out. He succeeded in obtaining the consent of the people to come out of their place of refuge and return to the agency. Thus the remaining portion of the Indians who started from Rosebud were brought back into the agency. Mr Commissioner, during the days of the great whirlwind out there, those good men tried to hold up a counteracting power, and that was "Peace." We have now come to realize that peace has prevailed and won the day. While we were engaged in bringing about peace our property was left behind, of course, and most of us have lost everything, even down to the matter of guns with which to kill ducks, rabbits, etc.shotguns, and guns of that order. When Young-Man-Afraid brought the people in and their guns ware asked for both men who were called hostile and men who stood loyal to the government delivered up their guns.

Document 14.5 The Messiah Letter of Wovoka

This document contains the message of the Piaute prophet Wovoka. Wovoka is credited with starting the Ghost Dance that found so many followers among the Plains tribes. It was collected by James Mooney and used to illustrate his 1896 Smithsonian Institution Bureau of American Ethnology. Pay attention to the message itself, what it promises, and how that vision can be achieved.

James Mooney, The Ghost-dance Religion and the Sioux Outbreak of 1890, 14th Annual Report of the Bureau of American Ethnology, Part 2 (1896).

When you get home you must make a dance to continue five days. Dance four successive nights, and the last night keep up the dance until the morning of the fifth day, when all must bathe in the river and then disperse to their homes. You must all do in the same way. I, Jack Wilson [Wovoka], love you all, and my heart is full of gladness for the gifts you have brought me. When you get home I shall give you a good cloud [rain?] which will make you feel good. I give you a good spirit and give you all good paint. I want you to come again in three months, some from each tribe there [the Indian Territory]. There will be a good deal of snow this year and some rain. In the fall there will be such a rain as I have never given you before.

Grandfather [a universal title of reverence among Indians and here meaning the messiah] says, when your friends die you must not cry. You must not hurt anybody or do harm to anyone. You must not fight. Do right always. It will give you satisfaction in life. This young man has a good father and mother. [Possibly this refers to Casper Edson, the young Arapaho who wrote down this message of Wovoka for the delegation].

Do not tell the white people about this. Jesus is now upon the earth. He appears like a cloud. The dead are still alive again. I do not know when they will be here; maybe this fall or in the spring. When the time comes there will be no more sickness and everyone will be young again.

Do not refuse to work for the whites and do not make any trouble with them until you leave them. When the earth shakes [at the coming of the new world] do not be afraid. It will not hurt you.

I want you to dance every six weeks. Make a feast at the dance and have food that everybody may eat. Then bathe in the water. That is all. You will receive good words again from me some time. Do not tell lies.

Document 14.6 A Piaute Account of the Ghost Dance Message

This document contains the testimony of Captain Dick, a Piaute, and some observations by Lieutenant K. P. Phister. James Mooney collected the information for his 1896 Smithsonian Institution Bureau of American Ethnology. Both are discussing the Ghost Dance. Does the message seem the same as that given by Wovoka? What will happen, and how can it be brought about?

We may now consider details of the doctrine as held by different tribes, beginning with, the Piaute, among whom it originated. The best account of the Piaute belief is contained in a report to the War Department by Captain J. M. Lee, who was sent out in the autumn of 1890 to investigate the temper and fighting strength, of the Piaute and other Indians in the vicinity of Fort Bidwell in northeastern California. We give the statement obtained by him from Captain Dick, a Piaute, as delivered one day in a conversational way and apparently without reserve, after nearly all the Indians had left the room:

Long time, twenty years ago, Indian medicine-man in Mason's valley at Walker lake talk same way, same as you hear now. In one year, maybe, after he begin talk he die. Three years ago another medicine-man begin same talk. He talk all time. Indians hear all about it everywhere. Indians come from long' way off to hear him. They come from the east; they make signs. Two years ago me go to Winnemucca and Pyra-mid lake, me Bee Indian Sam, a head man, and Johnson Sides. Sam he tell me he just been to see Indian medicine-man to hear him talk. Sam say medicine-man talk this way :

"All Indians must dance, everywhere, keep on dancing. Pretty soon in next spring Big Man [Great Spirit] come. He bring back all game of every kind. The game be thick everywhere. All dead Indians come back and live again. They all be strong just like young men, be young again. Old blind Indian see again and get young and have fine time. When Old-man [God] comes this way, then all the Indians go to mountains, high up away from whites. "Whites can't hurt Indians then. Then while Indians way up high, big flood comes like water and all white people die, get drowned. After that water go way and then nobody but Indians everywhere and game all kinds thick. Then medicine-man tell Indians to send word to all Indians to keep up dancing and the good time will come. Indians who don't dance, who don't believe in this word, will grow little, just about a foot high, and stay that way. Some of them will be turned into wood and be burned in fire." That's the way Sam tell me the medicine-man talk.

Lieutenant K. P. Phister, who gathered a part of the material embodied in Captain Lee's report, confirms this general statement and gives a few additional particulars. The flood is to consist of mingled mud and water, and when the faithful go up into the mountains, the skeptics will be left behind and will be turned to stone. The prophet claims to receive these revelations directly from God and the spirits of the dead Indians during his trances. He asserts also that he is invulnerable, and that if soldiers should attempt to kill him they would fall down as if they had no bones and die, while he would still live, even though cut into little pieces.

Document 14.7 Kuwapi's Account of the Ghost Dance

This document provides an account of the Ghost Dance given to the Sioux. Kuwapi was promoting the religion among the Sioux. Historians disagree about whether or not the Sioux developed a different version from other tribes. In particular, the issue is whether or not they abandoned Wavoka's insistence upon living peacefully with the Whites. Again, look at the message and promise of the Ghost Dance. How was it to be brought about?

Selwyns Interview with Kuwapi

On November 21,1890, it was reported to Agent B. W. Foster, in charge of Yankton agency, South Dakota, that an Indian named Kuwapi, from Rosebud agency, was on the reservation teaching the doctrine and ceremony of the Ghost dance. He at once had the man arrested by a force in charge of William T. Selwyn, a full-blood Tank-ton Sioux, who had received a fair education under the patronage of a gentleman in Philadelphia, and who had for several years been employed in various capacities at different Sioux agencies. Selwyn had recently come from Pine Ridge, where he had learned and reported to Agent Gallagher something of the religious excitement among the western Sioux, and had afterward repeated this information to the agent at Yankton. While Kuwapi was in his custody Selwyn questioned him at length concerning the new doctrine, and forwarded filed following report.

YANKTON AGENCY, SOUTH DAKOTA
NOVEMBER 1890. COLONEL B.W. FOSTER

United States Indian Agent, Yankton Agency South Dakota

DEAR SIR: It has been reported here a few days ago that there was an Indian visitor up at White Swan from Rosebud agency who has teen telling or teaching the doctrines of the new messiah, and has made some agitation among the people up there. According to the request of Captain Conrad, United States Army, of Fort Randall, South Dakota, and by your order of the 21st instant, I went up to White Swan and have arrested the wanted man (Kuwapi, or One they chased after). On my way to the agency with the prisoner I have made little interview with him on the subject of the new messiah. The following are the facts which he corroborated concerning the new messiah, his laws and doctrines to the Indians of this continent:

Q. Do you believe in the new messiah?
—A. I somewhat believe it.
Q. What made you believe it?
—-A. Because I ate some of the buffalo meat that he (the new messiah) sent to the Rosebud Indians through Short Bull.
Q. Did Short Bull say that he saw the living herd of roaming buffaloes while he was with the son of the Great Spirit?
—A. Short Bull told the Indian at Rosebud that the Buffalo and other wild game will be restored to the

G. D, Document 38861—1890 of the interview to Agent Foster.

Indians at the same time when, the general resurrection in favor of the Indians takes place.

Q. You said a general resurrection in favor of the Indians takes place;" when or how soon will this be?

—A. The father sends word to us that he will have all these earned to be so in the spring, when the grass is knee high.

Q. You said "father;" who is this father?

—A. It is the new messiah. He has ordered his children (Indians) to call him "father."

Q. You said the father is not going to send the buffalo until the resurrection takes place. Would he be able to send a few buffaloes over this way for a sort of a sample, so as to have his children (Indians) to have a taste of the meat?

—A. The father wishes to do things all at once, even in destroying the white race.

Q. You said something about the destroying of the white race. Do you mean to say that all mankind except the Indians will killed?

—A. Yes.

Q. How, and who is going to kill the white people?

—A. The father is going to cause a big cyclone or whirlwind, by which he will have all the white people to perish.

Q. If it should be a cyclone or whirlwind, what are we going to do to protect ourselves?

—A. The father will make some kind of provisions by which we will he saved,

Q. You said something about the coming destruction on the white people by your father. Supposing your father is sick, tired out, forget, or some other accidental cause by which he should not be able to accomplish his purpose, what would be the case about the destroying of the white people?

—A. There is no doubt about these things, as the miracle performer or the father is going to do just as what he said he would do.

Q. What other object could you come to by which you are led to believe that there is such a new messiah on earth at present?

—A. The ghost dancers are fainted whenever the dance goes on.

Q. Do you believe that they are really fainted?

—A. Yes.

Q. What makes you believe that the dancers have really fainted?

—A. Because when they wake or come back to their senses they sometimes bring back some news from the unknown world, and some little trinkets, such as buffalo tail, buffalo meat, etc.

Q. What did the fainted ones see when they fainted?

—A. They visited the happy hunting ground, the camps, multitudes of people, and a great many strange people.

Q. What did the ghost or the strange people tell the fainted one or ones?

— A. When the fainted one goes to the camp, he is welcomed by the relatives of the visitor (the fainted one), and he is also invited to several feasts.

Q. Were the people at Rosebud agency anxiously waiting or expecting to see all of their dead relatives who have died several years ago?

—A. Yes.

Q. We will have a great many older folks when all the dead people come back would we not?

—A. The visitors all say that there is not a single old man nor woman in the other world—all changed to young.

Q. Are we going to die when the dead ones come back?

—A. No; we will be just the same as we are today.

Q. Did the visitor say that there are any white men in the other world?

—A. No, no white people.

Q. If there is no white people in the other world, where did they get their provisions and clothing!

—A. In the other world, the messenger tells us that they have depended altogether for their food on the flesh of buffalo and other wild game; also, they were all clad in skins of wild animals.

Q. Did the Rosebud agency Indians believe the new messiah, or the son of the Great Spirit?

—A. Yes.

Q. How do they show that they have a belief in the new messiah?

—A. They show themselves by praying to the father by looking up to heaven, and call him "father," just the same as you would in a church.

Q. Have you ever been in a church?

—A. No.

Q. Do you faithfully believe in the new messiah?

—A. I did not in the first place, but as I became more acquainted with the doctrines of the new messiah that I really believe in him.

Q. How many people at Rosebud, in your opinion, believe this new messiah?

—A. Nearly every one.

Q. Did you know the Rosebud people prepare to attack the white people this summer? While I was at Pine Ridge agency this summer the Olalla Sioux Indians say they will resist against the government if the latter should try to put a stop to the messiah question. Did your folks at Rosebud say the same thing?

—A. Yes.

Q. Are they still preparing and thinking to attack the white people should the government send our soldiers with orders to put a stop to your new business of the messiah?

—A. I do not know, but I think that the Wojaji band at Rosebud agency will do some harm at any time.

Q. You do not mean to say that the Rosebud Indians will try and cause an outbreak?

—A. That seems to be the case.

Q. You said something about the "son of the Great Spirit," or "the father." What do you mean by the son of the Great Spirit?

—A. This father, as he is called, said himself that he is the son of the Great Spirit.

Q. Have you talked to or with any Indian at White Swan about the new messiah, his laws and doctrines, or have you referred this to anyone while there?

—A. I have told a few of them. I did not voluntarily express my wish for them to know and follow the doctrines of the new messiah.

Q. Yes, but you have explained the matter to the Indians, did you not?

—A. Yes, I have.

Q. Do the Yankton Indians at White Swan believe in your teaching of the new messiah?

—A. I did not intend to teach them, but as I have been questioned on the subject, I have said something about it.

Q. Did any of them believe in you?

—A. Some have already believed it, and some of them did not believe it.

Q. Those that have believed in you must be better men than the others, are they not?

—A. I do not know.

Q. Do you intend to introduce the doctrines of the new messiah from Rosebud to this agency as a missionary of the gospel?

—A. *No,* I did not.

Q. What brings you here, then?

—A. I have some relatives here that I wanted to see, and this was the reason why I came here.

Q. Where does this new messiah question originate? I mean from the first start of it.

—A. This has originated in White Mountains.

Q. Where is this White mountain?

—A. Close to the big Rocky mountains, near the country that belong to the Mexicans.

Q. Do you think that there will lie a trouble in the west by next spring?

—A. Yes.

Q. What makes you think so?

—A. Because that is what I have heard people talk of.

This is all that I have questioned Ktnrapi an the subject of the new messiah.

Respectfully, your obedient servant,
Selwyn

Document 14.8 Commissioner Morgan on the Causes of Wounded Knee

This document contains the conclusions about why Wounded Knee took place, described by the Commissioner of Indian Affairs. Focus on his analysis of why events took place. What were the most important reasons? What role did the Ghost Dance play?

Causes of the Outbreak

Commissioner Morgan's statement

In stating the events which led to this outbreak among the Sioux, the endeavor too often has been merely to find some opportunity for locating blame. The causes are complex, and many are obscure and remote. Among them may be named the following:

First. A feeling of unrest and apprehension in the mind of the Indian has naturally grown out of the rapid advance in civilization and the great changes which this advance has necessitated in their habits and mode of life.

Second. Prior to the agreement of 1876 buffalo and deer were the main support of the Sioux. Food, tents, bedding were the direct outcome of hunting, and with furs and pelts as articles of barter or

From Report of the Commissioner of Indian Affairs for 189?, Vol I, 232–135.

exchange, it was easy for the Sioux to procure whatever constituted for them the necessaries, the comforts, or even the luxuries of life. Within eight years from the agreement of 1876 the buffalo had gone and the Sioux had left to them, alkali land and government rations. It is hard to overestimate the magnitude of the calamity, as they viewed it, which, happened to these people by the sudden disappearance of the buffalo and the large diminution in the numbers of deer and other wild animals. Suddenly, almost without warning, they were expected at once and without previous training to settle down to the pursuits of agriculture in a land largely unfitted for such use. The freedom of the chase was to be exchanged for the idleness of the camp. The boundless range was to be abandoned for the circumscribed reservation, and abundance of plenty to be supplanted by limited and decreasing government subsistence and supplies. Under these circumstances it is not in human nature not to be discontented and restless, even turbulent and violent.

Third. During a long series of years, treaties, agreements, cessions of land and privileges, and removals of bands and agencies have kept many of the Sioux, particularly those at Pine Ridge and Rosebud, in an unsettled condition, especially as some of the promises made them were fulfilled tardily or not at all.

Fourth. The very large reduction of the great Sioux reservation, brought about by the Sioux commission through the consent of the large majority of the adult males, was bitterly opposed by a large, influential minority. For various reasons, they regarded the cession as unwise, and did all in their power to prevent its consummation, and afterwards were constant in their expressions of dissatisfaction and in their endeavors to awaken a like feeling in the minds of those who signed the agreement.

Fifth. There was diminution and partial failure of the crops for 1889, by reason of their neglect by the Indians, who were congregated in large numbers at the council with the Sioux commission, and a further diminution of ordinary crops by the drought of 1890. Also, in 1888, the disease of black leg appeared among the cattle of the Indians.

Sixth. At this time, by delayed and reduced appropriations, the Sioux rations were temporarily cut down. Rations were not diminished to such an. extent as to bring the Indians to starvation or even extreme suffering, as has been often reported but short rations came just after the Sioux commission had negotiated the agreement for the cession of lands, and, as a condition of securing the signatures of

the majority had assured the Indians that their rations would be continued unchanged. To this matter the Sioux commission called special attention in their report dated December 34th, 1889, as follows:

"During our conference at the different agencies who were repeatedly asked whether the acceptance or rejection of the act of Congress would influence the action of the government with reference to their rations, and in every instance the Indians were assured that subsistence was furnished in accordance with former treaties, and that signing would not affect their rations, and that they would continue to receive them as provided in former treaties. Without our assurances to this effect it would have been impossible to have secured their consent to the cession of their lands. Since our visit to the agencies it appears that large reductions have been made in the amounts of beef furnished for issues, amounting at Rosebud to 2,000,000 pounds and at Pine Ridge to 1,000,000 pounds, and lesser amounts at the other agencies. This action of the Department, following immediately after the successful issue of our negotiations, can not fail to have an injurious effect. It will be impossible to convince the Indians that the reduction is not due to the fact that the government, having obtained their land, has less concern in looking after their material interests than before. It will be looked upon as a breach of faith and especially as a violation of the express statements of the commissioners. Already this action is being used by the Indians opposed to the bill, notably at Pine Ridge, as an argument in support of the wisdom of their opposition."

In forwarding this report to Congress the Department called special attention to the above-quoted statements of the commission and said: "The commission further remarks that as to the quality of the rations furnished there seems to be no just cause for complaint, but that it was particularly to be avoided that there should be any diminution of the rations promised under the former treaties at this time, as the Indians would attribute it to their assent to the bill. Such diminution certainly should not be allowed, as the government is bound in good faith to carry into effect the former treaties where not directly and positively affected by the act, and if under the provisions of the treaty itself the ration is at any time reduced, the commissioners recommend that the Indians should be notified before spring opens, so that crops may be cultivated. It is desirable that the recent reduction made should be restored, as it is now impossible to convince the Indians that it was not due to the fact that the government, having obtained their lands, had less concern to looking after their material interests."

Notwithstanding the plea of the commission and of the Department, the appropriation made for the subsistence and civilization of the Sioux for 1890 was only $950,000, or $50,000 less than the amount estimated and appropriated for 1888 and 1889, and the appropriation not having been made until August 19, rations had to be temporarily purchased and issued in limited quantities pending arrival of new supplies to be secured from that appropriation. It was not until January, 1891, after the troubles, that an appropriation of $100,000 was made by Congress for additional beef for the Sioux.

Seventh. Other promises made by the Sioux commission and the agreement were not promptly fulfilled; among them were increase of appropriations for education, for which this office had asked an appropriation of $150,000; the payment of $200,000 in compensation for ponies taken from the Sioux in 1876 and 1877; and the reimbursement of the Crow Creek Indians for a reduction made in their per capita allowance of land, as compared with the amount allowed other Sioux, which, called for an appropriation of $187,039. The fulfillment of all these promises except the last named was contained in the act of January 19, 1891.

Eighth. In 1889 and 1890 epidemics of la grippe, measles, and whooping cough, followed by many deaths, added to the gloom and misfortune which seemed to surround the Indians.

Ninth. The wording of the agreement changed the boundary line between the Rosebud and Pine Ridge diminished reservations and necessitated a removal of a portion of the Rosebud Indians from the lands which, by the agreement, were included in the Pine Ridge reservation to lands offered them in lieu thereof upon the diminished Rosebud reserve. This, although involving no great hardship to any considerable number, added to the discontent.

Tenth. Some of the Indians were greatly opposed to the census which Congress ordered should be taken. The census at Rosebud, as reported by Special Agent Lea and confirmed by a special census taken, by Agent Wxiglit, revealed the somewhat startling fact that rations had been issued to Indians very largely in excess of the number actually present, and this diminution of numbers as shown by the census necessitated a diminution of the rations, which was based, of course, upon the census.

Eleventh. The Messiah craze, which fostered the belief that ghost shirts would be invulnerable to bullets, and that the supremacy of the Indian race was assured, added to discontent the fervor of fanaticism and brought those who accepted the new faith into the attitude of sullen defiance, but defensive rather than aggressive.

Twelfth. The sudden appearance of military upon their reservation gave rise to the wildest rumors among the Indians of danger and disaster, which were eagerly circulated by disaffected Indians and corroborated by exaggerated accounts in the newspapers, and these and other influences connected with and inseparable from military movements frightened many Indians away from their agencies into the had lands and largely intensified whatever spirit of opposition to the government existed.

Chapter 14 Worksheet and Questions

1. Based on Documents 14.1–14.4, what was the U.S. Cavalry's strategy in conducting battle with the Sioux? How did it change between the Battle of Little Big Horn and the Battle of Wounded Knee? Was there reason to believe before the battle that Custer's strategy might not work?

_____

_____

_____

_____

_____

_____

_____

_____

_____

2. Based on Documents 14.1–14.3, was the Battle of Little Big Horn a massacre? What happened?

_____

_____

_____

_____

_____

_____

_____

_____

_____

3. Based on Documents 14.4, was the Battle of Wounded Knee a massacre? What happened?

_____

_____

_____

_____

_____

_____

_____

_____

_____

_____

4. Based on Documents 14.5–14.7, what was Wavoka's prophecy, and how was it to be achieved? Did the Sioux have a different understanding, especially about peaceful relations with Whites?

_____

_____

_____

_____

_____

_____

_____

_____

_____

_____

5. Based on Documents 14.4–14.8, was there reason for Whites to worry about the Ghost Dance? Did all Sioux believe in it? What did Commissioner Morgan think led to Wounded Knee?

_____

_____

_____

_____

_____

_____

_____

_____

_____

_____

6. Based on all documents and the Introduction to the chapter, why did the United States and the Sioux fight? Given the cultural differences between the two groups, and White settlement of the West, could conflict have been avoided?

_____

_____

_____

_____

_____

_____

_____

_____

_____

_____

_____

Chapter 15

Labor and Industry

System, system, system, observed Fred Colvin, editor of the *American Machinist*, in an article about Ford's new Highland Park factory. Such pronouncements impressed late nineteenth- and early twentieth-century inventors, engineers, and business people who believed that system constituted the hallmark of modern technology. The development of a wide range of technological systems during the era provided ample justification for their views. Engineers transformed methods for producing cars, petroleum products, steel, machinery, cigarettes, newspapers, food, and virtually any other commodity. They invented new technological systems for electrical lighting, telephone services, movies, radio, and mass transportation. Even old technologies, like railroads, were systematized with the adoption of air brakes, common rail gauges (the width between rails), and standard time zones.

Contemporaries celebrated these achievements. They also realized that the new systems introduced a number of problems; perhaps the most pressing involved the human element of labor. New industries required unprecedented numbers of workers. Census data suggest the number of jobs in manufacturing increased by four and one-half million between 1860 and 1890. Further, the new industrial systems brought thousands of workers together in factories. By 1910, Carnegie Steel employed 40,000, and McCormick Reaper 15,000. A few years later Ford Motor Company had over 33,000 workers. Nevertheless, engineers noted that technological systems made large-scale production possible. Consequently, they gave it paramount or highest importance when designing, constructing, and operating industrial facilities. The mechanical engineer Frederick W. Taylor wrote authoritatively on this crucial issue, in his *Principles of Scientific Management,* "In the past the man has been first; in the future the system must be first." Few in his audience would have disagreed that the design and arrangement of machinery took precedence over the human considerations of the laborers who tended them.

Nevertheless, the matter of how to rationalize workers with technological processes proved a vexing issue for engineers. For their part, laborers found the adjustment equally daunting. Their responses were as varied and complex as the systems themselves. Workers too were impressed by the systems. Many appreciated how they reduced heavy and difficult work. Others found the loss of autonomy even more disturbing, and sought to have a voice in the system by creating unions. It is this interface between technological systems and human workers that will be the focus of this chapter. We will be examining the arrangement of industrial systems and their consequences for workers in terms of work, working conditions, health, safety, and wages.

By **system**, engineers, business people, and workers meant a rationalized process that produced a standardized product. Engineers rationalized technology by approaching it as a process composed of discrete specialized parts, each of which they designed with reference to the part's specific function or task and to its position in the process as a whole. For example, Ford resolved the manufacture of the parts of the car into a series of separate steps by which engines, brakes, ignitions, and myriad other components were made and machined. Engineers developed special-purpose machines for each step of the process, and arranged the equipment sequentially so that parts moved from one machine to the next. Once completed, the parts moved to sub-assembly rooms, after which they were delivered to appropriate points on the assembly line, where they were attached to what became a Model T. Standardization was equally important. Products produced by rationalized technological processes were identical. Henry Ford described the Model Ts he produced, "as alike as pins." This was true of other systems as well, whether they involved electrical current, gasoline grades, candy bars, or cuts of meat. Clearly then, technological systems varied widely in application; however, all of them employed the fundamental principles of rationalization and standardization in their design and operation.

The example of electric lighting is illuminating. Thomas Edison is popularly credited with inventing the light bulb or electrical incandescent lighting, yet this was not the case. After 1840, several inventors, such as Joseph Swan in England, invented incandescent bulbs. Their lights, however, short-lived and powered by electric batteries, lacked utility. To be sure, Edison produced a functional bulb, but his real achievement lay in inventing an entire electrical lighting system. In fact, he began the project by exploring the possibility of developing a lighting system that would be an economical alternative to gas lighting. Only when he was satisfied that incandescent lighting would be cost-effective did he proceed. Edison then assigned specific tasks to his staff of mechanics, model makers, and engineers at the Menlo Park "invention factory." Edison conceived of the undertaking as one of creating a system composed of distinct parts, each with a specific function and place within the process as a whole.

According to plan, the team developed the generator to produce electricity, feeders and mains to deliver it, and (once inside buildings) the wiring, fuses, sockets, switches, and, of course, meters needed to make electrical lighting possible. Edison developed the light bulb relatively late in the process. As with other systems, the bulb represented one part of a rationalized process. Edison then needed to design it with respect to its *specific function*—that is, a bulb with a filament that lasted a reasonably long period of time—and its *role in the system,* or a bulb that worked with the voltage produced by the generator and transmitted by wiring. Once the Menlo Park wizards had invented and tested the system, they proceeded to standardize the components and market them to cities as a standardized product.

Meat packing underwent a similar transformation. In fact, Henry Ford cited slaughterhouses as one of his inspirations for the moving assembly line. Ford referred to meat packing as a "disassembly line" and simply reversed the process to make cars. In facilities like those of Gustavus Swift, hogs were shackled to overhead cables that moved them from one work station to the next. At each stop, a worker removed one particular piece of the carcass until none of the pig remained. After rationalizing the process, meat packers standardized cuts of meat-steaks, loins, ribs, filets, and the like.

The scale of operations at packing plants like those of Swift and of Armor & Company illustrates another aspect of late nineteenth-century technological systems. Swift introduced the refrigerator car, to move his products across the nation, but particularly to large industrial cities in the northeast. In addition, he used the new telephone system to rationalize his operations by coordinating the purchase of cattle in the western states through his packing houses in Kansas City, Omaha, and Chicago in order to meet demand in the east.

At the same time, Andrew Carnegie oversaw the systematization of steel production at plants in Homestead and Pittsburgh. Carnegie's operations are frequently used to exemplify a corporate strategy called **vertical integration**, in which a company owns and controls every stage of production, from raw materials to finished product. Such arrangements were a manifestation of systematization. Carnegie Steel Co. rationalized the process of steel production by extracting iron ore from the Mesabi Range in Minnesota and mining coal from Pennsylvania. Specialized Great Lakes steamships and railroads cars transported the raw materials to plants in and near Pittsburgh. Workers used the new Bessemer Converters to smelt the iron ore into steel. Subsequently, the metal was cast in molds, as cast steel, or as pigs that were rolled, worked, and cut into rods, wire, and bars.

Standardization typified the manufacture of products made from Carnegie steel as well. Carnegie marketed most of his steel in the form of rails for railroads and construction beams for bridges, like the Eads Bridge across the Mississippi River in St. Louis and the Hannibal Bridge across the Missouri River in Kansas City, as well as for buildings like the new skyscrapers rising in Chicago and New York. Like Armour and Swift in meat packing, Carnegie Steel operated on a huge scale. By 1900, estimates suggest that Carnegies produced 90 percent of the nation's steel, an amount that had grown from 850,000 tons in 1870 to 10,600,000 tons by 1900.

The technological systems represented by steel production, meat packing, and car manufacture constituted a new scale and complexity of operations that were made possible by applying the precepts of **rationalization** and **standardization**. Only when all of the specialized, individual components of the technological processes functioned—both with respect to their particular task and in relation to the other parts of the process—did the system work efficiently. Technologies themselves proved to be tractable, and could be designed with system requirements in mind.

However, labor too had to be rationalized or fitted within the same system. In order to maximize efficiency, laborers had to perform individual tasks optimally and in concert with others in the process. Failure to do so compromised the process and diminished efficiency. Engineers and managers developed a number of different approaches for solving this problem. Because they constructed the systems, they were largely responsible for defining the working conditions, safety, health, and wages: the environment that labor inhabited.

Managers and engineers saw their main purpose in managing labor as adapting workers to specific niches in the production process. Men were assigned to a particular place in the factory process, and were trained to carry out a specific task; they worked at a set rate, and remained for a set period of time. Another new technology, time clocks, recorded when the worker arrived and departed. Frequently, work rules or factory regulations prohibited conversations, drinking, singing, or unscheduled breaks of any sort.

Factories tended to be extraordinarily loud places. Depending upon what was produced, they could be filthy, with an atmosphere containing noxious industrial chemicals, coal smoke, and particles emitted into the air from machine operations. Steel and meat packing plants were notorious in this regard. Considerations of worker health and safety were assigned lower priorities by engineers, for whom rationalizing the system to achieve maximum efficiency was far more important. Legally, too, under "fellow worker rules," laborers assumed responsibility for their own health, welfare, and negligent acts of co-workers. Consequently, factories tended to be dangerous places as well. In railroad yards, men who switched cars to form trains recognized anyone with all of his fingers as a new hire.

The responses of labor to industrial systems were as complex as the systems themselves. Oral accounts given by Connecticut factory workers suggest that as many workers found advantages to the new systems as those who disliked it. The first generation of factory labor, however, reported that the changes were profound. Before systems, workers in manufacturing plants had a great deal of autonomy. They often set their own hours and agreed among themselves about production goals. In the factory itself, foremen, inside-contractors, and craftsmen negotiated and contracted with management for production allotments. Subsequently, they would oversee the work and assure its quality. Hiring, firing, and paying workers also fell within their purview. With the advent of systems, those arrangements ended; instead, managers and engineers assumed direct responsibility for personnel, work rules, production, scheduling, and factory supervision.

Different corporations devised different strategies for rationalizing labor relations. In the packing plants and steel industry, managers like Henry Frick at Carnegie Steel simply demanded that workers conform to the requirements as outlined for each particular job. Since labor was plentiful, workers who did not fit in well, could not perform the job, or resisted factory discipline were dismissed. Some employers, however, explored alternatives. In 1914 the Ford Motor Company introduced the Five Dollar Day. Managers had determined that workers disliked the factory regimen intensely and that they expressed their feelings by walking off the job, temporarily or permanently. In 1913 the turnover rate reached 320 percent; that is, Ford hired and trained slightly more than three work forces every year! By doubling the average wage for auto workers, the company slashed rates of turnover and absenteeism. (The plan had the added advantage of paying workers a wage large enough to afford the $380 Model T they built.)

Frederick W. Taylor initiated the most rigorous movement to achieve efficiency by researching and rationalizing workers interactions with technological systems. The program of Scientific Management was built upon Taylor's belief that workers were inefficient because they "soldiered" or did less work than they could, and because they simply did not know the most efficient ways to conduct work, relying instead upon traditional methods. Viewed from Taylor's perspective or that of a technological system, workers failed both to perform specific tasks well and to understand the overall requirements of the production process. Scientific Management would solve these problems. It would achieve the highest possible efficiency by determining the precise set of motions each worker should make to perform each specific task in the production process. Each job was then subjected to time-and-motion studies, in which stop-watches measured human movements in order to ascertain the ideal motions required for their completion. Workers would then be able to achieve the maximum amount of work in the least amount of time. Overall, managers could now apply scientific studies to determine the requirements of the production process, and could fit the worker to its needs.

Not all industries subscribed to Taylor's scientific approach. Further, while business people and engineers agreed about the necessity of systematization, they applied very different ideas about how to achieve rationalization and standardization. Making clothes vividly illustrates those differences. By 1900, there were two fundamentally different approaches to manufacturing clothes. One involved the use of factories where a centralized management strove to systematize production by rationalizing technological processes and standardizing the product. The other, referred to as the "sweating system" by its opponents, neglected to construct factories and instead rationalized technological processes by distributing clothing to laborers who used sewing machines alone at home or in small groups. In either case, work was performed in "sweatshops" located in the tenement buildings of poor, immigrant neighborhoods. As with factory systems, laborers were given specific tasks, like attaching sleeves or collars to shirts, linings to coats, or buttons to dresses. Upon completion, the "sweater" transferred the pieces to other workers, who completed the next step of the process until the clothing was complete. Workers received low wages, and were paid on a piecework basis.

Advocates of factory production argued that subsistence wages alone made the system competitive, and criticized it for being inefficient and abusive, and a threat to public health. Calling for legislation to regulate the sweating system, they pointed to factories as a remedy to these evils. From their perspective, factories alone were the appropriate place for modern technological systems that could at the same time make adequate provisions for the working conditions, health, safety, and compensation of workers.

Considering the Evidence in the Readings

The documents in this chapter provide a variety of different view points about industrial systems and labor. You will find accounts by workers, authors, social scientists, engineers, and reporters. Despite the variety of perspectives, you should note the similarities in the descriptions of industrial systems, that is a rationalized (each part is distinct but connected to all of the other parts in the system) process that produced standardized products in huge quantities. Further, you should note that all of the sources agree about the power and efficiency of these systems. Think about why the sources agree in their admiration of industrial production. The issue that confronts them then is a human one. How do humans or laborers fit into the system? Should the system be first, if so, what is the cost, in terms of human labor? Do laborers see it the same way?

Document 15.1 "Homestead and Its Perilous Trades"

Americans were fascinated by technological systems and the lives of the workers who toiled in them. This description of Andrew Carnegie's steel plant at Homestead, Pennsylvania presents an overview of the technology used to produce steel and steel products. It also explains how that system was rationalized. Alternatively, the piece provides an account of how workers understood and responded to their environment. The author, Hamlin Garland, was a popular author best known for his novels about the Midwest and for two autobiographical works. He was an advocate of reform who had serious concerns about industrialization. *McClures*, the magazine in which this article appeared, was a low-priced journal—fifteen cents an issue-that originally published pieces by popular authors. After 1900, it turned to "muckraking," or critical examinations of corporate and political corruption.

McClure's Magazine, Vol. III, June, 1894, No. 1.

Homestead and Its Perilous Trades— Impressions of a Visit

By Hamlin Garland

...The Carnegie mills stood down near the river at some distance from the ferry landing, and thither I took my way through the sticky yellow mud and the gray falling rain. I had secured for my guide a young man whose life had been passed in Homestead and who was quite familiar with the mills and workmen. I do not think he over-stated the hardships of the work-men, whose duties he thoroughly understood. He spoke frankly and without undue prejudice of the management and the work.

We entered the yard through the fence which was aggrandized into a stockade during the riots of a year ago. We were in the yard of the "finished beams." On every side lay thousands of tons of iron. There came toward us a group of men pushing a cart laden with girders for building. They were lean men, pale and grimy. The rain was falling upon them. They wore a look of stoical indifference, though one or two of the younger fellows were scuffling as they pushed behind the car. Farther on was heard the crashing thunder of falling iron plates, the hoarse coughing of great engines, and the hissing of steam. Suddenly through the gloom I caught sight of the mighty up-soaring of saffron and sapphire flame, which marked the draught of the furnace of the Bessemer steel plant far down toward the water. It was a magnificent contrast to the dusky purple of the great smoky roofs below. The great building which we entered first was a beam mill, "one of the finest in the world," my guide said. It was an immense shed, open at the sides, and filled with a mixed and intricate mass of huge machinery. On every side tumultuous action seemed to make every inch of ground dangerous. Savage little engines went rattling about among piles of great beams. Dimly on my left were huge engines, moving with thunderous pounding.

"Come to the starting point," said my guide. I followed him timidly far up toward the other end, my eyes fixed on the beautiful glow of a redhot bloom of metal saving high in the air. It lighted the interior with a glorious light.

I was looking at this beautiful light whey my guide pulled me suddenly behind some shelter. The furious scream of a saw broke forth, the monstrous exaggeration of a circular wood-saw—a saw that melted its way through a beam of solid iron with deafening outcry, producing a gigantic glowing wheel of spattering sparks of golden fire. While it lasted all else was hid from sight.

"That's the saw which cuts the beams of iron into lengths as ordered," my guide said, and we hurried past.

Everywhere in this pandemoniac shed was the thunder of reversing engines, the crash of falling iron, the rumbling growl of rollers, the howl of horrible saws, the deafening hiss of escaping steam, the wild vague shouts of workmen.

"Here are the ingots of steel, just as they come from the Bessemer converting mill," said my guide, pointing toward the mouth of the shed where some huge hunks of iron lay. "And there are the 'soaking pits,' or upright furnaces, where they are heated for rolling. They are perpendicular furnaces, or pits, you see."

We moved toward the mouths of the pits, where a group of men stood with long shovels and bars in their hands. They were touched with orange light, which rose out of the pits. The pits looked like wells or cis-terns of white-hot metal. The men signalled a boy, and the huge covers, which hung on wheels, were moved to allow them to peer in at the metal. They threw up their elbows before their eyes, to shield their faces from the heat, while they studied the ingots within.

"It takes grit to stand there in July and August," said my guide. "Don't it, Joe?" he said to one of the men whom he knew. The man nodded, but was too busy to do more.

"I'd as soon go to hell at once," I replied. He laughed.

"But that isn't all. Those pits have to have their bottoms made after every 'heat,' and they can't wait for 'em to cool. The men stand by and work over them when it's hot enough to burn your boot-soles. Still it beats the old horizontal furnace."

A huge crane swung round and dipped into one of the pits and rose again, bringing one of the ingots, which was heated to proper point for rolling. Its glow made the eye recoil, and threw into steel-blue relief the gray outside rain. It was about six feet long and twenty inches square.

The crane swung round and laid it upon a road-way of steel travellers that carried it up to the waiting jaws of the rollers. High up above it stood the chief "roller," with his hand upon a lever, and as the glow-ing mass ambled forward, his eyes gauged it, and his hand controlled it.

Like a bar of soap through a wringer it went, and as it passed it lowered and lengthened, exploding at the end into flaming scales of fire.

"The power of two thousand five hundred horses is in that engine," said my guide. "The actual squeez-ing power exerted is of course several thousand tons."

Back the bar came with the same jar and tumult, a little longer and a little thinner; back and forth, until it grew into a long band of pink and rose purple. A swift and dangerous dragon that engine, whose touch was deadly. Thence the bar passed to the monstrous saw whose ear-splitting howl rose at intervals as it cut the beams into fixed lengths. From this the pieces passed into a low flat oven flaming fiercely; there to be kept hot while waiting their turn in the next process.

They passed finally to the "finishing rollers," where they took the completed forth of building beams. A vast carrier which moved sidewise with rumbling roar conveyed them across the intervening space. A man rode this carrier like a mahout his elephant, occupying a small platform high on the pyramidal mass of machinery.

Up at the pits again I stood to watch the "heaters" at their task. The crane and the travellers handled these huge pieces of iron deftly and surely, and moulded them into shape, as a girl might handle a cake of dough. Machinery has certainly come in here to lessen the horrors of the iron-worker's life, to diminish the number of deaths by exploding metal or by the leap of curling or breaking beams.

I watched the men as they stirred the deeps beneath. I could not help admiring the swift and splendid action of their bodies. They had the silence and certainty one admires in the tiger's action. I dared not move for fear of flying metal, the swift swing of a crane, or the sudden lurch of a great carrier. The men could not look out for me. They worked with a sort of desperate attention and alertness.

"That looks like hard work," I said to one of them to whom my companion introduced me. He was breathing hard from his work.

"Hard! I guess it's hard. I lost forty pounds the first three months I came into this business. It sweats the life out of a man. I often drink two buckets of water during twelve hours; the sweat drips through my sleeves, and runs down my legs and fills my shoes."

"But that isn't the worst of it," said my guide; "it's a dog's life. Now, those men work twelve hours, and sleep and eat out ten more. You can see a man don't have much time for anything else. You can't see your friends, or do anything but work. That's why I got out of it. I used to come home so exhausted, staggering like a man with a 'jag.' It ain't any place for a sick man—is it, Joe?"

Joe was a tall young fellow, evidently an assistant at the furnace. He smiled. "It's all the work I want, and I'm no chicken—feel that arm."

I felt his arm, it was like a billet of steel. His abdomen was like a sheet of boiler iron. The hair was singed from his hands and arms by the heat of the furnace.

"The tools I handle weigh one hundred and fifty pounds, and four o'clock in August they weigh about a ton."

"When do you eat?"

"I have a bucket of 'grub'; I eat when I can. We have no let-up for eating. This job I'm on now isn't so bad as it might be, for we're running easy; but when we're running full, it's all I can stand."

One of the men made a motion, and the ponderous cover moved a little to one side, and the bottom-makers ran long bars down into the pit and worked desperately, manipulating the ganister which lined the sides. The vivid light seemed to edge them with flame.

"Yes, sir; that is a terrible job in summer," repeated my companion. "When the whole mill is hot, and you're panting for breath, it takes nerve to walk up to that soaking pit or a furnace door."

"Oh, well, when you get ready to go home, your carriage comes for you, I suppose." I said to Joe.

He looked at me with a look that was not humorous. "I pattered down here in the mud, and crawled through a hole in the fence. That's the way I'll crawl home to-morrow morning at six. That's the way we all do."

He turned suddenly and pointed at a pale, stoop-shouldered man in grimy clothes. " There's one of the best-paid men in the mill. See any kid gloves on him? He'd look gay in a carriage at six o'clock in the morning, wouldn't he?"

I watched the man as he climbed to his perch on the great carrier that handled the beams, passing them from the rough roller to the finishing roller. As he took his place a transformation took place in him. He became alert, watchful, and deft. He was a man heavily marked by labor.

We went on into the boiler-plate mills, still noisier, still more grandiose in effect. The rosy slabs of iron were taken from the white-hot furnaces by a crane (on which a man sat and swung, moving with it, guiding it) quite as in the beam mill. They were dropped upon a similar set of travellers; but as they passed through the rollers a man flung a shovelful of salt upon them, and each slab gave off a terrific exploding roar, like a hundred guns sounding together. As they passed to and fro, they grew thinner in form and richer in tone. The water which sprayed them ran about, fled and returned in dark spatters, like flocks of frightened spiders. The sheet warped and twisted, and shot forward with a menacing action which made me shiver.

Everywhere in this enormous building were pits like the mouth of hell, and fierce ovens giving off a glare of heat, and burning wood and iron, giving off horrible stenches of gases. Thunder upon thunder, clang upon clang, glare upon glare! Torches flamed far up in the dark spaces above. Engines moved to and fro, and steam sissed and threatened.

Everywhere were grimy men with sallow and lean faces. The work was of the inhuman sort that hardens and coarsens.

"How long do you work?" I asked of a young man who stood at the furnace near me.

"Twelve hours," he replied. "The night set go on at six at night and come off at six in the morning. I go on at six and off at six."

"For how much pay?"

"Two dollars and a quarter.

"How much do those men get shovelling there in the rain?"

"One dollar and forty cents." (A cut has since taken place.)

"What proportion of the men get that pay?"

"Two-thirds of the whole plant, nearly two thousand. There are thirty-five hundred men in the mills. They get all prices, of course, from a dollar and forty cents up to the tonnage men, who get five and ten dollars per day when the mills run smooth. "

"I suppose not many men make ten dollars per day."

"Well, hardly." He smiled. "Of course the 'rollers' and the 'heaters' get the most, but there are only two 'rollers' to each mill, and three 'heaters,' and they are responsible for their product. The most of the men get under two dollars per day."

"And it is twelve hours' work without stop?"

"You bet! And then again you see we only get this pay part of the time. The mills are liable to be shut down part of the year. They shut down part of the night sometimes, and of course we're docked. Then, again, the tendency of the proprietors is to cut down the tonnage men; that is, the 'rollers' and 'heaters' are now paid by the ton, but they'll some day be paid by the day, like the rest of us.″…

The converting mill was the most gorgeous and dangerous of all. Here the crude product is turned into steel by the Bessemer process. It also was a huge shed-like building open on two sides. In the centre stood supports for two immense pear-shaped pots, which swung on pivots ten or twelve feet from the floor. Over each pot was a huge chimney. Out of each pot roared alternately a ferocious geyser of saffron and sapphire flame, streaked with deeper yellow. From it a light streamed—a light that flung violet shadows everywhere and made the gray outside rain a beautiful blue.

A fountain of sparks arose, gorgeous as ten thousand rockets, and fell with a beautiful curve, like the petals of some enormous flower. Overhead the beams were glowing orange in a base of purple. The men were yellow where the light struck them, violet in shadow. Wild shouts resounded amid the rumbling of an overhead train, and the squeal of a swift little engine, darting in and out laden with the completed castings. The pot began to burn with a whiter flame. Its fluttering, humming roar silenced all else.

"It is nearly ready to pour," said my companion; "the carbon is nearly burnt away."

"Why does it burn so ferociously?"

"Through the pivot a blast of oxygen is delivered with an enormous pressure. This unites with the silicon and carbon and carries it away to the surface. He'd better pour now, or the metal will burn."

Underneath the other pot men were shovelling away slag in the rain of falling sparks. They worked with desperate haste. To their wrists dangled disks of leather to protect their hands from heat. It was impossible to see what manner of men they were. They resembled human beings only in form.

A shout was heard, and a tall crane swung a gigantic ladle under the converting vessel, which then mysteriously up-ended, exploding like a cannon a prodigious discharge of star-like pieces of white-hot slag. The "blowers" on their high platform across the shed sheltered themselves behind a wall.

I drew back into the rain. "They call this the death-trap," shouted my companion, smiling at my timid action.

Down came the vessel, until out of it streamed the smooth flow of terribly beautiful molten metal. As it ran nearly empty and the ladle swung away, the dripping slag fell to the ground exploding, leaping viciously, and the scene became gorgeous beyond belief, with orange and red and green flame.

Into this steam and smoke and shower of sparks the workmen leapt, and were dimly seen preparing for another blast, prying off crusted slag, spraying the ladle, and guiding the cranes. Meanwhile, high up above them in the tumult, an engine backed up with a load of crude molten iron, discharged into the converter, and the soaring saffron and orange and sapphire flames began again.

"Yes, the men call this the death-trap," repeated my guide, as we stood in the edge of the building; "they wipe a man out here every little while." "In what way does death come?" I asked. "Oh, all kinds of ways. Sometimes a chain breaks, and a ladle tips over, and the iron explodes—like that." He pointed at the newly emptied retort, out of which the drippings fell into the water which lay beneath like pools of green gold. As it fell, each drop exploded in a dull report. "Sometimes the slag falls on the workmen from that roadway up there. Of course, if everything is working all smooth and a man watches out, why, all right! But you take it after they've been on duty twelve hours without sleep, and running like hell, everybody tired and loggy, and it's a different story." My guide went on: "You take it back in the beam mill—you saw how the men have to scatter when the carriers or the cranes move—well, sometimes they don't get out of the way; the men who should give warning don't do it quick enough." "What do those men get who are shovelling slag up there?" "Fourteen cents an hour. If they worked eight hours, like a carpenter, they'd get one dollar and twelve cents."

"So a man works in peril of his life for fourteen cents an hour," I remarked....

My guide looked serious. "You don't notice any old men here." He swept his hand about the building. "It shortens life, just like mining; there is no question about that. That, of course, doesn't enter into the usual statement. But the long hours, the strain, and the sudden changes of temperature use a man up. He quits before he gets fifty. I can see lots of fellows here who are failing. They'll lay down in a few years. I went all over that, and I finally came to the decision that I'd peddle groceries rather than kill myself at this business."

"Well, what is the compensation? I mean, why do men keep on?"

"Oh, the common hands do it because they need a job, I suppose, and fellows like Joe expect to be one of the high-paid men."

"How much would that be per year?"

"Oh, three thousand or possibly four thousand a year."

"Does that pay for what it takes out of you?"

"No, I don't think it does," he confessed. "Still, a man has got to go into something."

As night fell the scene became still more grandiose and frightful. I hardly dared move without direction. The rosy ingots, looking like stumps of trees reduced to coals of living fire, rose from their pits of flame and dropped upon the tables, and galloped head on against the rollers, sending off flakes of rosy scale. As they went through, the giant engine thundered fin, reversing with a sound like a nearby cannon; and everywhere the jarring clang of great beams fell upon the ear. Wherever the saw was set at work, great wheels of fire rose out of the obscure murk of lower shadow.

"I'm glad I don't have to work here for a living," said the young man of Else village, who stood near me looking on.

"Oh, this is nothing," said my guide. "You should see it when they're running full in summer. Then it gets hot here. Then you should see 'em when they reline the furnaces and converting vessels. Imagine getting into that Bessemer pot in July, hot enough to pop corn; when you had to work like the devil and then jump out to breathe."

"I wouldn't do it," said the young villager; "I'd break into jail first." He had an outside job. He could afford to talk that way.

"Oh, no, you wouldn't; you'd do it. We all submit to such things, out of habit, I guess. There are lots of other jobs as bad. A man could stand work like this six hours a day. That's all a man ought to do at such work. They could do it, too; they wouldn't make so much, but the hands would live longer."

"They probably don't care whether the hands live or die," I said, "provided they do every ounce they can while they do live."

"I guess that's right," said the other young fellow with a wink. "Mill-owners don't run their mills for the benefit of the men."

"How do you stand on the late strike?" I asked another man.

"It's all foolishness; you can't do anything that way. The tonnage men brought it on; they could afford to strike, but we couldn't. The men working for less than two dollars can't afford to strike."

"While capital wastes, labor starves," I ventured to quote.

"That's the idea; we can't hurt Carnegie by six months' starving. It's *our* ribs that'll show through our shirts."

"Then the strikes do not originate among the men of lowest pay?"

"No; a man working for fourteen cents an hour hasn't got any surplus for a strike." He seemed to voice the general opinion.

A roar as of a hundred lions a thunder as of cannons, flames that made the electric light look like a twinkling blue star, jarring clang of falling iron, burst of spluttering flakes of fire, scream of terrible saws, shifting of mighty trucks with hiss of steam! This was the scene upon which I looked back; this tumult I was leaving. I saw men prodding in the deep soaking pits where the ingots glowed in white-hot chambers. I saw other men in the hot yellow glare from the furnaces. I saw men measuring the serpentine rosy beams. I saw them send the saw flying into them. I saw boys perched high in cages, their shrill voices sounding wild fund animal-like in the midst of the uproar: a place into which men went like men going into war for the sake of wives and children, urged on by necessity, blinded and dulled by custom and habit; an inhuman place to spend four-fifths of one's waking hours. I crawled dismally back to my boarding-place, in the deep darkness, the chill, and the falling rain. The farther I got from those thundering beams and screaming saws, the deeper I drew my breath. Oh, the peace and sweetness of the dim hills across the river!...

"The worst part of the whole business is this," said one of them, as I was about saying good-by. "It brutalizes a man. You can't help it. You start in to be a man, but you become more and more a machine, and pleasures are few and far between. It's like any severe labor. It drags you down mentally and morally, just as it does physically. I wouldn't mind it so much if it weren't for the long hours. Many a trade would be all right if the hours could be shortened. Twelve hours is too long."...

Document 15.2 The Jungle

In *The Jungle*, Upton Sinclair describes a meat packing plant, one of the most thoroughly systematized industries of the late nineteenth- and early twentieth-centuries. The scope of operations, technology, and processes is presented in detail. The role of workers in this system is clearly portrayed. Sinclair also examines the range and standardization of products rendered from steers and pork. The concept of efficiency is also used to justify a host of corrupt practices. Like Hamlin Garland in the previous essay, Upton Sinclair was a reformer. In 1906 he published *The Jungle* as an indictment of the meat packing industry. Sinclair hoped that the work would convince Americans to move toward Socialism. The book failed in that task, but stirred popular outrage about conditions in the industry. President Theodore Roosevelt and numerous members of Congress were also appalled. After two commissions investigating meat packing verified Sinclair's claims, Roosevelt called for, and Congress passed, the Pure Food and Drug Act of 1906.

Chapter 3

There is over a square mile of space in the yards, and more than half of it is occupied by cattle pens; north and south as far as the eye can reach there stretches a sea of pens. And they were all filled—so many cattle no one had ever dreamed existed in the world. Red cattle, black, white, and yellow cattle; old cattle and young cattle; great bellowing bulls and little calves not an hour born; meek-eyed milch cows and fierce, long-horned Texas steers. The sound of them here was as of all the barnyards of the universe; and as for counting them—it would have taken all day simply to count the pens. Here and there ran long alleys, blocked at intervals by gates; and Jokubas told them that the number of these gates was twenty-five thousand. Jokubas had recently been reading a newspaper article which was full of statistics such as that, and he was very proud as he repeated them and made his guests cry out with wonder. Jurgis too had a little of this sense of pride. Had he not just gotten a job, and become a sharer in all this activity, a cog in this marvelous machine?

Here and there about the alleys galloped men upon horseback, booted, and carrying long whips; they were very busy, calling to each other, and to those who were driving the cattle. They were drovers and stock raisers, who had come from far states, and brokers and commission merchants, and buyers for all the big packing houses.

Here and there they would stop to inspect a bunch of cattle, and there would be a parley, brief and businesslike. The buyer would nod or drop his whip, and that would mean a bargain; and he would note it in his little book, along with hundreds of others he had made that morning. Then Jokubas pointed out the place where the cattle were driven to be weighed, upon a great scale that would weigh a hundred thousand pounds at once and record it automatically. It was near to the east entrance that they stood, and all along this east side of the yards ran the railroad tracks, into which the cars were run, loaded with cattle. All night long this had been going on, and now the pens were full; by tonight they would all be empty, and the same thing would be done again....

"And what will become of all these creatures?" cried Teta Elzbieta.

"By tonight," Jokubas answered, "they will all be killed and cut up; and over there on the other side of the packing houses are more railroad tracks, where the cars come to take them away."

There were two hundred and fifty miles of track within the yards, their guide went on to tell them. They brought about ten thousand head of cattle every day, and as many hogs, and half as many sheep—which meant some eight or ten million live creatures turned into food every year. One stood and watched, and little by little caught the drift of the tide, as it set in the direction of the packing houses. There were groups of cattle being driven to the chutes, which were roadways about fifteen feet wide, raised high above the pens. In these chutes the stream of animals was continuous; it was quite uncanny to watch them, pressing on to their fate, all unsuspicious a very river of death. Our friends were not poetical, and the sight suggested to them no metaphors of human destiny; they thought only of the wonderful efficiency of it all. The chutes into which the hogs went climbed high up —to the very top of the distant buildings; and Jokubas explained that the hogs went up by the power of their own legs, and then their weight carried them back through all the processes necessary to make them into pork.

"They don't waste anything here," said the guide, and then he laughed and added a witticism, which he was pleased that his unsophisticated friends should take to be his own: "They use everything about the hog except the squeal." In front of Brown's General Office building there grows a tiny plot of grass, and this, you may learn, is the only bit of green thing in Packingtown; likewise this jest about the hog and his squeal, the stock in trade of all the guides, is the one gleam of humor that you will find there.

After they had seen enough of the pens, the party went up the street, to the mass of buildings which occupy the center of the yards. These buildings, made of brick and stained with innumerable layers of Packingtown smoke, were painted all over with advertising signs, from which the visitor realized suddenly that he had come to the home of many of the torments of his life. It was here that they made those products with the wonders of which they pestered him so—by placards that defaced the landscape when he traveled, and by staring advertisements in the newspapers and magazines—by silly little jingles that he could not get out of his mind, and gaudy pictures that lurked for him around every street corner. Here was where they made Brown's Imperial Hams and Bacon, Brown's Dressed Beef, Brown's Excelsior Sausages! Here was the headquarters of Durham's Pure Leaf Lard, of Durham's Breakfast Bacon,

Durham's Canned Beef, Potted Ham, Deviled Chicken, Peerless Fertilizer!

Entering one of the Durham buildings, they found a number of other visitors waiting; and before long there came a guide, to escort them through the place. They make a great feature of showing strangers through the packing plants, for it is a good advertisement. But Ponas Jokubas whispered maliciously that the visitors did not see any more than the packers wanted them to. They climbed a long series of stairways outside of the building, to the top of its five or six stories. Here was the chute, with its river of hogs, all patiently toiling upward; there was a place for them to rest to cool off, and then through another passageway they went into a room from which there is no returning for hogs.

It was a long, narrow room, with a gallery along it for visitors. At the head there was a great iron wheel, about twenty feet in circumference, with rings here and there along its edge. Upon both sides of this wheel there was a narrow space, into which came the hogs at the end of their journey; in the midst of them stood a great burly Negro, bare-armed and bare-chested. He was resting for the moment, for the wheel had stopped while men were cleaning up. In a minute or two, however, it began slowly to revolve, and then the men upon each side of it sprang to work. They had chains which they fastened about the leg of the nearest hog, and the other end of the chain they hooked into one of the rings upon the wheel. So, as the wheel turned, a hog was suddenly jerked off his feet and borne aloft.

At the same instant the car was assailed by a most terrifying shriek; the visitors started in alarm, the women turned pale and shrank back. The shriek was followed by another, louder and yet more agonizing - for once started upon that journey, the hog never came back; at the top of the wheel he was shunted off upon a trolley, and went sailing down the room. And meantime another was swung up, and then another, and another, until there was a double line of them, each dangling by a foot and kicking in frenzy—and squealing. The uproar was appalling, perilous to the eardrums; one feared there was too much sound for the room to hold—that the walls must give way or the ceiling crack. There were high squeals and low squeals, grunts, and wails of agony; there would come a momentary lull, and then a fresh outburst, louder than ever, surging up to a deafening climax. It was too much for some of the visitors—the men would look at each other, laughing nervously, and the women would stand with hands clenched, and the blood rushing to their faces, and the tears starting in their eyes.

Meantime, heedless of all these things, the men upon the floor were going about their work. Neither squeals of hogs nor tears of visitors made any difference to them; one by one they hooked up the hogs, and one by one with a swift stroke they slit their throats. There was a long line of hogs, with squeals and lifeblood ebbing away together; until at last each started again, and vanished with a splash into a huge vat of boiling water.

It was all so very businesslike that one watched it fascinated. It was porkmaking by machinery, porkmaking by applied mathematics....

The carcass hog was scooped out of the vat by machinery, and then it fell to the second floor, passing on the way through a wonderful machine with numerous scrapers, which adjusted themselves to the size and shape of the animal, and sent it out at the other end with nearly all of its bristles removed. It was then again strung up by machinery, and sent upon another trolley ride; this time passing between two lines of men, who sat upon a raised platform, each doing a certain single thing to the carcass as it came to him. One scraped the outside of a leg; another scraped the inside of the same leg. One with a swift stroke cut the throat; another with two swift strokes severed the head, which fell to the floor and vanished through a hole. Another made a slit down the body; a second opened the body wider; a third with a saw cut the breastbone; a fourth loosened the entrails; a fifth pulled them out - and they also slid through a hole in the floor. There were men to scrape each side and men to scrape the back; there were men to clean the carcass inside, to trim it and wash it. Looking down this room, one saw, creeping slowly, a line of dangling hogs a hundred yards in length; and for every yard there was a man, working as if a demon were after him. At the end of this hog's progress every inch of the carcass had been gone over several times; and then it was rolled into the chilling room, where it stayed for twenty-four hours, and where a stranger might lose himself in a forest of freezing hogs....

The party descended to the next floor, where the various waste materials were treated. Here came the entrails, to be scraped and washed clean for sausage casings; men and women worked here in the midst of a sickening stench, which caused the visitors to hasten by, gasping. To another room came all the scraps to be "tanked," which meant boiling and pumping off the grease to make soap and lard; below they took out the refuse, and this, too, was a region in which the visitors did not linger. In still other places men were engaged in cutting up the carcasses that had been through the chilling rooms. First there were the "splitters," the most expert workmen in the plant, who earned as high as fifty cents an hour, and did not a thing all day except chop hogs down the middle. Then there were "cleaver men," great giants with muscles of iron; each had two men to attend him—to slide the half carcass in front of him on the table, and hold it while he chopped it, and then turn each piece so that he might chop it once more. His cleaver had a blade about two feet long, and he never made but one cut; he made it so neatly, too, that his implement did not smite through and dull itself—there was just enough force for a perfect cut, and no more. So through various yawning holes there slipped to the floor below—to one room hams, to another forequarters, to another sides of pork. One might go down to this floor and see the pickling rooms, where the hams were put into vats, and the great smoke rooms, with their airtight iron doors. In other rooms they prepared salt pork—there were whole cellars full of it, built up in great towers to the ceiling. In yet other rooms they were putting up meats in boxes and barrels, and wrapping hams and bacon in oiled paper, sealing and labeling and sewing them. From the doors of these rooms went men with loaded trucks, to the platform where freight cars were waiting to be filled; and one went out there and realized with a start that he had come at last to the ground floor of this enormous building.

Then the party went across the street to where they did the killing of beef—where every hour they turned four or five hundred cattle into meat. Unlike the place they had left, all this work was done on one floor; and instead of there being one line of carcasses which moved to the workmen, there were fifteen or twenty lines, and the men moved from one to another of these. This made a scene of intense activity, a picture of human power wonderful to watch. It was all in one great room, like a circus amphitheater, with a gallery for visitors running over the center.

Along one side of the room ran a narrow gallery, a few feet from the floor; into which gallery the cattle were driven by men with goads which gave them electric shocks. Once crowded in here, the creatures were prisoned, each in a separate pen, by gates that shut, leaving them no room to turn around; and while they stood bellowing and plunging, over the top of the pen there leaned one of the "knockers," armed with a sledge hammer, and watching for a chance to deal a blow. The room echoed with the thuds in quick succession, and the stamping and kicking of the steers. The instant the animal had fallen, the "knocker" passed on to another; while a second man raised a lever, and the side of the pen was raised, and the animal, still kicking and struggling, slid out to the "killing bed." Here a man put shackles about one leg, and pressed another lever, and the body was jerked up into the air. There were fifteen or twenty such pens, and it was a matter of only a couple of minutes to knock fifteen or twenty cattle and roll them out. Then once more the gates were opened, and another lot rushed in; and so out of each pen there rolled a steady stream of carcasses, which the men upon the killing beds had to get out of the way.

The manner in which they did this was something to be seen and never forgotten. They worked with furious intensity, literally upon the run—at a pace with which there is nothing to be compared except a football game. It was all highly specialized labor, each man having his task to do; generally this would consist of only two or three specific cuts, and he would pass down the line of fifteen or twenty carcasses, making these cuts upon each. First there came the "butcher," to bleed them; this meant one swift stroke, so swift that you could not see it—only the flash of the knife; and before you could realize it, the man had darted on to the next line, and a stream of bright red was pouring out upon the floor. This floor was half an inch deep with blood, in spite of the best efforts of men who kept shoveling it through holes; it must have made the floor slippery, but no one could have guessed this by watching the men at work.

The carcass hung for a few minutes to bleed; there was no time lost, however, for there were several hanging in each line, and one was always ready. It was let down to the ground, and there came the "headsman," whose task it was to sever the head, with two or three swift strokes. Then came the "floorsman," to make the first cut in the skin; and then another to finish ripping the skin down the center; and then half a dozen more in swift succession, to finish the skinning. After they were through, the carcass was again swung up; and while a man with a stick examined the skin, to make sure that it had not been cut, and another rolled it tip and tumbled it through one of the inevitable holes in the floor, the beef proceeded on its journey. There were men to cut it, and men to split it, and men to gut it and scrape it clean inside. There were some with hose which threw jets of boiling water upon it, and others who removed the feet and added the final touches. In the end, as with the hogs, the finished beef was run into the chilling room, to hang its appointed time.

The visitors were taken there and shown them, all neatly hung in rows, labeled conspicuously with the tags of the government inspectors—and some, which had been killed by a special process, marked with the sign of the kosher rabbi, certifying that it was fit for sale to the orthodox. And then the visitors were taken to the other parts of the building, to see what became of each particle of the waste material that had vanished through the floor; and to the pickling rooms, and the salting rooms, the canning rooms, and the packing rooms, where choice meat was prepared for shipping in refrigerator cars, destined to be eaten in all the four corners of civilization. Afterward they went outside, wandering about among the mazes of buildings in which was done the work auxiliary to this great industry. There was scarcely a thing needed in the business that Durham and Company did not make for themselves. There was a great steam power plant and an electricity plant. There was a barrel factory, and a boiler-repair shop. There was a building to which the grease was piped, and made into soap and lard; and then there was a factory for making lard cans, and another for making soap boxes. There was a building in which the bristles were cleaned and dried, for the making of hair cushions and such things; there was a building where the skins were dried and tanned, there was another where heads and feet were made into glue, and another where bones were made into fertilizer. No tiniest particle of organic matter was wasted in Durham's. Out of the horns of the cattle they made combs, buttons, hairpins, and imitation ivory; out of the shinbones and other big bones they cut knife and toothbrush handles, and mouthpieces for pipes; out of the hoofs they cut hairpins and buttons, before they made the rest into glue. From such things as feet, knuckles, hide clippings, and sinews came such strange and unlikely products as gelatin, isinglass, and phosphorus, bone black, shoe blacking, and bone oil. They had curled-hair works for the cattle tails, and a "wool pullery" for the sheepskins; they made pepsin from the stomachs of the pigs, and albumen from the blood, and violin strings from the ill-smelling entrails. When there was nothing else to be done with a thing, they first put it into a tank and got out of it all the tallow and grease, and then they made it into fertilizer. All these industries were gathered into buildings near by, connected by galleries and railroads with the main establishment; and it was estimated that they had handled nearly a quarter of a billion of animals since the founding of the plant by the elder Durham a generation and more ago. If you counted with it the other big plants—and they were now really all one—it was, so Jokubas informed them, the greatest aggregation of labor and capital ever gathered in one place. It employed thirty thousand men; it supported directly two hundred and fifty thousand people in its neighborhood, and indirectly it supported half a million. It sent its products to every country in the civilized world, and it furnished the food for no less than thirty million people!

To all of these things our friends would listen openmouthed—it seemed to them impossible of belief that anything so stupendous could have been devised by mortal man. That was why to Jurgis it seemed almost profanity to speak about the place as did Jokubas, skeptically; it was a thing as tremendous as the universe—the laws and ways of its working no more than the universe to be questioned or understood. All that a mere man could do, it seemed to Jurgis, was to take a thing like this as he found it, and do as he was told; to be given a place in it and a share in its wonderful activities was a blessing to be grateful for, as one was grateful for the sunshine and the rain. Jurgis was even glad that he had not seen the place before meeting with his triumph, for he felt that the size of it would have overwhelmed him. But now he had been admitted—he was a part of it all! He had the feeling that this whole huge establishment had taken him under its protection, and had become responsible for his welfare. So guileless was he, and ignorant of the nature of business, that he did not even realize that he had become an employee of Brown's, and that Brown and Durham were supposed by all the world to be deadly rivals—were even required to be deadly rivals by the law of the land, and ordered to try to ruin each other under penalty of fine and imprisonment!

Chapter 9

There was said to be two thousand dollars a week hush money from the tubercular steers alone; and as much again from the hogs which had died of cholera on the trains, and which you might see any day being loaded into boxcars and hauled away to a place called Globe, in Indiana, where they made a fancy grade of lard.

Jurgis heard of these things little by little....

It seemed that they must have agencies all over the country, to hunt out old and crippled and diseased cattle to be canned. There were cattle which had been fed on "whisky-malt," the refuse of the breweries, and had become what the men called "steerly"—which means covered with boils. It was a nasty job killing these, for when you plunged your knife into them they would burst and splash foul-smelling stuff into your face; and when a man's sleeves were smeared with blood, and his hands steeped in it, how was he ever to wipe his face, or to

clear his eyes so that he could see? It was stuff such as this that made the "embalmed beef" that had killed several times as many United States soldiers as all the bullets of the Spaniards; only the army beef, besides, was not fresh canned, it was old stuff that had been lying for years in the cellars.

Then one Sunday evening, Jurgis sat puffing his pipe by the kitchen stove, and talking with an old fellow whom Jonas had introduced, and who worked in the canning rooms at Durham's; and so Jurgis learned a few things about the great and only Durham canned goods, which had become a national institution.

...

And then there was "potted game" and "potted grouse," "potted ham," and "deviled ham"—de-vyled, as the men called it. "De-vyled" ham was made out of the waste ends of smoked beef that were too small to be sliced by the machines; and also tripe, dyed with chemicals so that it would not show white; and trimmings of hams and corned beef; and potatoes, skins and all; and finally the hard cartilaginous gullets of beef, after the tongues had been cut out. All this ingenious mixture was ground up and flavored with spices to make it taste like something. Anybody who could invent a new imitation had been sure of a fortune from old Durham, said Jurgis' informant; but it was hard to think of anything new in a place where so many sharp wits had been at work for so long; where men welcomed tuberculosis in the cattle they were feeding, because it made them fatten more quickly; and where they bought up all the old rancid butter left over in the grocery stores of a continent, and "oxidized" it by a forced-air process, to take away the odor, rechurned it with skim milk, and sold it in bricks in the cities!

There was another interesting set of statistics that a person might have gathered in Packingtown—those of the various afflictions of the workers....

There were the men in the pickle rooms, for instance, where old Antanas had gotten his death; scarce a one of these that had not some spot of horror on his person. Let a man so much as scrape his finger pushing a truck in the pickle rooms, and he might have a sore that would put him out of the world; all the joints in his fingers might be eaten by the acid, one by one. Of the butchers and floorsmen, the beef-boners and trimmers, and all those who used knives, you could scarcely find a person who had the use of his thumb; time and time again the base of it had been slashed, till it was a mere lump of flesh against which the man pressed the knife to hold it. The hands of these men would be criss-crossed with cuts, until you could no longer pretend to count them or to trace them. They would have no nails,—they had worn them off pulling hides; their knuckles were swollen so that their fingers spread out like a fan. There were men who worked in the cooking rooms, in the midst of steam and sickening odors, by artificial light; in these rooms the germs of tuberculosis might live for two years, but the supply was renewed every hour. There were the beef-luggers, who carried two-hundred-pound quarters into the refrigerator-cars; a fearful kind of work, that began at four o'clock in the morning, and that wore out the most powerful men in a few years. There were those who worked in the chilling rooms, and whose special disease was rheumatism; the time limit that a man could work in the chilling rooms was said to be five years. There were the wool-pluckers, whose hands went to pieces even sooner than the hands of the pickle men; for the pelts of the sheep had to be painted with acid to loosen the wool, and then the pluckers had to pull out this wool with their bare hands, till the acid had eaten their fingers off. There were those who made the tins for the canned meat; and their hands, too, were a maze of cuts, and each cut represented a chance for blood poisoning. Some worked at the stamping machines, and it was very seldom that one could work long there at the pace that was set, and not give out and forget himself and have a part of his hand chopped off. There were the "hoisters," as they were called, whose task it was to press the lever which lifted the dead cattle off the floor. They ran along upon a rafter, peering down through the damp and the steam; and as old Durham's architects had not built the killing room for the convenience of the hoisters, at every few feet they would have to stoop under a beam, say four feet above the one they ran on; which got them into the habit of stooping, so that in a few years they would be walking like chimpanzees. Worst of any, however, were the fertilizer men, and those who served in the cooking rooms. These people could not be shown to the visitor,—for the odor of a fertilizer man would scare any ordinary visitor at a hun-

dred yards, and as for the other men, who worked in tank rooms full of steam, and in some of which there were open vats near the level of the floor, their peculiar trouble was that they fell into the vats; and when they were fished out, there was never enough of them left to be worth exhibiting, —sometimes they would be overlooked for days, till all but the bones of them had gone out to the world as Durham's Pure Leaf Lard!

Chapter 14

...It was only when the whole ham was spoiled that it came into the department of Elzbieta. Cut up by the two-thousand-revolutions-a-minute flyers, and mixed with half a ton of other meat, no odor that ever was in a ham could make any difference. There was never the least attention paid to what was cut up for sausage; there would come all the way back from Europe old sausage that had been rejected, and that was moldy and white—it would be dosed with borax and glycerine, and dumped into the hoppers, and made over again for home consumption. There would be meat that had tumbled out on the floor, in the dirt and sawdust, where the workers had tramped and spit uncounted billions of consumption germs. There would be meat stored in great piles in rooms; and the water from leaky roofs would drip over it, and thousands of rats would race about on it. It was too dark in these storage places to see well, but a man could run his hand over these piles of meat and sweep off handfuls of the dried dung of rats. These rats were nuisances, and the packers would put poisoned bread out for them; they would die, and then rats, bread, and meat would go into the hoppers together. This is no fairy story and no joke; the meat would be shoveled into carts, and the man who did the shoveling would not trouble to lift out a rat even when he saw one—there were things that went into the sausage in comparison with which a poisoned rat was a tidbit.

Document 15.3 The Principles of Scientific Management

Frederick Taylor's *Principles of Scientific Management* was the original and classic text on how to rationalize human labor with technological systems. In these selections, Taylor lists the principles of his system; in the second excerpt, he provides a basic example of how they were applied at the Bethlehem Steel Company. An expert machinist, Taylor believed that the methods of production he observed when learning the trade—work largely controlled by craftsmen and foremen who contracted with factory management—were extremely inefficient. He subsequently began to study and write about methods of improving worker productivity. The popularity of his ideas led to his election as president of the American Society of

Mechanical Engineers, and to the publication of a compilation of his essays as the *Principles* in 1911. His ideas were tried in a number of industries, and proved particularly important in the design of the Ford auto production plants.

Introduction

PRESIDENT ROOSEVELT, in his address to the Governors at the White House, prophetically remarked that "The conservation of our national resources is only preliminary to the larger question of national efficiency."

The whole country at once recognized the importance of conserving our material resources and a large movement has been started which will be effective in accomplishing this object. As yet, however, we have but vaguely appreciated the importance of "the larger question of increasing our national efficiency."…

As yet there has been no public agitation for "greater national efficiency," no meetings have been called to consider how this is to be brought about. And still there are signs that the need for greater efficiency is widely felt.

The search for better, for more competent men, from the presidents of our great companies down to our household servants, was never more vigorous than it is now. And more than ever before is the demand for competent men in excess of the supply.

What we are all looking for, however, is the ready made, competent man; the man whom some one else has trained. It is only when we fully realize that our duty, as well as our opportunity, lies in systematically cooperating to train and to make this competent man, instead of in hunting for a man whom some one else has trained, that we shall be on the road to national efficiency.

In the past the prevailing idea has been well expressed in the saying that "Captains of industry are born, not made"; and the theory has been that if one could get the right man, methods could be safely left to him. In the future it will be, appreciated that our leaders must be trained right as well as born right, and that no great man can (with the old system of personal management) hope to compete with a number of ordinary men who have been properly organized so as efficiently to cooperate.

In the past the man has been first; in the future the system must be first. This in no sense, however, implies that great men are not needed. On the contrary, the first object of any good system must be that of developing first-class men; and under systematic management the best man rises to the top more certainly and more rapidly than ever before.

This paper has been written:

First. To point out, through a series of simple illustrations, the great loss which the whole country is suffering through inefficiency in almost all of our daily acts.

Second. To try to convince the reader that the remedy for this inefficiency lies in systematic management, rather than in searching for some unusual or extraordinary man.

Third. To prove that the best management is a true science, resting upon clearly defined laws, rules, and principles, as a foundation. And further to show that the fundamental principles of scientific management are applicable to all kinds of human activities, from our simplest individual acts to the work of our great corporations, which call for the most elaborate cooperation. And, briefly, through a series of illustrations, to convince the reader that whenever these principles are correctly applied, results must follow which are truly astounding.

This paper was originally prepared for presentation to The American Society of Mechanical Engineers. The illustrations chosen are such as, it is believed, will especially appeal to engineers and to managers of industrial and manufacturing establishments, and also quite as much to all of the men who are working in these establishments. It is hoped, however, that it will be clear to other readers that the same principles can be applied with equal force to all social activities: to the management of our homes; the management of our farms; the management of the business of our tradesmen, large and small; of our churches, our philanthropic institutions, our universities, and our governmental departments.

Fredrick W. Taylor, *The Principles of Scientific Management*, 1911

The Bethlehem Steel Company had five blast furnaces, the product of which had been handled by a pig-iron gang for many years. This gang, at this time, consisted of about 75 men. They were good, average pig-iron handlers, were under an excellent foreman who himself had been a pig-iron handler, and the work was done, on the whole, about as fast and as cheaply as it was anywhere else at that time.

A railroad switch was run out into the field, right along the edge of the piles of pig iron. An inclined plank was placed against the side of a car, and each man picked up from his pile a pig of iron weighing about 92 pounds, walked up the inclined plank and dropped it on the end of the car.

We found that this gang were loading on the average about 12 1/2 long tons per man per day. We were surprised to find, after studying the matter, that a first-class pig-iron handler ought to handle between 47(3*) and 48 long tons per day, instead of 12 1/2 tons. This task seemed to us so very large that we were obliged to go over our work several times before we were absolutely sure that we were right. Once we were sure, however, that 47 tons was a proper day's work for a first-class pig-iron handler, the task which faced us as managers under the modern scientific plan was clearly before us. It was our duty to see that the 80,000 tons of pig iron was loaded on to the cars at the rate of 47 tons per man per day, in place of 12 1/2 tons, at which rate the work was then being done. And it was further our duty to see that this work was done without bringing on a strike among the men, without any quarrel with the men, and to see that the men were happier and better contented when loading at the new rate of 47 tons than they were when loading at the old rate of 12 1/2 tons.

Our first step was the scientific selection of the workman. In dealing with workmen under this type of management, it is an inflexible rule to talk to and deal with only one man at a time, since each workman has his own special abilities and limitations, and since we are not dealing with men in masses, but are trying to develop each individual man to his highest state of efficiency and prosperity. Our first step was to find the proper workman to begin with. We therefore carefully watched and studied these 75 men for three or four days, at the end of which time we had picked out four men who appeared to be physically able to handle pig iron at the rate of 47 tons per day. A careful study was then made of each of these men.

We looked up their history as far back as practicable and thorough inquiries were made as to the character, habits, and the ambition of each of them.

Finally we selected one from among the four as the most likely man to start with. He was a little Pennsylvania Dutchman who had been observed to trot back home for a mile or so after his work in the evening about as fresh as he was when he came trotting down to work in the morning. We found that upon wages of $1.15 a day he had succeeded in buying a small plot of ground, and that he was engaged in putting up the walls of a little house for himself in the morning before starting to work and at night after leaving. He also had the reputation of being exceedingly "close," that is, of placing a very high value on a dollar. As one man whom we talked to about him said, "A penny looks about the size of a cart-wheel to him." This man we will call Schmidt. The task before us, then, narrowed itself down to getting Schmidt to handle 47 tons of pig iron per day and making him glad to do it. This was done as follows. Schmidt was called out from among the gang of pig-iron handlers and talked to somewhat in this way:

"Schmidt, are you a high-priced man?"

"Vell, I don't know vat you mean."

"Oh yes, you do. What I want to know is whether you are a high-priced man or not."

"Vell, I don't know vat you mean."

"Oh, come now, you answer my questions. What I want to find out is whether you are a high-priced-man or one of these cheap fellows here. What I want to find out is whether you want to earn $1.85 a day or whether you are satisfied with $1.15, just the same as all those cheap fellows are getting."

"Did I vant $1.85 a day? Vas dot a high-priced man? Vell, yes, I vas a high-priced man."

"Oh, you're aggravating me. Of course you want $1.85 a day every one wants it! You know perfectly well that that has very little to do with your being a high-priced man. For goodness' sake answer my questions, and don't waste any more of my time. Now come over here. You see that pile of pig iron?"

"Yes."

"You see that car?"

"Yes."

"Well, if you are a high-priced man, you will load that pig iron on that car to-morrow for $1.85. Now do wake up and answer my question. Tell me whether you are a high-priced man or not."

"Vell—did I got $1.85 for loading dot pig iron on dot car to-morrow?"

"Yes, of course you do, and you get $1.85 for loading a pile like that every day right through the year. That is what a high-priced man does, and you know it just as well as I do."

"Vell, dot's all right. I could load dot pig iron on the car to-morrow for $1.85, and I get it every day, don't I?"

"Certainly you do—certainly you do."

"Vell, den, I vas a high-priced man."

"Now, hold on, hold on. You know just as well as I do that a high-priced man has to do exactly as he's told from morning till night. You have seen this man here before, haven't you?"

"No, I never saw him."

"Well, if you are a high-priced man, you will do exactly as this man tells you to-morrow, from morning till night. When he tells you to pick up a pig and walk, you pick it up and you walk, and when he tells you to sit down and rest, you sit down. You do that right straight through the day. And what's more, no back talk. Now a high-priced man does just what he's told to do, and no back talk. Do you understand that? When this man tells you to walk, you walk; when he tells you to sit down, you sit down, and you don't talk back at him. Now you come on to work here to-morrow morning and I'll know before night whether you are really a high-priced man or not."

This seems to be rather rough talk. And indeed it would be if applied to an educated mechanic, or even an intelligent laborer. With a man of the mentally sluggish type of Schmidt it is appropriate and not unkind, since it is effective in fixing his attention on the high wages which he wants and away from what, if it were called to his attention, he probably would consider impossibly hard work.

What would Schmidt's answer be if he were talked to in a manner which is usual under the management of "initiative and incentive"? say, as follows:

"Now, Schmidt, you are a first-class pig-iron handler and know your business well. You have been handling at the rate of 12 1/2 tons per day. I have given considerable study to handling pig iron, and feel sure that you could do a much larger day's work than you have been doing. Now don't you think that if you really tried you could handle 47 tons of pig iron per day, instead of 12 1/2 tons?"

What do you think Schmidt's answer would be to this?

Schmidt started to work, and all day long, and at regular intervals, was told by the man who stood over him with a watch, "Now pick up a pig and walk. Now sit down and rest. Now walk—now rest," etc. He worked when he was told to work, and rested when he was told to rest, and at half-past five in the afternoon had his 47 1/2 tons loaded on the car. And he practically never failed to work at this pace and do the task that was set him during the three years that the writer was at Bethlehem. And throughout this time he averaged a little more than $1.85 per day, whereas before he had never received over $1.15 per day, which was the ruling rate of wages at that time in Bethlehem. That is, he received 60 per cent higher wages than were paid to other men who were not working on task work. One man after another was picked out and trained to handle pig iron at the rate of 47 1/2 tons per day until all of the pig iron was handled at this rate, and the men were receiving 60 per cent more wages than other workmen around them.

The writer has given above a brief description of three of the four elements which constitute the essence of scientific management: first, the careful selection of the workman, and, second and third, the method of first inducing and then training and helping the workman to work according to the scientific method. Nothing has as yet been said about the science of handling pig iron. The writer trusts, however, that before leaving this illustration the reader will be thoroughly convinced that there is a science of handling pig iron, and further that this science amounts to so much that the man who is suited to handle pig iron cannot possibly understand it, nor even work in accordance with the laws of this science, without the help of those who are over him.

Document 15.4 Work Accidents and the Law

Between 1907 and 1908, Crystal Eastmen researched working and living conditions of steel workers in Pittsburgh. In this reading, she describes a few cases of worker injuries, and her methods for examining the subject. She then draws a few tentative conclusions, much different in tone from those of Hamlin Garland about Homestead. The work was typical of studies made after 1900, when concern for worker health and safety engaged local, state, and (to a far lesser degree) federal governments. Like the studies of meat packers that substantiated Upton Sinclair's claims, private and public commissions were established to investigate the conditions of work and workers' safety. In this case, the Russell Sage Foundation funded the investigation, which was published as the *Pittsburgh Survey*. The steel industry, which had started worker safety programs before the study, continued to develop them after it was published.

Editor's Foreword

The Slavs from Austro-Hungary, the Latins from the Mediterranean provinces, the Germans or the British-born, who come to Pittsburgh to do the heavy work of manufacture (and for Pittsburgh read the United States), from a region of law and order to a region of law-made anarchy so far as the hazards of industry are concerned.

...

Laggard as the American states have thus been in what Mr. William Hard has called the "law of the killed and injured," it is ours to profit by the experience of the countries which have from five to fifteen years' headway in this field. An American system should, none the less, be grounded firmly in American conditions. Toward the understanding of these conditions, of the common causes of accidents, and their consequences in the actual household experience of working people, this book is contributed. Miss Eastman presents the findings of the first systematic investigation of all cases occurring during a representative period in a representative American district. No such body of facts has hitherto been available, and the investigation could scarcely have been better timed in relation to constructive efforts towards the establishment of industrial justice.

...

Yet as this book is issued, the rank and file of workers in no American state are protected adequately against economic loss due to the accidents of their work.

An equally momentous change manifests itself in the attitude being taken by engineers, superintendents and mechanics toward the prevention of accidents. The fact that the cases studied by Miss Eastman fell in a period before recent developments in this direction makes them more truly a reflection of the unregulated industrial practice with which the American public has to deal. At the same time, in Mr. Beyer's article, we are able to present, as an illustration of methods of advance, the work of prevention extensively developed by the United States Steel Corporation under a central committee appointed in May, 1908.

This investigation, it should be borne in mind, was of fatalities and not of plants. ...Thus the method commonly employed by the physician or scientist in studying the occurrence of a disease with the hope of learning something as to its causes and effects was applied to the problem at hand. It is my belief that this outspoken, pioneer presentation will open up to public consideration, a situation which in our industrial districts has been weakly surrendered to inertia and trepidation.

The lives of men, the fair living of families—these are worth conserving to the uttermost against the risks of work. These the industries of America waste without tally.

Paul U. Kellogg
Director Pittsburgh Survey

The Problem Stated

I.   On December 4, 1906, James Brand a young structural iron worker, employed by the Fort Pitt Bridge Company, while passing over a scaffold to get to his work on the Walnut Street Bridge, fourteenth ward, Pittsburgh, fell 35 feet to the ground and was killed. Testimony at the coroner's inquest brought out the fact that a plank broke under him. The two pieces of the plank were picked up where they fell. At the broken end of each, the frost and dirt had worked into the wood several inches, testifying eloquently to an old crack, a crack of at least two weeks' existence according to the statements of those who looked at the pieces. Brand had nothing to do with the building of the scaffold.

II. On May 1, 1907, Frank Koroshic, a Lithuanian angle-shearman employed by the McClintic and Marshall Company, at Rankin, Pa., had finished his work for the day and, in order to get some waste with which to clean his hands, went over to

---

Crystal Eastman, Work Accidents and the Law (1910).

a big punching machine with which he was familiar. It had a heavy fast-revolving wheel, boxed in with iron down to within two or three inches of the floor, to guard the workmen from accident. At one corner of the machine, in a hole, was some waste. According to the statement of the superintendent, Koroshic got down on his knees and, leaning with his left hand on the greasy platform a few inches from the wheel, reached with his right hand for the waste. As he bore his weight on his left hand, it slipped and slid into the wheel. In a second the hand was crushed.

III. On October 17, 1906, Adam Rogalas, a Russian laborer employed at $1.60 a day by the Iron City Grain Elevator Company of Pittsburgh, was sent with two other men to do some work in an adjoining building, used by the company for storage. On the floor above them grain was stored in bags. The supports of the floor gave way and it fell. One of the workmen escaped, another was injured, Rogalas was killed. At the inquest a building inspector testified that the floor supports were obviously inadequate. Rogalas had a wife, and four children, aged ten, six, five, and two; but he had no savings. According to Mrs. Rogalas, the claim agent of the company offered to settle with her for $400, which she refused. She put her case in the hands of a lawyer, and suit was entered for $20,000. Mrs. Rogalas got some washing to do; the city poor relief gave her $6.00 worth of groceries a month; she begged at the door of her Catholic church on Sundays; her sister, with a family of six, did what little she could; an occasional $10 was advanced by her lawyer. She was seen in severe winter weather, with shoes so old that her feet were exposed. Six months after the accident another child was born; it was the end of the year before the suit came to trial. The court instructed the jury to return a verdict for the defendant. The woman had lost her case.

IV. On August 5, 1907, Robert Reeve, a United States postal clerk, was working the Baltimore and Ohio yards in Pittsburgh. The engine to which his car was attached collided slightly with another, so that by the jar he was thrown against one of the iron hooks on which mail pouches are hung and a bone behind his ear was injured. He was four days in the hospital, the charges for which the railroad company paid. He did not go back to work for four weeks. During this time his salary was paid in full by the government, $83.30.

He received in addition $64 from a Mail Clerks' Association to which he belonged and to which he paid dues. He settled with the railroad for $250, of which his lawyer's fee took $100. Thus Reeve's slight injury, resulting, so far as we know, in nothing permanent, gave him a month's vacation on full pay, with $150 thrown in.

A social investigation is justified when there are grounds for belief that wrong exists in certain relations between individuals, a wrong of sufficient importance and extent to warrant concerted interference on the part of the community. When to such a belief is added a general conviction that this wrong results in a great public tax, a drain upon the productive forces of the community, the need for investigation becomes urgent. With regard to the work-accident problem, such a belief and conviction has long existed,—based not only upon newspaper stories, magazine articles, and hearsay, but upon the common knowledge and experience of working people. On the strength of it, this investigation was undertaken. It should give us facts, not isolated and unrelated, but massed and classified.

The incidents related above are isolated facts, the first two bearing especially upon the causes of work-accidents, the third and fourth upon their economic cost to the workman and his family.

If adequate investigation reveals that most work-accidents happen because workmen are fools, like Frank Koroshic, who reached into danger in spite of every precaution taken to protect him, then there is no warrant for direct interference by society in the hope of preventing them. If, on the other hand, investigation reveals that a considerable proportion of accidents are due to insufficient concern for the safety of workmen on the part of their employers, as in the death of Brand, then social interference in some form is justified.

If, again, investigation of a large number of cases shows that workmen and their families do not suffer economically from work-accidents, and that they often make money out of injuries, as Reeve did, then we are not warranted in interfering between employers and employees for the sake of further protecting the rights of the latter. But if investigation shows that the majority of work-accidents result in serious deprivation to the workers' families and consequent cost to the community, and that the economic loss is inequitably distributed, as in the Rogalas case, then we shall be warranted in advocating interference to adjust that burden more wisely....

Document 15.5 The Sweating System

This study by Florence Kelly contrasts the two methods of manufacturing clothes: the factory system and the sweating system. She very much favors the former, and explains the advantages of that system. Very critical of the sweating system, Kelly explores the problems that attended it. Florence Kelly herself worked with Jane Addams at Hull House in Chicago. Settlement Houses were created to improve the lives of inhabitants in poor, immigrant neighborhoods. While they established a myriad of programs, Hull House also sponsored research of the surrounding neighborhoods that was used to argue for laws to remediate social problems.

The sweating-system is confined in Chicago to the garment trades, which employ some 25,000 to 30,000 people (as nearly as we can estimate), among whom this system is found in all its modes and tenses. The manufacture of garments is in the hands of wholesale firms. Their factories are grouped in the first ward of the city, within a radius of four blocks, where they have large, well-lighted, fairly wholesome workrooms, in which the garments for the entire trade are cut. The cutters, having a strong organization, refuse to work except under conditions more or less equal with the conditions of work usual in the well-organized trades. The hours and wages prevailing in the cutters' shops, therefore, do not differ much from the hours and wages usual in the well-organized trades. Some of the wholesale manufacturers have not only the cutters' shops, but also large workrooms, in which all the processes of clothing manufacture are carried on. These latter are known as "inside shops," or garment factories; and in them the employees work under conditions vastly better than are imposed upon the sweaters' victims, though still farther than the cutters below the standard of hours and wages maintained in the well-organized trades.

In the inside shops the sanitary conditions are fairly good; and power is frequently, though by no means uniformly, furnished for running machines. The same division of labor prevails as in the smaller shops; and the garment, after being cut, goes to the operator, who stitches the seams, to the buttonholer, the finisher, and the presser. In the inside shop the presser is usually also a skilled cleaner, and adds to his function of pressing the garment made on the premises the duty of removing grease and other soils from the garments returned from the sweaters' shops. There are also usually employed in these shops both basters and girls who pull bastings out of the finished garments. Formerly the operator was often an "all around worker," who received the garment from the cutters, and handed it finished to the examiner; but the competition of the sweaters has led to a very general introduction of hand-girls, one of whom works with each operator, doing the hand-finishing on the garment as it comes from the operator. The sweating-system has affected disastrously the condition of the employees in the inside shops, since any demand of the inside hands for increased wages or shorter hours is promptly met by transfer of work from the inside shop to a sweater; and the cutters alone remain secure from this competition.

A very important functionary in the inside clothing shops is the examiner, who receives finished garments both from the inside hands and the sweaters, and passes upon the satisfactoriness of the work. Incidentally, it is a painful duty of the examiner to find and destroy the vermin commonly infesting garments returned from outside workers....

With two exceptions, every manufacturer of garments in Chicago gives out clothing to be made in tenement houses. This is true of white underwear and custom-made outer wear, quite as much as of the ready-made clothing ordinarily associated in the public mind with the sweating-system. There are three common variations in the manner of giving out goods. Many manufacturers have closed their inside shops, and retain only their cutting-rooms. These

Florence Kelley, "The Sweating-System," *Hull-House Maps and Papers: A Presentation of Nationalities and Wages in a Congested District of Chicago, Together with Comments and Essays on Problems Growing Out of the Social Conditions* (New York: Thomas Y. Crowell, 1895): 27-45.

give garments directly to large numbers of individual employees, who make them up in their dwellings; or to sweaters, or to both. Manufacturers who retain their inside shops commonly give out garments in both these ways; and many of them also make a practice of requiring employees who work by day to take home garments at night, and on Saturday, to be made at home on Sunday.

Every manufacturer keeps a list of the names and addresses of the people to whom he gives out garments to be made up, and is required by law to show this list on demand to the factory and workshop inspectors.

It is the duty of the inspectors to follow up these lists, and examine the surroundings amidst which this work is done; and they report that the conditions in which garments are made that are given out from the inside shops for night work and Sunday work differ not a jot from the tenement house shops and the sweaters' home finishers' dwellings. Thus, a recent night inspection of work given out from one of the largest cloak manufactories in the West resulted as follows: The garment maker was found in his tenement dwelling in the rear of a factory. With his family, a wife and four indescribably filthy children, he occupies a kitchen and two bedrooms. The farther bedroom could be entered only by passing through the other rooms. This farther bedroom, where the man was found at work, was 7 X 7 X 8 feet, and contained a bed, a machine, one chair, a reeking lamp, and two men. The bed seemed not to have been made up in weeks; and in the bed, in a heap, there lay two overcoats, two hats, a mass of bed-covers, and nine fine tan-color capes trimmed with ecru lace, a tenth cape being on the machine in process of stitching. The whole dwelling was found to be crawling with vermin, and the capes were not free from it....

The Sweaters

The name of the sweaters is legion. More than a thousand of their shops have been inspected, and more than eight hundred licensed by the city; while it is an open secret that these numbers fall far below the total actually existing. It is well-nigh impossible to keep perfect lists of sweaters; since a man may be an operator to-day, a sweater on a small scale next week, may move his shop in the night to avoid the payment of rent, and may be found working as operator in an inside shop at the close of the season.

The sweaters differ from the cutters in their relation to the manufacturers, in that the sweaters have no organization, and are incapable of making any organized demand for a standard of prices. They are separated by differences of religion, nationality, language, and location. As individuals they haggle with the manufacturers, undercutting each other, and calculating upon their power to reduce the pay of their employees below any point to which the manufacturers may reduce theirs; and as individuals they tyrannize over the victims who have the misfortune to work in their shops. There has never been, and there is not now, in Chicago any association of sweaters of any kind whatsoever. There is, therefore, no standard price for the making of any garment, either for the sweater or his victim. With every change of style, there is a change of price, and the tendency of the change is always downward. The fashion and the change of seasons are an ever-ready excuse for the manufacturers, who constantly aim to concentrate the work of the year into the shortest possible season....

The Nineteenth Ward

In the nineteenth ward the sweaters are Russian Jews and Bohemians; and their employees in the shops are of the same nationality, while their home finishers are exclusively Italians,—the wives and daughters of the streets-sweepers and railroad gang hands, who form so large a part of the population of the ward. The garments made here are principally coats, cloaks, trousers, knee-pants, and shirts. There are one hundred and sixty-two shops, employing men, women, and children.

The shops are, without exception, in tenement houses or in the rear of tenement houses, in two-story buildings facing alleys that are usually unpaved and always noxious with the garbage and refuse of a tenement-house district. If the sweater's shop is in a tenement house, it is sometimes—but very rarely—in the ground floor front room, built for a store and lighted by large store windows. But far more commonly it is a basement, or an attic, or the flat over a saloon, or the shed over a stable. All the tenement houses selected either for shops or home finishers are of the worst and most crowded description. The staircases are narrow, and are used in common by tenants and garment workers, so that infectious diseases breaking out among the swarming children can scarcely fail to be communicated to garments anywhere under the same roof, because the utmost laxity prevails in the matter of isolation. The unsanitary condition of many of these tenement houses, and the ignorance and abject poverty of the tenants, insure the maximum probability of disease; and diphtheria, scarlet-fever, smallpox, typhoid, scabies, and worse forms of skin diseases, have been found in alarming proximity to garments of excellent quality in process of manufacture for leading firms.

There is not in the whole ward a clothing-shop in any building erected for the purpose; and in no case is steam-power supplied, but the use of foot-power is universal. In but one case known to me within this ward has a sweater acquired means sufficient to own the premises on which his shop is carried on. Employers of this class are usually tenants, who rent by the week or month, and move upon the shortest notice. To illustrate: There is at 165 West Twelfth Street a crowded tenement house, with a Chinese laundry in the ground floor front, and swarming families above. In the ground floor rear is a Jewish butcher-shop, where sausage (not of pork) is made during part of the year; but at midsummer, meat is roasted to supply the demand of a large surrounding colony of Russian Jews. Over this butcher-shop is a tailor-shop, into which the fumes and heat of the wholesale roasting below rise in the most overpowering manner. This shop possesses an irresistible attraction to sweaters of several varieties. It was occupied last summer by a firm of cloakmakers. When they were required to vacate by reason of its unsanitary condition, the shop stood empty but a short time, when two coat-making partners moved in with a large body of victims. As the landlord could not be induced to make any improvement, these also were required to move; and the shop is now occupied by a veteran knee-pants maker, who moved into it when required to separate his shop from his dwelling as a sanitary measure!

Under a clause of the law which prohibits the use of any bedroom or kitchen for the manufacture of garments by any person outside of the immediate family living therein, the inspectors are waging war upon contractors who employ help in kitchen or bedroom, or in any room accessible only by going through the living-rooms of the family. The law is loosely drawn, the difficulties are many, and progress is slow towards an entire separation of shop and dwelling. Nor will such separation ever be complete until all manufacture in any tenement house is prohibited by law.

Meanwhile, every tenement-house shop is ruinous to the health of the employees. Basement shops are damp, and entail rheumatism. They never afford proper accommodations for the pressers, the fumes of whose gasoline stoves and charcoal heaters mingle with the mouldy smell of the walls and the stuffiness, always found where a number of the very poor are crowded together. The light in basement shops is bad, and they are colder in winter and hotter in summer than workrooms in ordinary factories.

Attic shops are hot in summer, and usually foul by reason of the presence of closets to which the water does not rise. As these shops are often on the fifth floor of crowded tenement houses, with narrow wooden stairs, no fire-escapes, and no sufficient water supply, the danger of death by fire is greatly aggravated by the omnipresent presser's stove. Shops on the middle floors are ill-lighted, ill-ventilated, and share the smell from the kitchens and drains of surrounding tenement flats.

The dye from cheap cloth goods is sometimes poisonous to the skin; and the fluff from such goods inhaled by the operators is excessively irritating to the membranes, and gives rise to inflammations of the eye and various forms of catarrh. All these conditions, taken together with the exhaustion consequent upon driving foot-power machines at the highest possible rate of speed, make consumption, either of the lung or intestine, the characteristic malady of the sweaters' victim.

In the minds of the physicians, nurses, and inspectors best acquainted with the sweaters' victims of the nineteenth ward, there is no doubt that the substitution of steam-power for foot-power would do more to change this medical aspect of the case than any other one change that could be made. This is, however, entirely hopeless until tenement-house manufacture is prohibited. Meanwhile, the trade life of the garment worker is probably shorter than prevails in any other occupation; and the employees are always on the verge of pauperism, and fall into the abyss with every illness or particularly bad season.

If the sweaters' victim or any member of his family fall ill, his only hope is in the county doctor and the visiting nurse supported by charity, unless the patient be taken outright to the Michael Reese or County Hospital. If the illness prove a long one, recourse must be had to the various charities; and death brings a funeral ending in the potter's field, unless some prosperous brother of the faith provide for private burial.

A typical example is the experience of a cloakmaker who began work at his machine in this ward at the age of fourteen years, and was found, after twenty years of temperate life and faithful work, living in a rear basement, with four of his children apparently dying of pneumonia, at the close of a winter during which they had had, for weeks together, no food but bread and water, and had been four days without bread. The visiting nurse had two of the children removed to a hospital, and nursed the other two safely through their illness, feeding the entire family nearly four months. Place after place was found for the father; but he was too feeble to be of value to any sweater, and was constantly told that he was not worth the room he took up. A place being found for him in charge of an elevator, he could not stand; and two competent physicians, after a careful examination, agreed that he was suffering from old age. Twenty years at a machine had made him an old man at thirty-four. During these twenty years his earnings had ranged from $260 to $300 per annum.

Even without illness in his family, the sweaters' victim is regularly a pauper during a part of the year. The two seasons of the trade in each year are followed by long pauses, during which nothing can be earned, and debts are incurred. If the "slack" season is phenomenally short, in a year of unusual commercial prosperity, the sweaters' victim may perhaps live through it, by means of the credit given him by the landlord and grocer, without applying for aid to the Charities or the County Relief. But in the ordinary years of merely average prosperity, the sweaters' victim is inevitably an applicant for relief, to supplement, during three to five months, the earnings made during the busy season.

This fact effectively disposes of the favorite humanitarian argument on behalf of tenement-house manufacture; namely, that widows with children to support must be permitted to work at home. Even if these widows made a sufficient living for themselves and their children, the price paid for their prosperity, in the spread of disease and the demoralization of a vast trade, might be considered exorbitant. As a matter of fact, however, no tenement-house garment maker earns a sufficient living for a family, least of all the widow whose housework and care of her children interrupt her sewing, and whose very necessities are exploited by the sweater in his doling out of work and pay. What we really get in the case of the widow is the worst conceivable form of tenement-house manufacture, with full-fledged pauperism thrown into the bargain.

It is preposterous, on the face of it, that a trade employing from 25,000 to 30,000 persons in a single city, with an annual output of many millions of dollars, should be carried on with the same primitive machines which were used thirty years ago. In every other branch of manufacture the watchword of the present generation has been concentration. Everywhere steam, electricity, and human ingenuity have been pressed into service for the purpose of organization and centralization; but in the garment trades this process has been reversed, and the division of labor

has been made a means of demoralization, disorganization, and degradation, carried to a point beyond which it is impossible to go. While the textile mills in which the material for garments is spun and woven have been constantly enlarged and improved, both as to the machinery used and as to the healthfulness of the surroundings of the work-people, the garment trade has been enriched merely by the addition of the buttonhole machine; and this lone, lorn improvement has been made the means of deforming the illiterate children employed at it.

Thirty years ago the shoemaker and the tailor were more or less equally placed. Each went through the experience of the apprentice, the journeyman, the master, working for a limited market, and more or less in personal contact with the individual customer. Today the shoe industry possesses a wealth of perfected machinery, such that a tanned hide can be carried through all the processes of manufacture under a single roof and with incredible speed. The shoemaker's shop, with its little group of workers, has become the shoemaking town, with a vast organization, both of capital and of labor, and a very high degree of intelligence and class consciousness pervading the thousands of employees. The garment worker, on the contrary, still works in his kitchen, perhaps with the aid of his wife, performing one of the dozen subdivisions of the labor of making garments. He rarely belongs to an organization, and if he does it is so weak as to be almost useless to him either for education or defense. If he is an "all-round garment worker," whatever his skill may be, he has little use for it; since, in competition with him, the cutter cuts, the operator stitches, the seam-binder binds seams, the hand-girl fells, the presser presses, the buttonholer makes buttonholes by the thousand gross. Whatever the disadvantages of the division of labor, the garment worker suffers them all. Of its advantages he has never had a taste.

A curious example of the isolation of the garment worker is found in a crowded tenement house in Ewing Street, known as "Poverty Flat," where five different women were found sewing, each in her own kitchen, five different bundles of knee-pants for the same sweater. The knee-pants were of the same size and quality, with the same amount of work to be done upon them; but the prices paid were five cents, seven cents, nine cents, eleven and thirteen cents per dozen, rising in accordance with the skill in haggling of the home finisher, and with no relation to her skill in sewing on buttons.

A millionaire philanthropist, at the head of one of the largest clothing-houses in the world, was once asked why he did not employ directly the people who made his goods, and furnish them with steam-power, thus saving a heavy drain upon their health, and reducing the number of sweaters' victims found every winter in his pet hospital. "So far," he replied, "we have found leg-power and the sweater cheaper."

In the shoe industry the products have been cheapened by developing the plant, perfecting the machinery, and employing relatively well-paid, high-grade labor. In the garment trade there is no plant. Under the sweating-system, with the foot-power sewing-machine, cheapness is attained solely at the cost of the victim. Even the inside shops are often located in rented quarters, and frequently the operator is required to supply his own machine, or to pay the rent of a hired one; and even with these niggardly provisions the manufacturers find it profitable to shift the burden of rent upon the sweaters, who, in turn, reduce the size of their shops by giving out garments to the buttonholer and the home finisher.

The intimate connection between this decentralization of the trade and the danger of infecting the purchaser with disease prevalent in tenement-house districts, is too palpable to need comment, and emphasizes the question why the clothing manufacturer should be permitted to eliminate the item of rent from his expenses, at the cost of the trade and of the purchasing community. All other manufacturers have to include rent in their calculations, why not he?

The condition of the sweaters' victim is a conclusive refutation of the ubiquitous argument that poverty is the result of crime, vice, intemperance, sloth, and unthrift; for the Jewish sweaters' victims are probably more temperate, hard-working, and avaricious than any equally large body of wage-earners in America. Drunkenness is unknown among them. So great is their eagerness to improve the social condition of their children, that they willingly suffer the utmost privation of clothing, food, and lodging, for the sake of keeping their boys in school. Yet the reward of work at their trade is grinding poverty, ending only in death or escape to some more hopeful occupation. Within the trade there has been and can be no improvement in wages while tenement-house manufacture is tolerated. On the contrary, there seems to be no limit to the deterioration not in progress....

Document 15.6 The Triangle Shirtwaist Fire

This article from the *New York Times* provides a graphic description of a fire that killed 146 young workers at the Triangle Waist Company in New York City on March 25, 1911. The company finished women's shirts. This account, however, provides a different perspective from that of Florence Kelly about factory conditions in the cloth making industry.

---

141 Men and Girls Die in Waist Factory Fire; Trapped High Up in Washington Place Building; Street Strewn with Bodies; Piles of Dead Inside

Three stories of a ten-floor building at the corner of Greene Street and Washington Place were burned yesterday, and while the fire was going on 141 young men and women at least 125 of them mere girls were burned to death or killed by jumping to the pavement below.

The building was fireproof. It shows now hardly any signs of the disaster that overtook it. The walls are as good as ever so are the floors, nothing is the worse for the fire except the furniture and 141 of the 600 men and girls that were employed in its upper three stories.

Most of the victims were suffocated or burned to death within the building, but some who fought their way to the windows and leaped met death as surely, but perhaps more quickly, on the pavements below.

New York Times, March 26, 1911, p. 1.

All Over in Half an Hour

Nothing like it has been seen in New York since the burning of the General Slocum. The fire was practically all over in half an hour. It was confined to three floors the eighth, ninth, and tenth of the building. But it was the most murderous fire that New York had seen in many years.

The victims who are now lying at the Morgue waiting for some one to identify them by a tooth or the remains of a burned shoe were mostly girls from 16 to 23 years of age. They were employed at making shirtwaist by the Triangle Waist Company, the principal owners of which are Isaac Harris and Max Blanck. Most of them could barely speak English. Many of them came from Brooklyn. Almost all were the main support of their hard-working families.

There is just one fire escape in the building. That one is an interior fire escape. In Greene Street, where the terrified unfortunates crowded before they began to make their mad leaps to death, the whole big front of the building is guiltless of one. Nor is there a fire escape in the back.

The building was fireproof and the owners had put their trust in that. In fact, after the flames had done their worst last night, the building hardly showed a sign. Only the stock within it and the girl employees were burned.

A heap of corpses lay on the sidewalk for more than an hour. The firemen were too busy dealing with the fire to pay any attention to people whom they supposed beyond their aid. When the excitement had subsided to such an extent that some of the firemen and policemen could pay attention to this mass of the supposedly dead they found about half way down in the pack a girl who was still breathing. She died two minutes after she was found.

The Triangle Waist Company was the only sufferer by the disaster. There are other concerns in the building, but it was Saturday and the other companies had let their people go home. Messrs. Harris and Blanck, however, were busy and ?? their girls and some stayed.

Leaped Out of the Flames

At 4:40 o'clock, nearly five hours after the employees in the rest of the building had gone home, the fire broke out. The one little fire escape in the interior was resorted to by any of the doomed victims. Some of them escaped by running down the stairs, but in a moment or two this avenue was cut off by flame. The girls rushed to the windows and looked down at Greene Street, 100 feet below them. Then one poor, little creature jumped. There was a plate glass protection over part of the sidewalk, but she crashed through it, wrecking it and breaking her body into a thousand pieces.

Then they all began to drop. The crowd yelled "Don't jump!" but it was jump or be burned the proof of which is found in the fact that fifty burned bodies were taken from the ninth floor alone.

They jumped, they crashed through broken glass, they crushed themselves to death on the sidewalk. Of those who stayed behind it is better to say nothing except what a veteran policeman said as he gazed at a headless and charred trunk on the Greene Street sidewalk hours after the worst cases had been taken out:

"I saw the Slocum disaster, but it was nothing to this."

"Is it a man or a woman?" asked the reporter.

"It's human, that's all you can tell," answered the policeman.

It was just a mass of ashes, with blood congealed on what had probably been the neck.

Messrs. Harris and Blanck were in the building, but they escaped. They carried with them Mr. Blanck's children and a governess, and they fled over the roofs. Their employees did not know the way, because they had been in the habit of using the two freight elevators, and one of these elevators was not in service when the fire broke out.

Found Alive After the Fire

The first living victims, Hyman Meshel of 322 East Fifteenth Street, was taken from the ruins four hours after the fire was discovered. He was found paralyzed with fear and whimpering like a wounded animal in the basement, immersed in water to his neck, crouched on the top of a cable drum and with his head just below the floor of the elevator.

Meantime the remains of the dead it is hardly possible to call them bodies, because that would suggest something human, and there was nothing human about most of these were being taken in a steady stream to the Morgue for identification. First Avenue was lined with the usual curious east side crowd. Twenty-sixth Street was impassable. But in the Morgue they received the charred remnants with no more emotion than they ever display over anything.

Back in Greene Street there was another crowd. At midnight it had not decreased in the least. The police were holding it back to the fire lines, and discussing the tragedy in a tone which those seasoned witnesses of death seldom use.

"It's the worst thing I ever saw," said one old policeman.

Chief Croker said it was an outrage. He spoke bitterly of the way in which the Manufacturers' Association had called a meeting in Wall Street to take measures against his proposal for enforcing better methods of protection for employees in cases of fire.

No Chance to Save Victims

Four alarms were rung in fifteen minutes. The first five girls who jumped did go before the first engine could respond. That fact may not convey much of a picture to the mind of an unimaginative man, but anybody who has ever seen a fire can get from it some idea of the terrific rapidity with which the flames spread.

It may convey some idea too, to say that thirty bodies clogged the elevator shaft. These dead were all girls. They had made their rush there blindly when they discovered that there was no chance to get out by the fire escape. Then they found that the elevator was as hopeless as anything else, and they fell there in their tracks and died.

The Triangle Waist Company employed about 600 women and less than 100 men. One of the saddest features of the thing is the fact that they had almost finished for the day. In five minutes more, if the fire had started then, probably not a life would have been lost.

Last night District Attorney Whitman started an investigation not of this disaster alone but of the whole condition which makes it possible for a firetrap of such a kind to exist. Mr. Whitman's intention is to find out if the present laws cover such cases, and if they do not to frame laws that will.

Girls Jump To Sure Death

Fire Nets Prove Useless
Firemen Helpless to Save Life

The fire which was first discovered at 4:40 o'clock on the eighth floor of the ten-story building at the corner of Washington Place and Greene Street, leaped through the three upper stories occupied by the Triangle Waist Company with a sudden rush that left the Fire Department helpless.

How the fire started no one knows. On the three upper floors of the building were 600 employees of the waist company, 500 of whom were girls. The vic-tims mostly Italians, Russians, Hungarians, and Germans were girls and men who had been employed by the firm of Harris & Blanck, owners of the Triangle Waist Company, after the strike in which the Jewish girls, formerly employed, had been become unionized and had demanded better working conditions. The building had experienced four recent fires and had been reported by the Fire Department to the Building Department as unsafe in account of the insufficiency of its exits.

The building itself was of the most modern construction and classed as fireproof. What burned so quickly and disastrously for the victims were shirtwaists, hanging on lines above tiers of workers, sewing machines placed so closely together that there was hardly aisle room for the girls between them, and shirtwaist trimmings and cuttings which littered the floors above the eighth and ninth stories.

Girls had begun leaping from the eighth story windows before firemen arrived. The firemen had trouble bringing their apparatus into position because of the bodies which strewed the pavement and sidewalks. While more bodies crashed down among them, they worked with desperation to run their ladders into position and to spread firenets.

One fireman running ahead of a hose wagon, which halted to avoid running over a body spread a firenet, and two more seized hold of it. A girl's body, coming end over end, struck on the side of it, and there was hope that she would be the first one of the score who had jumped to be saved.

Thousands of people who had crushed in from Broadway and Washington Square and were screaming with horror at what they saw watched closely the work with the firenet. Three other girls who had leaped for it a moment after the first one, struck it on top of her, and all four rolled out and lay still upon the pavement.

Five girls who stood together at a window close the Greene Street corner held their place while a fire ladder was worked toward them, but which stopped at its full length two stories lower down. They leaped together, clinging to each other, with fire streaming back from their hair and dresses. They struck a glass sidewalk cover and went through it to the basement. There was no time to aid them. With water pouring in upon them from a dozen hose nozzles the bodies lay for two hours where they struck, as did the many others who leaped to their deaths.

One girl, who waved a handkerchief at the crowd, leaped from a window adjoining the New York University Building on the westward. Her dress caught on a wire, and the crowd watched her hang there till her dress burned free and she came toppling down.

Many jumped whom the firemen believe they could have saved. A girl who saw the glass roof of a sidewalk cover at the first-story level of the New York University Building leaped for it, and her body crashed through to the sidewalk.

On Greene Street, running along the eastern face of the building more people leaped to the pavement than on Washington Place to the south. Fire nets proved just as useless to catch them and the ladders to reach them. None waited for the firemen to attempt to reach them with the scaling ladders.

All Would Soon Have Been Out. Strewn about as the firemen worked, the bodies indicated clearly the preponderance of women workers. Here and there was a man, but almost always they were women. One wore furs and a muss, and had a purse hanging from her arm. Nearly all were dressed for the street. The fire had flashed through their workroom just as they were expecting the signal to leave the building. In ten minutes more all would have been out, as many had stopped work in advance of the signal and had started to put on their wraps.

What happened inside there were few who could tell with any definiteness. All those that escaped seemed to remember was that there was a flash of flames, leaping first among the girls in the southeast corner of the eighth floor and then suddenly over the entire room, spreading through the linens and cottons with which the girls were working. The girls on the ninth floor caught sight of the flames through the window up the stairway, and up the elevator shaft.

On the tenth floor they got them a moment later, but most of those on that floor escaped by rushing to the roof and then on to the roof of the New York University Building, with the assistance of 100 university students who had been dismissed from a tenth story classroom.

There were in the building, according to the estimate of Fire Chief Croker, about 600 girls and 100 men.

Chapter 15 Worksheet and Questions

1. Technological Systems: In order understand the relationship between workers and technological systems, we need a good understanding of that system, its process, and its products. How do the accounts of Garland (15.1) and Sinclair (15.2) describe the systems of smelting steel and meat packing? That is, what was produced, and what processes were used to produce it? (Be sure to consider standardization of products and rationalization of processes.)

_____

_____

_____

_____

_____

_____

_____

_____

_____

2. Technological Systems: How do Garland (15.1) and Sinclair (15.2) view the systems for steel production and meat packing? (Do they find anything admirable about them? Anything troubling? Are they impressed?)

_____

_____

_____

_____

_____

_____

_____

_____

_____

3. Rationalization of Labor in Technological Systems: In *The Principles of Scientific Management*, Frederick Taylor suggests that "the system must come first." Based upon the documents by Garland (15.1), Sinclair (15.2), and Taylor (15.3), was this an accurate statement about the rationalization of labor or how labor was fitted into production systems?

_____

_____

_____

_____

_____

_____

_____

_____

_____

_____

4. Rationalization of Labor in Technological Systems: Based upon the accounts by Garland (15.1), Sinclair (15.2), Taylor (15.3), and Kelly (15.5), how did laborers respond to their position in the processes of manufacturing products?

_____

_____

_____

_____

_____

_____

_____

_____

_____

5. Rationalization of Labor in Technological Systems: Based upon all of the readings, how would you describe the factory environment and the effects of technological systems upon laborers?

_____

_____

_____

_____

_____

_____

_____

_____

_____

_____

6. Systems of Making Clothes: Based upon the articles by Kelly (15.5) and the *New York Times* (15.6), which system of producing clothing evidenced more concern for the health and safety of workers? Would this be another example of "the system comes first?" (Consider the differences between the Sweating System and the Factory System, and what the Triangle Shirt Waist Factory fire suggests about conditions in clothing factories.)

_____

_____

_____

_____

_____

_____

_____

_____

_____

_____

_____

Chapter 16

The City: Diversity and Complexity

In its briefest version, U.S. history may be summed up by the statement: "America was born on the farm and grew up in the city." If so, the nation reached maturity between 1870 and 1920. Urban population increased from 8.2 million, or 20 percent of U.S. population, to 54 million, or a majority (55%) of Americans. At the same time, cities doubled, tripled, and in some cases quadrupled in size. While this growth is important and impressive, even more significantly, the understanding or very meaning of "city" changed. Prior to 1870, cities were quite literally walking cities, relatively compact, often densely populated areas, located in places with convenient access to water transportation like oceans, rivers, and lakes. Subsequently, cities became sprawling, heavily populated, industrial centers situated near and linked by rails more than waterways.

Contemporaries appreciated the transformation of the physical characteristics of cities, yet they cast their descriptions of them in terms of complexity and diversity, concepts they believed best characterized the new urban environment. That is, cities were not undifferentiated constellations of industries and people strewn haphazardly across a landscape. Instead they were made up of separate and distinctive areas dedicated to specific uses like industry, business, commerce, entertainment, and residence. The inhabitants too were grouped into specific locations, based upon what contemporaries perceived to be significant differences among them, like class, race, nationality, ethnicity, occupation, and religion. Their views about the complexity, but especially the diversity, of cities will provide the focus for this chapter.

Inhabitants of late nineteenth- and early twentieth-century cities recognized the various districts and neighborhoods that comprised their cities. In the new city, non-residential areas were differentiated by specialized use or function. For example, industrial districts, almost invariably placed near rail lines, housed the new industrial systems discussed in the previous chapter. For Kansas City, the "West Bottoms" served this purpose. The "Gateway to the West" became the second largest meat processor in the country, when Armour and Company, Swift and Company, and Cudahy Packing Company, among others, assembled beef packing plants with hundreds of acres of holding pens in the "Bottoms." Pillsbury and other companies situated wheat milling operations in the same vicinity. Similarly, railroads like the Chicago, Burlington and Quincy Railroad and the Missouri Pacific Railroad erected maintenance shops and switchyards in the same location. Some cities specialized in particular kinds of products. As mentioned in the last chapter, Pittsburgh became associated with steel, and Chicago with meat packing. Detroit moved from maritime engines to automobiles. Other cities grew around industries: Schenectady with electrical equipment, Battle Creek with grain products, and Hershey with chocolate.

Industrial districts were crucial to the new cities. In one respect, industrial plants employed millions of laborers and gave people a reason to emigrate. Similarly, they supplied the goods and services needed for life in a city. The new technological systems also connected people together in ways that made urban life possible. Electricity was an invaluable service for businesses and city dwellers. It also connected urbanites to an electrical generator and to one another through a distribution network of feeders and mains. In 1888, Frank Sprague used the utility to power the first electric trolley in Richmond, Virginia. Quickly adopted elsewhere, electrical street traction systems permitted the geographic expansion of cities by enabling people to live farther from the urban center. Furthermore, it connected residents of different neighborhoods to a variety of advantages offered by cities, such as shopping, business, work, or entertainment. Subsequently, overhead or elevated railways were introduced in New York but were used more extensively as the "El" in

Chicago, while subways employing electrical traction underground became common first in New York and Boston. Telephones, too, connected people through a system of lines and switches, but also through the communication that it made possible. Water and sewer systems established the same sort of connections. Railroads and the new Piggly Wiggly chain of grocery stores linked city dwellers with farmers. These urban technological systems also connected the diverse and specialized parts of cities.

In addition to industrial districts, cities almost invariably had areas dedicated to the use of business, commerce, and entertainment. The introduction of skyscrapers identified business districts while changing urban skylines. Chicago, with its "Chicago school" of architects, led the movement; by the turn of the century, buildings of 30 stories became common. Corporations, banks, and financial institutions found the towering and spacious structures ideal for centralizing business operations. Innovations in retail trade, like department stores, distinguished commercial districts. Among the first were Wanamaker's in Philadelphia, Marshall Fields' in Chicago, and Bloomingdale's in New York. Kansas Citians shopped along "Petticoat Lane" at stores like Doggett's, the self-proclaimed "representative department store of the West," and the Jones Store company, which became the principal destination of Christmas shoppers for decades. In addition to shopping, commercial districts featured restaurants and theaters. Residents looking for less savory pursuits or the opportunity to sin could patronize bars and dance halls that performed yet another specialized urban service in entertainment districts.

While cities were clearly typified by a functional use of space, their inhabitants, too, were arranged into a variety of distinct and separate neighborhoods. According to historian Alan Marcus, contemporaries viewed cities as "cauldrons of diversity." That is, in cities, they perceived a populace divided into a variety of types that reflected racial, national, ethnic, class, occupational, and religious differences. From this perspective, each type or group possessed distinct physical features, abilities, behaviors, and propensities. Academics, authors, and journalists of the time used the broad and inaccurate term "race" to ascribe to groups what are now understood as national, ethnic, racial, and religious differences. To be sure, classification schemes differed widely, and agreement about specific attributes proved rare. Nevertheless, contemporaries saw differences among groups like Italians, Poles, Africans, Jews, Anglo-Saxons, and even Americans as real and important, and as a basis for differential treatment. Furthermore, the social geography of the city, or the distribution of distinct types of people across the residential landscape, seemed to justify such beliefs. Just as cities were divided into districts, so too its inhabitants were distributed into a wide diversity of neighborhoods, each identified with a distinct group or type.

Wealth represented one more attribute upon which urbanites established neighborhoods. The most affluent city dwellers, who had lived near businesses at the center of walking cities, moved away, as immigrants and industries moved in. Frequently, the affluent made use of trolley systems in order to live in large, comfortable estates on the outskirts of cities. For example, Cincinnati's wealthy citizens relocated to the Hilltops, while Kansas City's went to Mission Hills. Both locations were far removed from the crowds, noise, dirt, and disease (among other problems) that the wealthy associated with the new urban core. In other cases, they established enclaves within the city, like Fifth Avenue in New York or Nob Hill in San Francisco. The middle class, too, relied upon electric railways to move farther from the center of the city; they purchased homes with yards. Many left the city entirely to live in the latest amenities in "street car suburbs." Wealthy and middle-class neighborhoods were based upon and distinguished by relative degrees of wealth. However, affluent urbanites also established separate communities based upon occupation and religion. Middle-class neighborhoods too were subdivided along occupational lines, skilled workers versus clerical workers, and religious affiliations.

As the exodus from the center of the city occurred, cities became even more diverse due to the emigration of the working class and poor into cities. The newcomers almost invariably took up residence in the inner city, or what became known in the late nineteenth century as the "slums." They settled into "colonies," a mosaic of diverse neighborhoods composed of discrete groups. Journalists like Jacob Riis expressed wonder at the variety of people living in the inner city. A *Chicago Tribune* reporter described the new neighborhoods as a "cosmopolis." Such characterizations reflected the use of the idea of social types common at the time, and indicated the origins of the new urbanites.

Since colonial times, the European immigration to the United States came primarily from the western part of the continent, which included the English, Irish, Germans, and Scots, and to a lesser degree the Dutch, French, and Spanish. Between 1870 and 1920, immigrants increasingly left southern and eastern European nations for the United States. Italians, Poles, Russian Jews, Poles, and Slavs arrived in the largest numbers during this period. By 1890, the immigrant population of Chicago equaled the total population of the city a decade earlier. Immigrants made up one third of Philadelphia's population, and one fourth of Boston's. In the same year, 80 percent of the people living in New York were immigrants or their first-generation children born in the city.

While a majority of new inhabitants originated in Europe, native-born Americans flowed into the cities as well. Emigrants from farms accounted for nearly one fourth of urban population growth. Among them were Southern blacks, the first of the great migration to Northern cities. By 1910, as many as 100,000 reached New York. Ten years later, 109,000 lived in Chicago. Foreign or native-born, the new ghettoes exemplified diversity.

The slums wedded diversity with geography. Living together in distinct groups, communities established their own institutions. Where sufficient numbers lived, local newspapers circulated, written in the language of the inhabitants and addressing their particular concerns. Restaurants serving native dishes thrived. Social clubs for the arts, debate, or other educational activities took shape. Political bosses appointed "ward healers," hacks who organized citizens of the neighborhoods in taverns. Churches, synagogues, and temples were built to hold Roman Catholic, Greek Orthodox, Jewish, and other religious rituals familiar to the worshippers. Benevolent groups and mutual aid societies were also created to provide assistance when needed to members of neighborhoods.

If different groups in the slums created similar institutions, they also experienced the same conditions of life. Poor, dilapidated, and overcrowded housing was a constant problem. The first wave of immigrants moving into cities occupied the mansions abandoned by wealthy families. Landlords offered single rooms as apartments for entire families. They subdivided and rented larger spaces as well. Ramshackle wooden buildings were erected in alleys and along backstreets. Dank cellars, subject to flooding with heavy rains, also served as family dwellings. Demand for housing led to the construction of tenements. Dumbbell tenements, named after the weights they resembled when viewed from above, usually rose five stories and contained twenty apartments.

Construction could not keep up with the influx of population. In one exceptional case, a New York tenement held four hundred people. Further adding to the crowding, already large families defrayed expenses by taking in lodgers. The new tenements were intended to provide a healthful setting infused with light and air, but the construction of one next to another defeated both purposes. Typically, housing in the inner cities tended to be dirty, poorly ventilated, dark, and inadequately heated. Running water did not become common until the early 1900s. The same was true of indoor toilets. Kansas City differed little from other cities in this regard. The Board of Public Welfare reported in 1910 that in backyards and behind buildings stood rows of as many as 20 privies intended to meet the needs of hundreds of people. Infrequently emptied, vaults overflowed, spilling urine and feces in the immediate area and, after rains, onto streets. Flies thrived, and complaints about them were common as well.

Living conditions did not improve outside of living quarters. For the three decades after 1870, the slums represented, in the views of contemporaries, public health menaces. Unpaved streets became muddy quagmires after rains. Lack of regular garbage collection resulted in piles of refuse on streets and walkways. The remains of decaying animal carcasses added to the usual detritus. Sewage was a constant problem. Existing sewers emptied into creeks and rivers. During summers when water flow was reduced, streams backed up, in the estimate of one observer, into a "fetid mass of sewage."

The disposal of sewage into rivers and lakes posed another problem to cities that used them to supply drinking water. Air pollution was yet another public health threat. Electrical utilities and industries burned coal to produce steam and heat. Railroads, too, burned coal to drive steam locomotives. As pictures of cities during the period illustrate, the atmosphere took on a gray, sooty appearance even during the day. By 1920, city governments had addressed many of these problems. Political bosses discovered that civic improvements, like regular garbage collection, generated good will and votes. Municipal governments proceeded to pave streets, build water treatment facilities, construct sewer systems, and encourage the use of indoor toilets.

Throughout the period, however, slum conditions threatened health. They promoted the growth of a number of bacterial strains that, when combined with immune systems weakened by poor diet, produced thousands of deaths each year. Diseases like tuberculosis and dysentery thrived in crowded, poorly ventilated rooms and repeated exposure to fecal matter. Some historians have noted that, while extremely dangerous and taking hundreds of lives annually, these diseases were endemic and consequently their occurrence did not seem exceptional. On the other hand, epidemics of yellow fever, typhoid, cholera, polio, and influenza represented a constant threat, one that city governments were very much alive to. Typically, epidemics started in inner city neighborhoods and progressed to the other parts of the city. In 1878 and 1879, yellow fever epidemics struck Memphis, a city of 70,000. Nearly 20,000 caught the disease, and over 5,700 died. Subsequent studies demonstrated that the outbreaks originated in New Orleans. Infected passengers traveling up the Mississippi carried the disease with them to Memphis, where it broke out in Italian and Black neighborhoods. Other groups in the inner city contracted the disease before it spread to middle-class and wealthy neighborhoods.

The improvements sponsored by city governments did reduce the incidence of disease. Clean water, sewage treatment, paved streets, and garbage collection reduced the sources of bacterial infection (and transmission by insects), which significantly reduced the number of cases of cholera, yellow fever, and dysentery. Tuberculosis, polio, and influenza remained lethal. In fact, the worldwide influenza epidemic of 1918-1919 killed almost 700,000 Americans, making it the worst in the nation's history. Consequently, public health remained a problem for urbanites, especially those in the inner city.

Public order represented an equally pressing issue for cities. Between 1870 and 1920 conflicts between diverse groups living as communities in distinct geographical locations were also endemic. Competition for jobs and living space exacerbated the problem. Youth who formed neighborhood gangs, which one journalist described as an "institution" in the slums, added another element of menace and source of violence. The changing composition of neighborhoods over time was a constant source of friction between communities. Urban dwellers commented, usually unfavorably, on the succession of inhabitants living in the same buildings. One New York neighborhood reflected the changing patterns of immigration when the original Irish community was replaced by Germans, followed by Bohemians, and then Italians. Slum residents commonly expressed their grievances and tried to settle their differences in riots and fights on election days. In Kansas City, immigrant groups clashed so often during elections that the sixth ward became known as the "Bloody Sixth." Still, neighborhoods changed and many inner-city dwellers were able to move into the "zone of emergence" or the middle-class neighborhoods that abutted the slums.

Of all the groups living in the inner city, Blacks faced the most persistent discrimination, strictly enforced segregation, and violent resistance to expansion. Blacks confronted what W.E.B. DuBois called the "color line," a term adopted and redefined by journalists, politicians, and academics. While boundaries of other neighborhoods proved fluid over time, those of Black communities, referred to as the "Black Belt" in Chicago and as Harlem in New York, were fixed. One consequence was that problems of overcrowding, dilapidated housing, public health threats, and unemployment were far more acute in Black neighborhoods than in other parts of the city. Another was that Blacks created communities that were socioeconomically different from other groups. Since segregation restricted movement to other parts of the city, Black neighborhoods included the full spectrum of economic classes, from wealthy to poor. Of course, Black neighborhoods did expand, but the process was far more difficult and violent.

The worst riot broke out in Chicago on July 27, 1919 when a Black youth, Eugene Smith, swimming in Lake Michigan, strayed into a beach used by Whites. With a barrage of rocks, a mob of Whites prevented his coming to shore. Whether from exhaustion or from being hit by a projectile (accounts differ), Smith drowned. Rioting broke out on the beach and continued for the next four days, claiming the lives of 23 Blacks and 15 Whites. Another 340 Blacks and 178 whites were seriously injured. The Coroner's Report gave a full account of the events and suggested why they had taken place. Peter Hoffman, the coroner, attributed the rioting to "race hatred." He noted that meat packer managers had recruited Blacks and brought them to Chicago, presumably to threaten workers who might consider joining unions. Sensational newspaper accounts accusing Blacks of committing crimes also stirred White resentment. However, he identified the expansion of Black neighborhoods as the most important factor. Hoffman observed that in the weeks before the riots, Blacks had moved into housing beyond the "agreed upon boundary" of Michigan Avenue and 39th Street. In his recommendations to avoid a reoccurrence of rioting, Chicago's coroner concluded that Black neighborhoods, of necessity, had to expand. Between 1915 and 1919, the Black population doubled from about 50,000 to as many as 125,000. Since the existing space simply could not hold that increase, Blacks began to move into surrounding neighborhoods. Furthermore, Hoffman counseled the city to improve the extremely poor housing and sanitary conditions. In the years that followed, Blacks expanded the size of the neighborhood but the city failed to address the issues raised in the report.

The problems of public order, public health, and conditions in inner-city neighborhoods reflected the complexity and diversity that contemporaries perceived as defining the new urban environment. American cities changed between 1870 and 1920, as did America's understanding of "city" itself.

Considering the Evidence in the Readings

The documents in this chapter explore the diversity of the new industrial cities from a variety of different perspectives. In this case the documents are primarily descriptions by reporters and social scientists. However, they examine the implications of the diverse neighborhoods for the city, young immigrant women, public health, and race. You should note how the varieties of neighborhoods are described, that is, what makes them so diverse? What kinds of people live in them? How has their composition changed over time? Once you have a sense of the diverse peoples making up the city, look at their employment (especially with respect to the new industrial systems) and conditions of life. Was there a relationship? One thing you should think about is what diversity meant to the authors of these documents. What assumptions do they make about race and ethnicity? Further, think about the health and safety implications of the new neighborhoods. Finally, consider the differences between the treatment of Blacks and other ethnic groups. What does this suggest?

Document 16.1 Diversity in the 19th Ward

This *Chicago Tribune* article examines the complexity and diversity of Chicago's 19th Ward. The descriptions of different groups of people and the characteristics attributed to them provide a nice insight into the meaning of diversity at the beginning of the twentieth century. The discussion of "race" is particularly important. In many respects, this article corresponds closely to the observations of Jacob Riis in the next reading.

WHAT Is the Nineteenth Ward?

It Has Features of Strange Interest.
Its People Are of Twenty-six Nations.

Beginning at West Van Buren street and the river, west on West Van Buren to Throop, south on Throop to West Harrison, west on Harrison to Sibley, south on Sibley to West Taylor, east on West Taylor to Center avenue, south on Center avenue to West Twelfth, east on West Twelfth to the river, and north on the river to place of beginning.

That is the Nineteenth Ward, a ward which contains many features of strange interest and that rises to the sensational whenever, as at present, John Powers is a candidate for reelection to the Common Council. Its citizenship embraces, according to the school census, Americans, Belgians, Bohemians, Canadians, Danes, English, French, Germans, Greeks, Hollanders, Hungarians, Irish, Italians, Lithuanians, Mexicans, Norwegians, Poles, Russians, Scots, Spaniards, Swedes, Swiss, Welsh, Negroes, Chinese, and divers [*sic*] odds and ends classified under the head of "other countries" and "mixed parents." Among these "others" at the present day the Arabs deserve specific mention because, although they are not numerous, they nevertheless outnumber some of those people who have been separately named.

"What is the Nineteenth Ward," *Chicago Tribune* (February 13, 1898): 25.

The most remarkable thing about this list is that it contains no blanks. Wards that have a much smaller American population than the Nineteenth fail to make such a generous showing of the nations. There is the Seventh, for example. It has only 900 American residents to set against 6,184 in the Nineteenth, but it draws two blanks, not to speak of the Arabs. Moreover, of the nationalities represented only four rank above the thousand mark, whereas there are eight that may claim this distinction in the Nineteenth.

A glance shows that twenty-six separate peoples have been ascribed to that cosmopolis. A searcher for languages might travel all over Europe in the Nineteenth Ward and take in parts of both eastern and western Asia. He would find himself in a world's fair where there was a continuous performance. If he were an old resident of the city, once familiar with the district but long absent from it, he would be amazed at its tremendous changes. His memory might go back to the time when even down to the river it was largely American. A little later came the great increase of the Irish. Then there were the Germans and Bohemians. The passing of the races was first from over the river, and during the great tides of immigration from abroad it was about the nucleus thus formed, here and there, that the big foreign settlements developed. Naturally the newcomers sought neighbors among those of their own race and language. But Irish, Bohemians, and Germans lived side by side without either being to the others a cause of general exodus. Many of them became well-to-do and it is probable that under any circumstances they would have bought homes further away from the business center of the city, as that center began to throw its factories and warehouses into the ward.

Race Crowding Race

But the entry of new races had its influence also. As the Italians and the Russian Jews poured into the section east of Halsted street, the former on the north, the latter on the south, the emigration of the old inhabitants westward increased. The glory of Bohemia passed to the Eighth, Ninth, and Tenth Wards, and there was a general withdrawal beyond Halsted street. Meantime the leaven of Americanism was working. American born children in their new homes had children of their own, and these children would consider the world's fair of the Nineteenth Ward quite as curious a spectacle as if their ancestors had fought at Bunker Hill. They make the same distinction between Americans and foreigners as do the lions of the Revolution and feel the superiority of natives over all recent arrivals.

But there is an occasional survival to be met with in the old quarters. There may be a Bohemian saloon among the Jews, an Irish grocery among the Italians, and a dwelling or flat owned and occupied by representatives of the vanishing races. Descend into the yard of some little cottage that bears unmistakable evidence of being an old settler and you will be surprised at a hearty Milesian greeting, though the signs across the street and on both sides are certainly Neapolitan. Likely as not you will be ushered into a room, small but comfortable and where a good fire is burning, and you will resolve that the outward appearance of the Nineteenth is deceptive, in some cases at least, and that the neighborhood is not half as bad as it has been painted. The good impression is deepened amid social amenities. You begin to feel like one who has reached home after being stranded on a foreign shore. Little differences are forgotten and Irish, Scotch, English, and Americans seem essentially one and the same. The only difference remaining that you are conscious of, if you belong to one of the three people last named, is that of superior urbanity in your host or hostess. The warm welcome is reinforced by a grace of manners that is irresistible, and you succumb to the flattering charm in the best of good feeling.

"Thirty years and more," says the hostess in response to your inquiry concerning the period of her residence in the ward. The accent is just pleasant, not pronounced enough to indicate in writing. Yes, she has seen many changes, but she is loath to confess to race prejudices. She was never harassed with doubts by Germans or Bohemians. She could get along with them just as well as with her own people.

But the hospitality and the sentiment of the universal brotherhood of man had received a rude shock with the advent of the Italians. Here the urbane expression gave way to a censorious one, and the change was reflected in the countenance of a sympathetic friend.

"'Tis a shame," said the friend. "I thought the laws had been passed to keep them out."

"They are a noisy, quarreling set," continued the first speakers. "They are not even friendly with one another." It appeared also that their conduct as tenants left much to be desired. To have them in the same building with you was a sorrow, and when they departed it was a mystery how much of the building would remain. The plaster stood no show at all. "There are enough people in this country, anyway," interposed the friend again. It was a fair inference from her conversation that she would have put up the bars not long after her own arrival, which was not so many years ago, but even the most gracious nature will some time indulge in extreme expression under persistent irritation.

Further investigations served to lend color to the intimation that repose was not the leading trait of the Italian character. At various popular resorts in the neighborhood the groups of regular contributors were always in action. But there was no quarreling. What appeared like an earnest, not to say a passionate, invitation to a duel with knives was the Italian for calm. The fierce gesticulation, the heated argument amounting to a general chorus, were but the gentle messengers of peace. A general Italian quarrel would beggar description, and it is more than probable that what the Milesian lady took for angry disputes were outpourings of love and friendship.

"How many Italians in the ward?" ruminated one in authority. He did not throw any unnecessary terminal a's into his speech, but talked fluently and correctly. His estimate was 15,000. Another greater authority, who had delved much in politics, was more conservative in his estimate and equally correct in his English. He was given the school census for a text, and perhaps some comparative statistics from that document may not be uninteresting before his comment is reported.

The Nineteenth Ward has a population of 48,190, ranking fourteenth in this regard. The division into nationalities has been recorded already, and it has been explained also that eight of them are represented by more than a thousand persons each. These eight are: Irish, 13,065; Germans, 6,721; Americans, 6,184; Italians, 5,784; Russians, 4,980; Bohemians, 2,944; Canadians, 2,006; English, 1,460. In the smallness of its American population the ward ranks thirteenth. The Seventh heads the list with its almost incredibly small number of 930. The Twenty-third on the North Side at the fork of the river has only 1,780. The Eighth and Ninth, which, with the Seventh, bound the Nineteenth on the south, rank fourth and ninth respectively, the former having 2,310 and the latter 4,893. To show the variations in the neighborhood, the Seventh Ward, with a population of 42,049, has four races with a representation of over 1,000—German, 12,370; Russians, 11,130; Irish, 5,474; Bohemians, 4143. The Eighth, with a population of 41,729, has five nationalities with a representation of over 1,000—Bohemians, 18,076; German 7,329; Irish, 6,057; Russians, 8,521; Americans, 2,310. The Ninth, with a population of 56,369, has six nationalities with a representation of over 1,000—Bohemians, 17,172; German, 15,389; Irish, 7,700; Polish, 5,049; American, 4,893. It will thus be seen that in diversity of distribution the Nineteenth beats them all.

But it must be remembered that the school census was taken nearly two years ago, and that the entire district is in a condition of unstable equilibrium. The Italian commenator [sic] laughed at the Italian figures for the Nineteenth Ward, and, to judge by visible signs and the testimony of Bohemians and Irish, the figures are a joke by this time. The most densely populated Italian section of the ward lies, roughly speaking, between Halsted and Canal streets and Harrison and Taylor streets. This is something less than half a mile square, but what cannot be done with half a mile square to a people from Naples? Numerically they could make a metropolis of it. There are many Italians also in the old Tilden avenue district and in the triangle lying between Halsted and Twelfth street and Blue Island avenue. The commentator's estimate of 8,000, justified as it was by convincing reference to the voting strength of his countrymen, was certainly moderate enough. There can be no doubt that the Italians outnumber all other nationalities in the east end of the ward and that they now rank next to the Irish in the ward as a whole.

All but a very few families among them come from the south of Italy. They represent for the most part a new immigration, very different from the old one that was responsible for that curious combination of bar, oyster-house, and ice cream parlor, which meant Italy in this city long years ago. The owners of the "combines" were from the north, and they have become owners of handsome saloons or are making money by handling fruit at wholesale. They are the aristocrats of their race in Chicago, and live not in colonies, but in all parts of town.

Now, a vast majority of the Nineteenth-Warders are far removed from this aristocracy. They are common laborers, some from Sicily, some from Calabria, some from Naples. They work on the streets when they can get a chance, and the chance has generally come through "Johnny" Powers' henchmen. Moreover, it was declared amid a circle of approving nods from a considerable concourse of the laborers themselves that the favor of the said henchmen depended upon something more substantial than political activity. It took political activity plus a commission of wages to win, and the henchmen are not popular. But most of these voters are Republican, anyway, and it should be added that their number is large in proportion to the total Italian population. That is because the immigration has brought in many more men than women. The former are waiting to establish themselves before sending for their wives or families, and the hard times have tended to put off the day of establishment and to raise doubts as to whether the agents of steamship companies who pictured America as an earthly paradise were men of the finest veracity. However, the wives and families are coming over gradually, and the Nineteenth promises to be even more Italian in the future than it has been in the past.

The Russian Jews, another persistent and increasing people, divide interest with the Italians. They have overflowed from their stronghold, the Seventh Ward, where it is probable that their representation now is greater than that of the Germans. The census credits them with a numerical strength of 4,981 in the Nineteenth, but that is probably considerably short of the truth today. Their own peculiar territory lies between Taylor and Twelfth streets and Halsted and Canal streets, but they may be found all along the southern border of the ward. These people are apart from all others. Any lines of division that may have been indicated hitherto are faint by comparison with the line that separates them from their neighbors of every kind and degree. Nor is this due entirely to the antipathy of the neighbors. Jewish shops are patronized by the people of all nations. Indeed, it appears that when it comes to trade the laws of trade are much stronger than blood with Irish, Bohemians, and Italians, and that they patronize one another indiscriminately. But the Jews hold themselves aloof. Their clannishness is a rock of ages, and they are sufficient unto themselves. It is a curious sight to see the Hebrew signs here in Chicago, and to see the big-bearded men smoking little cigarets. There are times when the cigaret does not suggest the dude, and when one doubts if the alluring sign "Shave 5 Cents," which abounds in this part of the ward, will prove sufficient to attract custom. It is a dismal outlook for the barbers.

These Russian Jews live well, it is said—that is, they have enough to eat. Their children certainly have the appearance of being well fed, since they are apt to be plump and unctuous of skin. The whole family should probably rank third in the ward by this time, following after the Irish and the Italians.

Great Bohemian Exodus

Today 6,721 for the Germans and 6,184 for the Americans would be an overestimate. They are scattered and diminishing quantities like the Bohemians and the English. Probably the Bohemian exodus is the most notable of all. The ward was once a great Bohemian stronghold. A big Bohemian hall is a monument of that day, but it is out of place as a Bohemian resort, and halls are wanted elsewhere to supply the needs of the forty or fifty thousand Bohemians farther west. A member of the race skilled in its politics and its migrations gives 2,000 as an outside estimate of its representation in the ward today.

It is at the west end of the ward that the Irish now predominate. There is Vernon Park, and near it reside rich Irish politicians like Powers, whose home is on Macalister place, facing the park. It is a pretty neighborhood, adorned with handsome residences that would confound a person who had heard only of the miseries of the Nineteenth. Indeed, there are many wards of much greater pretensions and far less unpleasant notoriety which have no spot as fine to compare with it. The Irish settlement here is very old. Not faraway, at May and Twelfth streets, the great Jesuit Church or Church of the Holy Family and St. Ignatius' College have stood for many years. At Harrison and Throop streets is the building of the Little Sisters of the Poor; in Taylor street is the convent of the Ladies of the Sacred Heart. It is a great center of Irish Catholic activity. But the handsome dwellings of the Vernon Park region do not extend very far eastward. There are streets in the vicinity of the Andrew Jackson School, half way down, that are much like those east of Halsted street. No doubt the fixed institutions of the church and social influences proceeding therefrom [sic] have been instrumental in holding the Irish to their old homes in the west end of the ward. There is another church circle whose influence is felt, too, that which has for its center the Church of Notre Dame, a French establishment at Vernon Park place and Sibley street, which is just across the boundary in the Eleventh Ward.

Document 16.2 Diversity in New York's Inner City

Jacob Riis' "The Mixed Crowd" describes the immigrant neighborhoods of New York. In language that is often offensive to a twenty-first-century reader, Riis examines the diverse constituents that comprised New York's ghettoes. In its treatment of the late-nineteenth-century understanding of diversity, he clearly describes the different attributes and abilities believed at the time to be common to members of each group. He also clearly correlates different groups to specific geographic locations. Riis migrated to the United States from Denmark and found work as a newspaper reporter and photographer, taking a keen interest in

New York's immigrants. In his best known book, *How the Other Half Lives* (1890), Riis used text and photographs to tell their story.

Chapter III
The Mixed Crowd

When once I asked the agent of a notorious Fourth Ward alley how many people might be living in it I was told: One hundred and forty families, one hundred Irish, thirty-eight Italian, and two that spoke the German tongue. Barring the agent herself, there was not a native-born individual in the court. The answer was characteristic of the cosmopolitan character of lower New York, very nearly so of the whole of it, wherever it runs to alleys and courts. One may find for the asking an Italian, a German, a French, African, Spanish, Bohemian, Russian, Scandinavian, Jewish, and Chinese colony. Even the Arab, who peddles "holy earth" from the Battery as a direct importation from Jerusalem, has his exclusive preserves at the lower end of Washington Street. The one thing you shall vainly ask for in the chief city of America is a distinctively American community. There is none; certainly not among the tenements. Where have they gone to, the old inhabitants? I put the question to one who might fairly be presumed to be of the number, since I had found him sighing for the "good old days" when the legend "no Irish need apply" was familiar in the advertising columns of the newspapers. He looked at me with a puzzled air. "I don't know," he said. "I wish I did. Some went to California in '49, some to the war and never came back. The rest, I expect, have gone to heaven, or somewhere. I don't see them 'round here."

Whatever the merit of the good man's conjectures, his eyes did not deceive him. They are not here. In their place has come this queer conglomerate mass of heterogeneous elements, ever striving and working like whiskey and water in one glass, and with the like result: final union and a prevailing taint of whiskey. The once unwelcome Irishman has been followed in his turn by the Italian, the Russian Jew, and the Chinaman, and has himself taken a hand at opposition, quite as bitter and quite as ineffectual, against these later hordes. Wherever these have gone they have crowded him out, possessing the block, the street, the ward with their denser swarms. But the Irishman's revenge is complete. Victorious in defeat over his

recent as over his more ancient foe, the one who opposed his coming no less than the one who drove him out, he dictates to both their politics, and, secure in possession of the offices, returns the native his greeting with interest, while collecting the rents of the Italian whose house he has bought with the profits of his saloon. As a landlord he is picturesquely autocratic. An amusing instance of his methods came under my notice while writing these lines. An inspector of the Health Department found an Italian family paying a man with a Celtic name twenty-five dollars a month for three small rooms in a ramshackle rear tenement—more than twice what they were worth—and expressed his astonishment to the tenant, an ignorant Sicilian laborer. He replied that he had once asked the landlord to reduce the rent, but he would not do it.

"Well! What did he say?" asked the inspector.

"'Damma, man!' he said; 'if you speaka thata way to me, I fira you and your things in the streeta.'" And the frightened Italian paid the rent.

In justice to the Irish landlord it must be said that like an apt pupil he was merely showing forth the result of the schooling he had received, re-enacting, in his own way, the scheme of the tenements. It is only his frankness that shocks. The Irishman does not naturally take kindly to tenement life, though with characteristic versatility he adapts himself to its conditions at once. It does violence, nevertheless, to the best that is in him, and for that very reason of all who come within its sphere soonest corrupts him. The result is a sediment, the product of more than a generation in the city's slums, that, as distinguished from the larger body of his class, justly ranks at the foot of tenement dwellers, the so-called "low Irish "

It is not to be assumed, of course, that the whole body of the population living in the tenements, of which New Yorkers are in the habit of speaking vaguely as "the poor," or even the larger part of it, is to be classed as vicious or as poor in the sense of verging on beggary.

New York's wage-earners have no other place to live, more is the pity. They are truly poor for having no better homes; waxing poorer in purse as the exorbitant rents to which they are tied, as ever was serf to soil, keep rising. The wonder is that they are not all corrupted, and speedily, by their surroundings. If, on the contrary, there be a steady working up, if not out of the slough, the fact is a powerful argument for the optimist's belief that the world is, after all, growing better, not worse, and would go far toward disarming apprehension, were it not for the steadier growth of the sediment of the slums and its constant menace. Such an impulse toward better things there certainly is. The German rag-picker of thirty years ago, quite as low in the scale as his Italian successor, is the thrifty tradesman or prosperous farmer of to-day.

The Italian scavenger of our time is fast graduating into exclusive control of the corner fruit-stands, while his black-eyed boy monopolizes the boot-blacking industry in which a few years ago he was an intruder. The Irish hod-carrier in the second generation has become a bricklayer, if not the Alderman of his ward, while the Chinese coolie is in almost exclusive possession of the laundry business. The reason is obvious. The poorest immigrant comes here with the purpose and ambition to better himself and, given half a chance, might be reasonably expected to make the most of it. To the false plea that he prefers the squalid houses in which his kind are housed there could be no better answer. The truth is, his half chance has too long been wanting, and for the bad result he has been unjustly blamed.

As emigration from east to west follows the latitude, so does the foreign influx in New York distribute itself along certain well-defined lines that waver and break only under the stronger pressure of a more gregarious race or the encroachments of inexorable business. A feeling of dependence upon mutual effort, natural to strangers in a strange land, unacquainted with its language and customs, sufficiently accounts for this.

The Irishman is the true cosmopolitan immigrant. All-pervading, he shares his lodging with perfect impartiality with the Italian, the Greek, and the "Dutchman," yielding only to sheer force of numbers, and objects equally to them all. A map of the city, colored to designate nationalities, would show more stripes than on the skin of a zebra, and more colors than any rainbow. The city on such a map would fall into two great halves, green for the Irish prevailing in the West Side tenement districts, and blue for the Germans on the East Side. But intermingled with these ground colors would be an odd variety of tints that would give the whole the appearance of an extraordinary crazy-quilt. From down in the Sixth Ward, upon the site of the old Collect Pond that in the days of the fathers drained the hills which are no more, the red of the Italian would be seen forcing, its way northward along the line of Mulberry Street to

the quarter of the French purple on Bleecker Street and South Fifth Avenue, to lose itself and reappear, after a lapse of miles, in the "Little Italy" of Harlem, east of Second Avenue. Dashes of red, sharply defined, would be seen strung through the Annexed District, northward to the city line. On the West Side the red would be seen overrunning the old Africa of Thompson Street, pushing the black of the negro rapidly uptown, against querulous but unavailing protests, occupying his home, his church, his trade and all, with merciless impartiality. There is a church in Mulberry Street that has stood for two generations as a sort of milestone of these migrations. Built originally for the worship of staid New Yorkers of the "old stock," it was engulfed by the colored tide, when the draft-riots drove the negroes out of reach of Cherry Street and the Five Points. Within the past decade the advance wave of the Italian onset reached it, and to-day the arms of United Italy adorn its front. The negroes have made a stand at several points along Seventh and Eighth Avenues; but the ermine body, still pursued by the Italian foe, is on the march yet, and the black mark will be found overshadowing to-day many blocks on the East Side, with One Hundredth Street as the centre, where colonies of them have settled recently.

Hardly less aggressive than the Italian, the Russian and Polish Jew, having over run the district between Rivington and Division Streets, east of the Bowery, to the point of suffocation, is filling, the tenements of the old Seventh Ward to the river front, and disputing with the Italian every foot of available space in the back alleys of Mulberry Street. The two races, differing hopelessly in much, have this in common: they carry their slums with them wherever they go, if allowed to do it. Little Italy already rivals its parent, the "Bend," in foulness. Other nationalities that begin at the bottom make a fresh start when crowded up the ladder. Happily both are manageable, the one by rabbinical, the other by the civil law. Between the dull gray of the Jew, his favorite color, and the Italian red, would be seen squeezed in on the map a sharp streak of yellow, marking the narrow boundaries of Chinatown. Dovetailed in with the German population, the poor but thrifty Bohemian might be picked out by the somber hue of his life as of his philosophy, struggling against heavy odds in the big human bee-hives of the East Side. Colonies of his people extend northward, with long lapses of space, from below the Cooper Institute more than three miles. The Bohemian is the only foreigner with any considerable representation in the city who counts no wealthy man of his race, none who has not to work hard for a living, or has got beyond the reach of the tenement.

Down near the Battery the West Side emerald would be soiled by a dirty stain, spreading rapidly like a splash of ink on a sheet of blotting paper, headquarters of the Arab tribe, that in a single year has swelled from the original dozen to twelve hundred, intent, every mother's son, on trade and barter. Dots and dashes of color here and there would show where the Finnish sailors worship their djumala (God), the Greek peddlers the ancient name of their race, and the Swiss the goddess of thrift. And so on to the end of the long register, all toiling together in the galling fetters of the tenement. Were the question raised who makes the most of life thus mortgaged, who resists most stubbornly its levelling tendency—knows how to drag even the barracks upward a part of the way at least toward the ideal plane of the home—the palm must be unhesitatingly awarded the Teuton. The Ital-ian and the poor Jew rise only by compulsion. The Chinaman does not rise at all; here, as at home, he simply remains stationary. The Irishman's genius runs to public affairs rather than domestic life; wherever he is mustered in force the saloon is the gorgeous centre of political activity. The German struggles vainly to learn his trick; his Teutonic wit is too heavy, and the political ladder he raises from his saloon usually too short or too clumsy to reach the desired goal. The best part of his life is lived at home, and he makes himself a home independent of the surroundings, giving the lie to the saying, unhappily become a maxim of social truth, that pauperism and drunkenness naturally grow in the tenements. He makes the most of his tenement, and it should be added that whenever and as soon as he can save up money enough, he gets out and never crosses the threshold of one again.

Document 16.3 The Immigrant Girl in Chicago

By viewing inner-city neighborhoods from the perspective of gender, Grace Abbott's "The Special Problems of the Immigrant Girl" adds another dimension to the complexity of urban life at the end of the nineteenth century. The article examines the reasons for immigration, as well as the meaning of diversity. The ways in which the girls fit into different immigrant communities is also important. Grace Abbot took a Master's Degree in political science from the University of Chicago. She became particularly interested in the lives of immigrants and children. After working with Jane Addams at Hull House in Chicago, she was appointed director of the Industrial Division of the Children's Bureau of the U.S. Department of Labor, and later head of the Children's Bureau in the Department of Labor. In both positions she worked to legislate and enforce child labor laws.

Few American women realize that in the past five years more than half a million immigrant girls have come to the United States to make their own way, to help the fathers and mothers they have left at home, and to see that their younger sisters and brothers are given some of the opportunities which poverty and isolation denied to them.

Reports from the Commissioner-General of Immigration show that during the five years from July 1, 1910, to June 30, 1915, more than one half a million non-English-speaking girls and women under thirty years of age came to the United States. This included one year of the war (1915), and in consequence one year of greatly decreased immigration. Of this num-ber more than a hundred thousand were Polish, and more than 84,000 of these Polish girls were under twenty-one years of age. Most American women have never heard of the Ruthenians, the representatives of the Ukrainians, who come from eastern Galicia and Hungary, and yet here are 23,101 of them under twenty-one years of age coming to the United States—more than the number of the Scandinavian girls whom we know so well.

As one thinks of this great stream of Polish, Russian, Jewish, Italian, Ruthenian, Lithuanian, and all the other girls who have been coming from the country districts of southern and eastern Europe, one wonders how they had the courage to undertake this

Grace Abbott, "The Special Problems of the Immigrant Girl," Chapter III in *The Immigrant in the Community* (New York: The Century Co., 1917): 55-80.

excursion into the unknown. Several years ago, while studying the districts in Galicia, in northern Hungary, and in Croatia, from which so many girls have come to the United States, I kept asking myself and those whom I met this one question. A professor in the Polish University of Lemberg, which Americans have learned since the war began is the capital of Galicia and the center of a large Polish and a larger Ruthenian population, told me that the first thing I needed to understand in any study of emigration from this region was that the peasants did not go because they needed work; there was plenty of work for them there; he knew landlords whose crops were rotting in the ground because the men and women of the neighborhood had all gone to America. It was a fever that was running through the entire peasantry, he explained. They went to the United States as he might go to the next street....

Forced labor was abolished in Austria in 1848; but it was not until 1867 and 1869 that the right of the peasant to divide his land was made general, so that serfdom remained, in a sense, until that time. As I talked with the landlords of the neighborhood, I found that, like the Southern white man in his attitude toward the Negro, they were indulgently tolerant of the faults of the peasantry but were convinced that these faults were due to the fact that the peasants were a quite different order of human beings from themselves. They laughed at us for taking the peasants so seriously and imagining we could make ladies and gentlemen of them. The peasants, they were sure, were all "spoiled" by an American experience. The older peasants are themselves sometimes equally conservative in their devotion to the old social order; so the ambitious young peasant has the opposition of his own class as well as the class prejudice of those above him to overcome.

Whether or not it is completely reasoned out by the peasant who undertakes the journey, this class feeling is an important cause of emigration. It is much simpler to break entirely with the past, to abandon the picturesque costume, the little farm, the dependence on the landlord of the neighborhood, and to stake everything on a possible success in America than to try to break down the century-old social barriers of the village. In other words, it was the fact that apparently nothing could change either for themselves or for their children, which sent many of these women from Austria and Hungary to America....

Whether or not immigration as a whole increases at the end of the war, there will undoubtedly be larger numbers of young unmarried women emigrating from eastern Europe to the United States. It is, therefore, important for us to consider the peculiar problems of the immigrant girl in order that those who have suffered so much in Europe may be prevented from further unnecessary suffering here.

During the years from 1910 to 1915 the Immigrants' Protective League received from the ports of entry the names of 26,909 women and girls who came alone from Europe to Chicago. These girls were visited as soon after their arrival as possible by visitors of the League who spoke the language of the girls and were prepared to help them in adjusting themselves to their Chicago environment. By far the largest number who have been coming to Chicago, as to the United States, are Polish, and it may be assumed that the needs which were discovered in the visits made to these immigrant girls of Chicago are typical of the needs of the girls who have come to other cities and industrial towns.

The foreign-born girls face no simple situation when here in the United States they become self-supporting and self-directing. Most of them begin their new life indebted to a relative or a friend who has paid for the steamship ticket that brought them here. To the nervous apprehensions about her ability to repay so large an obligation is added the general bewilderment every girl feels who is experiencing life in a city and as part of a great industry for the first time.

Many of those who come are so young that their only work at home had been to watch the sheep and the cattle in the fields or on the mountain slopes from sunrise to sunset. Others worked side by side with the men in the harvest fields or in the factories. Some of them were hod-carriers and toiled up the ladders with the heavy brick or stone which the masons—always men—laid....

The immigrant girls do not realize their handicaps, and usually begin work in the United States without any of the doubts and anxious fears which many of us have for them. Being young, they believe that the world must hold something good in store for them. In the faith that America feels kindly toward them they expect to find here among us that happy future to which all girls look forward. And in this expectation these young foreign women and girls undertake the great American adventure.

Those of us who can remember our own great expectations as we left college and the anxious fears of that first year of our "independence" can, perhaps, understand the greater crisis which the immigrant girl faces in her first year in the United States.

Most of them are, at first, homesick and disappointed. The streets of the city are not always broad and beautiful, and life not always gay and bright as they had hoped it would be. On the contrary, the experience of the Russian-Jewish girl who came to a cousin on Liberty Street in Chicago is not unusual. A returned immigrant translated to her the word "Liberty," and she imagined that she was coming to live on an avenue which would symbolize all that one bearing that precious name should. But she found her cousin living in a rear house on a short, narrow, unpaved, dirty street. The houses on Liberty Street are as poor as any Chicago knows, and there is no place where poverty seems more intimate and its ugliness more inevitable. After a short experience in a tailor shop, she had to give up the struggle. She did not live long enough to know anything about the United States except the disappointment of Liberty Street.

Sometimes it seems to the peasant girls as if they had exchanged the green fields and woods and the long, quiet winters for a hideous round of noise, heat, and bitter cold.

For the Polish girls, the change is often very sudden. Most of those who come to Chicago are young girls, and many of them have no near relatives to help them through their difficulties. Out of 2013 who arrived in Chicago during a period of eighteen months and were visited by the Immigrants' Protective League, 1107 were between the ages of sixteen and twenty, 751 between twenty and thirty years of age. Only 81 had parents in this country, and 626 came to cousins or friends. Sometimes these "friends" have never known the girls at home. When they were discussing their journey to America, some one in the village suggested that they could stay during the first few weeks after they arrived with a brother, cousin, or friend of the speaker who was living in the United States. In such cases, and often too when the girl comes to an uncle or an aunt of her own, as soon as she gets her first job and finds a place to board, all feeling of responsibility on the part of the relatives or friends is ended. For example, one girl of seventeen came to an uncle on the North Side of Chicago.

He took her to the Stockyards neighborhood, some twelve miles away, found her work and a place to board, and then regarded his duty to his niece as fully performed. When the girl was in the most serious trouble, six months later, she had no idea where he lived and had no one to turn to for advice or help.

More than one half of the Polish girls visited did farm work at home, one eighth were servants, while some had followed one of the sewing trades, and a few were clerks, factory workers, and teachers. In Chicago, about one fifth of them work in hotels, restaurants, or hospitals, scrubbing or washing dishes for ten hours a day. Before the enactment of the Ten-Hour Law for Women, they worked often as long as fifteen hours a day. They were given in payment from four to seven dollars a week and two meals a day.

One hundred and eleven of the 2013 referred to were already at work in the Stockyards when they were visited by the League's representatives, and practically all the others who came to that neighborhood and were not yet employed expected to get work at the Yards in a short time. One hundred and ten found employment as servants, eighty one were at work in laundries, sixty seven in tobacco factories, while the remainder were working in the corerooms of foundries, in the dusty twine mills of a harvester company, and in the tin can factories, where so many girls lose their fingers in the inadequately guarded machinery. In fact the Polish girls are found doing almost every kind of heavy or disagreeable work in Chicago. Because they are large and strong looking, there is a popular belief that they can do work which would be physically too heavy for others. But the belief is based on ignorance of what it costs the Polish girls to do these tasks.

How many of them give way under the strain of long hours, bad living conditions, and the confused excitement which comes with their new environment, few people realize. The tragedy of this physical breakdown was illustrated one summer when the service of the Immigrants' Protective League were asked on behalf of a young Polish girl. Although she seemed entirely well when she came and had been passed by the examining doctors at Ellis Island, she had developed tuberculosis after a few months of factory work in Chicago. She was taken to the County Hospital and soon learned that she had no chance of recovery. She was most wretchedly homesick when the visitor for the League saw her at the hospital. She had only a cousin in this country, who could not come to see her because it was the season of overtime work in his trade and the County Hospital was many miles away. She was unable to talk to those around her and found it impossible to eat the strange American food given her, and, worst of all, she realized that all her girlish plans to earn money, send for her mother, and marry well were to come to nothing. Polish food which we were able to procure for her did not comfort her, however, for she wanted only one thing—to be sent back home so that she might die with her mother. In this, too, she was disappointed, for although she improved somewhat when she learned that she was to he deported, she died alone at sea.

The Lithuanian girls, who come from the country districts near Kovno and Wilna, and the Ruthenian and the Little Russian girls, who come from near Lemberg in Austria and across the Russian boundary to the south of Kiev, and the White Russian and Great Russian peasant girls, who have just begun to come from Central and Northern Russia, confront much the same problem. Like the Polish girls, more than one half of them have done farm work at home, and in Chicago they, too, find employment principally in the hotels and restaurants, at the heavier factory work, and in the Stockyards, although all these nationalities are also represented in the sewing trades and in domestic service.

With the Bohemians and Slovaks, the industrial movement is different. About one half of them have done housework at home, and in Chicago about the same proportion still do housework and the others find employment at tailoring, in the restaurants, laundries, and factories.

The Bohemian or Slovak girls who have worked in English-speaking families are, of course, more Americanized than those who have lived among their own people and worked in a factory. Still, the immigrant girl in the latter situation is usually safer than in the former. A too rapid Americanization is dangerous, and the girl who leaves her own people and eats strange American food, learns a new language, and gives up her old country clothes and manners, often wrongly concludes that all her old-world ideals are to be abandoned and that in America she is to live under a very different moral code from the one her mother taught her.

Of the Jewish women and girls who came during the same period, 613 were Russian. Most of them were unmarried and under twenty-five years of age. Four hundred and twelve had followed one of the sewing trades at home, and in Chicago the great majority are also employed at tailoring or dressmaking. But whatever their industrial experience in Russia may have been, the Jewish girls have never known the large, crowded workshop and the pace which piece work always demands in the United States. Probably 90 percent of them come on prepaid tickets and they all expect to repay this loan and be able soon to send for some relative or friend.

The Jewish girls come expecting to make America their permanent home, and they are, therefore, eager to learn English and to become Americanized. They attend night school more regularly than the girls of any other nationality, and in a year they usually make rapid progress if they are strong enough to keep up the day and evening work.

There is much greater diversity in the ages of the Italian girls who come than of the others. They seldom come unaccompanied by their mothers. The work they prefer is home finishing, but they do all kinds of home work, most often cracking nuts and making artificial flowers—until state regulation compels them to break reluctantly with their traditions and follow the work to the factory. The Italian girl, because of jealous parental supervision, is less frequently in trouble than are the girls of other nationalities, but this supervision means that she cannot attend night school or take part in the American recreations of her neighborhood, and that she must marry young so that, before her father dies, she will have a husband to protect her virtue. These traditions, which cannot live when the girl goes to the American factory, often make the Italian girl's adjustment to her American social environment a difficult family problem.

The conditions under which most of these immigrant girls must live are far from satisfactory. While many of them come to relatives or friends who can give them the care and protection they need, many of them must live among strangers upon whom they have no claim. Because more men than women emigrate to this country, the families with whom they live usually have, in addition to the girl, three or four men lodgers. The Immigrants' Protective League has found in its visits to the newly arrived immigrant girls that about one half of the Polish, Lithuanian, Slovak, and Russian girls who come to live with relatives find themselves one more in a group of boarders. Sometimes all the other boarders are men; and the girl innocently does not see that because of the congestion and the consequent lack of privacy and of the restraints which privacy exercises, she is quite unprotected against herself and the people with whom she lives. The following examples of boarding conditions which are all too common among the Polish girls may help to explain the difficulties which are met.

A nineteen-year-old girl, without relatives in Chicago, was found living with a man and his wife, who have in their three-room flat four men and three other women boarders. This girl paid two dollars a month for her part of a room—the usual price. It is customary for each boarder to select and pay for his or her own food, which is usually cooked by the landlady. The landlady is not often paid for her work, but whatever is left belongs to her and this supplies the family needs for the most part. Another eighteen-year-old girl and a friend live with a family of four in a four-room flat where there are six men and four women boarders. Occasionally a group of women rent rooms and live together. Five Polish girls, all under twenty, were found living in two rooms. They all worked in factories and each one did some part of their simple housekeeping.

The Lithuanians have no safer conditions. One girl lived with a married cousin who had a four-room flat in which she accommodated six men and two women boarders. The girl and the other boarders all worked in the Stockyards. Another Lithuanian girl of twenty, who cleans street cars at night, boards in a four-room flat which houses, in addition to the four members of the family, five men and one other woman boarder. These conditions are frequently met.

Immigrant men sometimes live in non-family groups, using the ordinary flat building which is so ill adapted for group housekeeping. This mode of living is generally regarded as so demoralizing to the men that it cannot be recommended as a way out of the lodging difficulty unless buildings especially constructed for that purpose are provided. In this kind of overcrowding, which every housing investigation shows to be common, the lack of privacy and of the restraints which privacy brings may be, with the complete absence of evil intent on the part of either the man or the girl, the sole cause of her ruin. There are also cases where, under some special strain or excitement, as for example, after a wedding or some other celebration, when liquor has been freely used, the moral barriers are broken down. This occurs most frequently in the homes that are overcrowded, and where, in consequence, an easy familiarity has been developed.

These living conditions follow inevitably from the fact that large numbers of young men and smaller but still large numbers of young women are coming into our industrial neighborhoods where no lodging provisions are made for them. The "company-owned boarding house" cannot be looked to as the solution of this problem. For long and often bitter experience has convinced employers, employees, and the interested public that it is undesirable to combine the functions of employer and landlord. It is true that the employers might provide the buildings and allow them to be controlled by an independent body of trustees, so that the workers could not be evicted in cases of industrial disputes or feel that they were too completely under the tutelage of their employers during normal times.

The solution usually suggested for these conditions is a good housing law vigorously enforced. But this will not meet the social need. The enforcement of decent housing standards will reduce the overcrowding, but it will still leave the immigrant girl open to a kind of temptation to which no girl should be exposed. It will leave the non-family groups of men with no social relationships, so that abnormal vice will almost surely develop among them. Municipal building, the final remedy, will probably not be undertaken until we have gone much further in accepting the simpler propositions for municipal ownership. Private philanthropy should, in the meantime, experiment with lodging houses for these men and women so that we could learn the best type to build. Such building would also perform the valuable purpose of calling attention to the needs of these large groups of young men and women and so make ready for a real solution.

There are many explanations for the fact that the immigrant girls sometimes become unmarried mothers. There is the greater helplessness which is due to their ignorance of English; there is also the more dangerous environment in which they live, for it is near an immigrant, or colored neighborhood that disreputable dancehalls and hotels are usually tolerated. Moreover, their recreational needs are less understood than those of the native-born American, and the break with the old-world traditions has left them with fewer standards of discrimination.

At home, the girls have been accustomed to out-of-door dances and sports. In Chicago, when Saturday night comes, the demand for some sort of excitement after a hard and uneventful week, has become too strong to be ignored. But the danger is that because of her physical and nervous exhaustion and her demand for acute sense stimulation, the girl will become an easy victim for the unscrupulous. The neighboring saloon keeper, alert to the business side of her needs, is constantly seeking to attract her to the dance hall which he conducts in the rear of his saloon. At its best, such a dance adds to the nervous demoralization which began with the girl's overfatigue. At its worst, it leaves her disgraced and ruined. An extension of Chicago's admirable system of parks and playgrounds or a wider use of the public schools while helpful, is not enough to meet this situation. For these girls must first be given sufficient leisure to enable them to enjoy the wholesome recreation and opportunities for self-advancement which the city is offering them. This, they are not able to do after ten hours of scrubbing or coremaking six days in a week.

Sometimes the girl is not morally safe in her place of work. The Polish girls who work in restaurants seem to be in special danger. They usually resist at first, but often in the end find themselves unfortified against the combination of force and persuasion which is exerted sometimes against them by the restaurant keeper or a fellow employee. This occurs most frequently in the Greek restaurants, in which, usually, only one girl is employed and there is, in consequence, not the protection which a group always affords. Many of the proprietors of the Greek restaurants are men whose families have not yet joined them in the United States or who have few opportunities to marry, as the number of Greek girls in the United States is small. These men have, in consequence, no normal social relationships.

But it is not always a restaurant employee. American foremen in factories sometimes abuse a power which is more absolute than any man should have the right to exercise over others, and on threat of dismissal the girl submits to familiarities which if they do not ruin her cannot fail to break down her self-respect. One does not need to be told how serious the situation is when a young immigrant girl explains that she has learned how to "get on with the boss" and "take care of herself" at the same time.

Occasionally a girl who has preferred housework in the belief that it would give her a "good home" is ruined by some man in the family for whom she has worked. One young Bohemian girl comes to my mind in this connection. She had had a very hard life at home where a drunken and brutal father's control had been followed by that of a brother no more considerate. She came to America before she was twenty, expecting to earn enough to send for her mother so that the old woman might spend her last years free from the sort of abuse she suffered at home. The fulfilment of this dream was delayed by the great misfortune that came to the girl, although her dream did in fact eventually come true. With a courage that humbled those of us who listened, she explained that she must have a good job so that she could support her baby and bring her mother to America. During the years that we watched her in her successful struggle to accomplish this great task, we realized that although, as the girl mourns, the baby "hasn't got a name" it has at least a good mother.

Promise of marriage may, of course, be a factor in cases of the betrayal of American girls, and the foreign girl, whose village experience has not prepared her for the easy way in which men can disappear in the United States, is more easily victimized through her affections.

A study of the pathetic stories of the betrayal or the weakness of these girls makes it clear that the prevention of delinquency among immigrant girls presents no entirely new or indeed unusual problems. It is the same story of the desire for affection, together with loneliness, lack of knowledge of herself, and long hours of hard, monotonous work. The difference between the temptations which meet the American country girl who comes to the city and those of the immigrant girl, is in the main, one of degree and not of kind.

Those who see race differences as the explanation of all social facts have attempted to discover whether the girls of one nationality more than those of another "go wrong." Statistics on this subject are generally unreliable, especially when in their interpretation no account is taken of general population statistics, the length of time that the nationality has been coming to the United States, and the peculiar temptations to which, because of employment, environment, or prejudice, the girls of a particular nationality are subjected.

Much more important, however, than the relative numbers of girls of the various nationalities who "go wrong" is the question whether any girl has suffered in this way when such suffering could have been prevented.

Much official attention has been given to the means of preventing immoral women and girls from coming into this country. Stirred by the stories that oriental women were being brought into the United States under contract for immoral purposes, Congress passed an Act in 1873 aimed especially at breaking up this "trade." The Immigration Law of 1903 excluded "prostitutes and persons who procure or attempt to bring in prostitutes or women for the purpose of prostitution." The language of the law was made more inclusive in 1907.[1] Those entering in violation of this law were made deportable if their presence in the country was discovered within three years after their coming. In 1910, in accordance with the agreement reached at the Paris Conference on the suppression of the "White Slave Traffic" of 1904 and in part as a result of the investigation of the United States Immigration Commission, a further act was passed making it a felony "to persuade, induce, or coerce" any girl or woman to come to the United States for any immoral purpose or to assist in its being done, and making it a misdemeanor to "keep, maintain, control, support, or harbor in any place used for immoral purposes any alien girl or woman who has been in the United States less than three years."[2] These provisions, it is apparent, are intended primarily to reach those who profit from the illegal earnings of the girls. The Immigration Law was also amended the same year so that any alien girl or woman who is an inmate of a house of prostitution or is employed in any place frequented by prostitutes, may be deported regardless of the length of time she has been in the United States.[3]

These laws applied the double standard of morality in the tests for exclusion and deportation. The man who profits by the social evil or who brings a girl into the country for immoral purposes is subject to punishment, but the man who is himself immoral is not regarded as an "undesirable" immigrant.

In so far as the Immigration Law breaks up the trade in women, in so far as it sends back home girls whose mothers and friends are in Europe and whose reformation, in consequence, will be more probable in Europe than in the United States, we can feel that the law is both useful and humane. But in its enforcement, it often means that we deny girls who have made some serious mistake at home the chance which they need to begin a new life here in the United States. For example, a few years ago, a young Austrian whose military service was uncompleted could not, therefore, marry the girl with whom he had lived and who was about to become a mother. They came to the United States that they might marry and their child be legitimate. The man was admitted but the girl was excluded. She was unmarried and her condition apparent, and as a matter of routine ruling she was denied admission. The young man had no relatives in this country. He was coming to Chicago because his one acquaintance in the United States lived in Chicago. He was overwhelmed by the excluding decision and told his story to the first sympathetic listener he met in Chicago. Special appeals from Chicago women resulted in reversing the decision. The woman was admitted and married on the day of her arrival in Chicago. And most people would probably agree that the moral level of the United States is not raised by the kind of harshness in judging others which an excluding decision such as this one showed.

Under this law, it is also possible to deport girls who are not citizens, although they have been in the United States since they were little children, whose ruin has been accomplished here, whose parents and all those who might help them back into an honest life are in the United States. Some Russian-Jewish girls, under exactly these circumstances, were recommended for deportation. Added to the family separation, these girls were ordered returned to a country in which religious prejudice made their outlook the more uncertain. In such cases, the United States was merely insuring that the girls would continue their immoral life by sending them away from any possible sources of help to live in what was to them, in spite of their citizenship, an alien country. And after these girls had been banished, could any one feel that the country was safer when the men and the conditions responsible for their ruin were left here in the United States—a menace to other girls, both immigrant and American?

There is no reason to feel that the moral health of the country will be promoted by special severity in dealing with the immigrant girl who has gone wrong. From the standpoint of the welfare of the community, attention could be much more profitably directed toward helping her to meet the difficulties she now encounters in the United States.

For this reason, it is to be regretted that the administration of the immigration law is so entirely in the hands of men. The women in the Immigration Service are "matrons"—the cross between a housekeeper and a chaperon who is rapidly disappearing in the best public and private institutions. Without the same pay as inspectors, these matrons are not expected to measure up with the men in intelligence and ability, although they often do. But they have, largely for these reasons, not been able to make much impression on the "Service" and have not secured the adoption of standards of comfort and consideration which trained women could institute in a place like Ellis Island, where so many thousands of women and children are detained each year.

Investigation of girls on charges of immorality should be made by women inspectors. Anonymous reports are investigated by the Department, and it often means serious injury to the reputation of a respectable girl to have a man inspector call to "investigate" her.

A woman's department has recently been organized in the Immigration Service, but there are no indications that these old traditions about the position of women in the Service are to be abolished. The "presence" of a woman in an Immigration Station is sentimentally supposed to give protection, but any practical person knows that ability, training, and resourcefulness on the part of women officials are necessary if they are to render the services which the immigrant women and girls really need.

The same measures have not been taken by private as well as public agencies to safeguard the immigrant that have been taken to protect the American girl. Boarding clubs, which are among the first kindly expressions of interest in the American girl, have not, except in a very few instances, been provided for the immigrant. Agencies which are trying to help girls who have made some misstep have usually not felt it necessary to employ women able to speak the language of the immigrant or to understand her social traditions.

The immigrant girl has a long and hard road to travel. She suffers from the industrial and legal discriminations which are the common lot of working women. In addition, she must overcome the stupid race prejudice which leads many Americans to conclude that she suffers less from shame and humiliation than do other women and girls. Without trade training and with little education, as a rule, she begins at the bottom industrially, where, if the wages of the men are low, the wages of the girls are still lower.

And yet, in this struggle in which they are so handicapped, these girls are winning little by little—often at a terrible cost to their health and, in consequence, to the health, of the children they will bear in the future. There are many who are moved only by

this danger to the future generations. But for the girls of this generation, we should ask more leisure, better pay, better homes, and more sympathy before they are too old and broken to enjoy the fruits of their toil and of their eager sacrifices

Notes

1. It provides that "prostitutes or women or girls coming into the United States for the purpose of prostitution, or for other immoral purposes; persons who procure or attempt to bring in prostitutes or women or girls for the purpose of prostitution or for any other immoral purpose" are to be excluded.

2. Act of June 25, 1910, 36 United States Statutes, 825.

3. Act of March 26, 1910.

Document 16.4 Public Health in the Inner City

Published as a Hull House study, "An Inquiry into the Causes of the Recent Epidemic of Typhoid Fever in Chicago" describes the public health conditions found in the inner-city neighborhoods and their relationship to the 1902 typhoid epidemic. The essay also notes a correlation among the incidence of the disease, its causes, and immigrant groups. Jane Addams established Hull House to address the problems of immigrant communities. Conducting research and developing responses to urban problems were two of several directions she took to achieve that goal.

During July, August and September of 1902 there was an unusually severe epidemic of typhoid fever in Chicago, which raised the death rate to 402 from this disease alone, as against 212 during the same three months of the previous year.

In discussing the causes for this outbreak of typhoid Dr. Reynolds, Commissioner of Health, speaks as follows:

"There was no sewer-flushing rainfall during the entire period from October, 1902, to March, 1903, and the city sewer-flushing, always inadequate, was wholly suspended in January on account of the lack of funds. The sewers were congested with filth, of which typhoid stools formed a component part, and the surface of the earth, in city and country alike, was covered with the five months' accumulations. From March to July inclusive was the wettest season on record. The sewers were repeatedly flushed out, and the accu-

mulated surface filth was washed away into streams, ponds and the lake. In August a succession of high variable winds set in, the strongest being from the west. The lake bottom was vigorously stirred up by high-wave action, the sewage was drifted to the intakes, and the water-supply from all sources became so contaminated that it averaged only 38 percent good for the month."

This pollution of the water-supply was undoubtedly the greatest causative factor in the epidemic of the past summer, but there are one or two subsidiary factors which are not brought out in the report of the Board of Health and which may serve to explain the peculiar localization of this epidemic. The mortality statistics of the Board of Health show that a comparatively small area on the West Side was the region most severely affected. Within the limits of the Nineteenth Ward, which contains only one thirty-sixth of the total population of the city, there were between

---

Hull-House Residents, "An Inquiry Into The Causes Of The Recent Epidemic Of Typhoid Fever In Chicago," *Commons* 81, no. 8 (April 1903): 3-7.

one-sixth and one-seventh of all the deaths from this disease. This part of the city is inhabited, largely by working people. It contains one of the largest Italian quarters, most of the Greek colony, a small Bohemian colony, the northern end of the Jewish quarter, and the western part is chiefly American-Irish. As far as the general intelligence of the inhabitants is concerned, their knowledge of the laws of hygiene, their general housing conditions, cleanliness, overcrowding, etc., this part of the city does not differ from the other semi-foreign quarters, yet it suffered much more than any in this epidemic. Evidently there must have been some local conditions which favored the spread of the infection. The drinking-water alone could not be responsible, for this part of the city is supplied from the Chicago avenue and Fourteenth street tunnels, the same water supply as that for the whole region between Forty seventh and Lake streets, Canal street and Western avenue. Nor could the milk be chargeable, for though in this neighborhood the milk is often badly diluted, yet it averaged quite as good as that supplied to a prosperous residence district to the west, as shown by analyses made of the milk of both districts by the University of Illinois in 1898.

To those who studied the distribution of the cases of typhoid fever it soon became evident that the number was greatest in those streets where removal of sewage is most imperfect. This is an old part of the city; the sewers in many of the streets were laid before the great fire, at a time when the neighborhood was more sparsely settled, and when usually not more than one family occupied each house. Adequate at that time, they are far from adequate now, and it takes only a moderate increase in the rainfall to make the sewage back up into vaults and closets, while clogging is of common occurrence in dry weather. The yards and closets are often below the level of the street, and are therefore easily overflowed. Last spring during the flooding rains it was no uncommon thing to see one of these yards, from six to fourteen feet below the level of the street, covered with several inches of foul water which in the neighborhood of the privy was distinctly sewage-contaminated. In this way the earth of the yards and that under the basement tenements became soaked with diluted excreta.

This condition of things is made possible by the primitive arrangements for the disposal of dejecta which prevail in this part of the city. Two of the residents of Hull House, which is situated almost in the center of the typhoid district, made a careful house-to-house investigation, noting the conditions as to drainage in each house and also the number of cases of typhoid fever which had appeared in each during the three months in question. Two thousand and two dwellings were thus investigated. A few extracts from the notebooks of the Hull House residents will give an idea of some of the conditions found:

DeKoven street (Jewish): Vault, said to be connected, but full; basement full of sewage contaminated water from backing-up of sewer.

Law avenue (Greek): Seventy six persons using three small closets under the house; very filthy; apparently no sewer connection

Bunker street (Bohemian and Polish): Unconnected vaults; very foul; ten cases of typhoid with four deaths; in this tenement; sixteen families.

Law avenue (colored): Connected, but out of order; full to the floor; boards at back are broken away so that cesspool is quite exposed.

Ewing street (Italian): Cesspool, said to have sewer connection, but full and running over, so that stream of sewage runs down the yard.

Taylor street (Italian): Old-fashioned privy; no sewer connection; one of six privies in a yard between a four-story front tenement and a three-story rear tenement. While we were inspecting it, a woman came down with a vessel filled with discharge from a typhoid patient, which she emptied into the vault. No disinfectant was used.

Aberdeen street (Irish): One large vault used by sixteen families; very foul-smelling; unconnected. This was cleaned by a scavenger during August, and the filth left standing in an open barrow in the alley between two houses for a week. It was so offensive that the tenants in these two houses were obliged to keep their windows on that side closed. Complaints to the Health Department and Garbage Inspector were fruitless, and finally the personal influence of a physician prevailed over the landlord and he removed it, but not until it had stood there during a week of warm weather, when, naturally, the place swarmed with flies. There were five cases of typhoid fever in each of the two houses next to the alley.

Blue Island avenue (French, German, Irish and Greek): One vault for ten families; overflows into the yard at every heavy rainfall, so that the yard is impassable for two or three days and tenants must reach the closets from the alley.

It was found that only 967 dwellings, or 48 per cent, of the whole number investigated, had modern sanitary plumbing, as was made obligatory for all buildings by an ordinance passed in 1896. One hundred and forty-eight dwellings, or 7 per cent of the whole number, had plumbing so badly out of order as to be a menace to health. Four hundred and thirty-three, or 22 per cent, had out-of-door water-closets supplied from the waste water from the kitchen sink and the rain-water from the roof. Two hundred and eighteen dwellings, or 11 per cent, had privy vaults with sewer connection but without water supply; vaults which are cleaned either by a scavenger or by means of a hose connected with the hydrant, and which, if not frequently cleaned, cannot be distinguished from the undrained, old-fashioned privies which form the fifth variety, and of which there are still 236 in this neighborhood, or 12 per cent, of the whole number.

Now, if there is any causative relation between the conditions described above and the distribution of the cases of typhoid fever, it must be largely through the agency of flies, since we know that typhoid infection cannot be breathed in but must be taken in through the mouth. It is true that germ-laden dust blown by the wind may also be a mode of conveyance of the infection. The typhoid bacillus has been shown to retain its vitality in dry soil for over sixty days. However, it was only after the middle of August that this agency could have come into play to any great extent, for up to that time there had been constant rains, and there was practically no dust.

...

There is no doubt that the influence of politics or wealth often intervenes in favor of the landlord, who does not wish to incur the expense of sanitary plumbing, and the Board of Health gives as an excuse for the existence of many of these illegal vaults that their prosecutions have been non-suited, although here again the Board of Health records show nothing. The following instances show the results of such influences:

There are only open vaults attached to certain houses on Jefferson street, owned by the brother of a well-known politician.[1]

When these vaults were overfilled during the last summer and the tenants were unable to secure the scavenger from the landlord, they made two complaints to the Board of Health, but with absolutely no result, save the visit of an inspector. Another case of politician's ownership is found on Forquer street, where, in a row of houses sheltering sixteen families, there is provided only one large open vault. Repeated complaints have been unavailing to secure anything beyond the mere visits of an inspector.

In another instance a tenement was owned by an ex-alderman. The main waste-pipe of the building was broken for more than five months, to the knowledge of the investigator. The basement was flooded with filth for that period. At the same time the closet on the second floor, separated from the living-rooms of a tenant by a loose-hanging door, was clogged, so that on the floor there was a puddle which the woman daily swept down the front stairway. This liquid filth also seeped through the ceiling and dripped down on the floor below, occupied by a Greek. The condition of this building has been reported to the Department of Health at least five times during this period, as can be proved by affidavits. Yet nothing was done, and the records of the department show no complaints. In the meantime the water-supply pipe was broken, so that for the last three weeks of this period water could not be drawn on the second floor for any purpose. Finally a personal appeal to the head of the department secured the visit of an inspector, whose report was truthful and showed the need of instant action. Nothing was done, however, until, ten days later, after repeated inquiries over the telephone and a threat of publicity, a suit was begun. It has been found that suits of this character frequently result either in a trifling fine (which it is much cheaper to pay than to make repairs) or in an appeal which may postpone the matter for two years or longer. At this point the corporation counsel was appealed to personally, and under his vigorous orders the suit was pressed and repairs were at once made on the one house in question, but of so flimsy a character that, although the requirements of the law were ostensibly complied with, in a month the condition was worse than before. It remains to be said, further, that the owner has adjacent property, also in shameful condition, which is untouched. This property is in litigation and, as the title is uncertain, there is a point of view from which it seems a hardship that a nominal owner may be compelled to pay heavy repair bills for which he may be unable to secure reimbursement. From this point of view, also, a certain leniency at the City Hall may seem only a decent courtesy. On the other hand, the tenant keeps on paying full rent in advance. His little business is established at this point and would be injured or destroyed by removal, as it is constantly injured to some degree by the bad state of the building. He pays for what he does not get, his interests are prejudiced, his health and that of his family are injured, and he has no redress. The law, official courtesy, and official supervision are all exerted in favor of the owner of the real estate as against the tenant and against the third and most important interest, the public health.

The law's delays, the carelessness, or worse, of inspectors, the indifference of landlords, each alone or combined, may put off the most essential repairs for months and even for years, as is frequently seen. Yet, in fact, the city ordinances are full and explicit in affording to the Department of Public Health complete power to summarily abate nuisances and adequately protect the health and lives of tenants, so far as they are threatened by unwholesome sanitary arrangements.

As the investigation showed, occupants of property where there is the most scrupulous compliance with sanitary ordinances cannot safeguard their own health or their lives if near them are such nuisances as have been described above. What is thus true of this district is true of the whole city. The river wards cannot be isolated from the other resident portions of the town. In this district are the stables of various large firms whose delivery wagons are sent throughout the city and suburbs; many of the teams doing city contract work are kept here; the peddlers' carts which carry fruit and vegetables in every direction within a day's journey start in large numbers from this region and their supplies are stored here. With all these go the houseflies, bearing, as we may believe, the typhoid germ.

Notes

1. For obvious reasons, the exact locations of houses mentioned are not given, but full and exact details have been obtained and are preserved at Hull House.

Document 16.5 Blacks in Chicago's Inner City

Sophonisba Breckinridge's examination of the "Color Line in Chicago" provides a clear contrast between Black neighborhoods and those occupied by other immigrants. In the article, she defines the "Color Line" and explores its consequences for Black neighborhoods. In particular she describes the disparity of wealth among the inhabitants, their conditions of life, and the role of racism in creating them. The essay is taken from a larger public health survey she conducted in Chicago. The Public Health Department had instructed her to ignore the Black neighborhoods, but Breckinridge carried out the survey to bring wider attention to the problems raised by the "Color Line." Earlier, Breckinridge received a doctorate in political economy and law at the University of Chicago and worked with Jane Addams at Hull House for over 15 years.

One of the many serious problems that now confront the Negro not only in southern communities but also in many a northern city is the difficulty he experiences in finding decent housing accommodations for his family. In the face of increasing manifestations of race prejudice, he has come to acquiesce silently, as various civil rights are withheld from him in the old "free North," which was once the Mecca of his race. He rarely protests, for example, at being excluded from restaurants and hotels or at being virtually refused entertainment at the theater or the opera. There are three points, however, which he cannot yield and in regard to which he should not be allowed to yield. He must claim a decent home for his family in a respectable neighborhood and at a reasonable rental, an equal chance of employment with the white man, and education for his children. We will consider here only the first of these three demands.

In a recent investigation of general housing conditions in Chicago,[1] the problem of the Negro was found to be quite different from that of immigrants. With the Negro, the housing dilemma was found to be an acute problem not only among the poor, as in the case of the Polish, the Jewish, or the Italian immigrant, but also among the well-to-do. The man who is poor as well as black must face the special evil of dilapidated insanitary dwellings and the lodger evil in its worst form. But for every man who is black, whether rich or poor, there is also the problem of extortionate rents and of dangerous proximity to segregated vice. The Negro is not only compelled to live in a segregated black district, but this region of Negro homes is almost invariably the one in which vice is tolerated by the police. That is, the segregation of the Negro quarter is only a segregation from respectable white people. The disreputable white element is

Sophonisba P. Breckinridge, "The Color Line in the Housing Problem," *Survey* 29, no. 18 (February 1, 1913): 575-76.

forced upon him. It is probably not too much to say that no colored family can long escape the presence of disreputable or disorderly neighbors. Respectable and well-to-do Negroes may by subterfuge succeed in buying property in a decent neighborhood, but they are sure to be followed soon by those disreputable elements which are allowed to exist outside the so-called "levee" district.

In no other part of Chicago, not even in the Ghetto, was there found a whole neighborhood so conspicuously dilapidated as the black belt on the South Side. No other group suffered so much from decaying buildings, leaking roofs, doors without hinges, broken windows, insanitary plumbing, rotting floors, and a general lack of repairs. In no other neighborhood were landlords so obdurate, so unwilling to make necessary improvements or to cancel leases so that tenants might seek better accommodations elsewhere. Of course, to go elsewhere was often impossible because nowhere is the prospective colored tenant or neighbor welcome. In the South Side black belt 74 per cent of the buildings were in a state of disrepair; in a more fortunate neighborhood, partly colored, only 65 per cent of the buildings were out of repair, but one-third were absolutely dilapidated.

Not only does the Negro suffer from this extreme dilapidation, but he pays a heavy cost in the form of high rent. A careful house-to-house canvass showed that in the most run down colored neighborhoods in the city, the rent for an ordinary four-room apartment was much higher than in any other section of the city. In crowded immigrant neighborhoods in different parts of the city, the median rental for the prevailing four-room apartment was between $8 and $8.50; in South Chicago near the steel mills it was between $9 and $9.50; and in the Jewish quarter, between $10 and $10.50 was charged. But in the great black belt of the South Side the sum exacted was between $12 and $12.50. That is, while half of the people in the Bohemian, Polish, and Lithuanian districts were paying less than $8.50, for their four-room apartments; the steel-mill employees less than $9.50, and the Jews in the Ghetto less than $10.50, the Negro, in the midst of extreme dilapidation and crowded into the territory adjoining the segregated vice district, pays from $12 to $12.50. This is from $2 to $4 a month more than the immigrant is paying for an apartment of the same size in a better state of repair.

It seemed worth while to collect and to present the facts relating to housing conditions in the Negro districts of Chicago because one must hope that they would not be tolerated if the great mass of white people knew of their existence. Most people stand for fair play. The persecutions which the Negro endures because of race prejudice undoubtedly express the feeling of but a small minority of his fellow-citizens of the white race. Their continuance must be due to the fact that the great majority are completely ignorant of the heavy burden of injustice that the Negro carries. Ignorance is the bulwark of prejudice, and race prejudice is singularly dependent upon an ignorance which is, to be sure, sometimes willful but which more often is unintentional and accidental. It has come about, however, that the small minority who cherish their prejudices have had the power to make life increasingly hard for the black man. Today they not only refuse to sit in the same part of the theater with him and to let him enter a hotel which they patronize, but they also refuse to allow him to live on the same street with them or in the same neighborhood. Even in the North where the city administration does not recognize a black "ghetto" or "pale," the real estate agents who register and commercialize what they suppose to be a universal race prejudice are able to enforce one in practice. It is out of this minority persecution that the special Negro housing problem has developed.

But while it is true that the active persecution of the Negro is the work of a small minority, its dangerous results are rendered possible only by the acquiescence of the great majority who want fair play. This prejudice can be made effective only because of the possible use of the city administration, and the knowledge that legal action intended to safeguard the rights of the Negro is both precarious and expensive. The police department, however, and the courts of justice are, in theory at least, the agents of the majority. It comes about therefore that while the great body of people desire justice, they not only become parties to gross injustice but must be held responsible for conditions demoralizing to the Negro and dangerous to the community as a whole.

Those friends of the Negro who have tried to understand the conditions of life as he faces them are very familiar with these facts. But it is hoped that those who have been ignorant of the heavy costs paid in decent family life for the ancient prejudice that persists among us, will refuse to acquiesce in its continuance when the facts are brought home to them.

Notes

1. See Housing Conditions in Chicago, VI. *American Journal of Sociology*, Vol. XVIII, p. 241.

Chapter 16 Worksheet and Questions

1. The Diversity of the City: In the introduction to the chapter, the author argued that beginning in the late 1800s the concept of diversity was used to describe the inhabitants of cities. That is, observers described

    > a populace divided into a variety of types that reflected racial, national, ethnic, class, occupational, and religious differences. From this perspective, each type or group possessed distinct physical features, abilities, behaviors, and propensities. Academics, authors, and journalists of the time used the broad and inaccurate term "race" to ascribe to groups what are now understood as national, ethnic, racial, and religious differences.

    Does the evidence in Document 16.1, "What is the 19th Ward?"; and Document 16.2, "The Mixed Crowd" support this definition of diversity? Why or why not? Be sure to cite specific examples.

    _____

    _____

    _____

    _____

    _____

    _____

    _____

    _____

2. Diversity and Geography: In the introduction to the chapter, the author suggested that diversity was expressed by geographical location: "The social geography of the city, or the distribution of distinct types of people across the urban landscape, seemed to justify such beliefs. Just as cities were divided into districts, so too its inhabitants were distributed into a wide diversity of neighborhoods, each identified with distinct groups or types." Does the evidence in Document 16.1, "What is the 19th Ward?"; and Document 16.2, "The Mixed Crowd" support this claim? Why or why not? Be sure to cite specific examples.

    _____

    _____

    _____

    _____

    _____

3. The Immigrant Girl: Based upon Document 16.3, "The Special Problems of the Immigrant Girl,"; Document 16.1, "What is the 19th Ward?"; and Document 16.2, "The Mixed Crowd," why did immigrant girls come to the United States, and what problems did they face when they arrived? Is the treatment of diversity in the document the same as or different from Documents 16.1 and 16.2? Why?

_____

_____

_____

_____

_____

_____

_____

_____

_____

4. Conditions of Life: Based upon Document 16.4 , "An Inquiry Into The Causes Of The Recent Epidemic Of Typhoid Fever In Chicago"; Document 16.1, "What is the 19th Ward?"; and Document 16.2, "The Mixed Crowd," what conclusions can you draw about conditions of life and health in the inner city neighborhoods? Why was disease so prevalent?

_____

_____

_____

_____

_____

_____

_____

_____

_____

5. Blacks in the Cities:

Based upon Document 16.5, "The Color Line in the Housing Problem"; Document 16.1, "What is the 19th Ward?"; and Document 16.2, "The Mixed Crowd," in what ways were Black neighborhoods different from other immigrant neighborhoods? In what ways were they similar? What factors account for the differences?

_____

_____

_____

_____

_____

_____

_____

_____

_____

6. Diversity: Based upon all of the readings, what is your understanding of diversity, and how does it compare to the meaning of diversity in the early 1900s?

_____

_____

_____

_____

_____

_____

_____

_____

_____

_____

Progressives

Progressive reformers embraced America. They prized advances in science, technology, and management that generated the new industrial systems and modern conveniences of urban life. They cherished the idea of American history: a country settled by religiously steeped Puritans, who in rebellion, created a democratic republic, preserved it through a civil war, and, in its latest stage, reaped the benefits of science and technology. Yet in the 1890s and early 1900s, Progressives concluded that the country was moving in the wrong direction. Corporate venality, abuse of workers, widespread poverty, abysmal physical and public health conditions in cities, and rampant political corruption—all threatened to derail the promise of future progress. In response, they undertook wide-ranging reforms to correct what they saw as problems in otherwise admirable and historically tested systems. Hardly revolutionaries, the reformers intended to adjust industrial, urban, and political institutions and put the nation back on a progressive course.

In the process, Progressives judged some problems to be more important than others. Segregation, poverty, inequality, disenfranchisement, discrimination, and, in particular, lynching experienced by Blacks throughout America would seem to be crucial issues requiring Progressive reform. Certainly, the nearly two thousand African Americans lynched between 1882 and 1900 demanded a response from Progressives who led in the enactment of over 56 laws after 146 deaths in the Triangle Shirtwaist fire. Yet, White reformers were, at best, ambivalent about the circumstances confronting Blacks. Some, like Jane Addams, Mary Ovington, and John Dewey, joined African Americans like W.E.B. DuBois and Ida B. Wells-Barnett to address them. Most White reformers, however, refused. They insisted upon segregation even when the two camps worked for common goals like voting rights for women, better working conditions, and more consumer protection. Furthermore, they justified their actions on the grounds of commonly accepted Progressive methods and principles. Coalitions of Black and White reformers then pursued a course that paralleled other Progressive initiatives. United behind efforts to end lynching, they also developed different approaches to bring about change. For example, industrial education at Booker T. Washington's Tuskegee Institute represented one favored by many Progressives. W.E.B. Dubois preferred to work through the Niagara Movement and NAACP to achieve equal rights. These efforts achieved few of their stated goals, but by the 1920s many Blacks argued that in fact there was now a "New Negro." This chapter will focus on these issues, starting with an overview of Progressivism.

Who were the Progressives? Answering that question is difficult. Essentially they were people who worked toward, and achieved, a wide range of reforms during the three decades after 1890. Socioeconomically, they were middle class; compared to the general population, a disproportionate number attended colleges and universities; the majority were white and female. However, they did not share a common identity as "Progressives," and they did not create or congregate in any specifically "Progressive" institutions. Nevertheless, Theodore Roosevelt sought their support for the Progressive Party in his 1912 presidential campaign. He appealed to them by seizing upon their shared beliefs and offering them a version of American history that ennobled them. In Roosevelt's view, Americans shared a history of progress populated by Puritans, founders and preservers of democracy, generals, inventors, and industrial leaders. He then outlined an array of problems that threatened America's future. Many reformers heard themselves in Roosevelt's narrative. They shared religious beliefs and values, democratic convictions, and an appreciation for the methods of science. They also subscribed to his larger conception of historical progress. Roosevelt then called upon the "Progressives" to do what they had already been doing—join him in solving problems that threatened the future.

The threats were legion. Rogue corporations, debased citizens living in uninhabitable cities, and political corruption topped the list. From the Progressive perspective, many corporations had abandoned competition, in which technological systems gained advantage from increased efficiency. Instead, "malefactors of great wealth" sought profit, monopoly, and power. Their rapacious behavior savaged workers and consumers while corrupting city, state, and national governments. In response, Progressives introduced a number of reforms. Presidents Roosevelt, Harding, and Wilson broke up monopolies, regulated corporate activities, and encouraged competition. A self-proclaimed "trust buster," Roosevelt's administration dismantled the Standard Oil Company, the Sugar Trust and, in the Northern Securities case, a railroad monopoly. In the Anthracite Coal Strike, Roosevelt used the power of government to threaten owners with armed seizure to arbitrate a settlement between coal companies and the United Mine Workers. The federal government introduced regulations for pure food and drugs in response to Upton Sinclair's *The Jungle*. All levels of government legislated work place safety requirements, workmen's compensation laws, consumer protection regulations, child labor laws, and laws limiting the hours of work for women. Woodrow Wilson created the Federal Reserve System, reducing the power of private banks like J.P. Morgan, which was reputed to own or control one fourth of the nation's wealth. Roosevelt and Taft sponsored the first conservation laws to protect pristine forests and make them available to the public.

Progressives also addressed the conditions of cities. They attributed urban problems to a combination of factors, but stressed corporate abuse of labor and malfeasance by politicians. Reformers tackled urban problems on a number of fronts. Jane Addams established Hull House in the immigrant neighborhoods of west Chicago. She saw it as a way for poor immigrants to achieve "better local government and a wider social and intellectual life." The settlement house functioned as a community center for immigrants to gain social skills and educations, learn American customs, and find help solving domestic problems. It provided employment and child care services. The middle-class women who managed the facilities also functioned as advocates to secure garbage collection and other city services. Reformers also promoted paved streets, clean water, sewage systems, housing regulations, and other improvements to the health and conditions of the urban poor. In these efforts, they confronted existing city governments or political machines led by bosses who found it to their advantage to provide the services themselves. As often as not, the much reviled machine politicians assumed the role of reformer and, with it, what became the politics of urban liberalism.

Carrying out reforms did not exonerate machine politicians. Exposés uncovered corruption and betrayal at all levels of government. Politicians seemed regularly to place corporate and personal interests above those of the people. From the reformers' perspective, urban political machines were perhaps the worst offenders. City bosses, like George B. Cox in Cincinnati or Jim and Tom Pendergast in Kansas City, were not only in the thrall of corporate interests, but they even manipulated and deceived newcomers, especially immigrants, into voting for them. State and national politicians were similarly debased.

As they did with corporate and urban problems, Progressives sponsored a host of changes. To deal with the urban political machines, they promoted city-wide elections that would deny bosses their strength in the poorer wards. The larger solution, however, lay in introducing new forms of city offices, like city commissions and city managers, staffed by professionals and experts. By modeling city government on corporate structures, where city commissions functioned like boards of directors and city managers like presidents, reformers hoped to achieve the same levels of efficiency. The first success came with the creation of a city commission style of government in Galveston, Texas that organized the city's recovery from a hurricane in 1900. Thirteen years later, Dayton, Ohio put a city manager into place. By 1919, some 130 other cities followed suit.

To deal with the problems of state officials, reformers called for more democracy. They advocated taking the selection of nominees for political office out of the hands of party parties through popular elections in direct primaries. Similarly, they called for, and achieved, the direct election of U.S. senators, with the 17th

Amendment to the U.S. Constitution. With the passage of the 19th Amendment in 1920, the work of Carrie Chapman Catt and Alice Paul was realized, and women were guaranteed the right to vote.

This list of corporate, urban, and political reforms only begins to enumerate the breadth of Progressive activity and accomplishments, but it does indicate what reformers shared in the way they cast problems and solutions to them. Roosevelt's historical appeal suggested that Progressives shared an appreciation for the methods of science, religion, and morality, and a democratic system of government; with respect to science and technology, they definitely did. Insofar as they were middle class, they were employed in the new industries, services, universities, and corporations. In particular, Progressives placed a high value upon expertise and professionalism. They referred to their methods as "scientific."

To be effective, reforms rested upon the collection and analysis of data. For example, in the area of law, Louis Brandies filed a brief in *Muller v. Oregon* (1908), on behalf of women in the Consumers League, arguing for the constitutionality of a ten-hour work day. In a document of over a hundred pages, two pages gave the legal argument, while the rest presented data illustrating the ill effects of long working days upon women's health, families, and morals. Progressives studied cities and their inhabitants extensively. In the Pittsburgh Survey conducted between 1911 and 1914, several researchers examined working and living conditions in the city's steel district. The Russell Sage Foundation commissioned a study of poverty that ran six volumes in length. Similarly, journalists (denoted Muckrakers by their critics) published well detailed accounts of corporate abuses, as in Ida M. Tarbell's *History of Standard Oil*; the conditions found in slums, as in Jacob Riis' *How the Other Half Lives*; and political abuses, as in Lincoln Steffens' *The Shame of the Cities*. Overall, then, the Progressive Method, or the collection and analysis of data, was evident in all areas of progressive reform.

A second commonality marking the Progressive approach is a concern for morality, often in the form of religious convictions. On one hand, reformers appreciated Christian traditions as an historical legacy from the Puritans who settled New England. On the other, many belonged to churches, and saw their religious beliefs as underlying reform activities. Roosevelt reminded Progressives of their living heritage of religiously based reform, in his 1912 address to the Bull Moose Party. He concluded the speech by claiming that our cause "is based on the eternal principles of righteousness," and that, "We stand at Armageddon, and we battle for the Lord." Some, like Walter Raushenbusch, were ministers who preached a "Social Gospel," calling it a Christian responsibility to minister to the needs of the poor. Others were less tied to specific religious outlooks, but thought that morality was crucial and was threatened. Jane Addams sought to address both the moral and material needs of the poor. Frederick W. Taylor saw efficiency itself as a moral value, and scientific management as a way to do good and be good. Certainly the Progressive condemnation of corporate, urban, and political abuses rested upon moral convictions. Roosevelt distinguished between good and bad corporations based upon their treatment of workers, customers, and government. Morality mattered; Progressives viewed themselves as moral agents, and viewed reform as having a moral dimension.

Historians generally agree that Progressives shared a commitment to democratic systems of government as well. Their convictions had both historical and contemporary aspects. Many believed that the nation's progress stemmed from the establishment of a democracy that guaranteed the rights of its citizens. Voicing perhaps an even more common theme, reformers invoked Lincoln's preservation of the Union in the Civil War because they believed the threats posed by industrial monopolies and machine politics called for an equally strong response. From this perspective, nothing less than "the right of the people to rule" was at stake. Consequently, Progressives spoke of restoring democracy, or of returning the country to its democratic heritage; they instituted reforms like direct primaries and direct election of senators. Modern conditions, they realized, required a proper understanding of the democratic system.

In this respect, reformers focused upon two related aspects of American government. First, it was a republic—voters elected representatives to conduct the business of government. From the reform perspective, representatives needed to understand modern circumstances; that is, politicians themselves had to be professionals or experts. If not, they should be open to the advice of professionals, and ready to appoint them to positions where the work of government was carried out. Second, a democracy could only function with qualified voters. At a minimum, they had to be educable. Voters needed to be able to recognize the best candidates and best ideas, which meant representatives with the expertise to govern an urban, industrial nation—or Progressives. To that end, political reformers instituted a variety of restrictions on voter eligibility, denying the franchise to those they deemed incompetent.

Progressives then shared views about expertise, morality, and democracy. They instituted a wide range of corporate, urban, and political reforms. However, with respect to African Americans, a very different picture emerges. In city slums, Blacks' experience of poverty, inadequate housing, and public health hazards was more severe, as judged at the time, than that of other immigrants. Employers paid Blacks less than other groups, gave them the least desirable jobs, and set them against other workers by recruiting them as strikebreakers. Certainly the political system failed Blacks, whose rights were ignored. Things differed little in the South, where most Blacks, employed as sharecroppers, were impoverished, had little access to education, were denied the vote, were severely segregated, and were subjected to racial violence. All of these circumstances invited the types of reforms that engaged Progressives elsewhere. Yet Progressives split over the issue of joining Blacks in programs of reform.

Certainly the rise of lynching after Reconstruction represented one horrific practice around which reformers could unite. Ida B. Wells-Barnett and Jane Addams attempted to enlist the Progressives' coalition to the cause. Wells-Barnett, a Black Progressive and part owner of Memphis' *Free Speech and Headlight*, became involved with the issue after the lynching of three friends. When she protested editorially in her paper, a mob burned the offices and threatened her with lynching. Unable to return to Memphis, Wells-Barnett began a campaign against lynching. In typical Progressive fashion, she began by researching the problem, and published her findings in *Horrors: Lynch Law in All Its Phases* (1892) and in an expanded version, *A Red Record* (1895). Other studies followed, including an annual report in the *Chicago Tribune*. The figures painted an appalling picture. One commission concluded that between 1889 and 1930, some 3,724 people were lynched in the United States. Approximately 75 percent were Blacks. While classified as lynching, many of the individuals were burned to death. In other cases, victims were first tortured and mutilated. (For further discussion, turn to Document 13.11 in chapter 13.) Entire communities attended lynchings, yet few perpetrators faced criminal indictment and fewer still (four by 1930) were sent to prison. Wells-Barnett combined this evidence with moral condemnation and demanded political reform in the form of the enactment and enforcement of laws against lynching. Addressing Progressive interests and applying Progressive methods, she looked for support. While initially distancing themselves from her, the National Association of Colored Women (NACW) made its primary mission an end to lynching.

Jane Addams, the founder of Hull House in Chicago, enlisted in the effort as well. During the late 1890s she visited with members of the NACW and began writing and speaking against lynching. In 1900 she brought Wells-Barnett together with co-founder and president of the NACW, Mary Church Terrell, at the group's annual convention in Chicago. Addams next moved to bring Black organizations into the National Federation of Women's Clubs (NFWC), an organization that promoted many Progressive reforms. The plan would potentially put the support of a national reform organization behind the cause of ending lynching. As Document 17.5 will show, the strategy failed.

When Progressives could not find common cause to end lynching, it became clear that they would not do so in other areas of reform, either. Subsequently, Progressivism followed separate courses. Black and White reformers did struggle to reform conditions confronting Blacks, but the majority of Progressives followed the segregationist direction of the NFWC. Oddly, reformers justified their actions in terms of their common Progressive methods and values.

Addams views illustrate some of the issues that led White reformers to separate themselves from Blacks. Wells-Barnett and Addams agreed about using Progressive methods to investigate the incidences and causes of lynching as well as to condemn its moral repugnance. Addams, however, disagreed about the efficacy of lynching laws, a critical objective to Black reformers and typical in the standard Progressive approach. Instead, she believed the only real reform lay in changing public sentiment. With respect to a national law, she argued that lynching fell under state jurisdiction and, consequently, Congress had no legal authority over it. As a practical matter, she doubted that the federal government would pass legislation, because Southern states would block it. (Congress has yet to pass a law against lynching, although a resolution to apologize for this inaction has recently been proposed.) Addams expressed one other reservation about lynching (see Document 17.1) She noted that Southerners were unanimous in asserting that lynching was necessary in cases where Black men raped White women. If true, that produced for Addams and other reformers the moral dilemma of choosing between two evils.

The majority of white Progressives appear to have accepted the rationale of rape that Southerners offered to justify lynching. Despite tremendous pressure to condemn lynching and call for legislation against it, Progressive presidents Roosevelt, Taft, and Wilson were reluctant to speak to the issue. During World War I, Wilson, without mentioning Blacks, pointed out that lynching and mob violence could easily be used in German propaganda against America. Perhaps Roosevelt typified Progressive attitudes in his 1906 State of the Union address, where he contended, "The greatest existing cause of lynching is the per-petration, especially by Black men, of the hideous crime of rape—the most abominable in all the category of crimes, even worse than murder." Further, he argued, that the lynching of rapists incited people to resort to lynching to punish lesser crimes and misbehavior. For Roosevelt then, the spirit of mob violence became the issue, and he called upon every "Christian patriot" to condemn it.

This lack of sympathy for and understanding of issues affecting Blacks was reflected in the findings of Progressive research into human diversity. Progressives interpreted diversity in terms of fundamentally dif-ferent types of humans, each possessing different physical attributes, moral beliefs, capabilities, and behav-iorial tendencies. To reformers, Italians, Africans, English, and Chinese were fundamentally different types of people. Frequently, they referred to different groups of people—national, racial, ethnic, or reli-gious—as different "races." Josiah Strong's *Our Country* attributed these differences to natural selection operating on human societies, or the workings of social Darwinism. Madison Grant's *The Passing of the Great Race* applied Mendelian genetics to explain the differences among human groups. Like others, Edward A. Ross' *The Old World in the New* listed the attributes of different groups in great detail. Charles Davenport's eugenic science, which called for selective breeding of humans, lent further legitimacy to this view of diversity.

In applications, these theorists warned of the evils of racial intermixing. Intermarriage would dilute the genetics of the better races, like the Anglo-Saxons, American, and Teutons. Similarly, they advised that even regular social interaction among different groups would impair morality, manners, and even the working of democratic institutions. Such Progressive theories applied to all types of humans, but drew especially insidious conclusions about African Americans. They were widely accepted among Progres-sives, and found expression in their policies and reforms. The consequences for Blacks were especially pernicious.

Application of the Progressive method provided a rationale for segregation, and suggested that White groups of reformers should not work with Blacks. White women's clubs in the South publicly criticized Jane Addams for dining with members of Black progressive women's clubs. She then "had the audacity to accept entertainment from the White ladies of Memphis as though she had not lost caste by actually eat-ing at the same table with colored women." She was warned against expecting hospitality in the future. Similarly, White women's groups like the National American Woman Suffrage Association denied mem-bership to Black women's clubs. Consequently, Ida Wells-Barnett established the Equal Suffrage League for Blacks. The NACW also took up the cause. Segregation also characterized Progressive Settlement Houses. If Whites refused to cooperate with Blacks to bring about common goals, in the field of politics their conception of diversity led to reforms directly inimical to Blacks.

Reformers coupled their commitment to democracy with concerns about the competence of voters. Their conception of diversity led them to conclude that several groups were not capable of exercising the franchise. Consequently, in the name of reform, Progressives proceeded to disenfranchise all people of color—Blacks as well as Hispanics, Indians, Arabs, and Asians...The favored mechanisms were literacy tests, which purported to determine voters' ability to read and their understanding of government; and poll taxes, which required voters to pay a tax and produce the receipt for it at the polls. These requirements excluded Blacks more than any other group. Direct primaries, too, provided an avenue to exclude voters. Lafollette's reform of Wisconsin elections was intended to return government to the people, but it had a very different purpose in the South, where seven states adopted it before Wisconsin, and all but three had by 1916. Since the 13th Amendment guaranteed Blacks the right to vote, states could not discriminate against Blacks in election law. However, this legal restriction did not apply to the direct primary where voters selected the party's candidates to run in the general election. In the South where Democrats dominated politics, the selection of the Democratic candidates effectively placed them in office. Southern states then passed laws prohibiting Blacks from voting in primaries, thereby ending their participation in the selection of representatives. North or South, Progressives approved of these changes. President William Howard Taft expressly approved disenfranchisement of Blacks. Many, however, were appalled by the racism and segregation practiced by Progressive groups. Some opted to work with Blacks in creating a set of parallel reform organizations.

In February 1905, W.E.B. DuBois and William Trotter called for a meeting of Black and White reformers to discuss the possibility of establishing an organization dedicated to achieving Black equality. In October at a public convention on the Canadian side of Niagara Falls (hotels on the American side would not accommodate Blacks), the Niagara Movement began. DuBois became General Secretary and the group issued a Declaration of Principles. The Conference's first mandate was "progress." The next 18 points laid out a plan to achieve full political and civic equality.

In taking these steps, the Niagara Movement directly challenged the course of improvement charted by Booker T. Washington. Washington had founded the Tuskegee Institute in 1881 just as Jim Crow segregation was taking form in Alabama. The college rested on a philosophy of industrial education, which would provide students with job skills. Washington believed that economic success was the best route to reforming race relations in the South. In time, he expected that the green of money would become the only color of consequence. To establish the school, he generated a wide interracial base of donors and supporters. In the process, Washington became a nationally known figure and spokesman for Blacks. In 1905 he met and dined with president Theodore Roosevelt. (The president was afterwards accused of race treason.) Washington's critics, however, believed that in promoting Tuskegee, he had made too many concessions to Whites. In what became known as the Atlanta Compromise Speech, Washington spoke to a largely White audience at the Cotton States and International Exposition in Atlanta. His topic was "In Industry the Foundation Must Be Laid." In the speech he conceded that for the time being, "In all things that are purely social we can be as separate as the fingers, yet one as the hand in all things essential to mutual progress." (The entire speech is found in chapter 13, Document 13.12.) Dubois and the members of the Niagara Movement called this Accommodationism, meaning that Washington had accepted segregation and the loss of rights, in order to please the Whites who supported him.

Blacks established two other national and interracial reform organizations. A New York settlement-house worker, Mary Ovington, whom DuBois invited to join the Niagara group, proposed an alliance of Black and White Progressives. She called a meeting in 1911 to create the National Association for the Advancement of Colored People (NAACP). DuBois and Wells-Barnett attended, as did Addams and two other nationally known Progressives, philosopher John Dewey, and author Theodore Dreiser. Together they agreed on a mission to "promote equality of rights and to eradicate caste or race prejudice." DuBois assumed the position of editor of the *Crisis*, the NAACP's journal. The coalition made securing a lynching law one of its priorities. It also challenged the constitutionality of discriminatory laws in the courts.

The National Urban League also coalesced in 1911. The interracial organization arose out of the merger of the Committee on Urban Conditions Among Negroes, the National League for the Protection of Colored Women, and the Committee for Improving the Committee on Urban Conditions Among Negroes. Similar to settlement houses, the organization was created to help Black immigrants adjust to city life. It operated social programs to familiarize clients with urban lifestyles and manners. The Urban League also offered employment services, and pressured employers to hire more Blacks.

Tuskegee, Niagara, the NAACP, and the Urban League all represented reform organizations. Due to the persistent refusal of exclusively white Progressive groups, they were forced to pursue a parallel course of reform, which no doubt reduced their effectiveness. During the 1920s, however, Blacks like Alain Locke, who lived through the Progressive Era, found that much had been accomplished, although in ways that reformers had not expected.

Considering the Evidence in the Readings

The documents in this chapter tell the story of Progressives' efforts at the turn of the twentieth century to stop lynching and achieve civil rights. All of them are by or about leaders of the movement. When reading them, keep in mind that Progressives were a disparate group of reformers who agreed that the new industrial systems and cities were necessary to the nation's future progress. To that end they sought to sustain them, but change them in ways that produced a more just, democratic, and humane society. In contrast to this, the issue of race divided the Progressives. They could not even agree about the need to end the vicious practice of lynching. As you proceed through the documents, focus on the authors' arguments for preventing lynching and realizing civil rights. You will find differences in the way the authors approach the subjects, especially the value they place on northern and southern unity within the Progressive movement. Also note the price that Progressives who supported civil rights paid for their actions. Further, even Progressives disagreed about how to achieve equality for Blacks. You should notice the different approaches they advocate and think about how they were carried out over time.

Document 17.1 A Progressive Attack on Lynching

With the turn of the twentieth century, Jane Addams decided that the time had come for Progressives to address the ugly practice of lynching. In this article, she provides a good Progressive analysis of the issue, delving into its history, its effects on government, and its moral repugnance. Note also the Southern explanation for lynching, which hinges on a moral argument. Ask yourself whether Addams rejects that argument. In these efforts, she was joined by Ida B. Wells-Barnett. (whose essays you will read next). The two began their association in the 1890s and continued with the National Association of Colored Women, the Chicago Association for the Advancement of Colored People, and the NAACP. Addams is better known for her work at Hull House in Chicago, and as a nationally known advocate for many Progressive reforms. She and Ellen Gates Starr established the settlement house in 1889 in the slums of west Chicago. The middle-class women who operated it addressed the problems of poor immigrants in a number of ways. The house itself served as a community center, with rooms for education, arts, bathing, and other activities. The group also advocated for reforms like garbage collection, while performing wide-ranging studies of the immigrant neighborhoods.

Each nation, and each section of a nation so large as ours; has its own problems and difficulties, many of them so subtle and intricate that it is almost impossible for an outsider to judge of them fairly. It is, moreover, the essence of self-government that it shall be local in administration, in order that special difficul-ties shall be met by the people who live among them, and who thus understand them better than an out-sider possibly could.

We are obliged to remember all this when we speak of the problems which face the present genera-tion of Southern men. Added to all the difficulties of

---

Jane Addams, "Respect for Law," *The Independent* 53, no. 2718 (January 3, 1901): 18–20.

reconstruction and the restoration of a country devastated by war, they must deal with that most intricate of all problems—the presence of two alien races. Admitting all this, and making due allowances for differences of standpoint, it still remains true that certain well established principles underlie all self-government, and that to persistently disregard these principles is to endanger self-government itself. When this disregard constantly occurs any section of a self-governing country has a right to enter its protest against any other section just as the civilized nations interfere with any one nation whose public acts throw back the whole of civilized progress.

Before entering this protest, however, in regard to the increasing number of negro lynching occurring in the South, we must remember that many of the most atrocious public acts recorded in history have been committed by men who had convinced themselves that then were doing right. They either proceeded upon a false theory of conduct, or—what is much worse—they later invented a theory of conduct to cover and support their deeds.

One of these time-honored false theories has been that criminality can be suppressed and terrorized by exhibitions of brutal punishment; that crime can be prevented by cruelty.

Let us then assume that the Southern citizens who take part in and abet the lynching of negroes honestly believe that that is the only successful method of dealing with a certain class of crimes; that they have become convinced that the Southern negro in his present undeveloped state must be frightened and subdued by terror; that, acting upon this theory, they give each lynching full publicity and often gather together numerous spectators. We know that at least on one occasion excursion trains carried thousands of people to view a carefully planned lynching, in order that as many people as possible might be thoroughly frightened by the spectacle, and terrorized from committing the same crime. Oft this same assumption the living victim is sometimes horribly mutilated and his body later exhibited.

Let us give the Southern citizens the full benefit of this position, and assume that they have set aside trial by jury and all processes of lair because they have become convinced that this brutal method of theirs is the most efficient method in dealing with a peculiar class of crime committed by one race against another.

A most superficial study of history will discover that the method of deterring crime by horrible punishment has been trial many times and that it particularly distinguishes the dealing with those crimes which a so-called lower class has committed against its superior.

It betrays the existence of the essentially aristocratic attitude, founded upon a contempt for the inferior class—a belief that they cannot be appealed to by reason and fair dealing, but must be treated upon the animal plane, bullied and terrorized.

This attitude is particularly discernible when the lower class evinces a tendency toward democratic development, toward asserting their human claim as such, when they assert their rights rather than ask for privileges.

We, recall that the years preceding the French Revolution were the years in which the most revolting public executions were common in all parts of Paris. Fifty spots are still pointed out as the sedges of horrible public exposures. A man would be taken to one place, where his hand would be chopped off, then carried on a cart to another where lie would be broken alive on a wheel; and at still another his body would be burned, and his ashes scattered to the winds. So late as 1780 a workingman for stealing some linen was condemned to be hung on a gibbet and strangled by the public executioner; certainly not because of the value of the linen, but because he had dared to touch the property of the class above his own. He must be made all example of, his temerity must be well punished and a repetition prevented among his fellows. And who was responsible for this torture, strangling and burning? The old nobility and monarchists, who honestly believed that this method of terrorizing was the only possible way to control the common people, who were so far inferior to themselves that they could not be appealed to by humane methods.

It is thus the people were prepared for the guillotine, and it was only because they were hardened by such scenes as these that they could leave endured the sights of the Revolution.

The English records of crime were never so full as when the penalties were most severe; when poaching—that arch crime against the upper classes—was punished by death; when the grinning skulls of thieves were exposed upon London Bridge; when, in short, the nobility made and executed the laws for the populace whose uprisings they feared.

It was because the gentle folk heard the rumblings of the Chartist movement that they were thus incensed and they went so far that they even succeeded in stirring up the law abiding country Englishman so that he went to burning hay ricks and attacking the houses of the country gentry in his desire to get even with the atrocities committed against him.

Punishments of this sort rise to unspeakable atrocities when the crimes of the so-called inferior class affect the property and persons of the superior; and when the situation is complicated by race animosity, as it is at present in the South, by the feeling of the former slave owner to his former slave, whom he is not bidden to regard as his fellow citizen, we have the worst possible situation for attempting this method of punishment. But, whether tried at its best or worst, this method has always failed and—more than that—has reacted to the moral degradation of all concerned.

We would send this message to our fellow citizens of the South who are once more trying to suppress vice by violence: That the bestial in man, that, which leads him to pillage and rape, can never be controlled by public cruelty and dramatic punishment, which too often cover fury and revenge. That violence is the most ineffectual method of dealing with crime, the most preposterous attempt to inculcate lessons of self control. A community has a right to protect itself from the criminal, to restrain him, to segregate him from the rest of society. But when it attempts revenge, when it persuades itself that exhibitions of cruelty result in reform, it shows itself ignorant of all the teachings of history; it allows itself to be thrown back into the savage state of dealing with criminality.

It further runs a certain risk of brutalizing each spectator, of shaking his belief in law and order, of sowing seed for future violence. It is certainly doubtful whether these scenes could be enacted over and over again, save in a community in which the hardening drama of slavery lead once been seen, in which the devastation of war had taken place; and we may be reasonably sure that the next generation of the South cannot escape the result of the lawlessness and violence which are now being indulged in.

Brutality begets brutality; and proceeding on the theory that the negro is undeveloped, and therefore must be treated in this primitive fashion, is to forget that the immature pay little attention to statements, but quickly imitate what they see. The nuder-developed [sic] are never helped by such methods as these, for they learn only by imitation. The child who is managed by a system of bullying and terrorizing is almost sure to be the vicious and stupid child.

And to those Southern citizens who claim that this method has been successful, that in certain localities a lynching has, in point of fact, been followed by a cessation of the crime of which the lynched man was guilty, we would quote the psychologist who tells us that, under the influence of certain strong emotions, such as fear, certain elements of the self can be prevented from coming into action, "inhibited," as they technically call it; but that these elements are thus only stupefied, or drugged, and sooner or later assert themselves with all of their old power, if the fuller self be aroused. All such inhibitive measures must in the end lie futile, and, altho they may for a fleeting moment appear successful, they are philosophically and historically unsound.

To those who say that most of these hideous and terrorizing acts have been committed in the name of chivalry, in order to make the lives and honor of women safe, perhaps it is women themselves who can best reply that bloodshed and arson and ungoverned anger have never yet controlled lust. On the contrary, that lust has always been the handmaid of these, and is prone to be found where they exist; that the suppression of the bestial cannot be accomplished by the counter exhibition of the brutal only.

Perhaps it is woman who can best testify that the honor of women is only secure in those nations and those localities where law and order and justice prevail; that the sight of human blood and the burning of human flesh has historically been the signal for lust; that an attempt to allay and control it by scenes such as those is as ignorant as it is futile and childish.

And if a woman might venture to add another word on behalf of her sex, that the woman who is protected by violence allows herself to be protected as the woman of the savage is, and she must still be regarded as the possession of man. As her lord and master is strong or weak, so is the protection which she receives; that if she takes brute force as her protection, she must also accept the status she held when brute force alone prevailed.

I have purposely treated this subject on the theory of its ablest defenders; I have said nothing of the innumerable chances of punishing the wrong man; of the many other results of lawless methods; I have avoided confusing the main issue.

CHICAGO, ILL.

Document 17.2 Jane Addams Speaks Against Lynching

This document is a newspaper account of Jane Addams' talk before a women's club. In the discussion she applies Progressive methods and criticizes lynching in ways that would be appreciated by other Progressives. As noted in the title, her themes were democracy and social ethics. The choice was no doubt careful, as Addams was trying to convince members of the National Federation of Women's Clubs to admit Black women's groups. This effort is discussed.

Decries Brute Force

Says Violent Methods in Punishment Beget Brutality.

Uses Burning of Negro in Colorado as an Example—Praises Democracy.

"Democracy and Social Ethics" was the theme selected by Miss Jane Addams for an address delivered yesterday afternoon before the Chicago Woman's club. Miss Addams' talk was in the nature of a plea for the abandonment of brute forces in dealing with law breakers, or rather, that it be rendered unnecessary by a general development of the best human qualities.

"Brutality begets brutality," declared the speaker. "Notwithstanding all our law-and-order government, we are continually committing the most undemocratic acts. No attempt is paid to developing the higher morals of man; it is believed the only way criminally inclined persons can be conquered and ruled is to terrorize and brutalize them. This is the accepted step toward restoring order, and it is accepted because it is thought to be for law and order. Result is wanted, not process of development. A splendid example of this is what happened yesterday in Colorado, when a colored man was burned at the stake because he killed a white child.

Lynching Undemocratic

"Lynching is undemocratic. It would seem that you cannot get at a colored man who has tendencies toward committing crime unless he is terrorized, brutally treated, and harshly forced into submission. It is the same today as it was in the early ages, when bar-barism had not died out, in dealing with offenders. There is no effort made to find out what is wanted, but instead all the force of the government is put on the negative side.

"This is exactly what happened in Colorado yesterday. This horrible affair, when a colored man was bound hand and foot to an iron rail, a fire built under him, and the miserable victim slowly burned to death, was made as public as possible. The avengers wanted the people to know what was being done. It was desired that the public know what was the end of the colored man who would murder another person—and that a white person, and, furthermore, a white child.

"This incident in Colorado was not the result of passion, as was that which drove the victim to commit the crime. Instead, it was done on the line of theory. It is the general belief that people in the second stages of civilization must be brutalized in order to restore order, but again I say brutality begets brutality and the impression left in the minds of those people who witnessed that fearful act yesterday will require years to overcome."

Violence Is Great

"Break the laws is the order," continued Miss Addams, "and furthermore, shoot the man who attempts to steal your property, the cry is. But why should you? It seems to me a greater offense to shoot the man who steals than the act of stealing itself. Is there any reason why it is necessary to commit a greater wrong to make a lesser wrong right?

"In the old town meetings of the early New England days the several persons went there to discuss some common need of the people. It was not

---

"Jane Addams Talks: Addresses Club Women on Democracy and Social Ethics," *Chicago Inter-Ocean* (November 18, 1900).

expected that some one was there to bring up his own selfish needs. These meetings were successful. But when several persons get together for other purposes than common interest, it is the extreme limit of incongruity."

In speaking of what is needed to correct existing evils, Miss Addams said:

"It is government by the people. It may not be good government at first, but it's going to do away with many things, but will improve and in the end will be satisfactory. The trouble is we lay too much stress on the negative side. The purpose is not considered, but an effort is made to terrorize.

"People go into politics for what there is in it. To go into it for any other reason than popular government, they think, is all right. As, for instance, one alderman in our ward hasn't much to do with setting the standard of life. A clever cartoonist once made a picture of the candidates in that ward running for alderman. One of them was a well-dressed man sitting at a fine table drinking champagne, the other was a bricklayer, sitting on a half-finished wall, eating his lunch from a dinner-pail. Ordinarily, it would be supposed that the people, especially when the district is made up almost exclusively of such, would favor the poor man. But they didn't, as was seen as the election. The man drinking the champagne was the successful candidate."

Document 17.3 Ending Lynching

Much like other "Muckrakers" who investigated and revealed the scandalous behavior of politicians and businessmen, Ida B. Wells-Barnett applied the same techniques to lynching. In this article, she utilizes Progressive methods and brings Progressive moral and political values to bear upon the sordid practice. Wells-Barnett made her first priority an end to lynching. She started her crusade after three of her friends, the owners of Peoples Grocery in Memphis, were lynched. Many suspected the store was competing successfully with a White-owned store. During an attempt to destroy the store, one White male was shot. All three owners of the grocery were arrested and taken to jail, where a mob stormed the building and lynched them. Another Memphis paper, to justify the murders, accused the three of raping a White woman. Wells-Barnett, who was a partner in the *Free Speech and Headlight*, used the newspaper as a forum, and published a series of articles decrying the murder, demanding a law against lynching, and calling for a boycott of the White-owned store. Some unidentified Whites in Memphis proceeded to burn the offices and threaten her with lynching. Wells-Barnett could not return to Memphis, and so began her work against lynching. She published two books on the subject, and worked through the National Association of Colored Women as well as the NAACP, to bring an end to it.

The closing month of the year 1912 witnessed an incident which probably could not happen in any other civilized country. The governor of one of the oldest states of the Union in an address before the Conference of Governors defended the practice of lynching, and declared that he would willingly lead a mob to lynch a Negro who had assaulted a white woman. Twenty years ago, another governor of the same state not only made a similar statement, but while he was in office actually delivered to a mob a Negro who had merely been charged with this offense—it was unproven—and who had taken refuge with the governor for protection.

It is gratifying to know that the governors' meeting formally condemned these expressions, and that a leading Georgia citizen has undertaken to refute the sentiment expressed by Governor Blease. However, while no other official has thus officially encouraged this form of lawlessness, yet, because of the widespread acquiescence in the practice, many governors have refused to deal sternly with the leaders of mobs or to enforce the law against lynchers.

Ida B. Wells-Barnett, "Our Country's Lynching Record," *Survey* 29, (February 1, 1913): 573-74.

To the civilized world, which has demanded an explanation as to why human beings have been put to death in this lawless fashion, the excuse given has been the same as that voiced by Governor Blease a short month ago. Yet statistics show that in none of the thirty years of lynching has more than one-fourth of the persons hung, shot and burned to death, been even charged with this crime. During 1912, sixty-five persons were lynched.

Up to November 15 the distribution among the states was as follows:

Alabama—5, Arkansas—3, Florida—3, Georgia—11, Louisiana—4, Mississippi—5, Montana—1, North Carolina—1, North Dakota—1, Oregon—1, Oklahoma—1, South Carolina—5, Tennessee—5, Texas—3, Virginia—1, West Virginia—1, Wyoming—1.

Fifty of these were Negroes; three were Negro women. They were charged with these offenses:

Murder—26, Rape—10, Murderous Assault—2, Complicity in murder—3, Arson—3, Insults to white women—3, Attempted rape—2, Assault and robbery—1, Race prejudice—1, No cause assigned—1.

Because the Negro has so little chance to be heard in his own defense and because those who have participated in the lynching have written most of the stories about them, the civilized world has accepted almost without question the excuse offered.

From this table it appears that less than a sixth of these persons were lynched because the mob believed them to be guilty of assaulting white women. In some cases the causes have been trivial. And it appears that the northern states have permitted this lawless practice to develop and the lives of hapless victims to be taken with as much brutality, if not as frequently, as those of the South—witness, Springfield, Ill., a few years ago, and Coatesville, Pa., only last year.

The lynching mania, so far as it affects Negroes, began in the South immediately after the Emancipation Proclamation fifty years ago. It manifested itself through what was known as the Ku Klux Klan, armed bodies of masked men, who during the period between 1865 and 1875, killed Negroes who tried to exercise the political rights conferred on them by the United States until by such terrorism the South regained political control. The aftermath of such

practices is displayed in the following table giving the number of Negroes lynched in each year since 1885:

1885—184,	1886—138,	1887—122,
1888—142,	1889—176,	1890—127,
1891—192,	1892—235,	1893—200,
1894—190,	1895—171,	1896—131,
1897—106,	1898—127,	1899—107,
1900—115,	1901—135,	1902—96,
1903—104,	1904—87,	1905—66,
1906—60,	1907—63,	1908—100,
1909—87,	1910—74,	1911—71,
1912—64.		

With the South in control of its political machinery, the new excuse was made that lynchings were necessary to protect the honor of white womanhood. Although black men had taken such good care of the white women of the South during the four years their masters were fighting to keep them in slavery, this calumny was published broadcast. The world believed it was necessary for white men in hundreds to lynch one defenseless Negro who had been accused of assaulting a white woman. In the thirty years in which lynching has been going on in the South, this falsehood has been universally accepted in all sections of our country, and has been offered by thousands as a reason why they do not spew out against these terrible outrages.

It is charged that a ceaseless propaganda has been going on in every northern state for years, with the result that not only is there no systematic denunciation of these horrible barbarisms, but northern cities and states have been known to follow the fashion of burning human beings alive. In no one thing is there more striking illustration of the North's surrender of its position on great moral ideas than in its lethargic attitude toward the lynching evil.

The belief is often expressed that if the North would stand as firmly for principle as the South does for prejudice, lynching and many other evils would be checked. It seems invariably true, however, that when principle and prejudice come into collision, principle retires and leaves prejudice the victor.

In the celebration of the fiftieth year of the Negro's freedom, does it seem too much to ask white civilization, Christianity and Democracy to be true to themselves on this as all other questions? They can not then be false to any man or race of men. Our democracy asserts that the people are fighting for the time when all men shall be brothers and the liberty of each shall be the concern of all. If this is true, the struggle is bound to take in the Negro. We cannot remain silent when the lives of men and women who are black are lawlessly taken, without imperiling the foundations of our government.

Civilization cannot burn human beings alive or justify others who do so; neither can it refuse a trial by jury for black men accused of crime, without making a mockery of the respect for law which is the safeguard of the liberties of white men. The nation cannot profess Christianity, which makes the golden rule its foundation stone, and continue to deity equal opportunity for life, liberty and the pursuit of happiness to the black race.

When our Christian and moral influences not only concede these principles theoretically but work for them practically, lynching will become a thing of the past, and no governor will again make a mockery of all the nation holds dear in the defense of lynching for any cause.

Appreciating the helpful influences of such a dispassionate and logical argument as that made by the writer referred to, I earnestly desire to say nothing to lessen the force of the appeal. At the same time an unfortunate presumption used as a basis for her argument works so serious, tho doubtless unintentional, an injury to the memory of thousands of victims of mob law, that it is only fair to call attention to this phase of the writer's plea. It is unspeakably infamous to put thousand of people to death without a trial by jury; it adds to that infamy to charge that these victims were moral monsters, when, in fact, four-fifths of them were not so accused even by the fiends who murdered them.

Document 17.4 Ida B. Wells Barnett on Lynching

In this article, Ida B. Wells-Barnett comments on Jane Addams' remarks in "Respect for the Law" (Document 17.1). She appreciates Addam's efforts and some of her arguments on the hideous matter of lynching. She also finds an area of disagreement that is vital to understanding Addams' approach to Progressivism, and explains why other White progressives would not join with African Americans in demanding laws against lynching.

IT was eminently befitting that THE INDEPENDENT'S first number in the new century should contain a strong protest against lynching. The deepest dyed infamy of the nineteenth century was that which, in its supreme contempt for law, defied all constitutional guaranties of citizenship, and during the last fifteen years of the century put to death two thousand men, women, and children, by shooting, hanging and burning alive. Well would it have been if every preacher in every pulpit in the land had made so earnest a plea as that which came from Miss Addams's forceful pen.

Appreciating the helpful influences of such a dispassionate and logical argument as that made by the writer referred to, I earnestly desire to say nothing to lessen the force of the appeal. At the same time an unfortunate presumption used as a basis for her argument works so serious, tho doubtless unintentional, injury to the memory of thousands of victims of mob law, that it is only fair to call attention to this phase of the writer's plea. It is unspeakably infamous to put thousands of people to death without a trial by jury; it adds to that infamy to charge that these victims were moral monsters, when, in fact, four-fifths of them were not so accused even by the fiends who murdered them.

Almost a the beginning of her discussion, the distinguished writer says:

> "Let us assume that the Southern citizens who take part in and abet the lynching of Negroes honestly believe that that is the only successful method of dealing with a certain class of crimes."

Ida B. Wells Barnett, "Lynching and the Excuse for It," *The Independent* 53, no. 2737 (May 16, 1901): 1133-1136.

It is this assumption, this absolutely unwarrantable assumption, that vitiates every suggestion which it inspires Miss Addams to make. It is the same baseless assumption which influences ninety-nine out of every one hundred persons who discuss this question. Among many thousand editorial clippings I have received in the past five years, ninety-nine per cent discuss the question upon the presumption that lynchings are the desperate effort of the Southern people to protect their women from black monsters, and while the large majority condemn lynching, the condemnation is tempered with a plea for the lyncher—that human nature gives way under such awful provocation and that the mob, insane for the moment, must be pitied as well as condemned. It is strange that an intelligent, law-abiding and fair minded people should so persistently shut their eyes to the facts in the discussion of what the civilized world now concedes to be America's national crime.

This almost universal tendency to accept as true the slander which the lynchers offer to civilization as an excuse for their crime might be explained if the true facts were difficult to obtain. But not the slightest difficulty intervenes. The associated Press dispatches, the press clipping bureau, frequent book publications and the annual summary of a number of influential journals give the lynching record every year. This record, easily within the reach of every one who wants it, makes inexcusable the statement and cruelly unwarranted the assumption that Negroes are lynched only because of their assaults upon womanhood.

For an example in point: For fifteen years past, on the first day of each year, the Chicago Tribune has given to the public a carefully compiled record of all the lynchings of the previous year. Space will not permit a resume of these fifteen years, but as fairly representing the entire time, I desire to briefly tabulate here the record of the five years last past. The statistics of the ten years preceding do not vary, they simply emphasize the record here presented.

The record gives the name and nationality of the man or woman lynched, the alleged crime, the time and place of the lynching. With this is given a resume of the offenses charged, with the number of persons lynched for the offenses named. That enables the reader to see at a glance the causes assigned for the lynchings, and leaves nothing to be assumed. The lynchers, at the time and place of the lynching, are the best authority for the causes which actuate them. Every presumption is in favor of this record, especially as it remains absolutely unimpeached. This record gives the following statement of the colored persons lynched and the causes of the lynchings for the years named:

1896

Murder.... 24
Attempted Murder.... 4
Rape.... 31
Incendiarism.... 2
No cause.... 2
Alleged rape.... 2
Cattle stealing.... 1
Miscegenation.... 2
Attempted rape.... 4
Murderous assault.... 1
Arson.... 2
Assault.... 3
Unknown cause.... 1
Slapping a child.... 1
Shooting an officer.... 1
Alleged murder.... 2
Threats.... 1
Passing counterfeit money.... 1
Theft.... 1

1897

Murder.... 55
Attempted rape.... 8
Mistaken identity.... 1
Arson.... 3
Murderous assault.... 2
Running quarantine.... 1
Burglary.... 1
Bad reputation.... 1
Unknown offense.... 3
Killing white cap.... 1
Attempted murder.... 1
Insulting white woman.... 1
Suspected arson.... 1
Giving evidence.... 2
Refusing to give evidence.... 1
Writing insulting letter.... 1
Cattle Thief.... 1
Train wrecking.... 1
Rape.... 22
Rape prejudice.... 1
Alleged arson.... 1
Robbery.... 6

Assault.... 2
Disobeying Fed. Regulations.... 1
Theft.... 2
Elopement.... 1
Concealing murder.... 1

1898

Murder.... 42
Rape.... 14
Attempted rape.... 7
Complicity in rape.... 1
Highway robbery.... 1
Burglary.... 1
Mistaken identity.... 1
Arson.... 1
Murderous assault.... 1
Theft.... 6
Miscegenation.... 1
Unknown offense.... 2
Violation of contract.... 1
Insults.... 2
Race prejudice.... 3
Resisting arrest.... 1
Suspected murder.... 13
Assaults upon whites.... 4

1899

Murder.... 23
Robbery.... 6
Inflammatory language.... 1
Desperado.... 1
Complicity in murder.... 3
Rape.... 11
Attempted rape.... 8
Arson.... 8
Unknown offense.... 4
Resisting arrest.... 1
Mistaken identity.... 1
Aiding escape of murderer.... 3

1900

Murder.... 30
Rape.... 16
Attempted assault.... 12
Race prejudice.... 9
Plot to kill whites.... 2
Suspected robbery.... 1

Giving testimony.... 1
Attacking white men.... 3
Attempted murder.... 4
Threats to kill.... 1
Suspected murder.... 2
Unknown offense.... 2
No offense.... 1
Arson.... 2
Suspicion of arson.... 1
Aiding escape of murderer.... 1
Unpopularity.... 1
Making threats.... 1
Informer.... 1
Robbery.... 2
Burglary.... 4
Assault.... 2

With this record in view there should be no difficulty in ascertaining the alleged offenses given as justification for lynchings during the last five years. If the Southern citizens lynch Negroes because "that is the only successful method of dealing with a certain class of crimes," then that class of crimes should be shown unmistakably by this record. Now consider the record.

It would be supposed that the record would show that all, or nearly all, lynchings were cause by outrageous assaults upon women; certainly that this particular offense would outnumber all other causes for putting human beings to death without a trial by jury and the other safeguards of our Constitution and laws.

But the record makes no such disclosure. Instead, it shows that five women have been lynched, put to death with unspeakable savagery, during the past five years. They certainly were not under the ban of the outlawing crime. It shows that men, not a few, but hundreds, have been lynched for misdemeanors, while others have suffered death for no offense known to the law, the causes assigned being "mistaken identity," "insult," "bad reputation," "unpopularity," "violating contract," "running quarantine," "giving evidence," "frightening child by shooting at rabbits," etc. Then, strangest of all, the record shows that the sum total of lynchings for these offenses—not crimes—and for the alleged offenses which are only misdemeanors, greatly exceeds the lynchings for the very crime universally declared to be the cause of lynching.

A careful classification of the offenses which have caused lynchings during the past five years shows that contempt for law and race prejudice constitute the real cause of all lynching. During the past five years 147 white persons were lynched. It may be argued that fear of the "law's delays" was the cause of their being lynched. But this is not true. Not a single white victim of the mob was wealthy or had friends or influence to cause a miscarriage of justice. There was no such possibility—it was contempt for law which incited the mob to put so many white men to death without a complaint under oath, much less a trial.

In the case of the negroes lynched the mobs' incentive was race prejudice. Few white men were lynched of any such trivial offenses as are detailed in the causes for lynching colored men. Negroes are lynched for "violating contracts," "unpopularity," "testifying in court," and "shooting at rabbits." As only negroes are lynched for "no offense," "unknown offenses," offenses not criminal, misdemeanors and crimes not capital, it must be admitted that the real cause of lynching in all such cases is race prejudice, and should be so classified. Grouping these lynchings under that classification and excluding rape, which in some States is made a capital offense, the record for the five years, so far as the negro is concerned, reads as follows:

Year,	Race Prejudice,	Murder	Rape	Total Lynchings
1896	31	24	31	86
1897	46	55	22	123
1898	39	47	16	102
1899	56	23	11	90
1900	57	30	16	103
Total	229	179	96	504

This table tells its own story, and shows how false is the excuse which lynchers offer to justify their fiendishness. Instead of being the sole cause of lynching, the crime upon which lynchers build their defense furnishes the least victims for the mob. In 1896 less than thirty-nine percent of the negroes lynched were charged with this crime; in 1897, less than eighteen percent; in 1898, less than sixteen percent; in 1899, less than fourteen percent; and in 1900, less than fifteen per cent were so charged.

No good result can come from any investigation which refuses to consider the facts. A conclusion that is based on upon a presumption, instead of the best evidence, is unworthy of a moment's consideration. The lynching record, as it is compiled from day to day by unbiased, reliable and responsible public journals, should be the basis of every investigation which seeks to discover the cause and suggest the remedy for lynching. The excuses of lynchers and the specious pleas of their apologists should be considered in the light of the record, which they invariably misrepresent or ignore. The Christians and moral forces of the nation should insist that misrepresentation should have no place in the discussion of this all important question, that the figures of the lynching record should be allowed to plead, trumpet tongued, in defense of the slandered dead, that the silence of concession be broken, and that truth, swift-winged and courageous, summon, this nation to do its duty to exalt justice and preserve inviolate the sacredness of human life.

CHICAGO, ILL.

Document 17.5 Keeping the Women's Clubs Segregated

This article, from the *New York Herald*, reports that the National Federation of Women's Clubs defeated an effort to admit Black women's clubs. As the article notes, this had been a project of Jane Addams and the Massachusetts club women. Note that the Federation did not vote on a proposal to admit Black groups, but rather on a procedural matter that would have made their entry possible. Also, pay attention to the reason given by those who wanted to remain segregated, and ask yourself if you think that was the whole explanation. Women's clubs played a crucial role in reform. Hundreds of thousands of women joined the organizations, focused on a number of reform issues like schools, factory safety, child labor, libraries, public parks, and women's suffrage. The National Association of Colored Women placed a priority on ending lynching.

Los Angeles, Cal., Tuesday

Massachusetts club women to-day saw the plans for which they have been fighting two years go down before the vote of the National Federation.

The final defeat was administered to the proposal for the admission of colored women's clubs, and the effort to down the individual club as a step toward reorganization through State federations only failed as did the plan to reduce the per capita tax from ten to five cents.

There is no element of bitterness in the defeat, and the union of the South and the North, as far as the women's clubs are concerned, promises to stay cemented for some time.

Massachusetts was first obliged to bow to adverse fate when it was discovered that her cherished series of amendments were illegal in that they disfranchised members already in the Federation.

The Convention turned its attention to compromise amendments, considering section 9 article 1. After several efforts to change it was accepted as proposed by the Compromise Committee. Then came consideration of section of article 2, the second feature in the color matter.

Miss Jane Addams, of Chicago, who believes in the admission of colored clubs, wished this section amended so that two instead of one vote of the membership committee of vie would be necessary to keep an unwelcome club out. Miss Addams made a worthy plea, but the amendment went down before a large vote.

Document 17.6 Different Approaches to Reform

In this excerpt from *The Souls of Black Folks,* W.E.B. DuBois evaluates the work of Booker T. Washington in bringing about change in the conditions of Blacks. He clearly agrees with Washington about the importance of education, and admires his life of work. However, he finds areas of disagreement as well, particularly what he calls Washington's Accommodationism, and his limited conception of education. The article also explains what direction DuBois would prefer to take. Like many Progressives, DuBois was college-educated; he was the first African American to receive a doctorate from Harvard. His reform program focused on the immediate recognition and enforcement of equal rights. He also emphasized the importance of higher education. Dubois was a founder of both the Niagara Movement and the NAACP. He edited The *Crisis* for the latter organization, and supported the pursuit of a legal strategy of court challenges to laws and conduct that violated the rights of African Americans.

Chapter III
Of Mr. Booker T. Washington and Others

From birth till death enslaved;
in word, in deed, unmanned!

. . . .

Hereditary bondsmen! Know ye not
Who would be free themselves must strike the blow?
BYRON.

Easily the most striking thing in the history of the American Negro since 1876 is the ascendancy of Mr.

Booker T. Washington. It began at the time when war memories and ideals were rapidly passing; a day of astonishing commercial development was dawning; a sense of doubt and hesitation overtook the freedmen's sons,—then it was that his leading began. Mr. Washington came, with a simple definite programme, at the psychological moment when the nation was a little ashamed of having bestowed so much sentiment on Negroes, and was concentrating its energies on Dollars. His programme of industrial education, conciliation of the South, and submission and silence as to civil and political rights, was not wholly original; the Free Negroes from 1830 up to wartime had

---

"Women Vote to Keep Color Line: National Federation of Clubs Also Defends Reorganization Plan by States," *New York Herald* (May 7, 1902) Jane Addams Papers, Clippings file, reel 55-0672, Special Collections, The University Library, The University of Illinois at Chicago.

striven to build industrial schools, and the American Missionary Association had from the first taught various trades; and Price and others had sought a way of honorable alliance with the best of the Southerners. But Mr. Washington first indissolubly linked these things; he put enthusiasm, unlimited energy, and perfect faith into this programme, and changed it from a by-path into a veritable Way of Life. And the tale of the methods by which he did this is a fascinating study of human life.

It startled the nation to hear a Negro advocating such a programme after many decades of bitter complaint; it startled and won the applause of the South, it interested and won the admiration of the North; and after a confused murmur of protest, it silenced if it did not convert the Negroes themselves.

To gain the sympathy and cooperation of the various elements comprising the white South was Mr. Washington's first task; and this, at the time Tuskegee was founded, seemed, for a black man, well-nigh impossible. And yet ten years later it was done in the word spoken at Atlanta: "In all things purely social we can be as separate as the five fingers, and yet one as the hand in all things essential to mutual progress." This "Atlanta Compromise" is by all odds the most notable thing in Mr. Washington's career. The South interpreted it in different ways: the radicals received it as a complete surrender of the demand for civil and political equality; the conservatives, as a generously conceived working basis for mutual understanding. So both approved it, and to-day its author is certainly the most distinguished Southerner since Jefferson Davis, and the one with the largest personal following.

Next to this achievement comes Mr. Washington's work in gaining place and consideration in the North. Others less shrewd and tactful had formerly essayed to sit on these two stools and had fallen between them; but as Mr. Washington knew the heart of the South from birth and training, so by singular insight he intuitively grasped the spirit of the age which was dominating the North. And so thoroughly did he learn the speech and thought of triumphant commercialism, and the ideals of material prosperity, that the picture of a lone black boy poring over a French grammar amid the weeds and dirt of a neglected home soon seemed to him the acme of absurdities. One wonders what Socrates and St. Francis of Assisi would say to this.

And yet this very singleness of vision and thorough oneness with his age is a mark of the successful man. It is as though Nature must needs make men narrow in order to give them force. So Mr. Washing-

ton's cult has gained unquestioning followers, his work has wonderfully prospered, his friends are legion, and his enemies are confounded. To-day he stands as the one recognized spokesman of his ten million fellows, and one of the most notable figures in a nation of seventy millions. One hesitates, therefore, to criticise a life which, beginning with so little, has done so much. And yet the time is come when one may speak in all sincerity and utter courtesy of the mistakes and shortcomings of Mr. Washington's career, as well as of his triumphs, without being thought captious or envious, and without forgetting that it is easier to do ill than well in the world.

The criticism that has hitherto met Mr. Washington has not always been of this broad character. In the South especially has he had to walk warily to avoid the harshest judgments,—and naturally so, for he is dealing with the one subject of deepest sensitiveness to that section. Twice—once when at the Chicago celebration of the Spanish-American War he alluded to the color-prejudice that is "eating away the vitals of the South," and once when he dined with President Roosevelt—has the resulting Southern criticism been violent enough to threaten seriously his popularity. In the North the feeling has several times forced itself into words, that Mr. Washington's counsels of submission overlooked certain elements of true manhood, and that his educational programme was unnecessarily narrow. Usually, however, such criticism has not found open expression, although, too, the spiritual sons of the Abolitionists have not been prepared to acknowledge that the schools founded before Tuskegee, by men of broad ideals and self-sacrificing spirit, were wholly failures or worthy of ridicule. While, then, criticism has not failed to follow Mr. Washington, yet the prevailing public opinion of the land has been but too willing to deliver the solution of a wearisome problem into his hands, and say, "If that is all you and your race ask, take it."

Among his own people, however, Mr. Washington has encountered the strongest and most lasting opposition, amounting at times to bitterness, and even to-day continuing strong and insistent even though largely silenced in outward expression by the public opinion of the nation. Some of this opposition is, of course, mere envy; the disappointment of displaced demagogues and the spite of narrow minds. But aside from this, there is among educated and thoughtful colored men in all parts of the land a feeling of deep regret, sorrow, and apprehension at the wide currency and ascendancy which some of Mr. Washington's theories have gained. These same men admire his sincerity of purpose, and are willing to forgive much to honest endeavor which is doing something worth the doing. They cooperate with Mr. Washington as far as they conscientiously can; and, indeed, it is no ordinary tribute to this man's tact and power that, steering as he must between so many diverse interests and opinions, he so largely retains the respect of all.

But the hushing of the criticism of honest opponents is a dangerous thing. It leads some of the best of the critics to unfortunate silence and paralysis of effort, and others to burst into speech so passionately and intemperately as to lose listeners. Honest and earnest criticism from those whose interests are most nearly touched,—criticism of writers by readers, of government by those governed, of leaders by those led,—this is the soul of democracy and the safeguard of modern society. If the best of the American Negroes receive by outer pressure a leader whom they had not recognized before, manifestly there is here a certain palpable gain. Yet there is also irreparable loss,—a loss of that peculiarly valuable education which a group receives when by search and criticism it finds and commissions its own leaders. The way in which this is done is at once the most elementary and the nicest problem of social growth. History is but the record of such group-leadership; and yet how infinitely changeful is its type and character! And of all types and kinds, what can be more instructive than the leadership of a group within a group?— that curious double movement where real progress may be negative and actual advance be relative retrogression. All this is the social student's inspiration and despair.

Now in the past the American Negro has had instructive experience in the choosing of group leaders, founding thus a peculiar dynasty which in the light of present conditions is worth while studying. When sticks and stones and beasts form the sole environment of a people, their attitude is largely one of determined opposition to and conquest of natural forces. But when to earth and brute is added an environment of men and ideas, then the attitude of the imprisoned group may take three main forms,—a feeling of revolt and revenge; an attempt to adjust all thought and action to the will of the greater group; or, finally, a determined effort at self-realization and self-development despite environing opinion. The influence of all of these attitudes at various times can be traced in the history of the American Negro, and in the evolution of his successive leaders.

Before 1750, while the fire of African freedom still burned in the veins of the slaves, there was in all leadership or attempted leadership but the one motive of revolt and revenge,—typified in the terrible Maroons, the Danish blacks, and Cato of Stono, and veiling all the Americas in fear of insurrection. The liberalizing tendencies of the latter half of the eighteenth century brought, along with kindlier relations between black and white, thoughts of ultimate adjustment and assimilation. Such aspiration was especially voiced in the earnest songs of Phyllis, in the martyrdom of Attucks, the fighting of Salem and Poor, the intellectual accomplishments of Banneker and Derham, and the political demands of the Cuffes.

Stern financial and social stress after the war cooled much of the previous humanitarian ardor. The disappointment and impatience of the Negroes at the persistence of slavery and serfdom voiced itself in two movements. The slaves in the South, aroused undoubtedly by vague rumors of the Haytian revolt, made three fierce attempts at insurrection,—in 1800 under Gabriel in Virginia, in 1822 under Vesey in Carolina, and in 1831 again in Virginia under the terrible Nat Turner. In the Free States, on the other hand, a new and curious attempt at self-development was made. In Philadelphia and New York color-prescription led to a withdrawal of Negro communicants from white churches and the formation of a peculiar socio-religious institution among the Negroes known as the African Church,—an organization still living and controlling in its various branches over a million of men.

Walker's wild appeal against the trend of the times showed how the world was changing after the coming of the cotton-gin. By 1830 slavery seemed hopelessly fastened on the South, and the slaves thoroughly cowed into submission. The free Negroes of the North, inspired by the mulatto immigrants from the West Indies, began to change the basis of their demands; they recognized the slavery of slaves, but insisted that they themselves were freemen, and sought assimilation and amalgamation with the nation on the same terms with other men. Thus, Forten and Purvis of Philadelphia, Shad of Wilmington, Du Bois of New Haven, Barbadoes of Boston, and others, strove singly and together as men, they said, not as slaves; as "people of color," not as "Negroes." The trend of the times, however, refused them recognition save in individual and exceptional cases, considered them as one with all the despised blacks, and they soon found themselves striving to keep even the rights they formerly had of voting and working and moving as freemen. Schemes of migration and colonization arose among them; but these they refused to entertain, and they eventually turned to the Abolition movement as a final refuge.

Here, led by Remond, Nell, Wells-Brown, and Douglass, a new period of self-assertion and self-development dawned. To be sure, ultimate freedom and assimilation was the ideal before the leaders, but the assertion of the manhood rights of the Negro by himself was the main reliance, and John Brown's raid was the extreme of its logic. After the war and emancipation, the great form of Frederick Douglass, the greatest of American Negro leaders, still led the host. Self-assertion, especially in political lines, was the main programme, and behind Douglass came Elliot, Bruce, and Langston, and the Reconstruction politicians, and, less conspicuous but of greater social significance Alexander Crummell and Bishop Daniel Payne.

Then came the Revolution of 1876, the suppression of the Negro votes, the changing and shifting of ideals, and the seeking of new lights in the great night. Douglass, in his old age, still bravely stood for the ideals of his early manhood,—ultimate assimilation *through* self-assertion, and on no other terms. For a time Price arose as a new leader, destined, it seemed, not to give up, but to re-state the old ideals in a form less repugnant to the white South. But he passed away in his prime. Then came the new leader. Nearly all the former ones had become leaders by the silent suffrage of their fellows, had sought to lead their own people alone, and were usually, save Douglass, little known outside their race. But Booker T. Washington arose as essentially the leader not of one race but of two,—a compromiser between the South, the North, and the Negro. Naturally the Negroes resented, at first bitterly, signs of compromise which surrendered their civil and political rights, even though this was to be exchanged for larger chances of economic development. The rich and dominating North, however, was not only weary of the race problem, but was investing largely in Southern enterprises, and welcomed any method of peaceful cooperation. Thus, by national opinion, the Negroes began to recognize Mr. Washington's leadership; and the voice of criticism was hushed.

Mr. Washington represents in Negro thought the old attitude of adjustment and submission; but adjustment at such a peculiar time as to make his programme unique. This is an age of unusual economic development, and Mr. Washington's programme naturally takes an economic cast, becoming a gospel of Work and Money to such an extent as apparently almost completely to overshadow the higher aims of life. Moreover, this is an age when the more advanced races are coming in closer contact with the less developed races, and the race-feeling is therefore intensi-fied; and Mr. Washington's programme practically accepts the alleged inferiority of the Negro races. Again, in our own land, the reaction from the sentiment of war time has given impetus to race-prejudice against Negroes, and Mr. Washington withdraws many of the high demands of Negroes as men and American citizens. In other periods of intensified prejudice all the Negro's tendency to self-assertion has been called forth; at this period a policy of submission is advocated. In the history of nearly all other races and peoples the doctrine preached at such crises has been that manly self-respect is worth more than lands and houses, and that a people who voluntarily surrender such respect, or cease striving for it, are not worth civilizing.

In answer to this, it has been claimed that the Negro can survive only through submission. Mr. Washington distinctly asks that black people give up, at least for the present, three things,—

First, political power,
Second, insistence on civil rights,
Third, higher education of Negro youth,—

and concentrate all their energies on industrial education, the accumulation of wealth, and the conciliation of the South. This policy has been courageously and insistently advocated for over fifteen years, and has been triumphant for perhaps ten years. As a result of this tender of the palm-branch, what has been the return? In these years there have occurred:

1. The disfranchisement of the Negro.
2. The legal creation of a distinct status of civil inferiority for the Negro.
3. The steady withdrawal of aid from institutions for the higher training of the Negro.

These movements are not, to be sure, direct results of Mr. Washington's teachings; but his propaganda has, without a shadow of doubt, helped their speedier accomplishment. The question then comes: Is it possible, and probable, that nine millions of men can make effective progress in economic lines if they are deprived of political rights, made a servile caste, and allowed only the most meagre chance for developing their exceptional men? If history and reason give any distinct answer to these questions, it is an emphatic *No*. And Mr. Washington thus faces the triple paradox of his career:

1. He is striving nobly to make Negro artisans business men and property-owners; but it is utterly impossible, under modern competitive methods,

for workingmen and property-owners to defend their rights and exist without the right of suffrage.

2. He insists on thrift and self-respect, but at the same time counsels a silent submission to civic inferiority such as is bound to sap the manhood of any race in the long run.

3. He advocates common-school and industrial training, and depreciates institutions of higher learning; but neither the Negro common-schools, nor Tuskegee itself, could remain open a day were it not for teachers trained in Negro colleges, or trained by their graduates.

This triple paradox in Mr. Washington's position is the object of criticism by two classes of colored Americans. One class is spiritually descended from Toussaint the Savior, through Gabriel, Vesey, and Turner, and they represent the attitude of revolt and revenge; they hate the white South blindly and distrust the white race generally, and so far as they agree on definite action, think that the Negro's only hope lies in emigration beyond the borders of the United States. And yet, by the irony of fate, nothing has more effectually made this programme seem hopeless than the recent course of the United States toward weaker and darker peoples in the West Indies, Hawaii, and the Philippines,—for where in the world may we go and be safe from lying and brute force?

The other class of Negroes who cannot agree with Mr. Washington has hitherto said little aloud. They deprecate the sight of scattered counsels, of internal disagreement; and especially they dislike making their just criticism of a useful and earnest man an excuse for a general discharge of venom from small-minded opponents. Nevertheless, the questions involved are so fundamental and serious that it is difficult to see how men like the Grimkes, Kelly Miller, J. W. E. Bowen, and other representatives of this group, can much longer be silent. Such men feel in conscience bound to ask of this nation three things:

1. The right to vote.
2. Civic equality.
3. The education of youth according to ability.

They acknowledge Mr. Washington's invaluable service in counselling patience and courtesy in such demands; they do not ask that ignorant black men vote when ignorant whites are debarred, or that any reasonable restrictions in the suffrage should not be applied; they know that the low social level of the mass of the race is responsible for much discrimination against it, but they also know, and the nation knows, that relentless color-prejudice is more often a cause than a result of the Negro's degradation; they seek the abatement of this relic of barbarism, and not its systematic encouragement and pampering by all agencies of social power from the Associated Press to the Church of Christ. They advocate, with Mr. Washington, a broad system of Negro common schools supplemented by thorough industrial training; but they are surprised that a man of Mr. Washington's insight cannot see that no such educational system ever has rested or can rest on any other basis than that of the well-equipped college and university, and they insist that there is a demand for a few such institutions throughout the South to train the best of the Negro youth as teachers, professional men, and leaders.

This group of men honor Mr. Washington for his attitude of conciliation toward the white South; they accept the "Atlanta Compromise" in its broadest interpretation; they recognize, with him, many signs of promise, many men of high purpose and fair judgment, in this section; they know that no easy task has been laid upon a region already tottering under heavy burdens. But, nevertheless, they insist that the way to truth and right lies in straightforward honesty, not in indiscriminate flattery; in praising those of the South who do well and criticising uncompromisingly those who do ill; in taking advantage of the opportunities at hand and urging their fellows to do the same, but at the same time in remembering that only a firm adherence to their higher ideals and aspirations will ever keep those ideals within the realm of possibility. They do not expect that the free right to vote, to enjoy civic rights, and to be educated, will come in a moment; they do not expect to see the bias and prejudices of years disappear at the blast of a trumpet; but they are absolutely certain that the way for a people to gain their reasonable rights is not by voluntarily throwing them away and insisting that they do not want them; that the way for a people to gain respect is not by continually belittling and ridiculing themselves; that, on the contrary, Negroes must insist continually, in season and out of season, that voting is necessary to modern manhood, that color discrimination is barbarism, and that black boys need education as well as white boys.

In failing thus to state plainly and unequivocally the legitimate demands of their people, even at the cost of opposing an honored leader, the thinking classes of American Negroes would shirk a heavy responsibility,—a responsibility to themselves, a responsibility to the struggling masses, a responsibility to the darker races of men whose future depends so largely on this american experiment, but especially a responsibility to this nation,—this common Fatherland. It is wrong to encourage a man or a people in evil-doing; it is wrong to aid and abet a national crime simply because it is unpopular not to do so. The growing spirit of kindliness and reconciliation between the North and South after the frightful differences of a generation ago ought to be a source of deep congratulation to all, and especially to those whose mistreatment caused the war; but if that reconciliation is to be marked by the industrial slavery and civic death of those same black men, with permanent legislation into a position of inferiority, then those black men, if they are really men, are called upon by every consideration of patriotism and loyalty to oppose such a course by all civilized methods, even though such opposition involves disagreement with Mr. Booker T. Washington. We have no right to sit silently by while the inevitable seeds are sown for a harvest of disaster to our children, black and white.

First, it is the duty of black men to judge the South discriminatingly. The present generation of Southerners are not responsible for the past, and they should not be blindly hated or blamed for it. Furthermore, to no class is the indiscriminate endorsement of the recent course of the South toward Negroes more nauseating than to the best thought of the South. The South is not "solid"; it is a land in the ferment of social change, wherein forces of all kinds are fighting for supremacy; and to praise the ill the South is to-day perpetrating is just as wrong as to condemn the good. Discriminating and broad-minded criticism is what the South needs,—needs it for the sake of her own white sons and daughters, and for the insurance of robust, healthy mental and moral development.

To-day even the attitude of the Southern whites toward the blacks is not, as so many assume, in all cases the same; the ignorant Southerner hates the Negro, the workingmen fear his competition, the money-makers wish to use him as a laborer, some of the educated see a menace in his upward development, while others—usually the sons of the masters—wish to help him to rise. National opinion has enabled this last class to maintain the Negro common schools, and to protect the Negro partially in property, life, and limb. Through the pressure of the money-makers, the Negro is in danger of being reduced to semi-slavery, especially in the country districts; the workingmen, and those of the educated who fear the Negro, have united to disfranchise him, and some have urged his deportation; while the passions of the ignorant are easily aroused to lynch and abuse any black man. To praise this intricate whirl of thought and prejudice is nonsense; to inveigh indis-

criminately against "the South" is unjust; but to use the same breath in praising Governor Aycock, exposing Senator Morgan, arguing with Mr. Thomas Nelson Page, and denouncing Senator Ben Tillman, is not only sane, but the imperative duty of thinking black men.

It would be unjust to Mr. Washington not to acknowledge that in several instances he has opposed movements in the South which were unjust to the Negro; he sent memorials to the Louisiana and Alabama constitutional conventions, he has spoken against lynching, and in other ways has openly or silently set his influence against sinister schemes and unfortunate happenings. Notwithstanding this, it is equally true to assert that on the whole the distinct impression left by Mr. Washington's propaganda is, first, that the South is justified in its present attitude toward the Negro because of the Negro's degradation; secondly, that the prime cause of the Negro's failure to rise more quickly is his wrong education in the past; and, thirdly, that his future rise depends primarily on his own efforts. Each of these propositions is a dangerous half-truth. The supplementary truths must never be lost sight of: first, slavery and race-prejudice are potent if not sufficient causes of the Negro's position; second, industrial and common-school training were necessarily slow in planting because they had to await the black teachers trained by higher institutions,—it being extremely doubtful if any essentially different development was possible, and certainly a Tuskegee was unthinkable before 1880; and, third, while it is a great truth to say that the Negro must strive and strive mightily to help himself, it is equally true that unless his striving be not simply seconded, but rather aroused and encouraged, by the initiative of the richer and wiser environing group, he cannot hope for great success.

In his failure to realize and impress this last point, Mr. Washington is especially to be criticised. His doctrine has tended to make the whites, North and South, shift the burden of the Negro problem to the Negro's shoulders and stand aside as critical and rather pessimistic spectators; when in fact the burden belongs to the nation, and the hands of none of us are clean if we bend not our energies to righting these great wrongs.

The South ought to be led, by candid and honest criticism, to assert her better self and do her full duty to the race she has cruelly wronged and is still wronging. The North—her co-partner in guilt—cannot salve her conscience by plastering it with gold. We cannot settle this problem by diplomacy and suaveness, by "policy" alone. If worse come to worst, can the moral fibre of this country survive the slow throttling and murder of nine millions of men?

The black men of America have a duty to perform, a duty stern and delicate,—a forward movement to oppose a part of the work of their greatest leader. So far as Mr. Washington preaches Thrift, Patience, and Industrial Training for the masses, we must hold up his hands and strive with him, rejoicing in his honors and glorying in the strength of this Joshua called of God and of man to lead the headless host. But so far as Mr. Washington apologizes for injustice, North or South, does not rightly value the privilege and duty of voting, belittles the emasculating effects of caste distinctions, and opposes the higher training and ambition of our brighter minds,—so far as he, the South, or the Nation, does this,—we must unceasingly and firmly oppose them. By every civilized and peaceful method we must strive for the rights which the world accords to men, clinging unwaveringly to those great words which the sons of the Fathers would fain forget: "We hold these truths to be self-evident: That all men are created equal; that they are endowed by their Creator with certain unalienable rights; that among these are life, liberty, and the pursuit of happiness."

Document 17.7 The "New Negro"

In this article, Alain Locke argues that a "New Negro" had emerged. A self-aware and self-confident individual , the New Negro was nurtured by the Black community in Harlem. Locke's focus on culture was certainly different from the typical Progressives; raised and educated during the Progressive Era, he discusses reform themes like the scientific method of study as well. Note also what he believes has happened to the old idea of Blacks, as well as what he sees as the essentially Black culture of the South. This article appeared in a special edition of the *Survey Graphic*, a journal with a long Progressive pedigree dating back to the scientific charities movement of the 1870s. The *Harlem* issue has been referred to as the manifesto of the New Negro Movement. Locke re-edited it and published it as the *New Negro*. Locke himself graduated from Harvard with a degree in philosophy. He became the first Black Rhodes Scholar, studied three years at Oxford in England and returned to teach at Howard University for the rest of his life.

Alain Locke

In the last decade something beyond the watch and guard of statistics has happened in the life of the American Negro and the three norns who have traditionally presided over the Negro problem have a changeling in their laps. The Sociologist, The Philanthropist, the Race-leader are not unaware of the New Negro but they are at a loss to account for him. He simply cannot be swathed in their formulae. For the younger generation is vibrant with a new psychology; the new spirit is awake in the masses, and under the very eyes of the professional observers is transforming what has been a perennial problem into the progressive phases of contemporary Negro life.

Could such a metamorphosis have taken place as suddenly as it has appeared to? The answer is no; not because the New Negro is not here, but because the Old Negro had long become more of a myth than a man. The Old Negro, we must remember, was a creature of moral debate and historical controversy. His has been a stock figure perpetuated as an historical fiction partly in innocent sentimentalism, partly in deliberate reactionism. The Negro himself has contributed his share to this through a sort of protective social mimicry forced upon him by the adverse circumstances of dependence. So for generations in the mind of America, the Negro has been more of a formula than a human being —a something to be argued about, condemned or defended, to be "kept down," or "in his place," or "helped up," to be worried with or worried over, harassed or patronized, a social bogey or a social burden. The thinking Negro even has been induced to share this same general attitude, to focus his attention on controversial issues, to see himself in the distorted perspective of a social problem. His shadow, so to speak, has been more real to him than his personality. Through having had to appeal from the unjust stereotypes of his oppressors and traducers to those of his liberators, friends and

Alain Locke, "Enter the New Negro." The *Survey Graphic*. Harlem Number (March 1925) 631-634 benefactors he has subscribed to the traditional positions from which his case has been viewed. Little true social or self-understanding has or could come from such a situation.

But while the minds of most of us, black and white, have thus burrowed in the trenches of the Civil War and Reconstruction, the actual march of development has simply flanked these positions, necessitating a sudden reorientation of view. We have not been watching in the right direction; set North and South on a sectional axis, we have not noticed the East till the sun has us blinking.

Recall how suddenly the Negro spirituals revealed themselves; suppressed for generations under the stereotypes of Wesleyan hymn harmony, secretive, half-ashamed, until the courage of being natural brought them out—and behold, there was folk-music. Similarly the mind of the Negro seems suddenly to have slipped from under the tyranny of social intimidation and to be shaking off the psychology of imitation and implied inferiority. By shedding the old chrysalis of the Negro problem we are achieving something like a spiritual emancipation. Until recently, lacking self-understanding, we have been almost as much of a problem to ourselves as we still are to others. But the decade that found us with a problem has left us with only a task. The multitude perhaps feels as yet only a strange relief and a new vague urge, but the thinking few know that in the reaction the vital inner grip of prejudice has been broken.

With this renewed self-respect and self-dependence, the life of the Negro community is bound to enter a new dynamic phase, the buoyancy from within compensating for whatever pressure there may be of conditions from without. The migrant masses, shifting from countryside to city, hurdle several generations of experience at a leap, but more important, the same thing happens spiritually in the life-attitudes and self-expression of the Young Negro, in his poetry, his art, his education and his new outlook, with the additional advantage, of course, of the poise and greater certainty of knowing what it is all about. From this comes the promise and warrant of a new leadership. As one of them has discerningly put it:

We have tomorrow
Bright before us
Like a flame.

Yesterday, a night-gone thing
A sun-down name.

And dawn today
Broad arch above the road we came.
We march!

This is what, even more than any "most creditable record of fifty years of freedom," requires that the Negro of today be seen through other than the dusty spectacles of past controversy. The day of "aunties," "uncles" and "mammies" is equally gone. Uncle Tom and Sambo have passed on, and even the "Colonel" and "George" play barnstorm roles from which they escape with relief when the public spotlight is off. The popular melodrama has about played itself out, and it is time to scrap the fictions, garret the bogeys and settle down to a realistic facing of facts.

FIRST we must observe some of the changes which since the traditional lines of opinion were drawn have rendered these quite obsolete. A main change has been, of course, that shifting of the Negro population which has made the Negro problem no longer exclusively or even predominantly Southern. Why should our minds remain sectionalized, when the problem itself no longer is? Then the trend of migration has not only been toward the North and the Central Midwest, but city-ward and to the great centers of industry—the problems of adjustment are new, practical, local and not peculiarly racial. Rather they are an integral part of the large industrial and social problems of our present-day democracy. And finally, with the Negro rapidly in process of class differentiation, if it ever was warrantable to regard and treat the Negro en masse it is becoming with every day less possible, more unjust and more ridiculous.

The Negro too, for his part, has idols of the tribe to smash. If on the one hand the white man has erred in making the Negro appear to be that which would excuse or extenuate his treatment of him, the Negro, in turn, has too often unnecessarily excused himself because of the way he has been treated. The intelligent Negro of today is resolved not to make discrimination an extenuation for his shortcomings in performance, individual or collective; he is trying to hold himself at par, neither inflated by sentimental allowances nor depreciated by current social discounts. For this he must know himself and be known for precisely what he is, and for that reason he **welcomes the new scientific rather than the old sentimental interest**. Sentimental interest in the Negro has ebbed. We used to lament this as the falling off of our friends; now we rejoice and pray to be delivered both from self-pity and condescension. The mind of each racial group has had a bitter weaning, apathy or hatred on one side matching disillusionment or resentment on the other; but they face each other today with the possibility at least of entirely new mutual attitudes.

It does not follow that if the Negro were better known, he would be better liked or better treated. But mutual understanding is basic for any subsequent cooperation and adjustment. The effort toward this will at least have the effect of remedying in large part what has been the most unsatisfactory feature of our present stage of race relationships in America, namely the fact that the more intelligent and representative elements of the two race groups have at so many points got quite out of vital touch with one another.

The fiction is that the life of the races is separate and increasingly so. The fact is that they have touched too closely at the unfavorable and too lightly at the favorable levels.

While inter-racial councils have sprung up in the South, drawing on forward elements of both races, in the Northern cities manual laborers may brush elbows in their everyday work, but the community and business leaders have experienced no such interplay or far too little of it. These segments must achieve contact or the race situation in America becomes desperate. Fortunately this is happening. There is a growing realization that in social effort the cooperative basis must supplant long-distance philanthropy, and that the only safeguard for mass relations in the future must be provided in the carefully maintained contacts of the enlightened minorities of both race groups. In the intellectual realm a renewed and keen curiosity is replacing the recent apathy; the Negro is being carefully studied, not just talked about and discussed. In art and letters, instead of being wholly caricatured, he is being seriously portrayed and painted .

To all of this the New Negro is keenly responsive as an augury of a new democracy in American culture. He is contributing his share to the new social understanding. But the desire to be understood would never in itself have been sufficient to have opened so completely the protectively closed portals of the thinking Negro's mind. There is still too much possibility of being snubbed or patronized for that. It was rather the necessity for fuller, truer, self-expression, the realization of the unwisdom of allowing social discrimination to segregate him mentally, and a counter-attitude to cramp and fetter his own living— and so the "spite-wall" that the intellectuals built over the "color-line" has happily been taken down. Much of this reopening of intellectual Contacts has Entered in New York and has been richly fruitful not merely in the enlarging of personal experience, but in the definite enrichment of American art and letters and in the clarifying of our common vision of the social tasks ahead.

The particular significance in the reestablishment of contact between the more advanced and representative classes is that it promises to offset some of the unfavorable reactions of the past, or at least to re-surface race contacts somewhat for the future. Subtly the conditions that are moulding a New Negro are moulding a new American attitude.

However, this new phase of things is delicate; it will call for less charity but more justice; less help, but infinitely closer understanding. This is indeed a critical stage of race relationships because of the likelihood, if the new temper is not understood, of engendering sharp group antagonism and a second crop of more calculated prejudice. In some quarters, it has already done so. Having weaned the Negro, public opinion cannot continue to paternalize. The Negro today is inevitably moving forward under the control largely of his own objectives. What are these objectives? Those of his outer life are happily already well and finally formulated, for they are none other than the ideals of American institutions and democracy. Those of his inner life are yet in process of formation, for the new psychology at present is more of a consensus of feeling than of opinion, of attitude rather than of program. Still some points seem to have crystallized.

Up to the present one may adequately describe the Negro's "inner objectives" as an attempt to repair a damaged group psychology and reshape a warped social perspective. Their realization has required a new mentality for the American Negro. And as it matures we begin to see its effects; at first, negative, iconoclastic, and then positive and constructive. In this new group psychology we note the lapse of sentimental appeal, then the development of a more positive self-respect and self-reliance; the repudiation of social dependence, and then the gradual recovery from hyper-sensitiveness and "touchy" nerves, the repudiation of the double standard of judgment with its special philanthropic allowances and then the sturdier desire for objective and scientific appraisal; and finally the rise from social disillusionment to race pride, from the sense of social debt to the responsibilities of social contribution, and offsetting the necessary working and commonsense acceptance of restricted conditions, the belief in ultimate esteem and recognition. Therefore the Negro today wishes to be known for what he is, even in his faults and shortcomings, and scorns a craven and precarious survival at the price of seeming to be what he is not. He resents being spoken for as a social ward or minor, even by his own, and to being regarded a chronic patient for the sociological clinic, the sick man of American Democracy. For the same reasons he himself is through with those social nostrums and panaceas, the so-called "solutions" of his "problem," with which he and the country have been so liberally dosed in the past. Religion, freedom, education, money—in turn, he has ardently hoped for and peculiarly trusted these things; he still believes in them, but not in blind trust that they alone will solve his life-problem.

Each generation, however, will have its creed and that of the present is the belief in the efficacy of collective efforts in race cooperation. This deep feeling of race is at present the mainspring of Negro life. It seems to be the outcome of the reaction to proscription and prejudice; an attempt, fairly successful on the whole, to convert a defensive into an offensive position, a handicap into an incentive. It is radical in tone, but not in purpose and only the most stupid forms of opposition, misunderstanding or persecution could make it otherwise. Of course, the thinking Negro has shifted a little toward the left with the world-trend, and there is an increasing group who affiliate with radical and liberal movements. But fundamentally for the present the Negro is radical on race matters, conservative on others, in other words, a "forced radical," a social protestant rather than a genuine radical. Yet under further pressure and injustice iconoclastic thought and motives will inevitably increase. Harlem's quixotic radicalisms call for their ounce of democracy today lest tomorrow they be beyond cure.

The Negro mind reaches out as yet to nothing but American wants, American ideas. But this forced attempt to build his Americanism on race values is a unique social experiment, and its ultimate success is impossible except through the fullest sharing of American culture and institutions. There should be no delusion about this. American nerves in sections unstrung with race hysteria are often fed the opiate that the trend of Negro advance is wholly separatist, and that the effect of its operation will be to encyst the Negro as a benign foreign body in the body politic. This cannot be—even if it were desirable. The racialism of the Negro is no limitation or reservation with respect to American life; it is only a constructive effort to build the obstructions in the stream of his progress into an efficient dam of social energy and power. Democracy itself is obstructed and stagnated to the extent that any of its channels are closed. Indeed they cannot be selectively closed. So the choice is not between one way for the Negro and another way for the rest, but between American institutions frustrated on the one hand and American ideals progressively fulfilled and realized on the other.

There is, of course, a warrantably comfortable feeling in being on the right side of the country's professed ideals. We realize that we cannot be undone without America's undoing. It is within the gamut of this attitude that the thinking Negro faces America, but the variations of mood in connection with it are if anything more significant than the attitude itself. Sometimes we have it taken with the defiant ironic challenge of McKay:

Mine is the future grinding down today
Like a great landslip moving to the sea,
Bearing its freight of debris far away
Where the green hungry waters restlessly
Heave mammoth pyramids and break and roar
Their eerie challenge to the crumbling shore.

Sometimes, perhaps more frequently as yet, in the fervent and almost filial appeal and counsel of Weldon Johnson's:

O Southland, dear Southland!
Then why do you still cling
To an idle age and a musty page,
To a dead and useless thing.

But between defiance and appeal, midway almost between cynicism and hope, the prevailing mind stands in the mood of the same author's To America, an attitude of sober query and stoical challenge:

How would you have us, as we are?
Or sinking neath the load we bear,
Our eyes fixed forward on a star,
Or gazing empty at despair?

Rising or falling? Men or things?
With dragging pace or footsteps fleet?
Strong, willing sinews in your wings,
Or tightening chains about your feet?

More and more, however, an intelligent realization of the great discrepancy between the American social creed and the American social practice forces upon the Negro the taking of the moral advantage that is his. Only the steadying and sobering effect of a truly characteristic gentleness of spirit prevents the rapid rise of a definite cynicism and counter-hate and a defiant superiority feeling. Human as this reaction would be, the majority still deprecate its advent, and would gladly see it forestalled by the speedy amelioration of its causes. We wish our race pride to be a healthier, more positive achievement than a feeling based upon a realization of the shortcomings of others. But all paths toward the attainment of a sound social attitude have been difficult; only a relatively few enlightened minds have been able as the phrase puts it "to rise above" prejudice. The ordinary man has had until recently only a hard choice between the alternatives of supine and humiliating submission and stimulating but hurtful counter-prejudice. Fortunately from some inner, desperate resourcefulness has recently sprung up the simple expedient of fighting prejudice by mental passive resistance, in other words by trying to ignore it. For the few, this manna may perhaps be effective, but the masses cannot thrive on it.

FORTUNATELY there are constructive channels opening out into which the balked social feelings of the American Negro can flow freely.

Without them there would be much more pressure and danger than there is. These compensating interests are racial but in a new and enlarged way. One is the consciousness of acting as the advance-guard of the African peoples in their contact with Twentieth Century civilization; the other, the sense of a mission of rehabilitating the race in world esteem from that loss of prestige for which the fate and conditions of slavery have so largely been responsible. Harlem, as we shall see, is the center of both these movements; she is the home of the Negro's "Zionism." The pulse of the Negro world has begun to beat in Harlem. A Negro newspaper carrying news material in English, French and Spanish, gathered from all quarters of America, the West Indies and Africa has maintained itself in Harlem for over five years. Two important magazines, both edited from New York, maintain their news and circulation consistently on a cosmopolitan scale. Under American auspices and backing, three pan-African congresses have been held abroad for the discussion of common interests, colonial questions and the future cooperative development of Africa. In terms of the race question as a world problem, the Negro mind has leapt, so to speak, upon the parapets of prejudice and extended its cramped horizons. In so doing it has linked up with the growing group consciousness of the dark-peoples and is gradually learning their common interests. As one of our writers has recently put it: "It is imperative that we understand the white world in its relations to the nonwhite world." As with the Jew, persecution is making the Negro international.

As a world phenomenon this wider race consciousness is a different thing from the much asserted rising tide of color. Its inevitable causes are not of our making. The consequences are not necessarily damaging to the best interests of civilization. Whether it actually brings into being new Armadas of conflict or argosies of cultural exchange and enlightenment can only be decided by the attitude of the dominant races in an era of critical change. With the American Negro his new internationalism is primarily an effort to recapture contact with the scattered peoples of African derivation. Garveyism may be a transient, if spectacular, phenomenon, but the possible role of the American Negro in the future development of Africa is one of the most constructive and universally helpful missions that any modern people can lay claim to.

Constructive participation in such causes cannot help giving the Negro valuable group incentives, as well as increased prestige at home and abroad. Our greatest rehabilitation may possibly come through such channels, but for the present, more immediate hope rests in the revaluation by white and black alike of the Negro in terms of his artistic endowments and cultural contributions, past and prospective. It must be increasingly recognized that the Negro has already made very substantial contributions, not only in his folk-art, music especially, which has always found appreciation, but in larger, though humbler and less acknowledged ways. For generations the Negro has been the peasant matrix of that section of America which has most undervalued him, and here he has contributed not only materially in labor and in social patience, but spiritually as well. The South has unconsciously absorbed the gift of his folk-temperament. In less than half a generation it will be easier to recognize this, but the fact remains that a leaven of humor, sentiment, imagination and tropic nonchalance has gone into the making of the South from a humble, unacknowledged source. A second crop of the Negro's gifts promises still more largely. He now becomes a conscious contributor and lays aside the status of d beneficiary and ward for that of a collaborator and participant in American civilization. The great social gain in this is the releasing of our talented group from the arid fields of controversy and debate to the productive fields of creative expression. The especially cultural recognition they win should in turn prove the key to that revaluation of the Negro which must precede or accompany any considerable further betterment of race relationships. But whatever the general effect, the present generation will have added the motives of self-expression and spiritual development to the old and still unfinished task of making material headway and progress. No one who understandingly faces the situation with its substantial accomplishment or views the new scene with its still more abundant promise can be entirely without hope. And certainly, if in our lifetime the Negro should not be able to celebrate his full initiation into American democracy, he can at least, on the warrant of these things, celebrate the attainment of a significant and satisfying new phase of group development, and with it a spiritual Coming of Age.

Chapter 17 Worksheet and Questions

1. Progressive Methods and Values: Based upon Document 17.1 (Jane Addams, "Respect for Law"), Document 17.2 ("Jane Addams Talks: Addresses Club Women on Democracy and Social Ethics"), Document 17.3 (Ida B. Wells-Barnett, "Our Country's Lynching Record"), and Document 17.4 (Ida B. Wells-Barnett, "Lynching and the Excuse for It"), how do Addams and Wells-Barnett use Progressive approaches to analyze the problem of lynching? That is, how do they employ Progressive methods, values, and democratic beliefs to explain the need for reforms to end lynching?

_____

_____

_____

_____

_____

_____

_____

_____

2. Comparing Progressive Views about Lynching: Based upon Documents 17.1-17.4, and Document 17.5 ("Women Vote to Keep the Color Line"). Addams and Wells-Barnett both agreed and disagreed in their analysis of lynching. How do they agree and how do they differ? While it is not explicitly stated, how could women's clubs, like the National Federation of Women's Clubs, use Addams discussion of lynching as a rationale for excluding Black women's clubs?

_____

_____

_____

_____

_____

_____

_____

_____

3. Different Approaches to Reform: Based upon Document 17.6 (W.E.B. DuBois, "Of Mr. Booker T. Washington and Others") and Document 17.7 (Alain Locke, "Enter the New Negro"). Compare and contrast Booker T. Washington's and W.E.B. DuBois' approaches to reforming the conditions faced by Blacks. In what ways did Alain Locke agree with Washington and DuBois? How did he believe the "New Negro" changed everything?

_____

_____

_____

_____

_____

_____

_____

_____

_____

_____

4. Based upon Documents 17.6 and 17.7: Washington started his work very early in the Progressive period, while Locke conducted his very late. Were they Progressives? Why or why not?

_____

_____

_____

_____

_____

_____

_____

_____

_____

5. Based upon all of the readings: In the introduction to this chapter, the author argued that Progressives like Theodore Roosevelt viewed American history as a history of progress, in which a religious people originally settled the country, proceeded to establish a democratic government, and mastered science and technology. Is this a fair summary of U.S. history, especially in light of the experiences of Blacks in America?

_____

_____

_____

_____

_____

_____

_____

_____

_____

_____

_____

_____

_____

_____

_____

_____

_____

_____

_____

_____

Scopes Trial

America's way of life hangs in the balance. The stakes seemed that high in the Scopes "Monkey Trial." For his closing argument, prosecutor William Jennings Bryan wrote, "The case has assumed the proportions of a battle-royal between unbelief that attempts to speak through so-called science and the defenders of the Christian faith, speaking through the legislators of Tennessee. It is again a choice between God and Baal." On the second day of the trial, defense attorney Clarence Darrow contended that "it is the setting of man against man and creed against creed until with flying banners and beating drums we are marching backward to the glorious ages of the sixteenth century when bigots lighted fagots to burn the men who dared to bring any intelligence and enlightenment and culture to the human mind."

In July 1925, Dayton teacher John T. Scopes stood accused of violating Tennessee's Butler Act, which prohibited teaching evolution in public schools. The events that put him there are complex. Charles Darwin had written *On the Origin of Species* more than half a century before the trial. Christian Fundamentalists had organized more than 20 years earlier as a response to biblical scholarship introduced by liberal Protestants. During that time, they became familiar with evolutionary thought, but did not express much concern about it. In fact, conservative Christians developed three different approaches to the relationship between Genesis and evolution.

However, after World War I, Fundamentalists began to perceive the theory in a very different way. Darwinian thought now seemed to threaten Christianity, morality, and the future of the nation. This change in sensibilities led them to support legislation banning the teaching of evolution. Led by William Jennings Bryan, they first succeeded in Tennessee. Still, the trial would not have taken place, were it not for the decision of a group of town boosters to put Dayton, Tennessee on the map with a test case. It did. In the weeks leading to the trial, the entire nation engaged in a debate about religion and science. The trial itself proved to be less dramatic, and did not tip the balance of America's way of life in either direction. The story begins with evolutionary science.

During the 1920s biologists established what became known as the classical synthesis, or Classical Evolutionary Theory. They placed Darwinian thought into an interdisciplinary context, organizing the sciences of biology, zoology, botany, comparative anatomy, paleontology, Mendelian genetics, and embryology according to evolutionary principles. Furthermore, the evidence developed by each of those sciences was harmonized in support of the theory. Classical Evolution went far beyond Darwin's conception and actually dispensed with many of his ideas and hypotheses. It did, however, retain his central conception: **natural selection.**

Darwin introduced the idea in *On the Origins of Species* (1858). He pointed first to the fact that far more offspring of any plant or animal are produced than survive to old age. From his perspective, the limiting factor was the environment; that is, the resources in any given environment could not feed or support all of the offspring produced; consequently, plants and animals competed with one another and with members of their own species to survive. The question then became why some survived and others did not. This led to his consideration of **variation.**

Within any species, individuals exhibited a number of variations. For example, humans vary in terms of height, weight, hair color, arm length, leg strength, and any number of other attributes. Plants and animals exhibited the same range of variation. In the competition for survival, some of those variations prove to be useful. That is, they "fit" better with their environment and resulted in the "survival of the fittest"—not necessarily the biggest or strongest, but plants and animals whose variations were better suited to the conditions in which they lived. In this manner, nature selected creatures that would survive, because they were better adapted to their environment. Natural Selection worked to the detriment of those creatures lacking the useful variation. They did not compete as well, and so died in greater numbers. Plants and animals possessing the advantageous trait not only survived in greater numbers, but they also reproduced in greater numbers, giving their offspring the useful trait. For example, at the time of the industrial revolution in England two varieties of a moths, silver and dark gray, inhabited forests near Birmingham. The smoke and soot from industrial processes began to coat trees, leaving them dark and sooty in appearance. Dark silver moths remained well camouflaged, while the white moths became increasingly more exposed. Predators preyed on the lighter-colored moths, leaving the dark silver moths to reproduce. Over time, the lighter moths became rare in a predominantly dark silver population. Over even longer periods of time, small variations that "fit" plants and animals to their environment resulted in even cumulatively larger changes, ultimately resulting in different species altogether. Darwin admitted that the process required enormous amounts of time. Given that, he had explained the evolutionary origin of "species"—why there are different *kinds* of the same creature.

Examining the fossil record, Darwin described the large number of, and wide differences between, species that once existed but were now extinct, and those living in the present. These fossilized plants and animals were ancestors to existing species. He noted also how fossilized species changed over time. The oldest species, those in the oldest strata of rock, were not as complex as their more recent counterparts. Darwin concluded that, at some point, all life probably evolved from simple, single-celled creatures. Still, the fossil record was clear enough to show that existing forms of life evolved from ancestral forms.

In *The Descent of Man* (1871), Darwin added humans to this evolutionary framework. Given their similarities, zoologists classified humans and primates into a common group. From the evolutionary perspective, this classification suggested that the two shared a common (now extinct) ancestor. (This point has often been misunderstood to mean that humans evolved *from* apes or monkeys, hence such terms as the "Monkey Trial" or the "missing link" between and humans. Darwin did not suggest this kind of a relationship; rather, he thought that apes, monkeys, and humans had a common ancestor.) By the 1920s, scientists had collected fossil evidence establishing that link.

Some conservative Christians responded to Darwinian evolution in a variety of ways, but the issue did not seem particularly pressing. In fact, Fundamentalists first began to organize in response to "higher criticism," a new approach to understanding the Bible proposed by some Protestant theologians. During the late 1800s, biblical scholars and ministers applied the new methods of science and history to study the Bible. Examining the text as a historical document, they investigated the origins and authorship of the Old and New Testaments, as well as the historical accuracy of the events found in them. The Liberal Protestants, as they became known, concluded that the description of events given in the Bible reflected the knowledge that people possessed at the time it was recorded. Consequently, modern readers did not have to accept those accounts as literally true or binding upon them. For example, the Book of Joshua reports that the sun and the moon stood still in the sky. Clearly, the author believed the sun orbited the earth. However, people living in the nineteenth century knew that to be false and, according to the Liberals, did not have to believe that the earth was at the center of the solar system as required by a literal understanding of the text. Similarly, while slavery was practiced in the Bible, modern Americans could abolish the practice because they understood it better than their ancient ancestors. The Liberals concluded that the biblical foundations of morality and religious belief had to be derived from the expressions of God's truth found in the ethical and moral meanings of the stories contained in the Bible. By the late 1800s, the Liberal perspective, or Higher Criticism, flourished in Protestant colleges, seminaries, and churches of the northeastern and midwestern states.

Conservatives Christians rejected the Liberal interpretation. Instead, they advocated an approach based upon the literal truth of the Bible. In their view, the Bible represented the revealed Word of God, so every word in the text had to be true. By the turn of the century, conservative Baptists, Presbyterians, Methodists, and Pentecostals began to organize and articulate a response to the Higher Criticism. In 1909, A.C. Dixon established a committee to compile and edit a 12-volume set of essays, *The Fundamentals,* that would outline and explain the basic beliefs of Christianity. Containing a sustained critique of Higher Criticism, the contributions Dixon's group selected for *The Fundamentals* presented the conservatives' core or essential beliefs. These beliefs included the literal truth of the Bible, or **biblical inerrancy**; the authenticity of miracles; and several principles explaining the nature and role of Jesus.

In the same year, Congregationalist minister C.I. Scofield issued the *Scofield Reference Bible*. Like the *Fundamentals*, the work was intended to correct liberal Christianity by explaining the text's meaning through annotated guides accompanying the text. Both sets of works were enormously popular. As Conservative Christians (as they were called) joined the movement, Fundamentalists became dominant in Southern and Western religious institutions. To unite Fundamentalists in one overarching organization, William B. Riley established the World Christian Fundamentals Association in 1919. Riley hoped that bringing together millions of Christians would lead to a second Reformation or new Protestantism, one expressing the new Fundamentalism.

Engaged in proselytizing and contesting biblical interpretation, Fundamentalists were at first ambivalent about Darwinian evolution. During the early 1900s the subject did not attract much attention. Several church-supported colleges, Wake Forest and Baylor among them, hired evolutionary biologists. Other Conservative Christians allowed that, if Darwin's notion could be proven, they would accept the theory. To be sure, many attacked Darwinism as being in conflict with the Genesis account of creation; however, other schools of thought developed as well. Historian Ronald Numbers, in *The Creationists*, has identified three Fundamentalist approaches to the biblical accounts of creation and their relation to evolution: Flood geology (or Creation science), Day Age theology, and Gap theory.

The concept of **Flood geology**, or **Creation science**, was diametrically opposed to Darwin's theory. Where the Bible enumerated God's creation of the universe, earth, life, and humans over the course of six days, evolutionary science posited the slow development of all forms of life from a common one-celled ancestor over a great length of time. To Flood geologists, the differences could hardly be clearer. First of all, in Genesis, God created each type of life whole and entire. This view had the added advantage of explaining the origin of species. Second, humans represented a special creation made in God's image, imbued with spirit, and having a singular relationship with the Creator; evolution portrayed humans evolving from human-like ancestors. Finally, evolutionary development of life required enormous lengths of time not found in biblical genealogy. Most in the Creation camp took the six days of creation to mean 24-hour days. (Some allowed for an indeterminate period of time before the creation of Eden when God—and again here there were different positions—fashioned the inanimate parts of the universe.) Further, they cited the work of Anglican archbishop James Usher who, in the 1650s, calculated, based upon the generations of the Bible, that God created the earth on October 22, 4004 BCE. Confronted with the contradictions between science and religion, Creation scientists opted for the authority of the revealed Word and concluded that Darwin's theory had to be in error. Amateur geologist George McCready Price, in *Evolutionary Geology and the New Catastrophism* (1911), was one of the principal advocates of this Flood geology or Creation science.

Two other Fundamentalist schools of thought, similarly committed to literal interpretation, reconciled science and religion differently. **Day Age theology** held that each of the six days of creation lasted for an indeterminate length of time, or an age. Since time no longer constrained the creation process, Day Age thinkers believed that the biblical description of God's creation each day could correspond to evolutionary development of life conducted over long periods of time. In the Day Age account, historical time or human history began with God's creation of Adam and Eve. William Jennings Bryan subscribed to this view. While averse to admitting it in public for fear of encouraging evolutionists, he had no problem with an evolutionary account of plants and animals. However, Bryan drew the line at humans, believing that God invested humans with souls and, therefore, the potential for salvation. Another interpretation, the **Gap theory**, agreed about the necessity of God's creation of man and woman, but they differed in interpreting the first verse of Genesis to admit the occurrence of a long period of time, or Gap, during which God formed the universe, earth, and the fossil record. From this perspective, the Genesis account of the six days of creation described what took place in the Garden of Eden. The most notable advocate of the Gap account was the widely read *Scofield Reference Bible*, where an explanation was appended to the first verse of Genesis. Like the Day Age school, Gap thought could be perfectly consistent with an evolutionary account, up to the point of humans.

Fundamentalists took issue with Liberal Protestant views about evolution as well. Since Liberals drew upon science to understand the Bible, and did not try to interpret the text literally, many did not see a conflict between evolutionary theory and Genesis. Others combined science and religion in the form of **theism**. Asa Gray, Darwin's principal advocate in the United States, argued that evolution was the way God carried out creation and operated in nature. Needless to say, Conservatives disagreed with both approaches. Yet, as with the Darwinian account itself, disputes remained relatively mild until the 1920s, when Fundamentalists began to find in evolution a threat to human morality, dignity, and religious belief.

Numerous cultural conflicts took place during the "Roaring Twenties" regarding moral standards. Americans expressed concern about Prohibition, immigration, movies, jazz music, flappers, dancing, and dating, to mention a few controversies. Fundamentalists expressed the same concerns as other conservatives, and focused on the relationship between science and religion. They found their review of evolutionary science and its effects chilling. If evolution had previously seemed benign, it now seemed poised to destroy morality and religion itself. Fundamentalists found evidence of moral decline everywhere they looked. The fact that they perceived a need to look into the issue at all illustrates a profound change in sensibilities among Conservative Christians. When they reflected upon the recently ended war, they discovered the insidious agency of science. Not only had advances in knowledge made possible the hideous weapons of the war like poison gas, machine guns, submarines, and airplanes, but (in their view) the widespread acceptance of evolutionary thought by Germans generated the militaristic spirit that caused the war. In the realm of religion, Fundamentalists, like WCFA leader William B. Riley, shifted criticism of Liberal Protestant Higher Criticism to a focus on what Riley now saw as its evolutionary foundations. Other Christian Conservatives turned their attention to education. Far from being institutions of higher learning, they discovered, colleges and universities were, in reality, factories using the machinery of evolutionary theory to churn out atheists from the raw material of naïve, Christian youth. Evolution infected high schools as well. T.T. Martin's *Hell and the High School* (1925) contended that teaching evolution "stripped them (the students) of their religious beliefs, leaving their souls prey to the devil." For the Fundamentalists, the contradictions between Darwin's theory and Genesis were no longer merely a matter of intellectual interest. Evolutionary thought challenged the foundations of Christian belief. By teaching the doctrine, high schools and universities encouraged students to give up their faith as part of the process of becoming educated. The implications could only be imagined, but the impending destruction of religion and, by extension, all morality threatened the very existence of democracy, society, and the nation itself. Something had to be done.

Fundamentalists took up the challenge. Among Conservative religious leaders enlisting in the crusade, William Jennings Bryan assumed a central role. In 1920, Bryan was already a well known national figure. His formidable skills as a public speaker, widely recognized, came into national prominence in 1896 when he delivered the "Cross of Gold" speech at the Democratic National Convention. The party nominated the Populist (and later Progressive) as their presidential candidate. Bryan lost the election to William McKinley and lost two subsequent campaigns, in 1900 and 1908. Democrat President Woodrow Wilson appointed him Secretary of State in 1915. Bryan, however, resigned in protest of Wilson's decision to enter World War I. A lifelong Conservative Christian, Bryan, like other Fundamentalists, became convinced of the evils of evolution early in the 1920s. Taking action against the threat in 1921, he crafted a diatribe, "The Menace of Darwinism," and toured the country speaking against evolution.

A year later the Kentucky Baptist State Board of Missions provided a focus for the diffuse anti-evolution movement. It passed a resolution for a law to prohibit the teaching of evolution in public schools. In *Summer of the Gods*, Edward J. Larson describes how Bryan, the WCFA, and other Fundamentalist leaders supported the Baptists. Bryan went to Kentucky and addressed a joint session of the legislature. While the measure lost on a close vote in the state legislature, Fundamentalists adopted the idea and introduced similar teaching bans in states across the country. In 1923, the movement scored two limited victories. Oklahoma passed an amendment to its education law, prohibiting the purchase of texts that challenged biblical history. Florida adopted a nonbinding resolution against teaching evolution as a true account of natural history. Bryan and his followers proceeded to select Tennessee and North Carolina as the two best prospects for passing a ban on the teaching of evolution.

Bryan and Riley of the WCFA, as well as others, visited Tennessee, where they began to speak and organize. In 1924, Bryan gave a major address attacking evolution, in the capitol at Nashville. The state seemed promising because a year earlier, bills to forbid evolution in public schools had been introduced but died in committee. One of them had been offered by farmer, Baptist lay minister, and Democratic State Representative John Butler. A year earlier, after hearing a minister describe the plight of a woman whose faith had been shattered by exposure to evolutionary thought at a university, he had decided to act. Campaigning on the issue, he was re-elected and in 1925 introduced another bill, "AN ACT prohibiting the teaching of the Evolution Theory in all the Universities, Normals and all other public schools of Tennessee." Specifically, the act would make it illegal "to teach any theory that denies the story of the Divine Creation of man as taught in the Bible, and to teach instead that man has descended from a lower order of animals." Conviction for the misdemeanor would result in "a fine of not less than one hundred and not more than five hundred dollars." Butler's bill passed the Tennessee House with little opposition and, after three hours of debate, the Senate approved the measure. Governor Austin Peay thought the legislature should have defeated the bill. Before signing it into law, he reviewed the texts approved by the state for use in public schools. He failed to find anything covered by the law, and so thought he had protected the teachers of Tennessee from prosecution. Further, he doubted the act would ever be enforced. So Peay signed the bill, proclaiming it as an affirmation of Christian principles. Bryan took a similar view. He saw the measure as exactly the kind of symbolic victory the movement against evolution needed. In fact, he had urged members of the legislature against including a penalty, to discourage the possibility of prosecutions.

Peay and Bryan might well have been right, were it not for a group of town boosters in the small town of Dayton, Tennessee who saw a small advertisement in a Memphis paper. Passage of the Butler Act had concerned the American Civil Liberties Union (ACLU). The group's leaders believed the law violated the First Amendment clause guaranteeing religious freedom, and wanted to try its constitutionality in court. To do that, the ACLU needed a teacher to volunteer for a test case. So ACLU paid for ads seeking such an educator and offering to cover all costs of litigation and legal representation. In Dayton, George Rappleyea, a coal mine manager, brought the ad to the attention of School Board Chair and drug store owner, Fred Robinson and Walter White, school superintendent. The three agreed that the test case might very well receive national attention, put Dayton on the map, and bring thousands of people to the city. It would certainly stimulate the local economy, and perhaps attract new residents to a town that had lost nearly half of its population over the last 25 years. They doubted that the school's principal and regular biology teacher would agree to the scheme, so they approached John Scopes, a physical science teacher and coach. Scopes admitted that he had once served as a substitute teacher for the biology class. As he recalled, it had been a review session, and evolution had been one of the subjects covered. Scopes proceeded to show them the text used in the course. George W. Hunter's *Civic Biology* (1919) contained an entire section about human evolution. After some further discussion, Scopes agreed to participate, and was subsequently arrested and arraigned for violating the Butler Act.

The defense and prosecution organized quickly. The ACLU agreed to the arrangement with Rappleyea and formed a legal team to represent Scopes. They also promised to handle publicity for the event. One of the releases caught the attention of the nationally known Chicago defense attorney Clarence Darrow, who offered to join the defense at no expense. Darrow specialized in criminal law, although he took several cases to establish precedents for labor and the poor. The ACLU thought he would be difficult, and preferred that Darrow remain in Chicago. Only after Scopes asked that he be part of the defense did the ACLU agree to bring the 70-year-old Darrow to Dayton. The prosecution, too, found a nationally know counsel. Initially they assembled a team consisting of two local lawyers and two past attorneys general; however, when the WCFA's William Riley heard about the case, he contacted William Jennings Bryan. The Fundamentalist leader who had worked so hard to pass the Butler Act now volunteered to work with the prosecution on a case he would have preferred never took place. Although Bryan had not practiced law in 30 years, the prosecution readily accepted his offer.

Darrow's and Bryan's participation virtually guaranteed a national audience for *Tennessee v. Scopes*. In the months before the trial, both sides, as well as the entrepreneurial Dayton boosters, publicized their arguments in newspapers across the country, to sway the court of public opinion. The ACLU brought

Scopes to New York for a series of photo opportunities, and scheduled the lawyers to address church and civic groups. Working closely with the WCFA, Bryan coordinated public relations for the prosecution. He also spoke frequently, and wrote a series of articles about the case. Newspapers and radios carried the speeches and published the essays. Reporters converged on Dayton and sent out a daily stream of stories about the trial. The courthouse was wired, and the trial would be the first one carried on national radio stations. In this fashion, The Trial of the Century, or the Final Debate between Science and Religion, was actually conducted before the parties ever met in Dayton. The "Duel to the Death" engaged the nation's media and produced tremendous sales of books on both sides of the issue.

In the weeks preceding the trial, the defense team agreed to emphasize three lines of argument in the public forum. First, they wanted to show that the Butler Act was unconstitutional; by passing the law, the state had endorsed the beliefs of one Christian sect. Furthermore, the law committed the Tennessee courts to enforcing those religious convictions with the full authority of the law and the police power of the state. Consequently, the provisions of the law violated the First Amendment—initially by "establishing" a religion (in this case the state gave preference to one religion over all others), and then by denying the "free exercise" of religion by the members of those not affiliated to the preferred church.

Second, speakers like Darrow argued that the act threatened the progress of human knowledge. The growth of science rested upon the free inquiry of scientists to examine any aspect of nature they chose, and to do so in the way they saw fit. Darwin's discovery of natural selection itself was a product of free thought. The subsequent growth of evolutionary knowledge and the evidence for it followed from the unrestricted explorations of scientist. The Butler Act destroyed science and knowledge by forcing scientists to observe, in the defense's portrayal, a narrow-minded, religiously sectarian standard of knowledge based upon the Bible. Once science submitted, Fundamentalists would force history, literature, and ultimately all human knowledge to conform to their particular interpretation of the Bible. America would then begin a march back to the "Dark Ages."

The last point the defense stressed was that evolution and the Book of Genesis did not conflict. To that end, they promoted the Liberal Protestant approach to the Bible.

While Darrow and the ACLU made their cases to the public, Bryan and the WCFA pressed the prosecution's arguments. Like the defense, Byran's strategy to win over public opinion emphasized three points. Patterned after his "Menace of Darwin" speech, Bryan first attacked the plausibility of the evolutionary "hypothesis" and compared it to the truth of the revealed Word of God found in the Bible. He ridiculed the credulity of scientists who could believe without evidence that one species became something else, or that apes could become humans. Only the Bible provided both evidence for and assurance of the true origin of humans in God's creation. Second, Bryan and the advocates of Fundamentalism also stressed the profoundly destructive consequences of accepting Darwinian ideas. The evolutionary account reduced humans to brutes. Since it contradicted Genesis, it discredited the Bible, led to disbelief and atheism, destroyed any foundation for morality, and consequently made permissible any human act—murder would be acceptable. No society could long survive without an established moral code. It would collapse into anarchy and violence. Bryan's third line of argument rested on the principle of democracy. The people established public schools through laws, and paid for them with taxes. In a democracy the people had a right to decide what the schools would teach. Instead, a small group of academics had corrupted the democratic system, introducing evolution into public schools against the will of the majority of citizens.

After the pyrotechnics of the national debate, the trial itself proved anticlimactic. If the press attended en masse, the crowds of three to five thousand did not meet expectations of tens of thousands. The boost to the local economy was disappointing, a fact many attributed to the "tight," miserly behavior of the press. The anticipated clash of great issues also failed to materialize during the trial.

The reason lay in the strategies adopted by the defense and prosecution. From the outset, the four principal defense attorneys agreed that they would lose the case. Their primary goal was to challenge the constitutionality of the Butler Act. Successful in that, all similar laws would be declared illegal as well. They doubted that the presiding Judge, John T. Raulston, would accept their constitutional arguments against prosecuting Scopes. Consequently, the defense could only win through an appeal to a higher court, where the constitutionality of the law would be the focus of deliberation. The defense would still present a strong case on Scopes' behalf. They planned to prove in court that evolution was true, and that it did not contradict the Bible. Consequently, teaching evolution did not violate the Butler Act. This strategy required the support of expert testimony; the defense planned to call eight authorities in biology, zoology, anthropology, religion, and philosophy.

For his part, Bryan originally planned to contest every argument offered by the defense. He, too, planned to bring experts to the stand. However, as the trial neared, he discovered that there were few Fundamentalists who possessed the credentials or authority to dispute evolution in court. Few of them were willing to assist him. In the end, only two agreed to testify. In light of the shortage of experts, the prosecutors decided to change their strategy. Rather than address the larger issues of religion and science, they would focus the case exclusively on the guilt of John Scopes, that is, prove that he taught evolution in a public school, a fact conceded by the defense. For the prosecutors, that alone put Scopes in violation of the law. They would also have to prevent the defense from introducing expert testimony; the prosecutors simply could not match the defense experts. Potentially, although very unlikely, the expert authorities could even convince the jury that evolution did not conflict with Genesis, and consequently that teaching the theory did not violate the law. Consequently, and paradoxically, the issues concerning the truth of evolution, the consequences of teaching it, and its relationship to the Bible would not come up in the trial, if the prosecution could prevent it.

The parties met before Judge Raulston in Dayton's large County Courthouse on Friday, July 10, 1925. They addressed a few procedural matters and selected a jury. The following Wednesday the Prosecution presented its case. They called the first witness, school superintendent Walther White, one of the three original conspirators. White testified that Scopes told him he had taught evolution in a biology class at the public school, and had shown him the chapter of the text on evolution. Two students proceeded to swear that Scopes had taught them evolution in class. School board chair, Frank Robinson, another of the three original plotters, then gave his opinion that anyone teaching from Hunter's *Civic Biology* had violated the law. Testimony completed, the prosecution rested.

Despite the best efforts of the defense, the trail followed the course plotted by the prosecutors.

On Monday, July 13, Raulston heard Darrow make defense motions to dismiss the case on constitutional grounds. He denied them the following morning. The parties then wrangled over the propriety of starting each session with a prayer. The judge continued the prayers but alternated between Conservative and Liberal ministers. According to those present, the Thursday session was memorable. Prosecutors had objected to hearing the testimony of expert witnesses for the defense. Both sides presented arguments. For the first time in the trial, Bryan spoke, and gave a much admired oration. Dudley F. Malone presented the defense position, in a speech that drew a standing ovation from everyone present. Before deciding the matter, Raulston had the jury removed, and listened to the defense question zoologist Maynard Metcalf for two hours. On Friday, he ruled against admitting expert testimony but, after more argument, allowed the experts to append written statements to the official trial transcript. The court adjourned for the weekend and most of the press left, thinking the trial done and seeking to escape the heat of Dayton. On Monday, few remained to watch Clarence Darrow cross-examine William Jennings Bryan. The defense lawyer tried to discredit Bryan's literalist interpretation of the Bible, while the prosecutor attempted to ridicule the effort and present the consequences of evolutionary thought. Subsequently the defense rested its case and opted against making a closing argument. The move prevented Bryan from giving his own closing speech, which he had been working on for months.

While the jury found John Scopes guilty of violating the Butler Act, the verdict failed to resolve much. The ACLU appealed the case, asking the appellate court to declare the law unconstitutional. Instead, the judges dismissed *Tennessee v. Scopes* on a technicality. In accord with the statute, Raulston fined Scopes $100, the lowest amount allowed. However, the Appeals Court held that, according to the Tennessee Constitution, all fines over $50 had to be set by a jury, not the judge. Rather than re-try the case, the Court decided to end all further legal action. This left the Butler Act in place. Similar prohibitions against teaching evolution, enacted in Louisiana, Texas, Arkansas, and Mississippi, remained standing as well. However, no other states passed teaching bans. By 1930, the Fundamentalist anti-evolution movement ground to an end. The country would not revisit the question for another four decades.

Considering the Evidence in the Readings

The documents in this chapter are taken from the main, or at least nationally known, actors in the trial of John Scopes. Two of them are William Jennings Bryan, who supported the law banning the teaching of evolution in Tennessee and served on the prosecution team, and Clarence Darrow, an attorney on Scope's defense team. The last document contains the famous cross-examination of Bryan by Darrow. A representative of the way the press reported the case, H.L. Mencken covered the trial for the *Baltimore Sun*. In all of these documents look for the arguments the authors and speakers are making for and against the teaching of evolution in public schools. What effects do they believe teaching evolution has on the students and the society? Is this a case of preserving religion or knowledge, or is it a case of who decides what should be taught in the schools? Also pay attention to how the two sides characterize each other. Does it look like there is much room for compromise?

Document 18.1 Bryan's "The Menace of Darwinism"

William Jennings Bryan wrote "The Menace of Darwinism" in 1921. In the article, he makes his case against evolution as a science and in relation to the Bible. He also describes the consequences of widespread acceptance of Darwinian ideas. Note also how he characterizes his opposition, or the image he creates of them. Bryan brought these ideas into the Fundamentalist efforts to ban the teaching of evolution. For a biography of Jennings, see the chapter introduction.

God and Evolution

Charge that American teachers of Darwinism "make the Bible a scrap of paper"

by William Jennings Bryan

I appreciate your invitation to present the objections to Darwinism, or evolution applied to man, and beg to submit to your readers the following:

The only part of evolution in which any considerable interest is felt is evolution applied to man. A hypothesis in regard to the rocks and plant life does not affect the philosophy upon which one's life is built. Evolution applied to fish, birds and beasts would not materially affect man's view of his own responsibilities except as the acceptance of an unsupported hypothesis as to these would be used to support a similar hypothesis as to man. The evolution that is harmful—distinctly so—is the evolution that destroys man's family tree as taught by the Bible and makes him a descendant of the lower forms of life. This, as I shall try to show, is a very vital matter.

I deal with Darwinism because it is a definite hypothesis. In his *Descent of Man* and *Origin of Species* Darwin has presumed to outline a family tree that begins, according to his estimates, about 200 million years ago with marine animals. He attempts to trace man's line of descent from this obscure beginning up through fish, reptile, bird and animal to man. He has us descend from European, rather than American, apes and locates our first ancestors in Africa. Then he says, "but why speculate?"—a very significant phrase because it applies to everything that he says. His entire discussion is speculation.

Darwin's "Laws"

Darwin set forth two (so-called) laws by which he attempts to explain the changes which he thought had taken place in the development of life from the earlier forms to man. One of these is called 'natural selection' or 'survival of the fittest,' his argument being that a form of life which had any characteristic that was beneficial had a better chance of survival than a form of life that lacked that characteristic. The second law that he assumed to declare was called 'sexual selection,' by which he attempted to account for every change that was not accounted for

Bryan, 20 December 2000, *New York Times,* 26 February 1922, Section 7, 1: 6–9, 11: 1.

by natural selection. Sexual selection has been laughed out to of the classroom. Even in his day Darwin said (see note 2 *Descent of Man* 1874 edition, p. 625) that it aroused more criticism than anything else he had said, when he used sexual selection to explain how man became a hairless animal. Natural selection is being increasingly discarded by scientists. John Burroughs, just before his death, registered a protest against it. But many evolutionists adhere to Darwin's conclusions while discarding his explanations. In other words, they accept the line of descent which he suggested without any explanation whatever to support it.

Other scientists accept the family tree which he outlined, but would have man branch off at a point below, or above, the development of apes and monkeys instead of coming through them. So far as I have been able to find, Darwin's line of descent has more supporters than any other outlined by evolutionists. If there is any other clearly defined family tree supported by a larger number of evolutionists, I shall be glad to have information about it that I may investigate it.

The first objection to Darwinism is that it is only a guess and was never anything more. It is called a 'hypothesis,' but the word 'hypothesis,' though euphonious, dignified and highsounding, is merely a scientific synonym for the old-fashioned word 'guess.' If Darwin had advanced his views as a guess they would not have survived for a year, but they have floated for half a century, buoyed up by the inflated word 'hypothesis.' When it is understood that 'hypothesis' means 'guess,' people will inspect it more carefully before accepting it.

No Support in the Bible

The second objection to Darwin's guess is that it has not one syllable in the Bible to support it. This ought to make Christians cautious about accepting it without thorough investigation. The Bible not only describes man's creation, but it gives a reason for it: man is a part of God's plan and is placed on earth for a purpose. Both the Old and New Testament deal with man and man only. They tell of God's creation of him, of God's dealing with him and of God's plan for him. Is it not strange that a Christian will accept Darwinism as a substitute for the Bible when the Bible not only does not support Darwin's hypothesis but directly and expressly contradicts it?

Third—neither Darwin nor his supporters have been able to find a fact in the universe to support their hypothesis. With millions of species, the investigators have not been able to find one single instance in which one species has changed into another, although, according to the hypothesis, all species have developed from one or a few germs of life, the development being through the action of 'resident forces' and without outside aid. Wherever a form of life, found in the rocks, is found among living organisms, there is no material change from the earliest form in which it is found. With millions of examples, nothing imperfect is found—nothing in the process of change. This statement may surprise those who have accepted evolution without investigation, as most of those who call themselves evolutionists have done. One preacher who wrote to me expressing great regret that I should dissent from Darwin said that he had not investigated the matter for himself, but that nearly all scientists seemed to accept Darwinism.

The latest word that we have on this subject comes from Professor Bateson, a high English authority, who journeyed all the way from London to Toronto, Canada, to address the American Association for the Advancement of Science the 28th day of last December. His speech has been published in full in the January issue of *Science*.

Professor Bateson is an evolutionist, but he tells with real pathos how every effort to discover the origin of species has failed. He takes up different lines of investigation, commenced hopefully but ending in disappointment. He concludes by saying, 'let us then proclaim in precise and unmistakable language that our faith in evolution is unshaken,' and then he adds, 'our doubts are not as to the reality or truth of evolution, but as to the origin of species, a technical, almost domestic problem. Any day that mystery may be solved.' Here is optimism at its maximum. They fall back on faith. They have not yet found the origin of species, and yet how can evolution explain life unless it can account for change in species? Is it not more rational to believe in creation of man by separate act of God than to believe in evolution without a particle of evidence?

Fourth—Darwinism is not only without foundation, but it compels its believers to resort to explanations that are more absurd than anything found in the *Arabian Nights*. Darwin explains that man's mind became superior to woman's because, among our brute ancestors, the males fought for the females and thus strengthen their minds. If he had lived until now, he would not have felt it necessary to make so ridiculous an explanation, because woman's mind is not now believed to be inferior to man's.

As to Hairless Man

Darwin also explained that the hair disappeared from the body, permitting man to become a hairless animal because, among our brute ancestors, the females preferred males with the least hair and thus, in the course of ages, bred the hair off. It is hardly necessary to point out that these explanations conflict: the males and the females could not both select at the same time.

Evolutionists, not being willing to accept the theory of creation, have to explain everything, and their courage in this respect is as great as their efforts are laughable. The eye, for instance, according to evolutionists, was brought out by 'the light beating upon the skin;' the ear came out in response to 'air waves;' the leg is the development of a wart that chanced to appear on the belly of an animal; and so the tommy-rot runs on ad infinitum, and sensible people are asked to swallow it.

Recently a college professor told an audience in Philadelphia that a baby wiggles its big toe without wiggling its other toes because its ancestors climbed trees; also that we dream of falling because our forefathers fell out of trees 50,000 years ago, adding that we are not hurt in our dreams of falling because we descended from those that fell and were not killed. 'If we descended from animals at all, we certainly did not descend from those that were killed in falling.' A professor in Illinois has fixed as a great day in history the day when a water puppy crawled upon the land and decided to stay there, thus becoming man's first progenitor. A dispatch from Paris recently announced that an eminent scientists had reported having communicated with the soul of a dog and learned that the dog was happy.

I simply mention these explanations to show what some people can believe who cannot believe the Bible. Evolution seems to close the heart of some to the plainest spiritual truths while it opens the mind to believe the wildest of guesses advanced in the name of science.

Guessing Is Not Science

Guesses are not science. Science is classified knowledge, and a scientist ought to be the last person to insist upon a guess being accepted until proof removes it from the field of hypothesis into the field of demonstrated truth. Christianity has nothing to fear from any truth; no fact disturbs the Christian religion or the Christian. It is the unsupported guess that is substituted for science to which opposition is made, and I think the objection is a valid one.

But, it may be asked, why should one object to Darwinism even though it is not true! This is a proper question and deserves a candid answer. There are many guesses which are perfectly groundless and at the same time entirely harmless; and it is not worth while to worry about a guess or to disturb the guesser so long as his guess does not harm others.

The objection to Darwinism is that it is harmful, as well as groundless. It entirely changes one's view of life and undermines faith in the Bible. Evolution has no place for the miracle or the supernatural. It flatters the egotist to be told that there is nothing that his mind cannot understand. Evolution proposes to bring all the processes of nature within the comprehension of man by making it the explanation of everything that is known. Creation implies a Creator, and the finite mind cannot comprehend the Infinite. We can understand some things, but we run across mystery at every point. Evolution attempts to solve the mystery of life by suggesting a process of development commencing 'in the dawn of time' and continuing uninterrupted up until now. Evolution does not explain creation: it simply diverts attention from it by hiding it behind eons of time. If a man accepts Darwinism, or evolution applied to man, and is consistent, he rejects the miracle and the supernatural as impossible. He commences with the first chapter of Genesis and blots out the Bible story of man's creation, not because the evidence is insufficient, but because the miracle is inconsistent with evolution. If he is consistent, he will go through the Old Testament step by step and cut out all the miracles and all the supernatural. He will then take up the New Testament and cut out all the supernatural—the virgin birth of Christ, His miracles and His resurrection, leaving the Bible a story book without binding authority upon the conscience of man. Of course, not all evolutionists are consistent; some fail to apply their hypothesis to the end just as some Christians fail to apply their Christianity to life.

Evolution and God

Most of the evolutionists are materialists; some admitting that they are atheists, others calling themselves agnostics. Some call themselves 'theistic evolutionists,' but the theistic evolutionist puts God so far away that He ceases to be a present influence in the life. Canon Barnes of Westminster, some two years ago, interpreted evolution as to put God back of the time when the electrons came out of 'stuff' and combined (about 1,740 of them) to form an atom. Since then, according to Canon Barnes, things have been developing to God's plan but without God's aid.

It requires measureless credulity to enable one to believe that all that we see about us came by chance, by a series of happy-go-lucky accidents. If only an infinite God could have formed hydrogen and oxygen and united them in just the right proportions to produce water—the daily need of every living thing—scattered among the flowers all the colors of the rainbow and every variety of perfume, adjusted the mocking bird's throat to its musical scale, and fashioned a soul for man, why should we want to imprison God in an impenetrable past? This is a living world.

Why not a living God upon the throne? Why not allow Him to work now?

Theistic evolutionists insists that they magnify God when they credit Him with devising evolution as a plan of development. They sometimes characterize the Bible God as a 'carpenter God,' who is described as repairing his work from time to time at man's request. The question is not whether God could have made the world according to the plan of evolution—of course, an all powerful God could make the world as he pleased. The real question is, did God use evolution as His plan? If it could be shown that man, instead of being made in the image of God, is a development of beasts we would have to accept it, regardless of its effect, for truth is truth and must prevail. But when there is no proof we have a right to consider the effect of the acceptance of an unsupported hypothesis.

Darwin's Agnosticism

Darwinism made an agnostic out of Darwin. When he was a young man he believed in God; before he died he declared that the beginning of all things is a mystery insoluble by us. When he was a young man he believed in the Bible; just before his death he declared that he did not believe that there had ever been any revelation; that banished the Bible as the inspired Word of God, and, with it, the Christ of whom the Bible tells. When Darwin was young he believed in a future life; before he died he declared that each must decide the question for himself from vague, uncertain probabilities. He could not throw any light upon the great questions of life and immortality. He said that he 'must be content to remain an agnostic.'

And then he brought the most terrific indictment that I have read against his own hypothesis. He asks (just before his death): "can the mind of man, which has, as I fully believe, been developed from a mind as low as that possessed by the lowest animal, be trusted when it draws such grand conclusions?' He brought man down to the brute level and then judged man's mind by brute standards.

This is Darwinism. This is Darwin's own testimony against himself. If Darwinism could make an agnostic of Darwin, what is its effect likely to be upon students to whom Darwinism is taught at the very age when they are throwing off parental authority and becoming independent? Darwin's guess gives the student an excuse for rejecting the authority of God, an excuse that appeals to him more strongly at this age than at any other age in life. Many of them come back after a while as Romanes came back. After feeding upon husks for twenty-five years, he began to feel his way back, like a prodigal son, to his father's house, but many never returned.

Professor Leuba, who teaches psychology at Bryn Mawr, Pennsylvania, wrote a book about six years ago entitled *Belief in God and immortality* (it can be obtained from the Open Court Publishing Company, Chicago), in which he declared that belief in God and immortality is dying out among the educated classes. As proof of this he gave the results which he obtained by submitting questions to prominent scientists in the United States. He says that he found that more than half of them, according to their own answers, do not believe in a personal God or a personal immortality. To reinforce his position, he sent questions to students of nine representative colleges and found that unbelief increases from 15 percent in the freshman year to 30 percent in the junior class, and to 40 to 45 percent (among the man) at graduation. This he attributes to the influence of the scholarly men under whose instruction they pass in college.

Religion Waning Among Children

Any one desiring to verify these statistics can do so by inquiry at our leading State institutions and even among some of our religious denominational colleges. Fathers and mothers complain of their children losing their interest in religion and speaking lightly of the Bible. This begins when they, under the influence of a teacher who accepts Darwin's guess, ridicules the Bible story of creation and instructs the child upon the basis of the brute theory. In Columbia a teacher began his course in geology by telling the children to lay aside all that they had learned in Sunday school. A teacher of philosophy in the University of Michigan tells students that Christianity is a state of mind and that there are only two books of literary value in the Bible.

Another professor in that university tells students that no thinking man can believe in God or in the Bible. A teacher in the University of Wisconsin tells his students that the Bible is a collection of myths. Another state University professor diverts a dozen young men from the ministry and the President of a prominent state University tells his students in a lecture on religion to throw away religion if it does not harmonize with the teaching of biology, psychology, and etc.

The effect of Darwinism is seen in the pulpits; men of prominent denominations deny the virgin birth of Christ and some even His resurrection. Two Presbyterians, preaching in New York State, recently told me that agnosticism was the natural attitude of old people. Evolution naturally leads to agnosticism and, if continued, finally to atheism. Those who teach Darwinism are undermining the faith of Christians; they are raising questions about the Bible as an authoritative source of truth; they are teaching materialistic views that rob the life of the young of spiritual values.

Christians do not object to freedom of speech; they believe that Biblical truth can hold its own in a fair field. They concede the right of ministers to pass from belief to agnosticism or atheism, but they contend that they should be honest enough to separate themselves from the ministry and not attempt to debase the religion which they profess.

And so in the matter of education. Christians do not dispute the right of any teacher to be agnostic or atheistic, but Christians do deny the right of agnostics and atheists to use the public school as a forum for the teaching of their doctrines.

The Bible has in many places been excluded from the schools on the ground that religion should not be taught by those paid by public taxation. If this doctrine is sound, what right have the enemies of religion to teach irreligion in the public schools? If the Bible cannot be taught, why should Christians taxpayers permit the teaching of guesses that make the Bible a lie? A teacher might just as well write over the door of his room, 'Leave Christianity behind you, all ye who enter here,' as to ask his students to accept an hypothesis directly and irreconcilably antagonistic to the Bible.

Our opponents are not fair. When we find fault with the teaching of Darwin's unsupported hypothesis, they talk about Copernicus and Galileo and ask whether we shall exclude science and return to the dark ages. Their evasion is a confession of weakness.

We do not ask for the exclusion of any scientific truth, but we do protest against an atheist teacher being allowed blow his guesses in the face of the student. The Christians who want to teach religion in their schools furnish the money for denominational institutions. If atheists want to teach atheism, why do they not build their own schools and employ their own teachers? If a man really believes that he has brute blood in him, he can teach that to his children at home or he can send them to atheistic schools, where his children will not be in danger of losing their brute philosophy, but why should he the allowed to deal with other peoples children as if they were little monkeys?

We stamp upon our coins 'in God we trust'; we administer to witnesses an oath in which God's name appears; our President takes his oath of office upon the Bible. Is it fanatical to suggest that public taxes should not be employed for the purpose of undermining the nation's God?

When we defend the Mosaic account of man's creation and contend that man has no brute blood in him, but was made in God's image by separate act and placed on earth to carry out a divine decree, we are defending the God of the Jews as well as the God of the Gentiles, the God of the Catholics as well as the God of the Protestants. We believe that faith in a Supreme Being is essential to civilization as well as to religion and that abandonment of God means ruin to the world and chaos to society.

Let these believers in 'the tree man' come down out of the trees and meet the issue. Let them defend the teaching of agnosticism or atheism if they dare. If they deny that the natural tendency of Darwinism is to lead many to a denial of God, let them frankly point out the portions of the Bible which they regard as consistent with Darwinism, or evolution applied to man. They weaken faith in God, discourage prayer, raise doubt as to a future life, reduce Christ to the stature of a man, and make the Bible a 'scrap of paper.' As religion is the only basis of morals, it is time for Christians to protect religion from its most insidious enemy.

Document 18.2 Bryan at the Scopes Trial

This document, taken from the trial transcript of *Tennessee v. Scopes*, is a verbatim transcription of Bryan's words. In this speech, Bryan summarized his arguments against evolutionary thought, its relation to religion, the effects of evolution, and the reasons it should not be taught in schools. He also discusses whether or not religion should be taught in schools. As Bryan notes at the beginning of the speech, he had not spoken until this, the fifth day of the trial. However, since this was a crucial matter for the prosecution team, they called upon him to make a powerful case. At this point in the trial, the defense had called its first expert witness. The prosecutors could not allow this testimony, because they lacked similar experts. Those attending the trial believed that this was one of Bryan's very best speeches.

William Jennings Bryan's Speech

If the court please we are now approaching the end of the first week of this trial and I haven't thought it proper until this time to take part in the discussions. . . . . I have been tempted to speak at former times, but I have been able to withstand the temptation. I have been drawn into the case by, I think nearly all the lawyers on the other side. The principal attorney has often suggested that I am the arch-conspirator and that I am responsible for the presence of this case and I have almost been credited with leadership of the ignorance and bigotry which he thinks could alone inspire a law like this. Then Mr. Malone has seen fit to honor me by quoting my opinion on religious liberty. I assume he means that that is the most important opinion on religious liberty that he has been able to find in this country and I feel complimented that I should be picked out from all the men living and dead as the one whose expressions are most vital to the welfare of our country. And this morning I was credited with being the cause of the presence of these so-called experts.

Duel to the Death?

Mr. Hays says that before he got here he read that I said this was to be a duel to the death, between science—was it? and revealed religion. I don't know who the other duelist was, but I was representing one of them and because of that they went to the trouble and the expense of several thousand dollars to bring down their witnesses. Well, my friend, if you said that this was important enough to be regarded as a duel between two great ideas or groups I certainly will be given credit for foreseeing what I could not then know and that is that this question is so important between religion and irreligion that even the invoking of the divine blessing upon it might seem partisan and partial. I think when we come to consider the importance of this question, that all of us who are interested as lawyers on either side, could claim what we— what your honor so graciously grants—a hearing. I have got down here for fear I might forget them, certain points that I desire to present for your honor's consideration. In the first place, the statute—our position is that the statute is sufficient. The statute defines exactly what the people of Tennessee desired and intended and did declare unlawful and it needs no interpretation. The caption speaks of the evolutionary theory and the statute specifically states that teachers are forbidden to teach in the schools supported by taxation in this state, any theory of creation of man that denies the divine record of man's creation as found in the Bible, and that there might be no difference of opinion— there might be no ambiguity—that there might be no such confusion of thought as our learned friends attempt to inject into it, the legislature was careful to define what it meant by the first part of the statute. It says to teach that man is a descendant of any lower form of life—if that had not been there—if the first sentence had been the only sentence in the statute, then these gentlemen might come and ask to define what that meant or to explain whether the thing that was taught was contrary to the language of the statute in the first sentence, but the second sentence removes all doubt, as has been stated by my colleague. The second sentence points out specifically what is meant, and that is the teaching that man is the descendant of any lower form of life, and if the defendant taught that as we have proven by the textbook that he used and as we have proven by the students that went to hear him—if he taught that man is a descendant of any lower form of life, he violated the statute, and more than that we have his own confession that he knew he was violating the statute. We have the testimony here of Mr. White, the superintendent of schools, who says that Mr. Scopes told him he could not teach that hook without violating the law. We have the testimony of Mr. Robertson— Robinson—the head of the Board of Education, who talked with Mr. Scopes just at the time the schools closed, or a day or two afterward, and Mr. Scopes told him that he had reviewed that book just before the school closed, and that he could not teach it without teaching evolution and without violating the law, and we have Mr. Robinson's statement that Mr. Scopes told him that he and one of the teachers, Mr. Ferguson, had talked it over after the law was passed and had decided that they could not teach it without the violation of the law, and yet while Mr. Scopes knew what the law was and knew what evolution was, and knew that it violated the law, he proceeded to violate the law. That is the evidence before this court, and we do not need any expert to tell us what that law means. An expert cannot be permitted to come in here and try to defeat the enforcement of a law by testifying that it isn't a bad law and it isn't—I mean a bad doctrine—no matter how these people phrase the doctrine—no matter how they eulogize it. This is not the place to try to prove that the law ought never to have been passed. The place to prove that, or teach that, was to the legislature. If these people were so anxious to keep the state of Tennessee from disgracing itself, if they were so afraid that by this action taken by the legislature, the state would put itself before the people of the nation as ignorant people and bigoted people—if they had half the affection for Tennessee that you would think they had as they come here to testify, they would have come at a time when their testimony would have been valuable and not at this time to ask you to refuse to enforce a law because they did not think the law ought to have been passed. And, my friends, if the people of Tennessee were to go into a state like New York—the one from which this impulse comes to resist this law, or go into any state—if they went into any state and tried to the people that a law they had passed ought not to be enforced, just because the people who went there didn't think it ought to have been passed, don't you think it would be resented as an impertinence? They passed a law up in New York repealing the enforcement of prohibition. Suppose the people of Tennessee had sent attorneys up there to fight that law, or to oppose it after it was passed, and experts to testify how good a thing prohibition is to New York and to the nation, I wonder if there would have been any lack of determination in the papers in speaking out against the offensiveness of such testimony. The people of this state passed this law, the people of this state knew what they were doing when they passed the law, and they knew the dangers of the doctrine—that they did not want it taught to their children, and my friends, it isn't—your honor, it isn't proper to bring experts in here to try to defeat (lie purpose of the people of this state by trying to show that this thing that they denounce and outlaw is a beautiful thing that everybody ought to believe in. If, for instance—I think this is a fair illustration—if a man had made a contract with somebody to bring rain in a dry season down here, and if he was to have $500 for an inch of rain, and if the rain did not come and he sued to enforce his contract and collect the money, could he bring experts in to prove that a drought was better than a rain? (Laughter in the courtroom.) And get pay for bringing a drought when he contracted to bring rain. These

people want to come here with experts to make your honor believe that the law should never have been passed and because in their opinion it ought not to have been passed, it ought not to be enforced. It isn't a place for expert testimony. We have sufficient proof in the book—doesn't the book state the very thing that is objected to, and outlawed in this state? Who has a copy of that book?

The Court—Do you mean the Bible?

Mr. Bryan—No, sir; the biology. (Laughter in the courtroom.)

A Voice—Here it is; Hunter's Biology.

Cannot Teach Bible in State

Mr. Bryan—No, not the Bible, you see in this state they cannot teach the Bible. They can only teach things that declare it to be a lie, according to the learned counsel. These people in the state—Christian people—have tied their hands by their constitution. They say we all believe in the Bible for it is the overwhelming belief in the state, but we will not teach that Bible, which we believe even to our children through teachers that we pay with our money. No, no, it isn't the teaching of the Bible, and we are not asking it. The question is can a minority in this state come in and compel a teacher to teach that the Bible is not true and make the parents of these children pay the expenses of the teacher to tell their children what these people believe is false and dangerous? Has it come to a time when the minority can take charge of a state like Tennessee and compel the majority to pay their teachers while they take religion out of the heart of the children of the parents who pay the teachers? This is the book that is outlawed if we can judge from the questions asked by the counsel for the defense. They think that because the board of education selected this book, four or five years ago, that, therefore, he had to teach it, that he would be guilty if he didn't teach it and punished if he does. Certainly not one of these gentlemen is unlearned in the law and if I, your honor, who have not practiced law for twenty-eight years, know enough to know it, I think those who have been as conspicuous in the practice as these gentlemen have been, certainly ought to know it and that is no matter when that law was passed; no matter what the board of education has done; no matter whether they put their stamp of approval upon this book or not, the moment that law became a law anything in these books contrary to that law was prohibited and nobody knew it better than Mr. Scopes himself. It doesn't matter anything about who ordered these books—the law supercedes all boards of education for the legislature is the Supreme Court on this subject from which there is no appeal.

Christian Believes Man from Above—Evolutionist from Below

So, my friends, if that were true, if man and monkey were in the same class, called primates, it would mean they did not come up from the same order. It might mean that instead of one being the ancestor of the other they were all cousins. But it does not mean that they did not come up from the lower animals, if this is the only place they could come from, and the Christian believes man came from above, but the evolutionist believes he must have come from below,

(Laughter in the courtroom.)

And that is from a lower order of animals.

Your honor, I want to show you that we have evidence enough here, we do not need any experts to come in here and tell us about this thing. Here we have Mr. Hunter. Mr. Hunter is the author of this biology and this is the man who wrote the book Mr. Scopes was teaching. And here we have the diagram. Has the court seen this diagram?

The Court—No, sir, I have not.

Bryan Shows "Tree of Life" to Court

Mr. Bryan—Well, you must see it (handing book to the court.) (Laughter in the courtroom.) On page 194—I take it for granted that counsel for the defense have examined it carefully?

Mr. Darrow—We have examined it.

Mr. Bryan—On page 194, we have a diagram, and this diagram purports to give some one's family tree. Not only his ancestors but his collateral relatives. We are told just how many animal species there are, 518,900. And in this diagram, beginning with protozoa we have the animals classified. We have circles differing in size according to the number of species in them and we have the guess that they give.

Of course, it is only a guess, and I don't suppose it is carried to a one or even to ten. I see they are round numbers, and I don't think all of these animals breed in round numbers, and so I think it must be a generalization of them.

(Laughter in the courtroom.)

The Court—Let us have order.

Mr. Bryan—8,000 protozoa, 3,500 sponges.

Must Be More Than 35,000 Sponges

I am satisfied from some I have seen there must be more than 35,000 sponges.

(Laughter in the courtroom.) Mr. Bryan—And then we run down to the insects, 360,000 insects. Two-thirds of all the species of all the animal world are insects. And sometimes, in the summer time we feel that we become intimately acquainted with them—a large percentage of the species are mollusks and fishes. Now, we are getting up near our kinfolks, 13,000 fishes. Then there are the amphibia. I don't know whether they have not yet decided to come out, or have almost decided to go back.

(Laughter in the courtroom.) But they seem to be somewhat at home in both elements. And then we have the reptiles, 3,500; and then we have 13,000 birds. Strange that this should be exactly the same as the number of fishes, round numbers. And then we have mammals, 3,500, and there is a little circle and man is in the circle, find him, find man.

There is that book! There is the book they were teaching your children that man was a mammal and so indistinguishable among the mammals that they leave him there with thirty-four hundred and ninety-nine other mammals.

(Laughter and applause.)

Including elephants?

Has Daniel Story Beaten

Talk about putting Daniel in the lion's den? How dared those scientists put man in a little ring like that with lions and tigers and everything that is bad! Not only the evolution is possible, but the scientists possibly think of shutting man up in a little circle like that with all these animals, that have an odor, that extends beyond the circumference of this circle, my friends.

(Extended laughter.)

He tells the children to copy this, copy this diagram. In the notebook, children are to copy this diagram and take it home in their notebooks. To show their parents that you cannot find man. That is the great game to put in the public schools to find man among animals, if you can.

Tell me that the parents of this day I have not any right to declare that children are not to be taught this doctrine? Shall not be taken down from the high plane upon which God put man? Shall be detached from the throne of God and be compelled to link their ancestors with the jungle, tell that to these children? Why, my friend, if they believe it, they go back to scoff at the religion of their parents! And the parents have a right to say that no teacher paid by their money shall rob their children of faith in God and send them back to their homes, skeptical, infidels, or agnostics, or atheists.

This doctrine that they want taught, this doctrine that they would force upon the schools, where they will not let the Bible be read!

Why, up in the state of New York they are now trying to keep the schools from adjourning for one hour in the afternoon, not that any teacher shall teach them the Bible, but that the children may go to the churches to which they belong and there have instruction in the work. And they are refusing to let the school do that. These lawyers who are trying to force Darwinism and evolution on your children, do not go back to protect the children of New York in their right to even have religion taught to them outside of the schoolroom, and they want to bring their experts in here.

As we have one family tree this morning given to us, I think you are entitled to have a more authentic one. My friend, my esteemed friend from New York, gave you the family tree according to Linnaeus.

Mr. Malone—Beg pardon, Mr. Bryan?

Hits at Darwinism

Mr. Bryan—I will give you the family tree according to Darwin. If we are going to have family trees here, let us have something that is reliable. I will give you the only family tree that any believer in evolution has ever dared to outline—no other family tree that any evolutionist has ever proposed has as many believers as Darwin has in his family tree. Some of them have discarded his explanations. Natural selections! People confuse evolution with Darwinism. They did not use to complain. It was not until Darwin was brought out into the open; it was not until the absurdities of Darwin had made his explanations the laughing stock that they began to try to distinguish between Darwinism and evolution. They explained that evolutionists had discarded Darwin's idea of sexual selection—I should think they would discard it, and they are discarding the doctrine of natural selection.

But, my friends, when they discard his explanations, they still teach his doctrines. Not one of these evolutionists have discarded Darwin's doctrine that makes life begin with one cell in the sea and continue in one unbroken line to man. Not one of them has discarded that.

Let me read you what Darwin says, if you will pardon me. If I have to use some of these long words —I have been trying all my life to use short words, and it is kind of hard to turn scientist for a moment.

(Laughter in the courtroom.)

And try to express myself in their language.

Here is the family tree of Darwin and remember that is the Darwin that is spoken of in Hunter's biology, that is Darwin he has praised. That is the Darwin who has series—

Mr. Malone—What is the book, Mr. Bryan?

Mr. Bryan—*The Descent of Man*, by Charles Darwin.

Mr. Malone—That has not been offered as evidence?

Mr. Bryan—I should be glad to offer it.

Mr. Malone—No, no, no. No, no.

Mr. Bryan—Let me know if you want it, and it will go in.

Mr. Malone—I would be glad to have it go in.

(Laughter in the courtroom.)

Mr. Bryan—Let us have it put in now so that there will be no doubt about it.

Mr. Malone—If you will let us put our witnesses on to show what the works are—

Mr. Hays—If you will let us put evidence in about it, perhaps we can settle the questions of what it is. I would be satisfied.

Mr. Bryan—If you attach that condition to it, I may not be willing.

Mr. Hays—No.

Mr. Bryan—You seemed to be so anxious about Darwin, I thought you would be content.

Mr. Malone—I merely wanted to know whether it was a hook offered by the prosecution; that was the purpose of my question.

Mr. Bryan—No. It was just referred to and Mr. Hays quoted from Linnaeus on the family tree. I will read this.

Reads from *Descent of Man*. "The most ancient progenitors in the kingdom of the Vertebrata, at which we are able to obtain an obscure glance, apparently consisted of a group of marine animals, resembling the larvae of existing Ascidians. These animals probably gave rise to a group of fishes, as lowly organized as the lancelet, and from these the Ganoids, and other fishes like the Lepidosiren must have been developed. From such fish a very small advance would carry us on to the amphibians. We have seen that birds and reptiles were once intimately connected together; and the Monotremata now connect mammals with reptiles in a slight degree. But no one can at present say by what line of descent the three higher and related classes, namely, mammals, birds and reptiles were derived from the two lower vertebrate classes, namely, amphibians and fishes. In the class of mammals the steps are not difficult to conceive which led from the ancient Monotremata to the ancient Marsupials, and from these to the early progenitors of the placental mammals. We may thus ascend to the Lemuridae, and the interval is not very wide from these to the Simiadae. The Simiadae then branched off into two great stems, the new world and the old world monkeys, and from the latter, at a remote period, man, the wonder and glory of the universe, proceeded."

"Not Even from American Monkeys"

Not even from American monkeys, but from old world monkeys. (Laughter.) Now, here we have our glorious pedigree, and each child is expected to copy the family tree and take it home to his family to be submitted for the Bible family tree—that is what Darwin says. Now, my friends—I beg pardon, if the court please, I have been so in the habit of talking to an audience instead of a court, that I will sometimes say "my friends," although I happen to know not all of them are my friends. (Laughter.)

The Court—Let me ask you a question: Do you understand the evolution theory to involve the divine birth of divinity, or Christ's virgin birth, in any way or not?

Mr. Bryan—I am perfectly willing to answer the question. My contention is that the evolutionary hypothesis is not a theory, your honor.

The Court—Well, hypothesis.

Mr. Bryan—The legislature paid evolution a higher honor than it deserves. Evolution is not a theory, but a hypothesis. Huxley said it could not raise to the dignity of a theory until they found some species that had developed according to the hypothesis, and at that time, Huxley's time, there had never been found a single species, the origin of which could be traced to another species. Darwin himself said he thought it was strange that with two or three million species they had not been able to find one that they could trace to another. About three years ago, Bateson, of London, who came all the way to Toronto at the invitation of the American Academy for the Advancement of Sciences—which, if the gentlemen will brace themselves for a moment, I will say I am a member of the American Academy for the Advancement of Science—they invited Mr. Bateson to come over and speak to them on evolution, and he came, and his speech on evolution was printed in Science magazine, and Science is the organ of the society and I suppose is the outstanding organ of science in this country, and I bought a copy so that if any of the learned counsel for the plaintiff had not had the pleasure of reading Bateson's speech that they could regale themselves during the odd hours. And Bateson told those people after having taken up every effort that had been made to show the origin of species and find it, he declared that every one had failed—every one—every one. And it is true today; never have they traced one single species to any other, and that is why

it was that this so-called expert staled that while the fact of evolution, they think, is established, that the various theories of how it come about, that every theory has failed, and today there is not a scientist in all the world who can trace one single species to any other, and yet they call us ignoramouses and bigots because we do not throw away our Bible and accept it as proved that out of two or three million species not a one is traceable to another. And they say that evolution is a fact when they cannot prove that one species came from another, and if there is such a thing, all species must have come, commencing as they say, commencing in that one lonely cell down there in the bottom of the ocean that just evolved and evolved until it got to be a man. And they cannot find a single species that came from another, and yet they demand that we allow them to teach this stuff to our children, that they may come home with their imaginary family tree and scoff at their mother's and father's Bible.

Bryan Refers to Own Degrees

Now, my friends, I want you to know that they not only have no proof, but they cannot find the beginning. I suppose this distinguished scholar who came here shamed them all by his number of degrees—he did not shame me, for I have more than he has, but I can understand how my friends felt when he unrolled degree after degree. Did he tell you where life began? Did he tell you that back of all these that there was a God? Not a word about it. Did he tell you how life began? Not a word; and not one of them can tell you how life began. The atheists say it came some way without a God; the agnostics say it came in some way, they know not whether with a God or not. And the Christian evolutionists say we come away back there somewhere, but they do not know how far back—they do not give you the beginning—not that gentleman that tried to qualify as an expert; he did not tell you how life began. He did not tell you whether it began with God or how. No, they take up life as a mystery that nobody can explain, and they want you to let them commence there and ask no questions. They want to come in with their little padded up evolution that commences with nothing and ends nowhere. They do not dare to tell you that it ended with God. They come here with this bunch of stuff that they call evolution, that they tell you that everybody believes *in,* but do not know that everybody knows as a fact, and nobody can tell how it came, and they do not explain the great riddle of the universe—they do not deal with the problems of life—they do not teach the great science of how to live—and yet they would undermine the faith of these little children in that God who stands back of everything and whose promise we have that we shall live with Him forever bye and bye. They shut God out of the world. They do not talk about God. Darwin says the beginning of all things is a mystery unsolvable by us. He does not pretend to say how these things started.

The Court—Well, if the theory is, Col. Bryan, that God did not create the cell, then it could not be reconcilable with the Bible?

Mr. Bryan—Of course, it could not be reconcilable with the Bible.

The Court—Before it could be reconcilable with the Bible it would have to be admitted that God created the cell?

Evolution Not Reconcilable with Bible

Mr. Bryan—There would be no contention about that, but our contention is, even if they put God back there, it does not make it harmonious with the Bible. The court is right that unless they put God back there, it must dispute the Bible, and this witness who has been questioned, whether he has qualified or not, and they could ask him every question they wanted to, but they did not ask him how life began, they did not ask whether back of it all, whether if in the beginning there was God. They did not tell us where immortality began. They did not tell us where in this long period of time, between the cell at the bottom of the sea and man, where man became endowed with the hope of immortality. They did not, if you please, and most of them do not go to the place to hunt for it, because more than half of the scientists of this country—Prof. James H. Labell, one of them, and he bases it on thousands of letters they sent to him, says more than half do not believe there is a God or personal immortality, and they want to teach that to these children, and take that from them, to take from them their belief in a God who stands ready to welcome his children.

Discusses Virgin Birth, Resurrection, and Atonement

And your honor asked me whether it has anything to do with the principle of the virgin birth. Yes, because this principle of evolution disputes the miracle; there is no place for the miracle in this train of evolution, and the Old Testament and the New are filled with miracles, and if this doctrine is true, this logic eliminates every mystery in the Old Testament and the New, and eliminates everything supernatural, and that means they eliminate the virgin birth—that means that they eliminate the resurrection of the body— that means that they eliminate the doctrine of atonement and they believe man has been rising all the time, that man never fell, that when the Savior came there was not any reason for His coming, there was no reason why He should not go as soon as He could, that He was born of Joseph or some other co-respondent, and that He lies in his grave, and when the Christians of this state have tied their hands and said we will not take advantage of our power to teach religion to our children, by teachers paid by us, these people come in from the outside of the state and force upon the people of this state and upon the children of the taxpayers of this state a doctrine that refutes not only their belief in God, but their belief in a Savior and belief in heaven, and takes from them every moral standard that the Bible gives us. It is this doctrine that gives us Nietzsche, the only great author who tried to carry this to its logical conclusion, and we have the testimony of my distinguished friend from Chicago in his speech in the Loeb and Leopold case that 50,000 volumes had been written about Nietzsche, and he is the greatest philosopher in the last hundred years, and have him pleading that because Leopold read Nietzsche and adopted Nietzsche's philosophy of the superman, that he is not responsible for the taking of human life. We have the doctrine— I should not characterize it as I should like to characterize it—the doctrine that the universities that had it taught, and the professors who taught it, are much more responsible for the crime that Leopold committed than Leopold himself. That is the doctrine, my friends, that they have tried to bring into existence, they commence in the high schools with their foundation in the evolutionary theory, and we have the word of the distinguished lawyer that this is more read than any other in a hundred years, and the statement of that distinguished man that the teachings of Nietzsche made Leopold a murderer.

Mr. Darrow—Your honor, I want to object; there is not a word of truth in it. Nietzsche never taught that. Anyhow, there was not a word of criticism of the professors, nor of the colleges in reference to that, nor was there a word of criticism of the theological colleges when that clergyman in southern Illinois killed his wife in order to marry someone else. But, again, I say, the statement is not correct, and I object.

Mr. Bryan—We do not ask to have taught in the schools any doctrine that teaches a clergyman killed his wife—

The Court—Of course, I can not pass on the question of fact.

Mr. Darrow—I want to take an exception.

Mr. Bryan—I will read you what you said in that speech here.

Mr. Darrow—If you will read it all.

Mr. Bryan—I will read that part I want; you read the rest. (Laughter.) This book is for sale.

Mr. Darrow—First, of all I want to say, of course this argument is presumed to be made to the court, but it is not, I want to object to injecting any other case into this proceeding, no matter what the case is. I want to take exception to it, if the court permits it.

The Court—Well, Col. Bryan, I doubt you are making reference to what Col. Darrow has said in any other case, since, since he has not argued this case, except to verify what you have said, it can not be an issue here, perhaps you have the right—Mr. Bryan—Yes, I would like very much to give you this.

Mr. Darrow—If your honor permits, I want to take an exception.

The Court—You may do so.

Mr. Bryan—If I do not find what I say, I want to tender an apology, because I have never in my life misquoted a man intentionally.

Mr. Darrow—I am intimating you did. Mr. Bryan, but you will find a thorough explanation in it. I am willing for him to refer to what he wants, to look it up, and I will refer the court to what I want to later.

The Court—All right.

Mr. Darrow—It will only take up time.

Mr. Bryan—I want to find what he said, where he says the professors and universities were more responsible than Leopold was.

Mr. Darrow—All right, I will show you what I said, that the professors and the universities were not responsible at all.

Mr. Bryan—You added after that you did not believe in excluding the reading of it, that you thought that was one of the things—

Mr. Darrow—The fellow that invented the printing press did some mischief as well as some good.

Mr. Bryan—Here it is, Page 84, and this is on sale here in town. *I* got four copies the other day; cost me $2; anybody can get it for 50 cents apiece, but he cannot buy mine. They are valuable.

Mr. Malone—I will pay $1.50 for yours. (Laughter.)

Bryan Quotes Darrow in Loeb-Leopold Case

Mr. Bryan (Reading)—"I will guarantee that you can go down to the University of Chicago today—into its big library and find over 1,000 volumes of Nietzsche, and I am sure I speak moderately. If this boy is to blame for this, where did he get it? Is there any blame attached because somebody took Nietzsche's philosophy seriously and fashioned his life on it? And there is no question in this case but what it is true. Then who is to blame? The university would be more to blame than he is. The scholars of the world would be more to blame than he is. The publishers of the world—and Nietzsche's books are published by one of the biggest publishers in the world—are more to blame than he. Your honor, it is hardly fair to hang a 19-year-old boy for the philosophy that was taught him at the university." Now, there is the university and there is the scholar.

Mr. Darrow—Will you let me see it?

Mr. Bryan—Oh, yes, but let me have it back.

Mr. Darrow—I'll give you a new one autographed for you. (Laughter.)

Mr. Bryan—Now, my friends, Mr. Darrow asked Howard Morgan, "Did it hurt you? Did it do you any harm? Did it do you any harm?" Why did he not ask the boy's mother?

Mr. Darrow—She did not testify. Mr. Bryan—No, but why did you not bring her here to testify?

Mr. Darrow—I fancy that his mother might have hurt him.

Mr. Bryan—Your honor, it is the mothers who find out what is being done, and it is the fathers who find out what is being done. It is not necessary that a boy, whose mind is poisoned by this stuff, poisoned by the stuff administered—without ever haying the precaution to write poison on the outside, it is the parents that are doing that, and here we have the testimony of the greatest criminal lawyer in the United States, stating that the universities—

Mr. Darrow—I object, your honor, to an injection of that case into this one.

The Court—It is argument before the court period. I do not see how—Mr. Darrow—If it does not prejudice you, it does not do any good.

The Court—No, sir; it does not prejudice me.

Mr. Darrow—Then, it does not do any good.

The Court—Well. (Loud laughter and great applause.)

Mr. Bryan—If your honor, please, let me submit, we have a different idea of the purpose of argument, my idea is that it is to inform the court, not merely to prejudice the court.

The Court—Yes.

Mr. Darrow—I am speaking of this particular matter.

The Court—Suppose you get through with Col. Darrow as soon as you can, Mr. Bryan.

Mr. Bryan—Yes, I will. I think I am through with the colonel now. The gentleman was called as an expert, I say, did not tell us where life began, or how. He did not tell us anything about the end of this series, he did not tell us about the logical consequences of it, and the implications based upon it. He did not qualify even as an expert in science, and not at all as an expert in the Bible. If a man is going to come as an expert to reconcile this definition of evolution with the Bible, he must be an expert on the Bible also, as well as on evolution, and he did not qualify as an expert on the Bible, except to say he taught a Sunday School class.

Mr. Malone—We were not offering him for that purpose. We expect to be able to call experts on the Bible.

Mr. Bryan—Oh, you did not count him as an expert?

Mr. Malone—We count him as a Christian, possibly not as good as Mr. Bryan.

Mr. Bryan—Oh, you have three kinds to be called.

Mr. Malone—No, just Americans. It is not a question of citizenship and not a distinction.

Mr. Bryan—We are to have three kinds of people called. We are to have the expert scientist, the expert Bible men and then just Christians.

Mr. Malone—We will give you all the information you want, Mr. Bryan.

Mr. Bryan—Thank you, sir. I think we have all we want now.

(Applause.) Now, your honor, when it comes to Bible experts, do (you) think that they can bring them in here to instruct the members of the jury, eleven of whom are members of the church? I submit that of the eleven members of the jury, more of the jurors are experts on what the Bible is than any Bible expert who does not subscribe to the true spiritual influences or spiritual discernments of what our Bible says. (Voice in audience, "Amen!")

Must Be a Christian to Understand the Bible

Mr. Bryan—(Continuing) and the man may discuss the Bible all he wants to, but he does not find out anything about the Bible until he accepts God and the Christ of whom He tells.

Mr. Darrow—I hope the reporters got the amens in the record. I want somewhere, at some point, to find some court where a picture of this will be painted. (Laughter.)

Mr. Bryan—Your honor, we first pointed out that we do not need any experts in science. Here is one plain fact, and the statute defines itself, and it tells the kind of evolution it does not want taught, and the evidence says that this is the kind of evolution that was taught, and no number of scientists could come in here, my friends, and override that statute or take from the jury its right to decide this question, so that all the experts that they could bring would mean nothing. And, when it comes to Bible experts, every member of the jury is as good an expert on the Bible as any man that they could bring, or that we could bring. The one beauty about the Word of God is, it does not take an expert to understand it. They have translated that Bible into five hundred languages, they have carried it into nations where but few can read a word, or write, to people who never saw a book, who never read, and yet can understand that Bible, and they can accept the salvation that that Bible offers, and they can know more about that book by accepting Jesus and feeling in their hearts the sense of their sins forgiven than all of the skeptical outside Bible experts that could come in here to talk to the people of Tennessee about the construction that they place upon the Bible, that is foreign to the construction that the people here place upon it. Therefore, your honor, we believe that this evidence is not competent, it is not a mock trial, this is not a convocation brought here to allow men to come and stand for a time in the limelight, and speak to the world from the platform at Dayton. If we must have a mock trial to give these people a chance to get before the public with their views, then let us convene it after this case is over, and let people stay as long as they want to listen, but let this court, which is here supported by the law, and by the taxpayers, pass upon this law, and when the legislature passes a law and makes it so plain that even though a fool need not err therein, let us sustain it in our interpretations. We have a book here that shows everything that is needed to make one understand evolution, and to show that the man violated the law. Then why should we prolong this case. We can bring our experts here for the Christians; for every one they can bring who does not believe in Christianity, we can bring more than one who believes in the Bible and rejects evolution, and our witnesses will be just as good experts as theirs on a question of that kind. We could have a thousand or a million witnesses, but this case as to whether evolution is true or not, is not going to be tried here, within this city; if it is carried to the state's courts, it will not be tried there, and if it is taken to the great court at Washington, it will not be tried there. No, my friends, no court or the law, and no jury, great or small, is going to destroy the issue between the believer and the unbeliever. The Bible is the Word of God; the Bible is the only expression of man's hope of salvation. The Bible, the record of the Son of God, the Savior of the world, born of the virgin Mary, crucified and risen again. That Bible is not going to be driven out of this court by experts who come hundreds of miles to testify that they can reconcile evolution, with its ancestor in the jungle, with man made by God in His image, and put here for purposes as a part of the divine plan. No, we are not going to settle that question here, and I think we ought to confine ourselves to the law and to the evidence that can be admitted in accordance with the law. Your court is an office of this state, and we who represent the state as counsel are officers of the state, and we cannot humiliate the great state of Tennessee by admitting for a moment that people can come from anywhere and protest against the enforcement of this state's laws on the ground that it does not conform with their ideas, or because it banishes from our schools a thing that they believe in and think ought to be taught in spite of the protest of those who employ the teacher and pay him his salary.

The facts are simple, the case is plain, and if those gentlemen want to enter upon a larger field of educational work on the subject of evolution, let us get through with this case and then convene a mock court for it will deserve the title of mock court if its purpose is to banish from the hearts of the people the Word of God as revealed. (Great applause.)

The Court—We will take a short recess.

Document 18.3 Darrow Addresses the Court for the Defense

Scopes' defense team feared Bryan's oratorical skills. In the usual course of a trial in Tennessee, the prosecution spoke last. The defense worried that Bryan would be very effective in convincing the jury of his case. Consequently, they designed a strategy in which, after they finished making their case, they would ask the jury for a directed verdict; that is, they would ask the jury to find Scopes guilty. (The defense expected to lose and wanted to appeal the case to a higher court that would determine the constitutionality of the law.) Since they asked for a guilty plea, there would be no need for either side to make a closing argument. The maneuver would prevent Bryan from speaking and swaying the jury. The defense team also wanted to use Darrow's considerable skills as a speaker. So, rather than a closing argument, Darrow made the defense arguments as part of a hearing about the constitutionality of the law. This document contains that speech. Most of the people who heard it said it was the best of his entire life. One newspaper, however, noted that it was meant to be heard, not read.

Darrow's Speech— Holds Bryan Responsible

Mr. Darrow—... This case we have to argue is a case at law, and hard as it is for me to bring my mind to conceive it, almost impossible as it is to put my mind back into the sixteenth century, I am going to argue it as if it was serious, and as if it was a death struggle between two civilizations.

Let us see, now what there is about it. We have been informed that the legislature has the right to prescribe the course of study in the public schools. Within reason, they no doubt have, no doubt. They could not prescribe it, I am inclined to think, under your constitution, if it omitted arithmetic and geography and writing, neither under the rest of the constitution if it shall remain in force in the state, could they prescribe it if the course of study was only to teach religion, because several hundred years ago, when our people believed in freedom, and when no men felt so sure of their own sophistry that they were willing to send a man to jail who did not believe them. The people of Tennessee adopted a constitution, and they made it broad and plain, and said that the people of Tennessee should always enjoy religious freedom in its broadest terms, so I assume that no legislature could fix a course of study which violated that. For instance, suppose the legislature should say, we think the religious privileges and duties of the citizens of Tennessee are much more important than education, we agree "with the distinguished governor of the state, if religion must go, or learning must go, why, let learning go, I do not know how much it would have to go, but let it go, and therefore we will establish a course in the public schools of teaching that the Christian religion as unfolded in the Bible, is true, and that every other religion, or mode or system of ethics is false and to carry that out, no person in the public schools shall be permitted to read or hear anything except Genesis, Pilgrims Progress, Baxter's Saint Rest, and In His Image. Would that be constitutional? If it is, the constitution is a lie and a snare and the people have forgot what liberty means.

I remember, long ago, Mr. Bancroft wrote this sentence, which is true: "That it is all right to preserve freedom in constitutions, but when the spirit of freedom has fled, from the hearts of the people, then its matter is easily sacrificed under law," And so it is, unless there is left enough of the spirit of freedom in the state of Tennessee, and in the United States, there is not a single line of any constitution that can withstand bigotry and ignorance when it seeks to destroy the rights of the individual; and bigotry and ignorance are ever active. Here, we find today as brazen and as bold an attempt to destroy learning as was ever made in the middle ages, and the only difference is we have not provided that they shall be burned at the stake, but there is time for that, Your Honor, we have to approach these things gradually.

If This Law Holds—Reverts to Wicked Ancient Laws

... I am going to begin with some of the simpler reasons why it is absolutely absurd to think that this statute, indictment, or—any part of the proceedings in this case are legal, and I think the sooner we get rid of it in Tennessee the better for the peace of Tennessee, and the better for the pursuit of knowledge in the world, so let me begin at the beginning.

... Here is what it is: "Be it enacted by the general assembly of the state of Tennessee, that it shall be unlawful for any teacher in any of the universities, normals and all other public schools in the state, which are supported in whole or in part by the public school funds of the state, to teach"—what, teach evolution? Oh! no—"to teach the theory that denies the story of the divine creation of man, as taught in the Bible, and to teach instead that man has descended from a lower order of animals." That is what was foisted on the people of this state, ... that it should be a crime in the state of Tennessee to teach any theory

of the origin of man, except that contained in the divine account as recorded in the Bible. But the state of Tennessee under an honest and fair interpretation of the constitution has no more right to teach the Bible as the divine book than that the Koran is one, or the book of Mormons, or the book of Confucius, or the Buddha, or the Essays of Emerson, or any one of the 10,000 books to which human souls have gone for consolation and aid in their troubles. Are they going to cut them out? They . . . could not pick it put without violating the constitution, which is as old and as wise as Jefferson.

Certainly Violates Constitution

...Now, as to the statute itself. It is full of weird, strange, impossible and imaginary provisions. Driven by bigotry and narrowness they come together and make this statute and bring this litigation. I cannot conceive anything greater.

What is this law? What does it mean? ...

The statute should be comprehensible. It should not be written in Chinese anyway. It should be in passing English. As you say, so that common, human beings would understand what it meant, and so a man would know whether he is liable to go to jail when he is teaching not so ambiguous as to be a snare or a trap to get someone who does not agree with you. It should be plain, simple and easy. Does this statute state what you shall teach and what you shall not? Oh, no! Oh, no! Not at all. Does it say you cannot teach the earth is round? Because Genesis says it is flat? No. Does it say you cannot teach that the earth is millions of ages old, because the account in Genesis makes it less than six thousand years old? Oh, no. It doesn't state that. If it did you could understand it. It says you shan't teach any theory of the origin of man that is contrary to the divine theory contained in the Bible.

No Legislature Can Say What Is Divine—Discusses Bible

Now let us pass up the word "divine!" No legislature is strong enough in any state in the Union to characterize and pick any book as being divine. Let us take it as it is. What is the Bible? Your Honor, I have read it myself. I might read it more or more wisely. Others may understand it better. Others may think they understand it better when they do not. But in a general way I know what it is. I know there are millions of people in the world who look on it as being a divine book, and I have not the slightest objection to it. I know there are millions of people in the world who derive consolation in their times of trouble and solace in times of distress from the Bible. I would be pretty near the last one in the world to do anything or take any action to take it away. I feel just exactly the same toward the religious creed of every human being who lives. If anybody finds anything in this life that brings them consolation and health and happiness I think they ought to have it whatever they get. I haven' any fault to find with them at all. But what is it? The Bible is not one book. The Bible is made up of sixty-six books written over a period of about one thousand years, some of them very early and some of them comparatively late. It is a book primarily of religion and morals. It is not a book of science. Never was and was never meant to be. Under it there is nothing prescribed that would tell you how to build a railroad or a steamboat or to make anything that would advance civilization. It is not a textbook or a text on chemistry. It is not big enough to be. It is not a book on geology; they knew nothing about geology. It is not a book on biology; they knew nothing about it. It is not a work on evolution; that is a mystery. It is not a work on astronomy. The man who looked out at the universe and studied the heavens had no thought but that the earth was the center of the universe. But we know better than that. We know that the sun is the center of the solar system. And that there are an infinity of other systems around about us. They thought the sun went around the earth and gave us light and gave us night. We know better. We know the earth turns on its axis to produce days and nights. They thought the earth was created 4,004 years before the Christian Era. We know better. I doubt if there is a person in Tennessee who does not know better. They told it the best they knew. And while suns may change all you may learn of chemistry, geometry and mathematics, there are no doubt certain primitive, elemental instincts in the organs of man that remain the same, he finds out what he can and yearns to know more and supplements his knowledge with hope and faith.

Bible Is in Province of Religion— Accounts of Creation Conflict

That is the province of religion and I haven't the slightest fault to find with it. Not the slightest in the world. One has one thought and one another, and instead of fighting each other as in the past, they should support and help each other. Let's see now. Can your Honor tell what is given as the origin of man as shown in the Bible? Is there any human being who can tell us? There are two conflicting accounts in the first two chapters. There are scattered all through it various acts and ideas, but to pass that up for the sake of argument no teacher in any school in the state of Tennessee can know that he is violating a law, but must test every one of its doctrines by the Bible, must he not? You cannot say two times two equals four or a man an educated man if evolution is forbidden. It does not specify what you cannot teach, but says you cannot teach anything that conflicts with the Bible. Then just imagine making it a criminal code that is so uncertain and impossible that every man must be sure that he has read everything in the Bible and not only read it but understands it, or he might violate the criminal code. Who is the chief mogul that can tell us what the Bible means? He or they should write a book and make it plain and distinct, so we would know. Let us look at it. There are in America at least five hundred different sects or churches, all of which quarrel with each other and the importance and non-importance of certain things or the construction of certain passages. All along the line they do not agree among themselves and cannot agree among themselves. They never have and probably never will. There is a great division between the Catholics and the Protestants. There is such a disagreement that my client, who is a school-teacher, not only must know the subject he is teaching, but he must know everything about the Bible in reference to evolution. And he must be sure that he expresses his right or else some fellow will come along here, more ignorant perhaps than he and say, "You made a bad guess and I think you have committed a crime." No criminal statute can rest that way. There is not a chance for it, for this criminal statute and every criminal statute must be plain and simple. If Mr. Scopes is to be indicted and prosecuted because he taught a wrong theory of the origin of life why not tell him what he must teach. Why not say that you must teach that man was made of the dust; and still stranger not directly from the dust, without taking any chances on it, whatever, that Eve was made out of Adam's rib. You will know what I am talking about.

No Man Could Obey Law—No Court Could Enforce It

Now my client must be familiar with the whole book, and must know all about all of these warring sects of Christians and know which of them is right and which wrong, in order that he will not commit crime. Nothing was heard of all that until the fundamentalists got into Tennessee. I trust that when they prosecute their wildly made charge upon the intelligence of some other sect they may modify this mistake and state in simple language what was the account contained in the Bible that could not be taught. So, unless other sects have something to do with it, we must know just what we are charged with doing. This statute, I say, your Honor, is indefinite and uncertain. No man could obey it, no court could enforce it and it is bad for indefiniteness and uncertainty. Look at that indictment up there. If that is a good indictment I never saw a bad one. Now, I do not expect, your honor, my opinion to go because it is my opinion, because I am like all lawyers who practice law; I have made mistakes in my judgment of law. I will probably make more of them. I insist that you might just as well hand my client a piece of blank paper and then send the sheriff after him to jail him. Let me read this indictment.

Reads from Newspaper

I am reading from a newspaper. I forget what newspaper it was, but am sure it was right: "That John Thomas Scopes on April, 1925, did unlawfully and willfully teach in the public schools of Rhea County, Tennessee, which public schools are supported in part and in whole —" I don't know how that is possible, but we will pass that up — "In part or in whole by the public school funds of the state a certain theory and theories that deny the story of the divine creation of man as taught in the Bible and did teach instead thereof that man is descended from a lower order of animals." Now, then there is something that is very elementary. That is one of them and very elementary, because the constitutions of Tennessee provides and the constitution of pretty near every other state in the United States provide that an indictment must state in sufficient terms so that a man may be appraised of what is going to be the character of charge against him. Tennessee said that my friend the attorney-general says that John Scopes knows what he is here for. Yes, I know what he is here for, because the fundamentalists are after everybody that thinks. I know why he is here. I know who is here because ignorance and bigotry are rampant, and it is a mighty strong combination, your Honor, it makes him fearful. But the state is bringing him here by indictment, and several things must be stated in the indictment; indictments must state facts, not law nor conclusions of law. It is all well enough to show that the indictment is good if it charges the offense in the language of the statute. In our state of Illinois, if one man kills another with malice aforethought, he would be guilty of murder, but an indictment would not be good that said John Jones killed another. It would not be good. It must

tell more about it and how. It is not enough in this indictment to say that John Scopes taught something contrary to the divine account written by Moses—maybe—that is not enough. There are several reasons for it. First, it is good and right to know. Secondly, after the shooting is all over here and Scopes has paid his fine if he can raise his money, or has gone to jail if he cannot, somebody else will come along and indict him over again. But there is one thing I cannot account for, that is the hatred and the venom and feeling and the very strong religious combination. That I never could account for. There are a lot of things I cannot account for. Somebody' may come along next week and indict him again, on the first indictment. It must be so plain that a second case will never occur. He can say to him, "I have cleared that off." ...

Violates Right of Worship—Does Not Understand Religious Hatred

The state by constitution is committed to the doctrine of education, committed to schools. It is committed to teaching and I assume when it is committed to teaching it is committed to teaching the truth—ought to be anyhow—plenty of people to do the other. It is committed to teaching literature and science. My friend has suggested that literature and science might conflict. I cannot quite see how, but that is another question. But that indicates the policy of the state of Tennessee and wherever it is used in construing the unconstitutionality of this act it can only be used as an indication of what the state meant and you could not pronounce a statute void on it, but we insist that this statute is absolutely void because it contravenes Section 3, which is headed "the right of worship free." Now, let's see, your Honor, there isn't any court in the world that can uphold the spirit of the law by simply upholding its letters. I read somewhere—I don't know where—that the letter killeth, but the spirit giveth life. I think I read it out of "The Prince of Peace." I don't know where I did, but I read it. If this section of the constitution which guarantees religious liberty in Tennessee cannot be sustained in the spirit it cannot be sustained in the letter. What does it mean? What does it mean? I know two intelligent people can agree only for a little distance, like a company walking along in a road. They may go together a few blocks and then one branches off. The remainder go together a few more blocks and another branches off and still further some one else branches off and the human minds are just that way, provided they are free, of course, the fundamentalists may be put in a trap so they cannot think differently if at all, probably not at all, but leave two free minds and they may go together a certain distance, but not all the way together. There are no two human machines alike and no two human beings have the same experiences and their ideas of life and philosophy grow out of their construction of the experiences that we meet on our journey through life. It is impossible, if you leave freedom in the world, to mold the opinions of one man upon the opinions of another—only tyranny can do it—and your constitutional provision, providing a freedom of religion, was meant to meet that emergency. I will go further—there is nothing else—since man—I don't know whether I dare say evolved—still, this isn't a school—since man was created out of the dust of the earth —out of hand—there is nothing else your Honor that has caused the difference of opinion, of bitterness, of hatred, of war, of cruelty, that religion has caused. With that, of course, it has given consolation to millions.

But it is one of those particular things that should be left solely between the individual and his Maker, or his God, or whatever takes expression with him, and it is no one else's concern.

500 Different Christian Creeds—Darrow Pseudo-Scientist

How many creeds and cults are there this whole world over? No man could enumerate them? At least as I have said, 500 different Christian creeds, all made up of differences, your honor, every one of them, and these subdivided into small differences, until they reach every member of every congregation. Because to think is to differ, and then there are any number of creeds older and any number of creeds younger, than the Christian creed, any number of them, the world has had them forever. They have come and they have gone, they have abided their time and have passed away, some of them are here still, some may be here forever, but there has been a multitude, due to the multitude and manifold differences in human beings, and it was meant by the constitutional convention of Tennessee to leave these questions of religion between man and whatever he worshiped, to leave him free. Has the Mohammedan any right to stay here and cherish his creed? Has the Buddhist a right to live here and cherish his creed? Can the Chinaman who comes here to wash our clothes, can he bring his joss and worship it? Is there any man that holds a religious creed, no matter where he came from, or how old it is or how false it is, is there any man that can be prohibited by any act of the legislature of Tennessee?

Impossible? The constitution of Tennessee, as I understand, was copied from the one that Jefferson wrote, so clear, simple, direct, to encourage the freedom of religious opinion, said in substance, that no act shall ever be passed to interfere with complete religious liberty. Now is this it or is not this it? What do you say? What does it do? We will say I am a Scientist, no, I will take that back, I am a pseudo-scientist, because I believe in evolution, pseudo-scientist named by somebody, who neither knows or cares what science is, except to grab it by the throat and throttle it to death. I am a pseudo-scientist, and I believe in evolution. Can a legislative body say, "You cannot read a book or take a lesson, or make a talk on science until you first find out whether you are saying against Genesis." It can unless that constitutional provision protects me. It can. Can it say to the astronomer, you cannot turn your telescope upon the infinite planets and suns and stars that fill space, lest you find that the earth is not the center of the universe and there is not any firmament between us and the heaven. Can it? It could—except for the work of Thomas Jefferson, which has been woven into every state constitution of the Union, and has stayed there like the flaming sword to protect the rights of man against ignorance and bigotry, and when it is permitted to overwhelm them, then we are taken in a sea of blood and ruin that all the miseries and tortures and carrion of the middle ages would be as nothing. They would need to call back these men once more. But are the provisions of the constitutions that they left, are they enough to protect you and me, and every one else in a land which we thought was free? Now, let us see what it says: "All men have a natural and indefeasible right to worship Almighty God according to the dictates of their own conscience."

That takes care, even of the despised modernist, who dares to be intelligent. "That no man can of right be compelled to attend, erect or support any place of worship, or to maintain any minister against his consent; that no human authority can in any case whatever control or interfere with the rights of conscience in any case whatever"—that does not mean whatever, that means barring fundamentalist propaganda. It does not mean whatever at all times, sometimes may be—and that "no preference shall be given by law to any religious establishment or mode of worship." Does it? Could you get any more preference, your honor, by law? Let us see. Here is the state of Tennessee, living peacefully, surrounded by its beautiful mountains, each one of which contains evidence that the earth is millions of years old,— people quiet, not all agreeing upon any one subject, and not necessary.

If I could not live in peace with people I did not agree with, why, what? I could not live. Here is the state of Tennessee going along in its own business, teaching evolution for years, state boards handing out books on evolution, professors in colleges, teachers in schools, lawyers at the bar, physicians, ministers, a great percentage of the intelligent citizens of the state of Tennessee evolutionists, have not even thought it was necessary to leave their church. They believed that they could appreciate and understand and make their own simple and human doctrine of the Nazarene, to love their neighbor, be kindly with them, not to place a fine on and not try to send to jail some man who did not believe as they believed, and got along all right with it, too, until something happened. They have not thought it necessary to give up their church, because they believed that all that was here was not made on the first six days of creation, or that it had come by a slow process of developments extending over the ages, that one thing grew out of another. There are people who believed that organic life and the plants and the animals and man and the mind of man, and the religion of man are the subjects of evolution, and they have not got through, and that the God in which they believed did not finish creation on the first day, but that he is still working to make something better and higher still out of human beings, who are next to God, and that evolution has been working forever and will work forever—they believe it.

A Crime in the State to Get Learning

And along comes somebody who says—we have got to believe it as I believe it. It is a crime to know more than I know. And they publish a law to inhibit learning. Now, what is in the way of it? First, what does the law say? This law says that it shall be a criminal offense to teach in the public schools any account of the origin of man that is in conflict with the divine account in the Bible. It makes the Bible the yard stick to measure every man's intellect, to measure every man's intelligence and to measure every man's learning. Are your mathematics good? Turn to I Elijah ii, is your philosophy good? See II Samuel iii, is your astronomy good? See Genesis, Chapter 2, Verse 7, is your chemistry good? See—well, chemistry, see Deuteronomy iii-6, or anything that tells about brimstone. Every bit of knowledge that the mind has, must be submitted to a religious test. Now, let us see, it is a travesty upon language, it is a travesty upon justice, it is a travesty upon the constitution to say that any citizen of Tennessee can be deprived of his rights by a legislative body in the face of the constitution. Tell me, your honor, if this is not good, then what? Then, where are we coming out? I want to argue that in connection with another question here which is equally plain. Of course, I used to hear when I was a boy you could lead a horse to water, but you could not make him drink—water. I could lead a man to water, but I could not make him drink, either. And you can close your eyes and you won't see, cannot see, refuse to open your eyes—stick your fingers in your ears and you cannot hear— if you want to. But your life and my life and the life of every American citizen depends after all upon the tolerance and forbearance of his fellowman. If men are not tolerant, if men cannot respect each other's opinions, if men cannot live and let live, then no man's life is safe, no man's life is safe.

Here is a country made up of Englishmen, Irishmen, Scotch, German, Europeans, Asiatics, Africans, men of every sort and men of every creed and men of every scientific belief; who is going to begin this sorting out and say, "I shall measure you; I know you are a fool, or worse; I know and I have read a creed telling what I know and I will make people go to Heaven even if they don't want to go with me, I will make them do it." Where is the man that is wise enough to do it?

Statute Under Police Power

This statute is passed under the police power of this state. Is there any kind of question about that? Counsel have argued that the legislature has the right to say what shall be taught in the public school. Yes, within limits, they have. We do not doubt it, but they probably cannot say writing and arithmetic could not be taught, and certainly they cannot say nothing can be taught unless it is first ascertained that it agrees with the Scriptures; certainly they cannot say that.

But this is passed under the police power. Let me call your honor's attention to this. This is a criminal statute, nothing else. It is not any amendment to the school law of the state. It makes it a crime in the caption to teach evolution and in the body of the act to teach something else, purely and simply a criminal statute.

There is no doubt about the law in this state. Show me that Barber's case will you? (Taking book from counsel.)

There isn't the slightest doubt about it, or in any other state. Your honor, I have got a case there, but I have not got my glasses.

Associate Counsel—Here they are.

Mr. Darrow—Thank you.

There isn't the slightest doubt about it. Can you pass a law under the police powers of the state; that a thing cannot be done in Dayton, but they can do it down in Chattanooga? Oh, no. What is good for Chattanooga is good for Dayton; I would not be sure that what is good for Dayton is good for Chattanooga, but I will put it the other way.

Any law passed under the police power must be uniform in its application; must be uniform. What do you mean by a police law? Well, your honor, that calls up visions of policemen and grand juries and jails and penitentiaries and electrocutionary establishments, and all that, and wickedness of heart; that is police power. True, it may extend to public health and public morals, and a few other things. I do not imagine evolution hurts the health of anyone, and probably not the morals, excepting as all enlightenment may and the ignorant think, of course, that it does, but it is not passed for them, your honor, oh, no. It is not passed because it is best for the public morals, that they shall not know anything about evolution, but because it is contrary to the divine account contained in Genesis, that is all, that is the basis of it.

Now let me see about that. Any police statute must rest directly upon crime, or what is analogous to it; it has that smack, anyhow. Talk about the police power and the policemen and all the rest of them with their clubs and so on, you shudder and wonder what you have been doing, and that is the police power.

Now, any such law must be uniform in its application, there cannot be any doubt about that, not the slightest. Here, for instance, the good people of— well, I guess these are good people, Nashville, wasn't it? Whether the common people down there—

Mr. Neal—That is a Tennessee case.

Is Bath on Sunday Wicked?

Mr. Darrow—Anyhow, it is a Tennessee case. Good people stirred up the community, by somebody, I don't know who, passed a law which said it was a misdemeanor to carry on barbering on Sunday, and that it should be a misdemeanor for anyone engaged in the business of barbering to shave, shampoo and cut hair or to keep open the bath rooms on Sunday. (Laughter in courtroom.)

Mr. Darrow—Well, of course, I suppose it would be wicked to take a bath on Sunday, I don't know, but that was not the trouble with this statute. It would have been all right to forbid the good people of Tennessee from taking a bath on Sunday, but that was not the trouble. A barber could not give a bath on Sunday, anybody else could. No barber shall be permitted to give a bath on Sunday, and the Supreme Court seemed to take judicial notice of the fact that people take a bath on Sunday just the same as any other day.

Foreigners come in there in the habit of bathing on Sundays just as any other time, and they could keep shops open, but a barber shop, no. The Supreme Court said that would not do, you could not let a hotel get away with what a barber shop can't. (Laughter.)

And so they held that this law was unconstitutional, under the provision of the constitution which says laws must be uniform. There is no question about the theory of it. If there were not, why, they would be passing laws against—the fundamentalists would be passing laws against the Congregationalists and Unitarians—I cannot remember all the names—Universalists—they might graduate the law according to how orthodox or unorthodox the church was. You cannot do it; they have to be general. The supreme court of this state has decided it and it does not admit of a doubt.

Now, I will just read one section of the opinion: The act is for the benefit of all individuals, barbers excepted; we know that all of the best hotels have bathrooms for the use of guests, that they accept pay for baths and permit them on Sunday.

Charges Class Legislation

(Reading from Barbers case, 2 Pickle, beginning with "that in many cases the barber has bathroom" to "for this and other things the act is held void.")

That in the case in 2 Pickle that I read from. Why they named this Pickle I have not found out yet.

But there is another in 16 Gates, page 12. This is a case, your honor, where they passed a law:

(Reading from above book beginning with words "that it shall be unlawful for any jobbing," to "It shall be unlawful.")

If it is unlawful for these corporations to discharge an individual because they didn't vote a certain ticket, this must have been passed against the wicked democrats up here. Up in our state it is the republicans who do all that, but still, it shall be unlawful to discharge any man if he don't vote a certain way or buy at a certain place if he did buy at a certain place, that only applied to corporations; if John Smith had a little ranch upon the mountain or had hired a man he could discharge him all right if he didn't vote the right ticket or go to the right church or any old reason. And the supreme court of the state said, "Oh, no, you cannot pass that sort of a law." What is sauce for the goose must be sauce for the gander. You cannot pass a law making it a crime for a corporation to discharge a man because he voted differently and leave private individuals to do it. And they passed this law.

Let us look at this act, your honor. Here is a law which makes it a crime to teach evolution in the caption. I don't know whether we have discussed that or not, but it makes it a crime in the body of the act to teach any theory of the origin of man excepting that contained in the divine account, which we find in the Bible. All right. Now that act applies to what? Teachers in the public schools. Now I have seen somewhere a statement of Mr. Bryan's that the fellow that made the pay check had a right to regulate the teachers. All right, let us see. I do not question the right of the legislature to fix the courses of study, but the state of Tennessee has no right under the police power of the state to carve out a law which applies to schoolteachers, a law which is a criminal statute and nothing else; which makes no effort to prescribe the school law or course of study. It says that John Smith who teaches evolution is a criminal if he teaches it in the public schools. There is no question about this act; there is no question where it belongs; there is no question of its origin. Nobody would claim that the act could be passed for a minute excepting that teaching evolution was in the nature of a criminal act; that it smacked of policemen and criminals and jails and grand juries; that it was in the nature of something that was criminal and, therefore, the state should forbid it.

It cannot stand a minute in this court on any theory than that it is a criminal act, simply because they say it contravenes the teaching of Moses without telling us what those teachings are. Now, if this is the subject of a criminal act, then it cannot make a criminal out of a teacher in the public schools and leave a man free to teach it in a private school. It cannot make it criminal for a teacher in the public schools to teach evolution, and for the same man to stand among the hustings and teach it. It cannot make it a criminal act for this teacher to teach evolution and permit books upon evolution to be sold in every store in the state of Tennessee and to permit the newspapers from foreign cities to bring into your peaceful community the horrible utterances of evolution. Oh, no, nothing like that. If the state of Tennessee has any force in this day of fundamentalism, in this day when religious bigotry and hatred is being kindled all over our land, see what can be done?

Now, your honor, there is an old saying that nits make lice. I don't know whether you know what it makes possible down here in Tennessee? I know, I was raised in Ohio. It is a good idea to clear the nits, safer and easier.

To Strangle Puppies Is Good When They Grow Into Mad Dogs, Maybe

To strangle puppies is good when they grow up into mad dogs, maybe. I will tell you what is going to happen, and I do not pretend to be a prophet, but I do not need to be a prophet to know. Your honor knows the fires that have been lighted in America to kindle religious bigotry and hate. You can take judicial notice of them if you cannot of anything else. You know that there is no suspicion which possesses the minds of men like bigotry and ignorance and hatred.

If today—

The Court—Sorry to interrupt your argument, but it is adjourning time.

Mr. Darrow—If I may I can close in five minutes. I can close in five minutes in the morning, only a few.

If today, your honor—give me five minutes more, I will not talk five minutes.

The Court—Proceed tomorrow.

Mr. Darrow—I shall not talk long, your honor, I will tell you that.

If today you can take a thing like evolution and make it a crime to teach it in the public school, tomorrow you can make it a crime to teach it in the private schools, and the next year you can make it a crime to teach it to the hustings or in the church. At the next session you may ban books and the newspapers. Soon you may set Catholic against Protestant and Protestant against Protestant, and try to foist your own religion upon the minds of men. If you can do one you can do the other. Ignorance and fanaticism is ever busy and needs feeding. Always it is feeding and gloating for more. Today it is the public school teachers, tomorrow the private. The next day the preachers and the lecturers, the magazines, the books, the newspapers. After while, your honor, it is the setting of man against man and creed against creed until with flying banners and beating drums we are marching backward to the glorious ages of the sixteenth century when bigots lighted fagots to burn the men who dared to bring any intelligence and enlightenment and culture to the human mind.

Tomorrow I will say a few words.

The Court—You gentlemen send down your authorities to my room at the hotel—, on both sides, and your briefs, if you have such.

Court is adjourned to 9:00 o'clock tomorrow morning.

Document 18.4 Darrow Cross-Examines Bryan

This document, taken directly from the trial transcripts of *Tennessee v. Scopes*, is the stenographic transcription of the event. In this confrontation between defense attorney Clarence Darrow and prosecution attorney William Jennings Bryan, both lawyers try to discredit the other's case throughout the cross-examination. Through his questions, Darrow attacks a "literal" interpretation of the Bible. Conversely, Bryan ridicules the attacks, and tries to show how a Christian can provide convincing answers for any question asked by the advocates of evolution. The event took place at the end of the trial. When completed, the defense rested, refused to make a closing argument, and asked the jury for a guilty verdict. Their intention was to appeal the case.

Darrow's Examination of Bryan

Hays—The defense desires to call Mr. Bryan as a witness, and, of course, the only question here is whether Mr. Scopes taught what these children said he taught, we recognize what Mr. Bryan says as a witness would not be very valuable. We think there are other questions involved, and we should want to take Mr. Bryan's testimony for the purpose of our record, even if your honor thinks it is not admissible in general, so we wish to call him now.

The Court—Do you think you have a right to his testimony or evidence like you did these others?

McKenzie—I don't think it is necessary to call him, calling a lawyer who represents a client.

The Court—If you ask him about any confidential matter, I will protect him, of course.

Darrow—On scientific matters, Col. Bryan can speak for himself.

Bryan—If your honor please, I insist that Mr. Darrow can be put on the stand, and Mr. Malone and Mr. Hays.

The Court—Call anybody you desire. Ask them any questions you wish.

Bryan—Then, we will call all three of them.

Darrow—Not at once?

Bryan—Where do you want me to sit?

The Court—Mr. Bryan, you are not objecting to going on the stand?

Bryan—Not at all.

The Court—Do you want Mr. Bryan sworn?

Darrow—No.

Bryan—I can make affirmation; I can say "So help me God, I will tell the truth."

Darrow—No, I take it you will tell the truth, Mr. Bryan.

Examination of **W. J. Bryan** by **Clarence Darrow**, of counsel for the defense:

Q—You have given considerable study to the Bible, haven't you, Mr. Bryan?

A—Yes, sir, I have tried to.

Q—Then you have made a general study of it?

A—Yes, I have; I have studied the Bible for about fifty years, or sometime more than that, but, of course, I have studied it more as I have become older than when I was but a boy.

Q—You claim that everything in the Bible should be literally interpreted?

A—I believe everything in the Bible should be accepted as it is given there: some of the Bible is given illustratively. For instance: "Ye are the salt of the earth." I would not insist that man was actually salt, or that he had flesh of salt, but it is used in the sense of salt as saving God's people.

Q—But when you read that Jonah swallowed the whale—or that the whale swallowed Jonah— excuse me please—how do you literally interpret that?

A—When I read that a big fish swallowed Jonah—it does not say whale....That is my recollection of it. A big fish, and I believe it, and I believe in a God who can make a whale and can make a man and make both what He pleases.

Q—Now, you say, the big fish swallowed Jonah, and he there remained how long—three days— and then he spewed him upon the land. You believe that the big fish was made to swallow Jonah?

A—I am not prepared to say that; the Bible merely says it was done.

Q—You don't know whether it was the ordinary run of fish, or made for that purpose?

A—You may guess; you evolutionists guess.....

Q—You are not prepared to say whether that fish was made especially to swallow a man or not?

A—The Bible doesn't say, so I am not prepared to say.

Q—But do you believe He made them—that He made such a fish and that it was big enough to swallow Jonah?

A—Yes, sir. Let me add: One miracle is just as easy to believe as another.

Q—Just as hard?

A—It is hard to believe for you, but easy for me. A miracle is a thing performed beyond what man can perform. When you get within the realm of miracles; and it is just as easy to believe the miracle of Jonah as any other miracle in the Bible.

Q—Perfectly easy to believe that Jonah swallowed the whale?

A—If the Bible said so; the Bible doesn't make as extreme statements as evolutionists do....

Q—The Bible says Joshua commanded the sun to stand still for the purpose of lengthening the day, doesn't it, and you believe it?

A—I do.

Q—Do you believe at that time the entire sun went around the earth?

A—No, I believe that the earth goes around the sun.

Q—Do you believe that the men who wrote it thought that the day could be lengthened or that the sun could be stopped?

A—I don't know what they thought.

Q—You don't know?

A—I think they wrote the fact without expressing their own thoughts.

Q—Have you an opinion as to whether or not the men who wrote that thought—

Gen. Stewart—I want to object, your honor; it has gone beyond the pale of any issue that could possibly be injected into this lawsuit, except by imagination. I do not think the defendant has a right to conduct the examination any further and I ask your honor to exclude it.

The Witness—It seems to me it would be too exacting to confine the defense to the facts; if they are not allowed to get away from the facts, what have they to deal with?

The Court—Mr. Bryan is willing to be examined. Go ahead.

Mr. Darrow—I read that years ago. Can you answer my question directly? If the day was lengthened by stopping either the earth or the sun, it must have been the earth?

A—Well, I should say so.

Q—Now, Mr. Bryan, have you ever pondered what would have happened to the earth if it had stood still?

A—No.

Q—You have not?

A—No; the God I believe in could have taken care of that, Mr. Darrow.

Q—I see. Have you ever pondered what would naturally happen to the earth if it stood still suddenly?

A—No.

Q—Don't you know it would have been converted into molten mass of matter?

A—You testify to that when you get on the stand, I will give you a chance.

Q—Don't you believe it?

A—I would want to hear expert testimony on that.

Q—You have never investigated that subject?

A—I don't think I have ever had the question asked.

Q—Or ever thought of it?

A—I have been too busy on things that I thought were of more importance than that.

Q—You believe the story of the flood to be a literal interpretation?

A—Yes, sir.

Q—When was that Flood?

A—I would not attempt to fix the date. The date is fixed, as suggested this morning.

Q—About 4004 B.C.?

A—That has been the estimate of a man that is accepted today. I would not say it is accurate.

Q—That estimate is printed in the Bible?

A—Everybody knows, at least, I think most of the people know, that was the estimate given.

Q—But what do you think that the Bible, itself says? Don't you know how it was arrived at?

A—I never made a calculation.

Q—A calculation from what?

A—I could not say.

Q—From the generations of man?

A—I would not want to say that.

Q—What do you think?

A—I do not think about things I don't think about.

Q—Do you think about things you do think about?

A—Well, sometimes.

(Laughter in the courtyard.)

Policeman—Let us have order....

Stewart—Your honor, he is perfectly able to take care of this, but we are attaining no evidence. This is not competent evidence.

Witness—These gentlemen have not had much chance—they did not come here to try this case. They came here to try revealed religion. I am here to defend it and they can ask me any question they please.

The Court—All right.

(Applause from the court yard.)

Darrow—Great applause from the bleachers.

Witness—From those whom you call "Yokels."

Darrow—I have never called them yokels.

Witness—That is the ignorance of Tennessee, the bigotry.

Darrow—You mean who are applauding you? (Applause.)

Witness—Those are the people whom you insult.

Darrow—You insult every man of science and learning in the world because he does believe in your fool religion.

The Court—I will not stand for that.

Darrow—For what he is doing?

The Court—I am talking to both of you....

Q—Wait until you get to me. Do you know anything about how many people there were in Egypt 3,500 years ago, or how many people there were in China 5,000 years ago?

A—No.

Q—Have you ever tried to find out?

A—No, sir. You are the first man I ever heard of who has been in interested in it. (Laughter.)

Q—Mr. Bryan, am I the first man you ever heard of who has been interested in the age of human societies and primitive man?

A—You are the first man I ever heard speak of the number of people at those different periods.

Q—Where have you lived all your life?

A—Not near you. (Laughter and applause.)

Q—Nor near anybody of learning?

A—Oh, don't assume you know it all.

Q—Do you know there are thousands of books in our libraries on all those subjects I have been asking you about?

A—I couldn't say, but I will take your word for it....

Q—Have you any idea how old the earth is?

A—No.

Q—The Book you have introduced in evidence tells you, doesn't it?

A—I don't think it does, Mr. Darrow.

Q—Let's see whether it does; is this the one?

A—That is the one, I think.

Q—It says B.C. 4004?

A—That is Bishop Usher's calculation.

Q—That is printed in the Bible you introduced?

A—Yes, sir....

Q—Would you say that the earth was only 4,000 years old?

A—Oh, no; I think it is much older than that.

Q—How much?

A—I couldn't say.

Q—Do you say whether the Bible itself says it is older than that?

A—I don't think it is older or not.

Q—Do you think the earth was made in six days?

A—Not six days of twenty-four hours.

Q—Doesn't it say so?

A—No, sir....

The Court—Are you about through, Mr. Darrow?

Darrow—I want to ask a few more questions about the creation.

The Court—I know. We are going to adjourn when Mr. Bryan comes off the stand for the day. Be very brief, Mr. Darrow. Of course, I believe I will make myself clearer. Of course, it is incompetent testimony before the jury. The only reason I am allowing this to go in at all is that they may have it in the appellate court as showing what the affidavit would be.

Bryan—The reason I am answering is not for the benefit of the superior court. It is to keep these gentlemen from saying I was afraid to meet them and let them question me, and I want the Christian world to know that any atheist, agnostic, unbeliever, can question me anytime as to my belief in God, and I will answer him.

Darrow—I want to take an exception to this conduct of this witness. He may be very popular down here in the hills....

Bryan—Your honor, they have not asked a question legally and the only reason they have asked any question is for the purpose, as the question about Jonah was asked, for a chance to give this agnostic an opportunity to criticize a believer in the world of God; and I answered the question in order to shut his mouth so that he cannot go out and tell his atheistic friends that I would not answer his questions. That is the only reason, no more reason in the world.

Malone—Your honor on this very subject, I would like to say that I would have asked Mr. Bryan—and I consider myself as good a Christian as he is—every question that Mr. Darrow has asked him for the purpose of bringing out whether or not there is to be taken in this court a literal interpretation of the Bible, or whether, obviously, as these questions indicate, if a general and literal construction cannot be put upon the parts of the Bible which have been covered by Mr. Darrow's questions. I hope for the last time no further attempt will be made by counsel on the other side of the case, or Mr. Bryan, to say the defense is concerned at all with Mr. Darrow's particular religious views or lack of religious views. We are here as lawyers with the same right to our views. I have the same right to mine as a Christian as Mr. Bryan has to his, and we do not intend to have this case charged by Mr. Darrow's agnosticism or Mr. Bryan's brand of Christianity. (A great applause.)

Mr. Darrow:

Q—Mr. Bryan, do you believe that the first woman was Eve?

A—Yes.

Q—Do you believe she was literally made out of Adams's rib?

A—I do.

Q—Did you ever discover where Cain got his wife?

A—No, sir; I leave the agnostics to hunt for her.

Q—You have never found out?

A—I have never tried to find.

Q—You have never tried to find?

A—No.

Q—The Bible says he got one, doesn't it? Were there other people on the earth at that time?

A—I cannot say.

Q—You cannot say. Did that ever enter your consideration?

A—Never bothered me.

Q—There were no others recorded, but Cain got a wife.

A—That is what the Bible says.

Q—Where she came from you do not know. All right. Does the statement, "The morning and the evening were the first day," and "The morning and the evening were the second day," mean anything to you?

A— I do not think it necessarily means a twenty-four-hour day.

Q—You do not?

A—No.

Q—What do you consider it to be?

A—I have not attempted to explain it. If you will take the second chapter—let me have the book. (Examining Bible.) The fourth verse of the second chapter says: "These are the generations of the heavens and of the earth, when they were created in the day that the Lord God made the earth and the heavens," the word "day" there in the very next chapter is used to describe a period. I do not see that there is

any necessity for construing the words, "the evening and the morning," as meaning necessarily a twenty-four-hour day, "in the day when the Lord made the heaven and the earth."

Q—Then, when the Bible said, for instance, "and God called the firmament heaven. And the evening and the morning were the second day," that does not necessarily mean twenty-four hours?

A—I do not think it necessarily does.

Q—Do you think it does or does not?

A—I know a great many think so.

Q—What do you think?

A—I do not think it does.

Q—You think those were not literal days?

A—I do not think they were twenty-four-hour days.

Q—What do you think about it?

A—That is my opinion—I do not know that my opinion is better on that subject than those who think it does.

Q—You do not think that?

A—No. But I think it would be just as easy for the kind of God we believe in to make the earth in six days as in six years or in 6,000,000 years or in 600,000,000 years. I do not think it important whether we believe one or the other.

Q—Do you think those were literal days?

A—My impression is they were periods, but I would not attempt to argue as against anybody who wanted to believe in literal days.

Q—I will read it to you from the Bible: "And the Lord God said unto the serpent, because thou hast done this, thou art cursed above all cattle, and above every beast of the field; upon thy belly shalt thou go and dust shalt thou eat all the days of thy life." Do you think that is why the serpent is compelled to crawl upon its belly?

A—I believe that.

Q—Have you any idea how the snake went before that time?

A—No, sir.

Q—Do you know whether he walked on his tail or not?

A—No, sir. I have no way to know. (Laughter in audience).

Q—Now, you refer to the cloud that was put in heaven after the flood, the rainbow. Do you believe in that?

A—Read it.

Q—All right, Mr. Bryan, I will read it for you.

Bryan—Your Honor, I think I can shorten this testimony. The only purpose Mr. Darrow has is to slur at the Bible, but I will answer his question. I will answer it all at once, and I have no objection in the world, I want the world to know that this man, who does not believe in a God, is trying to use a court in Tennessee—

Darrow—I object to that.

Bryan—(Continuing) to slur at it, and while it will require time, I am willing to take it.

Darrow—I object to your statement. I am exempting you on your fool ideas that no intelligent Christian on earth believes.

The Court—Court is adjourned until 9 o'clock tomorrow morning.

Document 18.5 The Press Covers the Trial

This document is one of H.L. Mencken's reports from the trial. In it Mencken discusses his impressions of the religious beliefs in Dayton's citizens, and the effects those beliefs are likely to have on the trial. He also discusses the relationship between religious belief and knowledge. Mencken is hardly an objective observer—like most of the press at the trial, he was a partisan supporter of the defense. Darrow discussed the case with him before offering to join the defense team. Mencken was a nationally known correspondent for the *Baltimore Sun*; his reporting, editorials, and observations are still widely admired for their wit and incisiveness.

Mencken Likens Trial to a Religious Orgy, with Defendant a Beelzebub

by H.L. Mencken

Chattanooga, Tenn., July 11.

Life down here in the Cumberland mountains realizes almost perfectly the ideal of those righteous and devoted men, Dr. Howard A. Kelly, the Rev. Dr. W.W. Davis, the Hon. Richard H. Edmonds and the Hon. Henry S. Dulaney. That is to say, evangelical Christianity is one hundred per cent triumphant. There is, of course, a certain subterranean heresy, but it is so cowed that it is almost inarticulate, and at its worst it would pass for the strictest orthodoxy in such Sodoms of infidelity as Baltimore. It may seem fabulous, but it is a sober fact that a sound Episcopalian or even a Northern Methodist would be regarded as virtually an atheist in Dayton. Here the only genuine conflict is between true believers. Of a given text in Holy Writ one faction may say this thing and another that, but both agree unreservedly that the text itself is impeccable, and neither in the midst of the most violent disputation would venture to accuse the other of doubt.

To call a man a doubter in these parts is equal to accusing him of cannibalism. Even the infidel Scopes himself is not charged with any such infamy. What they say of him, at worst, is that he permitted himself to be used as a cat's paw by scoundrels eager to destroy the anti-evolution law for their own dark and hellish ends. There is, it appears, a conspiracy of scientists afoot. Their purpose is to break down religion, propagate immorality, and so reduce mankind to the level of the brutes. They are the sworn and sinister agents of Beelzebub, who yearns to conquer the world, and has his eye especially upon Tennessee. Scopes is thus an agent of Beelzebub once removed, but that is as far as any fair man goes in condemning him. He is young and yet full of folly. When the secular arm has done execution upon him, the pastors will tackle him and he will be saved.

The selection of a jury to try him, which went on all yesterday afternoon in the atmosphere of a blast furnace, showed to what extreme lengths the salvation of the local primates has been pushed. It was obvious after a few rounds that the jury would be unanimously hot for Genesis. The most that Mr. Darrow could hope for was to sneak in a few men bold enough to declare publicly that they would have to hear the evidence against Scopes before condemning

---

him. The slightest sign of anything further brought forth a peremptory challenge from the State. Once a man was challenged without examination for simply admitting that he did not belong formally to any church. Another time a panel man who confessed that he was prejudiced against evolution got a hearty round of applause from the crowd.

The whole process quickly took on an air of strange unreality, at least to a stranger from heathen parts. The desire of the judge to be fair to the defense, and even polite and helpful, was obvious enough—in fact, he more than once stretched the local rules of procedure in order to give Darrow a hand. But it was equally obvious that the whole thing was resolving itself into the trial of a man by his sworn enemies. A local pastor led off with a prayer calling on God to put down heresy; the judge himself charged the grand jury to protect the schools against subversive ideas. And when the candidates for the petit jury came up Darrow had to pass fundamentalist after fundamentalist into the box—some of them glaring at him as if they expected him to go off with a sulphurous bang every time he mopped his bald head.

In brief this is a strictly Christian community, and such is its notion of fairness, justice and due process of law. Try to picture a town made up wholly of Dr. Crabbes and Dr. Kellys, and you will have a reasonably accurate image of it. Its people are simply unable to imagine a man who rejects the literal authority of the Bible. The most they can conjure up, straining until they are red in the face, is a man who is in error about the meaning of this or that text. Thus one accused of heresy among them is like one accused of boiling his grandmother to make soap in Maryland. He must resign himself to being tried by a jury wholly innocent of any suspicion of the crime he is charged with and unanimously convinced that it is infamous. Such a jury, in the legal sense, may be fair. That is, it may be willing to hear the evidence against him before bumping him off. But it would certainly be spitting into the eye of reason to call it impartial.

The trial, indeed, takes on, for all its legal forms, something of the air of a religious orgy. The applause of the crowd I have already mentioned. Judge Raulston rapped it down and threatened to clear the room if it was repeated, but he was quite unable to still its echoes under his very windows. The courthouse is surrounded by a large lawn, and it is peppered day and night with evangelists. One and all they are fundamentalists and their yells and bawlings fill the air with orthodoxy. I have listened to twenty of them and had private discourse with a dozen, and I have yet to find one who doubted so much as the

typographical errors in Holy Writ. They dispute raucously and far into the night, but they begin and end on the common ground of complete faith. One of these holy men wears a sign on his back announcing that he is the Bible champion of the world. He told me today that he had studied the Bible four hours a day for thirty-three years, and that he had devised a plan of salvation that would save the worst sinner ever heard of, even a scientist, a theater actor or a pirate on the high seas, in forty days. This gentleman denounced the hard-shell Baptists as swindlers. He admitted freely that their sorcerers were powerful preachers and could save any ordinary man from sin, but he said that they were impotent against iniquity. The distinction is unknown to city theologians, but is as real down here as that between sanctification and salvation. The local experts, in fact, debate it daily. The Bible champion, just as I left him, was challenged by one such professor, and the two were still hard at it an hour later.

Most of the participants in such recondite combats, of course, are yokels from the hills, where no sound is heard after sundown save the roar of the catamount and the wailing of departed spirits, and a man thus has time to ponder the divine mysteries. But it is an amazing thing that the more polished classes also participate actively. The professor who challenged the Bible champion was indistinguishable, to the eye, from a bond salesman or city bootlegger. He had on a natty palm beach suit and a fashionable soft collar and he used excellent English. Obviously, he was one who had been through the local high school and perhaps a country college. Yet he was so far uncontaminated by infidelity that he stood in the hot sun for a whole hour debating a point that even bishops might be excused for dodging, winter as well as summer.

The Bible champion is matched and rivaled by whole herds of other metaphysicians, and all of them attract good houses and have to defend themselves against constant attack. The Seventh Day Adventists, the Campbellites, the Holy Rollers and a dozen other occult sects have field agents on the ground. They follow the traveling judges through all this country. Everywhere they go, I am told, they find the natives ready to hear them and dispute with them. They find highly accomplished theologians in every village, but even in the county towns they never encounter a genuine skeptic. If a man has doubts in this immensely pious country, he keeps them to himself.

Dr. Kelly should come down here and see his dreams made real. He will find a people who not only accept the Bible as an infallible handbook of history, geology, biology and celestial physics, but who also practice its moral precepts—at all events, up to the limit of human capacity. It would be hard to imagine a more moral town than Dayton. If it has any bootleggers, no visitor has heard of them. Ten minutes after I arrived a leading citizen offered me a drink made up half of white mule and half of coca cola, but he seems to have been simply indulging himself in a naughty gesture. No fancy woman has been seen in the town since the end of the McKinley administration. There is no gambling. There is no place to dance. The relatively wicked, when they would indulge themselves, go to Robinson's drug store and debate theology.

In a word, the new Jerusalem, the ideal of all soul savers and sin exterminators. Nine churches are scarcely enough for the 1,800 inhabitants: many of them go into the hills to shout and roll. A clergyman has the rank and authority of a major-general of artillery. A Sunday-school superintendent is believed to have the gift of prophecy. But what of life here? Is it more agreeable than in Babylon? I regret that I must have to report that it is not. The incessant clashing of theologians grows monotonous in a day and intolerable the day following. One longs for a merry laugh, a burst of happy music, the gurgle of a decent jug. Try a meal in the hotel; it is tasteless and swims in grease. Go to the drug store and call for refreshment: the boy will hand you almost automatically a beaker of coca cola. Look at the magazine counter: a pile of *Saturday Evening Posts* two feet high. Examine the books: melodrama and cheap amour. Talk to a town magnifico; he knows nothing that is not in Genesis.

I propose that Dr. Kelly be sent here for sixty days, preferably in the heat of summer. He will return to Baltimore yelling for a carboy of pilsner and eager to master the saxophone. His soul perhaps will be lost, but he will be a merry and a happy man.

Chapter 18 Worksheet and Questions

1. The Case for the Prosecution: Based upon Document 18.1 (Bryan, "God and Evolution") and Document 18.2 (Bryan at the Scopes Trial), what is Bryan's case or argument against the teaching of evolution in public schools? Be sure to mention his reasons for doubting the truth of evolution, the effects of teaching evolution, and his views of who should decide what is taught in the public schools.

_____

_____

_____

_____

_____

_____

_____

_____

2. The Case for the Defense: Based upon Document 18.3 (Darrow Addresses the Court for the Defense), and Document 18.5 (Mencken, "Mencken Likens Trial to a Religious Orgy, with Defendant a Beelzebub"), what is Darrow's and the defense team's case against banning the teaching of evolution in the public schools? Be sure to discuss the role of religion, the progress of human knowledge, and the effects of prohibiting the teaching of evolution.

_____

_____

_____

_____

_____

_____

_____

_____

3. Characterizing the Opposition: Based upon Documents 18.1, 18.2, 18.3, and 18.5. Both Bryan and Darrow believed that, in addition to winning the Scopes Trial, it was crucial to win over popular opinion. One way they did that was to create an image or characterization of their opponents. Compare the way the defense and prosecution describe their opponents.

_____

_____

_____

_____

_____

_____

_____

_____

_____

4. The Constitution and the Trial: Based upon Documents 18.1, 18.2, 18.3, and 18.5. Darrow and the defense expected to lose the Scopes Trial and appeal the decision to a higher court. In the appeal, they expected the court to declare that the Butler Act was unconstitutional because it expressed a particular religious view, which violated the First Amendment. The defense never had an opportunity to make that argument, because the appeals court dismissed the case. Both the defense and the prosecution did discuss religion during the trial, however. Do either Darrow or Bryan believe that religion should be taught in the public schools? Why or why not?

_____

_____

_____

_____

_____

_____

_____

_____

5. Religion and Science: Based upon Document 18.4 (Darrow Cross-Examines Bryan).
    Look carefully at the kinds of questions Darrow asks Bryan, and the way Bryan responds to them. Is the main issue the "literal truth" of the Bible? Could you conclude that the defense team took the position of Liberal Protestants? What position did Bryan take–Day Age, Gap theory, or Flood geology? Why? Would it be fair to say that the position Christians take in the debate about evolution is based upon the way they interpret the Bible?

    _____

    _____

    _____

    _____

    _____

    _____

    _____

    _____

6. Conclusions: Based upon all the documents. Assume you were asked to serve as a judge in the debate between science and religion. Would you side with Bryan and the prosecution, or with Darrow and the defense? Why?

    _____

    _____

    _____

    _____

    _____

    _____

    _____

    _____

The Era of the Great Depression and the New Deal: The Impact on American Society

The Great Depression was an economic catastrophe that crippled the entire industrialized world in the early twentieth century. Spanning ten years, it was the longest and most devastating depression experienced in the Western World. Although other nations were affected by the economic shock, America felt the brunt of the Depression. Americans lost their life savings; young people, known as hobos and sisters of the road, took to the streets, as a cloud of hopelessness loomed over American communities.

In October 1929, the U.S. stock market collapsed, sending a catastrophic wave throughout the country. From 1929 to1931, the stock prices in America continued to plummet, and by 1932 stocks were worthless, having dropped to roughly 20 percent of their value before the Crash. Banks were collapsing at record rates. America's manufacturing output had fallen to 54 percent of its capacity in 1929, and the unemployment rate consisted of 25 to 30 percent of the work force. By 1933 nearly 50 percent of the U.S. banks had failed. This failure, coupled with the general loss of confidence in the economy, led to reduced spending, resulting in low demand and production, thus creating a downward spiral.

Americans tended to lay the blame for the Great Depression on President Herbert Hoover's passivity. At the onset of the Depression, Hoover believed that high and steady wages would usher in recovery. Overall, he believed that it was the duty of state and local governments to handle the brunt of the responsibility for recovery. The workforce held steady for a few months, but soon there was a decline in wages and output. Hoover's recovery initiative in 1932, the establishment of the Reconstruction Finance Corporation (RFC), provided a means for banks to extend loans to clients. However, some felt that giving government credit to banks for extending loans was more beneficial to bankers than to the average citizen. Ultimately, Hoover's attempt to restore confidence in the American economy failed—there simply was not enough money available to support such massive undertakings.

The election of 1932 marked a new beginning in American history and politics. The presidential debate focused on the causes and potential remedies for the Great Depression. Franklin D. Roosevelt, then governor of New York, believed that the Depression stemmed from flaws in the economy, stirred by Republican politics during the decade of the 1920s. Roosevelt, unlike Hoover, anticipated full use of the federal government's power and authority to provide courageous, experimental remedies to cure the country's economic woes.

By the time the election took place in 1932, the American people were engrossed in a paralyzing fear because of economic conditions. Roosevelt won the election by a landslide, and in the spring of 1933, attempted to restore confidence in the American people through reforms. "The only thing we have to fear is fear itself," FDR declared in his inaugural address to the nation. Ushering in an air of optimism, Roosevelt rallied the American public to embrace his program, known as the "New Deal."

Endearing himself to the American people, FDR communicated with the American public through a series of radio addresses known as the "Fireside Chats." He used this medium feverishly to implement program after program in an attempt to provide relief, create jobs, and stimulate the economy. Although FDR's acts were well intentioned, they were not enough; the economy failed to emerge from the Great Depression. From 1932 to 1938, there was public debate regarding the New Deal policies and their effects on politics and economics. Americans wanted the government to take more responsibility for the recovery of the nation, but there were those who were leery of granting too much power to the federal government. By the end of FDR's second term, domestic issues were overshadowed by the horrors of war in Europe and Asia. It wasn't until World War II that the American economy began to recover.

As a result of the Japanese attack on Pearl Harbor, Congress declared war on Japan; three days later, Germany and Italy declared war on the United States. Americans heeded the call to national defense. The United States geared itself for mobilization. Resources related to farming, manufacturing, communications, and other undertakings were in part placed under the auspices of the federal government. By 1943, some 65 million men and women were in uniform, and the official unemployment rate fell below 10 percent.

The following documents include primary sources covering the era of the Great Depression and the New Deal.

Considering the Evidence in the Readings

It is important for the reader to evaluate the effects of the Great Depression on all American citizens. The documents in this chapter have been selected from two groups the Executive branch of Franklin Delano Roosevelt's administration and the African American response to the New Deal. The readings, including FDR's inaugural address and his outline for the New Deal initiatives, address Roosevelt's philosophy of hope and prosperity as he attempts to restore the American confidence both politically and economically.

Other selections, from the African American perspective, reflect on the experiences of minorities under FDR's administration. A narrative by Luther C. Wandall shares his experience in the Civilian Conservation Corps. Noted author and poet, Langston Hughes, responds to the times in his poem, entitled "Ballad of Roosevelt."

One of the criticisms of the New Deal was that the programs did not go far enough in relieving the economic burden under which the people labored, and that there were inequities in the treatment of white and black Americans. As you read the documents, ask yourself whether or not Roosevelt restored America's confidence. Were there shortcomings in the New Deal initiatives? If so, what were they?

Document 19.1 FDR's First Inaugural Address

On March 4, 1933, Franklin D. Roosevelt addressed the nation, inspiring and giving hope; the most famous line from his speech is… "the only thing we have to fear is fear itself." FDR attempts to galvanize the American public to move beyond fear of the Great Depression. Roosevelt commits himself and the administration to take necessary action and put people to work. There is also a plan to bring order to the nation's banking system. Roosevelt affirms the administration's responsibility in "putting our own national house in order" over international issues which "are in point of time and necessity secondary."

First Inaugural Address
Franklin Delano Roosevelt

(Saturday, March 4, 1933: Washington, DC)

I am certain that my fellow Americans expect that on my induction into the Presidency I will address them with a candor and a decision which the present situation of our Nation impels. This is preeminently the time to speak the truth, the whole truth, frankly and boldly. Nor need we shrink from honestly facing conditions in our country today. This great Nation will endure as it has endured, will revive and will prosper. So, first of all, let me assert my firm belief that the only thing we have to fear is fear itself— nameless, unreasoning, unjustified terror which paralyzes needed efforts to convert retreat into advance. In every dark hour of our national life a leadership of frankness and vigor has met with that understanding and support of the people themselves which is essential to victory. I am convinced that you will again give that support to leadership in these critical days.

In such a spirit on my part and on yours we face our common difficulties. They concern, thank God, only material things. Values have shrunken to fantastic levels; taxes have risen; our ability to pay has fallen; government of all kinds is faced by serious curtailment of income; the means of exchange are frozen in the currents of trade; the withered leaves of industrial enterprise lie on every side; farmers find no markets for their produce; the savings of many years in thousands of families are gone.

More important, a host of unemployed citizens face the grim problem of existence, and an equally great number toil with little return. Only a foolish optimist can deny the dark realities of the moment.

Yet our distress comes from no failure of substance. We are stricken by no plague of locusts. Compared with the perils which our forefathers conquered because they believed and were not afraid, we have still much to be thankful for. Nature still offers her bounty and human efforts have multiplied it. Plenty is at our doorstep, but a generous use of it languishes in the very sight of the supply. Primarily this is because the rulers of the exchange of mankind's goods have failed, through their own stubbornness and their own incompetence, have admitted their failure, and abdicated. Practices of the unscrupulous money changers stand indicted in the court of public opinion, rejected by the hearts and minds of men.

True they have tried, but their efforts have been cast in the pattern of an outworn tradition. Faced by failure of credit they have proposed only the lending of more money. Stripped of the lure of profit by which to induce our people to follow their false leadership, they have resorted to exhortations, pleading tearfully for restored confidence. They know only the rules of a generation of self-seekers. They have no vision, and when there is no vision the people perish.

The money changers have fled from their high seats in the temple of our civilization. We may now restore that temple to the ancient truths. The measure of the restoration lies in the extent to which we apply social values more noble than mere monetary profit.

Happiness lies not in the mere possession of money; it lies in the joy of achievement, in the thrill of creative effort. The joy and moral stimulation of work no longer must be forgotten in the mad chase of evanescent profits. These dark days will be worth all they cost us if they teach us that our true destiny is not to be ministered unto but to minister to ourselves and to our fellow men.

Recognition of the falsity of material wealth as the standard of success goes hand in hand with the abandonment of the false belief that public office and high political position are to be valued only by the standards of pride of place and personal profit; and there must be an end to a conduct in banking and in business which too often has given to a sacred trust the likeness of callous and selfish wrongdoing. Small wonder that confidence languishes, for it thrives only on honesty, on honor, on the sacredness of obligations, on faithful protection, on unselfish performance; without them it cannot live.

Restoration calls, however, not for changes in ethics alone. This Nation asks for action, and action now.

Our greatest primary task is to put people to work. This is no unsolvable problem if we face it wisely and courageously. It can be accomplished in part by direct recruiting by the Government itself, treating the task as we would treat the emergency of a war, but at the same time, through this employment, accomplishing greatly needed projects to stimulate and reorganize the use of our natural resources.

Hand in hand with this we must frankly recognize the overbalance of population in our industrial centers and, by engaging on a national scale in a redistribution, endeavor to provide a better use of the land for those best fitted for the land. The task can be helped by definite efforts to raise the values of agricultural products and with this the power to purchase the output of our cities. It can be helped by preventing realistically the tragedy of the growing loss through foreclosure of our small homes and our farms. It can be helped by insistence that the Federal, State, and local governments act forthwith on the demand that their cost be drastically reduced. It can be helped by the unifying of relief activities which today are often scattered, uneconomical, and unequal. It can be helped by national planning for and supervision of all forms of transportation and of communications and other utilities which have a definitely public character. There are many ways in which it can be helped, but it can never be helped merely by talking about it. We must act and act quickly.

Finally, in our progress toward a resumption of work we require two safeguards against a return of the evils of the old order; there must be a strict supervision of all banking and credits and investments; there must be an end to speculation with other people's money, and there must be provision for an adequate but sound currency.

There are the lines of attack. I shall presently urge upon a new Congress in special session detailed measures for their fulfillment, and I shall seek the immediate assistance of the several States.

Through this program of action we address ourselves to putting our own national house in order and making income balance outgo. Our international trade relations, though vastly important, are in point of time and necessity secondary to the establishment of a sound national economy. I favor as a practical policy the putting of first things first. I shall spare no effort to restore world trade by international economic readjustment, but the emergency at home cannot wait on that accomplishment.

The basic thought that guides these specific means of national recovery is not narrowly nationalistic. It is the insistence, as a first consideration, upon the interdependence of the various elements in all parts of the United States—a recognition of the old and permanently important manifestation of the American spirit of the pioneer. It is the way to recovery. It is the immediate way. It is the strongest assurance that the recovery will endure.

In the field of world policy I would dedicate this Nation to the policy of the good neighbor—the neighbor who resolutely respects himself and, because he does so, respects the rights of others—the neighbor who respects his obligations and respects the sanctity of his agreements in and with a world of neighbors.

If I read the temper of our people correctly, we now realize as we have never realized before our interdependence on each other; that we can not merely take but we must give as well; that if we are to go forward, we must move as a trained and loyal army willing to sacrifice for the good of a common discipline, because without such discipline no progress is made, no leadership becomes effective. We are, I know, ready and willing to submit our lives and property to such discipline, because it makes possible a leadership which aims at a larger good. This I propose to offer, pledging that the larger purposes will bind upon us all as a sacred obligation with a unity of duty hitherto evoked only in time of armed strife.

With this pledge taken, I assume unhesitatingly the leadership of this great army of our people dedicated to a disciplined attack upon our common problems.

Action in this image and to this end is feasible under the form of government which we have inherited from our ancestors. Our Constitution is so simple and practical that it is possible always to meet extraordinary needs by changes in emphasis and arrangement without loss of essential form. That is why our constitutional system has proved itself the most superbly enduring political mechanism the modern world has produced. It has met every stress of vast expansion of territory, of foreign wars, of bitter internal strife, of world relations.

It is to be hoped that the normal balance of executive and legislative authority may be wholly adequate to meet the unprecedented task before us. But it may be that an unprecedented demand and need for undelayed action may call for temporary departure from that normal balance of public procedure.

I am prepared under my constitutional duty to recommend the measures that a stricken nation in the midst of a stricken world may require. These measures, or such other measures as the Congress may build out of its experience and wisdom, I shall seek, within my constitutional authority, to bring to speedy adoption.

But in the event that the Congress shall fail to take one of these two courses, and in the event that the national emergency is still critical, I shall not evade the clear course of duty that will then confront me. I shall ask the Congress for the one remaining instrument to meet the crisis—broad Executive power to wage a war against the emergency, as great as the power that would be given to me if we were in fact invaded by a foreign foe.

For the trust reposed in me I will return the courage and the devotion that befit the time. I can do no less.

We face the arduous days that lie before us in the warm courage of the national unity; with the clear consciousness of seeking old and precious moral values; with the clean satisfaction that comes from the stern performance of duty by old and young alike. We aim at the assurance of a rounded and permanent national life.

We do not distrust the future of essential democracy. The people of the United States have not failed. In their need they have registered a mandate that they want direct, vigorous action. They have asked for discipline and direction under leadership. They have made me the present instrument of their wishes. In the spirit of the gift I take it.

In this dedication of a Nation we humbly ask the blessing of God. May He protect each and every one of us. May He guide me in the days to come.

Document 19.2 Greeting to the Civilian Conservation Corps

The New Deal is a general term used by FDR outlining his programs that attempted to provide domestic relief during the Great Depression. The Civilian Conservation Corp (CCC) was created within the first 100 days of Roosevelt's administration, to provide work for America's young men. The goal of the CCC was for the young men to undertake a multitude of conservation and forestry projects. The following document expresses FDR's gratitude for their role in fighting the Depression.

Franklin D. Roosevelt

Greetings to the Civilian Conservation Corps

July 8, 1933

I welcome the opportunity to extend, through the medium of the columns of Happy Days, a greeting to the men who constitute the Civilian Conservation Corps.

Congratulations are due those responsible for the successful accomplishment of the gigantic task of creating the camps, arranging for the enlistments and launching the greatest peacetime movement this country has ever seen.

It is my belief that what is being accomplished will conserve our natural resources, create future national wealth and prove of moral and spiritual value not only to those of you who are taking part, but to the rest of the country as well.

You young men who are enrolled in this work are to be congratulated as well. It is my honest conviction that what you are doing in the way of constructive service will bring to you, personally and individually, returns the value of which it is difficult to estimate. Physically fit, as demonstrated by the examinations you took before entering the camps, the clean life and hard work in which you are engaged cannot fail to help your physical condition and you should emerge from this experience strong and rugged and ready for a reentrance into the ranks of industry, better equipped than before. Opportunities for employment in work; for which individually you are best suited are increasing daily and you should emerge from this experience splendidly equipped for the competitive fields of endeavor which always marl; the industrial life of America.

I want to congratulate you on the opportunity you have and to express to you my appreciation for the hearty cooperation which you have given this movement which is so vital a step in the Nation's fight against the depression and to wish you all a pleasant, wholesome and constructively helpful stay in the woods.

Document 19.3 "Waitin' on Roosevelt"

"Paradox" and "bitter-sweet" are terms that can describe the relationship between President Roosevelt and the African-American community. Roosevelt was not a Civil Rights president—segregation was an accepted practice in this country, and discrimination was commonplace; however, he won the African American vote. Some Blacks were critical of Roosevelt. Langston Hughes, a literary figure during the time, was a Socialist, and had spent time in the Soviet Union publishing works that supported the Communist cause. The following poem criticizes FDR for his broken promises to the poor.

From *New Republic*, November 14, 1934 by Langston Hughes.

"Waitin' on Roosevelt"

Langston Hughes's "Ballad of Roosevelt"

Ballad of Roosevelt
The pot was empty,
The cupboard was bare.
I said, Papa,
What's the matter here?
I'm waitin' on Roosevelt, son,
Roosevelt, Roosevelt,
Waitin' on Roosevelt, son.
The rent was due,
And the lights was out.
I said, Tell me, Mama,
What's it all about?
We're waitin' on Roosevelt, son,
Roosevelt, Roosevelt,
Just waitin' on Roosevelt.
Sister got sick
And the doctor wouldn't come
Cause we couldn't pay him
The proper sum—
A-waitin on Roosevelt,
Roosevelt, Roosevelt,
A-waitin' on Roosevelt.
Then one day
They put us out o' the house.
Ma and Pa was Meek as a mouse
Still waitin' on Roosevelt,

Roosevelt, Roosevelt.
But when they felt those
Cold winds blow
And didn't have no
Place to go
Pa said, I'm tired
O'waitin' on Roosevelt,
Roosevelt, Roosevelt.
Damn tired o' waitin' on Roosevelt.
I can't git a job
And I can't git no grub.
Backbone and navel's
Doin' the belly-rub—
A-waitin' on Roosevelt,
Roosevelt, Roosevelt.
And a lot o' other folks
What's hungry and cold
Done stopped believin'
What they been told
By Roosevelt,
Roosevelt, Roosevelt—
Cause the pot's still empty,
And the cupboard's still bare,
And you can't build a
bungalow
Out o' air—
Mr. Roosevelt, listen!
What's the matter here?

Document 19.4 "The Problem of Unemployment"

In January 1935, Aubrey Williams, Assistant Works Progress Administrator and executive Director of the National Youth Administration (NYA), gave a status report on the New Deal initiatives. Williams expresses his gratitude to the various agencies for their roles in helping America during a time of crisis. In addition to discussing the success of the NYA and other New Deal initiatives, Williams also points out the shortcomings. One of the strategies outlined is "the program of economic assurance against unemployment, old age, and sickness." Pay attention to the statistical data that is offered.

The Problem of Unemployment

Aubrey Williams

The full text of an address by Aubrey W. Williams, Assistant Works Progress Administrator and executive Director of the National Youth Administration, before the Buffalo Council of Social Agencies, Wednesday night, January 15, in the Statler Hotel, follows:

I am pleased with the opportunity of speaking before the Buffalo Council Agencies, for yours is a group with which I feel at home. By your training and the character of your work, I feel that you are gifted with the clearest perception of any professional group in the country of the problems which face America's millions of unemployed. By virtue of that fact I can approach you this evening on a basis of common understanding, for we are all working with the same tools toward common goal.

You and I know that the problem of unemployment does not stem directly from industrial depression. Depression aggravates unemployment and in the present instance has brought it to a nearly unbearable intensity. We know instead that it was spawned in an era of giddy expansionism; that it is an inescapable concomitant of our type of civilization, and that its roots are now sunk in the very bedrock of our capitalist society.

I do not think you will accuse me of pessimism when I say that unemployment—or better, disemployment—is, like the airplane, the radio, the weather and taxes, here to stay. Millions of those now out of jobs will never find jobs again. Thousands of young men and women leaving our schools each year are destined never to become self-supporting and independent in the sense that your and my generation were led to believe was our due.

The supply of workers exceeds the demand. Man power is a drag on the market. The productive forces of this country, are glutted with brawn and brain which they cannot use. And what can't be utilized, is simply laid aside to moulder and decay. Look about you and you'll see what I mean, Look at the case histories in your files and see the splendid, capable, intelligent workers for whom there are no jobs. Thumb through the cards in the National Reemployment Service. Look into the haggard faces of those who haunt the factory gates and the employment offices.

Civilization has done a great job of marching ahead in the last fifty years but it has been to the harsh, metallic beat of engines. Man has been thrust aside to make way for the machines, and the human carnage has not been reckoned. The stretch-out, the speed-up, and the soul-destroying regimentation of the production line are the grim symbols of our progress, and as they have been applied, a toll in human values has been taken.

Equally distorted has been the distribution of our national income, giving to our country today that inhumane paradox of need in the midst of plenty.

Is proof of these phenomena lacking? Turn to the United States Department of Labor, the files of the A. F. of L., the research findings of the Brookings Institution, the National Industrial Conference, and scores of the most able economists and sociologists in the land. Cumulative, progressive unemployment has been in progress since before the World War. Production methods have been steadily in favor of the machines as against human labor in practically any field you can name. Production ratios have doubled, trebled, and quadrupled while employment indices have remained static.

Incomes and the national wealth, meanwhile, have funneled into the coffers of the few. While 70 percent of our people are obliged to live in poverty on incomes of less than $1,500 a year—a sum insufficient to maintain health and decency for a family of five— a mere one-sixth of one percent of our people are privileged to enjoy the luxuries and good things of life which can be bought with incomes of $7,500 a year or more. Even in 1929, that false-faced Nirvana toward which the Bourbons still yearn, the Brookings Institution has revealed not more than ten percent of all our people were financially able to enjoy a liberal diet.

Now, these distressing conditions were not built up over night. They have been accumulating for the last fifty years when our physical frontiers were reached and overrun. Unseen for the most part save by a few inspired prophets whose warnings we scorned, they hung like the sword of Damocles over our heads, until the slender thread snapped in the fall of 1929.

Similarly, the damage is not to be repaired off hand. We have a long job of reconstruction ahead and as we build anew we must build for permanence. We must recognize that our cherished American liberties are but a pretense so long as three-fourths of our people do not know the meaning of security; when ten millions of our workers are denied the right to earn a living; while thousands of parents sit with helpless, folded hands while their children waste away from hunger.

It is along the line of a permanent correction of these inequalities that the Roosevelt New Deal has moved. Our efforts were clumsy at first, as naturally would result from attempting so momentous a task with not a single precedent or pattern to go by. But at least the direction was clear: it was not to spend the government's millions in salvaging railroads, banks, and insurance companies alone, but to spend them as well for the salvaging of human beings. For the first time in any national administration, President Roosevelt has thrown the spotlight of emphasis on human rather than material values.

The wails of protest from Park Avenue and Wall Street have, as you know, been piteous. I am fascinated by the glib wizardry of those who would care for these dispossessed millions and at the same time balance the budget, reduce taxes, end the war in Ethiopia and produce prosperity like a long eared rabbit from an opera hat. Theirs is the wistful, wishful thinking of adolescence.

You will be interested in some of the details of the very comprehensive picture we have been able to draw concerning our relief population. The trend of unemployment, the natural precursor of relief status, leaped upward from approximately 3,000,000 in March 1929, to an all-time high of 15,000,000 in the same month of 1933, when the present administration came into power. Last March, the estimates had dropped to 12,000,000, and today most reliable sources place the number of jobless at 10,000,000.

Relief trends followed those of unemployment, increasing from somewhere in the neighborhood of 400,000 in March 1929—a figure which we will never know with exactness—to about 18,000,000 in March 1933. With the introduction of organized Federal aid in that year, and as family resources among the unemployed finally broke under the long strain of joblessness, the number continued to increase until in January 1935, we had our maximum relief burden of 20,654,000 men, women and children, As of last May, one in every six persons in the cities, and one in every eight persons in the rural areas, were dependent upon public funds for support. The greatest proportion of these were under 20 years of age, while the next largest age group was that from 20 to 40—the period of greatest employability. Twenty-seven percent of all persons on relief were at that age when vitality and earning capacity should have been at its very peak, yet they were broke and without jobs, facing a hopeless future.

We have learned a great many other things about our relief group—where and in what sort of houses they live; their former usual occupations; the extent of their training and education; their general health status; their present employability, and many other details of their lives, character and capacities. We are able to answer with a defiant and emphatic "No!" those scornful critics who would make out our relief people to be idlers, wasters, and malingerers. We know that there are triflers in the lot, but by and large they are the same honest, industrious workers who contributed to America's prosperity of the 1920's. There are bankers, lawyers, architects, and ministers in the group as well as carpenters, bricklayers, farmers and laborers. A cross section of the relief rolls today would reveal a hardly discernible difference from any other segment of American life save for the one factor of dependence.

It was a tremendous statistical job to develop this picture on a national scale, but it had to be done if we were to use intelligent, long-range planning. This planning has assumed two general forms—employment at security wages for those who have been on relief, and the program of economic assurance against unemployment, old age, and sickness as embodied in the Social Security Act. Let's consider them separately and see to what extent they meet the needs imposed by the inequalities of civilization today.

Four billion, eight hundred million dollars were made available at the last session of Congress to take 3,500,000 Americans off the relief rolls. The dole was to be obliterated and relief clients were to be given jobs on constructive public works at wages on which they could decently support themselves and their families. That appropriation was bitterly fought when it was proposed and has been bitterly fought ever since, particularly by those who persist in thinking in terms of their own pocketbooks instead of the lives and welfare of other people. They would have perpetuated the dole because it was cheaper and would have ignored the waste of human values, the degradation, the smouldering resentment in honest hearts which such a system cannot help but inspire.

Now, what has the WPA done with its money? How much of it has gone into "boondoggling" and other channels of waste, inefficiency, or graft?

It should be borne in mind that the WPA did not get the entire four billion dollar fund. Not by any means. Only about 37 percent, or $1,082,900,000, went to that agency. The balance was distributed between the CCC, which got over $500,000,000, and certain other regular Government departments. Among the latter, the Department of Agriculture received over $500,000,000, the Public Works Administration $444,000,000 the Department of the Interior $118,000,000, the War Department $142,000,000, and so on.

As for the WPA's share, it is a simple matter to see to what purpose it is being put. Forty-two and one-half per cent of the entire fund has been earmarked for highway, road, and street projects. There are 20,950 such projects with an aggregate cost of $455,055,892 already in operation or soon to be begun. Parks and playgrounds account for another 11.8 per cent, public buildings for 9.2 per cent, water supply and sewer systems for 9.1 per cent, flood control and other conservation projects for 5.9 per cent, sewing rooms and other production projects for 6.1 per cent, and white collar projects for 5.8 per cent.

Well, that list accounts for 90 per cent of all the funds allotted to the WPA and we haven't even touched on the health and sanitation projects, the airports, and a number of other groups of equal importance. I don't think any fair observer could complain of public funds being, spent for such meritorious purposes as these.

Now think what these undertakings mean to the communities in which they are operating. In practically every case you will find that the work being done is some essential construction or service which the community has long wanted but been unable to accomplish out of its own budget. Take your own state of New York, exclusive of New York City, and let's see what the program is doing here. One hundred fifty-eight thousand of your people have been given employment at wages ranging from $44 to $103 per month. One hundred thirty-four thousand of them are working for the WPA 16,000 of them are in the CCC and approximately 8,000 of them are engaged on projects sponsored by regular Governmental departments.

Forty-seven million, one hundred thirty-eight thousand dollars have been set aside to carry on the WPA program here, again, remember, exclusive of New York City. Forty-three per cent of this money is going into the building of new roads and streets and the maintenance of those already built. Farm-to-market roads, feeders from the hinterlands to the main arteries of traffic which will be passable throughout the year, constitute a large part of this highway work. Fourteen and one-half per cent of the money is being spent in the development of parks, playgrounds, swimming pools, not only for the children of such cities as Buffalo but for those in smaller towns and rural districts as well. Public building projects, which means, predominantly, schools, account for nine per cent of the funds. Not only are new schools being built, but thousands of gallons of paint, miles of roofing, millions of feet of lumber, and tons of brick, cement and steel are being used to make repairs and alterations which your school boards have long desired, but been unable to have.

A little over six per cent of the funds to be spent in New York State are going into projects for professional and non-manual workers—white-collar people. Old, worn out court records are being recopied to withstand hard use, tax maps remade and brought up to date, surveys and studies of a dozen different kinds being carried or which will add materially to the value of services rendered by your various public bodies.

In Buffalo alone, $137,000 is being spent to provide much needed additional personnel in your public libraries. Another $44,000 is being used to employ extra help at the City Hospital in order to expand the services of its out-patient department. Many of your unemployed writers, artists, and musicians have been placed on projects where their talents will add to the cultural value of life. Such a list as this hardly scratches the surface of the varied activities which are being carried on in this field, yet it has been called "boondoggling," and as such is the favorite target of the critics.

Turning to the national scene again, we see that the youth of the country has not been forgotten. Fifty million dollars of WPA funds were set aside last June for the creation of the National Youth Administration so that young people in this particularly difficult period might not come to their majority under the blight of joblessness and destitution.

Up to this time we are maintaining more than 300,000 young people between the ages of 16 and 25 in high schools and colleges throughout the nation. Four thousand of them are pursuing graduate work on benefits averaging $25 a month. One hundred thousand are undergraduate students in some 1,600 colleges and universities and are receiving average benefits of $15 a month. Another 200,000 are students in high schools and are receiving $6 a month each. These, as you know, are not honorariums, but represent wages earned for constructive work in or about the schools and communities.

A little more than half of our $50,000,000 is being thus expended. The remainder is being applied as wages on work projects for those young people for whom further schooling is impossible or inadvisable. Special projects designed for young people have been set up in every state. Many of these have training as the predominant element. In other cases, young people are being employed part-time on regular WPA projects at one-third of the regular security wage. Many offices of the United States Employment Service have added young people to their staffs to seek particularly those jobs which are generally recognized as belonging to youth, and we are co-operating in full with the Federal Committee on Apprentice Training to place unemployed young people in apprentice jobs.

General control of the WPA program is retained in Washington. This, you will agree, is essential where one and not 48 separate objectives are sought. But the administration of the program, the shaping and fitting of plans and policies to the needs of individual localities, has been left with the various state and district administrators. Contrary to a belief which seems to have become general, there is no autocratic control vested in Washington. The greatest flexibility has been allowed the states to fit the program to their own needs, and it is, essentially, a state program in each state.

Localities design the types of projects they want. They are built around community needs and the abilities of the young people on relief. The communities contribute what they can toward the cost, and the project application is forwarded through local WPA headquarters to Washington. There it is judged in the light of certain essential requirements as to social and economic desirability, employment value, and cost. If these specifications are met, it is turned over to the Comptroller General for financial inspection, and finally to the Treasury for the actual allocation of funds. All along the line, greatest care is exerted to see that each project not only provides the requisite number of jobs, but constitutes a work or service of definite public value.

The WPA set out to remove the curse of the dole from American life and to substitute in its place honest jobs at honest rates of pay in which the unemployed might not only achieve a decent standard of living but retain their self-respect as well. In this I believe we are succeeding and I do not believe that a one of you here will tell me that our philosophy is wrong.

As to social security, the other half of our long-range program, I shall not go into detail. Briefly, it embodies unemployment compensation, old-age security, security for dependent children, aid to the blind, extension of public health services and vocational rehabilitation. It is much in the public prints at this time and most of you are familiar with its general procedure. I do wish to point out, however, how it and the WPA program of providing jobs for the unemployed complement one another and work to the greater security of the average American citizen.

I think I can be as lusty in my praise of America and American form of government as any professional patriot who ever waved a flag or damned a Communist, but I cannot blind myself to the abuses which have arisen about us. I cannot condone the inequalities, the injustices or the mass social crimes which have been perpetuated under the guise of American freedom and liberty. I get small consolation in counting the digits of our national wealth or hearing described our celestial standard of living when I know that these blessings have clogged up at the top of the social structure.

But it is not our part to concern ourselves overmuch with the forms and processes of government. Ours must be the objective point of view. We must take hunger, destitution, and the mal-adjustments of society as we find them, and mitigate their effects as best we can within the limitations of the existing scheme of things.

But there is no law or rule or ethical precept which says we cannot exult when we see government concern itself with the problems in which we deal. And we must give our counsel and support to any political regime which says, as President Roosevelt said last June in submitting the draft of the Social Security Act, "Among our objectives I place the security of the men and women and children of the Nation first."

That, all along, has been the objective of those of us who have viewed unemployment and need as a professional problem. Now it has the sanction of a strong government and a courageous President and I think we may well be encouraged over the promise of fulfillment which they give.

Document 19.5 "Outlining the New Deal Program"

President Roosevelt was an active legislator, responsible for much of the New Deal legislation. His plan was to put Americans back to work under the auspices of the federal government. It is important to remember that the New Deal programs did not usher in an era of recovery; on the contrary, many poor and middle-class families continued to face economic uncertainties. The following speech outlines Roosevelt's plan for recovery.

Outlining the New Deal Program

Franklin D. Roosevelt
Sunday, May 7, 1933

On a Sunday night a week after my Inauguration I used the radio to tell you about the banking crisis and the measures we were taking to meet it. I think that in that way I made clear to the country various facts that might otherwise have been misunderstood and in general provided a means of understanding which did much to restore confidence.

Tonight, eight weeks later, I come for the second time to give you my report—in the same spirit and by the same means to tell you about what we have been doing and what we are planning to do.

Two months ago we were facing serious problems. The country was dying by inches. It was dying because trade and commerce had declined to dangerously low levels; prices for basic commodities were such as to destroy the value of the assets of national institutions such as banks, savings banks, insurance companies, and others. These institutions, because of their great needs, were foreclosing mortgages, calling loans, refusing credit. Thus there was actually in process of destruction the property of millions of people who had borrowed money on that property in terms of dollars which had had an entirely different value from the level of March, 1933. That situation in that crisis did not call for any complicated consideration of economic panaceas or fancy plans. We were faced by a condition and not a theory.

There were just two alternatives: The first was to allow the foreclosures to continue, credit to be withheld and money to go into hiding, and thus forcing liquidation and bankruptcy of banks, railroads and insurance companies and a re-capitalizing of all business and all property on a lower level. This alternative meant a continuation of what is loosely called "deflation", the net result of which would have been extraordinary hardship on all property owners and, incidentally, extraordinary hardships on all persons working for wages through an increase in unemployment and a further reduction of the wage scale.

It is easy to see that the result of this course would have not only economic effects of a very serious nature but social results that might bring incalculable harm. Even before I was inaugurated I came to the conclusion that such a policy was too much to ask the American people to bear. It involved not only a further loss of homes, farms, savings and wages but also a loss of spiritual values—the loss of that sense of security for the present and the future so necessary to the peace and contentment of the individual and of his family. When you destroy these things you will find it difficult to establish confidence of any sort in the future. It was clear that mere appeals from Washington for confidence and the mere lending of more money to shaky institutions could not stop this downward course. A prompt program applied as quickly as possible seemed to me not only justified but imperative to our national security. The Congress, and when I say Congress I mean the members of both political parties, fully understood this and gave me generous and intelligent support. The members of Congress realized that the methods of normal times had to be replaced in the emergency by measures which were suited to the serious and pressing requirements of the moment. There was no actual surrender of power, Congress still retained its constitutional authority and no one has the slightest desire to change the balance of these powers. The function of Congress is to decide what has to be done and to select the appropriate agency to carry out its will. This policy it has strictly adhered to. The only thing that has been happening has been to designate the President as the agency to carry out certain of the purposes of the Congress. This was constitutional and in keeping with the past American tradition.

The legislation which has been passed or in the process of enactment can properly be considered as part of a well-grounded plan.

First, we are giving opportunity of employment to one-quarter of a million of the unemployed, especially the young men who have dependents, to go into the forestry and flood prevention work. This is a big task because it means feeding, clothing and caring for nearly twice as many men as we have in the regular army itself. In creating this civilian conservation corps we are killing two birds with one stone. We are clearly enhancing the value of our natural resources and second, we are relieving an appreciable amount of actual distress. This great group of men have entered upon their work on a purely voluntary basis, no military training is involved and we are conserving not only our natural resources but our human resources. One of the great values to this work is the fact that it is direct and requires the intervention of very little machinery.

Second, I have requested the Congress and have secured action upon a proposal to put the great properties owned by our Government at Muscle Shoals to work after long years of wasteful inaction, and with this a broad plan for the improvement of a vast area in the Tennessee Valley. It will add to the comfort and happiness of hundreds of thousands of people and the incident benefits will reach the entire nation.

Next, the Congress is about to pass legislation that will greatly ease the mortgage distress among the farmers and the home owners of the nation, by providing for the easing of the burden of debt now bearing so heavily upon millions of our people.

Our next step in seeking immediate relief is a grant of half a billion dollars to help the states, counties and municipalities in their duty to care for those who need direct and immediate relief.

In addition to all this, the Congress also passed legislation authorizing the sale of beer in such states as desired. This has already resulted in considerable reemployment and, incidentally, has provided much needed tax revenue.

Now as to the future

We are planning to ask the Congress for legislation to enable the Government to undertake public works, thus stimulating directly and indirectly the employment of many others in well-considered projects.

Further legislation has been taken up which goes much more fundamentally into our economic problems. The Farm Relief Bill seeks by the use of several methods, alone or together, to bring about an increased return to farmers for their major farm products, seeking at the same time to prevent in the days to come disastrous over-production which so often in the past has kept farm commodity prices far below a reasonable return. This measure provides wide powers for emergencies. The extent of its use will depend entirely upon what the future has in store.

Well-considered and conservative measures will likewise be proposed which will attempt to give to the industrial workers of the country a more fair wage return, prevent cut-throat competition and unduly long hours for labor, and at the same time to encourage each industry to prevent over-production.

One of our bills falls into the same class, the Railroad Bill. It seeks to provide and make certain definite planning by the railroads themselves, with the assistance of the Government, to eliminate the duplication and waste that is now results in railroad receiverships and in continuing operating deficits.

I feel very certain that the people of this country understand and approve the broad purposes behind these new governmental policies relating to agriculture and industry and transportation. We found ourselves faced with more agricultural products than we could possibly consume ourselves and surpluses which other nations did not have the cash to buy from us except at prices ruinously low. We found our factories able to turn out more goods than we could possibly consume, and at the same time we have been faced with a falling export demand. We have found ourselves with more facilities to transport goods and crops than there were goods and crops to be transported. All of this has been caused in large part by a complete failure to understand the danger signals that have been flying ever since the close of the World War. The people of this country have been erroneously encouraged to believe that they could keep on increasing the output of farm and factory indefinitely and that some magician would find ways and means for that increased output to be consumed with reasonable profit to the producer.

But today we have reason to believe that things are a little better than they were two months ago. Industry has picked up, railroads are carrying more freight, farm prices are better, but I am not going to indulge in issuing proclamations of over-enthusiastic assurance. We cannot ballyhoo ourselves back to prosperity. I am going to be honest at all times with the people of the country. I do not want the people of this country to take the foolish course of letting this improvement come back on another speculative wave. I do not want the people to believe that because of unjustified optimism we can resume the ruinous practice of increasing our crop output and our factory output in the hope that a kind providence will find buyers at high prices. Such a course may bring us immediate and false prosperity but it will be the kind of prosperity that will lead us into another tailspin.

It is wholly wrong to call the measure that we have taken Government control of farming, control of industry, and control of transportation. It is rather a partnership between Government and farming and industry and transportation, not partnership in profits, for the profits would still go to the citizens, but rather a partnership in planning and partnership to see that the plans are carried out.

Let me illustrate with an example. Take the cotton goods industry. It is probably true that ninety per cent of the cotton manufacturers would agree to eliminate starvation wages, would agree to stop long hours of employment, would agree to stop child labor, would agree to prevent an overproduction that would result in unsaleable surpluses. But, what good is such an agreement if the other ten per cent of cotton manufacturers pay starvation wages, require long hours, employ children in their mills and turn out burdensome surpluses? The unfair ten per cent could produce goods so cheaply that the fair ninety per cent would be compelled to meet the unfair conditions. Here is where government comes in. Government ought to have the right and will have the right, after surveying and planning for an industry to prevent, with the assistance of the overwhelming majority of that industry, unfair practice and to enforce this agreement by the authority of government. The so-called anti-trust laws were intended to prevent the creation of monopolies and to forbid unreasonable profits to those monopolies. That purpose of the anti-trust laws must be continued, but these laws were never intended to encourage the kind of unfair competition that results in long hours, starvation wages and overproduction.

And my friends, the same principle that is illustrated by that example applies to farm products and to transportation and every other field of organized private industry.

We are working toward a definite goal, which is to prevent the return of conditions which came very close to destroying what we call modern civilization. The actual accomplishment of our purpose cannot be attained in a day. Our policies are wholly within purposes for which our American Constitutional Government was established 150 years ago.

I know that the people of this country will understand this and will also understand the spirit in which we are undertaking this policy. I do not deny that we may make mistakes of procedure as we carry out the policy. I have no expectation of making a hit every time I come to bat. What I seek is the highest possible batting average, not only for myself but for the team. Theodore Roosevelt once said to me: "If I can be right 75 per cent of the time I shall come up to the fullest measure of my hopes."

Much has been said of late about Federal finances and inflation, the gold standard, etc. Let me make the facts very simple and my policy very clear. In the first place, government credit and government currency are really one and the same thing. Behind government bonds there is only a promise to pay. Behind government currency we have, in addition to the promise to pay, a reserve of gold and a small reserve of silver. In this connection it is worth while remembering that in the past the government has agreed to redeem nearly thirty billions of its debts and its currency in gold, and private corporations in this country have agreed to redeem another sixty or seventy billions of securities and mortgages in gold. The government and private corporations were making these agreements when they knew full well that all of the gold in the United States amounted to only between three and four billion and that all of the gold in all of the world amounted to only about eleven billion.

If the holders of these promises to pay started in to demand gold the first comers would get gold for a few days and they would amount to about one twenty-fifth of the holders of the securities and the currency. The other twenty-four people out of twenty-five, who did not happen to be at the top of the line, would be told politely that there was no more gold left. We have decided to treat all twenty-five in the same way in the interest of justice and the exercise of the constitutional powers of this government. We have placed every one on the same basis in order that the general good may be preserved.

Nevertheless, gold, and to a partial extent silver, are perfectly good bases for currency and that is why I decided not to let any of the gold now in the country go out of it.

A series of conditions arose three weeks ago which very readily might have meant, first, a drain on our gold by foreign countries, and secondly, as a result of that, a flight of American capital, in the form of gold, out of our country. It is not exaggerating the possibility to tell you that such an occurrence might well have taken from us the major part of our gold reserve and resulted in such a further weakening of our government and private credit as to bring on actual panic conditions and the complete stoppage of the wheels of industry.

The Administration has the definite objective of raising commodity prices to such an extent that those who have borrowed money will, on the average, be able to repay that money in the same kind of dollar which they borrowed. We do not seek to let them get such a cheap dollar that they will be able to pay back a great deal less than they borrowed. In other words, we seek to correct a wrong and not to create another wrong in the opposite direction. That is why powers are being given to the Administration to provide, if necessary, for an enlargement of credit, in order to correct the existing wrong. These powers will be used when, as, and if it may be necessary to accomplish the purpose.

Hand in hand with the domestic situation which, of course, is our first concern, is the world situation, and I want to emphasize to you that the domestic situation is inevitably and deeply tied in with the conditions in all of the other nations of the world. In other words, we can get, in all probability, a fair measure of prosperity return in the United States, but it will not be permanent unless we get a return to prosperity all over the world.

In the conferences which we have held and are holding with the leaders of other nations, we are seeking four great objectives. First, a general reduction of armaments and through this the removal of the fear of invasion and armed attack, and, at the same time, a reduction in armament costs, in order to help in the balancing of government budgets and the reduction of taxation. Secondly, a cutting down of the trade barriers, in order to re-start the flow of exchange of crops and goods between nations. Third, the setting up of a stabilization of currencies, in order that trade can make contracts ahead. Fourth, the reestablishment of friendly relations and greater confidence between all nations.

Our foreign visitors these past three weeks have responded to these purposes in a very helpful way. All of the Nations have suffered alike in this great depression. They have all reached the conclusion that each can best be helped by the common action of all. It is in this spirit that our visitors have met with us and discussed our common problems. The international conference that lies before us must succeed. The future of the world demands it and we have each of us pledged ourselves to the best joint efforts to that end.

To you, the people of this country, all of us, the Members of the Congress and the members of this Administration owe a profound debt of gratitude. Throughout the depression you have been patient. You have granted us wide powers, you have encour-

aged us with a wide-spread approval of our purposes. Every ounce of strength and every resource at our command we have devoted to the end of justifying your confidence. We are encouraged to believe that a wise and sensible beginning has been made. In the present spirit of mutual confidence and mutual encouragement we go forward.

And in conclusion, my friends, may I express to the National Broadcasting Company and to the Columbia Broadcasting System my thanks for the facilities which they have made available to me tonight.

Document 19.6 African Americans in the CCC

Luther C. Wandall was a participant in the Civilian Conservation Corp. He provides a first-hand account of his experience as an African American. How does his account compare or contrast to the general concepts of the CCC?

A Negro in the CCC

By Luther C. Wandall

The author is a New Yorker and gives here a first hand picture of CCC life

During the two years of its previous existence I had heard many conflicting reports concerning the Civilian Conservation Corps, President Roosevelt's pet project. One boy told me that he almost froze to death one night out in Washington. Some said that the colored got all the leftovers. Others said that everything was all right. But my brother, who is a World War veteran, advised me emphatically: "I wouldn't be in anything connected with the Army."

So it was with some apprehension that I surveyed the postal card instructing me to see Miss A. at the Home Relief Bureau the following Friday. At this Bureau I signed a paper, of which I kept two copies, and the Bureau one. This paper asserted that I was "accepted for enrollment," and should report the following Monday "to U. S. Army authorities for further registration."

One thing I saw at the Bureau increased my apprehension. So many of the boys who appeared in answer to cards were excused because they had been "dishonorably discharged" in a previous enlistment. It was impossible to tell whether they were disappointed or not, but they were not always discreditable-looking persons.

According to instructions, I went Monday morning at 8 o'clock to Pier I, North River. There were, I suppose, more than 1,000 boys standing about the pier. And here I got another shock. Many of the boys carried suitcases. I had not been instructed that we would leave that day. But still, I reasoned, we would be given time to go home and tell our folks goodbye.

The colored boys were a goodly sprinkling of the whole. A few middle-aged men were in evidence. These, it turned out, were going as cooks. A good many Spaniards and Italians were about. A good-natured, lively, crowd, typical of New York.

At eight o'clock we were rapidly admitted to the pier, given papers and herded into the warehouse, out on the water. And here the "fun" began. A few boys were being admitted from time to time to a lower platform through a small gate in the center. And of

The author wishes to thank the Crisis Publishing Co., Inc., the publisher of the magazine of the National Association for the Advancement of Colored People, for the use of material first published in the August 1935 issue of Crisis.

course, everyone in that mob was anxious to get there.

At first there was a semblance of order. The men in charge of us formed us into companies of fifty as we came up. But suddenly a U. S. Army officer in full uniform entered the door. A mighty roar went up from the boys, who surged forward, evidently thinking that they could follow him. But the officer, a tall handsome fellow, moving with easy grace, completely ignored them, and passed on through.

With some effort we were finally forced back into a so-called line. But a newspaper photographer appeared. The line broke again, and after that confusion reigned for the most part.

There were no seats where we were. So I stood about until two o'clock before I finally got through that little gate. We answered questions, and signed papers, and then a group of us marched over to U. S. Army headquarters on Whitehall Street in charge of an Army officer.

Here we stripped for a complete physical examination. Then we were grouped into busloads. Each busload of 35 ate a meal at South Ferry before boarding the bus. This meal consisted of beans, pickles, bread, coffee and butter, and was eaten out of Army mess-kits.

So there I was, on a bus bound for Camp Dix, New Jersey, without having prepared or told anyone goodbye. Our bus was comfortable, and equipped with a radio, so the ride was a very enjoyable one.

Jim Crow at Camp Dix

We reached Camp Dix about 7:30 that evening. As we rolled up in front of headquarters an officer came out to the bus and told us: "You will double-time as you leave this bus, remove your hat when you hit the door, and when you are asked questions, answer 'Yes, sir,' and 'No, sir.'"

And here it was that Mr. James Crow first definitely put in his appearance. When my record was taken at Pier I, a "C" was placed on it. When the busloads were made up at Whitehall street an officer reported as follows: "35, 8 colored." But until now there had been no distinction made.

But before we left the bus the officer shouted emphatically: "Colored boys fall out in the rear. The colored from several buses were herded together, and stood in line until after the white boys had been registered and taken to their tents. This seemed to be the established order of procedure at Camp Dix.

This separation of the colored from the whites was completely and rigidly maintained at this camp.

One Puerto Rican, who was darker than I, and who preferred to be with the colored, was regarded as pitifully uninformed by the officers.

While we stood in line there, as well as afterwards, I was interested to observe these officers. They were contradictory, and by no means simple or uniform in type. Many of them were southerners, how many I could not tell. Out of their official character they were usually courteous, kindly, refined, and even intimate. They offered extra money to any of us who could sing or dance. On the other hand, some were vicious and ill-tempered, and apparently restrained only by fear.

Southerners at West Point! Emotional, aristocratic, with refined features and soft blue eyes. And paradoxically they choose the Army for a career. Slaves to traditions and fetishes....

We were finally led away to our tents. And such tents! They were the worst in Camp Dix. Old, patched, without floors or electric lights. It was dark already, so we went to bed immediately, by candlelight. And since it was cold, we slept in most, and in some cases all, of our clothes.

The bedding was quite ample: four blankets, two sheets, and a pillowcase. But Camp Dix is a cold place, and the condition of our tents didn't help. Then, too, it was raining.

Next day we rose at 6:15; There was roll call and "mess." A few minutes later we were shocked to see snow falling, on April 16! The boys built a fire, so we were able to keep somewhat warm. Then there was another questionnaire, and more papers to sign.

Southerners Plentiful

By now only one thought occupied my mind: When do I leave this place? I understood that Camp Dix was only a replacement camp, and that we would be leaving, probably within a week. So you can imagine my feelings when an officer, a small quiet fellow, obviously a southerner, asked me how I would like to stay in Camp Dix permanently as his clerk! This officer was very courteous, and seemed to be used to colored people, and liked them. I declined his offer.

We slept six in a tent. And right here I might attempt to describe the class of young men I found myself with. Two things surprised me: that out of the whole crowd, I had known not one in New York, and that almost without exception they were of a very low order of culture. Such low ideals. Of course many were plainly ignorant and underprivileged, while others were really criminal. They cursed with every breath, stole everything they could lay hands on, and fought over their food, or over nothing at all.

That same day we got another complete physical examination, two vaccinations and one "shot." They were for typhoid fever, parathyroid and smallpox.

The following day, which was a Wednesday, we got our first clothes, a complete outfit. They were Army clothes, and fitted as well as could be expected. That afternoon we worked. I was on a truck hauling lumber. The next two days we sampled several different kinds of work, none of it very hard. We also heard a very edifying health lecture, chiefly on venereal diseases.

Food at Camp Dix was poor in quality and variety, and barely sufficient in quantity. A typical breakfast: boiled eggs, corn flakes, milk, bread, coffee, butter. Lunch: frankfurters, sauerkraut, potatoes, gravy, bread, apple-butter, coffee. Dinner: bologna, applesauce, potato salad, bread, coffee, cake.

We stayed at Camp Dix eight days. We were never told officially where we were going. Just before we boarded the train we were split into two companies. I was placed in Company Y.

The ride was quite enjoyable. On through Jersey, with the sun setting like a ball of fire on golden Delaware. Maryland, with night falling like a shroud.

We were taken to permanent camp on a site rich in Colonial and Revolutionary history, in the upper South. This camp was a dream compared with Camp Dix. There was plenty to eat, and we slept in barracks instead of tents. An excellent recreation hall, playground, and other facilities.

I am still in this camp. At the "rec" we have a radio, a piano, a store called a "canteen," a rack of the leading New York papers, white and colored, as well as some from elsewhere. There is a little library with a variety of books and magazines. All sports are encouraged. We have a baseball team, boxing squad etc. An orchestra has been formed, and classes in various arts and crafts.

Colored People Unfriendly

In fact, the setup is quite ideal. The rest is left with the officers and the men. But the final result leaves much to be desired. Things are not always run efficiently, food is often poorly cooked.

During the first week we did no work outside camp, but only hiked, drilled, and exercised. Since then we have worked five days a week, eight hours a day. Our bosses are local men, southerners, but on the whole I have found nothing to complain of. The work varies, but is always healthy, outdoor labor. As the saying goes, it's a great life, if only you don't weaken!

There are colored people living on farms on all sides of this camp. But they are not very friendly toward CCC boys in general, and toward the northerners in particular. (There are four companies here: two of southerners, one of veterans, and our own.) So that, socially, the place is "beat."

Our officers, who, of course, are white, are a captain, a first lieutenant, a doctor, and several sergeants. Our athletic director is colored, as is our vocational teacher. Discipline is maintained by imposing extra duty and fines on offenders. The fines are taken only from the $5 a month which the men receive directly.

On the whole, I was gratified rather than disappointed with the CCC. I had expected the worst. Of course it reflects, to some extent, all the practices and prejudices of the U. S. Army. But as a job and an experience, for a man who has no work, I can heartily recommend it.

Chapter 19 Worksheet and Questions

1. What is President Roosevelt's approach for economic recovery, what is the greatest task, and what is the role of the federal government?

    _____

    _____

    _____

    _____

    _____

    _____

    _____

    _____

    _____

2. What is the role of the Civilian Conservation Corp? Be sure to describe the treatment of African Americans as described by Luther Wandall.

    _____

    _____

    _____

    _____

    _____

    _____

    _____

    _____

    _____

    _____

3. What is the "paradox" regarding the relationship between African Americans and President Roosevelt? What similarities can be inferred regarding the relationship between FDR and the poor in general?

_____

_____

_____

_____

_____

_____

_____

_____

_____

_____

4. Unemployment was one of the concerns during the New Deal era. Roosevelt's administration attempted to correct the internal problems of society. In his address to the Buffalo Council of Social Agencies, Aubrey Williams discussed unemployment—problems and strategies. What was the objective, and what statistical examples did he provide supporting the idea that the road to recovery must be permanent?

_____

_____

_____

_____

_____

_____

_____

_____

_____

The Decision to Drop the Atomic Bomb

Preparations in the desert at Alamagordo, New Mexico proceeded at a feverish pace during May and June of 1945. The original test date for the giant "firecracker" was scheduled for July 4, 1945, but that was delayed. Electrical wiring and telephone lines were strung, shelters built, and scientific measuring equipment installed; a 100-foot-tall steel tower was built at Ground Zero. Then, to add to the strain, a ferocious thunderstorm struck the area at 2:00 A.M. the morning of the "Trinity" test. Rescheduled for 5:30 A.M., the countdown proceeded and the first atomic bomb exploded on July 16, 1945.

The noise of the blast, sounding like speeding trains, rolled through the testing grounds for five minutes. The concussion from the shock waves broke windows 125 miles away. Observers gazed in awe at the mushroom-shaped fireball cloud, rising up to a height of eight miles. Others noted the light from the blast, a light so intense that a blind woman on the edge of the testing area saw the light. Dr. Robert Oppenheimer, who led the team that constructed and tested the bombs, recited a line from the Bhagavad-Gita: "I am become death, the shatterer of worlds." This test was followed by the dropping of the only atomic weapons in history: August 6, 1945 on Hiroshima, and August 9 on Nagasaki.

Historians, philosophers and religious leaders have tried ever since to answer the questions: Was it necessary to drop the atomic bombs on Japan, and if so, was it necessary to drop the second one? Were the atomic bombs necessary to end the war, and did they speed the cause of peace in 1945? Was there any way to reduce the destruction and loss of lives? What was the decision-making process that led our national leaders to explode the only atomic weapons ever used in wartime? That last question is the primary focus of this chapter.

Why did the United States decide to build the atomic bomb? The earliest breakthroughs in nuclear physics came in Germany, but when the Nazis took over they favored biological sciences, looking suspiciously on "Jewish Physics" because of who the leading researchers were. Many scientists fled to England and the United States as persecutions increased, among them Leo Szilard, the Hungarian-born physicist who first conceived of the chain reaction. But in 1939 German physicists successfully triggered nuclear fission, and informed the German War Office of its potential. At the beginning of World War II, only Nazi Germany had an office focused on developing nuclear energy. The Soviet Union and Great Britain started similar research, aware that if a controlled chain reaction was possible, then powerful explosives could be the end result.

Leo Szilard and Enrico Fermi, now both at Columbia University, worried that the Nazis had a research lead, and that no coordinated efforts to research and develop nuclear energy existed in the United States. Szilard and Albert Einstein drafted a letter to President Franklin Roosevelt warning him of the dangers. FDR quickly grasped the importance of this issue and created the Advisory Committee on Uranium. A few scientists were first granted $6,000 to continue research, the start of a project that would eventually build 37 factories, employ over 150,000 people, and cost over $2 billion. This project is driven by the belief that in 1941–1942 the Nazis were ahead of us, and would be first to perfect atomic battlefield weapons. Scientists and government collaborated across the country: Szilard and Fermi built "piles" (nuclear reactors) at the University of Chicago to create controlled chain reactions; plants were built in Oak Ridge, Tennessee and Hanford, Washington to produce uranium and plutonium by two different methods, and the bomb builders gathered at isolated Los Alamos, New Mexico to complete the project.

As the task neared completion in 1945, important changes were occurring outside the program. President Roosevelt died and Harry Truman took over. Thrust into the difficult situation of bringing the world war to an end, planning for the postwar world without returning to the depression years, and competing with the Roosevelt legacy, Truman also faced questions over using this new weapon. As a vice president and senator, Truman was uninformed about the project, which was kept on a strict need-to-know basis. He would thus need to rely on advisors and those entrenched in the project for advice. When Secretary of War Henry L. Stimson first fully briefed the president on April 25, 1945, he told Truman that "within four months we shall in all probability have completed the most terrible weapon ever known in human history, one bomb of which could destroy a whole city." He also warned Truman that if handled unwisely, atomic weapons could mean the end of western civilization. At Stimson's urging, President Truman established an Interim Committee to advise him on all things relating to the atomic bomb, with members both from the military and from the scientific community that was creating the weapon.

President Roosevelt's goal in the war was essentially this: achieve total victory at the lowest cost in American lives. Use material and technological superiority, take time, but achieve total victory. He also required "unconditional surrender" by our enemies in Germany and Japan. Harry Truman made clear to his White House Chief of Staff, Admiral William Leahy, that these were his committed goals also. There was a growing concern about the cost of fighting Japan to the end. The use of kamikaze attacks on our ships, suicide assaults by ground troops, and the growing American casualty figures on Okinawa created an impression that the Japanese were fanatics. If they defended their homeland as they had Iwo Jima and Okinawa, how high would American casualties be?

Some of the scientists involved in the Manhattan Project (as it was called) were beginning to have doubts by late 1944. Allied victory seemed assured by now, so was there still a need for nuclear weapons in this war? Secret papers captured by General Patton's' forces showed that the Germans were at least two years behind us in developing nuclear weapons, and the Japanese were beginning to contact the Soviet Union about negotiating peace. Scientists were divided on the issue of continuing. Some suggested turning over all nuclear information to international control to avert a nuclear arms race. The Franck Report warned that if the United States used this weapon we would lose "the moral high ground" we claimed we were fighting for. Szilard and Einstein sent another letter to FDR in March 1945 discussing the political, moral, and postwar implications of atomic weapons, but the president died before reading it. Secretary-of-State designate James F. Byrnes, firmly committed to using the weapon, denied the scientists access to President Truman.

By late spring of 1945 the issue boiled down to how to finish the war with Japan at the lowest cost in American lives. The first option was to continue the blockade and bombardment of Japan. Raw materials for their factories, food, and medical supplies were already cut off, and they faced massive starvation by early 1946. We could bombard them at will, and had long since stopped worrying about rules regarding bombarding civilians. Following the instructions of General Curtis LeMay that there "are no innocent civilians in Japan," the Air Force began using incendiary bombs on large cities. The firebombing of Tokyo on March 9, 1945 took 87,000 lives and left over 1,000,000 homeless. Air officials and the Navy preferred this method, both for saving American lives and enhancing their service reputations for the inevitable postwar appropriations fights. But would this approach really cause the Japanese to surrender? Secretary of War Stimson and Army Chief-of-Staff George C. Marshall doubted that anything short of an invasion would defeat the Japanese, and that any invasion would be costly. Marshall especially doubted that anything in history proved you could "bomb people into submission."

A second option, frequently tied to invasion plans, was hoping for Soviet aid. If the Soviet Union declared war on Japan they could tie down over 2,000,000 troops in China. Their mere entrance into the war might convince Japan that they had no hope of winning. The joint chiefs and President Truman both thought this was a good policy to pursue in early spring, but as postwar problems with the Soviets began to appear in Europe, the idea pushed ahead of ending the Pacific war before the USSR became a factor in the region.

The third option was invasion of the Japanese home islands, tentatively scheduled for November 1, 1945. The Joint Chiefs estimated that the Army and Marines would face at least 2,000,000 Japanese troops, in addition to local militia trained for suicide attacks, while the Navy could expect heavy casualties from attacks by 5,000 to 7,000 *kamikaze* planes. The operation would not be completed until the end of 1946, and would cost at least 220,000 Americans killed and wounded. These casualty estimates fluctuated as different leaders made their estimates. (There is, however, no evidence that anyone ever suggested to President Truman that casualties would range from 500,000 to one million.) The Army, sure of the cost of invading, was stockpiling officers at the rank of 2nd Lieutenants, to replace those killed in the first weeks of the invasion, while the Navy assembled hospital ships for the operation.

The fourth option open to President Truman was to deploy the atomic bomb, which (if it worked) could end the war quickly and at a lower cost than the other options. Sparing American lives was always the president's first priority, not just because of the announced wartime goals, but because of his personal experience in World War I. No matter if 10,000 or 250,000 Japanese died, he would use the bomb if American lives were saved. Using the bomb might also impress and intimidate the Soviets, making postwar life easier for the United States. This was the position of Secretary-of-State designate James Byrnes. Using the bomb would also justify the immense cost in dollars and manpower spent developing the weapon, and would avoid embarrassing questions in Congress about costs after the war. Winning the war against the Japanese would be politically popular also, since Americans hated the Japanese with an intensity surpassing our other wartime enemies. The attack on Pearl Harbor, the Bataan Death March, atrocities committed by the Imperial Army against our prisoners and the Chinese, and the rape and murder of nuns in Hong Kong all fueled national hatred. Truman demonstrated these values when he wrote to the head of the Federal Council of Churches "when you have to deal with a beast you have to treat him as a beast."

Truman's closest advisors promoted the use of the bomb as well. The Interim Committee ruled against a demonstration bomb to scare the Japanese, for fear it would misfire, or that they would move key industries or move American prisoners-of-war into the target areas. They insisted on combining military targets with civilian areas, to create the greatest psychological impact of bombing, and convince the Japanese people they cannot win. Scientists on the committee also warned against informing the Soviets, for fear matters would be complicated if they protested the bomb's use. They also suggested that the bomb would save Japanese lives, by ending the "terror bombing" with incendiaries, slow starvation from the blockade, and deaths from invasion.

Most of those involved in completing the Manhattan Project never doubted the bomb would or should be used. Robert Oppenheimer stated "we always assumed if they were needed, they would be used." Secretary of War Stimson stated that the "entire purpose was the production of a military weapon." Finally, President Truman said in his memoirs "I regarded the bomb as a military weapon and never had any doubt it should be used."

But not all advisors supported using the bomb. General Eisenhower told Secretary Stimson that he believed Japan was already defeated and the atomic bomb was unnecessary, but deferred to commanders in the Pacific. Admiral Leahy believed using the bomb against civilians was immoral, and the bomb was unnecessary to insure victory. General MacArthur claimed he was against dropping the bombs, although he later called for their extensive use in Korea and China.

Three B-29s flew to Hiroshima on August 6, 1945; the *Enola Gay* carried the bomb, and the other two carried photographers and scientific equipment to document the blast. At 8:15 A.M. (Hiroshima time) the bomb detonated about 1,900 feet above Hiroshima, rocking the *Enola Gay* with shock waves 30,000 feet high and 11 miles away. An area about 4.4 miles surrounding Ground Zero was completely devastated, killing over 135,000 people either instantly or from exposure to radiation over the next few months. President Truman's press release, simultaneously announcing the creation and the use of atomic weapons to the nation, declared that the Japanese had been repaid for Pearl Harbor, and threatened total annihilation if they did not surrender at once. Three days later, August 9, 1945, the *Bock's Car* dropped a plutonium bomb on Nagasaki after failing to acquire its primary target of Kokura. Between 60,000 and 70,000 people perished. A day later, leaflets were dropped on Nagasaki warning the people about further atomic attacks. On August 15th, Truman announced the surrender of Japan.

Reaction to dropping the bombs was mixed. Stalin was convinced the bomb would be turned against him next, so he made the Soviet bomb project a top priority. A survey of *Time* magazine readers found

Americans condemning the use of atomic bombs as "simple mass murder, sheer terrorism," or that "the United States has this day become the new master of brutality, infamy, atrocity." *Christian Century* called this "America's Atomic Atrocity." But most Americans felt differently. The troops preparing for invasion of Japan, and the POWs under Japanese control, were sure the bombs saved their lives, and continue to express those feelings today. Opinion polls taken in fall 1945 showed almost 54 percent of Americans fully supported dropping the bombs, and 23 percent wished more atomic bombs could have struck Japan before it surrendered. Senator Brian McMahon of Connecticut declared "the bombing of Hiroshima was the greatest event in world history since the birth of Jesus Christ." In private, President Truman responded differently. Seeing the pictures of the destruction, he issued an executive order placing the use of atomic weapons under direct presidential control.

Considering the Evidence in the Readings

In this chapter you are considering the decision-making that led to dropping the atomic bombs. As you read through the documents, remember that while many are official papers, others are private documents written with an eye on history. Who might be phrasing ideas, or making suggestions, to clear themselves of charges and accusations by other civilized nations in the future? What is their audience, and are the writers focused on current (i.e., 1945) issues or on their future reputations?

Document 20.1 Minutes of the Second Meeting of the Target Committee, Los Alamos, May 10–11, 1945

The Target Committee assembled to determine potential uses of the bomb, and to focus on overcoming potential problems with each target site, from mechanical issues to the weather. The Committee consisted of four military officers and nine scientists, mostly from the Los Alamos site where the bomb was being assembled. Dr. Robert Oppenheimer chaired the committee and sent reports to General Groves. As you read the proceedings, look for what factors the committee considered when choosing targets—military, geographical, psychological, and so on. Why are some targets downgraded by the military, while others remain "A" targets? What recommendations are forwarded to General Groves, and then to the president?

---

12 May 1945

Memorandum For: Major General L. R. Groves
Subject: Summary of Target Committee Meetings on 10 and 11 May 1945

1. The Meeting

The second meeting of the Target Committee convened at 9:00 A.M. 10 May in Dr. Oppenheimer's office at Site Y with the following present:

General Farrell	Dr. C. Lauritsen
Colonel Seeman	Dr. Ramsey
Captain Parsons	Dr. Dennison

Major Derry	Dr. von Neumann
Dr. Stearns	Dr. Wilson
Dr. Tolman	Dr. Penney
Dr. Oppenheimer	

Dr. Bethe and Dr. Brode were brought into the meeting for discussion of Item A of the agenda. During the course of the meeting panels were formed from the committee members and others to meet in the afternoon and develop conclusions to items discussed in the agenda. The concluding meeting was held at 10:00 A.M. 11 May in Dr. Oppenheimer's office with the following present:

Colonel Seeman	Dr. Stearns
Captain Parsons	Dr. Von Neumann
Major Derry	Dr. Dennison

Dr. Tolman   Dr. Penney
Dr. Oppenheimer Dr. Ramsey
Dr. Wilson

2. The Agenda

The agenda for the meetings presented by Dr. Oppenheimer consisted of the following:

A. Height of Detonation
B: Report on Weather and Operations
C: Gadget Jettisoning and Landing
D: Status of Targets
E: Psychological Factors in Target Selection
F: Use Against Military Objectives
G: Radiological Effects
H: Coordinated Air Operations
I: Rehearsals
J: Operating Requirements for Safety of Airplanes
K: Coordination with 21st Program

3. Height of Detonation

A. The criteria for determining height selection were discussed. It was agreed that conservative figures should be used in determining the height since it is not possible to predict accurately the magnitude of the explosion and since the bomb can be detonated as much as 40% below the optimum with a reduction of 25% in area of damage whereas a detonation 14% above the optimum will cause the same loss in area. It was agreed that fuses should be prepared to meet the following possibilities:

(1) For the Little Boy the detonation heights should correspond to a pressure of 5 psi, a height of the Mach-stem of 100 feet and a magnitude of detonation of either 5,000 or 15,000 tons of H.E. equivalent. With present knowledge the fuse setting corresponding to 5,000 tons equivalent would be used but fusing for the other should be available in case more is known at the time of delivery. The height of detonation corresponding to 5,000 and 15,000 tons are 1550 feet and 2400 feet, respectively.

(2) For the Fat Man the detonation heights should correspond to a pressure of 5 psi, a height of the Mach-stem of 100 feet, and a magnitude of explosion of 700, 2,000, or 5,000 tons of H.E. equivalent. With the present information the fuse should be set at 2,000 tons equivalent but fusing for the other values should be available at the time of final delivery. The heights of detonation corresponding to 700, 2,000, and 5,000 tons are 580 feet, 1,000 feet and

1,550 feet, respectively. Trinity data will be used for this gadget.

B. In the case of the Fat Man delay circuits are introduced into the unit for purposes which make the detonation of the bomb 400 feet below the height at which the fuse is set. For this reason as far as the Fat Man is concerned the fuse settings should be 980 feet, 1,400 feet, or 1,950 feet.

C. In view of the above it was agreed by all present that fuses should be available at four (4) different height settings. These heights are 1,000 feet, 1,400 feet, 2,000 feet and 2,400 feet. With present information the 1,400 feet fuse would be most likely to be used for both the Fat Man and the Little Boy. (Later data presented by Dr. Brode modify the above conclusions on fusing and detonating heights; the differential height for the Little Boy is 210 feet and for the Fat Man 500 feet. For this reason some of the above figures must be revised).

4. Report on Weather and Operations

A. Dr. Dennison reported on the above subject. His report essentially covered the materials in his Top Secret memo of 9 May—Subject: "Preliminary report on Operational Procedures." For this reason his report will not be repeated here but is attached as an appendix. It was agreed by those present that the mission if at all possible should be a visual bombing mission. For this we should be prepared to wait until there is a good weather forecast in one or more of three alternative targets. There is only a 2% chance in this case that we will have to wait over two weeks. When the mission does take place there should be weather spotter aircraft over each of three alternative targets in order that an alternative target may be selected in the last hour of the flight if the weather is unpromising over the highest priority target.

B. In case the aircraft reaches the target and finds, despite these precautions that visual bombing is impossible, it should return to its base provided that it is in good operating condition. Only if the aircraft is in sufficiently bad shape that it is unlikely that it can return to base and make a safe landing or if it is essential that the drop be made that day should the drop be made with radar equipment. For this purpose it may be desirable to have an Eagle radar equipped plane accompany the mission in order that formation bombing with the Eagle plane in the lead can be made to obtain the increased accuracy from Eagle. A final decision as to the desirablity of this emergency procedure can only be made after further combat experience is obtained with Eagle aircraft. In any case every effort should be made to have the mission such that blind bombing will be unnecessary.

C. It was agreed that Dr. Stearns and Dr. Dennison should keep themselves continuously informed as to radar developments. If at any time new developments are available which show in combat a marked improvement of accuracy the basic plan may be altered.

D. It was agreed that Shoran was a very promising development for the 21st Bomber Command but that we should make no plans to use Shoran until its success is fully confirmed in normal bombing missions in that area.

E. The plan to use the gadget with visual bombing even though this may require a one day to three weeks delay requires that the gadget be such that for a period of at least three weeks it can be held in readiness in such a state that on twelve hours notice it can be prepared for a combat mission. No difficulty in this regard was foreseen by those present.

5. Gadget Jettisoning and Landing

A. It was agreed that if the aircraft has to return to its base with the gadget and if it is in good condition when it has reached there, it should make a normal landing with the greatest possible care and with such precautions as stand-by fire equipment being held in readiness on the ground. This operation will inevitably involve some risks to the base and to the other aircraft parked on the field. However, the chance of a crash when the aircraft is in good condition and the chances of a crash initiating a high order explosion are both sufficiently small that it was the view of those present that the landing operation with the unit under these circumstances was a justifiable risk. Frequent landings with inert and H.E. filled units have been made in the past. Training in landing with the unit should be given to all crews who carry an active unit.

B. In case the aircraft returns to its base and then finds that it cannot make a normal landing it may be necessary to jettison the bomb. In the case of the Fat Man this can probably best be accomplished by dropping the bomb into shallow water from a low altitude. Tests on this will be carried out with both inert and live units. In the case of the Little Boy the situation is considerably more complicated since water leaking into the Little Boy will set off a nuclear reaction, and since the American held territory in the vicinity of the base is so densely filled that no suitable jettisoning

ground for the Little Boy has been found which is sufficiently devoid of moisture, which is sufficiently soft that the projectile is sure not to seat from the impact, and which is sufficiently remote from extremely important American installations whose damage by a nuclear explosion would seriously affect the American war effort. The best emergency procedure that has so far been proposed is considered to be the removal of the gunpowder from the gun and the execution of a crash landing. In this case there is no danger of fire setting off the gun and the accelerations should be sufficiently small to prevent seating of the projectile by the impact. Tests on the feasibility of unloading the gun powder in flight will be conducted.

C. It was agreed that prior to actual delivery some form of instructions should be prepared as a guide to the senior man on the aircraft as to procedures to be followed in cases of different types of disasters.

6. Status of Targets

A. Dr. Stearns described the work he had done on target selection. He has surveyed possible targets possessing the following qualification: (1) they be important targets in a large urban area of more than three miles in diameter, (2) they be capable of being damaged effectively by a blast, and (3) they are unlikely to be attacked by next August. Dr. Stearns had a list of five targets which the Air Force would be willing to reserve for our use unless unforeseen circumstances arise. These targets are:

(1) **Kyoto**—This target is an urban industrial area with a population of 1,000,000. It is the former capital of Japan and many people and industries are now being moved there as other areas are being destroyed. From the psychological point of view there is the advantage that Kyoto is an intellectual center for Japan and the people there are more apt to appreciate the significance of such a weapon as the gadget. (Classified as an AA Target)

(2) **Hiroshima**—This is an important army depot and port of embarkation in the middle of an urban industrial area. It is a good radar target and it is such a size that a large part of the city could be extensively damaged. There are adjacent hills which are likely to produce a focussing effect which would considerably increase the blast damage. Due to rivers it is not a good incendiary target. (Classified as an AA Target)

(3) **Yokohama**—This target is an important urban industrial area which has so far been untouched.

Industrial activities include aircraft manufacture, machine tools, docks, electrical equipment and oil refineries. As the damage to Tokyo has increased additional industries have moved to Yokohama. It has the disadvantage of the most important target areas being separated by a large body of water and of being in the heaviest anti-aircraft concentration in Japan. For us it has the advantage as an alternate target for use in case of bad weather of being rather far removed from the other targets considered. (Classified as an A Target)

(4) **Kokura Arsenal**—This is one of the largest arsenals in Japan and is surrounded by urban industrial structures. The arsenal is important for light ordnance, anti-aircraft and beach head defense materials. The dimensions of the arsenal are 4100' x 2000'. The dimensions are such that if the bomb were properly placed full advantage could be taken of the higher pressures immediately underneath the bomb for destroying the more solid structures and at the same time considerable blast damage could be done to more feeble structures further away. (Classified as an A Target)

(5) **Niigata**—This is a port of embarkation on the N.W. coast of Honshu. Its importance is increasing as other ports are damaged. Machine tool industries are located there and it is a potential center for industrial dispersion. It has oil refineries and storage. (Classified as a B Target)

(6) The possibility of bombing the Emperor's palace was discussed. It was agreed that we should not recommend it but that any action for this bombing should come from authorities on military policy. It was agreed that we should obtain information from which we could determine the effectiveness of our weapon against this target.

B. It was the recommendation of those present at the meeting that the first four choices of targets for our weapon should be the following:

   a. Kyoto
   b. Hiroshima
   c. Yokohama
   d. Kokura Arsenal

C. Dr. Stearns agreed to do the following: (1) brief Colonel Fisher thoroughly on these matters, (2) request reservations for these targets, (3) find out more about the target area including exact locations of the strategic industries there, (4) obtain further photo information on the targets, and (5) to determine the nature of the construction, the area, heights, contents and roof coverage of buildings. He also agreed to keep in touch with the target data as it develops and to keep the committee advised of other possible target areas. He will also check on locations of small military targets and obtain further details on the Emperor's palace.

7. Psychological Factors in Target Selection

A. It was agreed that psychological factors in the target selection were of great importance. Two aspects of this are (1) obtaining the greatest psychological effect against Japan and (2) making the initial use sufficiently spectacular for the importance of the weapon to be internationally recognized when publicity on it is released.

B. In this respect Kyoto has the advantage of the people being more highly intelligent and hence better able to appreciate the significance of the weapon. Hiroshima has the advantage of being such a size and with possible focussing from nearby mountains that a large fraction of the city may be destroyed. The Emperor's palace in Tokyo has a greater fame than any other target but is of least strategic value.

8. Use Against "Military" Objectives

A. It was agreed that for the initial use of the weapon any small and strictly military objective should be located in a much larger area subject to blast damage in order to avoid undue risks of the weapon being lost due to bad placing of the bomb.

9. Radiological Effect

A. Dr. Oppenheimer presented a memo he had prepared on the radiological effects of the gadget. This memo will not be repeated in this summary but it is being sent to General Groves as a separate exhibit. The basic recommendations of this memo are (1) for radiological reasons no aircraft should be closer than 2-1/2 miles to the point of detonation (for blast reasons the distance should be greater) and (2) aircraft must avoid the cloud of radio-active materials. If other aircraft are to conduct missions shortly after the detonation a monitoring plane should determine the areas to be avoided.

10. Coordinated Air Operations

A. The feasibility of following the raid by an incendiary mission was discussed. This has the great advantage that the enemies' fire fighting ability will probably be paralyzed by the gadget so that a very serious conflagration should be capable of being started. However, until more is learned about the phenomena associated with a detonation of the gadget, such as the extent to which there will be radio-active clouds, an incendiary mission immediately after the delivery of the gadget should be avoided. A coordinated incendiary raid should be feasible on the following day at which time the fire raid should still be quite effective. By delaying the coordinated raid to the following day, the scheduling of our already contemplated operations will not be made even more difficult, photo reconnaissance of the actual damage directly caused by our device can be obtained without confusion from the subsequent fire raid, and dangers from radio-active clouds can be avoided.

B. Fighter cover should be used for the operation as directed by the 21st Bomber Command.

11. Rehearsals

A. It was agreed by all that very complete rehearsals of the entire operation are essential to its success. It is possible for thirty (30) pumpkin units for this purpose to be shipped from this country in June with perhaps sixty (60) being shipped in July. These rehearsals overseas should take place beginning in July. At least some of the rehearsals should be very complete including the placing of spotter aircraft over the alternative targets, use of fighter cover, etc. Even though it is hoped that radar will not be used some rehearsals of radar operations are required in order that the operations may be carried out successfully if emergency arises for which they are required.

12. Operating Requirements for Safety of Aircraft

A. Dr. Penney reported some very encouraging information he had just received from England in this respect. His previous information was that no one could guarantee the safety of a large aircraft at blast pressures greater than 1/2 lb. per square inch. However, in some recent experiments in England large

aircraft have been flown over detonations of 2,000 lbs. of TNT and pilots have not objected to going as low as 900 feet. On this basis with a 100,000 ton total equivalent energy release or a 64,000 ton equivalent blast energy 23,000 feet would be a safe altitude on the basis of these experiments if allowance is made for the rarefaction of the atmosphere at high altitudes. However, due to the greater duration of the blast in our case, the safe height will probably be somewhat greater.

13. Coordination with 21st Program

A. This matter was included as part of the other discussion and is included in previous paragraphs of this summary.

14. The Next Meeting

It was agreed that the next meeting of the Target Committee should take place at 9:00 AM EWT on 28 May in Room 4E200 of the Pentagon Building in Washington. Dr. Oppenheimer recommended and others agreed that either Captain Parsons and/or Dr. Ramsey should attend this meeting.

15. High Classification

In view of the high classification of the minutes of this meeting it was agreed that copies should not be sent to those present but that instead one copy should be kept on file in General Groves' office, one copy in Dr. Oppenheimer's office, and one copy in Captain Parson's office.

[signature]
[signature]
Major J. A. Derry
Dr. N. F. Ramsey

dc

Distribution:
Copy 1: Maj Gen L. R. Groves
Copy 2: Capt. Parsons
Copies 3 & 4: J. R. Oppenheimer

Document 20.2 Recommendations of the Immediate Use of Nuclear Weapons, June 16, 1945

As the Manhattan Project neared completion, some scientists began considering and questioning the long-term impact of this project, both for the war with Japan and the postwar world. The "Franck Report" coming out of the University of Chicago warned about long-term radiation impacts and a nuclear arms race that could harm the United States. They suggested the United States demonstrate the bomb to Japanese and other world leaders on a deserted island before using it in combat. In response, the Interim Committee of scientists and governmental leaders recommended immediate use of the bomb. Most of the scientists on this panel were at Los Alamos, involved in the construction of the weapon. Why do they recommend immediate use of the weapon? What codicils do they recommend the government employ before bombing Japan?

Recommendations on the Immediate Use of Nuclear Weapons, June 16, 1945

Recommendations on the Immediate Use of Nuclear Weapons, by the Scientific Panel of the Interim Committee on Nuclear Power, June 16, 1945.

TOP SECRET

THIS PAGE REGRADED UNCLASSIFIED
Order Sec Army By TAG per 720564

THIS DOCUMENT CONSISTS OF 2 PAGE(S)
NO. 1 OF 12 COPIES, SERIES A

RECOMMENDATIONS ON THE IMMEDIATE USE OF NUCLEAR WEAPONS

A. H. Compton
E. O. Lawrence
J. R. Oppenheimer
E. Fermi

[signature]
J. R. Oppenheimer
For the Panel

June 16, 1945

You have asked us to comment on the initial use of the new weapon. This use, in our opinion, should be such as to promote a satisfactory adjustment of our international relations. At the same time, we recognize our obligation to our nation to use the weapons to help save American lives in the Japanese war.

(1) To accomplish these ends we recommend that before the weapons are used not only Britain, but also Russia, France, and China be advised that we have made considerable progress in our work on atomic weapons, that these may be ready to use during the present war, and that we would welcome suggestions as to how we can cooperate in making this development contribute to improved international relations.

(2) The opinions of our scientific colleagues on the initial use of these weapons are not unanimous: they range from the proposal of a purely technical demonstration to that of the military application best designed to induce surrender. Those who advocate a purely technical demonstration would wish to outlaw the use of atomic weapons, and have feared that if we use the weapons now our position in future negotiations will be prejudiced. Others emphasize the opportunity of saving American lives by immediate military use, and believe that such use will improve the international prospects, in that they are more concerned with the prevention of war than with the elimination of this specific weapon. We find ourselves closer to

---

Source: U. S. National Archives, Record Group 77, Records of the Office of the Chief of Engineers, Manhattan Engineer District, Harrison-Bundy File, Folder #76.

these latter views; we can propose no technical demonstration likely to bring an end to the war; we see no acceptable alternative to direct military use.

(3) With regard to these general aspects of the use of atomic energy, it is clear that we, as scientific men, have no proprietary rights. It is true that we are among the few citizens who have had occasion to give thoughtful consideration to these problems during the past few years. We have, however, no claim to special competence in solving the political, social, and military problems which are presented by the advent of atomic power.

Document 20.3 Meeting Held at the White House on Monday, 18 June 1945

The wartime goal of both the Roosevelt and Truman administrations was to win a decisive victory as quickly as possible, at the lowest cost in American lives. This thinking prompted the building and use of the atomic bomb, and is a point Harry Truman constantly referred to years later. President Truman also pointed to the White House meeting of June 18, 1945 as the place and time his advisors clearly warned about the human costs of continuing the war with Japan. Many of the plans discussed here, including relying on Russia's entry into the war, all discuss ways to cut American casualties. What are the expected casualties, and why is there such a range debated? What options are discussed for ending the war? What major concerns do the Joint Chiefs have for an invasion of Japan? Why do you think dropping the bomb was not discussed here?

Meeting held at the White House on Monday, 18 June 1945 at 1530

PRESENT

The President
Fleet Admiral William D. Leahy
General of the Army G.C. Marshall
Fleet Admiral E. J. King
Lieut. General I.C. Eaker (Representing
  General of the Army H.H. Arnold)
The Secretary of War, Mr. Stinsom
The Secretary of the Navy, Mr. Forrestal
The Assistant Secretary of War, Mr. McCloy

SECRETARY

Brig. General A.J. McFarland

1. Details of the Campaign Against Japan

THE PRESIDENT stated that he had called the meeting for the purpose of informing himself with respect to the details of the campaign against Japan set out in Admiral Leahy's memorandum to the Joint Chiefs of Staff of 14 June. He asked General Marshall if he would express his opinion.

GENERAL MARSHALL pointed out that the present situation with respect to operations against Japan was practically identical with the situation which had existed in connection with the operations proposed against Normandy He then read, as an expression of his views, the following digest of a memorandum prepared by the joint Chiefs of Staff for presentation to the President (J.C.S. 1388):

Our air and sea power has already greatly reduced movement of Jap shipping south of Korea and should in the next few months cut it to a trickle if not choke it off entirely. Hence, there is no need for seizing further positions in order to block Japanese communications south of Korea.

General MacArthur and Admiral Nimitz are in agreement with the Chiefs of Staff in selecting 1 November as the target date to go into Kyushu because by that time:

a. If we press preparations we can be ready.

b. Our estimates are that our air action will have smashed practically every industrial target worth hitting in Japan as well as destroying huge areas in the Jap cities.

c. The Japanese Navy, if any still exists, will be completely powerless.

d. Our sea action and air power will have cut Jap reinforcement capabilities from the mainland to negligible proportions.

Important considerations bearing on the 1 November date rather than a later one are the weather and cutting to a minimum Jap time for preparation of defenses. If we delay much after the beginning of November the weather situation in the succeeding months may be such that the invasion of Japan, and hence the end of the war, will be delayed for up to 6 months.

An outstanding military point about attacking Korea is the difficult terrain and beach conditions which appear to make the only acceptable assault areas Fusan in the southeast corner and Keijo, well up the western side. To get to Fusan, which is a strongly fortified area, we must move large and vulnerable assault forces past heavily fortified Japanese areas. The operation appears more difficult and costly than assault on Kyushu. Keijo appears an equally difficult and costly operation. After we have undertaken either one of them we still will not be as far forward as going into Kyushu.

The Kyushu operation is essential to a strategy of strangulation and appears to be the least costly worth-while operation following Okinawa. The basic point is that a lodgement in Kyushu is essential, both to tightening our strangle hold of blockade and bombardment on Japan, and to forcing capitulation by invasion of the Tokyo Plain.

We are bringing to bear against the Japanese every weapon and all the force we can employ and there is no reduction in our maximum possible application of bombardment and blockade, while at the same time we are pressing invasion preparations. It seems that if the Japanese are ever willing to capitulate short of complete military defeat in the field they will do it when faced by the completely hopeless prospect occasioned by (1) destruction already wrought by air bombardment and sea blockade, coupled with (2) a landing on Japan indicating the firmness of our resolution, and also perhaps coupled with (3) the entry or threat of entry of Russia into the war.

With reference to clean-up of the Asiatic mainland, our objective should be to get the Russians to deal with the Japs in Manchuria (and Korea if necessary) and to vitalize the Chinese to a point where, with assistance of American air power and some supplies, they can mop out their own country.

Casualties. Our experience in the Pacific war is so diverse as to casualties that it is considered wrong to give any estimate in numbers. Using various combinations of Pacific experience, the War Department staff reaches the conclusion that the cost of securing a worthwhile position in Korea would almost certainly be greater than the cost of the Kyushu operation. Points on the optimistic side of the Kyushu operation are that: General MacArthur has not yet accepted responsibility for going ashore where there would be disproportionate casualties. The nature of the objective area gives room for maneuver, both on the land and by sea. As to any discussion of specific operations, the following data are pertinent:

Campaign	U.S. Casualties Killed, wounded, missing	Jap Casualties Killed and Prisoners (Not including wounded)	Ratio U.S. to Jap
Leyto	17,000	78,000	1:4.6
Luzon	31,000	156,000	1:5.0
Iwo Jima	20,000	25,000	1:1.25
Okinawa	34,000 (Ground) 7,700 (Navy)	81,000 (not a complete count)	1:2
Normandy (1st 30 days)	42,000		

The record of General MacArthur's operations from 1 March 1944 through 1 May 1945 shows 13,742 U.S. killed compared to 310,165 Japanese killed, or a ratio of 22 to 1.

There is reason to believe that the first 30 days in Kyushu should not exceed the price we have paid for Luzon. It is a grim fact that there is not an easy, bloodless way to victory in war and it is the thankless task of the leaders to maintain their firm outward front which holds the resolution of their subordinates. Any irresolution in the leaders may result in costly weakening and indecision in the subordinates. It was this basic difficulty with the Prime Minister which clouded and hampered all our preparations for the cross channel operation now demonstrated as having been essential to victory in Europe.

An important point about Russian participation in the war is that the impact of Russian entry on the already hopeless Japanese may well be the decisive action levering them into capitulation at that time or shortly thereafter if we land in Japan.

In considering the matter of command and control in the Pacific war which the British wish to raise at the next conference, we must bear in mind the point that anything smacking of combined command in the Pacific might increase the difficulties with Russia and perhaps with China. Furthermore the obvious inefficiencies of combined command may directly result in increased cost in resources and American lives.

GENERAL MARSHALL said that he had asked General MacArthur's opinion on the proposed operation and had received from him the following telegram, which General Marshall then read:

"I believe the operation presents less hazards of excessive loss than any other that has been suggested and that its decisive effect will eventually save lives by eliminating wasteful operations of nondecisive character. I regard the operation as the most economical one in effort and lives that is possible. In this respect it must be remembered that the several preceeding months will involve practically no losses in ground troops and that sooner or later a decisive ground attack must be made. The hazard and loss will be greatly lessened if an attack is launched from Siberia sufficiently ahead of our target date to commit the enemy to major combat. I most earnestly recommend no change in OLYMPIC. Additional subsidiary attacks will simply build up our final total casualties."

GENERAL MARSHALL said that it was his personal view that the operation against Kyushu was the only course to pursue. He felt that air power alone was not sufficient to put the Japanese out of the war. It was unable alone to put the Germans out. General Eaker and General Eisenhower both agreed to this. Against the Japanese, scattered through mountainous country, the problem would be much more difficult that it had been in Germany. He felt that this plan offered the only way the Japanese could be forced into a feeling of utter helplessnes. The operation would be difficult but not more so than the assault in Normandy. He was convinced that every individual moving to the Pacific should be indoctrinated with a firm determination to see it through.

ADMIRAL KING agreed with General Marshall's views and said that the more he studied the matter, the more he was impressed with the strategic location of Kyushu, which he considered the key to the success of any siege operations. He pointed out that within three months the effects of air power based on Okinawa will begin to be felt strongly in Japan. It seemed to him that Kyushu followed logically after Okinawa. It was a natural setup. It was his opinion that we should do Kyushu now, after which there would be time to judge the effect of possible operations by the Russians and the Chinese. The weather constituted quite a factor. So far as preparation was concerned, we must aim now for Tokyo Plain; otherwise we will never be able to accomplish it. If preparations do not go forward now, they cannot be arranged for later. Once started, however, they can always be stopped if desired.

GENERAL MARSHALL agreed that Kyushu was a necessity and pointed out that it constituted a landing in the Japanese homeland. Kyushu having been arranged for, the decision as to further action could be made later.

THE PRESIDENT inquired if a later decision would not depend on what the Russians agree to do. It was agreed that this would have considerable influence.

THE PRESIDENT then asked Admiral Leahy for his views of the situation.

ADMIRAL LEAHY recalled that the President had been interested in knowing what the price in casualties for Kyushu would be and whether or not that price could be paid. He pointed out that the troops on Okinawa had lost 35 percent in casualties. If this percentage were applied to the number of troops to be employed in Kyushu, he thought from the similarity of the fighting to be expected that this would give a good estimate of the casualties to be expected. He was interested therefore in finding out how many troops are to be used in Kyushu.

ADMIRAL KING called attention to what he considered an important difference in Okinawa and Kyushu. There had been only one way to go on Okinawa. This meant a straight frontal attack against a highly fortified position. On Kyushu, however, landings would be made on three fronts simultaneously and there would be much more room for maneuver. It was his opinion that a realistic casualty figure for Kyushu would lie somewhere between the number experienced by General MacArthur in the operations on Luzon and the Okinawa casualties.

GENERAL MARSHALL pointed out that the total assault troops for the Kyushu campaign were shown in the memorandum prepared for the President as 766,700. He said, in answer to the President's question as to what opposition could be expected on Kyushu, that it was estimated at eight Japanese divisions or about 350,000 troops. He said that divisions were still being raised in Japan and that reinforcement from other areas was possible but it was becoming increasingly difficult and painful.

THE PRESIDENT asked about the possibility of reinforcements for Kyushu moving south from the other Japanese islands.

GENERAL MARSHALL said that it was expected that all communications with Kyushu would be destroyed.

ADMIRAL KING described in some detail the land communications between the other Japanese islands and Kyushu and stated that as a result of operations already planned, the Japanese would have to depend on sea shipping for any reinforcement.

ADMIRAL LEAHY stressed the fact that Kyushu was an island. It was crossed by a mountain range, which would be difficult for either the Japanese or the Americans to cross. The Kyushu operation, in effect, contemplated the taking of another island from which to bring increased air power against Japan.

THE PRESIDENT expressed the view that it was practically creating another Okinawa closer to Japan, to which the Chiefs of Staff agreed.

THE PRESIDENT then asked General Eaker for his opinion of the operation as an air man.

GENERAL EAKER said that he agreed completely with the statements made by General Marshall in his digest of the memorandum prepared for the President. He had just received a cable in which General Arnold also expressed complete agreement. He stated that any blockade of Honshu was dependent upon airdromes on Kyushu; that the air plan contemplated employment of 40 groups of heavy bombers against Japan and that these could not be deployed without the use of airfields on Kyushu. He said that those who advocated the use against Japan of air power alone overlooked the very impressive fact that air casualties are always much heavier when the air faces the enemy alone and that these casualties never fail to drop as soon as the ground forces

come in. Present air casualties are averaging 2 percent per mission, about 30 percent per month. He wished to point out and to emphasize that delay favored only the enemy and he urged that there be no delay.

THE PRESIDENT said that as he understood it the Joint Chiefs of Staff, after weighing all the possibilities of the situation and considering all possible alternative plans were still of the unanimous opinion that the Kyushu operation was the best solution under the circumstances.

The Chiefs of Staff agreed that this was so.

THE PRESIDENT then asked the Secretary of War for his opinion.

MR. STIMSON agreed with the Chiefs of Staff that there was no other choice. He felt that he was personally responsible to the President more for political than for Military considerations. It was his opinion that there was a large submerged class in Japan who do not favor the present war and whose full opinion and influence had never yet been felt. He felt sure that this submerged class would fight and fight tenaciously if attacked on their own ground. He was concerned that something should be done to arouse them and to develop any possible influence they might have before it became necessary to come to grips with them.

THE PRESIDENT stated that this possibility was being worked on all the time. He asked if the invasion of Japan by white men would not have the effect of more closely uniting the Japanese.

MR. STIMSON thought there was every prospect of this. He agreed with the plan proposed by the Joint Chiefs of Staff as being the best thing to do, but he still hoped for some fruitful accomplishment through other means.

THE PRESIDENT then asked for the views of the Secretary of the Navy.

MR. FORRESTAL pointed out that even if we wished to besiege Japan for a year or a year and a half, the capture of Kyushu would still be essential. Therefore, the sound decision is to proceed with the operation against Kyushu. There will still be time thereafter to consider the main decision in the light of subsequent events.

MR. McCLOY said he felt that the time was propitious now to study closely all possible means of bringing out the influence of the submerged group in Japan which had been referred to by Mr. Stimson.

THE PRESIDENT stated that one of his objectives in connection with the coming conference would be to get from Russia all the assistance in the war that was possible. To this end he wanted to know all the decisions that he would have to make in advance in order to occupy the strongest possible position in the discussions.

ADMIRAL LEAHY said that he could not agree with those who said to him that unless we obtain the unconditional surrender of the Japanese that we will have lost the war. He feared no menace from Japan in the foreseeable future, even if we were unsuccessful in forcing unconditional surrender. What he did fear was that our insistence on unconditional surrender would result only in making the Japanese desperate and thereby increase our casualty lists. He did not think that this was at all necessary.

THE PRESIDENT stated that it was with that thought in mind that he had left the door open for Congress to take appropriate action with reference to unconditional surrender. However, he did not feel that he could take any action at this time to change public opinion on the matter.

THE PRESIDENT said he considered the Kyushu plan all right from the military standpoint and, so far as he was concerned, the Joint Chiefs of Staff could go ahead with it; that we can do this operation and then decide as to the final action later.

The conversation then turned on the situation in China.

GENERAL MARSHALL stated that General Wedemeyer's operations were pointing towards Canton. He thought it was already evident that the Japanese would hold fortress troops there and in other places. It might be necessary to go around these fortress troops as had been done in France or to take other courses with respect to them.

In reply to a question from the President, GENERAL MARSHALL outlined the present status of Chinese divisions as to completeness of personnel and equipment. He said the military ability of the Chinese generals was not very good. He had already asked General Wedemeyer whether it would be possible to use with the Chinlese troops one or more of the U.S. Army commanders with their staffs, who were now returning from France. General Wedemeyer's reply, while not conclusive, had been, in general, favorable. General Marshall thought that if the Generalissimo would accept the use of these commanders for control of Chinese groups, it would be a very excellent thing.

THE PRESIDENT then inquired as to the possibility of getting an over-all commander in the Pacific.

GENERAL MARSHALL and ADMIRAL KING both agreed that under the circumstances existing in the Pacific there was little prospect of it. ADMIRAL KING pointed out that it was undesir-

able to accept divided command with the British and that we would lose more than we would gain if we brought about in the Pacific the situation that had existed in France.

GENERAL MARSHALL stated the American commander would always have to think of his government's policies. In connection with this, he recounted the difficulty experienced in Malta in obtaining British agreement to General Eisenhower's plan for the invasion of Germany. Their reluctance in the matter was due to their belief that General Eisenhower was influenced by the American commanders.

THE PRESIDENT said he was simply interested in finding out whether an over-all commander for the Pacific would be an advantage or a liability.

GENERAL MARSHALL said that from the large point of view there was no question about its being a liability.

In connection with British participation in the Pacific, General Marshall said that the President would find the Prime Minister very articulate. He is interested in showing that the British Government has played a full part in the defeat of Japan and that it had not been necessary for them to wait for the United States to recapture Singapore for them. The Americans, of course, were glad to have any real help or any assistance that would result in striking a real blow, but that British participation in some ways would constitute an embarrassment. However, the British were under American over-all command in the Pacific.

THE PRESIDENT referred to the Portuguese participation in the Southwest Pacific and stated that he wished to get the air program definitely settled with the Portuguese before we do anything more about Timor.

THE PRESIDENT reiterated that his main reason for this conference with the Chiefs of Staff was his desire to know definitely how far we could afford to go in the Japanese campaign. He had hoped that there was a possibility of preventing an Okinawa from one end of Japan to the other. He was clear on the situation now and was quite sure that the Joint Chiefs of Staff should proceed with the Kyushu operation.

With reference to operations in China, GENERAL MARSHALL expressed the opinion that we should not seek an over-all commander in China. The present situation in which the Geraralissimo was supporting General Wedemeyer, acting as his Chief of Staff, was entirely satisfactory. The suggestion of the appointment of an over-all commander might cause some difficulty.

ADMIRAL KING said he wished to emphasize the point that, regardless of the desirability of the Russians entering the war, they were not indispensable and he did not think we should go so far as to beg them to come in. While the cost of defeating Japan would be greater, there was no question in his mind but that we could handle it alone. He thought that the realization of this fact should greatly strengthen the President's hand in the forthcoming conference.

THE PRESIDENT and the Chiefs of Staff then discussed certain other matters.

2. Reinstatement of Lend-Lease Supplies to the French

ADMIRAL LEAHY read a telegram in which General McNarney recommended that Lend-Lease supplies to the French be reinstated after the French withdrawal from northern Italy had been completed. He asked the President's views.

THE PRESIDENT stated that he agreed with General McNarney's recommendations and felt that he should be supported.

THE PRESIDENT expressed his appreciation of the results of his conference with the Joint Chiefs of Staff. He said it cleared up a great many points in his mind and that he now felt satisfied and reassured.

Document 20.4 Leo Szilard: A Petition to the President of the United States, July 17, 1945

Leo Szilard was born in Hungary in 1898, studied physics under and later collaborated with Albert Einstein at the University of Berlin, and fled Germany in 1933 to escape Nazi persecution. That same year he conceived the idea of a nuclear chain reaction. Moving to the United States in 1939, he convinced Albert Einstein to sign a letter he drafted, warning President Roosevelt about the dangers of the Nazis' developing an atomic bomb, thus triggering the development of the Manhattan Project. Working with Enrico Fermi at the University of Chicago, he achieved the first self-sustaining nuclear reaction in 1942. Worried about the immorality of atomic weapons, and foreseeing the nuclear arms race of the Cold War, he first co-authored the Franck Report, and then unsuccessfully sought personal meetings with the president. This petition, signed by 69 other scientists in the Manhattan Project working at the University of Chicago, reflected the growing concern in the scientific community that their research would be used for strictly military objectives. According to the petition, why do the signers feel the atomic bomb should not be used? If used, what guidelines for its use should be established? What do they fear in the future?

A Petition to the President of the United States

On July 17, 1945, Leo Szilard and 69 co-signers at the Manhattan Project "Metallurgical Laboratory" in Chicago petitioned the President of the United States.

July 17, 1945

Discoveries of which the people of the United States are not aware may affect the welfare of this nation in the near future. The liberation of atomic power which has been achieved places atomic bombs in the hands of the Army. It places in your hands, as Commander-in-Chief, the fateful decision whether or not to sanction the use of such bombs in the present phase of the war against Japan.

We, the undersigned scientists, have been working in the field of atomic power. Until recently, we have had to fear that the United States might be

---

Source: U.S. National Archives, Record Group 77, Records of the Chief of Engineers, Manhattan Engineer District, Harrison-Bundy File, folder #76.

attacked by atomic bombs during this war and that her only defense might lie in a counterattack by the same means. Today, with the defeat of Germany, this danger is averted and we feel impelled to say what follows:

The war has to be brought speedily to a successful conclusion and attacks by atomic bombs may very well be an effective method of warfare. We feel, however, that such attacks on Japan could not be justified, at least not unless the terms which will be imposed after the war on Japan were made public in detail and Japan were given an opportunity to surrender.

If such public announcement gave assurance to the Japanese that they could look forward to a life devoted to peaceful pursuits in their homeland and if Japan still refused to surrender our nation might then, in certain circumstances, find itself forced to resort to the use of atomic bombs. Such a step, however, ought not to be made at any time without seriously considering the moral responsibilities which are involved.

The development of atomic power will provide the nations with new means of destruction. The atomic bombs at our disposal represent only the first step in this direction, and there is almost no limit to the destructive power which will become available in the course of their future development. Thus a nation which sets the precedent of using these newly liberated forces of nature for purposes of destruction may have to bear the responsibility of opening the door to an era of devastation on an unimaginable scale.

If after this war a situation is allowed to develop in the world which permits rival powers to be in uncontrolled possession of these new means of destruction, the cities of the United States as well as the cities of other nations will be in continuous danger of sudden annihilation. All the resources of the United States, moral and material, may have to be mobilized to prevent the advent of such a world situation. Its prevention is at present the solemn responsibility of the United States—singled out by virtue of her lead in the field of atomic power.

The added material strength which this lead gives to the United States brings with it the obligation of restraint and if we were to violate this obligation our moral position would be weakened in the eyes of the world and in our own eyes. It would then be more difficult for us to live up to our responsibility of bringing the unloosened forces of destruction under control.

In view of the foregoing, we, the undersigned, respectfully petition: first, that you exercise your power as Commander-in-Chief, to rule that the United States shall not resort to the use of atomic bombs in this war unless the terms which will be imposed upon Japan have been made public in detail and Japan knowing these terms has refused to surrender; second, that in such an event the question whether or not to use atomic bombs be decided by you in light of the considerations presented in this petition as well as all the other moral responsibilities which are involved.

Leo Szilard and 69 co-signers

Signers listed in alphabetical order, with position identifications added:

1. DAVID S. ANTHONY, Associate Chemist
2. LARNED B. ASPREY, Junior Chemist, S.E.D.
3. WALTER BARTKY, Assistant Director
4. AUSTIN M. BRUES, Director, Biology Division
5. MARY BURKE, Research Assistant
6. ALBERT CAHN, JR., Junior Physicist
7. GEORGE R. CARLSON, Research Assistant-Physics
8. KENNETH STEWART COLE, Principal Bio-Physicist
9. ETHALINE HARTGE CORTELYOU, Junior Chemist
10. JOHN CRAWFORD, Physicist
11. MARY M. DAILEY, Research Assistant
12. MIRIAM P. FINKEL, Associate Biologist
13. FRANK G. FOOTE, Metallurgist
14. HORACE OWEN FRANCE, Associate Biologist
15. MARK S. FRED, Research Associate-Chemistry
16. SHERMAN FRIED, Chemist
17. FRANCIS LEE FRIEDMAN, Physicist
18. MELVIN S. FRIEDMAN, Associate Chemist
19. MILDRED C. GINSBERG, Computer
20. NORMAN GOLDSTEIN, Junior Physicist
21. SHEFFIELD GORDON, Associate Chemist
22. WALTER J. GRUNDHAUSER, Research Assistant
23. CHARLES W. HAGEN, Research Assistant
24. DAVID B. HALL, position not identified
25. DAVID L. HILL, Associate Physicist, Argonne
26. JOHN PERRY HOWE, JR., Associate Division Director, Chemistry
27. EARL K. HYDE, Associate Chemist

28. JASPER B. JEFFRIES, Junior Physicist, Junior Chemist
29. WILLIAM KARUSH, Associate Physicist
30. TRUMAN P. KOHMAN, Chemist-Research
31. HERBERT E. KUBITSCHEK, Junior Physicist
32. ALEXANDER LANGSDORF, JR., Research Associate
33. RALPH E. LAPP, Assistant to Division Director
34. LAWRENCE B. MAGNUSSON, Junior Chemist
35. ROBERT JOSEPH MAURER, Physicist
36. NORMAN FREDERICK MODINE, Research Assistant
37. GEORGE S. MONK, Physicist
38. ROBERT JAMES MOON, Physicist
39. MARIETTA CATHERINE MOORE, Technician
40. ROBERT SANDERSON MULLIKEN, Coordinator of Information
41. J. J. NICKSON, [Medical Doctor, Biology Division]
42. WILLIAM PENROD NORRIS, Associate Biochemist
43. PAUL RADELL O'CONNOR, Junior Chemist
44. LEO ARTHUR OHLINGER, Senior Engineer
45. ALFRED PFANSTIEHL, Junior Physicist
46. ROBERT LEROY PLATZMAN, Chemist
47. C. LADD PROSSER, Biologist
48. ROBERT LAMBURN PURBRICK, Junior Physicist
49. WILFRED RALL, Research Assistant-Physics
50. MARGARET H. RAND, Research Assistant, Health Section
51. WILLIAM RUBINSON, Chemist
52. B. ROSWELL RUSSELL, position not identified
53. GEORGE ALAN SACHER, Associate Biologist
54. FRANCIS R. SHONKA, Physicist
54. ERIC L. SIMMONS, Associate Biologist, Health Group
56. JOHN A. SIMPSON, JR., Physicist
57. ELLIS P. STEINBERG, Junior Chemist
58. D. C. STEWART, S/SGT S.E.D.
59. GEORGE SVIHLA, position not identified [Health Group]
60. MARGUERITE N. SWIFT, Associate Physiologist, Health Group
61. LEO SZILARD, Chief Physicist
62. RALPH E. TELFORD, position not identified
63. JOSEPH D. TERESI, Associate Chemist
64. ALBERT WATTENBERG, Physicist
65. KATHERINE WAY, Research Assistant
66. EDGAR FRANCIS WESTRUM, JR., Chemist
67. EUGENE PAUL WIGNER, Physicist
68. ERNEST J. WILKINS, JR., Associate Physicist
69. HOYLANDE YOUNG, Senior Chemist
70. WILLIAM F. H. ZACHARIASEN, Consultant

Source note: The position identifications for the signers are based on two undated lists, both titled "July 17, 1945," in the same file as the petition in the National Archives. From internal evidence, one probably was prepared in late 1945 and the other in late 1946. Signers were categorized as either "Important" or "Not Important," and dates of termination from project employment were listed in many cases. It is reasonable to conclude that the lists were prepared and used for the purpose of administrative retaliation against the petition signers.

Document 20.5 Memorandum for General Arnold, Subject: Groves Project, July 24, 1945

General H.H. Arnold commanded the Army Air Force in World War II. This memorandum is essentially the order from President Truman to use the bomb. The target list was revised by Secretary of War Stimson to eliminate any cultural centers that could incite further resistance from Japan. Compare the new target list with the one created earlier, and note the justifications for each target. How detailed are the tactics and planning getting now?

Memorandum for General Arnold

SUBJECT: Groves Project

1. The following plan and schedule for initial attacks using special bombs have been worked out:

   a. The first bomb (gun type) will be ready to drop between August 1 and 10 and plans are to drop it the first day of good weather following readiness.

   b. The following targets have been selected: Hiroshima, Kokura, Niigata and Nagasaki.

      (1) Hiroshima (population 350,000) is an "Army" city; a major POE; has large QM and supply depots; has considerable industry and several small shipyards.

      (2) Nagasaki (population 210,000) is a major shipping and industrial center of Kyushu.

      (3) Kokura (population 178,000) has one of the largest army arsenals and ordnance works; has the largest railroad shops on Kyushu: and has large munitions storage to the south.

      (4) Niigata (population 150,000) is an important industrial city, building machine tools, diesel engines, etc., and is a key port for shipping to the mainland.

   c. All four cities are believed to contain large numbers of key Japanese industrialists and political figures who have sought refuge from major destroyed cities.

   d. The attack is planned to be visual to insure accuracy and will await favorable weather. The four targets give a very high probability of one being open even if the weather varies from that forecast, as they are considerably separated.

   e. The bomb will be carried in a master airplane accompanied by two other project B-29's with observers and special instruments.

   f. The three B-29's will take off from North Field Tinian, and fly via Iwo Jima. The use of fighter escort will be determined by General Spaatz upon consideration of all operational factors.

   g. The master plane will attack the selected target from [?] feet plus altitude will immediately upon release of the bomb make a steep diving turn away from the target to achieve maximum slant range distance as quickly as possible. Recording planes and fighters if employed will be kept several miles from the target. The participating planes are believed to be safe from the effects of the bomb.

   h. The bomb will be detonated by radar proximiter fuze about 2,000 feet above the ground.

   i. Emergency arrangements have been provided at Iwo Jima for handling the bomb if required.

2. Two tested type bombs are expected to be available in August, one about the 6th and another the 24th. General Groves expects to have more information on future availabilities in a few days which will be furnished you when received.

3. The above has been discussed with Generals Spaatz and Eaker who concur.

JOHN N. STONE
Colonel, GSC

Document 20.6 Pages from President Truman's Diary; July 17, 18, and 25, 1945

The Potsdam Conference was the last major meeting between the World War II Coalition leaders. They were supposed to iron out differences on managing postwar Europe, rebuilding the continent, and concluding the war with Japan. President Truman postponed the meeting so that the "Trinity" test of the atomic bomb could occur while he was there. He hoped having a successful bomb test would give him more bargaining power. When he left for the conference, most of his advisors concluded he should tell both Winston Churchill and Joseph Stalin about the bomb. How do plans about telling Stalin about the bomb change during the conference? How does President Truman describe the test? What is his announced military goal for using the weapon?

July 17, '45

Just spent a couple of hours with Stalin. Joe Denis called on Maiski and made the date last night for noon today. Promptly a few minutes before twelve I looked up from the desk and there stood Stalin in the doorway. I got to my feet and advanced to meet him. He put out his hand and smiled. I did the same, we shook, I greeted Molotov and the interpreter and we sat down. After the usual polite remarks we got down to business. I told Stalin that I am no diplomat but usually said yes or no to questions after hearing all the argument. It pleased him. I asked him if he had the agenda for the meeting. He said he had some more questions to present. I told him to fire away. He did and it is dynamite—but I have some dynamite too which I'm not exploding now. He wants to fire Fianco, to which I wouldn't object and divide up the Italian colonies and other mandates, some no doubt that the British have. Then he got on the Chinese situation told us what agreements had been reached and what was in abeyance. Most of the big points are settled. He'll be in the Jap War on August 15th. Fini Japs when that comes about. We had lunch, talked socially, put on a real sham drinking toasts to everyone, then had pictures made in the back yard. I can deal with Stalin. He is honest—but smart as hell.

July 18, [19]45

Ate breakfast with nephew Harry, a sergeant in the Field Artillery. He is a good soldier and a nice boy. They took him off Queen Elizabeth at Glasco and flew him here. Sending him home Friday. Went to lunch with P.M., at 1:30 walked around to British Hqrs. Met at the gate by Mr. Churchill. Guard of honor drawn up. Fine body of men Scottish Guards. Band played Star Spangled Banner. Inspected Guard and went in for lunch. P.M. and I ate alone. Discussed Manhattan (it is a success). Decided to tell Stalin about it. Stalin had told P.M. of telegram from Jap Emperor asking for peace. Stalin also read his answer to me. It was satisfactory. Believe Japs will fold up before Russia comes in.

I am sure they will when Manhattan appears over their homeland. I shall inform Stalin about it at an opportune time. Stalin's luncheon was a most satisfactory meeting. I invited him to come to the U.S. Told him I'd send the Battleship Missouri for him if he'd come. He said he wanted to cooperate with U.S. in peace as we had cooperated in war but it would be harder. Said he was grossly misunderstood in U.S. and I was misunderstood in Russia. I told him that we

each could help to remedy that situation in our home countries and that I intended to try with all I had to do my part at home. He gave me a most cordial smile and said he would do as much in Russia.

We then went to the conference and it was my job to present the Ministers proposed agenda. There were three proposals and I banged them through in short order, much to the surprise of Mr. Churchill. Stalin was very much pleased. Churchill was too after he had recovered. I'm not going to stay around this terrible place all Sunday just to listen to speeches. I'll go home to the Senate for that.

July 20, '45

Jim Blair now Lt. Col. came in for breakfast. Harry left for Paris & N.Y. Sure hated to see him go. Discussed German situation with Jim. He had been in command of clean up detail which prepared the area for American occupation especially for our conference delegation. Said it was the filthiest place imaginable. No sanitary arrangement whatever. Toilets all full and all stopped up. Basements used as outdoor toilets. Said the sewer system evidently hadn't worked for months. Same all over town. Said Germans are sore and sullen. That we would not treat them rough enough. Russians treated 'em too rough and too kindly. Anyway it's a hell of a mess any way it's taken.

Saw Gen. Omar Bradley about taking over the Vets. bureau. Will take over Aug. 15th. Talked to Gen. Eisenhower about government of Germany along same lines as I'd talked to Gen. Clay. Got a concrete program to present.

Raised a flag over our area in Berlin. It is the flag raised in Rome, North Africa and Paris. Flag was on the White House when Pearl Harbor happened. Will be raised over Tokyo.

Uncle Joe looked drawn and tired today and the P.M. seemed lost. I told 'em U.S. had ceased to give away its assets without returns.

July 25, 1945

We met at 11 A.M. today. That is Stalin, Churchill, and the U.S. President. But I had a most important session with Lord Mountbatten and General Marshall before that. We have discovered the most terrible bomb in the history of the world. It may be the fire distruction [destruction] prophesied in the Euphrates Valley Era, after Noah and his fabulous Ark. Anyway we think we have found the way to cause a disintegration of the atom. An experiment in the New Mexican desert was startling—to put it mildly. Thirteen pounds of the explosive caused the complete disintegration of a steel tower 60 feet high, created a crater 6 feet deep and 1200 feet in diameter, knocked over a steel tower 1/2 mile away and knocked men down 10,000 yards away. The explosion was visible for more than 200 miles and audible for 40 miles and more.

This weapon is to be used against Japan between now and August 10th. I have told the Sec. of War, Mr. Stimson to use it so that military objectives and soldiers and sailors are the target and not women and children. Even if the world for the common welfare cannot drop this terrible bomb on the old Capitol or the new.

He and I are in accord. The target will be a purely military one and we will issue a warning statement asking the Japs to surrender and save lives. I'm sure they will not do that, but we will have given them the chance. It is certainly a good thing for the world that Hitler's crowd or Stalin's did not discover this atomic bomb. It seems to be the most terrible thing ever discovered, but it can be made the most useful.

At 10:15 I had Gen. Marshall come in and discuss with me the tactical and political situation. He is a level headed man—so is Mountbatten.

At the conference Poland and the Bolshiriki land grant came up. Russia liked herself to a slice of Poland and gave Poland a nice slice of Germany taking also a good slice of East Prussia for herself. Poland has moved in up to the Oder and the west Nilsse, taking Stettin and Silesia as a fact accomplished. My position is that according to commitments made at Yalta by my predecessor, Germany was to be divided into four occupation zones, one each for Britain, Russia and France and the U.S. If Russia chooses to allow Poland to occupy a part of her zone I am agreeable but title to territory cannot and will not be settled here. For the fourth time I've stated my position and explained that territorial sessions had to be made by treaty and ratified by the Senate.

We discussed reparations and movement of populations from East Germany, Czechoslovakia, Austria, Italy and elsewhere. Churchill said Maisky had so defined war booty as to include the German fleet and Merchant Marine. It was a bomb shell and sort of paralyzed the Ruskies, but it has a lot of merit.

July 16, 1945

Last night talked to Gen. Somersville on time for universal military training. Regular Army wants a straight year. I am very sure it cannot be put into

effect. Talked to McCaffery about France. He is scared stiff of Communism, the Russian society which isn't communism at all but just police government pure and simple. A few top hands just take clubs, pistols and concentration camps and rule the people on the lower levels.

The Communist Party in Moscow is no different in its methods and actions toward the common man than were the Czar and the Russian Noblemen (so called: they were anything but noble) Nazis and Facists were worse. It seems that Sweden, Norway, Denmark and perhaps Switzerland have the only real peoples government on the Continent of Europe. But the rest are a bad lot from the standpoint of the people who do not believe in tyranny.

July 30, 1945

Sent Capt. Vardaman to ship at Portsmouth, Eng. to get ready for departure to US some day soon. Secretary of Navy Joe Forestal came to breakfast with me and we discussed universal military service after the war and navy policy on office training etc. Gen. Eisenhower and son were also at breakfast with us. His boy is a nice fellow. Adm. Cochran and several other naval officers were present.

Conference is delayed. Stalin and Molotov were to call on me yesterday to discuss Polish question and Reparations. Molotov came but no Stalin. Said he is sick. No big three meeting yesterday and none today as a result of Stalins indisposition. Sent him a note expressing regret at his illness. Sent Churchill a note of consolation, telling him we regretted his failure to return and wishing him a long and happy life.

If Stalin should suddenly cash in it would end the original Big Three. First Roosevelt by death, then Churchill by political failure and then Stalin. I am wondering what would happen to Russia and central Europe if Joe suddenly passed out. If some demagogue on horse back gained control of the efficient Russian military machine he could play havoc with European peace for a while. I also wonder if there is a man with the necessary strength and following to step into Stalin's place and maintain peace and solidarity at home. It isn't customary for dictators to train leaders to follow them in power. I've seen no one at this Conference in the Russian line up who can do the job. Molotov is not able to do it. He lacks sincerity. Vishinsky same thing and Maisky is short on honesty. Well we shall see what we shall see. Uncle Joe's pretty tough mentally and physically but there is an end to every man and we can't help but speculate.

We are at an impasse on Poland and its western boundary and on Reparations Russia and Poland have agreed on the Oder and West Niesse to the Czechoslovakian border. Just a unilateral arrangement without so much a by your lease. I don't like it. Roosevelt let Maisky mention twenty billions as reparations—half for Russia and half for everybody else. Experts say no such figure is available.

I've made it plain that the United States of America does not intend to pay reparations this time. I want the German war industry machine completely dismantled and far as U.S. is concerned the other allies can divide it up on any basis they choose. Food and other necessities we send into the restored countries and Germany must be first lein on export before reparation. If Russian strip country and carry off population of course there'll be no reparations.

I have offered a waterway program and a suggestion for free intercourse between Central European nations which will help keep future peace. Our only hope for good from the European War is restored prosperity to Europe and future trade with them. It is a sick situation at best.

Document 20.7 Draft of a White House Press Release, August 6, 1945

This is the statement from President Truman to the American people announcing the building and use of the first atomic bomb on Hiroshima. How does he describe the weapon to our citizens? How does President Truman justify its use? Considering all you have read, are there some important things missing from this announcement that he did not tell the American people?

THE WHITE HOUSE
Washington, D.C.

IMMEDIATE RELEASE

STATEMENT BY THE PRESIDENT OF THE UNITED STATES

Sixteen hours ago an American airplane dropped one bomb on _____ and destroyed its usefulness to the enemy. That bomb had more power than 20,000 tons of T.N.T. It has more than two thousand times the blast power of the British "Grand Slam" which is the largest bomb ever yet used in the history of warfare.

The Japanese began the war from the air at Pearl Harbor. They have been repaid many fold. And the end is not yet. With this bomb we have now added a new and revolutionary increase in destruction to supplement the growing power of our armed forces. In their present form these bombs are now in production and even more powerful forms are in development.

It is an atomic bomb. It is a harnessing of the basic power of the universe. The force from which the sun draws its power has been loosed against those who brought war to the Far East.

Before 1939, it was the accepted belief of scientists that it was theoretically possible to release atomic energy. But no one knew any practical method of doing it. By 1942, however, we knew that the Germans were working feverishly to find a way to add atomic energy to the other engines of war with which they hoped to enslave the world. But they failed. We may be grateful to Providence that the Germans got the V-1's and V-2's late and in limited quantities and even more grateful that they did not get the atomic bomb at all.

The battle of the laboratories held fateful risks for us as well as the battles of the air, land and sea, and we have now won the battle of the laboratories as we have won the other battles.

Beginning in 1940, before Pearl Harbor, scientific knowledge useful in war was pooled between the United States and Great Britain, and many priceless helps to our victories have come from that arrangement. Under that general policy the research on the atomic bomb was begun. With American and British scientists working together we entered the race of discovery against the Germans.

The United States had available the large number of scientists of distinction in the many needed areas of knowledge. It had the tremendous industrial and financial resources necessary for the project and they could be devoted to it without undue impairment of other vital war work. In the United States the laboratory work and the production plants, on which a substantial start had already been made, would be out of reach of enemy bombing, while at that time Britain was exposed to constant air attack and was still threatened with the possibility of invasion. For these reasons Prime Minister Churchill and President Roosevelt agreed that it was wise to carry on the project here. We now have two great plants and many lesser works devoted to the production of atomic power. Employment during peak construction numbered 125,000 and over 65,000 individuals are even now engaged in operating the plants. Many have worked there for two and a half years. Few know what they have been producing. They see great quantities of material going in and they see nothing coming out of these plants, for the physical size of the explosive change is exceedingly small. We have spent two billion dollars on the greatest scientific gamble in history—and won.

But the greatest marvel is not the size of the enterprise, its secrecy, nor its cost, but the achievement of scientific brains in putting together infinitely complex pieces of knowledge held by many men in different fields of science into a workable plan. And hardly less marvelous has been the capacity of industry to design, and of labor to operate, the machines and methods to do things never done before so that the brain child of many minds came forth in physical shape and performed as it was supposed to do. Both science and industry worked under the direction of the United States Army, which achieved a unique success in managing so diverse a problem in the advancement of knowledge in an amazingly short time. It is doubtful if such another combination could be got together in the world. What has been done is the greatest achievement of organized science in history. It was done under high pressure and without failure.

We are now prepared to obliterate more rapidly and completely every productive enterprise the Japanese have above ground in any city. We shall destroy their docks, their factories, and their communications. Let there be no mistake; we shall completely destroy Japan's power to make war.

It was to spare the Japanese people from utter destruction that the ultimatum of July 26 was issued at Potsdam. Their leaders promptly rejected that ulti-matum. If they do not now accept our terms they may expect a rain of ruin from the air, the like of which has never been seen on this earth. Behind this air attack will follow sea and land forces in such numbers and power as they have not yet seen and with the fighting skill of which they are already well aware.

The Secretary of War, who has kept in personal touch with all phases of the project, will immediately make public a statement giving further details.

His statement will give facts concerning the sites at Oak Ridge near Knoxville, Tennessee, and at Richland near Pasco, Washington, and an installation near Santa Fe, New Mexico. Although the workers at the sites have been making materials to be used in producing the greatest destructive force in history, they have not themselves been in danger beyond that of many other occupations, for the utmost care has been taken of their safety.

The fact that we can release atomic energy ushers in a new era in man's understanding of nature's forces. Atomic energy may in the future supplement the power that now comes from coal, oil, and falling water, but at present it cannot be produced on a basis to compete with them commercially. Before that comes there must be a long period of intensive research.

It has never been the habit of the scientists of this country or the policy of this Government to withhold from the world scientific knowledge. Normally, therefore, everything about the work with atomic energy would be made public.

But under present circumstances it is not intended to divulge the technical process of production or all the military applications, pending further examination of possible methods of protecting us and the rest of the world from the danger of sudden destruction.

I shall recommend that the Congress of the United States consider promptly the establishment of an appropriate commission to control the production and use of atomic power within the United States. I shall give further consideration and make further recommendations to the Congress as to how atomic power can become a powerful and forceful influence towards the maintenance of world peace.

Chapter 20 Worksheet and Questions

1. According to most of the people involved, the decision to drop the atomic bomb on Japan was very difficult and involved. According to the documents in the chapter, what issues were considered in choosing targets? What did the early advisory committee and other persons close to the president recommend as targets, and why were those locations selected? Consider if there were viable alternatives. Was the dropping of a demonstration bomb in a largely uninhabited area a viable option?

    _____

    _____

    _____

    _____

    _____

    _____

    _____

    _____

2. On July 17, 1945 Leo Szilard and 69 other scientists petitioned President Truman to not drop the atomic bomb on Japan. What reasons did they have for not using the weapon? Were they right? In 1960 Szilard, in an interview with *U.S. News and World Report*, claimed Harry Truman did not understand the moral issues of using the bomb, the destruction it would cause, or the impact on the postwar world. Based on President Truman's papers, diaries, and public statements in this chapter, either support or refute that claim.

    _____

    _____

    _____

    _____

    _____

    _____

    _____

    _____

3. Who besides the scientists are opposed to dropping the atomic bomb, and why? Many historians claim racism and hatred of the Japanese prompted the decision to bomb Japan, and that we would never have used the weapons against the "white" Germans. Present the evidence of racism or hatred of the Japanese in the private and public documents in this chapter. Is the argument convincing?

_____

_____

_____

_____

_____

_____

_____

_____

_____

4. By the 1950s Harry Truman crafted a consistent response to why the bomb was dropped, a response that appears in his memoirs and public interviews. He claimed he did it to save American and Japanese lives, that more people would have died in an invasion of Japan, and that he could never have looked a mother in the eye if he could have saved her son's life and did not just because of the type of weapon used. What evidence of this goal do you see in his 1945 meetings and writings? What other factors seem to be just as important in 1945?

_____

_____

_____

_____

_____

_____

_____

_____

_____

5. The ultimate question always needing to be answered is this: Was it necessary to drop the atomic bombs on Hiroshima and Nagasaki to end World War II? Answer this question from one of the following perspectives: as one of Truman's former advisors two years after the war, as the parent of a soldier scheduled to be part of the invasion force, or as a veteran of the Pacific War 50 years later.

_____

_____

_____

_____

_____

_____

_____

_____

_____

_____

_____

_____

_____

_____

_____

_____

_____

_____

_____

_____

_____

The Cold War

The relationship between the United States and the Soviet Union at the close of World War II had deteriorated, resulting in hostilities that would last nearly half a century. A series of events following the convening of the Yalta Conference, early in 1945, would foreshadow the coming of the Cold War. Promises were broken, and trust among the "Big Three" was weakened. The Soviets broke their promise with regard to holding free elections. Other events, such as the Communist coup in Czechoslovakia, the Soviet blockade of West Berlin; the fall of China, the Korean conflict, and the Soviet's atomic bomb confirmed the "free world's greatest threat": the spread of Communism.

The United States, perceiving Soviet expansionism as a threat to its own interests, ushered in the era of the Cold War. American diplomat George Kennan submitted a telegram from the U.S. Embassy in Moscow, known as the "Long Telegram," warning that the Soviet Union was taking the path toward Communism. This news helped to substantiate the United States' fears.

During the Cold War, both the United States and Russia stockpiled nuclear weapons, but their motivation was slightly different. The Soviets maintained that a nuclear war could be fought and won, while the United States adopted a policy of deterrence, even though the United States was capable of delivering the "first strike." To convince the American public and the world that the Soviet threat was real, the United States developed and deployed several types of delivery systems for attacking the Soviets with nuclear weapons. These delivery systems emerged as the basis for U.S. strategic deterrence: (1) long-range manned aircraft carrying nuclear weapons, (2) land-based intercontinental ballistic missiles with nuclear capabilities, and (3) nuclear-powered submarines armed with nuclear weapons. Each capable of acting independently, any one of these three systems, also known as the Nuclear Triad, was powerful enough to deter an attack.

The Cold War affected many aspects of American life—socially, culturally, and politically. The Cold War left its mark on areas such as entertainment, education, politics, and the military. Almost anyone who dared to voice an opinion contrary to the status quo, or to engage in activities considered "suspect" was labeled "Communist." Many allegations of Communist connections and Communist activities surfaced in America.

In the forefront of such accusations was the House Un-American Activities Committee (HUAC), established in 1938. Although the committee's efforts were aimed primarily at German-American involvement in the Nazi movement, the committee also investigated alleged Communist practices in government programs, especially in various New Deal initiatives. Senator Joseph McCarthy of Wisconsin continued this war against suspected Communists, who were, according to popular belief, attempting to overthrow the American government from within.

In June of 1950, with the outbreak of the Korean War, the United States' suspicions of the expansion of Communism were confirmed. President Harry S. Truman committed U.S. ground, air, and naval forces to the region. Douglas MacArthur, commander of the United Nations military forces in South Korea, was able to drive North Korean forces beyond the 38th Parallel. He also received permission to advance toward the Yule River—the border area between North Korea and China. China intervened on behalf of the North Koreans, leaving the U.N. forces in disarray. MacArthur requested permission to bomb Chinese bases in Manchuria. When Truman refused, MacArthur submitted a letter expressing his disagreement with President Truman to Joseph Martin, U.S. House minority leader. The letter was made public, and Truman relieved MacArthur of his command. An armistice was signed, bringing about an end to the hostilities in Korea in 1953. However, armed forces build-up throughout Europe and Asia became permanent, and defense spending began long years of unremitting growth.

Considering the Evidence in the Readings

The nature of the Cold War can best be understood by examining the conferences at Yalta (February 1945) and Potsdam (summer of 1945). As the war was nearing an end, Roosevelt, Churchill, and Stalin attempted to outline the post-war settlements, but much of what was agreed upon was left to broad interpretation. Roosevelt and Churchill agreed to a Soviet sphere of influence in Eastern Europe based upon Stalin's agreement to hold fair democratic elections. Although Stalin agreed in principle, he fell short on practice. The aftermath was the ushering in of Communism throughout Eastern Europe, and subsequently Asia.

The phrase "iron curtain" typified the growing conflict between the Soviet Union and its former allies, Great Britain and the United States. In his 1946 speech in Fulton, Missouri, Churchill warned of the divisions between West and East. This division had been sparked by a series of events dating back to the Atlantic Charter, Teran, Yalta, and the Potsdam conferences.

The readings included in this chapter are divided into three parts. Part One contains documents detailing America's position regarding the spread of Communism and the policy of "containment." Part Two includes a reading from the Korean War era, a description of the events leading to the dismissal of General Douglass MacArthur from his position as commander of U.S. troops. The readings in Part Three deal with McCarthyism—Senator Joseph McCarthy's fear of the "threat of communism."

As you read the documents, keep in mind that the initial events of the Cold War helped to shape American politics and aspects of American socio-economic culture. Think about America's position. Was it that of containment, response, or first strike? Also consider the legacy of the Cold War and the position of the two major players during the Cold War.

Document 21.1 George F. Kennan, The "Long Telegram," 1946

As U.S. diplomat and advisor, George Kennan was in charge of long-range planning for the State Department after World War II. He became the architect of the policy of "containment"—a strategy to keep Soviet influence from expanding. While stationed at the U.S. embassy in Moscow, Kennan submitted an analysis of Soviet intentions to the State Department in Washington. This document illustrates America's anti-Communist views and general suspicion of Soviet aspirations. Kennan later published his telegram in *Foreign Affairs* magazine, under the pseudonym, Mr. X.

From *Memoirs* by George F. Kennan. Copyright © 1967 by George F. Kennan. Reprinted by permission of Little, Brown and Co., Inc.

*Not printed; in this telegram the Department informed the Chargé: "We should welcome receiving from you an interpretive analysis of what we may expect in the way of future implementation of these announced policies . . ." (861.00/2–1246). The policies referred to were those contained in the pre-election speeches of Stalin and his associates.

The Chargé in the Soviet Union (Kennan) to the Secretary of State

George F. Kennan

SECRET

Moscow, February 22, 1946—9 p.m.
[Received February 22 3:52 p.m.]

511. Answer to Dept's 284, Feb 3 [*13*]** involves questions so intricate, so delicate, so strange to our form of thought, and so important to analysis of our international environment that I cannot compress answers into single brief message without yielding to what I feel would be dangerous degree of oversimplification. I hope, therefore, Dept will bear with me if I submit in answer to this question five parts, subjects of which will be roughly as follows:

(1) Features of postwar Soviet outlook.
(2) Background of this outlook.
(3) Its projection in practical policy on official level.
(4) Its projection on unofficial level.
(5) Practical deductions from standpoint of U.S. policy.

I apologize in advance for this burdening of telegraphic channel; but questions involved are of such urgent importance, particularly in view of recent events, that our answers to them, if they deserve attention at all, seem to me to deserve it at once. There follows

Part 1: Basic Features of Post War Soviet Outlook, as Put Forward by Official Propaganda Machine, Are as Follows:

(a) USSR still lives in antagonistic "capitalist encirclement" with which in the long run there can be no permanent peaceful coexistence. As stated by Stalin in 1927 to a delegation of American workers:

> "In course of further development of international revolution there will emerge two centers of world significance: a socialist center, drawing to itself the countries which tend toward socialism, and a capitalist center, drawing to itself the countries that incline toward capitalism. Battle between these two centers for command of world economy will decide fate of capitalism and of communism in entire world."

(b) Capitalist world is beset with internal conflicts, inherent in nature of capitalist society. These conflicts are insoluble by means of peaceful compromise. Greatest of them is that between England and U.S.

(c) Internal conflicts of capitalism inevitably generate wars. Wars thus generated may be of two kinds: intra-capitalist wars between two capitalist states, and wars of intervention against socialist world. Smart capitalists, vainly seeking escape from inner conflicts of capitalism, incline toward latter.

(d) Intervention against USSR, while it would be disastrous to those who undertook it, would cause renewed delay in progress of Soviet socialism and must therefore be forestalled at all costs.

(e) Conflicts between capitalist states, though likewise fraught with danger for USSR, nevertheless hold out great possibilities for advancement of socialist cause, particularly if USSR remains militarily powerful, ideologically monolithic and faithful to its present brilliant leadership.

(f) It must be borne in mind that capitalist world is not all bad. In addition to hopelessly reactionary and bourgeois elements, it includes (1) certain wholly enlightened and positive elements united in acceptable communistic parties and (2) certain other elements (now described for tactical reasons as progressive or democratic) whose reactions, aspirations and activities happen to be "objectively" favorable to interests of USSR. These last must be encouraged and utilized for Soviet purposes.

(g) Among negative elements of bourgeois-capitalist society, most dangerous of all are those whom Lenin called false friends of the people, namely moderate-socialist or social-democratic leaders (in other words, non-Communist left-wing). These are more dangerous than out-and-out reactionaries, for latter at least march under their true colors, whereas moderate left-wing leaders confuse people by employing devices of socialism to serve interests of reactionary capital.

So much for premises. To what deductions do they lead from standpoint of Soviet policy? To following:

(a) Everything must be done to advance relative strength of USSR as factor in international society. Conversely, no opportunity must be missed to reduce strength and influence, collectively as well as individually, of capitalist powers.

(b) Soviet efforts, and those of Russia's friends abroad, must be directed toward deepening and exploiting of differences and conflicts between capitalist powers. If these eventually deepen into an "imperialist" war, this war must be turned into revolutionary upheavals within the various capitalist countries.

(c) "Democratic-progressive" elements abroad are to be utilized to maximum to bring pressure to bear on capitalist governments along lines agreeable to Soviet interests.

(d) Relentless battle must be waged against socialist and social-democratic leaders abroad.

Part 2: Background of Outlook

Before examining ramifications of this party line in practice there are certain aspects of it to which I wish to draw attention.

First, it does not represent natural outlook of Russian people. Latter are, by and large, friendly to outside world, eager for experience of it, eager to measure against it talents they are conscious of possessing, eager above all to live in peace and enjoy fruits of their own labor. Party line only represents thesis which official propaganda machine puts forward with great skill and persistence to a public often remarkably resistant in the stronghold of its innermost thoughts. But party line is binding for outlook and conduct of people who make up apparatus of power-party, secret police and Government—and it is exclusively with these that we have to deal.

Second, please note that premises on which this party line is based are for most part simply not true. Experience has shown that peaceful and mutually profitable coexistence of capitalism and socialist states is entirely possible. Basic internal conflicts in advanced countries are no longer primarily those arising out of capitalist ownership of means of production, but are ones arising from advanced urbanism and industrialism as such, which Russia has thus far been spared not by socialism but only by her own backwardness. Internal rivalries of capitalism do not always generate wars; and not all wars are attributable to this cause. To speak of possibility of intervention against USSR today, after elimination of Germany and Japan and after example of recent war, is sheerest nonsense. If not provoked by forces of intolerance and subversion "capitalist" world of today is quite capable of living at peace with itself and with Russia. Finally, no sane person has reason to doubt sincerity of moderate socialist leaders in Western countries. Nor is it fair to deny success of their efforts to improve conditions for working population whenever, as in Scandinavia, they have been given chance to show what they could do.

Falseness of these premises, every one of which pre-dates recent war, was amply demonstrated by that conflict itself. Anglo-American differences did not turn out to be major differences of Western World. Capitalist countries, other than those of Axis, showed no disposition to solve their differences by joining in crusade against USSR. Instead of imperialist war turning into civil wars and revolution, USSR found itself obliged to fight side by side with capitalist powers for an avowed community of aims.

Nevertheless, all these theses, however baseless and disproven, are being boldly put forward again today. What does this indicate? It indicates that Soviet party line is not based on any objective analysis of situation beyond Russia's borders: that it has, indeed, little to do with conditions outside of Russia; that it arises mainly from basic inner-Russian necessities which existed before recent war and exist today.

At bottom of Kremlin's neurotic view of world affairs is traditional and instinctive Russian sense of insecurity. Originally, this was insecurity of a peaceful agricultural people trying to live on vast exposed plain in neighborhood of fierce nomadic peoples. To this was added, as Russia came into contact with economically advanced West, fear of more competent, more powerful, more highly organized societies in that area. But this latter type of insecurity was one which afflicted rather Russian rulers than Russian people; for Russian rulers have invariably sensed that their rule was relatively archaic in form, fragile and artificial in its psychological foundation, unable to stand comparison or contact with political systems of Western countries. For this reason they have always feared foreign penetration, feared direct contact between Western world and their own, feared what would happen if Russians learned truth about world without or if foreigners learned truth about world within. And they have learned to seek security only in patient but deadly struggle for total destruction of rival power, never in compacts and compromises with it.

It was no coincidence that Marxism, which had smouldered ineffectively for half a century in Western Europe, caught hold and blazed for first time in Russia. Only in this land which had never known a friendly neighbor or indeed any tolerant equilibrium of separate powers, either internal or international, could a doctrine thrive which viewed economic conflicts of society as insoluble by peaceful means. After establishment of Bolshevist regime, Marxist dogma, rendered even more truculent and intolerant by Lenin's interpretation, became a perfect vehicle for sense of insecurity with which Bolsheviks, even more than previous Russian rulers, were afflicted. In this dogma, with its basic altruism of purpose, they found justification for their instinctive fear of outside world, for the dictatorship without which they did not know how to rule, for cruelties they did not dare not to inflict, for sacrifices they felt bound to demand. In the name of Marxism they sacrificed every single ethical value in their methods and tactics. Today they cannot dispense with it. It is fig leaf of their moral and intellectual respectability. Without it they would stand before history, at best, as only the last of that long succession of cruel and wasteful Russian rulers who have relentlessly forced country on to ever new heights of military power in order to guarantee external security of their internally weak regimes. This is why Soviet purposes must always be solemnly clothed in trappings of Marxism, and why no one should underrate importance of dogma in Soviet affairs. Thus Soviet leaders are driven [by?] necessities of their own past and present position to put forward a dogma which [apparent omission] outside world as evil, hostile and menacing, but as bearing within itself germs of creeping disease and destined to be wracked with growing internal convulsions until it is given final *coup de grace* by rising power of socialism and yields to new and better world. This thesis provides justification for that increase of military and police power of Russian state, for that isolation of Russian population from outside world, and for that fluid and constant pressure to extend limits of Russian police power which are together the natural and instinctive urges of Russian rulers. Basically this is only the steady advance of uneasy Russian nationalism, a centuries old movement in which conceptions of offense and defense are inextricably confused. But in new guise of international Marxism, with its honeyed promises to a desperate and war-torn outside world, it is more dangerous and insidious than ever before.

It should not be thought from above that Soviet party line is necessarily disingenuous and insincere on part of all those who put it forward. Many of them are too ignorant of outside world and mentally too dependent to question [apparent omission] self-hypnotism, and who have no difficulty making themselves believe what they find it comforting and convenient to believe. Finally we have the unsolved mystery as to who, if anyone, in this great land actually receives accurate and unbiased information about outside world. In atmosphere of oriental secretiveness and conspiracy which pervades this Government, possibilities for distorting or poisoning sources and currents of information are infinite. The very disrespect of Russians for objective truth—indeed, their disbelief in its existence—leads them to view all stated facts as instruments for furtherance of one ulterior purpose or another. There is good reason to suspect that this Government is actually a conspiracy within a conspiracy; and I for one am reluctant to believe that Stalin himself receives anything like an objective picture of outside world. Here there is ample scope for the type of subtle intrigue at which Russians are past masters. Inability of foreign governments to place their case squarely before Russian policy makers—extent to which they are delivered up in their relations with Russia to good graces of obscure and unknown advisers whom they never see and cannot influence—this to my mind is most disquieting feature of diplomacy in Moscow, and one which Western statesmen would do well to keep in mind if they would understand nature of difficulties encountered here.

Part 3: Projection of Soviet Outlook in Practical Policy on Official Level

We have now seen nature and background of Soviet program. What may we expect by way of its practical implementation?

Soviet policy, as Department implies in its query under reference, is conducted on two planes: (1) official plane represented by actions undertaken officially in name of Soviet Government; and (2) subterranean plane of actions undertaken by agencies for which Soviet Government does not admit responsibility.

Policy promulgated on both planes will be calculated to serve basic policies (a) to (d) outlined in part 1. Actions taken on different planes will differ considerably, but will dovetail into each other in purpose, time and effect.

On official plane we must look for following:

(a) Internal policy devoted to increasing in every way strength and prestige of Soviet state: intensive military-industrialization; maximum development of armed forces; great displays to impress outsiders; continued secretiveness about internal matters, designed to conceal weaknesses and to keep opponents in dark.

(b) Wherever it is considered timely and promising, efforts will be made to advance official limits of Soviet power. For the moment, these efforts are restricted to certain neighboring points conceived of here as being of immediate strategic necessity, such as Northern Iran, Turkey, possibly Bornholm. However, other points may at any time come into question, if and as concealed Soviet political power is extended to new areas. Thus a "friendly" Persian Government might be asked to grant Russia a port on Persian Gulf. Should Spain fall under Communist control, question of Soviet base at Gibraltar Strait might be activated. But such claims will appear on official level only when unofficial preparation is complete.

(c) Russians will participate officially in international organizations where they see opportunity of extending Soviet power or of inhibiting or diluting power of others. Moscow sees in UNO not the mechanism for a permanent and stable world society founded on mutual interest and aims of all nations, but an arena in which aims just mentioned can be favorably pursued. As long as UNO is considered here to serve this purpose, Soviets will remain with it. But if at any time they come to conclusion that it is serving to embarrass or frustrate their aims for power expansion and if they see better prospects for pursuit of these aims along other lines, they will not hesitate to abandon UNO. This would imply, however, that they felt themselves strong enough to split unity of other nations by their withdrawal, to render UNO ineffective as a threat to their aims or security, and to replace it with an international weapon more effective from their viewpoint. Thus Soviet attitude toward UNO will depend largely on loyalty of other nations to it, and on degree of vigor, decisiveness and cohesion with which these nations defend in UNO the peaceful and hopeful concept of international life, which that organization represents to our way of thinking. I reiterate, Moscow has no abstract devotion to UNO ideals. Its attitude to that organization will remain essentially pragmatic and tactical.

(d) Toward colonial areas and backward or dependent peoples, Soviet policy, even on official plane, will be directed toward weakening of power and influence and contacts of advanced Western nations, on theory that in so far as this policy is successful, there will be created a vacuum which will favor Communist-Soviet penetration. Soviet pressure for participation in trusteeship arrangements thus represents, in my opinion, a desire to be in a position to complicate and inhibit exertion of Western influence at such points rather than to provide major

channel for exerting of Soviet power. Latter motive is not lacking, but for this Soviets prefer to rely on other channels than official trusteeship arrangements. Thus we may expect to find Soviets asking for admission everywhere to trusteeship or similar arrangements and using levers thus acquired to weaken Western influence among such people.

(e) Russians will strive energetically to develop Soviet representation in, and official ties with, countries in which they sense strong possibilities of opposition to Western centers of power. This applies to such widely separated points as Germany, Argentina, Middle Eastern countries, etc.

(f) In international economic matters, Soviet policy will really be dominated by pursuit of autarchy for Soviet Union and Soviet-dominated adjacent areas taken together. That, however, will be underlying policy. As far as official line is concerned, position is not yet clear. Soviet Government has shown strange reticence since termination hostilities on subject foreign trade. If large scale long term credits should be forthcoming, I believe Soviet Government may eventually again do lip service, as it did in 1930s to desirability of building up international economic exchanges in general. Otherwise I think it possible Soviet foreign trade may be restricted largely to Soviet's own security sphere, including occupied areas in Germany, and that, a cold official shoulder may be turned to principle of general economic collaboration among nations.

(g) With respect to cultural collaboration, lip service will likewise be rendered to desirability of deepening cultural contacts between peoples, but this will not in practice be interpreted in any way which could weaken security position of Soviet peoples. Actual manifestations of Soviet policy in this respect will be restricted to arid channels of closely shepherded official visits and functions, with superabundance of vodka and speeches and dearth of permanent effects.

(h) Beyond this, Soviet official relations will take what might be called "correct" course with individual foreign governments, with great stress being laid on prestige of Soviet Union and its representatives and with punctilious attention to protocol, as distinct from good manners.

Part 4: Following May Be Said as to What We May Expect by Way of Implementation of Basic Soviet Policies on Unofficial, or Subterranean Plane, i.e., on Plane for Which Soviet Government Accepts no Responsibility

Agencies utilized for promulgation of policies on this plane are following:

1. Inner central core of Communist Parties in other countries. While many of persons who compose this category may also appear and act in unrelated public capacities, they are in reality working closely together as an underground operating directorate of world communism, a concealed Comintern* tightly coordinated and directed by Moscow. It is important to remember that this inner core is actually working on underground lines, despite legality of parties with which it is associated.

2. Rank and file of Communist Parties. Note distinction is drawn between these and persons defined in paragraph 1. This distinction has become much sharper in recent years. Whereas formerly foreign Communist Parties represented a curious (and from Moscow's standpoint often inconvenient) mixture of conspiracy and legitimate activity, now the conspiratorial element has been neatly concentrated in inner circle and ordered underground, while rank and file—no longer even taken into confidence about realities of movement—are thrust forward as bona fide internal partisans of certain political tendencies within their respective countries, genuinely innocent of conspiratorial connection with foreign states. Only in certain countries where communists are numerically strong do they now regularly appear and act as a body. As a rule they are used to penetrate, and to influence or dominate, as case may be, other organizations less likely to be suspected of being tools of Soviet Government, with a view to accomplishing their purposes through [apparent omission] organizations, rather than by direct action as a separate political party.

3. A wide variety of national associations or bodies which can be dominated or influenced by such penetration. These include: labor unions, youth leagues, women's organizations, racial societies, religious societies, social organizations, cultural groups, liberal magazines, publishing houses, etc.

4. International organizations which can be similarly penetrated through influence over various national components. Labor, youth and women's organizations are prominent among them. Particular, almost vital, importance is attached in this connection to international labor movement. In this, Moscow sees possibility of sidetracking western governments in world affairs and building up international lobby capable of compelling governments to take actions favorable to Soviet interests in various countries and of paralyzing actions disagreeable to USSR.

5. Russian Orthodox Church, with its foreign branches, and through it the Eastern Orthodox Church in general.

6. Pan-Slav movement and other movements (Azerbaijan, Armenian, Turcoman, etc.) based on racial groups within Soviet Union.

7. Governments or governing groups willing to lend themselves to Soviet purposes in one degree or another, such as present Bulgarian and Yugoslav Governments, North Persian regime, Chinese Communists, etc. Not only propaganda machines but actual policies of these regimes can be placed extensively at disposal of USSR.

It may be expected that component parts of this far-flung apparatus will be utilized, in accordance with their individual suitability, as follows:

(a) To undermine general political and strategic potential of major western powers. Efforts will be made in such countries to disrupt national self confidence, to hamstring measures of national defense, to increase social and industrial unrest, to stimulate all forms of disunity. All persons with grievances, whether economic or racial, will be urged to seek redress not in mediation and compromise, but in defiant violent struggle for destruction of other elements of society. Here poor will be set against rich, black against white, young against old, newcomers against established residents, etc.

(b) On unofficial plane particularly violent efforts will be made to weaken power and influence of Western Powers of [on] colonial backward, or dependent peoples. On this level, no holds will be barred. Mistakes and weaknesses of western colonial administration will be mercilessly exposed and exploited. Liberal opinion in Western countries will be mobilized to weaken colonial policies. Resentment

---

*The Third (Communist) International, founded by the Bolsheviks at Moscow in March 1919, announced as having been dissolved in May 1943; see *Foreign Relations,* 1943, vol. Ill, pp. 531–532, and 542–543.

among dependent peoples will be stimulated. And while latter are being encouraged to seek independence of Western Powers, Soviet dominated puppet political machines will be undergoing preparation to take over domestic power in respective colonial areas when independence is achieved.

(e) Where individual governments stand in path of Soviet purposes pressure will be brought for their removal from office. This can happen where governments directly oppose Soviet foreign policy aims (Turkey, Iran), where they seal their territories off against Communist penetration (Switzerland, Portugal), or where they compete too strongly, like Labor Government in England, for moral domination among elements which it is important for Communists to dominate. (Sometimes, two of these elements are present in a single case. Then Communist opposition becomes particularly shrill and savage.

(d) In foreign countries Communists will, as a rule, work toward destruction of all forms of personal independence, economic, political or moral. Their system can handle only individuals who have been brought into complete dependence on higher power. Thus persons who are financially independent—such as individual businessmen, estate owners, successful farmers, artisans and all those who exercise local leadership or have local prestige, such as popular local clergymen or political figures, are anathema. It is not by chance that even in USSR local officials are kept constantly on move from one job to another, to prevent their taking root.

(c) Everything possible will be done to set major Western Powers against each other. Anti-British talk will be plugged among Americans, anti-American talk among British. Continentals, including Germans, will be taught to abhor both Anglo-Saxon powers. Where suspicions exist, they will be fanned; where not, ignited. No effort will be spared to discredit and combat all efforts which threaten to lead to any sort of unity or cohesion among other [apparent omission] from which Russia might be excluded. Thus, all forms of international organization not amenable to Communist penetration and control, whether it be the Catholic [apparent omission] international economic concerns, or the international fraternity of royalty and aristocracy. must expect to find themselves under fire from many, and often [apparent omission].

(f) In general, all Soviet efforts on unofficial international plane will be negative and destructive in character, designed to tear down sources of strength beyond reach of Soviet control. This is only in line with basic Soviet instinct that there can be no compromise with power and that constructive work can start only when Communist power is dominant. But behind all this will be applied insistent, unceasing pressure for penetration and command of key positions in administration and especially in police apparatus of foreign countries. The Soviet regime is a police regime par excellence, reared in the dim half world of Tsarist police intrigue, accustomed to think primarily in terms of police power. This should never be lost sight of in gauging Soviet motives.

Part 5: [Practical Deductions from Standpoint of U.S. Policy]

In summary, we have here a political force committed fanatically to the belief that with U.S. there can be no permanent *modus vivendi*, that it is desirable and necessary that the internal harmony of our society be disrupted, our traditional way of life be destroyed, the international authority of our state be broken, if Soviet power is to be secure. This political force has complete power of disposition over energies of one of world's greatest peoples and resources of world's richest national territory, and is borne along by deep and powerful currents of Russian nationalism. In addition, it has an elaborate and far flung apparatus for exertion of its influence in other countries, an apparatus of amazing flexibility and versatility, managed by people whose experience and skill in underground methods are presumably without parallel in history. Finally, it is seemingly inaccessible to considerations of reality in its basic reactions. For it, the vast fund of objective fact about human society is not, as with us, the measure against which outlook is constantly being tested and re-formed, but a grab bag from which individual items are selected arbitrarily and tendentiously to bolster an outlook already preconceived. This is admittedly not a pleasant picture. Problem of how to cope with this force in [*is*] undoubtedly greatest task our diplomacy has ever faced and probably greatest it will ever have to face. It should be point of departure from which our political general staff work at present juncture should proceed. It should be approached with same thoroughness and care as solution of major strategic problem in war, and if necessary, with no smaller outlay in planning effort. I cannot attempt to suggest all answers here. But I would like to record my conviction that problem is within our power to solve—and that without recourse to any general military conflict. And in support of this conviction there are certain observations of a more encouraging nature I should like to make:

(1) Soviet power, unlike that of Hitlerite Germany, is neither schematic nor adventuristic. It does not work by fixed plans, It does not take unnecessary risks. Impervious to logic of reason, and it is highly sensitive to logic of force. For this reason it can easily withdraw—and usually does—when strong resistance is encountered at any point. Thus, if the adversary has sufficient force and makes clear his readiness to use it, he rarely has to do so. If situations are properly handled there need be no prestige-engaging showdowns.

(2) Gauged against Western World as a whole, Soviets are still by far the weaker force. Thus, their success will really depend on degree of cohesion, firmness and vigor which Western World can muster. And this is factor which it is within our power to influence.

(3) Success of Soviet system, as form of internal power is not yet finally proven. It has yet to be demonstrated that it can survive supreme test of successive transfer of power from one individual or group to another. Lenin's death was first such transfer, and its effects wracked Soviet state for 15 years, After Stalin's death or retirement will be second. But even this will not be final test. Soviet internal system will now be subjected, by virtue of recent territorial expansions, to series of additional strains which once proved severe tax on Tsardom. We here are convinced that never since termination of civil war have mass of Russian people been emotionally farther removed from doctrines of Communist Party than they are today. In Russia, party has now become a great and—for the moment—highly successful apparatus of dictatorial administration; but it has ceased to be a source of emotional inspiration. Thus internal soundness and permanence of movement, need not yet be regarded as assured.

(4) All Soviet propaganda beyond Soviet security sphere is basically negative and destructive. It should therefore be relatively easy to combat it by any intelligent and really constructive program.

For these reasons I think we may approach calmly and with good heart problem of how to deal with Russia. As to how this approach should be made, I only wish to advance, by way of conclusion, following comments:

(1) Our first step must be to apprehend, and recognize for what it is, the nature of the movement with which we are dealing. We must study it with same courage, detachment, objectivity, and same determination not to be emotionally provoked or unseated by it, with which doctor studies unruly and unreasonable individual.

(2) We must see that our public is educated to realities of Russian situation. I cannot over-emphasize importance of this. Press cannot do this alone. It must be done mainly by Government, which is necessarily more experienced and better informed on practical problems involved. In this we need not be deterred by [ugliness?] of picture. I am convinced that there would be far less hysterical anti-Sovietism in our country today if realities of this situation were better understood by our people. There is nothing as dangerous or as terrifying as the unknown. It may also be argued that to reveal more information on our difficulties with Russia would reflect unfavorably on Russian-American relations. I feel that if there is any real risk here involved, it is one which we should have courage to face, and sooner the better. But I cannot see what we would be risking. Our stake in this country, even coming on heels of tremendous demonstrations of our friendship for Russian people, is remarkably small. We have here no investments to guard, no actual trade to lose, virtually no citizens to protect, few cultural contacts to preserve. Our only stake lies in what we hope rather than what we have; and I am convinced we have better chance of realizing those hopes if our public is enlightened and if our dealings with Russians are placed entirely on realistic and matter-of-fact basis.

(3) Much depends on health and vigor of our own society. World communism is like malignant parasite which feeds only on diseased tissue. This is point at which domestic and foreign policies meet. Every courageous and incisive measure to solve internal problems of our own society, to improve self-confidence, discipline, morale and community spirit of our own people, is a diplomatic victory over Moscow worth a thousand diplomatic notes and joint communiqués. If we cannot abandon fatalism and indifference in face of deficiencies of our own ;society, Moscow will profit—Moscow cannot help profiting by them in its foreign policies.

(4) We must formulate and put forward for other nations a much more positive and constructive picture of sort of world we would like to see than we have put forward in past. It is not enough to urge people to develop political processes similar to our own. Many foreign peoples, in Europe at least, are tired and frightened by experiences of past, and are less interested in abstract freedom than in security. They are seeking guidance rather than responsibilities. We should be better able than Russians to give them this. And unless we do, Russians certainly will.

(5) Finally we must have courage and self-confidence to cling to our own methods and conceptions of human society. After all, the greatest danger that can befall us in coping with this problem of Soviet communism, is that we shall allow ourselves to become like those with whom we are coping.

KENNAN

Document 21.2 "Are We Only Paying Lip Service to Peace?"

In 1933, President Roosevelt appointed Henry Wallace as his Secretary of Agriculture. For the 1940 elections, Roosevelt selected Wallace as his vice president. During World War II, Wallace's left-wing views made him unpopular in the Democratic party, and FDR came under pressure to drop him as his vice-resident in the 1944 election campaign. After the war, Wallace served as Secretary of Commerce; he favored cooperation with the Soviet Union. His private feelings regarding President Truman's foreign policy were made public in 1946. After complaints from members of his cabinet, Truman released Wallace as Secretary of Commerce. The following document is an excerpt from a letter Wallace wrote to President Truman in 1946.

Henry A. Wallace

I have been increasingly disturbed about the trend of international affairs since the end of the war, and I am even more troubled by the apparently growing feeling among the American people that another war is coming and the only way that we can head it off is to arm ourselves to the teeth. Yet all of past history indicates that an armaments race does not lead to peace but to war. The months just ahead may well be the crucial period which will decide whether the civilized world will go down in destruction after the five or ten years needed for several nations to arm themselves with atomic bombs. Therefore, I want to give you my views on how the present trend toward conflict might be averted. . . .

How do American actions since VJ Day [Victory in Japan Day, i.e., the end of World War II] appear to other nations? I mean by actions the concrete things like $13 billion for the War and Navy Departments, the Bikini tests of the atomic bomb and continued production of bombs, the plan to arm Latin America with our weapons, production of B29s and planned production of B-36s, and the effort to secure air bases spread over half the globe from which the other half of the globe can be bombed. I cannot but feel that these actions must make it look to the rest of the world as if we were only paying lip service to peace at the conference table.

These facts rather make it appear either (1) that we are preparing ourselves to win the war which we regard as inevitable or (2) that we are trying to build up a predominance of force to intimidate the rest of mankind. How would it look to us if Russia had the atomic bomb and we did not, if Russia had 10,000-mile bombers and air bases within a thousand miles of our coastlines, and we did not?

Some of the military men and self-styled "realists" are saying: "What's wrong with trying to build up a predominance of force? The only way to preserve peace is for this country to be so well armed that no one will dare attack us. We know that America will never start a war." The flaw in this policy is simply that it will not work. In a world of atomic bombs and other revolutionary new weapons, such as radioactive poison gases and biological warfare, a peace maintained by a predominance of force is no longer possible.

Why is this so? The reasons are clear:

FIRST. Atomic warfare is cheap and easy compared with old-fashioned war. Within a very few years several countries can have atomic bombs and other atomic weapons. Compared with the cost of large armies and the manufacture of old-fashioned weapons, atomic bombs cost very little and require only a relatively small part of a nation's production plant and labor force.

SECOND. So far as winning a war is concerned, having more bombs—even many more bombs—than the other fellow is no longer a decisive advantage. If

From *A History of Our Time* by Henry A. Wallace. Published by Oxford University Press, Inc.

another nation had enough bombs to eliminate all of our principal cities and our heavy industry, it wouldn't help us very much if we had ten times as many bombs as we needed to do the same to them.

THIRD. And most important, the very fact that several nations have atomic bombs will inevitably result in a neurotic, fear-ridden, itching-trigger psychology in all the peoples of the world, and because of our wealth and vulnerability we would be among the most seriously affected. Atomic war will not require vast and time-consuming preparations, the mobilization of large armies, the conversion of a large proportion of a country's industrial plants to the manufacture of weapons. In a world armed with atomic weapons, some incident will lead to the use of those weapons.

There is a school of military thinking which recognizes these facts, recognizes that when several nations have atomic bombs, a war which will destroy modern civilization will result and that no nation or combination of nations can win such a war. This school of thought, therefore, advocates a "preventive war," an attack on Russia now before Russia has atomic bombs.

This scheme is not only immoral, but stupid. If we should attempt to destroy all the principal Russian cities and her heavy industry, we might well succeed. But the immediate countermeasure which such an attack would call forth is the prompt occupation of all Continental Europe by the Red Army. Would we be prepared to destroy the cities of all Europe in trying to finish what we had started? This idea is so contrary to all the basic instincts and principles of the American people that any such action would be possible only under a dictatorship at home. . . .

Our basic distrust of the Russians, which has been greatly intensified in recent months by the playing up of conflict in the press, stems from differences in political and economic organization. For the first time in our history defeatists among us have raised the fear of another system as a successful rival to democracy and free enterprise in other countries and perhaps even our own. I am convinced that we can meet that challenge as we have in the past by demonstrating that economic abundance can be achieved without sacrificing personal, political and religious liberties. We cannot meet it as Hitler tried to by an anti-Comintern alliance.

It is perhaps too easy to forget that despite the deep-seated differences in our cultures and intensive anti-Russian propaganda of some twenty-five years' standing, the American people reversed their attitudes during the crisis of war. Today, under the pressure of seemingly insoluble international problems and continuing deadlocks, the tide of American public opinion is again turning against Russia. In this reaction lies one of the dangers to which this letter is addressed. I should list the factors which make for Russian distrust of the United States and of the Western world as follows. The first is Russian history, which we must take into account because it is the setting in which Russians see all actions and policies of the rest of the world. Russian history for over a thousand years has been a succession of attempts, often unsuccessful, to resist invasion and conquest—by the Mongols, the Turks, the Swedes, the Germans and the Poles. The scant thirty years of the existence of the Soviet Government has in Russian eyes been a continuation of their historical struggle for national existence. The first four years of the new regime, from 1917 through 1921, were spent in resisting attempts at destruction by the Japanese, British and French, with some American assistance, and by the several White Russian armies encouraged and financed by the Western powers. Then, in 1941, the Soviet State was almost conquered by the Germans after a period during which the Western European powers had apparently acquiesced in the rearming of Germany in the belief that the Nazis would seek to expand eastward rather than westward. The Russians, therefore, obviously see themselves as fighting for their existence in a hostile world.

Second, it follows that to the Russians all of the defense and security measures of the Western powers seem to have an aggressive intent. Our actions to expand our military security system—such steps as extending the Monroe Doctrine to include the arming of the Western Hemisphere nations, our present monopoly of the atomic bomb, our interest in outlying bases and our general support of the British Empire—appear to them as going far beyond the requirements of defense. I think we might feel the same if the United States were the only capitalistic country in the world, and the principal socialistic countries were creating a level of armed strength far exceeding anything in their previous history. From the Russian point of view, also, the granting of a loan to Britain and the lack of tangible results on their request to borrow for rehabilitation purposes may be regarded as another evidence of strengthening of an anti-Soviet bloc.

Finally, our resistance to her attempts to obtain warm-water ports and her own security system in the form of "friendly" neighboring states seems, from the Russian point of view, to clinch the case. After twenty-five years of isolation and after having achieved the status of a major power, Russia believes that she is entitled to recognition of her new status. Our interest in establishing democracy in Eastern Europe, where democracy by and large has never existed, seems to her an attempt to re-establish the encirclement of unfriendly neighbors which was created after the last war, and which might serve as a springboard of still another effort to destroy her.

If this analysis is correct, and there is ample evidence to support it, the action to improve the situation is clearly indicated. The fundamental objective of such action should be to allay any reasonable Russian grounds for fear, suspicion and distrust. We must recognize that the world has changed and that today there can be no "One World" unless the United States and Russia can find some way of living together. For example, most of us are firmly convinced of the soundness of our position when we suggest the internationalization and de-fortification of the Danube or of the Dardanelles, but we would be horrified and angered by any Russian counterproposal that would involve also the internationalizing and disarming of Suez or Panama. We must recognize that to the Russians these seem to be identical situations. . . .

We should make an effort to counteract the irrational fear of Russia, which is being systematically built up in the American people by certain individuals and publications. The slogan that communism and capitalism, regimentation and democracy, cannot continue to exist in the same world is, from a historical point of view, pure propaganda. Several religious doctrines, all claiming to be the only true gospel and salvation, have existed side by side with a reasonable degree of tolerance for centuries. This country was for the first half of its national life a democratic island in a world dominated by absolutist governments.

We should not act as if we too felt that we were threatened in today's world. We are by far the most powerful nation in the world, the only Allied nation which came out of the war without devastation and much stronger than before the war. Any talk on our part about the need for strengthening our defenses further is bound to appear hypocritical to other nations. . . .

This proposal admittedly calls for a shift in some of our thinking about international matters. It is imperative that we make this shift. We have little time to lose. Our postwar actions have not yet been adjusted to the lesions to be gained from experience of Allied cooperation during the war and the facts of the atomic age.

It is certainly desirable that, as far as possible, we achieve unity on the home front with respect to our international relations; but unity on the basis of building up conflict abroad would prove to be not only unsound but disastrous. I think there is some reason to fear that in our earnest efforts to achieve bipartisan unity in this country we may have given way too much to isolationism masquerading as tough realism in international affairs.

The real test lies in the achievement of international unity. It will be fruitless to continue to seek solutions for the many specific problems that face us in the making of the peace and in the establishment of an enduring international order without first achieving an atmosphere of mutual trust and confidence. The task admittedly is not an easy one.

There is no question, as the Secretary of State has indicated, that negotiations with the Russians are difficult because of cultural differences, their traditional isolationism, and their insistence on a visible quid pro quo in all agreements. But the task is not an insuperable one if we take into account that to other nations our foreign policy consists not only of the principles that we advocate but of the actions we take.

Fundamentally, this comes down to the point discussed earlier in this letter, that even our own security, in the sense that we have known it in the past, cannot be preserved by military means in a world armed with atomic weapons. The only type of security which can be maintained by our own military force is the type described by a military man before the Senate Atomic Energy Commission—a security against invasion after all our cities and perhaps 40 million of our city population have been destroyed by atomic weapons. That is the best that "security" on the basis of armaments has to offer us. It is not the kind of security that our people and the people of the other United Nations are striving for.

Document 21.3 "The United States Must Be Firm"

Clark Clifford served as Naval Aide to the President in 1946 and as Special Counsel to the President from 1946 to 1950. Clifford supported the idea of containment, as he believed that the Soviet danger was potentially a military threat against the United States. Clifford continued to serve as an advisor to Presidents Kennedy and Johnson. The following document is from a memorandum Clifford wrote for President Truman.

Clark Clifford

It is perhaps the greatest paradox of the present day that the leaders of a nation, now stronger than it has ever been before, should embark on so aggressive a course because their nation is "weak." And yet Stalin and his cohorts proclaim that "monopoly capitalism" threatens the world with war and that Russia must strengthen her defenses against the danger of foreign attacks. The USSR, according to Kremlin propaganda, is imperilled so long as it remains within a "capitalistic encirclement." This idea is absurd when adopted by so vast a country with such great natural wealth, a population of almost 200 million and no powerful or aggressive neighbors. But the process of injecting this propaganda into the minds of the Soviet people goes on with increasing intensity.

The concept of danger from the outside is deeply rooted in the Russian people's haunting sense of insecurity inherited from their past. It is maintained by their present leaders as a justification for the oppressive nature of the Soviet police state. The thesis, that the capitalist world is conspiring to attack the Soviet Union, is not based on any objective analysis of the situation beyond Russia's borders. It has little to do, indeed, with conditions outside the Soviet Union, and it has risen mainly from basic inner-Russian necessities which existed before the Second World War and which exist today. . . .

The Kremlin acknowledges no limit to the eventual power of the Soviet Union, but it is practical enough to be concerned with the actual position of the USSR today. In any matter deemed essential to the security of the Soviet Union, Soviet leaders will prove adamant in their claims and demands. In other matters they will prove grasping and opportunistic, but flexible in proportion to the degree and nature of the resistance encountered.

Recognition of the need to postpone the "inevitable" conflict is in no sense a betrayal of the Communist faith. Marx and Lenin encouraged compromise and collaboration with non-Communists for the accomplishment of ultimate communistic purposes. The USSR has followed such a course in the past. In 1939 the Kremlin signed a nonaggression pact with Germany and in 1941 a neutrality pact with Japan. Soviet leaders will continue to collaborate whenever it seems expedient, for time is needed to build up Soviet strength and weaken the opposition. Time is on the side of the Soviet Union, since population growth and economic development will, in the Soviet view, bring an increase in its relative strength. . . .

A direct threat to American security is implicit in Soviet foreign policy which is designed to prepare the Soviet Union for war with the leading capitalistic nations of the world. Soviet leaders recognize that the United States will be the Soviet Union's most powerful enemy if such a war as that predicted by Communist theory ever comes about and therefore the United States is the chief target of Soviet foreign and military policy. . . .

The most obvious Soviet threat to American security is the growing ability of the USSR to wage an offensive war against the United States. This has not hitherto been possible, in the absence of Soviet long-range strategic air power and an almost total lack of sea power. Now, however, the USSR is rapidly developing elements of her military strength which she hitherto lacked and which will give the Soviet Union great offensive capabilities. Stalin has declared his intention of sparing no effort to build up the military strength of the Soviet Union. Development of atomic weapons, guided missiles, materials for biological warfare, a strategic air force, submarines of great cruising range, naval mines and mine craft, to name the most important, are extending the effective range of Soviet military power well into areas which the United States regards as vital to its security. . . .

The primary objective of United States policy toward the Soviet Union is to convince Soviet leaders

---

The United States Must be Firm by Clark Clifford, Secretary of Defense.

that it is in their interest to participate in a system of world cooperation, that there are no fundamental causes for war between our two nations, and that the security and prosperity of the Soviet Union, and that of the rest of the world as well, is being jeopardized by the aggressive militaristic imperialism such as that in which the Soviet Union is now engaged. However, these same leaders with whom we hope to achieve an understanding on the principles of international peace appear to believe that a war with the United States and the other leading capitalistic nations is inevitable. They are increasing their military power and the sphere of Soviet influence in preparation for the "inevitable" conflict, and they are trying to weaken and subvert their potential opponents by every means at their disposal. So long as these men adhere to these beliefs, it is highly dangerous to conclude that hope of international peace lies only in "accord" "mutual understanding," or "solidarity" with the Soviet Union.

Adoption of such a policy would impel the United States to make sacrifices for the sake of Soviet-U.S. relations, which would only have the effect of raising Soviet hopes and increasing Soviet demands, and to ignore alternative lines of policy, which might be much more compatible with our own national and international interests.

The Soviet government will never be easy to "get along with." The American people must accustom themselves to this thought, not as a cause for despair, but as a fact to be faced objectively and courageously. If we find it impossible to enlist Soviet cooperation in the solution of world problems, we should be prepared to join with the British and other Western countries in an attempt to build up a world of our own which will pursue its own objectives and will recognize the Soviet orbit as a distinct entity with which conflict is not predestined but with which we cannot pursue common aims.

As long as the Soviet government maintains its present foreign policy, based upon the theory of an ultimate struggle between communism and capitalism, the United States must assume that the USSR might fight at any time for the two-fold purpose of expanding the territory under Communist control and weakening its potential capitalist opponents. The Soviet Union was able to flow into the political vacuum of the Balkans, Eastern Europe, the Near East, Manchuria and Korea because no other nation was both willing and able to prevent it. Soviet leaders were encouraged by easy success, and they are now preparing to take over new areas in the same way.

The Soviet Union, as Stalin euphemistically phrased it, is preparing "for any eventuality."

Unless the United States is willing to sacrifice its future security for the sake of "accord" with the USSR now, this government must, as a first step toward world stabilization, seek to prevent additional Soviet aggression. . . . This government should be prepared, while scrupulously avoiding any act which would be an excuse for the Soviets to begin a war, to resist vigorously and successfully any efforts of the USSR to expand into areas vital to American security.

The language of military power is the only language which disciples of power politics understand. The United States must use that language in order that Soviet leaders will realize that our government is determined to uphold the interests of its citizens and the rights of small nations. Compromise and concessions are considered, by the Soviets, to be evidences of weakness, and they are encouraged by our "retreats" to make new and greater demands. The main deterrent to Soviet attack on the United States, or to attack on areas of the world which are vital to our security, will be the military power of this country. It must be made apparent to the Soviet government that our strength will be sufficient to repel any attack and sufficient to defeat the USSR decisively if a war should start. The prospect of defeat is the only sure means of deterring the Soviet Union.

The Soviet Union's vulnerability is limited due to the vast area over which its key industries and natural resources are widely dispersed, but it is vulnerable to atomic weapons, biological warfare, and long-range power. Therefore, in order to maintain our strength at a level which will be effective in restraining the Soviet Union, the United States must be prepared to wage atomic and biological warfare. A highly mechanized army, which can be moved either by sea or by air, capable of seizing and holding strategic areas, must be supported by powerful naval and air forces. A war with the USSR would be "total" in a more horrible sense than any previous war, and there must be constant research for both offensive and defensive weapons.

Whether it would actually be in this country's interest to employ atomic and biological weapons against the Soviet Union in the event of hostilities is a question which would require careful consideration in the light of the circumstances prevailing at the time. The decision would probably be influenced by a number of factors, such as the Soviet Union's capacity to employ similar weapons, which can not now be estimated. But the important point is that the United States must be prepared to wage atomic and biological warfare if necessary. The mere fact of preparedness may be the only powerful deterrent to Soviet aggressive action and in this sense the only sure guaranty of peace.

The United States, with a military potential composed primarily of [highly] effective technical weapons, should entertain no proposal for disarmament or limitation of armament as long as the possibility of Soviet aggression exists. Any discussion on the limitation of armaments should be pursued slowly and carefully with the knowledge constantly in mind that proposals on outlawing atomic warfare and long-range offensive weapons would greatly limit United States strength, while only moderately affecting the Soviet Union. The Soviet Union relies primarily on a large infantry and artillery force, and the result of such arms limitation would be to deprive the United States of its most effective weapons without impairing the Soviet Union's ability to wage a quick war of aggression in Western Europe, the Middle East or the Far East. . . .

In addition to maintaining our own strength, the United States should support and assist all democratic countries which are in any way menaced or endangered by the USSR. Providing military support in case of attack is a last resort; a more effective barrier to communism is strong economic support. Trade agreements, loans and technical missions strengthen our ties with friendly nations and are effective demonstrations that capitalism is at least the equal of communism. The United States can do much to ensure that economic opportunities, personal freedom and social equality are made possible in countries outside the Soviet sphere by generous financial assistance. Our policy on reparations should be directed toward strengthening the areas we are endeavoring to keep outside the Soviet sphere. Our efforts to break down trade barriers, open up rivers and international waterways, and bring about economic unification of countries, now divided by occupation armies, are also directed toward the reestablishment of vigorous and healthy non-Communist economies.

In conclusion, as long as the Soviet government adheres to its present policy, the United States should maintain military forces powerful enough to restrain the Soviet Union and to confine Soviet influence to its present area. All nations not now within the Soviet sphere should be given generous economic assistance and political support in their opposition to Soviet penetration. Economic aid may also be given to the Soviet government and private trade with the USSR permitted provided the results are beneficial to our interests.

Even though Soviet leaders profess to believe that the conflict between Capitalism and Communism is irreconcilable and must eventually be resolved by the triumph of the latter, it is our hope that they will change their minds and work out with us a fair and equitable settlement when they realize that we are too strong to be beaten and too determined to be frightened.

Document 21.4 The Truman Doctrine

The Truman Doctrine was the basis for the U.S. position in the Cold War with the Soviet Union. In 1947, pro-American governments in Greece and Turkey were threatened with Communist rebellion. President Truman asked Congress to provide military and economic assistance to sustain the Greek and Turkish governments. He declared that the United States should "help free people to maintain their free institutions...against aggressive movements that seek to impose upon them totalitarian regimes." This measure to resist Communism provided the framework for the U.S. containment policy throughout the world.

President Truman Announces the Truman Doctrine

Harry S. Truman

Mr. President, Mr. Speaker, Members of the Congress of the United States:

The gravity of the situation which confronts the world today necessitates my appearance before a joint session of the Congress.

The foreign policy and the national security of this country are involved.

One aspect of the present situation, which I wish to present to you at this time for your consideration and decision, concerns Greece and Turkey.

The Truman Doctrine, Harry S. Truman

The United States has received from the Greek Government an urgent appeal for financial and economic assistance. Preliminary reports from the American Economic Mission now in Greece and reports from the American Ambassador in Greece corroborate the statement of the Greek Government that assistance is imperative if Greece is to survive as a free nation. I do not believe that the American people and the Congress wish to turn a deaf ear to the appeal of the Greek Government.

Greece is not a rich country. Lack of sufficient natural resources has always forced the Greek people to work hard to make both ends meet. Since 1940 this industrious and peace-loving country has suffered invasion, four years of cruel enemy occupation, and bitter internal strife. . . .

The very existence of the Greek state is today threatened by the terrorist activities of several thousand armed men, led by Communists, who defy the Government's authority at a number of points, particularly along the northern boundaries. A commission appointed by the United Nations Security Council is at present investigating disturbed conditions in northern Greece and alleged border violations along the frontier between Greece on the one hand and Albania, Bulgaria, and Yugoslavia on the other.

Meanwhile, the Greek Government is unable to cope with the situation. The Greek Army is small and poorly equipped. It needs supplies and equipment if it is to restore authority to the Government throughout Greek territory.

Greece must have assistance if it is to become a self-supporting and self-respecting democracy.

The United States must supply that assistance. We have already extended to Greece certain types of relief and economic aid, but these are inadequate.

There is no other country to which democratic Greece can turn.

No other nation is willing and able to provide the necessary support for a democratic Greek Government.

The British Government, which has been helping Greece, can give no further financial or economic aid after March 31. Great Britain finds itself under the necessity of reducing or liquidating its commitments in several parts of the world, including Greece.

We have considered how the United Nations might assist in this crisis. But the situation is an urgent one requiring immediate action, and the United Nations and its related organizations are not in a position to extend help of the kind that is required.

It is important to note that the Greek Government has asked for our aid in utilizing effectively the financial and other assistance we may give to Greece, and in improving its public administration. It is of the utmost importance that we supervise the use of any funds made available to Greece, in such a manner that each dollar spent will count toward making Greece self-supporting, and will help to build an economy in which a healthy democracy can flourish.

No government is perfect. One of the chief virtues of a democracy, however, is that its defects are always visible and under democratic processes can be pointed out and corrected. The Government of Greece is not perfect. Nevertheless it represents 85 percent of the members of the Greek Parliament who were chosen in an election last year. Foreign observers, including 692 Americans, considered this election to be a fair expression of the views of the Greek people. The Greek Government has been operating in an atmosphere of chaos and extremism. It has made mistakes. The extension of aid by this country does not mean that the United States condones everything that the Greek Government has done or will do. We have condemned in the past, and we condemn now, extremist measures of the right or the left, We have in the past advised tolerance, and we advise tolerance now.

Greece's neighbor, Turkey, also deserves our attention.

The future of Turkey as an independent and economically sound state is clearly no less important to the freedom-loving peoples of the world than the future of Greece. The circumstances in which Turkey finds itself today are considerably different from those of Greece. Turkey has been spared the disasters that have beset Greece. And during the war the United States and Great Britain furnished Turkey with material aid.

Nevertheless, Turkey now needs our support.

Since the war Turkey has sought additional financial assistance from Great Britain and the United States for the purpose of effecting that modernization necessary for the maintenance of its national integrity.

That integrity is essential to the preservation of order in the Middle East.

The British Government has informed us that, owing to its own difficulties, it can no longer extend financial or economic aid to Turkey.

As in the case of Greece, if Turkey is to have the assistance it needs, the United States must supply it. We are the only country able to provide that help.

I am fully aware of the broad implications involved if the United States is involved in the creation of conditions in which we and other nations will be able to work out a way of life free from coercion. This was a fundamental issue in the war with Germany and Japan. Our victory was won over countries which sought to impose their will, and their way of life upon other nations. To insure the peaceful development of nations, free from coercion, the United States has taken a leading part in establishing the United Nations.

The United Nations is designed to make possible lasting freedom and independence for all its members. We shall not realize our objectives, however, unless we are willing to help free peoples to maintain their free institutions and their national integrity against aggressive movements that seek to impose upon them totalitarian regimes. This is no more than a frank recognition that totalitarian regimes imposed upon free peoples, by direct or indirect aggression, undermine the foundations of international peace and hence the security of the United States. The peoples of a number of countries of the world have recently had totalitarian regimes forced upon them against their will. The Government of the United States has made frequent protests against agreement, in Poland, Rumania, and Bulgaria. I must also state that in a number of other countries there have been similar developments.

At the present moment in world history nearly every nation must choose between alternative ways of life. The choice is too often not a free one.

One way of life is based upon the will of the majority, and is distinguished by free institutions, representative government, free elections, guaranties of individual liberty, freedom of speech and religion, and freedom from political oppression.

The second way of life is based upon the will of a minority forcibly imposed upon the majority. It relies upon terror and oppression, a controlled press and radio, fixed elections, and the suppression of personal freedoms.

I believe that it must be the policy of the United States to support free peoples who are resisting attempted subjugation by armed minorities or by outside pressures.

I believe that we must assist free peoples to work out their own destinies in their own way.

I believe that our help should be primarily through economic and financial aid which is essential to economic stability and orderly political processes.

The world is not static, and the status quo is not sacred. But we cannot allow changes in the status quo in violation of the Charter of the United Nations by such methods as coercion, or by such subterfuges as political infiltration. In helping free and independent nations to maintain their freedom, the United States will be giving effect to the principles of the Charter of the United Nations.

It is necessary only to glance at a map to realize that the survival and integrity of the Greek nation are of grave importance in a much wider situation. If Greece should fall under the control of an armed minority, the effect upon its neighbor, Turkey, would be immediate and serious. Confusion and disorder might well spread throughout the entire Middle East.

Moreover, the disappearance of Greece as an independent state would have a profound effect upon those countries in Europe whose peoples are struggling against great difficulties to maintain their freedoms and their independence while they repair the damages of war.

It would be an unspeakable tragedy if these countries, which have struggled so long against overwhelming odds, should lose that victory for which they sacrificed so much. Collapse of free institutions and loss of independence would be disastrous not only for them but for the world. Discouragement and possibly failure would quickly be the lot of neighboring peoples striving to maintain their freedom and independence.

Should we fail to aid Greece and Turkey in this fateful hour, the effect will be far-reaching to the West as well as to the East.

We must take immediate and resolute action.

I therefore ask the Congress to provide authority for assistance to Greece and Turkey in the amount of $400,000,000 for the period ending June 30, 1948. In requesting these funds, I have taken into consideration the maximum amount of relief assistance which would be furnished to Greece out of the $350,000,000 which I recently requested that the Congress authorize for the prevention of starvation and suffering in countries devastated by the war.

In addition to funds, I ask the Congress to authorize the detail of American civilian and military personnel to Greece and Turkey, at the request of those countries, to assist in the tasks of reconstruction, and for the purpose of supervising the use of such financial and material assistance as may be furnished. I recommend that authority also be provided for the instruction and training of selected Greek and Turkish personnel.

Finally, I ask that the Congress provide authority which will permit the speediest and most effective use, in terms of needed commodities, supplies, and equipment, of such funds as may be authorized.

If further funds, or further authority, should be needed for purposes indicated in this message, I shall not hesitate to bring the situation before the Congress. On this subject the Executive and Legislative branches of the Government must work together.

This is a serious course upon which we embark.

I would not recommend it except that the alternative is much more serious.

The United States contributed $341,000,000,000 toward winning World War Il. This is an investment in world freedom and world peace.

The assistance that I am recommending for Greece and Turkey amounts to little more than one tenth of one percent of this investment. It is only common sense that we should safeguard this investment and make sure that it was not in vain.

The seeds of totalitarian regimes are nurtured by misery and want. They spread and grow in the evil soil of poverty and strife. They reach their full growth when the hope of a people for a better life has died.

We must keep that hope alive.

The free peoples of the world look to us for support in maintaining their freedoms.

If we falter in our leadership, we may endanger the peace of the world and we shall surely endanger the welfare of our own Nation.

Great responsibilities have been placed upon us by the swift movement of events.

I am confident that the Congress will face these responsibilities squarely.

Document 21.5 The Marshall Plan

The Marshall Plan was a program used to funnel U.S. economic aid to Europe during the years from 1948 to 1952. Secretary of State George Marshall proposed the plan in June 1947. He declared that the United States would provide economic assistance to Western Europe, and did provide $14 billion in assistance. The Marshall Plan was highly successful, and it was used as a basis of the U.S. containment policy during the Cold War.

George C. Marshall

I need not tell you, gentlemen, that the world situation is very serious. That must be apparent to all intelligent people. I think one difficulty is that the problem is one of such enormous complexity that the very mass of facts presented to the public by press and radio make it exceedingly difficult for the man in the street to reach a clear appraisement of the situation. Furthermore, the people of this country are distant from the troubled areas of the earth and it is hard for them to comprehend the plight and consequent reactions of the long-suffering peoples, and the effect of those reactions on their governments in connection with our efforts to promote peace in the world.

In considering the requirements for the rehabilitation of Europe, the physical loss of life, the visible destruction of cities, factories, mines, and railroads was correctly estimated, but it has become obvious during recent months that this visible destruction was probably less serious than the dislocation of the entire fabric of European economy. For the past ten years conditions have been highly abnormal. The feverish preparation for war and the more feverish maintenance of the war effort engulfed all aspects of national economies. Machinery has fallen into disrepair or is entirely obsolete. Under the arbitrary and destructive Nazi rule, virtually every possible enterprise was geared into the German war machine. Long-standing commercial ties, private institutions, banks, insurance companies, and shipping companies disappeared, through loss of capital, absorption through nationalization, or by simple destruction. In many countries, confidence in the local currency has been severely shaken. The breakdown of the business structure of Europe during the war was complete. Recovery has been seriously retarded by the fact that two years after the close of hostilities a peace settlement with Germany and Austria has not been agreed upon. But even given a more prompt solution of these difficult problems, the rehabilitation of the economic structure of Europe quite evidently will require a

---

The Marshall Plan by George C. Marshall.

much longer time and greater effort than had been foreseen.

There is a phase of this matter which is both interesting and serious. The farmer has always produced the foodstuffs to exchange with the city dweller for the other necessities of life. This division of labor is the basis of modern civilization. At the present time it is threatened with breakdown. The town and city industries are not producing adequate goods to exchange with the food-producing farmer. Raw materials and fuel are in short supply. Machinery is lacking or worn out. The farmer or the peasant cannot find the goods for sale which he desires to purchase. So the sale of his farm produce for money which he cannot use seems to him an unprofitable transaction. He, therefore, has withdrawn many fields from crop cultivation and is using them for grazing. He feeds more grain to stock and finds for himself and his family an ample supply of food, however short he may be on clothing and the other ordinary gadgets of civilization. Meanwhile people in the cities are short of food and fuel. So the governments are forced to use their foreign money and credits to procure these necessities abroad. This process exhausts funds which are urgently needed for reconstruction. Thus a very serious situation is rapidly developing which bodes no good for the world. The modern system of the division of labor upon which the exchange of products is based is in danger of breaking down.

The truth of the matter is that Europe's requirements for the next three or four years of foreign food and other essential products—principally from America—are so much greater than her present ability to pay that she must have substantial additional help or face economic, social, and political deterioration of a very grave character.

The remedy lies in breaking the vicious circle and restoring the confidence of the European people in the economic future of their own countries and of Europe as a whole. The manufacturer and the farmer throughout wide areas must be able and willing to exchange their products for currencies the continuing value of which is not open to question.

Aside from the demoralizing effect on the world at large and the possibilities of disturbances arising as a result of the desperation of the people concerned, the consequences to the economy of the United States should be apparent to all. It is logical that the United States should do whatever it is able to do to assist in the return of normal economic health in the world, without which there can be no political stability and no assured peace. Our policy is directed not against any country or doctrine but against hunger, poverty, desperation, and chaos. Its purpose should be the revival of a working economy in the world so as to permit the emergence of political and social conditions in which free institutions can exist. Such assistance, I am convinced, must not be on a piecemeal basis as various crises develop. Any assistance that this Government may render in the future should provide a cure rather than a mere palliative. Any government that is willing to assist in the task of recovery will find full cooperation, I am sure, on the part of the United States Government. Any government which maneuvers to block the recovery of other countries cannot expect help from us. Furthermore, governments, political parties, or groups which seek to perpetuate human misery in order to profit therefrom politically or otherwise will encounter the opposition of the United States.

It is already evident that, before the United States Government can proceed much further in its efforts to alleviate the situation and help start the European world on its way to recovery, there must be some agreement among the countries of Europe as to the requirements of the situation and the part those countries themselves will take in order to give proper effect to whatever action might be undertaken by this Government. It would be neither fitting nor efficacious for this Government to undertake to draw up unilaterally a program designed to place Europe on its feet economically. This is the business of the Europeans. The initiative, I think, must come from Europe. The role of this country should consist of friendly aid in the drafting of a European program and of later support of such a program so far as it may be practical for us to do so. The program should be a joint one, agreed to by a number, if not all, European nations.

An essential part of any successful action on the part of the United States is an understanding on the part of the people of America of the character of the problem and the remedies to be applied. Political passion and prejudice should have no part. With foresight, and a willingness on the part of our people to face up to the vast responsibility which history has clearly placed upon our country, the difficulties I have outlined can and will be overcome.

. . . This program will cost our country billions of dollars. It will impose a burden on the American taxpayer. It will require sacrifices today in order that we may enjoy security and peace tomorrow. Should the Congress approve the program for European recovery, as I urgently recommend, we Americans will have made an historic decision of our peacetime history.

A nation in which the voice of its people directs the conduct of its affairs cannot embark on an undertaking of such magnitude and significance for light or purely sentimental reasons. Decisions of this importance are dictated by the highest considerations of national interest. There are none higher, I am sure, than the establishment of enduring peace and the maintenance of true freedom for the individual. In the deliberations of the coming weeks I ask that the European Recovery Program be judged in these terms and on this basis. . . .

The program is not one of a series of piecemeal relief measures. I ask that you note this difference, and keep it in mind throughout our explanations. The difference is absolutely vital.

Document 21.6 The MacArthur Dismissal

In the spring of 1951, the American forces regained Seoul and pushed the North Koreans back to the 38th Parallel, resulting in a stalemate. After Chinese intervention in the Korean conflict, public support for the U.S. military activities had dropped. Truman and his advisors settled for a negotiated peace. MacArthur vehemently disagreed with Truman's actions. Not heeding the instructions of Truman, MacArthur traveled to Taiwan to drum up support for a new offensive—an attack on the mainland of China. MacArthur also requested permission to use the atomic bomb to intimidate the Chinese. His opposition to the stalemate was made public, and in April 1951, Truman relieved MacArthur of his command. The following document is a statement made by Truman regarding his Korean policy and his defense for firing MacArthur.

The Korean War and the Dismissal of MacArthur

Harry S. Truman

In the simplest terms, what we are doing in Korea is this:

We are trying to prevent a third world war.

I think most people in this country recognized that fact last June. And they warmly supported the decision of the Government to help the Republic of Korea against the Communist aggressors. Now, many persons, even some who applauded our decision to defend Korea, have forgotten the basic reason for our action. . . .

The Communists in the Kremlin are engaged in a monstrous conspiracy to stamp out freedom all over the world. If they were to succeed, the United States would be numbered among their principal victims. It must be clear to everyone that the United States cannot—and will not—sit idly by and await foreign conquest. The only question is: When is the best time to meet the threat and how? . . .

The aggression against Korea is the boldest and most dangerous move the Communists have yet made.

The attack on Korea was part of a greater plan for conquering all of Asia. . . .

They want to control all of Asia from the Kremlin.

This plan of conquest is in flat contradiction to what we believe. We believe that Korea belongs to the Koreans. We believe that India belongs to the Indians. We believe that all the nations of Asia should be free to work out their affairs in their own way. This is the basis of peace in the Far East and it is the basis of peace everywhere else.

The whole Communist imperialism is back of the attack on peace in the Far East. It was the Soviet Union that trained and equipped the North Koreans for aggression. The Chinese Communists massed forty-four well-trained and well-equipped divisions on the Korean frontier. These were the troops they threw into battle when the North Korean Communists were beaten.

The question we have to face is whether the Communist plan of conquest can be stopped without

Department of State Bulletin 24.

general war. Our Government and other countries associated with us in the United Nations believe that the best chance of stopping it without general war is to meet the attack in Korea and defeat it there.

That is what we have been doing. It is a difficult and bitter task.

But so far it has been successful.

So far, we have prevented World War III.

So far, by fighting a limited war in Korea, we have prevented aggression from succeeding and bringing on a general war. And the ability of the whole free world to resist Communist aggression has been greatly improved. . . .

But you may ask: Why can't we take steps to punish the aggressor? Why don't we bomb Manchuria and China itself? Why don't we assist nationalist Chinese troops to land on the mainland of China?

If we were to do these things we would be running a very grave risk of starting a general war. If that were to happen, we would have brought about the exact situation we are trying to prevent. . . .

I believe that we must try to limit the war to Korea for these vital reasons: to make sure that the precious lives of our fighting men are not wasted, to see that the security of our country and the free world is not needlessly jeopardized; and to prevent a third world war.

A number of events have made it evident that General MacArthur did not agree with that policy. I have therefore considered it essential to relieve General MacArthur so that there would be no doubt or confusion as to the real purpose and aim of our policy.

It was with the deepest personal regret that I found myself compelled to take this action. General MacArthur is one of our greatest military commanders. But the cause of world peace is more important than any individual.

The change in commands in the Far East means no change whatever in the policy of the United States.

We will carry on the fight in Korea with vigor and determination in an effort to bring the war to a speedy and successful conclusion.

The new commander, Lt. Gen. Matthew Ridgway, has already demonstrated that he has the great qualities of military leadership needed for this task. We are ready, at any time, to negotiate for a restoration of peace in the area. But we will not engage in appeasement. We are only interested in real peace. Real peace can be achieved through a settlement based on the following factors:

One: the fighting must stop.

Two: concrete steps must be taken to insure that the fighting will not break out again.

Three: there must be an end to the aggression. A settlement founded upon these elements would open the way for the unification of Korea and the withdrawal of all foreign forces.

In the meantime, I want to be clear about our military objective. We are fighting to resist an outrageous aggression in Korea. We are trying to keep the Korean conflict from spreading to other areas. But at the same time we must conduct our military activities so as to insure the security of our forces. This is essential if they are to continue the fight until the enemy abandons its ruthless attempt to destroy the Republic of Korea.

That is our military objective—to repel attack and to restore peace. In the hard fighting in Korea, we are proving that collective action among nations is not only a high principle but a workable means of resisting aggression. Defeat of aggression in Korea may be the turning point in the world's search for a practical way of achieving peace and security. . . .

We do not want to widen the conflict. We will use every effort to prevent that disaster. And in so doing, we know that we are following the great principles of peace, freedom, and justice.

Document 21.7 Address to Congress, April 19, 1951

After his dismissal, MacArthur returned to the United States. He was given a hero's welcome. In recognition of his being one of the nation's greatest living military leaders, Congress asked MacArthur to address a joint session in April 1951. His speech is best known for its final lines "Old soldiers never die; they fade away." In 1952, MacArthur tried to secure the Republican presidential nomination. His attempt was unsuccessful, as the nomination and election went to Dwight D. Eisenhower, his former aide.

Douglas MacArthur

. . . I do not stand here as an advocate for any partisan cause, for the issues are fundamental and reach quite beyond the realm of partisan consideration. They must be resolved on the highest plane of national interest if our course is to prove sound and our future protected. . . . I address you with neither rancor nor bitterness in the fading twilight of life with but one purpose in mind, to serve my country.

The issues are global and so interlocked that to consider the problems of one sector oblivious to those of another is but to court disaster for the whole.

While Asia is commonly referred to as the gateway to Europe, it is no less true that Europe is the gateway to Asia, and the broad influence of the one cannot fail to have its impact upon the other. . . .

The Communist threat is a global one. Its successful advance in one sector threatens the destruction of every other sector. You cannot appease or otherwise surrender to communism in Asia without simultaneously undermining our efforts to halt its advance in Europe. . . .

I now turn to the Korean conflict. While I was not consulted prior to the President's decision to intervene in the support of the Republic of Korea, that decision from a military standpoint proved a sound one . . . as we hurled back the invaders and decimated his forces. Our victory was complete and our objectives within reach when Red China intervened with numerically superior ground forces. This created a new war and an entirely new situation, a situation not contemplated when our forces were committed against the North Korean invaders, a situation which called for new decisions in the diplomatic sphere to permit the realistic adjustment of military strategy. Such decisions have not been forthcoming.

While no man in his right mind would advocate sending our ground forces into continental China and such was never given a thought—the new situation did urgently demand a drastic revision of strategic planning if our political aim was to defeat this new enemy as we had defeated the old. . . .

I felt that military necessity in the conduct of the war made necessary:

First, the intensification of our economic blockade against China.

Second, the imposition of a naval blockade against the China coast.

Third, removal of restrictions on air reconnaissance of China's coastal areas and of Manchuria.

Fourth, removal of restrictions on the forces of the Republic of China on Formosa with logistical support to contribute to their effective operation against the Chinese mainland.

For entertaining these views . . . I have been severely criticized in lay circles, principally abroad, despite my understanding that from a military standpoint the above views have been fully shared in the past by practically every military leader concerned with the Korean campaign, including our own Joint Chiefs of Staff.

I called for reinforcements, but was informed that reinforcements were not available. I made clear that if not permitted to utilize the friendly Chinese force of some 600,000 men on Formosa; if not permitted to blockade the China coast to prevent the Chinese Reds from getting succor from without; and if there were to be no hope for major reinforcements, the position of the command from the military standpoint forbade victory. We could hold in Korea . . . but we could hope at best for only an indecisive campaign, with its terrible and constant attrition upon our forces if the enemy utilized his full military potential. I have constantly called for the new political decisions essential to a solution. Efforts have been made to distort my position. It has been said in effect that I was a warmonger. Nothing could be further from the truth. I know war as few other men now living know it, and nothing to me is more revolting. . . .

But once war is forced upon us, there is no other alternative than to apply every available means to bring it to a swift end. War's very object is victory— not prolonged indecision. In war, indeed, there can be no substitute for victory.

There are some who for varying reasons would appease Red China. They are blind to history's clear lesson. For history teaches with unmistakable emphasis that appeasement but begets new and bloodier war. It points to no single instance where the end had justified the means—where appeasement has led to more than a sham peace. Like blackmail, it lays the basis for new and successively greater demands, until, as in blackmail, violence becomes the only other alternative. Why, my soldiers asked of me, surrender military advantages to an enemy in the field? I cannot answer. Some may say to avoid spread of the conflict into an all-out war with China; others, to avoid Soviet intervention. Neither explanation seems valid. For

---

Address to Congress, April 1951.

China is already engaging with the maximum power it can commit, and the Soviet will not necessarily mesh its actions with our moves. Like a cobra, any new enemy will more likely strike when ever it feels that relativity in military or other potential is in its favor on a worldwide basis. . . .

I have just left your fighting sons in Korea. They have met all the tests there and I can report to you without reservation that they are splendid in every way. It was my constant effort to preserve them and end this savage conflict honorably and with the least loss of time and a minimum sacrifice of life. Its growing bloodshed has caused me the deepest anguish and anxiety. Those gallant men will remain often in my thoughts and in my prayers always.

I am closing my fifty-two years of military service. When I joined the Army even before the turn of the century, it was the fulfillment of all my boyish hopes and dreams. The world has turned over many times since I took the oath on the Plain at West Point, and the hopes and dreams have long since vanished. But I still remember the refrain of one of the most popular barrack ballads of that day, which proclaimed most proudly that—

"Old soldiers never die, they just fade away."

And like the old soldier of that ballad, I now close my military career and just fade away—an old soldier who tried to do his duty as God gave him the light to see that duty.

Good-by.

Document 21.8 The Threat of Communism

In the 1950s, Senator Joseph McCarthy of Wisconsin gained notoriety for his accusations that high levels of the U.S. government had been infiltrated by Communists. President Truman denied McCarthy's charges. At a time when Americans viewed Communism as a serious threat, McCarthy became the center of attention. By 1954, he was conducting a series of televised hearings, claiming that there were Communists in the U.S. Army. The wild accusations and name-calling made McCarthy appear crude; his popularity declined and his fellow senators voted to censure him. He continued to work as a senator until his death in 1957.

Joseph R. McCarthy

Ladies and gentlemen, tonight as we celebrate the one hundred and forty-first birthday of one of the greatest men in American history, I would like to be able to talk about what a glorious day today is in the history of the world. As we celebrate the birth of this man who with his whole heart and soul hated war, I would like to be able to speak of peace in our time, of war being outlawed, and of world-wide disarmament. These would be truly appropriate things to be able to mention as we celebrate the birthday of Abraham Lincoln.

Five years after a world war has been won, men's hearts should anticipate a long peace, and men's minds should be free from the heavy weight that comes with war. But this is not such a period—for this is not a period of peace. This is a time of the "cold war." This is a time when all the world is split into two vast, increasingly hostile armed camps—a time of a great armaments race.

Today we can almost physically hear the mutterings and rumblings of an invigorated god of war. You can see it, feel it, and hear it all the way from the hills of Indochina, from the shores of Formosa, right over into the very heart of Europe itself.

The one encouraging thing is that the "mad moment" has not yet arrived for the firing of the gun or the exploding of the bomb which will set civilization about the final task of destroying itself. There is still a hope for peace if we finally decide that no longer can we safely blind our eyes and close our ears to those facts which are shaping up more and more clearly. And that is that we are now engaged in a show-down fight—not the usual war between nations for land areas or other material gains, but a war between two diametrically opposed ideologies.

The great difference between our western Christian world and the atheistic Communist world is not

The Threat of Communism, 81st Congress, 1950.

political, ladies and gentlemen, it is moral. There are other differences, of course, but those could be reconciled. For instance, the Marxian idea of confiscating the land and factories and running the entire economy as a single enterprise is momentous. Likewise, Lenin's invention of the one-party police state as a way to make Marx's idea work is hardly less momentous.

Stalin's resolute putting across of these two ideas, of course, did much to divide the world. With only those differences, however, the East and the West could most certainly still live in peace.

The real, basic difference, however lies in the religion of immoralism—invented by Marx, preached feverishly by Lenin, and carried to unimaginable extremes by Stalin. This religion of immoralism, if the Red half of the world wins—and well it may—this religion of immoralism will more deeply wound and damage mankind than any conceivable economic or political system.

Karl Marx dismissed God as a hoax, and Lenin and Stalin have added in clear-cut, unmistakable language their resolve that no nation, no people who believe in a God, can exist side by side with their communistic state.

Karl Marx, for example, expelled people from his Communist Party for mentioning such things as justice, humanity, or morality. He called this soulful ravings and sloppy sentimentality.

While Lincoln was a relatively young man in his late thirties, Karl Marx boasted that the Communist specter was haunting Europe. Since that time, hundreds of millions of people and vast areas of the world have fallen under Communist domination. Today, less than 100 years after Lincoln's death, Stalin brags that this Communist specter is not only haunting the world, but is about to completely subjugate it.

Today we are engaged in a final, all-out battle between communistic atheism and Christianity. The modern champions of communism have selected this as the time. And, ladies and gentlemen, the chips are down—they are truly down.

Lest there be any doubt that the time has been chosen, let us go directly to the leader of communism today—Joseph Stalin. Here is what he said—not back in 1928, not before the war, not during the war—but two years after the last war was ended: "To think that the Communist revolution can be carried out peacefully, within the framework of a Christian democracy, means one has either gone out of one's mind and lost all normal understanding, or has grossly and openly repudiated the Communist revolution."

And this is what was said by Lenin in 1919, which was also quoted with approval by Stalin in 1947:

"We are living," said Lenin, "not merely in a state, but in a system of states, and the existence of the Soviet Republic side by side with Christian states for a long time is unthinkable. One or the other must triumph in the end. And before that end supervenes, a series of frightful collisions between the Soviet Republic and the Bourgeois states will be inevitable."

Ladies and gentlemen, can there be anyone here tonight who is so blind as to say that the war is not on? Can there be anyone who fails to realize that the Communist world has said, "The time is now"—that this is the time for the show-down between the democratic Christian world and the Communist atheistic world?

Unless we face this fact, we shall pay the price that must be paid by those who wait too long.

Six years ago, at the time of the first conference to map out the peace—Dumbarton Oaks—there was within the Soviet orbit 180,000,000 people. Lined up on the anti-totalitarian side there were in the world at that time roughly 1,625,000,000 people. Today, only six years later, there are 800,000,000 people under the absolute domination of Soviet Russia—an increase of over 400 percent. On our side, the figure has shrunk to around 500,000,000. In other words, in less than six years the odds have changed from 9 to 1 in our favor to 8 to 5 against us. This indicated the swiftness of the tempo of Communist victories and American defeats in the cold war. As one of our outstanding historical figures once said, "When a great democracy is destroyed, it will not be because of enemies from without, but rather because of enemies from within."

The truth of this statement is becoming terrifyingly clear as we see this country each day losing on every front.

At war's end we were physically the strongest nation on earth and, at least potentially, the most powerful intellectually and morally. Ours could have been the honor of being a beacon in the desert of destruction, a shining living proof that civilization was not yet ready to destroy itself. Unfortunately, we have failed miserably and tragically to arise to the opportunity.

The reason why we find ourselves in a position of impotency is not because our only powerful potential enemy has sent men to invade our shores, but rather because of the traitorous actions of those who have been treated so well by this Nation. It has not been the less fortunate or members of minority groups who have been selling this Nation out, but rather those who have had all the benefits that the wealthiest nation on earth has had to offer—the finest homes, the finest college education, and the finest jobs in Government we can give.

This is glaringly true in the State Department. There the bright young men who are born with silver spoons in their mouths are the ones who have been worst.

Now I know it is very easy for anyone to condemn a particular bureau or department in general terms. Therefore, I would like to cite one rather unusual case—the case of a man who has done much to shape our foreign policy.

When Chiang Kai-shek was fighting our war, the State Department had in China a young man named John S. Service. His task, obviously, was not to work for the communization of China. Strangely, however, he sent official reports back to the State Department urging that we torpedo our ally Chiang Kai-shek and stating, in effect, that communism was the best hope of China.

Later, this man—John Service—was picked up by the Federal Bureau of Investigation for turning over to the Communists secret State Department information. Strangely, however, he was never prosecuted. However, Joseph Grew, the Under Secretary of State, who insisted on his prosecution, was forced to resign. Two days after Grew's successor, Dean Acheson, took over as Under Secretary of State, this man—John Service—who had been picked up by the FBI and who had previously urged that communism was the best hope of China, was not only reinstated in the State Department but promoted. And finally, under Acheson, placed in charge of all placements and promotions.

Today, ladies and gentlemen, this man Service is on his way to represent the State Department and Acheson in Calcutta—by far and away the most important listening post in the Far East.

Now, let's see what happens when individuals with Communist connections are forced out of the State Department. Gustave Duran, who was labeled as (I quote) "a notorious international Communist," was made assistant to the Assistant Secretary of State in charge of Latin American affairs. He was taken into the State Department from his job as a lieutenant colonel in the Communist International Brigade. Finally, after intense congressional pressure and criticism, he resigned in 1946 from the State Department—and, ladies and gentlemen, where do you think he is now? He took over a high-salaried job as Chief of Cultural Activities Section in the office of the Assistant Secretary General of the United Nations.

Then there was a Mrs. Mary Jane Kenny, from the Board of Economic Warfare in the State Department, who was named in an FBI report and in a House committee report as a courier for the Communist Party while working for the Government. And where do you think Mrs. Kenny is—she is now an editor in the United Nations Document Bureau.

Another interesting case was that of Julian H. Wadleigh, economist in the Trade Agreements Section of the State Department for 11 years and was sent to Turkey and Italy and other countries as United States representative. After the statute of limitations had run so he could not be prosecuted for treason, he openly and brazenly not only admitted but proclaimed that he had been a member of the Communist Party * * * that while working for the State Department he stole a vast number of secret documents * * * and furnished these documents to the Russian spy ring of which he was a part.

You will recall last spring there was held in New York what was known as the World Peace Conference—a conference which was labeled by the State Department and Mr. Truman as the sounding board for Communist propaganda and a front for Russia. Dr. Harlow Shapley was the chairman of that conference. Interestingly enough, according to the new release put out by the Department in July, the Secretary of State appointed Shapley on a commission which acts as liaison between UNESCO and the State Department.

This, ladies and gentlemen, gives you somewhat of a picture of the type of individuals who have been helping to shape our foreign policy. In my opinion the State Department, which is one of the most important government departments, is thoroughly infested with Communists.

I have in my hand 57 cases of individuals who would appear to be either card carrying members or certainly loyal to the Communist Party, but who nevertheless are still helping to shape our foreign policy.

One thing to remember in discussing the Communists in our Government is that we are not dealing with spies who get 30 pieces of silver to steal the blueprints of a new weapon. We are dealing with a far more sinister type of activity because it permits the enemy to guide and shape our policy.

In that connection, I would like to read to you very briefly from the testimony of Larry E. Kerley, a man who was with the counter espionage section of the FBI for eight years. And keep in mind as I read this to you that at the time he is speaking, there was in the State Department Alger Hiss, the convicted

Alger Hiss; John Service, the man whom the FBI picked up for espionage—

And for turning over secret documents—Julian Wadleigh, who brazenly admitted he was a spy and wrote newspaper articles in regard thereto, plus hundreds of other bad security risks.

The FBI, I may add, has done an outstanding job, as all persons in Washington, Democrats and Republicans alike, agree. If J. Edgar Hoover had a free hand, we would not be plagued by Hisses and Wadleighs in high positions of power in the State Department. The FBI has only power to investigate.

Here is what the FBI man said.

In accordance with instructions of the State Department to the FBI, the FBI was not even permitted to open an espionage case against any Russia suspect without State Department approval.

In other words they could not afford to let the whole ring which extended into the State Department be exposed.

This brings us down to the case of one Alger Hiss who is important not as an individual any more, but rather because he is so representative of a group in the State Department. It is unnecessary to go over the sordid events showing how he sold out the Nation which had given him so much. Those are rather fresh in all of our minds.

However, it should be remembered that the facts in regard to his connection with this international Communist spy ring were made known to the then Under Secretary of State Berle three days after Hitler and Stalin signed the Russo-German alliance pact. At that time one Whittaker Chambers—who was also part of the spy ring—apparently decided that with Russia on Hitler's side, he could no longer betray our Nation to Russia. He gave Under Secretary of State Berle—and this is all a matter of record—practically all, if not more, of the facts upon which Hiss's conviction was based.

Under Secretary Berle promptly contacted Dean Acheson and received word in return that Acheson (and I quote) "could vouch for Hiss absolutely"—at which time the matter was dropped. And this, you understand, was at a time when Russia was an ally of Germany. This condition existed while Russia and Germany were invading and dismembering Poland, and while the Communist groups here were screaming "warmonger" at the United States for their support of the allied nations.

Again in 1943, the FBI had occasion to investigate the facts surrounding Hiss's contacts with the Russian spy ring. But even after that FBI report was submitted, nothing was done.

Then late in 1948—on August 5—when the Un-American Activities Committee called Alger Hiss to give an accounting, President Truman at once issued a Presidential directive ordering all Government agencies to refuse to turn over any information whatsoever in regard to the Communist activities of any Government employee to a congressional committee.

Incidentally, even after Hiss was convicted . . . it is interesting to note that the President still labeled the exposé of Hiss as a "red herring."

If time permitted, it might be well to go into detail about the fact that Hiss was Roosevelt's chief adviser at Yalta when Roosevelt was admittedly in ill health and tired physically and mentally * * * and when, according to the Secretary of State, Hiss and Gromyko drafted the report on the conference.

According to the then Secretary of State Stettinius, here are some of the things that Hiss helped to decide at Yalta. (1) The establishment of a European High Commission; (2) the treatment of Germany— this you will recall was the conference at which it was decided that we would occupy Berlin with Russia occupying an area completely circling the city, which, as you know, resulted in the Berlin airlift which cost 31 American lives; (3) the Polish question; (4) the relationship between UNRRA and the Soviet; (5) the rights of Americans on control commissions of Rumania, Bulgaria, and Hungary; (6) Iran; (7) China—here's where we gave away Manchuria; (8) Turkish Straits question; (9) International trusteeships; (10) Korea.

Of the results of this conference, Arthur Bliss Lane of the State Department had this to say: "As I glanced over the document, I could not believe my eyes. To me, almost every line spoke of a surrender to Stalin."

As you hear this story of high treason, I know that you are saying to yourself, "Well, why doesn't the Congress do something about it?" Actually, ladies and gentlemen, one of the important reasons for the graft, the corruption, the dishonesty, the disloyalty, the treason in high Government positions—one of the most important reasons why this continues is a lack of moral uprising on the part of the 140,000,000 American people. In the light of history, however, this is not hard to explain.

It is the result of an emotional hang-over and a temporary moral lapse which follows every war. It is the apathy to evil which people who have been subjected to the tremendous evils of war feel. As the people of the world see mass murder, the destruction of defenseless and innocent people, and all of the crime and lack of morals which go with war, they become numb and apathetic. It has always been thus after war.

However, the morals of our people have not been destroyed. They still exist. This cloak of numbness and apathy has only needed a spark to rekindle them. Happily, this spark has finally been supplied.

As you know, very recently the Secretary of State proclaimed his loyalty to a man guilty of what has always been considered as the most abominable of all crimes—of being a traitor to the people who gave him a position of great trust. The Secretary of State in attempting to justify his continued devotion to the man who sold out the Christian world to the atheistic world, referred to Christ's Sermon on the Mount as a justification and reason therefore, and the reaction of the American people to this would have made the heart of Abraham Lincoln happy.

When this pompous diplomat in striped pants, with a phony British accent, proclaimed to the American people that Christ on the Mount endorsed communism, high treason, and betrayal of a sacred trust, the blasphemy was so great that it awakened the dormant indignation of the American people.

He has lighted the spark which is resulting in a moral uprising and will end only when the whole sorry mess of twisted, warped thinkers are swept from the national scene so that we may have a new birth of national honesty and decency in Government.

Document 21.9 Declaration of Conscience

In opposition to McCarthyism, Senator Margaret Chase Smith from Maine delivered the Declaration of Conscience speech before the Senate in June 1950, attacking the methods of Senator Joseph McCarthy.

Margaret Chase Smith

I would like to speak briefly and simply about a serious national condition. It is a national feeling of fear and frustration that could result in national suicide and the end of everything that we Americans hold dear. It is a condition that comes from the lack of effective leadership in either the Legislative Branch or the Executive Branch of our Government.

That leadership is so lacking that serious and responsible proposals are being made that national advisory commissions be appointed to provide such critically needed leadership.

I speak as a Republican. I speak as a woman. I speak as a United States Senator. I speak as an American. . . .

I think that it is high time that we remembered that we have sworn to uphold and defend the Constitution. I think that it is high time that we remembered that the Constitution, as amended, speaks not only of the freedom of speech but also of trial by jury instead of trial by accusation. . . .

Those of us who shout the loudest about Americanism in making character assassinations are all too frequently those who, by our own words and acts, ignore some of the basic principles of Americanism:

The right to criticize;
The right to hold unpopular beliefs;
The right to protest;
The right of independent thought.

The exercise of these rights should not cost one single American citizen his reputation or his right to a livelihood nor should he be in danger of losing his reputation or livelihood merely because he happens to know someone who holds unpopular beliefs. Who of us doesn't? Otherwise none of us could call our souls our own. Otherwise thought control would have set in.

The American people are sick and tired of being afraid to speak their minds lest they be politically smeared as "Communists" or "Fascists" by their opponents. Freedom of speech is not what it used to be in America. It has been so abused by some that it is not exercised by others. . . .

Today our country is being psychologically divided by the confusion and the suspicions that are bred in the United States Senate to spread like

From *The New York Times,* June 2, 1950. Reprinted with permission.

cancerous tentacles of "know nothing, suspect everything" attitudes. Today we have a Democratic Administration that has developed a mania for loose spending and loose programs. History is repeating itself—and the Republican Party again has the opportunity to emerge as the champion of unity and prudence.

The record of the present Democratic Administration has provided us with sufficient campaign issues without the necessity of resorting to political smears. America is rapidly losing its position as leader of the world simply because the Democratic Administration has pitifully failed to provide effective leadership. . . .

Yet to displace it with a Republican regime embracing a philosophy that lacks political integrity or intellectual honesty would prove equally disastrous to this nation. The nation sorely needs a Republican victory. But I don't want to see the Republican Party ride to political victory on the Four Horsemen of Calumny—Fear, Ignorance, Bigotry, and Smear.

I doubt if the Republican Party could-simply because 1 don't believe the American people will uphold any political party that puts Political exploitation above national interest. Surely we Republicans aren't that desperate for victory. . . .

As a United States Senator, I am not proud of the way in which the Senate has been made a publicity platform for irresponsible sensationalism. I am not proud of the reckless abandon in which unproved charges have been hurled from this side of the aisle. I am not proud of the obviously staged, undignified countercharges that have been attempted in retaliation from the other side of the aisle.

I don't like the way the Senate has been made a rendezvous for vilification, for selfish political gain at the sacrifice of individual reputations and national unity. I am not proud of the way we smear outsiders from the Floor of the Senate and hide behind the cloak of congressional immunity and still place ourselves beyond criticism on the Floor of the Senate.

As an American, I am shocked at the way Republicans and Democrats alike are playing directly into the Communist design of "confuse, divide, and conquer." As an American, I don't want a Democratic Administration "whitewash" or "cover-up" any more than I want a Republican smear or witch hunt.

As an American, I condemn a Republican "Fascist" just as much as I condemn a Democrat "Communist." I condemn a Democrat "fascist" just as much as I condemn a Republican "Communist." They are equally dangerous to you and me and to our country. As an American, I want to see our nation recapture the strength and unity it once had when we fought the enemy instead of ourselves.

It is with these thoughts that I have drafted what I call a "Declaration of Conscience." I am gratified that [six Republican senators] have concurred in that declaration and have authorized me to announce their concurrence.

Document 21.10 McCarthy's Charges Rebutted

In response to McCarthy's accusation of Communists within the U.S. State Department, the Senate appointed a committee, under the direction of Senator Millard Tydings from Maryland. It began hearings in March 1950. McCarthy failed to name a single State Department employee with Communist ties. On July 17, 1950, Tydings issued a report that found no grounds for McCarthy's allegations. The following report is from the Senate Committee on Foreign Relations, 81st Congress, 1950.

Senate Foreign Relations Committee

The Facts Behind the Charge of "Whitewash"

Seldom, if ever, in the history of congressional investigations has a committee been subjected to an organized campaign of vilification and abuse comparable to that with which we have been confronted throughout this inquiry. This campaign has been so acute and so obviously designed to confuse and confound the American people that an analysis of the factors responsible therefore is indicated.

The first of these factors was the necessity of creating the impression that our inquiry was not thorough and sincere in order to camouflage the fact that the charges made by Senator McCarthy were groundless and that the Senate and the American people had been deceived. No sooner were hearings started than the cry of "whitewash" was raised along with the chant "investigate the charges and not McCarthy."

This chant we have heard morning, noon, and night for almost four months from certain quarters for readily perceptible motives. Interestingly, had we elected to investigate Senator McCarthy, there would have been ample basis therefore, since we have been reliably informed that at the time he made the charges initially he had no information whatever to support them, and, furthermore, it early appeared that in securing Senate Resolution 231 a fraud had been perpetrated upon the Senate of the United States.

From the very outset of our inquiry, Senator McCarthy has sought to leave the impression that the subcommittee has been investigating him and not "disloyalty in the State Department." The reason for the Senator's concern is now apparent. He had no facts to support his wild and baseless charges, and lived in mortal fear that this situation would be exposed.

Few people, cognizant of the truth in even an elementary way, have, in the absence of political partisanship, placed any credence in the hit-and-run tactics of Senator McCarthy. He has stooped to a new low in his cavalier disregard of the facts.

The simple truth is that in making his speech at Wheeling [West Virginia],** Senator McCarthy was talking of a subject and circumstances about which he knew nothing. His extreme and irresponsible statements called for emergency measures. As Senator Wherry told Emmanuel S. Larsen, "Oh, Mac has gone out on a limb and kind of made a fool of himself and we have to back him up now." Starting with nothing, Senator McCarthy plunged headlong forward, desperately seeking to develop some information, which colored with distortion and fanned by a blaze of bias, would forestall a day of reckoning.

Certain elements rallied to his support, particularly those who ostensibly fight communism by adopting the vile methods of the Communists themselves and in so doing actually hinder the fight of all right-minded people who detest and abhor communism in all its manifestations. We cannot, however, destroy one evil by the adoption of another. Senator McCarthy and McCarthyism have been exposed for what they are—and the sight is not a pretty one. . . .

Another consideration is the oft-repeated and natural reaction of many good people that goes something like this—" Well, there must be something to the charges, or a United States Senator would never have made them!" The simple truth now is apparent, that a conclusion based on this premise, while normally true, is here erroneous; for we have the amazing spectacle of a United States Senator having made such charges with no facts or with discredited allegations of fact to support them.

Still, a third consideration has been the readiness of many people to believe charges of disloyalty in the State Department by reason of the Alger Hiss case. In this regard, we have been appalled by the studied effort to inject Hiss's name into our proceedings without any basis whatsoever therefor. The Hiss case was indeed despicable. The facts are, however, that Alger Hiss was convicted for perjury in connection with his associations with Whittaker Chambers back in 1938. To seek to translate that case to a setting 12 years later and employ it as a basis for charges of widespread disloyalty today in the State Department is not convincing of anything to thinking men and women.

A . . . final consideration has been the vague uneasiness of many Americans concerning the ascendancy of the Communists in China and the decline of the Nationalist Government. In such a setting, there was "fertile ground" to receive any charges to indicate that perhaps someone, somewhere in our own State Department may have been responsible for the Chinese situation. To those who would know the true facts concerning American diplomacy in China, we earnestly recommend to your reading the so-called white paper on China, being the story of our relations with China during the period 1944 to 1949, based on the files of the State Department. . . .

General Observations

In concluding our report, we are constrained to make observations which we regard as fundamental.

It is, of course, clearly apparent that the charges of Communist infiltration of and influence upon the State Department are false. This knowledge is reassuring to all Americans whose faith has been temporarily shaken in the security of their Government by perhaps the most nefarious campaign of untruth in the history of our Republic.

We believe, however, that this knowledge and assurance, while important, will prove ultimately of secondary significance in contemplating the salutary aspects of our investigation. For we believe that

Senate Committee on Foreign Relations, 81st Congress, 1950.
*A famous speech where McCarthy claimed that the State Department had 205 known Communists as employees.

inherent in the charges that have been made and the sinister campaign to give them ostensible verity are lessons from which the American people will find inspiration for a rededication to the principles and ideals that have made this Nation great.

We have seen the technique of the "Big Lie," elsewhere employed by the totalitarian dictator with devastating success, utilized here for the first time on a sustained basis in our history. We have seen how, through repetition and shifting untruths, it is possible to delude great numbers of people.

We have seen the character of private citizens and of Government employees virtually destroyed by public condemnation on the basis of gossip, distortion, hearsay, and deliberate untruths. By the mere fact of their associations with a few persons of alleged questionable proclivities an effort has been made to place the stigma of disloyalty upon individuals, some of whom are little people whose only asset is their character and devotion to duty and country. This has been done without the slightest vestige of respect for even the most elementary rules of evidence or fair play or, indeed, common decency. Indeed, we have seen an effort not merely to establish guilt by association but guilt by accusation alone. The spectacle is one we would expect in a totalitarian nation where the rights of the individual are crushed beneath the juggernaut of statism and oppression; it has no place in America where government exists to serve our people, not to destroy them.

We have seen an effort to inflame the American people with a wave of hysteria and fear on an unbelievable scale in this free Nation. Were this campaign founded in truth it would be questionable enough; where it is fraught with falsehood from beginning to end, its reprehensible and contemptible character defies adequate condemnation.

We sincerely believe that charges of the character which have been made in this case seriously impair the efforts of our agencies of Government to combat the problem of subversion. Furthermore, extravagant allegations, which cannot be proved and are not subject to proof, have the inevitable effect of dulling the awareness of all Americans to the true menace of communism. . . .

Communism represents the most diabolical concept ever designed to enslave mankind. Its stock and trade are deception, falsehood, and hate. The one hope of communism's success is to divide our people at home and our allies abroad. The false charges made in this case have succeeded in accomplishing to a great degree what the Communists themselves have been unable to do. These charges have created distrust and suspicion at home and raised serious doubts abroad. We can never hope to preserve for posterity the American dream of freedom by adopting totalitarian methods as an excuse to preserve that freedom. Our greatest weapon against communism is truth. If we lose that weapon, we shall have gone far toward that fate which has already brought sorrow, death, and degradation to millions of people upon this earth.

Chapter 21 Worksheets and Questions

1. Define "containment." Explain how the Truman Doctrine, the Marshall Plan, and the Long Telegram contribute to this policy.

_____

_____

_____

_____

_____

_____

_____

_____

_____

2. Wallace and Clifford viewed American Soviet policy differently. According to Wallace, what will result from the American policy toward the Soviet Union? According to Clifford, what is the Soviet threat to the United States?

_____

_____

_____

_____

_____

_____

_____

_____

_____

3. Explain the Truman-MacArthur controversy as it relates to Korea.

_____

_____

_____

_____

_____

_____

_____

_____

_____

_____

4. Explain the rise of McCarthyism in America.

_____

_____

_____

_____

_____

_____

_____

_____

_____

_____

5. What led to McCarthy's demise in the 1950s? Provide examples from the comments of his critics: Margaret Chase Smith and Millard Tydings.

_____

_____

_____

_____

_____

_____

_____

_____

_____

_____

_____

_____

_____

_____

_____

_____

_____

_____

_____

_____

_____

The Struggle for Equality and Civil Rights: American Transition in the 1950s and 1960s

The 1950s and 1960s brought America face-to-face with one of its greatest internal challenges since the Reconstruction Era (1865-1877). A change in race relations, which had far-reaching effects upon all aspects of society, appeared inevitable. America's African-American population could no longer endure the rising tide of injustice. The few changes that had occurred in the past—the 1896 decision in *Plessy v. Ferguson* regarding the separate but equal doctrine in schools, and the desegregation of the United States Armed Forces in 1947—had given the people a reason to hope. African Americans, weary of being disfranchised, wanted full suffrage and nothing less. Likewise, they believed they were entitled to equal access to housing, jobs, and educational opportunities without regard to race. In the twenty-first century, such aspirations may not appear revolutionary, but during the height of the civil rights movement, for African Americans to desire equal treatment under the law as Whites was tantamount to challenging the core of White authority. America's treatment of its African-American population would eventually lead to confrontation between Blacks and Whites and erupt into episodes of violence, especially in the South. Eventually, all branches of the government would be instrumental in the transition of millions of African Americans into mainstream American society.

During the sociopolitical revolution of the Eisenhower administration, the event that triggered the beginning of social change in America was the decision rendered in the 1954 *Brown v. Board of Education* case, in which the U.S. Supreme Court ruled that segregated schools were intrinsically unequal. This decision overturned *Plessy v. Ferguson* and its doctrine of "separate but equal" in public schools. Revitalized by the *Brown* decision, civil rights activists—Black and White—began to organize ways to overthrow the Jim Crow establishment *de facto* segregation that had reigned for too long in the South. Alabama became fertile ground for NAACP (National Association for the Advancement of Colored People) activity. On an eventful day in December of 1955, the actions of one nondescript African-American woman became the weapon that triggered the civil rights movement, which in turn reshaped and redefined America's struggle for equality among its people.

On December 1, 1955, in Montgomery, Alabama, Rosa Parks, a local seamstress on her way home from work, was arrested for refusing to give up her seat to a White man on a bus. This event would eventually lead to a planned boycott of the bus company in 1956. The bus boycott, under the leadership of the Reverend Martin Luther King, Jr., captured international attention. One year later, the segregated busing ordinance was declared invalid and the civil rights movement reorganized its leadership. The Reverend King organized an alliance of Black ministers, which became known as the Southern Christian Leadership Conference (SCLC). This organization would lead nonviolent civil rights campaigns in various locations in America.

The civil rights campaign was gaining momentum. In 1957, when nine African-American students attempted to enter Central High School in Little Rock, Arkansas, they were denied entrance. When President Dwight D. Eisenhower sanctioned the use of federal troops to enforce a court order admitting the Little Rock Nine to Central High, the message from the *Declaration of Independence* reverberated throughout the African American community—"created equal, created equal....Life, Liberty...."

By the 1960s, the civil rights movement had enlarged its territory to include other testing grounds. The campaign had moved from the schools to other places of public accommodation. On February 1, 1960, four African-American students from Greensboro, North Carolina staged a sit-in at a "Whites only" counter in a Woolsworth's department store, occupying all available seats and refusing to surrender them. Other students throughout the South were inspired by the nonviolent protest; shortly thereafter, students began to organize their efforts in order to be more effective.

By the spring of 1960, student leaders had organized the Student Nonviolent Coordinating Committee (SNCC). Other groups would follow. In 1961, the Congress of Racial Equality (CORE) organized Freedom Rides, in which groups of Black and White activists tested the desegregation laws by riding buses into the South. In Alabama, the Riders were met by angry mobs of Whites, who firebombed buses and assaulted the activists. A short time later, Attorney General Robert F. Kennedy ordered the state of Alabama to provide protection for the activists. The following year the federal court ordered the University of Mississippi to admit James Meredith, an African-American student. U.S. marshals were called in to guarantee Meredith's safety, as riots ensued. Members of the United States Air Force were brought in to end the violence.

In early spring of 1963, Martin Luther King, Jr. and SCLC launched a frontal assault on White supremacy. Aware of Police Commissioner Eugene "Bull" Conner's zero-tolerance rule, the activists staged a protest in the streets of downtown Birmingham, Alabama. The protesters included school-aged children. Television cameras captured the horrid scenes for the world to view as police assaulted the children with fire hoses, unleashed dogs on them, and carried them off to jail. As the protest continued, the fury of men who had long been denied their rights was unleashed, and Blacks bravely confronted the police and White mobs violently.

By August of 1963, several civil rights groups had organized what was to become known as one of the largest demonstrations in American history. Nearly a quarter of a million people converged on Washington, D.C. to join Martin Luther King, Jr. in his march for the rights of the poor and disfranchised. Words from King's famous "I Have a Dream Speech," delivered at the Lincoln Memorial, will forever linger in the hearts of the American people. Several weeks after the march on Washington, violence erupted in Birmingham, where the Ku Klux Klan was responsible for the bombing of a local church, killing four young girls. Two months later, on November 22, President John F. Kennedy was assassinated, and in December, the charismatic and outspoken Malcolm X, broke from the Nation of Islam and formed his own movement—Muslim Mosque, Inc. A pall of uncertainty hung over communities in America, the protests continued, but change would come. In 1964, America witnessed the legislation of the Civil Rights Act, prohibiting discrimination based on race, ethnic origin, religion, or sex. The Voting Rights Act followed in 1965. This legislation prohibited registration and voting discrimination.

The legal landmarks of 1964 and 1965 could not, however, prevent the increasing racial tension in this country. Violence had erupted in cities throughout America—racism was not a Southern problem but a national problem. In 1968, Martin Luther King, Jr. was assassinated in Memphis, Tennessee, and shortly after, riots erupted in cities across America.

Throughout the decades of the 1950s and 1960s, America witnessed "protest"—African Americans revolting against the *de facto* segregation that permeated all facets of American society but, for the most part, White America vehemently resisted change—change which would become inevitable. The faces and voices during the civil rights movement were many. The documents in this chapter will allow the reader to experience, vicariously, some of the struggles for equality during the 1950s and 1960s in America.

Considering the Evidence in the Readings

The Civil Rights movement of the 1950s and 1960s, often referred to as the second Reconstruction, forced America's recognition of the injustice that had been inflicted upon African Americans for centuries. The spokesman for the movement, the Reverend Martin Luther King, Jr., was able to articulate the experiences of African Americans, and later all Americans, and to eloquently present their struggle—not only to mainstream America, but the world as well.

King's philosophy, rooted in non-violent protest, helped to bring about change in America. Not all Americans were quick to respond, however, to Dr. King's call. Those who responded did so more reactively than proactively. Two of the following documents include oratory of Martin Luther King's "Letter from the Birmingham Jail" and "I Have a Dream." Readers should pay close attention to these two documents because they reveal defining moments in the Civil Rights movement. The other documents provide examples of African American youth activities during the 1960s, the political position of Southern Democrats following the *Brown v. Board of Education* decision of 1954, and President Eisenhower's address to the nation concerning the racial conflict in Little Rock, Arkansas.

Readers should assess the overall goals and strategies of those during the Civil Rights movement from three vantage points: (1) African Americans; (2) the presidential administration, and (3) Southern Democrats.

Document 22.1 The Congressional Response by Southerners to *Brown v. the Board of Education*

The Southern Manifesto was a counter to the Supreme Court decision in 1954 *Brown vs. Board of Education*. The document, written in 1956 by Southern legislators, opposed racial integration in public places. The Manifesto was signed by nearly 100 Southern Congressmen. Segregated schools were one of the most enduring of the Jim Crow laws that exemplified the American South during the first half of the twentieth century.

"The Southern Manifesto"

THE DECISION OF THE SUPREME COURT IN THE SCHOOL CASES DECLARATION OF CONSTITUTIONAL PRINCIPLES

Mr. [Walter F.] GEORGE. Mr. President, the increasing gravity of the situation following the decision of the Supreme Court in the so-called segregation cases, and the peculiar stress in sections of the country where this decision has created many difficulties, unknown and unappreciated, perhaps, by many people residing in other parts of the country, have led some Senators and some Members of the House of Representatives to prepare a statement of the position which they have felt and now feel to be imperative.

I now wish to present to the Senate a statement on behalf of 19 Senators, representing 11 States, and 77 House Members, representing a considerable number of States likewise. . . .

DECLARATION OF CONSTITUTIONAL PRINCIPLES

The unwarranted decision of the Supreme Court in the public school cases is now bearing the fruit always produced when men substitute naked power for established law.

The Founding Fathers gave us a Constitution of checks and balances because they realized the inescapable lesson of history that no man or group of men can be safely entrusted with unlimited power. They framed this Constitution with its provisions for change by amendment in order to secure the fundamentals of government against the dangers of temporary popular passion or the personal predilections of public officeholders.

From *Congressional Record*, 84th Congress Second Session. Vol. 102, part 4 (March 12, 1956). Washington, D.C.: Governmental Printing Office, 1956. 4459-4460.

We regard the decisions of the Supreme Court in the school cases as a clear abuse of judicial power. It climaxes a trend in the Federal Judiciary undertaking to legislate, in derogation of the authority of Congress, and to encroach upon the reserved rights of the States and the people.

The original Constitution does not mention education. Neither does the 14th Amendment nor any other amendment. The debates preceding the submission of the 14th Amendment clearly show that there was no intent that it should affect the system of education maintained by the States.

The very Congress which proposed the amendment subsequently provided for segregated schools in the District of Columbia.

When the amendment was adopted in 1868, there were 37 States of the Union. . . .

Every one of the 26 States that had any substantial racial differences among its people, either approved the operation of segregated schools already in existence or subsequently established such schools by action of the same law-making body which considered the 14th Amendment.

As admitted by the Supreme Court in the public school case (*Brown v. Board of Education*), the doctrine of separate but equal schools "apparently originated in *Roberts v. City of Boston* (1849), upholding school segregation against attack as being violative of a State constitutional guarantee of equality." This constitutional doctrine began in the North, not in the South, and it was followed not only in Massachusetts, but in Connecticut, New York, Illinois, Indiana, Michigan, Minnesota, New Jersey, Ohio, Pennsylvania and other northern states until they, exercising their rights as states through the constitutional processes of local self-government, changed their school systems.

In the case of *Plessy v. Ferguson* in 1896 the Supreme Court expressly declared that under the 14th Amendment no person was denied any of his rights if the States provided separate but equal facilities. This decision has been followed in many other cases. It is notable that the Supreme Court, speaking through Chief Justice Taft, a former President of the United States, unanimously declared in 1927 in *Lum v. Rice* that the "separate but equal" principle is "within the discretion of the State in regulating its public schools and does not conflict with the 14th Amendment."

This interpretation, restated time and again, became a part of the life of the people of many of the States and confirmed their habits, traditions, and way of life. It is founded on elemental humanity and commonsense, for parents should not be deprived by Government of the right to direct the lives and education of their own children.

Though there has been no constitutional amendment or act of Congress changing this established legal principle almost a century old, the Supreme Court of the United States, with no legal basis for such action, undertook to exercise their naked judicial power and substituted their personal political and social ideas for the established law of the land.

This unwarranted exercise of power by the Court, contrary to the Constitution, is creating chaos and confusion in the States principally affected. It is destroying the amicable relations between the white and Negro races that have been created through 90 years of patient effort by the good people of both races. It has planted hatred and suspicion where there has been heretofore friendship and understanding.

Without regard to the consent of the governed, outside mediators are threatening immediate and revolutionary changes in our public schools systems. If done, this is certain to destroy the system of public education in some of the States.

With the gravest concern for the explosive and dangerous condition created by this decision and inflamed by outside meddlers:

We reaffirm our reliance on the Constitution as the fundamental law of the land.

We decry the Supreme Court's encroachment on the rights reserved to the States and to the people, contrary to established law, and to the Constitution.

We commend the motives of those States which have declared the intention to resist forced integration by any lawful means.

We appeal to the States and people who are not directly affected by these decisions to consider the constitutional principles involved against the time when they too, on issues vital to them may be the victims of judicial encroachment.

Even though we constitute a minority in the present Congress, we have full faith that a majority of the American people believe in the dual system of government which has enabled us to achieve our greatness and will in time demand that the reserved rights of the States and of the people be made secure against judicial usurpation.

We pledge ourselves to use all lawful means to bring about a reversal of this decision which is contrary to the Constitution and to prevent the use of force in its implementation.

In this trying period, as we all seek to right this wrong, we appeal to our people not to be provoked by the agitators and troublemakers invading our States and to scrupulously refrain from disorder and lawless acts.

Signed by:

MEMBERS OF THE UNITED STATES SENATE

Walter F. George, Richard B. Russell, John Stennis, Sam J. Elvin, Jr., Strom Thurmond, Harry F. Byrd, A. Willis Robertson, John L. McClellan, Allen J. Ellender, Russell B. Long, Lister Hill, James O. Eastland, W. Kerr Scott, John Sparkman, Olin D. Johnston, Price Daniel, J.W. Fulbright, George A. Smathers, Spessard L. Holland.

MEMBERS OF THE UNITED STATES HOUSE OF REPRESENTATIVES

Alabama: Frank W. Boykin, George M. Grant, George W. Andrews, Kenneth A. Roberts, Albert Rains, Armistead I. Selden, Jr., Carl Elliott, Robert E. Jones, George Huddleston, Jr.

Arkansas: E.C. Gathings, Wilbur D. Mills, James W. Trimble, Oren Harris, Brooks Hays, W.F. Norrell.

Florida: Charles E. Bennett, Robert L.F. Sikes, A.S. Herlong, Jr., Paul G. Rogers, James A. Haley, D.R. Matthews.

Georgia: Prince H. Preston, John L. Pilcher, E.L. Forrester, John James Flynt, Jr., James C. Davis, Carl Vinson, Henderson Lanham, Iris F. Blitch, Phil M. Landrum, Paul Brown.

Louisiana: F. Edward Hebert, Hale Boggs, Edwin E. Willis, Overton Brooks, Otto E. Passman, James H. Morrison, T. Ashton Thompson, George S. Long.

Mississippi: Thomas G. Abernathy, Jamie L. Whitten, Frank E. Smith, John Bell Williams, Arthur Winstead, William M. Colmer.

North Carolina: Herbert C. Bonner, L.H. Fountain, Graham A. Barden, Carl T. Durham, F. Ertel Carlyle, Hugh Q. Alexander, Woodrow W. Jones, George A. Shuford.

South Carolina: L. Mendel Rivers, John J. Riley, W.J. Bryan Dorn, Robert T. Ashmore, James P. Richards, John L. McMillan.

Tennessee: James B. Frazier, Jr., Tom Murray, Jere Cooper, Clifford Davis.

Document 22.2 President Dwight D. Eisenhower Addresses the Nation Concerning Little Rock, Arkansas

Three years after the Supreme Court ruling in *Brown vs. Board of Education*, a landmark decision that challenged the "separate but equal doctrine" in *Plessy v. Ferguson*, Central High School in Little Rock, Arkansas became a battleground over the issue of desegregation. Rather than abiding by the court order, Arkansas Governor Orval Faubus fueled the flames of this crisis. President Eisenhower, angered by the events in Little Rock and the actions of Governor Faubus, federalized the Arkansas National Guard to prevent "mob rule" and to ensure that the nine black students could enter the school safely. This document is an excerpt from Eisenhower's address to the nation regarding his decision.

Address to the Nation about the situation in Little Rock, President Dwight D. Eisenhower.

President Eisenhower Speaks to the Nation about the Situation in Little Rock

Dwight D. Eisenhower

My Fellow Citizens. . . .

I must speak to you about the serious situation that has arisen in Little Rock. . . . In that city, under the leadership of demagogic extremists, disorderly mobs have deliberately, prevented the carrying out of proper orders from a federal court. Local authorities have not eliminated that violent opposition and, under the law, I yesterday issued a proclamation calling upon the mob to disperse.

This morning the mob again gathered in front of the Central High School of Little Rock, obviously for the purpose of again preventing the carrying out of the court's order relating to the admission of Negro children to that school.

Whenever normal agencies prove inadequate to the task and it becomes necessary for the executive branch of the federal government to use its powers and authority to uphold federal courts, the President's responsibility is inescapable.

In accordance with that responsibility, I have today issued an Executive Order directing the use of troops under federal authority to aid in the execution of federal law at Little Rock, Arkansas. This became necessary when my Proclamation of yesterday was not observed, and the obstruction of justice still continues. It is important that the reasons for my action be understood by all our citizens.

As you know, the Supreme Court of the United States has decided that separate public educational facilities for the races are inherently unequal and therefore compulsory school segregation laws are unconstitutional. . . .

During the past several years, many communities in our southern states have instituted public school plans for gradual progress in the enrollment and attendance of school children of all races in order to bring themselves into compliance with the law of the land.

They thus demonstrated to the world that we are a nation in which laws, not men, are supreme. I regret to say that this truth—the cornerstone of our liberties—was not observed in this instance. . . .

Here is the sequence of events in the development of the Little Rock school case. In May of 1955, the Little Rock School Board approved a moderate plan for the gradual desegregation of the public schools in that city. It provided that a start toward integration would be made at the present term in the high school, and that the plan would be in full operation by 1963. . . . Now this Little Rock plan was challenged in the courts by some who believed that the period of time as proposed in the plan was too long.

The United States Court at Little Rock, which has supervisory responsibility under the law for the plan of desegregation in the public schools, dismissed the challenge, thus approving a gradual rather than an abrupt change from the existing system. The court found that the school board had acted in good faith in planning for a public school system free from racial discrimination.

Since that time, the court has on three separate occasions issued orders directing that the plan be carried out. All persons were instructed to refrain from interfering with the efforts of the school board to comply with the law.

Proper and sensible observance of the law then demanded the respectful obedience which the nation has a right to expect from all its people. This, unfortunately, has not been the case at Little Rock. Certain misguided persons, many of them imported into Little Rock by agitators, have insisted upon defying the law and have sought to bring it into disrepute. The orders of the court have thus been frustrated.

The very basis of our individual rights and freedoms rests upon the certainty that the President and the Executive Branch of Government will support and insure the carrying out of the decisions of the federal courts, even, when necessary, with all the means at the President's command. . . .

Mob rule cannot be allowed to override the decisions of our courts.

Now, let me make it very clear that federal troops are not being used to relieve local and state authorities of their primary duty to preserve the peace and order of the community. . . .

The proper use of the powers of the Executive Branch to enforce the orders of a federal court is limited to extraordinary and compelling circumstances. Manifestly, such an extreme situation has been created in Little Rock. This challenge must be met and with such measures as will preserve to the people as a whole their lawfully protected rights in a climate permitting their free and fair exercise.

The overwhelming majority of our people in every section of the country are united in their respect for observance of the law—even in those cases where they may disagree with that law. . . . A foundation of our American way of life is our national respect for law.

In the South, as elsewhere, citizens are keenly aware of the disservice that has been done to the people of Arkansas in the eyes of the nation, and that has been done to the nation in the eyes of the world.

At a time when we face grave situations abroad because of the hatred that communism bears toward a system of government based on human rights, it would be difficult to exaggerate the harm that is being done to the prestige and influence, and indeed to the safety, of our nation and the world.

Our enemies are gloating over this incident and using it everywhere to misrepresent our whole nation. We are portrayed as a violator of those standards of conduct which the peoples of the world united to proclaim in the Charter of the United Nations. There they affirmed "faith in fundamental human rights" and "in the dignity and worth of the human person" and they did so "without distinction as to race, sex, language or religion."

And so, with deep confidence, I call upon the citizens of the State of Arkansas to assist in bringing to an immediate end all interference with the law and its processes. If resistance to the federal court orders ceases at once, the further presence of federal troops will be unnecessary and the City of Little Rock will return to its normal habits of peace and order and a blot upon the fair name and high honor of our nation in the world will be removed.

Thus will be restored the image of America and of all its parts as one nation, indivisible, with liberty and justice for all.

Document 22.3 Letter from the Birmingham City Jail

The letter from the Birmingham Jail was an open letter written by Martin Luther King, Jr. in response to White clergymen who denounced the tactics of the Southern Christian Leadership Conference (SCLC), which believed that the battles for social injustice should be resolved in the courts rather than protests and demonstrations in the streets. While King was imprisoned for leading demonstrations in Birmingham, he responded in his letter, stating why and how he and the other protesters did what they did. In essence, King outlined the Civil Rights Movement's defense by using logic and emotional appeal.

Letter from the Birmingham City Jail

Martin Luther King, Jr.

My dear Fellow Clergymen,

While confined here in the Birmingham city jail, I came across your recent statement calling our present activities "unwise and untimely [S]ince I feel that you are men of genuine good will and your criticisms are sincerely set forth, I would like to answer your statement in what I hope will be patient and reasonable terms.

I think I should give the reason for my being in Birmingham, since you have been influenced by the argument of "outsiders coming in." I have the honor of serving as president of the Southern Christian Leadership Conference, an organization operating in every southern state, with headquarters in Atlanta, Georgia. We have some eighty-five affiliate organizations all across the South. . . . Several months ago our local affiliate here in Birmingham invited us to be on call to engage in a nonviolent direct action program if such were deemed necessary. . . .

Beyond this, I am in Birmingham because injustice is here. . . . I cannot sit idly by in Atlanta and not be concerned about what happens in Birmingham. Injustice anywhere is a threat to justice everywhere. . . .

You deplore the demonstrations that are presently taking place in Birmingham. But I am sorry that your statement did not express a similar concern for the conditions that brought the demonstrations into being. . . .

Birmingham is probably the most thoroughly segregated city in the United States. Its ugly record of police brutality is known in every section of this country. Its unjust treatment of Negroes in the courts is a notorious reality. There have been more unsolved bombings of Negro homes and churches in Birmingham than any city in this nation. These are the hard, brutal and unbelievable facts. . . .

You may well ask, "Why direct action? Why sit-ins, marches, etc.? Isn't negotiation a better path?" You are exactly right in your call for negotiation. Indeed, this is the purpose of direct action. Nonviolent direct action seeks to create such a crisis and establish such creative tension that a community that has constantly refused to negotiate is forced to confront the issue. It seeks so to dramatize the issue that it can no longer be ignored. . . . So the purpose of the direct action is to create a situation so crisis packed that it will inevitably open the door to negotiation. . . .

One of the basic points in your statement is that our acts are untimely. . . . My friends, I must say to you that we have not made a single gain in civil rights without determined legal and nonviolent pressure. History is the long and tragic story of the fact that privileged groups seldom give up their privileges voluntarily. . . .

We know through painful experience that freedom is never voluntarily given by the oppressor; it must be demanded by the oppressed. Frankly, I have never yet engaged in a direct action movement that was "well timed," according to the timetable of those who have not suffered unduly from the disease of segregation. For years now I have heard the words "Wait!" It rings in the ear of every Negro with a piercing familiarity. This "Wait" has almost always meant "Never." . . . We have waited for more than 340 years for our constitutional and God-given rights. The nations of Asia and Africa are moving with jetlike speed toward the goal of political independence, and we still creep at horse and buggy pace toward the gaining of a cup of coffee at a lunch counter. I guess it is easy for those who have never felt the stinging darts of segregation to say, "Wait." But when you have seen vicious mobs lynch your mothers and fathers at will and drown your sisters and brothers at whim; when you have seen hate filled policemen curse, kick, brutalize and even kill your black brothers and sisters with impunity; when you see the vast majority of your twenty million Negro brothers smothering in an airtight cage of poverty in the midst of an affluent society; when you suddenly find your tongue twisted and your speech stammering as you seek to explain to your six-year-old daughter why she can't go to the public amusement park that has just been advertised on television, and see tears welling up in her little eyes when she is told that Funtown is closed to colored children, and see the depressing

clouds of inferiority begin to form in her little mental sky, and see her begin to distort her little personality by unconsciously developing a bitterness toward white people; when you have to concoct an answer for a five-year-old son asking in agonizing pathos: "Daddy, why do white people treat colored people so mean?"; when you take a cross-country drive and find it necessary to sleep night after night in the uncomfortable corners of your automobile because no motel will accept you; when you are humiliated day in and day out by nagging signs reading "white" and "colored"; when your first name becomes "nigger" and your middle name becomes "boy" (however old you are) and your last name becomes "John," and when your wife and mother are never given the respected title "Mrs."; when you are harried by day and haunted by night by the fact that you are a Negro, living constantly at tiptoe stance never quite knowing what to expect next, and plagued with inner fears and outer resentments; when you are forever fighting a degenerating sense of "nobodiness"; then you will understand why we find it difficult to wait. There comes a time when the cup of endurance runs over, and men are no longer willing to be plunged into an abyss of injustice where they experience the blackness of corroding despair. I hope, sirs, you can understand our legitimate and unavoidable impatience.

You express a great deal of anxiety over our willingness to break laws. This is certainly a legitimate concern. Since we so diligently urge people to obey the Supreme Court's decision of 1954 outlawing segregation in the public schools, it is rather strange and paradoxical to find us consciously breaking laws. One may well ask, "How can you advocate breaking some laws and obeying others?" The answer is found in the fact that there are two types of laws: there are just and there are unjust laws. I would agree with Saint Augustine that "An unjust law is no law at all."

Now what is the difference between the two? How does one determine when a law is just or unjust? A just law is a man-made code that squares with the moral law or the law of God. An unjust law is a code that is out of harmony with the moral law. To put it in the terms of Saint Thomas Aquinas, an unjust law is a human law that is not rooted in eternal and natural law. Any law that uplifts human personality is just. Any law that degrades human personality is unjust. All segregation statutes are unjust because segregation distorts the soul and damages the personality. It gives the segregator a false sense of superiority, and the segregated a false sense of inferiority. . . . So segregation is not only politically, economically and sociologically unsound, but it is morally wrong and sinful. . . . So I can urge men to disobey segregation ordinances because they are morally wrong. . . .

I hope you can see the distinction I am trying to point out. In no sense do I advocate evading or defying the law as the rabid segregationist would do. This would lead to anarchy. One who breaks an unjust law must do it openly, lovingly. . . and with a willingness to accept the penalty. I submit that an individual who breaks a law that conscience tells him is unjust, and willingly accepts the penalty by staying in jail to arouse the conscience of the community over its injustice, is in reality expressing the very highest respect for law.

Of course, there is nothing new about this kind of civil disobedience. . . . It was practiced superbly by the early Christians who were willing to face hungry lions and the excruciating pain of chopping blocks, before submitting to certain unjust laws of the Roman Empire.

I must make two honest confessions to You, my Christian and Jewish brothers. First, I must confess that over the last few years I have been gravely disappointed with the white moderate. I have almost reached the regrettable conclusion that the Negro's great stumbling block in the stride toward freedom is not the White Citizens' Councilor or the Ku Klux Klanner, but the white moderate who is more devoted to order than to justice; who prefers a negative peace which is the absence of tension to a positive peace which is the presence of justice; who constantly says, "I agree with you in the goal you seek, but I can't agree with your methods of direct action"; who paternalistically feels that he can set the timetable for another man's freedom; who lives by the myth of time and who constantly advised the Negro to wait until a "more convenient season." Shallow understanding from people of good will is more frustrating than absolute misunderstanding from people of ill will. Lukewarm acceptance is much more bewildering than outright rejection.

I had hoped that the white moderate would understand that law and order exist for the purpose of establishing justice, and that when they fail to do this they become dangerously structured dams that block the flow of social progress. I had hoped that the white moderate would understand that the present tension of the South is merely a necessary phase of the transition from an obnoxious negative peace, where the Negro passively accepted his unjust plight, to a substance-filled positive peace, where all men will respect the dignity and worth of human personality. Actually, we who engage in nonviolent direct action are not the creators of tension. We merely bring to the surface the hidden tension that is already alive. We bring it out in the open where it can be seen and dealt with. . . .

In your statement you asserted that our actions, even though peaceful, must be condemned because they precipitate violence. But can this assertion be logically made? Isn't this like condemning the robbed man because his possession of money precipitated the evil act of robbery?

You spoke of our activity in Birmingham as extreme. At first I was rather disappointed that fellow clergymen would see my nonviolent efforts as those of the extremist. I started thinking about the fact that I stand in the middle of two opposing forces in the Negro community. One is a force of complacency made up of Negroes who, as a result of long years of oppression, have been so completely drained of self-respect and a sense of "somebodiness" that they have adjusted to segregation, and, of a few Negroes in the middle class who, because of a degree of academic and economic security, and because at points they profit by segregation, have unconsciously become insensitive to the problems of the masses. The other force is one of bitterness and hatred, and comes perilously close to advocating violence. It is expressed in the various black nationalist groups that are springing up over the nation, the largest and best known being Elijah Muhammad's Muslim movement. This movement is nourished by the contemporary frustration over the continued existence of racial discrimination. It is made up of people who have lost faith in America, who have absolutely repudiated Christianity, and who have concluded that the white man is an incurable "devil." I have tried to stand between these two forces, saying that we need not follow the "do-nothingism" of the complacent or the hatred and despair of the black nationalist. There is the more excellent way of love and nonviolent protest. I'm grateful to God that, through the Negro church, the dimension of nonviolence entered our struggle. If this philosophy had not emerged, I am convinced that by now many streets of the South would be flowing with floods of blood. And I am further convinced that if our white brothers dismiss us as "rabble-rousers" and "outside agitators," those of us who are working through the channels of nonviolent direct action and refuse to support our nonviolent efforts, millions of Negroes, out of frustration and despair, will seek solace and security in black nationalist ideologies, a development that will lead inevitably to a frightening racial nightmare.

Oppressed people cannot remain oppressed forever. The urge for freedom will eventually come. This is what happened to the American Negro. . . .

But as I continued to think about the matter I gradually gained a bit of satisfaction from being considered an extremist. Was not Jesus an extremist in love—"Love your enemies, bless them that curse you, pray for them that despitefully use you." . . . Was not Abraham Lincoln an extremist? "This nation cannot survive half slave and half free." Was not Thomas Jefferson an extremist?—"We hold these truths to be self-evident, that all men are created equal." So the question is not whether we will be extremist but what kind of extremist will we be. Will we be extremists for hate or will we be extremists for love? Will we be extremists for the preservation of injustice—Or will we be extremists for the cause of justice? . . .

But before closing I am impelled to mention one other point in your statement that troubled me profoundly. You warmly commended the Birmingham police force for keeping "order" and "preventing violence." I don't believe you would have so warmly commended the police force if you had seen its angry violent dogs literally biting six unarmed, nonviolent Negroes. I don't believe you would so quickly commend the policemen if you would observe their ugly and inhuman treatment of Negroes here in the city jail; if you would watch them push and curse old Negro women and young Negro girls; if you would see them slap and kick old Negro men and young boys; if you will observe them, as they did on two occasions, refuse to give us

food because we wanted to sing our grace together. I'm sorry that I can't join you in your praise for the police department. . . .

I wish you had commended the Negro sit-inners and demonstrators of Birmingham for their sublime courage, their willingness to suffer and their amazing discipline in the midst of the most inhuman provocation. One day the South will recognize its real heroes. They will be the James Merediths courageously and with a majestic sense of purpose facing jeering and hostile mobs and the agonizing loneliness that characterizes the life of the pioneer. They will be old, oppressed, battered Negro women, symbolized in a seventy-two-year-old woman of Montgomery, Alabama, who rose up with a sense of dignity and with her people decided not to ride the segregated buses, and responded to one who inquired about her tiredness with ungrammatical profundity: "My feet is tired, but my soul is rested." They will be the young high school and college students, young ministers of the gospel and a host of their elders courageously and nonviolently sitting in at lunch counters and willingly going to jail for conscience's sake. One day the South will know that when these disinherited children of God sat down at lunch counters they were in reality standing up for the best in the American dream and the most sacred values in our Judeo-Christian heritage, and thusly, carrying our whole nation back to those great wells of democracy which were dug deep by the Founding Fathers in the formulation of the Constitution and the Declaration of Independence.

Document 22.4 "I Have a Dream"

Influenced by the *Declaration of Independence*, Martin Luther King's famous "I Have a Dream" speech suggested all of the natural rights that African Americans should have, such as life, liberty, and happiness. In this speech, delivered before a group of almost a quarter of a million people at the Lincoln Memorial in Washington D.C., King reaffirmed his position on Civil Rights and refused to back down from the negative aspects that he faced. King was able to affect people emotionally, using portions of the *Declaration of Independence* to speak of vision and a future not only for African Americans, but for all Americans.

"I Have a Dream"

Martin Luther King, Jr.

Delivered on the steps at the Lincoln Memorial in Washington D.C. on August 28, 1963

Five score years ago, a great American, in whose symbolic shadow we stand signed the Emancipation Proclamation. This momentous decree came as a great beacon light of hope to millions of Negro slaves who had been seared in the flames of withering injustice. It came as a joyous daybreak to end the long night of captivity.

But one hundred years later, we must face the tragic fact that the Negro is still not free. One hundred years later, the life of the Negro is still sadly crippled by the manacles of segregation and the chains of discrimination. One hundred years later, the Negro lives on a lonely island of poverty in the midst of a vast ocean of material prosperity. One hundred years later, the Negro is still languishing in the corners of American society and finds himself an exile in his own land. So we have come here today to dramatize an appalling condition.

In a sense we have come to our nation's capital to cash a check. When the architects of our republic wrote the magnificent words of the Constitution and the Declaration of Independence, they were signing a promissory note to which every American was to fall heir. This note was a promise that all men would be guaranteed the inalienable rights of life, liberty, and the pursuit of happiness.

It is obvious today that America has defaulted on this promissory note insofar as her citizens of color are concerned. Instead of honoring this sacred obligation, America has given the Negro people a bad check which has come back marked "insufficient funds." But we refuse to believe that the bank of justice is bankrupt. We refuse to believe that there are insufficient funds in the great vaults of opportunity of this nation. So we have come to cash this check—a check that will give us upon demand the riches of freedom and the security of justice. We have also come to this hallowed spot to remind America of the fierce urgency of now. This is no time to engage in the luxury of cooling off or to take the tranquilizing drug of gradualism. Now is the time to rise from the dark and desolate valley of segregation to the sunlit path of racial justice. Now is the time to open the doors of opportunity to all of God's children. Now is the time to lift our nation from the quicksands of racial injustice to the solid rock of brotherhood.

It would be fatal for the nation to overlook the urgency of the moment and to underestimate the determination of the Negro. This sweltering summer of the Negro's legitimate discontent will not pass until there is an invigorating autumn of freedom and equality. Nineteen sixty-three is not an end, but a beginning. Those who hope that the Negro needed to blow off steam and will now be content will have a rude awakening if the nation returns to business as usual. There will be neither rest nor tranquility in America until the Negro is granted his citizenship rights. The whirlwinds of revolt will continue to shake the foundations of our nation until the bright day of justice emerges.

But there is something that I must say to my people who stand on the warm threshold which leads into the palace of justice. In the process of gaining our rightful place we must not be guilty of wrongful deeds. Let us not seek to satisfy our thirst for freedom by drinking from the cup of bitterness and hatred.

We must forever conduct our struggle on the high plane of dignity and discipline. We must not allow our creative protest to degenerate into physical violence. Again and again we must rise to the majestic heights of meeting physical force with soul force. The marvelous new militancy which has engulfed the Negro community must not lead us to distrust of all white people, for many of our white brothers, as evidenced by their presence here today, have come to realize that their destiny is tied up with our destiny and their freedom is inextricably bound to our freedom. We cannot walk alone.

And as we walk, we must make the pledge that we shall march ahead. We cannot turn back. There are those who are asking the devotees of civil rights, "When will you be satisfied?" We can never be satisfied as long as our bodies, heavy with the fatigue of travel, cannot gain lodging in the motels of the highways and the hotels of the cities. We cannot be satisfied as long as the Negro's basic mobility is from a smaller ghetto to a larger one. We can never be satisfied as long as a Negro in Mississippi cannot vote and a Negro in New York believes he has nothing for which to vote. No, no, we are not satisfied, and we will not be satisfied until justice rolls down like waters and righteousness like a mighty stream.

I am not unmindful that some of you have come here out of great trials and tribulations. Some of you have come fresh from narrow cells. Some of you have come from areas where your quest for freedom left you battered by the storms of persecution and staggered by the winds of police brutality. You have been the veterans of creative suffering. Continue to work with the faith that unearned suffering is redemptive.

Go back to Mississippi, go back to Alabama, go back to Georgia, go back to Louisiana, go back to the slums and ghettos of our northern cities, knowing that somehow this situation can and will be changed. Let us not wallow in the valley of despair.

I say to you today, my friends, that in spite of the difficulties and frustrations of the moment, I still have a dream. It is a dream deeply rooted in the American dream.

I have a dream that one day this nation will rise up and live out the true meaning of its creed: "We hold these truths to be self-evident: that all men are created equal."

I have a dream that one day on the red hills of Georgia the sons of former slaves and the sons of former slave owners will be able to sit down together at a table of brotherhood.

I have a dream that one day even the state of Mississippi, a desert state, sweltering with the heat of injustice and oppression, will be transformed into an oasis of freedom and justice.

I have a dream that my four children will one day live in a nation where they will not be judged by the color of their skin but by the content of their character.

I have a dream today.

I have a dream that one day the state of Alabama, whose governor's lips are presently dripping with the words of interposition and nullification, will be transformed into a situation where little black boys and black girls will be able to join hands with little white boys and white girls and walk together as sisters and brothers.

I have a dream today.

I have a dream that one day every valley shall be exalted, every hill and mountain shall be made low, the rough places will be made plain, and the crooked places will be made straight, and the glory of the Lord shall be revealed, and all flesh shall see it together.

This is our hope. This is the faith with which I return to the South. With this faith we will be able to hew out of the mountain of despair a stone of hope. With this faith we will be able to transform the jangling discords of our nation into a beautiful symphony of brotherhood. With this faith we will be able to work together, to pray together, to struggle together, to go to jail together, to stand up for freedom together, knowing that we will be free one day.

This will be the day when all of God's children will be able to sing with a new meaning, "My country, 'tis of thee, sweet land of liberty, of thee I sing. Land where my fathers died, land of the pilgrim's pride, from every mountainside, let freedom ring."

And if America is to be a great nation this must become true. So let freedom ring from the prodigious hilltops of New Hampshire. Let freedom ring from the mighty mountains of New York. Let freedom ring from the heightening Alleghenies of Pennsylvania!

Let freedom ring from the snowcapped Rockies of Colorado!

Let freedom ring from the curvaceous peaks of California!

But not only that; let freedom ring from Stone Mountain of Georgia!

Let freedom ring from Lookout Mountain of Tennessee!

Let freedom ring from every hill and every molehill of Mississippi. From every mountainside, let freedom ring.

When we let freedom ring, when we let it ring from every village and every hamlet, from every state and every city, we will be able to speed up that day when all of God's children, black men and white men, Jews and Gentiles, Protestants and Catholics, will be able to join hands and sing in the words of the old Negro spiritual, "Free at last! free at last! thank God Almighty, we are free at last!"

Document 22.5 Black Power

From 1966 to 1968, Stokely Carmichael was the chairman of the Student Nonviolent Coordinating Committee (SNCC). Birthed out of the frustration regarding the progress of the nonviolent civil disobedient movement, Carmichael embraced the ideology of Black Power. Meaning different things to different people, one could surmise that Black Power was meant to empower and create a strong racial identity for Black people. Although considered anti-White, the followers of the Black Power movement acknowledged the role of White Americans in the Civil Rights Movement. Black Power meant that it was time for African Americans to fight for themselves, and it also gave Blacks a sense of self-worth during an oppressive time in American history. In this document, Carmichael provides an explanation of his concept.

Black Power

Stokely Carmichael

One of the tragedies of the struggle against racism is that up to now there has been no national organization which could speak to the growing militancy of young black people in the urban ghetto. There has been only a civil rights movement, whose tone of voice was adapted to an audience of liberal whites. It served as a sort of buffer zone between them and angry young blacks. None of its so-called leaders could go into a rioting community and be listened to. In a sense, I blame ourselves—together with the mass media—for what has happened in Watts, Harlem, Chicago, Cleveland, Omaha (where riots occurred in the 1960s). Each time the people in those cities saw Martin Luther King get slapped, they became angry; when they saw four little black girls bombed to death, they were angrier; and when nothing happened, they were steaming. We had nothing to offer that they could see, except to go out and be beaten again. We helped to build their frustration.

For too many years, black Americans marched and had their heads broken and got shot. They were saying to the country, "Look, you guys are supposed to be nice guys and we are only going to do what we are supposed to do—why do you beat us up, why don't you give us what we ask, why don't you straighten yourselves out?" After years of this, we are at almost the same point because we demonstrated from a position of weakness. We cannot be expected any longer to march and have our heads broken in order to say to whites: come on, you're nice guys. For you are not nice guys. We have found you out.

An organization which claims to speak for the needs of a community—as does the Student Nonviolent Coordinating Committee—must speak in the tone of that community, not as somebody else's buffer zone. This is the significance of black power as a slogan. For once, black people are going to use the words they want to use—not just the words whites want to hear. And they will do this no matter how often the press tries to stop the use of the slogan by equating it with racism or separatism.

An organization which claims to be working for the needs of a community—as SNCC does—must work to provide that community with a position of strength from which to make its voice heard. This is the significance of black power beyond the slogan.

Black power can be clearly defined for those who do not attach the fears of white America to their questions about it. We should begin with the basic fact that black Americans have two problems: they are poor and they are black. All other problems arise from this two-sided reality: lack of education, the so-called apathy of black men. Any program to end racism must address itself to that double reality.

Almost from its beginning, SNCC sought to address itself to both conditions with a program aimed at winning political power for impoverished Southern blacks. We had to begin with politics because black Americans are a propertyless people in a country where property is valued above all. We had to work for power, because this country does not function by morality, love, and nonviolence, but by power, Thus we determined to win political power, with the idea of moving on from there into activity that would have economic effects. With power, the masses could make or participate in making the decisions which govern destinies, and thus create basic change in day-to-day lives. . . .

SNCC today is working in both North and South on programs of voter registration and independent political organizing. In some places, such as Alabama, Los Angeles, New York, Philadelphia, and New Jersey, independent organizing under the black panther symbol is in progress. The creation of a national "black panther party" must come about; it will take time to build, and it is much too early to predict its success. We have no infallible master plan and we make no claim to exclusive knowledge of how to end racism; different groups will work in their own different ways. SNCC cannot spell out the full logistics of self-determination but it can address itself to the problem by helping black communities define their needs, realize their strength, and go into action along a variety of lines which they must choose for themselves. . . .

Ultimately, the economic foundations of this country must be shaken if black people are to control their lives. The colonies of the United States—and this includes the black ghettoes within its borders, north and south—must be liberated. For a century, this nation has been like an octopus of exploitation, its tentacles stretching from Mississippi and Harlem to South America, the Middle East, southern Africa, and Vietnam; the form of exploitation varies from area to area but the essential result has been the same—a powerful few have been maintained and enriched at the expense of the poor and voiceless colored masses. This pattern must be broken. As its grip loosens here and there around the world, the hopes of black Americans become more realistic. For racism to die, a totally different America must be born.

This is what the white society does not wish to face; this is why that society prefers to talk about integration. But integration speaks not at all to the problem of poverty, only to the problem of blackness. Integration today means the man who "makes it," leaving his black brothers behind in the ghetto as fast as his new sports car will take him. It has no relevance to the Harlem wino or to the cotton picker making three dollars a day. . . .

Integration, moreover, speaks to the problem of blackness in a despicable way. As a goal, it has been based on complete acceptance of the fact that in order to have a decent house or education, blacks must move into a white neighborhood or send their children to a white school. This reinforces, among both black and white, the idea that "white" is automatically better and "black" is by definition inferior. This is why integration is a subterfuge for the maintenance of white supremacy. It allows the nation to focus on a handful of Southern children who get into white schools, at great price, and to ignore the 94 percent who are left behind in unimproved all-black schools. Such situations will not change until black people have power—to control their own school boards, in this case. Then Negroes become equal in a way that means something, and integration ceases to be a one-way street. Then integration doesn't mean draining skills and energies from the ghetto into white neighborhoods; then it can mean white people moving from Beverly Hills into Watts. . . . Then integration becomes relevant. . . .

Whites will not see that I, for example, as a person oppressed because of my blackness, have common cause with other blacks who are oppressed because of blackness. This is not to say that there are no white people who see things as I do, but that it is black people I must speak to first. It must be the oppressed to whom SNCC addresses itself primarily, not to friends from the oppressing group.

From birth, black people are told a set of lies about themselves. We are told that we are lazy—yet I drive through the Delta area of Mississippi and watch black people picking cotton in the hot sun for fourteen hours. We are told, "If you work hard, you'll succeed"—but if that were true, black people would own this country. We are oppressed because we are black—not because we are ignorant, not because we

are lazy, not because we're stupid (and got good rhythm), but because we're black.

The need for psychological equality is the reason why SNCC today believes that blacks must organize in the black community. Only black people can convey the revolutionary idea that black people are able to do things themselves. Only they can help create in the community an aroused and continuing black consciousness that will provide the basis for political strength. In the past, white allies have furthered white supremacy without the whites involved realizing it—or wanting it, I think. Black people must do things for themselves; they must get poverty money they will control and spend themselves; they must conduct tutorial programs themselves so that black children can identify with black people. This is one reason Africa has such importance: The reality of black men ruling their own nations gives blacks elsewhere a sense of possibility, of power, which they do not now have.

This does not mean we don't welcome help, or friends. But we want the right to decide whether anyone is, in fact, our friend. In the past, black Americans have been almost the only people whom everybody and his momma could jump up and call their friends. We have been tokens, symbols, objects—as I was in high school to many young whites, who liked having "a Negro friend." We want to decide who is our friend, and we will not accept someone who comes to us and says: "If you do X, Y, and Z, then I'll help you." We will not be told whom we should choose as allies. We will not be isolated from any group or nation except by our own choice. We cannot have the oppressors telling the oppressed how to rid themselves of the oppressor. . . .

Black people do not want to "take over" this country. They don't want to "get whitey"; they just want to get him off their backs, as the saying goes. . . . The white man is irrelevant to blacks, except as an oppressive force. Blacks want to be in his place, yes, but not in order to terrorize and lynch and starve him. They want to be in his place because that is where a decent life can be had.

But our vision is not merely of a society in which all black men have enough to buy the good things of life. When we urge that black money go into black pockets, we mean the communal pocket. We want to see money go back into the community and used to benefit it. We want to see the cooperative concept applied in business and banking. We want to see black ghetto residents demand that an exploiting landlord or storekeeper sell them, at minimal cost, a building or a shop that they will own and improve cooperatively; they can back their demand with a rent strike, or a boycott, and a community so unified behind them that no one else will move into the building or buy at the store. The society we seek to build among black people, then, is not a capitalist one. It is a society in which the spirit of community and humanistic love prevail. The word love is suspect; black expectations of what it might produce have been betrayed too often. But those were expectations of a response from the white community, which failed us. The love we seek to encourage is within the black community, the only American community where men call each other "brother" when they meet. We can build a community of love only where we have the ability and power to do so: among blacks.

As for white America, perhaps it can stop crying out against "black supremacy," "black nationalism," "racism in reverse," and begin facing reality. The reality is that this nation, from top to bottom, is racist; that racism is not primarily a problem of "human relations" but of an exploitation maintained—either actively or through silence—by the society as a whole. . . .

We have found that they usually cannot condemn themselves, and so we have done it. But the rebuilding of this society, if at all possible, is basically the responsibility of whites—not blacks. We won't fight to save the present society, in Vietnam or anywhere else. We are just going to work in the way we see fit, and on the goals we define, not for civil rights but for all our human rights.

Chapter 22 Worksheet and Questions

1. Why was the civil rights movement a driving force from 1955 to 1968? What were the major groups in that movement? What role did Martin Luther King, Jr. play?

_____

_____

_____

_____

_____

_____

_____

_____

_____

2. What did Black Power and the civil rights movement have in common? How did they differ? What caused some activists to embrace Black Power?

_____

_____

_____

_____

_____

_____

_____

_____

_____

3. What types of specific demands and goals did the mass demonstrations and public campaigns have that King helped lead?

_____

_____

_____

_____

_____

_____

_____

_____

_____

_____

4. Describe President Eisenhower's role during the crisis of 1957. Did he act decisively? Explain why you agree or disagree with his actions in Little Rock.

_____

_____

_____

_____

_____

_____

_____

_____

_____

5. King wrote from jail, "Injustice anywhere is a threat to justice everywhere." Comment on this statement as it relates to the Civil Rights Movement.

_____

_____

_____

_____

_____

_____

_____

_____

_____

_____

6. What argument did Southern Whites make against integration, in the Southern Manifesto?

_____

_____

_____

_____

_____

_____

_____

_____

_____

_____

_____

Cultural Unrest and the Vietnam Conflict

The decade of the 1960s gave rise to several different movements in America's cultural, social, and political spheres. . . . The African-American protest for equality had culminated in the passage of a key piece of legislation, the Civil Rights Act of 1964. On the heels of the Civil Rights Act came the Voting Rights Act of 1965. Other groups, fanning the flame of protest, took to the streets through passive or aggressive means to express their discontent or to proclaim their support for a cause. The 1960s gave birth to the American Indian Movement (Native Americans asserting their cultural pride), the women's liberation movement, anti-war demonstrations against America's involvement in Southeast Asia, and other movements. Overall, the 1960s could be described as a period of unrest resulting from internal conflicts within American society that had not been adequately dealt with previously. In addition, the perceived threat in Vietnam did little to stabilize conditions in the United States.

During the 1960s, U.S. policymaker misinterpreted the ramifications of the conflict in Southeast Asia. The containment view was but one side of the issue. Viewing the conflict in Vietnam in relationship to the Cold War, policy makers envisioned a potential rise in Communism, which could lead to global supremacy. While their speculations may have held some truth, there were other views equally valid. In addition to global supremacy, the Vietnam conflict was a war rooted in nationalism, religious sentiment, and economics. The conflict was, in essence, a civil conflict.

The United States' involvement in Vietnam resulted, in part, from the void left by the French after their withdrawal from the region in 1954. During the Eisenhower and Kennedy administrations, the United States provided substantial military aid, and committed approximately 16,000 "military advisors" to the region. The United States' official entrance into the conflict occurred in August 1964, when Congress passed the Gulf of Tonkin Resolution, authorizing the president to take all necessary measures to repel any armed attack against the forces of the United States. By 1965, there was increased U.S. involvement, including air attacks on the north and the commitment of ground troops. Within two years, the number of U.S. troops had grown to more than 500,000.

Many Americans vehemently opposed America's involvement in Southeast Asia. The people turned to protest to substantiate the hatred they felt toward the war. The conflict alienated the working and poor classes in America, who saw their sons drafted into a war that did not make sense to them, while college students received deferments. Some groups, Blacks in particular, were disproportionately represented in fighting units. College campuses throughout the country staged protests against America's involvement in the war in Vietnam, and students openly defied the draft. The atrocities of war, the increasing numbers of troops, the large number of casualties sustained on a weekly basis, and the televised reports of bombing campaigns further exacerbated the American people's hatred toward the war. Dismayed by public sentiment, President Johnson announced that he would not seek re-election in the 1968 presidential campaign.

With the promise to bring the war to an end, Richard M. Nixon secured his election to the presidency in November 1968. Nixon's plan was to diffuse opposition to the war while averting defeat in South Vietnam. It would take four years, however, for him to live up to his commitment. Implementing his "Vietnamization" policy, Nixon withdrew American troops from the region and transferred combat duties to the South Vietnamese troops. By the fall of 1969, some 60,000 American troops had been withdrawn from the region. In January 1973, a peace agreement was signed in Paris; remaining troops were withdrawn and U.S.

prisoners of war were released. Over 47,000 Americans had lost their lives in combat, and over a quarter of a million had been wounded during the final eight years of the war.

Lasting over ten years, the Vietnamese conflict was America's longest war, claiming 350,000 casualties. This war also resulted in bitter division among America's people and its politicians. The war had been one of inheritance—from Truman to Nixon—but it forced American politicians and servicemen to search within for a reason for the horrific bombing campaigns and the war crimes committed. The My Lai Massacre in March 1968 would haunt them for a long time.

The war was over, and America had been defeated, both morally and politically; South Vietnam collapsed and fell to the Northern influence of Communism.

Considering the Evidence in the Readings

The struggle in Vietnam can be viewed as a "conflict" or a "war of inheritance"—Vietnamese Revolution and American intervention. The documents in this chapter may help dispel the ambivalence of those struggling to understand America's role in the conflict.

Beginning in 1946, under the leadership of Ho Chi Mihn, the Vietmihn began the struggle for self-determination against French rule. During the early years of the Cold War, America maintained the position of "containment" with regard to the spread of Communism. After the French withdrawal in 1954, America"s presence in Southeast Asia increased.

The documents include selections from President Lyndon B. Johnson's outlining the mission and vision for Vietnam. Oral histories of African American veterans serving during the Vietnam conflict help reflect a sense of time and place so that the reader better understands the socio-political and racial dynamics of the 1960s. Points to consider are the acts of discrimination African Americans faced while serving in the United States military in comparison to the discriminatory acts committed against black civilians. Students should also assess America's containment policy in Southeast Asia, both during and after the war with the fall of Saigon. Was the war worth the cost?

Document 23.1 Special Message to the Congress—The Gulf of Tonkin Resolution

President Johnson requested that the United States maintain its commitments in Southeast Asia as defined in the Southeast Asia Collective Defense Treaty. Early in August 1964, U.S. ships were attacked by North Vietnamese torpedo boats in the Gulf of Tonkin, situated off the coast of Vietnam. By authorizing the Johnson administration to "take all necessary measures to repel any armed attack against the forces of the United States," Congress gave its support, thereby expanding the role of the United States to include the use of military troops, both ground and air forces.

The Tonkin Gulf Incident, 1964

1. President Johnson's Message to Congress August 5, 1964

Last night I announced to the American people that the North Vietnamese regime had conducted further deliberate attacks against U.S. naval vessels operating in international waters, and I had therefore directed air action against gunboats and supporting facilities used in these hostile operations. This air action has now been carried out with substantial damage to the boats and facilities. Two U.S. aircraft were lost in the action.

After consultation with the leaders of both parties in the Congress, I further announced a decision to ask the Congress for a resolution expressing the unity and determination of the United States in supporting freedom and in protecting peace in southeast Asia.

These latest actions of the North Vietnamese regime has given a new and grave turn to the already serious situation in southeast Asia. Our commitments in that area are well known to the Congress. They were first made in 1954 by President Eisenhower. They were further defined in the **Southeast Asia Collective Defense Treaty** approved by the Senate in February 1955.

This treaty with its accompanying **protocol** obligates the United States and other members to act in accordance with their constitutional processes to meet Communist aggression against any of the parties or protocol states.

Our policy in southeast Asia has been consistent and unchanged since 1954. I summarized it on June 2 in four simple propositions:

America keeps her word. Here as elsewhere, we must and shall honor our commitments.

The issue is the future of southeast Asia as a whole. A threat to any nation in that region is a threat to all, and a threat to us.

Our purpose is peace. We have no military, political, or territorial ambitions in the area.

This is not just a jungle war, but a struggle for freedom on every front of human activity. Our military and economic assistance to South Vietnam and Laos in particular has the purpose of helping these countries to repel aggression and strengthen their independence.

The threat to the free nations of southeast Asia has long been clear. The North Vietnamese regime has constantly sought to take over South Vietnam and Laos. This Communist regime has violated the Geneva accords for Vietnam. It has systematically conducted a campaign of subversion, which includes the direction, training, and supply of personnel and arms for the conduct of guerrilla warfare in South Vietnamese territory. In Laos, the North Vietnamese regime has maintained military forces, used Laotian territory for infiltration into South Vietnam, and most recently carried out combat operations—all in direct violation of the Geneva Agreements of 1962.

In recent months, the actions of the North Vietnamese regime have become steadily more threatening. . . .

As President of the United States I have concluded that I should now ask the Congress, on its part, to join in affirming the national determination that all such attacks will be met, and that the United States will continue in its basic policy of assisting the free nations of the area to defend their freedom.

As I have repeatedly made clear, the United States intends no rashness, and seeks no wider war. We must make it clear to all that the United States is united in its determination to bring about the end of Communist subversion and aggression in the area. We seek the full and effective restoration of the **international agreements signed in Geneva in 1954**, with respect to South Vietnam, and again in Geneva in 1962, with respect to Laos. . . .

2. Joint Resolution of Congress H.J. RES 1145 August 7, 1964

Resolved by the Senate and House of Representatives of the United States of America in Congress assembled,

That the Congress approves and supports the determination of the President, as Commander in Chief, to take all necessary measures to repel any armed attack against the forces of the United States and to prevent further aggression.

Section 2. The United States regards as vital to its national interest and to world peace the maintenance of international peace and security in southeast Asia. Consonant with the **Constitution of the United States** and the **Charter of the United Nations** and in accordance with its obligations under the **Southeast Asia Collective Defense Treaty,** the United States is, therefore, prepared, as the President determines, to take all necessary steps, including the use of armed force, to assist any member or protocol state of the **Southeast Asia Collective Defense Treaty** requesting assistance in defense of its freedom.

Section 3. This resolution shall expire when the President shall determine that the peace and security of the area is reasonably assured by international conditions created by action of the United Nations or otherwise, except that it may be terminated earlier by concurrent resolution of the Congress.

Document 23.2 President Johnson's Vision for Vietnam

President Johnson reaffirmed America's commitment to Southeast Asia while delivering this address at Johns Hopkins University in 1965. His speech, reminiscent of the New Deal era, outlines Vietnam's transition in a similar fashion to the New Deal projects of the 1930s.

President Johnson's Vision for Vietnam

Lyndon B. Johnson

Our objective is the independence of South Vietnam, and its freedom from attack. We want nothing for ourselves, only that the people of South Vietnam be allowed to guide their own country their own way.

In recent months attacks on South Vietnam were stepped up. Thus, it became necessary for us to increase our response and to make attacks by air. This is not a change of purpose. It is a change in what we believe that purpose requires. . . .

We hope that peace will come swiftly. But that is in the hands of others besides ourselves. And we must be prepared for a long continued conflict. It will require patience as well as bravery, the will to endure as well as the will to resist. . . .

These countries of southeast Asia are homes for millions of impoverished people. Each day these people rise at dawn and struggle through until the night to wrestle existence from the soil. They are often racked by disease, plagued by hunger, and death comes at the early age of 40.

Stability and peace do not come easily in such a land. Neither independence nor human dignity will ever be won, though, by arms alone. It also requires the work of peace. The American people have helped generously in past times. Now there must be a much more massive effort to improve the life of man in that conflict-torn corner of the world. . . .

The task is nothing less than to enrich the hopes and existence of more than a hundred million people. And there is much to be done.

The vast Mekong River can provide food and water and power on a scale to dwarf even our own TVA.

The wonders of modern medicine can be spread through villages where thousands die every year from lack of care.

Schools can be established to train people in the skills that are needed to manage the process of development.

The ordinary men and women of North Vietnam, and South Vietnam . . . are brave people. They are filled with the same proportions of hate and fear, of love and hope. Most of them want the same things for themselves and their families. Most of them do not want their sons to die in battle, or to see their homes . . . destroyed.

Well, this can be their world yet. Man has the knowledge . . . to make this planet serve the real needs of the people who live on it.

Document 23.3 "Attention All Military Personnel"

The majority of people who fought in the Vietnam War were college age; ironically, as the anti-war movement grew, rapid growth came from college campuses. On the campus at Berkeley, California, students organized the Vietnam Day Committee and published a pamphlet opposing the war in Vietnam. With experience in the Free Speech Movement, students at Berkeley were viewed as freethinkers during this era of protests for civil and human rights. The following pamphlet was distributed to military personnel and draftees.

American Goals in Vietnam, President Lyndon B. Johnson.
From *American Issues,* Volume 2 by Unger, © 1994, Reprinted by permission of Pearson Education, Inc., Upper Saddle River, NJ.

Attention All Military Personnel (Pamphlet, May 1965)

Vietnam Day Committee

You may soon be sent to Vietnam. You have heard about the war in the news; your officers will give you pep talks about it. But you probably feel as confused and uncertain as most Americans do. Many people will tell you to just follow orders, and leave the thinking to others. But you have the right to know as much about this war as anyone. After all, it's you—not your Congressman—who might get killed.

Why Are We Fighting in Vietnam?

We are supposed to be fighting to protect democracy in Vietnam, and yet your own government admits that South Vietnam is run by a dictatorship.

General Ky, the latest military dictator, is as bad as they come. In a recent interview he said: "People ask me who my heroes are. I have only one—Hitler. I admire Hitler because he pulled his country together when it was in a terrible state" (*London Sunday Mirror*, July 4, 1965).

General Ky doesn't mean much to us; we're not even sure how to pronounce his name, but the South Vietnamese have lived under men like him for years. As far as the Vietnamese are concerned, we are fighting on the side of Hitlerism: and they hope we lose.

Who Is the Enemy?

U.S. military spokesmen have often said that their greatest problem is finding the enemy. The enemy, they say, is everywhere. The old woman feeding her chickens may have a stock of hand grenades in her hut. The little boy who trails after the American soldiers during the day slips out to give information to the guerrillas at night. The washerwoman at the American air base brings a bomb to work one day. It is impossible, say the military, to tell which are the Viet Cong and which are the civilians.

And so, because the whole Vietnamese people seem to be the enemy, the military is taking no chances. They use tear gas—a weapon designed for use against civilians. They order American troops to fire at women and children—because women and children, after all, are firing at American troops. American fighter planes destroy civilian villages with napalm; American B-52s are flattening whole regions. That is why the war in Vietnam is so often called a "dirty war."

When the South Vietnamese people see you in your foreign uniform, they will think of you as their enemy. You are the ones bombing their towns. They don't know whether you're a draftee or a volunteer, whether you're for the war or against it; but they're not taking any chances either.

Free Elections

The Vietnamese would like to vote the foreigners out of their country, but they have been denied the chance. According to the Geneva Agreement of 1954, there were supposed to be elections throughout Vietnam in 1956. But the U.S. government was certain that our man in Vietnam, Premier Diem, would lose. So we decided not to allow any election until we were sure we could win. Diem set up a political police force and put all political opposition—Communist and anti-Communist—in jail. By 1959, it was clear there weren't going to be any elections, and the guerrillas known as the Viet Cong began to fight back. By 1963 our government was fed up with Diem, but still wasn't willing to risk elections. Our CIA helped a group of Vietnamese generals to overthrow Diem and kill him. Since then there have been a series of "better" military dictators. General Ky—the man who admires Hitler—is the latest one.

Fighting for Democracy

Your job as a soldier is supposed to be "to win the people of South Vietnam." Win them to what—democracy? No, we keep military dictators in power. What then? The American way of life? But why should they care any more about our way of life than we care about theirs? We can't speak their language or even pronounce their names. We don't know anything about their religion or even what it is. We never even heard of Vietnam until Washington decided to run it.

You are supposed to be fighting "to save the Vietnamese people from Communism." Certainly Communist influence is very strong in the National Liberation Front, the rebel government. Yet most of the people support the NLF. Why? Many of the same people who now lead the NLF led the Vietnamese independence movement against the Japanese during World II, and then went on to fight against French colonial rule. Most Vietnamese think of the NLF leaders as their country's outstanding patriots. In fact, many anti-Communists have joined the guerrilla forces in the belief that the most important thing is to get rid of foreign domination and military dictators.

On the other hand, very few Vietnamese support the official government of General Ky. His army has low morale and a high desertion rate.

The Guerrillas

The newspapers and television have told us again and again what a tough fighter the Vietnamese guerrilla is. Short of ammunition and without any air cover, he can beat forces that outnumber him five or ten to one. Why do they have such high morale? They are not draftees; no draftees ever fight like that. They are not high-paid professional soldiers. Most of them are peasants who work their fields; they can't even spare the ammunition for target practice.

Their secret is that they know why they are fighting. They didn't hear about Vietnam in the newspapers; they've lived there all their lives. While we were in high school, they were living under the Diem regime and hating it. Now American planes are bombing their towns and strafing their fields; American troops have occupied their country; and if they complain out loud, an American-supported dictator sentences them to jail or the firing squad. Is it any wonder that they fight so fiercely?

Crushing the Resistance

The war in Vietnam is not being fought according to the rules. Prisoners are tortured. Our planes drop incendiary bombs on civilian villages. Our soldiers shoot at women and children. Your officers will tell you that it is all necessary, that we couldn't win the war any other way. *And they are right.* Americans are no more cruel than any other people; American soldiers don't enjoy this kind of war. But if you are going to wage war against an entire people, you have to become cruel.

The ordinary German soldier in occupied Europe wasn't especially cruel, either. But as the resistance movements grew, he *became* cruel. He shot at women and children because they were shooting at him; he never asked himself why they were shooting at him. When a certain town became a center of resistance activity, he followed his orders and destroyed the whole town. He knew that SS men were torturing captured resistance fighters, but it wasn't his business to interfere.

Following Orders

As a soldier you have been trained to obey orders, but as a human being you must take responsibility for your own acts. International and American law recognize that an individual soldier, even if acting under orders, must bear final legal and moral responsibility for what he does. This principle became a part of law after World War II, when the Allied nations, meeting in London, decided that German war criminals must be punished even if they committed war crimes under orders. This principle was the basis of the Nuremberg trials. We believe that the entire war in Vietnam is criminal and immoral. We believe that the atrocities which are necessary to wage this war against the people of Vietnam are inexcusable.

Oppose the War

We hope that you too find yourself, as a human being, unable to tolerate this nightmare war, and we hope that you will oppose it. We don't know what kind of risks we are taking in giving you this leaflet; you won't know what risk you will be taking in opposing the war. A growing number of GIs have already refused to fight in Vietnam and have been court-martialed. They have shown great courage. We believe that they, together with other courageous men who will join them, will have influence far out of proportion to their numbers.

There may be many other things you can do; since you are in the service, you know better than civilians what sorts of opposition are possible. But whatever you do, keep your eyes open. Draw your own conclusions from the things you see, read, and hear. At orientation sessions, don't be afraid to ask questions, and if you're not satisfied with the answers, keep asking. Take every chance you get to talk to your fellow soldiers about the war.

You may feel the war is wrong, and still decide not to face a court-martial. You may then find yourself in Vietnam under orders. You might be forced to do some fighting—but don't do any more than you have to. Good luck.

Document 23.4 Jeff Rogers, Letters from Vietnam, November 10, 1968—August 28, 1969

Letters chronicle the role of soldiers during the Vietnam war, and record impressions of this time period in American history. Historians rely on letters (and diaries) to gain insights into how people responded to situations—how they interacted with others, politically, socially, economically, and militarily. Letters capture a moment in time—often unedited, flowing with expression and sometimes emotion. Jeff Rogers' tour of duty in Vietnam was from November 1968 to October 1969. During that time he wrote letters home describing the horrors of war. The following letters written by Rogers depict the anger and shock shared by many American troops.

November 10, 1968

Jeff Rogers left Travis Air Force Base, northeast of San Francisco, California, on Friday, November 1, 1968, and after a series of airplane flights, he arrived in Vietnam on Tuesday, November 5, the day Richard Nixon was elected president. He devoted most of his first letter home to his parents to describing life aboard his hospital ship, the USS *Repose.*

Dear Mother and Dad,

. . . I'm quite impressed with and already proud of what this ship does. As they say, it's not about the traditional Navy—a lot of the stuff about secrecy, about protocol, about routine, and of course about weapons is irrelevant here. But it's obvious we do a vital job and a greatly appreciated one. Some statistics: in 1968 so far, 5,571 patients (2,624 battle casualties, 485 non-battle casualties, 2,590 disease) only 152 deaths and returned 2,834 to combat. We've had a total of 8,763 helicopter landings since we got on station in February, 1966 and not one accident.[1] . . . It's a little "heavy" at times directing down a helo [helicopter] that extends almost the full length of the landing pad onto a small area which is moving up and down ten feet or more, especially when you know that there may be someone close to dead already inside—minutes count. All kinds of patients are brought aboard—about 15–20 helos per day . . . [by boat] quite a few Vietnamese—some combat victims but many others for elective surgery or general care.

I feel good about doing something relatively positive in this war. But it's also a strange feeling of being almost farther from the war here. Standing on the bridge at night and watching flares, gunfire, and occasional ships firing in the distance while drinking coke or coffee, BS'ing with the men on watch, and thinking about going back to bed in an air conditioned room after eating a midnight breakfast if wanted—the two things contrast so much. And then supervising the carrying from the helos of bleeding, dying, sick patients. It's hard to know what my reaction to it all is yet. Mostly I've been too busy so far to have time to form a reaction. And we get so little news out here. Just occasional Armed Forces Radio and week or two old papers and magazines. Right now anyway somehow for me personally the war seemed worse when I was watching it on TV—maybe partly because of feeling frustrated to only be able to sit there. But for the guys brought aboard (and women civilians too), the war is *here* and a helluva lot worse than it is on TV. And for the doctors—they seem much more tired than the crew. . . . I was pleased with the outcome of the election. . . . I'm not surprised it was so close. Just like in '60. Another couple of weeks and it might have been reversed. Have you talked with Mr. Nixon, Dad? Must be kind of an awesome feeling for him now. . . .

Love, Jeff

1. Later in the letter, Rogers noted that he just learned that these statistics, though available in news magazines, were supposed to be secret, so he added, "HUSH HUSH."

The Source: Jeff Rogers's Letters from Vietnam, November 10, 1968–August 28, 1969

November 24, 1968

Dear Dale and Don [Jeff's older sister and her husband],

. . . You speak of having trouble imagining me over here. Well, in a way, it's difficult to comprehend being over here. The American presence is so overwhelming here, it doesn't seem halfway around the world. . . . in the military, it's as if a portion of the U.S. had been transplanted over here and stuck in amongst little bits and pieces of a foreign, oriental country called Vietnam. Here I live with Americans, eat American food, drink fresh water (distilled aboard ship), watch occasional taped U.S. TV, listen to U.S. radio . . . and watch American military power fire at an invisible enemy. Never once in three weeks here have I even been aware of hearing Vietnamese talked. . . . The Vietnamese I have interacted with so far are either fluent in English or are too wounded or sick to talk. It's a strange war, but as attested to by the 34 guys we flew out yesterday by helicopter on stretchers on their way back home—a real one.

Love, Jeff

December 7, 1968

Jeff's job was to position the USS *Repose* at offshore locations as close as possible to battle areas so that helicopters carrying the wounded had quick access to the hospital. He also helped to direct the highly skilled helicopter pilots on to the ship's small landing pad and aided in the transfer of the wounded from the helicopters to the operating room.

Dear Dad,

. . . I was pleased to hear that Chief Justice Warren agreed to stay on. I assume that was your work—congratulations.[1] My major news is that I have taken over as navigator of the *Repose*. This won't change my job much because I've been doing the navigator work anyway. But . . . this gives me more leeway in making decisions. . . . So the *Repose* has definate advantages for a junior officer. It is one of the very few large ships on which an Ensign can become OOD ("officer of the deck") after only a month aboard (this is nothing great to my credit, as other Ensigns have made it in equal or less time, though some in much more). . . . Other advantages of the *Repose* for officers are the good living conditions, and the preferred treatment you get on next duty. I toured the crew's living quarters the other day, really for the first time—and

they're pretty bad. Four small "bunks" in a stack, all very close together, and inadequate toilet and shower facilities. Compare to my two-room stateroom, bathroom shared by two people, and quiet. . . .

Disadvantages of the *Repose* are the full unbroken year over here and the unNavy-like nature of the ship—no weapons, unique organization, etc. . . . The biggest disadvantage of this ship is its monotonous and repetitious operating schedule. Pretty much the same times, same places, same operations. This simplifies navigation and much else but increases the tedium of a year over here. . . .

I really appreciate your letters too.

Love, Jeff

1. Chief Justice Earl Warren was appointed to the Supreme Court by President Eisenhower when William Rogers was attorney general. Warren led the court in the *Brown v. Board of Education* decision, which desegregated public schools in 1954. Rogers approved this decision, but it was one that created enforcement problems for the Eisenhower administration, in which Richard Nixon served as vice president.

December 30, 1968

Dear Mother and Dad,

. . . The *Newsweeks* just started arriving; getting here when they are still current, which is great . . . mail time both ways varies a lot. We've been spending three days in Da Nang harbor, where we get mail quickly; followed by three days off the DMZ,[1] where we get mail slowly or not at all. . . . We are scheduled to be off the DMZ on the 25th. We go to Subic [Bay Naval Base] in the Philippines on the 27th so at least we'll be in a little better shape for the New Year. On the way to Subic celestial navigation becomes important, so I should get some experience using a sextant with stars and the sun. We go to Subic four times a year for 5 or 6 days each time. But the ship hasn't gone anyplace else for 1 1/2 years . . . so unless the war changes, we stay right here. . . .

Since I stopped writing yesterday, the following things happened—all fairly typical of life on the *Repose*. I stood a 12 noon to 1600 OOD[2] watch during which we sent away various of the ship's boats to the Da Nang area for milk, mail, to take some of the crew to beach parties, to transport the Captain and other brass to play tennis or amuse themselves. . . . Like a lot on the *Repose,* things often seem to be done haphazardly and the little things sometimes seem more important to the brass aboard (5 captains, 4 medical) than the big things, which is frustrating. The captain gets much madder if you are 5 minutes late with a boat for tennis than if a helicopter with 16 seriously wounded medevac (medical evacuation patients) is mistakenly sent one hour out of its way—both have happened.

[*Rogers then described his first trip ashore with thirty other officers to have dinner and drinks at the Officers Club at the Naval base in Da Nang.*] You feel a little foreign walking from the boat to the club. Mud streets, dodging motor scooters, being saluted by little Vietnamese military men, and almost being run over by little Vietnamese civilians. Then into the club and back to the pseudo-America where the Vietnamese waiters and waitresses seem to be the foreigners there to serve the big Americans. These parties are cherished by the Captain, Exec, and the doctors—but they turn off almost all of the junior officers in the ship's company—including me definitely. They take up time better used sleeping and the "regulars" become so obsessed with their little ventures that they become a real burden for those who have to prepare boats for them and see that everyone gets there and back . . . quite a lot of trivia to take up the time we don't have between the important things . . . this month promised to be very quiet—just administrative, with lookout for small craft and swimmers (patrol boats in the harbor, after dropping percussion grenades to keep away any Viet Cong swimmers who have a liking for sabotaging ships). . . .

Being on the periphery of a hospital here. . . . I'm more convinced than ever that I was correct in leaving medicine. But I'm also less sure than ever of just what I want to do. One thing I've eliminated is a career in the Navy. . . .

Yes, we see some of the firing around Da Nang and near the DMZ. And we anchor close to the piers which have been shelled occasionally—but still we are relatively quite safe. . . .

Love, Jeff

1. The "DMZ" was the demilitarized zone, which marked the border between the northern and southern halves of the country.
2. According to the twenty-four-hour clock used in the military, "1600" is 4:00 P.M.; "OOD," as Jeff noted in a previous letter, means "officer of the deck."

February 18, 1969

Dear Mother and Dad,

Though it's been quite a while since I wrote, not much new has happened in the interim. . . . Thirty days straight of floating with only a sandy, bar-

ren, low coastline in the distance. . . . There have been some kind of depressing times for me since Subic in that the initial excitement of the ship and activity of learning has worn off and now it's the prospect of 8 ½ more months of the same plus questions still about what I want to do in the future and about myself in general. But my spirits are pretty good now. I've been spending some time with the nurses, which is something of a diversion, though even there the conversation often revolves around the frustration of one year at sea, the frustration of this war, and the condition of the dead and dying patients. . . .

Everyone has been prepared for a large Tet offensive (Tet began yesterday, the 17th), though so far only minor increases in fighting seem to have occurred.[1] I've doubted all along that they would have a major offensive at this time. They are too smart to do so when we are all prepared for one. We'll see.

Seems like Nixon is doing a good job so far. I've heard only positive comments even from self-proclaimed "liberals." Seems to me the two basic elements are his air of calm, quiet efficiency and his open honesty with the press and public about his opinion. I think the latter is *very* important. The fact that no one in the administration seems disturbed by such trivial things as everyone knowing who the cabinet would be a day or two early is a hugely refreshing contrast to Johnson. As is his directness about his hopes and himself: i.e. "hope to win the respect and eventually the friendship of Negroes." If he can just keep speaking openly and honestly and acting on his own beliefs even when he starts to be criticized, as is inevitable, he should be a damn good president, I think.

I received and enjoyed the tapes you sent. It was reassuring to know you're still having ice cream with butterscotch sauce for dinner. . . . In your last letter, it annoyed me a little what you said about Dad not being able to ask about job suggestions for me. I'm not asking any special favors, in fact I've made it clear I don't want them. All I'm asking is that you keep your eyes open for possibilities. . . . I can't believe that any mention of the subject [of Jeff's search for a post after Vietnam] would be taken as an "order" as Mother suggests. . . . Which brings me to the whole subject of not using pull. I agree in general, but I think it's easy to be so sensitive to it (as I've been in the past) as to pass up opportunities and thus perhaps the chance to do something worthwhile for others. . . . Dad and I were talking once about families and Dad pointed out that an alternative to rejecting the parents, in effect, and starting on your own was to build on what the parents are and have done, and he used the Kennedys as an example. Well, one of the reasons the Kennedys have done so much is that they haven't been afraid to use their own and each other's influence. Though I, too, find the extremes they carry it to distasteful, there is definitely something to be said for the good of all. . . . So I repeat my original request made months ago: I'd appreciate it if Dad would let me know if he hears of any good Junior Naval Officer billets that exist in the D.C. area . . . I don't think it's an unreasonable request to ask of my father, Secretary of State or not. Thanks. . . .

I found the following headline in the *Wall Street Journal* and it now is on my desk:

Cruise Ship Staves Off Ennui With Good Food and Endless Activities.

Love, Jeff

1. Tet Nguyen Dan is the lunar New Year festival and marks the most important holiday in Vietnamese culture. This celebration of the beginning of spring is a time for family visiting, feasting, and gift giving. A year earlier, in 1968, the North Vietnamese and Viet Cong had staged a dramatic assault on the south during Tet. They inflicted so much damage that polls showed a majority of the American public doubted the United States was making progress in the war.

March 14, 1969

Jeff wrote this letter just three days before Nixon ordered secret bombing of Cambodia.

Dear Mother and Dad,

Nothing much new to report. Things stay the same here—which is one of the most discouraging aspects of this war. No apparent motion or progress, just a steady influx of dead and dying men. For the first time, yesterday, I felt a little sick to my stomach watching a helo land with six Marines straight off the battlefield—they looked pretty badly mangled when they took them off the helo. Soon found out I was right: 5 out of 6 were dead on arrival, the 6th died shortly after. Not that I'm not expecting to see death in a war, but all of it we see here seems harder to accept because we see or sense no progress towards any goal.

Another thing that bothers me about the war is the so-called "intelligence." First of all it seems to have little relation to what really happens. A case in point is the intelligence about the recent offensive. We were told a month before Tet they expected a big attack on Quang Tri during Tet, etc., etc. As far as I know there has still been no sizeable attack on Quang Tri, and the offensive began after Tet, is not the same type of offensive as was predicted, etc. Every few days we get classified intelligence messages saying that "tonite will be the big attack." Never happens.

And on the other side our press releases both exaggerate and underplay events. *Newsweek* described the attack on Da Nang as something like: "bombs raining in on the city, fires and secondary explosions throughout the city." We got there several hours after the attack and saw three fires, widely scattered, and little else. In general, things looked normal and only moderate damage was done to several military installations. Or another example was the explosion in the landing craft in Da Nang—an explosion we could see, hear, smell. Military press releases as reported on American Forces Vietnam radio network said one killed and 30 inured. In truth, over 30 were killed instantly and the whole landing area was a shambles.

So if intelligence reports and press reports have such little relation to what really is happening, who does one believe? Worse, I really wonder if *anyone* knows what the true story is. The war is too fragmented, too spread out, and too multifaceted to really be understood as far as who is accomplishing what.

About income tax. We don't have to file as long as we're in the Vietnam combat zone, so I'll wait until I get back to do that.

Yes, we occasionally have beach parties and I've gotten to swim once or twice. But we just got word that there had been a sniper incident at the beach we've been using so beach parties may be out.

We have a change of command next month. Should be interesting to adjust to a new Captain. . . . This Captain now is quite lax and so we have things pretty easy, but I dislike him strongly, to be frank. His priority list is 1. His reputation and social status 2. Other niceties (but not necessities) like parties, uninterrupted church services, and short hair 3. The welfare and safety of patients. His attitude bothers me a lot. . . .

Love, Jeff

April 20, 1969

Secretary of State Rogers and his wife were scheduled to make an inspection trip to Vietnam in the spring of 1969. Though Rogers was often frozen out of strategic planning for the war, his trip was intended to demonstrate the Nixon administration's continuing support for the war even as it laid plans to announce the Vietnamization policy.

Dear Mother and Dad,

Needless to say, when writing from Vietnam, things are the same. . . . I've been navigating without a Chief, but my men have been very efficient and we've been getting along pretty well. In fact I was real pleased with our navigating on the way back from Subic—our star sights coming out good. Also the Captain let me take the ship alongside an oiler the other day and that went well, the Captain of the oiler saying it was one of the best approaches he'd seen this deployment.

So there are a few high spots, but much just sitting around waiting and thinking, both of which can get pretty depressing. It's funny that many of the situations I've been in the past several years seem somehow prison-like or other-worldly. Even at college (though I hardly felt it there) a common expression was "When we get to the outside world." At med school the same: everyone looks forward to going out in the "real world." At OCS to extremes: "Only 28 days to freedom, back to the outside." And in Vietnam you hear everywhere, on the radio, etc.: "when you go back to the world—wonder how things are in the world." Or just civilian life in general referred to as the "outside." And then there's the added confinement, even with the material luxuries of being on a floating football field.

That confinement is one reason I've been wondering, Dad, if you plan to travel at all around Vietnam when you're here—if you still plan to come. It's a shame to be over here a year and see only the coastline and bits of Da Nang. I don't know if it's possible or ethical for me to travel around with you (or your entourage, that is) for a day or so, but it would be great if it would. If it's impossible, I certainly understand.

The longer I'm over here, the more I think we should get out quickly, almost no matter how. Even an initial small unilateral withdrawal might both demonstrate our ultimate peace goal and scare the South Vietnamese into doing a little more for themselves. As I've said before the thing that bothers me most about it all are the sickening sameness of each day, of the news reports, of the "battles," of the intelligence briefings, of the dead and dying people— there seems to be *no* progress or even change—just more dead and destroyed. The other aspect that makes me doubt that we should stay is the very strong impression that NO ONE REALLY KNOWS what's happening over here. . . . Our Captain says "the allies have really been winning a gent victory in the A Shaw Valley" and Marines who have been wounded in the A Shaw Valley say we are getting wiped out there . . .

the government since '65 predicts changes that never occur, and doesn't predict the few that do, etc. It's not that there's a conspiracy to deceive, or a plan to keep the war going by the Vietnamese capitalists or the U.S. militarists or expansionist plans by the U.S.—as the radicals would have one believe. It's not that intentions are bad—it's just that knowledge of what's really happening is abysmal, and given the nature of the war and the country it's probably impossible to ever attain a complete, accurate picture. And if no one can really understand what's happening now, how can anyone decide what should happen or how to get there. Maybe I'm saying that the whole thing is beyond our control and we should stop trying to control it, because all we do meanwhile is waste men and money. The loss of men is obvious. The loss of money becomes clearer when you watch millions spent on the battleship *New Jersey,* then see it sit off the coast here, firing maybe 50 rounds a day far inland and read reports that it "destroyed 4 enemy bunkers and 2 tunnels, no known enemy killed." In fact, I think every U.S. Navy combatant ship over here could be pulled out without any noticeable effect on the war. (Supply ships and hospital ships are different.)

I like what the administration has been saying so far but, as you pointed out, it seems awfully important that results be "forthcoming," not just talk. Look forward to seeing maybe both of you next month.

Love, Jeff

P.S. If troops are pulled out of Vietnam, an excellent way to get them back would be on big white ships.

May 24, 1969

William and Adele Rogers made an official State Department visit to Vietnam between May 14 and May 19. On the first day of their visit, President Nixon went on national television to announce the new Viemamization policy. Jeff Rogers was able to travel around the country with his parents for three or four days. Today, Jeff recalls visiting Hue with them and seeing some young recruits preparing to go out on their mission, looking "petrified." He says his parents were deeply affected by the trip, including their visit on board the USS *Repose.*

Dear Dad,

I'm enclosing the death report on Forbes, the man with the blistered amputation you gave the purple heart to. They didn't think he would die, but he did.

The hospital people also wanted you to know so you could take it into account if you write letters to families.

Love, Jeff

May 31, 1969

Dear Mother and Dad,

Hope the rest of your trip went well. As I wrote to Dad earlier, it was great to see both of you and a really good chance to see more of the country . . . Am working on a collection of pictures of our trip to the *Repose,* some of which Mother would particularly like I suspect. Don't know if you ever heard, also, that just before you went into the Intensive Care Unit to give purple hearts another patient died. Apparently they just covered him with a sheet while you were there and removed him later. But to most of the men over here and to their families that's what this war is about—not the pacification resettlement stuff you were shown on your trip.[1]

Love, Jeff

1. "Pacification resettlement" was a wartime term for U.S. efforts to move South Vietnamese villagers away from areas controlled by the north or the Viet Cong and to persuade them that allegiance to the United States and Saigon promised greater political and economic freedom.

June 10, 1969

Dear Mother and Dad,

Generally things are the same. . . . Of course, people are standing by to see if there'll be any major changes in our operations with the beginning of withdrawal [crossed out] replacement, though it's probably doubtful I realize. If troops continue to be removed, it's going to be harder than ever for those who remain—and for the families of those wounded or killed. Also for those who are sent over here. Wonder if there's some way to stop sending any combat troops over here and use the natural end of men's tours to phase out our combat troops. Probably will be necessary to send replacement advisory and support military types for some time. But to send replacement frontline Marines, for example, who may have a 20% chance of getting killed or permanently maimed over here while troops are being withdrawn will be hard as hell on everyone. Anyway, I am

pleased about the first move and hope that the process goes as quickly as possible or quicker. . . .

Mother, let me put in a correction. As long as you think it's a good story (I do too) and are going to be telling it, let me tell you how it really goes: This nurse did not say, as you said, "No it doesn't matter to me that your father is Secretary of — what is he secretary of?" This implies that she didn't know his position. She did. What really was said is as follows: Me: "Does my father's position make any difference to you one way or the other?" Her: "No, it doesn't matter to me that your father is Secretary of—(brief pause while her mind went blank for a second before she completed the sentence) Me (interrupting quickly during the pause): "Okay, okay, you've convinced me." The point is not that she didn't know what Dad is Secretary of, but that her mind went blank for a second just at the appropriate time. (Which perhaps indicated indeed that Dad's position was not in the forefront of her impression of me, which is what I was trying to ascertain.)

Love, Jeff

June 23, 1969

Dear Mother and Dad,

As always, things are the same. So there really is no news. There is very little talk about the replacement <----> withdrawal—obviously it doesn't affect at all the lives of most people over here. As a matter of fact, there is in general little talk about the general situation over here and what should be done. People just seem to have given up on the whole mess and only look forward to finishing their year (this is not a new development, having been that way since I arrived). . . .

Love, Jeff

August 28, 1969

Dear Mother and Dad,

Got back from R&R a few days ago. It was great—especially the days of leave I took afterward to visit Pleiku. I was off the ship 13 days—somewhat longer than most R&R's to say the least. Six days in Tokyo . . . then back to Vietnam and up to the Pleiku area for three days. I was with an Army major I'd met in Saigon. He is really fine and was great to me—as were all his friends and associates, from the Commanding General on down (or "up" depending on what you think of Generals). I spent two days traveling in helicopters around the various Montagnard villages that the U.S. civic action people are working in.

It is one of the most fascinating things I've seen. The people are truly primitive, yet truly appreciative of the Americans—in both respects quite unlike Vietnamese. Again it confirmed my impression that one's attitude towards our involvement in Vietnam is conditioned *very* strongly by one's experience here, because there is a huge variety of possible types of experiences: from getting killed, which we see on the ship every day—to political involvement which I saw in Saigon—to the grateful smiles of some Montagnard chief—to obscene gestures towards and thievery from GI's that I see in Da Nang.

Watching the civic action work with the Montagnards raises again the moot question of whether we should be here at all—and the vital question of what to do now—abandoning some of these people too abruptly would be criminal now—but having Americans killed every day is equally criminal. . . . The

chance to go into the villages and talk to the people leisurely and actually see what's going on was a good complement to my field trips with Dad in which we saw a great variety of places—but one felt it was all staged in the showplaces of Vietnam. This visit was the real places where the war is going on. . . .

I, for one, have been really pleased with all the major directions that you and the President have been steering policy, as well as pleased with the President's domestic plans. Do hope though that the next withdrawal from here isn't postponed too long. I worry that the administration will fall into the LBJ trap of trying too hard to save face for the U.S., i.e., not withdrawing in the face of enemy action. When in reality "face" is much less important than lives.

See you in two months.

Love, Jeff

Document 23.5 Oral Histories of African-American Soldiers in Vietnam

Oral histories provide us with experiences of people from all walks of life. Their lives have intersected with an historic event. The spoken words of an individual can yield a deeper understanding of historical events. It is essential for students of history to appreciate and accept the value of oral histories. The following stories help to place the experience of Vietnam into historical and cultural context.

Specialist 5
Harold "Light Bulb" Bryant
East St. Louis, Illinois

Combat Engineer
1st Cavalry Division
U.S. Army
An Khe
February 1966–February 1967

We were in a fire fight one morning. We had our mad minute at six o'clock. We received some fire, and so we just started shooting. I guess maybe about eight o'clock a dust-off came in to take out a wounded guy. And they came and asked for me, and they told me that I was rotating. Going home right in the middle of the fire fight. I hadn't kept up with my days. I didn't have a short-time calendar. So I was a little surprised. So they took me back to An Khe for me to clear base camp.

I went downtown and bought a few trinkets to give people. A opium pipe. Four or five of those little jackets that said on the back, "I know I'm goin' to

heaven, 'cause I done spent my time in hell." I grabbed my stuff out of the connex and put it in two of those Air Vietnam suitcases and my two duffel bags. And I went to the airstrip for the Caribou that would fly me into Pleiku.

When I got to Pleiku, I guess it was about 4 p.m. They said the plane was gonna be comin' in about seven. Then Pleiku started gettin' hit, and the plane didn't come in. And they had us in a secure area with no weapons while Pleiku was being mortared. So we had to spend the night.

The plane to take us to Japan got there the next morning. And it picked up two rounds as we were leaving. And this white guy got hit. Killed. And he was rotating home, too. And his body, it stayed on the plane until we got to Japan.

From Japan, they flew us to Oakland. Then they gave us uniforms, 'cause when I left 'Nam I was still in jungle fatigues. And I took a shower, put on my Class A's, got my records. Finally they let us go, and I caught a bus over to the San Francisco airport and got home about three o'clock that morning.

My mother didn't keep up with my days left either, so she was surprised when I called from San Francisco. She met the plane. I said, "Mom, I'm happy to be home." And she said, "I'm happy to see you here with everything. It's God's blessing that you didn't get hurt." My father wasn't there 'cause he worked at night, driving eighteen-wheelers.

I went right out into the streets in my uniform and partied. Matter fact, got drunk.

I wasn't sleepy. I was still hyped up. And East St. Louis is a city that never closes. So I went to a place called Mother's, which was the latest jazz joint in town.

A lot of people knew me, so everybody was buying me drinks. Nobody was asking me how Vietnam was, what Vietnam was all about. They just was saying, "Hey, happy to see you back. Get you a drink?" They were happy I made it back, because a lot of my friends who had been over there from my city had came home dead in boxes, or disabled.

Finally, I got guys that asked me what it was really like. And when I was trying to explain it, after a while, I saw that they got disinterested. So I just didn't talk about it anymore. I was just saying, "I'm happy to be home. I hope I'll never have to go back."

I had six more months to go, so they sent me to Fort Carson in Colorado. There weren't any more airborne soldiers on post but me and maybe five or six. We either had come back from Vietnam or were getting ready to go.

Well, I ran into this officer. Second lieutenant. Just got out of OCS. He asked me if I was authorized to wear a combat infantryman's badge and jump wings. I told him, "You damn right. I earned them." He didn't like that answer. So I said, "You can harass me now, sir, but you can't go over in Vietnam and do that shit." So he ended up giving me a Article 15 for disrespect. And I got busted one rank and fined $25.

That was just another nail in the coffin to keep me from reuping. I didn't want career military nohow.

I told him taking my stripe away from me wasn't shit. And he couldn't do nothing to me, 'cause they couldn't send me back to Vietnam. He didn't enjoy that, so he tried to make it hard for me until *he* got shipped out. And when I heard he had orders for 'Nam, I went and found him and laughed at him and told him that he wasn't gon' make it back.

"Somebody's gon' kill you," I said. "One of your own men is gon' kill you."

I enlisted in the Army to stay out of the Marines. I had went to college for a semester at Southern Illinois University at Edwardsville. But the expenses had gotten too much for my family, so I went and got me a job at McDonnell Aircraft as a sheet-metal assembler. About eight months later, two guys I went to high school with got drafted by the Marines. So I joined the Army so I could get a choice.

It was August of '65. I was twenty.

My father was not too hot about it. He was in World War II, in France and Germany. He was a truck driver on the Red Ball Express, gettin' gas to Patton's tanks. He resented the Army because of how they treated black soldiers over there, segregated and not with the same support for white soldiers.

My left ear was pierced when I was nine just like my father's left ear was pierced when he was nine. Grandmother said all the male warriors in her mother's tribe in Africa had their ears pierced. Her mother was born in Africa. You can imagine the teasing I got in high school for wearing an earring. But I felt in this small way I carry on the African tradition. I would go in the Army wearing the mark of the African warriors I descend from.

I did my basic and my AIT at Fort Leonardwood, Missouri. "Lost in the Woods," yeah. Trained for combat engineer to build bridges, mountain roads. But we didn't build too many bridges. Cleared a lot of LZs. Did a lot of demolition work.

I was sent to An Khe, 8th Engineers Battalion, and attached to the 1st of the 9th of the Cav. It was in February, after the first battle of the Ia Drang Valley, when 300 Cav troops got wiped out in the first real fight anybody had with the NVA. I was one of those replacements.

We probed for mines, blew up mines, disarmed and blew up booby traps. If you saw a trip wire, you could take a look at what was happening. You could see where the booby trap was, then throw a grenade at the beginning of the booby trap. Or shoot up the trail to make 'em go off. The land mines, ones you had to dig up, was the big problem, 'cause they could have another one planted somewhere next to it.

And you had to worry about crimping right and taking your time. You squeeze the blasting cap and the fuse together so they won't come apart. Crimping, right. But if you don't crimp right, like an inch high from the bottom of the cap, it will blow you up. And you can't be rushed by some second lieutenant, telling you, "Hurry up, hurry up, so we can move on." If you rush, something wrong would happen. We lost three guys from rushing or crimping wrong.

One time I had to get a guy off a mine. It looked like it was impossible.

This infantry unit was on a little trail, west of Pleiku, makin' a sweep towards the Ia Drang Valley. This white dude had stepped on a mine. And knew it.

He felt the plunger go down. Everybody moved away from him, about 20 meters. So they called for the engineers, and somebody asked for Light Bulb.

I have a nickname from the streets of East St. Louis. Light Bulb. Came from a friend of mine when we were growing up, 'cause he said I was always full of ideas.

When I got there on the chopper, he's been standin' there for over an hour. He really wasn't in any panic. He was very calm. He knew if he alleviated any of the pressure, both of us would have got destroyed.

I dug all around the mine with my bayonet and found out that it was a Bouncin' Betty. I told him I was gonna try to diffuse it. But the three-prong primer on the Bouncin' Betty had gotten in between the cleats on his jungle boots, so there wasn't any way I could deal with it. So I said let's see if we could kind of change the pressure by him takin' his foot out of his boot and me keepin' the pressure by holding his boot down. That way he could get out uninjured. But when he started doin' that, I thought I was seein' the plunger rise, so I told him to stop.

I guess maybe I'd been working with him for maybe an hour now.

Then I got the idea. I knew when the plunger would depress, the Bouncin' Betty would bounce up about 3 feet and then explode. So I got the other members of his team together, and I tied a rope around his waist. And everybody, including me, moved off about 20 yards from the mine and him. And when I counted to three, everyone would pull on the rope and snatch him about 15 feet off the mine. And it would bounce up its 3 feet and then explode. And it did that. And the only damage that he received was the heel of his jungle boot was blown off. No damage to him.

This was somethin' that they never taught us in school. This guy thanked me for saving his life and the life of his squad. And whenever we were back in base camp, I would always go with them. And since a platoon would always carry three or four combat engineers with them in the bush, I would always go with them.

When I came to Vietnam, I thought we were helping another country to develop a nation. About three or four months later I found out that wasn't the case. In high school and in the papers I had been hearing about Indochina, but I couldn't find Indochina on the map. I didn't know anything about the country, about the people. Those kinds of things I had to learn on myself while I was there.

We had a Vietnamese interpreter attached to us. I would always be asking him questions. He had told me this war in Vietnam had been going on for hundreds of years. Before the Americans, they had been fighting for hundreds of years against the Chinese aggressors. I thought we had got into the beginning of a war. But I found out that we were just in another phase of their civil wars.

And we weren't gaining any ground. We would fight for a hill all day, spend two days or two nights there, and then abandon the hill. Then maybe two, three months later, we would have to come back and retake the same piece of territory. Like this Special Forces camp outside Dak To. The camp was attacked one evening. Maybe two or three platoons flew up to give them some assistance. Then somehow headquarters decided we should close down that camp. So they ended up closing down. Two or three months later, we went back to the same area to retake it. We lost 20 men the first time saving it, 30 or 40 men the next time retaking it.

And they had a habit of exaggerating a body count. If we killed 7, by the time it would get back to base camp, it would have gotten to 28. Then by the time it got down to Westmoreland's office in Saigon, it done went up to 54. And by the time it left from Saigon going to Washington, it had went up to about 125. To prove we were really out there doing our jobs, doing, really, more than what we were doing.

I remember a place called the Ashau Valley. The 7th went in there and got cut up real bad. They had underestimated the enemy's power. So they sent in the 9th, and we cleared the Ashau Valley out. All we was doing was making contact, letting the gunships know where they were, and then we would draw back. We had 25 gunships circling around, and jet strikes coming in to drop napalm. We did that all day, and the next day we didn't receive any other fire.

Stars and Stripes said we had a body count of 260 something. But I don't think it was true.

By then I had killed my first VC. It was two or three o'clock in the afternoon, somewhere in the Central Highlands. I was point man. I was blazing my own trail. I was maybe 40 meters in front of the rest of the squad. And I just walked up on him. He just stepped out of the bush. I didn't see him until he moved. I'd say maybe 50 meters. And then he saw me. We both had a look of surprise. And I cracked him, because it just ran through my mind it would be either him or me. I just fired from the hip. And he hadn't even brought his weapon down from port arms.

But what really got to me from the beginning was not really having any information, not knowing, what

I was gonna be doin' next. We might be pullin' guard for some artillery one night. Then the next day some choppers would come and get us. We would never know where we were going until in the air. Then we would get word that we were going to the LZ that was really hot. Or something ignorant, like the time we went over in Cambodia to pull guard on a helicopter that had been shot down. And we got stuck there.

It was in the latter part of '66, late in the afternoon. I think it got shot down probably in 'Nam and just ended up in Cambodia. So they sent out a squad of us combat engineers to cut around the shaft so a Chinook could come in, hook up, and pull it out. We didn't get there until six or seven, and it was getting dark. So the Chinook couldn't come in, so we had to stay there all night. The chopper had one door gunner and two pilots, and they were all dead. It wasn't from any rounds. They died from the impact of the chopper falling. I thought it made a lot more sense for us to get out of there and bring the bodies back with us.

When it got dark, we could see a fire maybe half a mile from us. We knew it had to be a VC camp. In the bamboo thicket right up on us we kept hearing this movement, these small noises. We thought if we fired, whoever was out there would attack us. We were so quiet that none of us moved all night. Matter of fact, one of the guy's hair turned stone gray. Because of the fear. He was just nineteen. He was a blond-headed kid when the sun went down, and when the sunlight came up, his hair was white.

We didn't find out they were monkeys until that morning.

That was about as crazy as the time we tryin' to take a shower in a monsoon rain. We had no shower for maybe ten days in the bush. We was standin' out there in the middle of a rice paddy, soapin' up. By the time all of us got soaped up, it stopped rainin'. So we had to lay down and roll around in the rice paddy to get the soap off of us. We never did call that a shower.

It seems like a lot of green guys got killed just coming in country by making a mistake. I remember this white guy from Oklahoma. We got to callin' him Okie. He said that the reason he had volunteered to come over to Vietnam was because he wanted to kill gooks. He was a typical example of a John Wayne complex.

It was a week after he had just gotten there that we got into any action. He was just itching to get into some. We went out and got pinned down by machine guns. They were on our right flank. He saw where the machine-gun net was, and he tried to do the John Wayne thing. He got up, trying to circle around the machine-gun net. Charge the machine gun. And never made it. Whoever was firing saw him move and turned the machine gun on him. We stayed down till we could call in some gunships. Then we moved back.

There was another guy in our unit who had made it known that he was a card-carrying Ku Klux Klan member. That pissed a lot of us off, 'cause we had gotten real tight. We didn't have racial incidents like what was happening in the rear area, 'cause we had to depend on each other. We were always in the bush.

Well, we got out into a fire fight, and Mr. Ku Klux Klan got his little ass trapped. We were goin' across the rice paddies, and Charlie just start shootin'. And he jumped in the rice paddy while everybody else kind of backtracked.

So we laid down a base of fire to cover him. But he was just immobile. He froze. And a brother went out there and got him and dragged him back. Later on, he said that action had changed his perception of what black people were about.

But I got to find out that white people weren't as tough, weren't the number one race and all them other perceptions that they had tried to ingrain in my head. I found out they got scared like I did. I found out a lot of them were a lot more cowardly than I expected. I found out some of them were more animalistic than any black people I knew. I found out that they really didn't have their shit together.

At that time we would carry our dog tags on a chain and tie it through the buttonholes of our fatigue jacket. Wearing them around our necks would cause a rash. Also, they would make noise unless you had 'em taped around your neck.

Well, these white guys would sometimes take the dog-tag chain and fill that up with ears. For different reasons. They would take the ear off to make sure the VC was dead. And to confirm that they had a kill. And to put some notches on they guns.

If we were movin' through the jungle, they'd just put the bloody ear on the chain and stick the ear in their pocket and keep on going. Wouldn't take time to dry it off. Then when we get back, they would nail 'em up on the walls to our hootch, you know, as a trophy. They was rotten and stinkin' after a while, and finally we make 'em take 'em down.

These two guys that I can specifically think of had about 12. I thought it was stupid. And spiritually, I was lookin' at it as damaging a dead body. After a while, I told them, "Hey, man, that's sick. Don't be around me with the ears hangin' on you."

One time after, a fire fight, we went for a body count. We wiped part of them out, and the rest of them took off. There were five known dead. And these two other guys be moanin'. One of them was trying to get to his weapon. One of the guys saw that and popped him. Then another guy went by and popped the other one to make sure that he was dead. Then this guy—one of the white guys—cut off the VC's dick and stuck it in his mouth as a reminder that the 1st Cavs had been through there. And he left the ace of spades on the body.

That happened all the time.

So did burnin' villages.

Sometimes we would get to villages, and fires would still be burnin', food still be cookin', but nobody was there. The commanding officer, this major, would say if no one is there in the village, then the village must not belong to anybody, so destroy it. But the people had probably ran off because they knew we were comin'.

If we didn't want people further down the road, like the VC, to know we were comin', we wouldn't fire the village. Or if we were movin' too fast, we wouldn't. Otherwise, you would strike your lighter. Torch it. All of 'em were thatched huts anyway. I looked at the major's orders as something he knew more about than I did.

And the villagers caught hell if they were Suspect, too.

I remember at this LZ. We could sit on our bunkers and look across the road at the POW compound. The MPs had them surrounded by barbed wire. We would see MPs go in there and get them and take 'em to another bunker. Then we'd hear the Vietnamese hollerin' and shit. The MPs would take the telephone wires and wrap it around the Vietnamese fingers and crank the phone so the charge would go through the wires. Papa san, mama san, would start talkin'. And then we'd see the MPs carry 'em back into the camp.

One day at the LZ we saw a chopper maybe a mile away, high up in the air. Maybe 300 feet. And we'd see something come out. I didn't think it was a body until I talked to the other guys. I had thought maybe the chopper had banked and then somebody had rolled out. That was a fear that we always had when we were ridin' in choppers 'cause there weren't any seat belts in the choppers at that time.

What happened was they were interrogating somebody. And the interrogation was over with.

Outside An Khe, the 1st Cav built an area for soldiers to go relieve theirselves. Bars, whorehouses. It would open at nine in the morning. We called it Sin City. And it had soul bars. A group of us would walk around to find a joint that would be playin' some soul music, some Temptations, Supremes, Sam and Dave.

I would want to do my drinking somewhere where I'd hear music that I liked rather than hillbilly. But a lot of gray guys who wasn't racially hung up would also be there.

The women were much more friendly there. We had heard that was because they thought of the black man as bein' more stronger, more powerful, because Buddha was black. Take a good look at a Buddha. You'll see that he has thick lips and has a very broad nose and very kinky hair. But I didn't know that until I got in country.

We would go to a Class 6 store and get two half-gallons of Gilby's gin for a $1.65 each. We take a bottle to papa san. Buy a girl for $5 or $10. Whatever came by, or whatever I liked. And still have a half a gallon of gin. We would have to leave the area at six o'clock.

Another good thing about the girls in Sin City was that the medical personnel in the camp would always go and check 'em once a week. And if they got disease, they'd get shots and wouldn't be able to work until they were clear. Nobody used rubbers because all the girls in Sin City were clean.

But the people got abused anyway. Like a lot of guys would have Vietnamese give them haircuts. And after papa san got through cuttin' the hair, this guy would tell him that he wouldn't like it and would walk off. He wouldn't pay papa san. And the haircut cost no more than thirty cents.

And it seemed the Vietnamese were always hung up on menthol cigarettes. Kools and things. And they knew brothers all smoked Kools. And they would always ask us for a cigarette. So a lot of guys would start givin' 'em loaded cigarettes to stop 'em from always askin' us. One of the guy's brothers had mailed him some loads from a trick shop. You take out some of the tobacco, then put in a small load of gunpowder. When the Vietnamese smokin' it, it just blow up in his face, and he wouldn't go back to that GI and ask him for a cigarette 'cause he was scared he'd get another loaded cigarette.

One night I saw a drunk GI just pull out his .45 and pop papa san. Papa san was irritatin' him or botherin' him or something. Right downtown in Sin City. After he fired, the MPs and a lot of soldiers grabbed him. They took him to the camp, and he got put up on some charges.

You could find plenty of women out in the field, too. We would set up our perimeter, and all of a sudden a little Coke girl would show up with Coca-Cola. And also some broads would show. We would set up lean-tos, or we'd put up bunkers. A guy would go outside the wire, take the broad through the wire to the bunker, knock her off, and take her back outside the wire. Normally, those kinds of deals was a C-ration deal. Or a couple of dollars. We would give the girl a C-ration meal. Ham and lima beans, 'cause nobody in the squad would want to eat ham and lima beans. You would never give up spaghetti and meatballs.

One morning, we were sweepin' a highway near Phu Cat. Four of us in a jeep with two M-60 machine guns mounted on the back. We were coming down the road, and we looked off on to a spur and we saw three black pajama bodies start runnin' away from us. So one of the two white guys turned his gun on automatic and knocked all three down. The three of them ran over there to see what was happening and found out that two of them were women, maybe eighteen or nineteen, and one of them was a man. I stayed with the Quad 60, just pullin' guard to make sure there might have been some more VC in the area.

As I was watching, I noticed one of the white guys take his pants down and just start having sex. That kind of freaked me out, 'cause I thought the broad was dead. The brother was just standin' guard watchin'. It kind of surprised him to see this guy get off. After about 20 minutes, I ended up saying, "Hey, man. Come on. Let's go."

When they got back in the jeep, they start tellin' me what was happenin'. They had told me that they had confirmed three KIA. And the brother asked the dude what was wrong with him, why did he fuck a dead woman. And he said he just wanted to get his rocks off. And that was the end of it.

Today I'm constantly thinking about the war. I walk down streets different. I look at places where individuals could hide. Maybe assault me or rob me or just harass me. I hear things that other people can't hear. My wife, she had a habit at one time of buying cheap watches and leaving them on top of the dresser. I could hear it ticking, so she would put it in a drawer. I could still hear it ticking. And I dream of helicopters coming over my house, comin' to pick me up to take me to a fire fight. And when we get to the fire fight, they were dropping napalm on our own men. And I have to shoot our own soldiers to put them out of their misery. After my discharge, I lived off my unemployment until it ran out, which was about 18 months. Then I decided to go back to school. I went two years, and then I got involved in veterans affairs. I was noticing that in my city, which is 95 percent black, that there were a lot of black combat veterans coming back not able to find any employment because of bad discharges, or killing theirselves or dopin' up. We started the Wasted Men Project at the university, and I have been counseling at veterans centers ever since.

In 1982 I transferred to the Vet Center in Tucson because I wanted to do some research on the Buffalo Soldiers. In 'Nam I didn't know they were part of the original 9th Cav. These are black boys who had just received their freedom from the United States government, and they had to go to the West and suppress the freedom from another race of people who were the Indians. I think they won 13 or 14 Congressional Medals of Honor. But they were really policing other people, just like we were in Vietnam.

When my son, Ronnie, turned sixteen, I had him sit down and watch all thirteen hours of this film documentary about the Vietnam War so he could have an understanding of what war really was about. He had asked had I did any killing. I told him, "Yes. I had to do it. I had to do it to keep myself alive."

I wouldn't want him to go and fight an unpopular war like I did. I wouldn't want him to go down to El Salvador. And if that means that I would have to pick up me and my family baggage and move somewhere out of the country, then I would do that.

America should have won the war. But they wouldn't free us to fight. With all the American GIs that were in Vietnam, they could have put us all shoulder to shoulder and had us march from Saigon all the way up to the DMZ. Just make a sweep. We had enough GIs, enough equipment to do that.

When I came to Washington to see the Vietnam Veterans Memorial, I looked through the book and there were about 15 guys from my hometown who were killed. And six of them I knew.

But I looked up the memorial for James Plummet first.

Plummer was a black guy from Cincinnati. We were the same age. Twenty. We were at Camp Alpha together. That's where they assign you when you first come to 'Nam. I was in C Company, a line company. He was a truck driver, so he was in Headquarters Company, where they had all the heavy equipment.

I liked Plummer's style. He was just so easygoing. We'd sit down and just rap. Rap about music, the girls, what was happening in the world. Get high. Plummer was a John Coltrane fan. And I'm bein' a Miles Davis fan, we just automatically fell in with each other.

He was my best friend.

One day we were at the airfield at the LZ. Plummer was out of the truck, over by the ammo dump. And the ammo dump received a mortar round. It blew him up.

It freaked me out. I mean that here I saw him, and five minutes later he's instantaneously dead.

Me and two other guys ran and grabbed what we could. We pulled on the jungle fatigues, which was full of blood. It looked like maybe a dog after it crossed the street and got hit by a truck. His head was gone, both his legs from about the knee down were both gone. One arm was gone. The other was a stump left. We finally got his trunk together. The rest of it we really couldn't find, 'cause that one mortar round, it started the ammo dump to steady exploding. It constantly blew up for about an hour.

What we found was probably sent back to the States. They probably had a closed-casket funeral.

I kind of cried. I was sayin' to myself that this was such a waste because we weren't really doin' anything at the time. And him just being such a nice fella, why did he have to go this way? Go in pieces?

Everybody knew that me and him was tight, so a couple of guys took me up over to a bunker and we rapped about him all night. 'Cause we were out in the bush, I really couldn't get no booze. But when I did get back, I bought me a half gallon of gin, and I knocked it off. And that didn't make me feel any better.

When I got back, I called his mother. His mother knew me from him writing to her. I told her I was close by when he did get killed. I just told her a ammo dump blew up. I'm pretty sure she didn't have no idea what that was.

Every year I send her a Christmas card. I just sign my name. When I saw Plummer on the memorial, I kind of cried again.

I guess deep down in my head now I can't really believe in God like I did because I can't really see why God would let something like this happen. Specially like to my friend Plummer. Why He would take such a good individual away from here.

Before I went to Vietnam, I was very active in the church, because of my mother's influence. She sent me a Bible, and I carried it in my pocket everywhere I went. When I couldn't find any *Playboys* or something like that, I would read it. Matter of fact, I read it from cover to cover, starting from Genesis.

I guess I got kind of really unreligious because of my Vietnam experience. Oh, I went to church once in my uniform to please my mother. But I haven't been back since except for a funeral. I've talked to chaplains, talked to preachers about Vietnam. And no one could give me a satisfactory explanation of what happened overseas.

But each year since I've been back I have read the Bible from cover to cover. I keep looking for the explanation.

I can't find it. I can't find it.

Staff Sergeant Don F. Browne Washington, D.C.

Security Policeman
31st Security Police Squadron
Tuy Hoa
November 1967—January 1968
Air Force Special Elements Activity
U.S. Air Force
Saigon
January 1968—November 1968

We thought we were really shit-hot.

There were eleven of us. All Air Force security police. It was a unique organization. It was called the Air Force Special Elements Activity. Our primary duty there in Saigon was to escort VIPs who worked in the American Embassy after curfew hours. But there were several other jobs.

The Army took care of the exterior of the American Embassy compound. The Marines took care of the lobby of the main building, the Chancery. We took care of everything else. So when the American Embassy was hit during the Tet Offensive and six Viet Cong got inside the Chancery, we had to go in and clean 'em out.

It was a suicide mission at the Embassy anyway. I don't see any other reason for it. What was the purpose of them blowing a hole through the wall in the building and going inside? They had to realize that once they went in, they'd never come out, I would think. But then, Asian philosophy is strange.

I was career Air Force when I got to South Vietnam in 1967. And I was rather pro-military. Vietnam, as I was told and as I read at the time, was about us trying to prevent the Domino Theory, you know, the Communists taking South Vietnam and then the Philippines and marching across the Pacific to Hawaii and then on to the shores of California.

My folks are both ministers in Washington, D.C., and they had always wanted me to go into the ministry. I started singing in the church where my mother was the pastor when I was very young. And I still sing. I've won the Air Force worldwide competition for top male vocalist four times. But I never felt the call to be a preacher.

I went to Howard University on a football scholarship, and I was starting fullback right away. We were rolling along there with a three-game winning streak, and we ran up against Morgan State. And they taught us how to play football.

I didn't do anything academically that first year and flunked out. After knocking around at a job as a laborer for a period of time, I decided that maybe the service could do something for me. It was July 1959. I'd always wanted to be in the Air Force. I was just fascinated with planes. I'm in seventh heaven when I'm flying even as a passenger. I wanted to be a pilot. But I could not pass the physical because of my eyes, and, truthfully, I couldn't pass the written exam. I became a security policeman.

My first job in Vietnam was bunker security guard out on the perimeter of the air base at Tuy Hoa. We were there for three months protecting the F-100s. Through some disagreement with the host commander, the Korean troops decided that they would no longer provide security on the outer perimeter, so that burden fell on the security police, too. And we had to formalize search and destroy teams, and go out looking for Viet Cong encampments. Because at night they would attempt to penetrate the base.

I remember the first night we went out. I guess maybe 15 of us. We were at least 1½ miles from base. And without any warning, you just begin to hear whistles go by you. Then you hear the shots. So the sarge told us we were being attacked.

I learned how to love mother earth. Not knowing from which direction the projectiles were coming, you just hug the ground and lay tight. And you shoot at sounds. If something moved in front of you—something caused by the wind, maybe some rodent running through—you fired at it.

I'm sure the incoming didn't last longer than five or six minutes. But it seemed like an eternity. Then we pressed on.

When we arrived at an encampment, it was totally empty. These VC were pretty smart. They weren't going to sit there and wait for us.

A couple of weeks later, we more or less surrounded a camp. There was a very brief fire fight. We went from hut to hut. All we found was these two guys sitting in the corner, all huddled up, in this hut. They were not armed. I'm almost ashamed to say these were very old warriors. In excess of forty years old, although to tell the age of a Vietnamese is difficult. I guess they simply couldn't escape fast enough. We just turned them over to the ARVN for interrogation.

When we reported to the special contingency at the Embassy, we wore fatigues with no insignia, no ranking. They didn't want your rank to be known. Our names were on an access roster with just your name and social security card number.

We worked out of the Embassy basement, and the civilian who was in charge of us had an ammo cache in the back of his home in downtown Saigon that would sink half the city.

Besides escorting the VIPs to their different homes around the city, we had several side jobs. Like running escorts, training guards for the homes of the VIPs, doing background investigations on Vietnamese employees.

Every week money was brought into the country at Tan Son Nhut airport which had to be delivered to the Embassy. It was one of those things you didn't ask questions about. But it was supposed to be millions of dollars for the Embassy payroll. I imagine they did other things with the money, too. We had an armored car in front and one in back. And here's this Volkswagen bus in the middle with the money. We're flashing lights and telling everybody to get out of the way and all that, escorting it downtown to the bank to be counted and then from the bank to the Embassy.

I had one special job. To train Chinese Vietnamese or Chinese Nungs to guard these homes of the VIPs. Most of the people that we recruited came up from the Cholon district, which was south of Saigon. The Nungs were supposed to be known for their fighting capability, their aggressiveness, their tenacity and whatever. And in the evening hours, we would make regular post checks on these folks when they became guards.

One day one individual walked into our training camp that we had in Gia Dinh. He was much taller than the average Vietnamese. This guy is almost 6 feet. But he's a super guy. Dressed well. We gave him the baggy fatigue uniforms, and he immediately went out and had them tailored. We were teaching hand-to-hand defense and combat techniques and weapons firing. The whole spectrum. And this guy was number one in everything. He was kicking *our* behinds in the hand-to-hand combat.

About the time that this guy graduated, the guard quit who was guarding the house occupied by this real big wheel who handled money for USAID. He had a chauffeured driven car, and the chauffeur had a shotgun. So what better troop to put on that house than this new 6-foot Vietnamese? So we put him on there.

The policy was then that when you hire these folks, you get a Vietnamese detective to run a background check. We had a Vietnamese detective firm on contract to the Embassy. Most of the people we caught were really just draft dodgers, trying to stay out of the South Vietnamese Army.

About two weeks after the tall Vietnamese went to work, I get a call from the detective agency. Their office is downstairs from mine in downtown Saigon.

The detective says, "We have a problem. Could you come down and see me?" I went right downstairs.

He says, "Would you believe that this man is a graduate of the North Vietnamese NCO academy?"

Of course I was flabbergasted.

I called the Embassy and passed the information on right away. They said, "We need to latch on to this guy?" Then I went to the Embassy to brief them directly. And they said, "Good Lord, let's get over there and get this guy."

From the time I left my office, went to the Embassy, and got to the USAID guy's home, the tall Vietnamese is gone. In the meantime the detective had taken it upon himself to call this individual and question him over the phone.

When we got the full record on this guy, we found out he was the top graduate of the North Vietnamese NCO academy. Trained in Hanoi. A North Vietnamese. Really one of their really shit-hot guys.

As I reflect back on that now, I think of how stupid we were.

The guys in the contingent were really pampered. Because of not wanting a lot of visibility, we were given extra money to do this and that. It was something like $500, $600 a month. So I just banked my military check.

And food and lodging was taken care of. We lived together in a villa about 2 miles from the Embassy. We were eating steaks all the time. And the little mama san who cooked for us had her little vegetable garden there. This other brother in the contingent who is from North Carolina wrote home and had some seeds sent back. For mustard greens, turnip greens. And he showed her how to fix greens Southern-style. So living there was a welcome change from a base. We enjoyed it.

We had access to any kind of weapon we wanted to carry. There was no kind of rule that you had to carry any particular kind. I usually carried the Swedish K that you can fold up and put in a briefcase and a 9-millimeter Colt.

Well, we had this white guy we called Brute. He was big, weighed at least 230 pounds, over 6 feet 4. He was the typical example of all brawn and no brains. We had an armored vehicle made with so much armor on it that it would only go about 20 miles an hour. That was our contingent vehicle. We titled it the Beast, but in parentheses we painted the word "Brute."

Well, Brute carried a little bit of everything. He would have a M-I carbine, a M-16. He'd have a .38 on one hip, a 9-millimeter on another. A pistol in a shoulder holster under each armpit. And he had a strap of grenades across his chest.

I said, "Brute, stop and think for a minute. You're carrying all these different kinds of weapons. How're you going to carry all the ammunition for them, too?"

One evening I had the VIP patrol with Brute. We were going to escort some secretaries home from the Embassy after the curfew. I got on the elevator in the Embassy with Brute, and the elevator would not move. That's how heavy he was. And this Marine guard said to Brute, "My God. If one round hits you, it would blow up half a block."

Down in the Cholon district, you had the American commissary. And outside the perimeter of the commissary there must have been hundreds of kids peddling whatever. You have to push them away to get in.

Brute kept saying how smart he is and how he's going down to Cholon to put one over on these little kids. What he had in mind, nobody knew. We kept telling Brute, "Leave those kids alone."

One day one little kid ran up to Brute and showed him what Brute thought was a couple of hundred dollars in Vietnamese money. He rammed it in Brute's pocket.

He says, "You number one GI. Don't look how much money I have. Police may arrest me. I tell you what. You can have all this money for twenty-dollar MPC."

All Brute saw was dollar signs.

So he reaches in his pocket and gives the kid the MPC note, and the kid turns his hand loose out of Brute's pocket and runs. Brute takes out the money to count. I think he had an equivalency of a dollar. Vietnamese money was highly worthless. There was one note worth less than a penny. No matter the quantity, you could get very little valuewise.

Now Brute wants to kill every Vietnamese kid.

When I first came to Saigon in January of '68, we kept receiving intel briefings that something was imminent. There was some indication that a big Communist push was coming. They had said there would probably be a lot of terrorist activity. They expected a lot of VC to infiltrate the city. Those who were already planted in the city would begin to do their thing insofar as setting off of massive rocket barrages. The purpose of that, as we were told, was to discredit the presence of the United States military. They wanted to show that even after all these years our presence really has not assured a safe environment, not even in the cities. The cities were the ultimate target for what we ended up calling the Tet Offensive.

In the afternoon on January 30, the Embassy guy came by and told us tomorrow's the day. We had heard this before, so I really didn't give it a whole lot of thought. But we were placed on immediate standby, which meant that we couldn't leave the villa.

It was funny. You always have power fluctuations. This particular day, the power went out. And just like any American, when the power goes out, you bitch and complain about the air conditioning. So you open up the windows, and you suffer. And there's no TV.

About four o'clock in the morning, the squawk came over the radio. There were some fire fights in various parts of the city. We were told to go to our various positions. I went up to the roof. We sat around looking out into the city, and you could see the rockets come in, the afterbursts and all.

Then around six-fifteen the emergency net went off, which entailed a recall of all security officers and related personnel to report to the Embassy. They said bring the Beast. When they added that, we knew something was wrong.

So we go rumbling down there with this three-quarter-ton truck with half-inch armor plate, tires looking like donuts, and two M-60s, one facing the front and one facing the back.

And the guys who stayed out at the training site in Gia Dinh, they came in from that area.

When I get there, I see this gaping hole in the big 8-foot-high wall that surrounds the Embassy compound. The hole is on the side that runs along the main thoroughfare in front of the Embassy. A Viet Cong sapper team of about 15 had attacked the Embassy around two-forty-five.

I thought to myself, They have really done it. Now they've gone too far.

By the time we got there, the Marine guys had already secured the lobby area of the Chancery. The Army had landed a helicopter right on the roof. And the Army had strung a ring of men up around the Chancery. I learned later four Army MPs and a Marine had been killed in the fighting.

Then I heard the Army guys saying, "I believe they got inside. I believe they got inside."

Then I saw this big powwow taking place of the powers that be. They said there must be some Viet Cong in the building, but we didn't know how many.

Then our boss came over and said, "Well, Brownie, the decision is that you and your guys have to go in and flush them out." There was no direct order to take them alive if you can, just get them out of there.

Knowing these sappers are suicidal, I just couldn't understand why the Army guys couldn't have done this. They are the experts. We're the Air Force. We're lovers.

It was about seven by then.

The plan was to start from the top floor and work down. So here comes Brute with all his equipment to get on the elevator with me and this other brother to go to the top three floors. Another team of our contingent would work the next three floors at the same time.

If you heard something, you were to yell "Score event." The guy would call it back to you, and you'd know the noise you heard came from a friendly.

We got to the top floor, and it seemed like there were a zillion offices. You could hide anywhere. This was going to be shaky. Checking all of those offices one at a time. All the closets. Behind every desk.

You talk about doing some tall praying. You didn't know what to look for. All you knew was that in this building there are some people bent on eliminating the breath in your body. And they know they got nowhere to go.

We would open the doors very carefully. One guy would go right, one would go left, and the last to come in would come up the middle. That would work fine as long as there were no desks right there at the door. Each room was different. And we didn't have time to get a floor plan—to know how the rooms were set up.

The top floor was very hair-shaking. It took us about a half-hour to clear it. I kept hoping that the other guys would run into those dudes.

So we take the elevator down to the next floor. When we went into the second room, I moved left, the other brother was on the right, and poor Brute came down the middle. Then we heard some scuffling over in the back corner. Everybody got quiet. Real quiet.

I threw a grenade over in the corner. And then we just started shooting in that area.

When we got through shooting, there was no more noise. So now the question becomes, Who's going to go over there and see what we have shot? Brute decides to be the hero.

He went from behind one desk to another until he found this one guy. He was wasted. He had been hiding more or less. He had an AK-47 with one banana clip. If he gets off a burst for five seconds, he's out of ammo. He had on black pajamas and those rubber-tire sandals. He looked to be maybe in his middle twenties.

Now it's for real. Until you come face to face with the VC, it doesn't seem so real. This is real. And who knows when you open this next door, there may be five or six guys there waiting. Or somebody not dumb like this one guy fumbling around behind a desk.

As we cleared the rest of the floor and the next floor, we heard gunshots from the other team. By the time we got down to the lobby, the five they killed were all stretched out in a row, lined up like ducks. We didn't bring our guy down. Left him up there for the medic folks. We shoot 'em, you drag 'em.

So we got six VC out of the Chancery. They never saw any classified material. They were just lookin' for a place to hide.

They had told Ambassador Bunker to stay away until the fighting was over. The rankingest guy that I saw there was a three-button Army general, Frederick Weyand, commander of the United States forces in the area, and this guy, Barry Zorthian, who spoke for the Embassy.

It would have been impossible to totally prevent what happened to the Embassy. But we did a lot of dumb-shit things over there. The wall around the Embassy was a barrier to honest folks. Just like a lock on your front door. But if a burglar wants to break in, he will. So who was watching the wall where the VC blew the hole. We needed more Marines than two on guard. And better equipped. This was a war zone.

And the VC would watch you all the time. They knew your pattern. And we would, most of us, do the same thing at the same time every day.

In Tuy Hoa they would set the claymore mines out in the daytime. The VC would be watching in the bush. They know exactly where they are so they can sneak up at night and turn them around against you. We would broadcast over an open airway. The Vietnamese would learn some English. So we're telling them when we were coming and what time and how many of us are coming. They'd sit back and wait. We would even bomb the same area the same time day in and day out. So the enemy would sit in their caves till the bombing is over. Then they would come back out and have a picnic. We won't be back until tomorrow. Same time. Creatures of habit.

I got so I enjoyed the city of Saigon. The real difficulties came mostly after curfew, when the Vietnamese police, the MPs, and our group were the only ones allowed on the city streets.

The guys in our outfit went to a club on Tu Do Street—"the street of flowers." We called it our club. Being favorite customers, we were accustomed to getting more than normal favors from the proprietor, which meant girls.

Not too far from the main gate of Tan Son Nhut was Soul Alley, where you could find Cambodian girls in bars who could readily pass for black females. And in the Soul Kitchen, which was run by this brother in the Air Force, you could buy soul food that tasted like back home. Chitlins, ham hocks, cornbread—the works.

If you could drive around Saigon in the daytime, you could drive in any city in the world. Saigon prepared me for driving in West Germany. Saigon had no speed limit.

The big thing during rush hour was to burn rubber from traffic light to traffic light. Especially guys who were driving jeeps and cars that had some pickup. What really aggravated you was waiting at this red light when, invariably, a Vietnamese guy would pull in front of you on a pedal bicycle, loaded with bricks.

One day, coming from the Embassy, I was drag racing this Vietnamese up the strip to the Saigon River. I was in a jeep. He was on this Honda. From red light to red light, he would win one, I would win the other.

When we got to the last traffic light before the bridge, I knew the one who got there first wouldn't have to give up the lane closest to the center. The four lanes would become two after the light.

When the light turned green, he zoomed off in the lane that would merge with mine. There was no blockade. The road just quit. At the bridge. He had to turn into my lane or go into the river. And that river was so thick with pollution it looked like syrup.

I don't think he realized what was happening until too late. The last I saw of that young fellow and his Honda, they were both airborne. And he was screaming "Ahhhhhh."

A lot of Army MPs who would go around checking on their people would go through a narrow alley or street and never come out. There's no way to turn around. And it's very easy to drop a grenade in the back seat of an open jeep. And that's how the MPs usually drove. Which I thought was ludicrous.

One time I was out checking cars in my closed jeep, and I had a grenade thrown at me. It bounced off the side. It was a dud.

Another time I was following an MP jeep, and for some reason, I stopped to talk to another guy who was on the road. The MP jeep went on. About three or four minutes later, we heard this tremendous explosion. Naturally, we responded. When we were about to run into this alley, this guy said, "Don't go up there. Let's get out and go on foot." We found the jeep blown up by a grenade or several grenades. The two Army guys, obviously dead.

Snipers were the biggest danger in the city, however. Especially at night. And sometimes a guy would ride up on a Honda next to a GI on a cycle or in a pedicab and just shot him right there on the spot. You learned to duck at any sound, watch the movement of anyone.

It got to the point where we were told to always be armed, even in daytime. And if a Vietnamese, be it man, woman, or child, refused to *di di mau* or tried to get away, the authorization was to go 'head and shoot 'em. We were told not to hesitate.

One guy in our contingency was traveling in the Cholon district. A girl on a Honda bike stopped beside him. He told her three times, *"Di di mau."* She didn't. Maybe it was difficult for her to get away through the traffic. Maybe she didn't understand the Vietnamese he was speaking. Well, he shot her. The white mice showed up, and just took the body away. She was not armed. There was no report. It was just one of those things.

During the spring and summer of '68, the Viet Cong were just shelling Saigon indiscriminately. I remember one night I was in bed and all of a sudden this tremendous explosion went off. My whole life passed before my eyes. I grabbed a helmet, flak vest, and my weapon. I went up to the roof, and this three-story building that stood next door was nothing but total rubble. There were several Vietnamese casualties, and one baby fatality.

One of our guys ran out the front of our villa and was shot in the leg by someone. Then the Army MPs showed up. This second lieutenant jumped out of his jeep and left it unattended with a M-60 machine gun and all the ammunition in the world on it. So he yells, "Go get my jeep. Go get my jeep." By that time, some Vietnamese or Viet Cong is standing by the jeep, just about ready to take off with it. They fired a couple of shots and he disappeared into the woodwork. Now everything is really tense.

Then this dumb-ass second lieutenant felt that the area wasn't lit up enough. He fires off a hand flare that sounds like an incoming round. Everybody just dives into the street or tries to grab something to pull over them. The second lieutenant is standing there looking dumb.

Needless to say, we wanted to kick the second lieutenant in the rear.

Then everything calmed down, and we took care of the wounded.

When I heard that Martin Luther King was assassinated, my first inclination was to run out and punch the first white guy I saw. I was very hurt. All I wanted to do was to go home. I even wrote Lyndon Johnson a letter. I said that I didn't understand how I could be trying to protect foreigners in their country with the possibility of losing my life wherein in my own country people who are my hero, like Martin Luther King, can't even walk the streets in a safe manner. I didn't get an answer from the President, but I got an answer from the White House. It was a wonderful letter, wonderful in terms of the way it looked. It wanted to assure me that the President was doing everything in his power to bring about racial equality, especially in the armed forces. A typical bureaucratic answer.

A few days after the assassination, some of the white guys got a little sick and tired of seeing Dr. King's picture on the TV screen. Like a memorial. It really got to one guy. He said, "I wish they'd take that nigger's picture off." He was a fool to begin with, because there were three black guys sitting in the living room when he said it. And we commenced to give him a lesson in when to use that word and when you should not use that word. A physical lesson.

With the world focused on the King assassination and the riots that followed in the United States, the North Vietnamese, being politically astute, schooled the Viet Cong to go on a campaign of psychological warfare against the American forces.

At the time, more blacks were dying in combat than whites, proportionately, mainly because more blacks were in combat-oriented units, proportionately, than whites. To play on the sympathy of the black soldier, the Viet Cong would shoot at a white guy, then let the black guy behind him go through, then shoot at the next white guy.

It didn't take long for that kind of word to get out. And the reaction in some companies was to arrange your personnel where you had an all-black or nearly all-black unit to send out.

Over the next months some of us in the contingency were sent on secret operations in the Delta similar to the Phoenix Program. We would get the word that certain people were no longer necessary or needed to be removed. Our group never got a high-ranking VC. It was always a local person in the village who was coerced by the VC into being a leader, to get the community to rise up in arms against the allied forces. ARVN troops engaged in everything we did, but when it came to the interrogation or the torture, we were specifically instructed not to do that. The ARVN troops did that.

I remember this one ARVN sergeant took one of these old guys into this hut and strung him up from his ankles. The guy wouldn't talk. So the sergeant built a fire underneath him. When his hair caught on fire, he started talking. Then they stopped the fire.

When we passed through those villages, we really had to watch out for the kids. They would pick up arms and shoot at you. And we had to fire right back.

When we were going out from an operation not very far from Vung Tau, we went through a hamlet we were told was friendly. Quite naturally, you see the women and the children. Never see the men. The men are out conducting the war.

We had hooked up with some Army guys, so it was about a company of us. As soon as we got about a half mile out down the road, we got hit from the rear. Automatic gunfire. It's the women and the children. They just opened up. And a couple of our guys got wasted.

The captain who was in charge of this so-called expeditionary group just took one squad back to the village. And they just melted the whole village. If women and children got in the way, then they got in the way.

In another village we sent an advance party to recon the place. It was fairly empty. But when we got there, this kid come running out of a hut. Looked to be about fourteen or fifteen years old. He was told to halt. And he didn't. He ran into another hut, and gunfire started coming from the hut. So two GIs took defensive measures. Dropped to the ground and fired into the hut. We went inside. And here's the kid with the gun. Dead. And then mama san comes out of the other hut boohooing and all.

I'm willing to bet that a lot of those grenades that were thrown in the back of Army jeeps were done by kids. The very kids the GIs befriended with candy or whatever.

When it was time for me to leave, my staff had a dinner in my honor at one of the restaurants. My secretary, my interpreter, and the clerk were there. And the Vietnamese who helped with the training. And they put me at the head of the table.

On the menu was pigeon soup. And each bowl had a pigeon head in it with the eye open and the beak. I ate the soup. I didn't eat the pigeon head.

And as custom goes, I had to toast each person at the table with what was like rice whiskey syrup. I made it to nine of the twenty sitting there. That was Saturday. I didn't gain full control of my senses until Tuesday.

And just before I left, one of our maids tried to sell me her baby boy for about the equivalent of $200. She wanted me to bring him back to the United States and raise him.

She had difficulty with English so I couldn't philosophize with her. I just told her that in American society we just don't buy children like that.

When the North Vietnamese started taking over South Vietnam in 1974 without too many shots being fired, I felt let down. But I never had any faith in the ARVN. As long as they knew that the American platoon was 2 feet behind them, they would fight like cats and dogs. But if they knew that they didn't have American support real close—like right behind them—they would not fight.

When I watched on TV the cowardly, shameful way we left Saigon and left the Embassy, I felt hurt. I felt betrayed. I didn't feel very proud to be an American.

We destroyed what we couldn't carry with us. We ducked our tails and ran.

Why wait ten years and thousands upon thousands of lives later to just turn it over to the Communists? We could have done that at the very beginning.

Late that year I got accepted to officers' candidate school, after failing six times. General David Jones, whom I worked for in race relations in West Germany when he commanded the Air Force in Europe, wrote a beautiful letter to make that appointment happen.

I've made captain and will retire at that rank. And I still sing when I can. Swing stuff. I don't do much disco. You could call it a cross between Lou Rawls and Johnny Mathis. When I was stationed in Nevada, I worked as a replacement in the lounges at the Sahara, the Dunes, the Landmark. That was great. That's the top of the line.

When I think back, there were a lot of things we did in that special contingency unit in Vietnam that we didn't get credit for. We couldn't talk about it. Or put in for commendations. In fact, we were even under oath not to talk about what we did for five years.

But we really wanted some kind of commendation for what we did at the Embassy during Tet. Some of the Marines and Army guys got medals. But that was out of the question for us. You weren't supposed to report our activities. They were secret.

All we got was the Vietnam campaign medal. Everybody got that. If you flew into the country and stayed overnight during the war, you were eligible for that.

So at the famous battle of the American Embassy, officially, we were not there.

Specialist 4
Richard J. Ford III
Washington, D.C.

LURP
25th Infantry Division
U.S. Army
Hill 54
June 1967—July 1968

I should have felt happy I was goin' home when I got on that plane in Cam Ranh Bay to leave. But I didn't exactly. I felt—I felt—I felt very insecure 'cause I didn't have a weapon. I had one of them long knives, like a big hacksaw knife. I had that. And had my cane. And I had a couple of grenades in my bag. They took them from me when I got to Washington, right? And I felt insecure. I just felt real bad.

You know, my parents never had a weapon in the house. Rifle, shotgun, pistol, nothing. Never had one. Never seen my father with one. And I needed a weapon. 'Cause of that insecurity. I never got over it.

It was Saturday evening when we landed. Nineteen sixty-eight. I caught a cab from Dulles and went straight to my church. The Way of the Cross Church. It's a Pentacostal holiest church. I really wasn't active in the church before I went overseas. But a lot of people from the church wrote me, saying things like "I'm praying for you." There was a couple of peoples around there. They had a choir rehearsal. And they said they were glad to see me. But I went to the altar and stayed there from seven o'clock to about eleven-thirty. I just wanted to be by myself and pray. At the altar.

I was glad to be home. Just to be stateside. I was thankful that I made it. But I felt bad because I had to leave some friends over there. I left Davis there, I couldn't say a prayer for people that was already gone. But I said a prayer for them guys to come back home safely. For Davis. Yeah, for Davis.

The first nights I came home I couldn't sleep. My room was the back room of my parents' house. I couldn't sleep in the bed, so I had to get on the floor. I woke up in the middle of the night, and looking out my back window, all you see is trees. So I see all these trees, and I'm thinkin' I'm still in Vietnam. And I can't find my weapon. And I can't find Davis. I can't find nobody. And I guess I scared my mother and father half to death 'cause I got to hollering, "Come on, where are you? Where are you? Davis. Davis. SIR DAVIS." I thought I had got captured or something.

The first thing I did Monday was went to the store and bought me a .38. And bought me a .22.

It was right after the Fourth of July, and kids were still throwing firecrackers. I couldn't deal with it. Hear the noise, I hit the ground. I was down on 7th and F, downtown. I had this little .22. A kid threw fire-crackers, and I was trying to duck. And some guys laughed at me, right? So I fired the pistol back at them and watched them duck. I said, "It's not funny now, is it?" I didn't go out of my way to mess with nobody, but I demanded respect.

One day, me and my mother and my wife were coming home from church, up Illinois Avenue. I made a left turn, and four white guys in a car cut in front of me and blew the horn. They had been drinking. They gave me the finger. And, man, I forgot all about my mother and wife was in the car. I took off after them. I had the .22 and was firing out the window at them. I just forgot where—and Vietnam does that to you—you forget where you are. It was open season. I'm shooting out the window. My mother said, "Oh, my God. Please, please help him."

Got home and it was, "You need help. You need help." But I was like that. I just couldn't adjust to it. Couldn't adjust to coming back home, and people think you dirty 'cause you went to Vietnam.

The Army sent me to Walter Reed Hospital for therapy. For two weeks. It was for guys who had been involved in a lot of combat. They said that I was hyper. And they pumped me up with a whole bunch of tranquilizers.

I'll never forget this goddamn officer. I'm looking at him. He's got a Good Conduct ribbon on. He's a major. He's reading my jacket, and he's looking with his glasses at me. I'm just sitting there. So he says, "Ford, you were very lucky. I see you got these com-mendations. You were very lucky, to come back." So I told him, "No, I'm not lucky. You're lucky. You didn't go. You sitting there with a Good Conduct Medal on your chest and haven't been outside the States. You volunteered for service. You should have went. I didn't volunteer for Vietnam. They made me go."

There was 12 guys in the therapy session up there at Walter Reed. It was six white, and it was six black. I was the only combat person up there in the class. These guys were having flashbacks and had no com-bat experience. I can relate to it now, but at that point I couldn't understand. I said, "What y'all talking 'bout? You was in artillery. At the base camp. You fired guns from five miles away and talking 'bout flashbacks?" Other guys was truck drivers or supply. Nobody done hand-to-hand combat. I said, "You bring me somebody in here with a CIB. We can sit down and talk. But I can't talk to none of y'all 'cause y'all wasn't there."

You know, they decorated me in Vietnam. Two Bronze Stars. The whiteys did. I was wounded three times. The officers, the generals, and whoever came out to the hospital to see you. They respected you and pat you on the back. They said, "'You brave. And you courageous. You America's finest. America's best." Back in the States the same officers that pat me on the back wouldn't even speak to me. They wanted that salute, that attention, 'til they holler at ease. I didn't get the respect that I thought I was gonna get.

I had six months to go. So now they trying to figure out where they can put me for six months. They said my time was too short to qualify for school. Then up pop my medical record. The one they couldn't find when they sent me to 'Nam. The one say I shouldn't even be runnin', my knees so bad. They tell me I can't learn no skill. Drive no jeep. 'Cause of my knees. So they put me in charge of the poolroom at Fort Meade.

They lost my medical records when they wanted to. Now they got 'em back when they wanted to. They just wanted another black in the field. Uncle Sam, he didn't give me no justice. You had a job to do, you did it, you home. Back where you started. They didn't even ask me to reenlist.

I graduated from Roosevelt High School in 1966 and was working for the Food and Drug Administration as a lab technician when I was drafted. My father was administrator of a halfway house for Lorton, and my mother was on the Board of Elections in D.C. I was nineteen, and they took me to Fort Bragg. Airborne.

We were really earmarked for Vietnam. Even the drill sergeant and the first sergeant in basic told us that we was going to Vietnam. From basic we went straight to jungle warfare AIT in South Carolina. Before I went to Vietnam, three medical doctors at Fort Dix examined my knees. They trained us so hard in Fort Bragg the cartilages were roughed up. The doctors signed the medical record. It was a permanent profile. Said they would find something in the rear for you. A little desk job, clerk, or medic aid. But they didn't. I was sent straight to the infantry.

I really thought Vietnam was really a civil war between that country, and we had no business in there. But it seems that by the Russians getting involved and supplying so many weapons to the North Vietnamese that the United States should send troops in.

When I stepped off the plane in Tan Son Nhut, that heat that was coming from the ground hit me in the face. And the odor from the climate was so strong. It hit me. I said, Goddamn, where am I? What is this?

While we was walking off the plane, guys were coming toward the plane. And guys said, "Happy Birthday, Merry Christmas, Happy Easter. I'll write your mom." They kept going. In other words, you gon' have Easter here, gonna have a birthday here, and you gonna have Christmas here. And good luck.

It was in June 1967. My MOS was mortarman, but they made me be a rifleman first and sent me to Company C, 3rd Brigade, 25th Infantry Division. We was operating in Chu Lai, but we was a floatin' battalion.

It was really weird how the old guys would ask you what you want to carry. It wasn't a thing where you get assigned an M-14, M-16. If you want to carry an M-16, they say how many rounds of ammo do you want to carry? If you want to carry 2,000, we got it for you. How many grenades do you want? It was really something. We were so in the spirit that we hurt ourself. Guys would want to look like John Wayne. The dudes would just get in the country and say, "I want a .45. I want eight grenades. I want a bandolier. I want a thousand rounds ammo. I want ten dips. I want the works, right?" We never knew what the weight of this ammo is gon' be.

A lot of times guys be walkin' them hills, choppin' through them mountains, and the grenades start gettin' heavy. And you start throwin' your grenades under bushes and takin' your bandoliers off. It wasn't ever questioned. We got back in the rear, and it wasn't questioned if you felt like goin' to get the same thing again next time.

Once I threw away about 200 rounds of ammo. They designated me to carry ammo for the M-60 machine gun. We was going through a stream above Chu Lai. I'm carrying my C rations, my air mattress, poncho, five quarts of water, everything that you own. The ammo was just too heavy. I threw away the ammo going through the river. I said it got lost. The terrain was so terrible, so thick, nobody could question that you lost it.

I come from a very religious family. So I'm carrying my sister's Bible, too. All my letters that I saved. And a little bottle of olive oil that my pastor gave me. Blessed olive oil. But I found it was a lot of guys in basic with me that were atheist. When we got to Vietnam there were no atheist. There was not one atheist in my unit. When we got hit, everybody hollered, "Oh, God, please help, please." And everybody want to wear a cross. Put a cross on their helmet. Something to psych you up.

Black guys would wear sunglasses, too. We would put on sunglasses walking in the jungle. Think about it, now. It was ridiculous. But we want to show how bad we are. How we're not scared. We be saying, "The Communists haven't made a bullet that can kill me." We had this attitude that I don't give a damn. That made us more aggressive, more ruthless, more careless. And a little more luckier than the person that was scared.

I guess that's why I volunteered for the LURPs and they brought me into Nha Trang. And it was six other black fellas to go to this school at the 5th Special Forces. And we would always be together in the field. Sometimes it would be Captain Park, this Korean, with us. Most of the time it was us, five or six black dudes making our own war, doing our thing alone.

There was Larry Hill from New York. Garland from Baltimore. Holmes from Georgia. Louis Ford from New Orleans. Moon from Detroit, too. They called him Sir Drawers, 'cause he wouldn't wear underwear. Said it gave him a rash. And this guy from Baton Rouge named Albert Davis. He was only 5 feet 9. Only 120 pounds. He was a terrific soldier. A lot of guts, a lot of heart. He was Sir Davis. I was Sir Ford. Like Knights of the Round Table. We be immortal. No one can kill us.

I didn't believe Nha Trang was still part of Vietnam, because they had barracks, hot water, had mess halls with three hot meals and air conditioning. Nha Trang was like a beach, a resort. They was ridin' around on paved streets. They be playing football and basketball. Nobody walked around with weapons. They were white. And that's what really freaked me out. All these white guys in the rear.

They told us we had to take our weapons to the armory and lock 'em up. We said naw. So they decided to let us keep our weapons till we went to this show.

It was a big club. Looked like 80 or 90 guys. Almost everybody is white. They had girls dancing and groups singin'. They reacted like we was some kind of animals, like we these guys from the boonies. They a little off. I don't know if I was paranoid or what. But they stare at you when you first come in. All of us got drunk and carryin' on. I didn't get drunk, 'cause I didn't drink. And we started firin' the weapons at the ceiling. Telling everybody to get out. "Y'all not in the war." We was frustrated because all these whites were in the back having a big show. And they were clerks. Next thing I know, about a hundred MPs all around the club. Well, they took our weapons. That was all.

The next day Davis got in trouble 'cause he wouldn't salute this little second lieutenant. See, we weren't allowed to salute anybody in the field. Officers didn't want you to. A sniper might blow his head off. The captain wanted to be average. He say, "I'm just like you, brother." When we got in the rear, it was hard for us to adjust to salutin' automatically.

When we got to be LURPs, we operated from Hill 54. Then they'd bring us in for like three days. They'd give you steak, all the beer you could drink. They know it's your last time. Some of us not coming back. We'd eat half the steaks, throw 'em away, have a ball. Go into town, and tear the town up.

Davis couldn't make no rank 'cause he got court-martialed for somethin' we do in town. We stole a jeep. Went to town. Tuy Hoa was off limits. Davis turned the jeep over comin' around one of them curves. But Davis was a born leader. He went back to the unit and got some more fools to get another jeep to push this jeep up. But he got court-martialed for stearin' the jeep. And for having United States currency.

Davis would take American money into town. Somebody send him $50, he get 3 to 1. Black market. First chance we go to town, he go get some cash. 'Cause he stayed high all the time. Smokin' marijuana, hashish. At mama san's house.

And some guys used to play this game. They would smoke this opium. They'd put a plastic bag over their head. Smoke all this smoke. See how long you could hold it. Lot of guys would pass out.

In the field most of the guys stayed high. Lot of them couldn't face it. In a sense, if you was high, it seemed like a game you was in. You didn't take it serious. It stopped a lot of nervous breakdown.

See, the thing about the field that was so bad was this. If I'm working on the job with you stateside and you're my friend, if you get killed, there's a compassion. My boss say, "Well, you better take a couple of days off. Get yourself together." But in the field, we can be the best of friends and you get blown away. They put a poncho around you and send you back. They tell 'em to keep moving.

We had a medic that give us a shot of morphine anytime you want one. I'm not takin' about for wounded. I'm talkin' about when you want to just get high. So you can face it.

In the rear sometimes we get a grenade, dump the gunpowder out, break the firing pin. Then you'll go inside one of them little bourgeois clubs. Or go in the barracks where the supply guys are, sitting around playing bid whist and doing nothing. We act real crazy. Yell out, "Kill all y'all motherfuckers." Pull the pin and throw the grenade. And everybody would haul ass and get out. It would make a little pop sound. And we would laugh. You didn't see anybody jumpin' on them grenades.

One time in the field, though, I saw a white boy jump on a grenade. But I believe he was pushed. It ain't kill him. He lost both his legs.

The racial incidents didn't happen in the field. Just when we went to the back. It wasn't so much that they were against us. It was just that we felt that we were being taken advantage of, 'cause it seemed like more blacks in the field than in the rear.

In the rear we saw a bunch of rebel flags. They didn't mean nothing by the rebel flag. It was just saying we for the South. It didn't mean that they hated blacks. But after you in the field, you took the flags very personally.

One time we saw these flags in Nha Trang on the MP barracks. They was playing hillbilly music. Had their shoes off dancing. Had nice, pretty bunks. Mosquito nets over top the bunks. And had the nerve to have this camouflaged covers. Air conditioning. Cement floors. We just came out the jungles. We dirty, we smelly, hadn't shaved. We just went off. Said, "Y'all the real enemy. We stayin' here." We turned the bunks over, started tearing up the stereo. They just ran out. Next morning, they shipped us back up.

In the field, we had the utmost respect for each other, because when a fire fight is going on and everybody is facing north, you don't want to see nobody looking around south. If you was a member of the Ku Klux Klan, you didn't tell nobody.

Take them guys from West Virginia, Kentucky. First time they ever seen blacks was when they went in the service. One of them told me that the only thing he hate about the service was he had to leave his sheep. He said he used to never wear boots or shoes. He tell us how he cut a stump, put the sheep across the stump, and he would rape the sheep. Those guys were dumb, strong, but with no problems about us blacks. Matter of fact, the whites catered to the blacks in the infantry in the field.

Captain one time asked Davis what kind of car he gonna have when he get back in the States. Davis told him, "I'm not gonna get a car, sir. I'm gonna get me a Exxon station and give gas away to the brothers. Let them finish burnin' down what they leave." It wasn't funny if he said it in the stateside. But all of 'em bust out laughing.

We used to bathe in the stream. Shave and everything. Captain was telling Davis he had some Ivory soap. Davis said, "I don't take baths. Water rusts iron and put knots on the alligator's back." Creole talk.

Everybody laugh. They know he don't bathe, but he was a terrific soldier. Small fella. He had one of the Napoleon complexes. Always had to prove something. He wasn't scared. He had more heart than anybody. They respected him, and they knew if you need fire cover or need help, he right there.

Right after Tet, the mail chopper got shot down. We moved to Tam Ky. We didn't have any mail in about three weeks. Then this lady by the name of Hanoi Helen come on the radio. She had a letter belong to Sir Drawers. From the chopper that was shot down. She read the letter from his wife about how she miss him. But that didn't unsettle the brothers as much as when she got on the air after Martin Luther King died, and they was rioting back home. She was saying, "Soul brothers, go home. Whitey raping your mothers and your daughters, burning down your homes. What you over here for? This is not your war. The war is a trick of the Capitalist empire to get rid of the blacks." I really thought—I really started believing it, because it was too many blacks than there should be in infantry.

And take the Montagnards, the brothers considered them brothers because they were dark. They had some of the prettiest ladies, pretty complexion, long hair, and they didn't wear no tops. Breasts would be exposed. And the Montagnard be walking with his water buffalo, his family, his crossbow. You waved at them, kept on walking. The people in Saigon didn't have anything to do with Montagnards. It was almost like white people in the States didn't have anything to do with blacks in the ghetto. So we would compare them with us.

I remember when we was stealing bananas in Pleiku and here come a bunch of Montagnards. Some white guys were talking about them: "Now I'd like to bang one of them." I remember Davis said, "Yeah. But you get that thought out your mind, 'cause I'll blow your brains out just for thinking it."

In the field, I wasn't about to do nothing crazy. Not like Davis. I got two Bronze Stars for valor by accident. It wasn't intentional.

The first time, it was really weird. We hadn't had any activity for about three weeks. Not even a sniper round. We was sitting at the bottom of this hill, sitting around joking. Some guys smoking, eating C-rations, talking about their homes. I saw this little animal run into this bush about 50 yards away. I told everybody, "Quiet. I saw a gook." Everybody grabbed their weapons, got quiet.

Well, I knew it wasn't no dink. I had the machine gun. I was just gon' play with the guys. I'ma get this little fox, little weasel, whatever, and bring him back down the hill. So I gets up to where I saw him runnin' in this real thick terrain. So I opened up with this M-60. About 20 rounds. Goddamn if three dinks ain't jump up. They was hiding in the terrain. I'm shooting at them on the joke, right? When they jumped up, I fell all the way back down the hill 'cause they scared me half to death. Then the rest of us moved on up. The dinks had about 100 rounds of ammo, 'bout 12 grenades. I had killed all three of them.

Anyway, the commendation read how I crawled 100 yards to attack three enemy scouts and killed them single-handedly. I joke about it, 'cause if I knew they was up there, I wouldn't have went up there by myself. Naw, everybody was going, and I'd be in the rear, 'cause I didn't walk point."

When I got the second Bronze Star, it was almost similar. I took some guys out on a listening post. At that time, Charlie would throw rocks at listening posts to find out where your location is and make you open up. He would find your claymore mines, turn them around to face you, for you to blow your own self away. I told the men, "If y'all hear something, y'all wake me up."

It was getting close to day, and this guy say he heard somethin'. I said to myself I know what it was. It was a water buffalo. That's what's messing with the trip wires. But I decided to have some fun, play with the captain. I told them to radio back we got activity, they coming toward us. And I just said, "Shit, I'ma have me a mad minute."

I saw the buffalo. And I opened up the M-60. I sprayed the area, threw a couple of grenades, and I got a couple of NVAs. I didn't know they were there either.

Davis wasn't scared even when he was hit. He would just go on encouragin' you.

I remember we was up in Chu Lai, going on an assault in this hot LZ. You got 30 choppers, and the first chopper got hit. It don't turn around 'cause the other choppers waitin' for you. We was in the first chopper. When he got to treetop level, the chopper gunner tell you hit it. If you not out, he'll throw you out. We was jumping out, and Davis got shot in the tail. He never paid it any mind. He was bleeding bad. No question. He was hard.

Another guy named Taylor got hit at the same time. Taylor cried like a baby. This black guy. Davis told him, "You cryin' 'cause you gettin' ready to die. You dying, and you know you dying. You might as well come on and take some of these gooks with us."

Taylor said, "I'm not gonna die."

He said, "Why you sittin' there crying if you not gon' die? You cryin' cause you a big faggot, and you gettin' ready to die."

And he put the spunk back in Taylor. Davis would intimidate you into not dying.

So Taylor got to fightin' until the medevac carried both of them back. Matter of fact, all of us went back. I got hit in the head. Five steps off the chopper. Trying to be cool, I had took my helmet off, put my soft cap on. It knocked me down. I saw this blood. It was burning: I said, "I'll be damned."

The weird thing, after we always have a little jive assault, these majors and these idiots in the back would say they want a body count. Go back out there and find the bodies. After we found the body count, then we had to bury them. Geneva Convention says we have to bury 'em. And I said, "What the hell y'all talkin' 'bout the Geneva Convention? We're not in a war."

I remember February 20. Twentieth of February. We went to this village outside Duc Pho. Search and destroy. It was suppose to have been VC sympathizers. They sent fliers to the people telling them to get out. Anybody else there, you have to consider them as a VC.

It was a little straw-hut village. Had a little church at the end with this big Buddha. We didn't see anybody in the village. But I heard movement in the rear of this hut. I just opened up the machine gun. You ain't wanna open the door, and then you get blown away. Or maybe they booby-trapped.

Anyway, this little girl screamed. I went inside the door. I'd done already shot her, and she was on top of the old man. She was trying to shield the old man. He looked like he could have been about eighty years old. She was about seven. Both of them was dead. I killed an old man and a little girl in the hut by accident.

I started feeling funny. I wanted to explain to someone. But everybody was there, justifying my actions, saying, "It ain't your fault. They had no business there." But I just—I ain't wanna hear it. I wanted to go home then.

It bothers me now. But so many things happened after that, you really couldn't lay on one thing. You had to keep going.

The flame throwers came in, and we burnt the hamlet. Burnt up everything. They had a lot of rice. We opened the bags, just throw it all over the street. Look for tunnels. Killing animals. Killing all the livestock. Guys would carry chemicals that they would put in the well. Poison the water so they couldn't use it. So they wouldn't come back to use it, right? And it was trifling.

They killed some more people there. Maybe 12 or 14 more. Old people and little kids that wouldn't leave. I guess their grandparents. See, people that were old in Vietnam couldn't leave their village. It was like a ritual. They figured that this'll pass. We'll come and move on.

Sometimes we went in a village, and we found a lot of weapons stashed, little tunnels. On the twentieth of February we found nothing.

You know, it was a little boy used to hang around the base camp. Around Hill 54. Wasn't no more than about eight years old. Spoke good English, a little French. Very sharp. His mother and father got killed by mortar attack on his village. I thought about that little girl. And I wanted to adopt him. A bunch of us wanted to. And we went out to the field, and then came back and he was gone.

We went in town looking for him, and we see these ARVNs pull up. We thought they was chasing Viet Congs. So the lieutenant and these two sergeants opened fire on these three guys running. Find out they weren't Viet Cong. They were draft dodgers. ARVNs would come to the city and snatch you if you eighteen, sixteen, fifteen, or however old you are. Put you in uniform. So a lots of mothers would hide their sons from the ARVNs. These guys looked like they wasn't no more than about fifteen. They killed all three of them. And Davis went up to the lieutenant and said, "Man, you fucked up again. Y'all can't do nothin' right."

We never found that boy.

Davis, this little guy. He was a private 'cause he kept gettin' court-martialed. But he was the leader with the LURPs. We was best friends, but I felt a little threatened. 'Cause he would always argue about who killed the last Viet Cong. "You got the last one, this one—these two are mine. I'ma jump 'em." Sometimes he would carry me.

Our main function was to try to see can we find any type of enemy element. They gave us a position, a area, and tell us to go out there and do the recon. We alone—these six black guys—roamin' miles from the base camp. We find them. We radio helicopter pick us up, take us to the rear. We go and bring the battalion out and wipe 'em out. You don't fire your weapon. That's the worse thing you do if you a LURP. Because if it's a large unit and it's just six of y'all, you fire your weapon and you by yourself. You try to kill 'em without firing your weapon. This is what they taught us in Nha Trang. Different ways of killing a person without using your weapon. Use your weapon, it give you away.

I wasn't suppose to carry a M-60 as a LURP. But I told them the hell with that. I'm carrying the firepower. Davis carried a shotgun. We would lay back, and then we'll jump one or two. Bust them upside the head, take their weapons.

Davis would do little crazy things. If they had gold in their mouth, he'd knock the gold out 'cause he saved gold. He saved a little collection of gold teeth. Maybe 50 or 60 in a little box. And he went and had about 100 pictures made of himself. And he used to leave one in the field. Where he got the gook.

One day we saw two gooks no more than 50 yards away. They was rolling cigarettes. Eating. Davis said, "They mine. Y'all just stay here and watch." He sneaked up on 'em real fast, and in one swing he had them. Hit one with the bayonet, hit the other one with the machete.

Wherever he would see a gook, he would go after 'em. He was good.

The second time I got wounded was with the LURPs. We got trapped. Near Duc Pho.

We saw a couple of Viet Congs. We dropped our packs, and chased them. The terrain was so thick there that we lost them. It was jungle. It was the wait-a-minute vines that grab you, tangles you as you move in the jungle. Start gettin' kind of dark, so we go on back to where we had dropped our packs.

And that's where they were.

All of a sudden, something said boop. I said I hope this is a rock. It didn't go off. Then three or four more hit. They were poppin' grenades. About ten. One knocked me down. Then I just sprayed the area, and Davis start hittin' with the shotgun. We called for the medevac, and they picked me up. We didn't see if we killed anybody. Only three grenades exploded. The good thing about the Viet Congs was that a lot of their equipment didn't go off.

I told them to give me a local anesthesia: "I want to watch everything you do on my legs." I don't want them to amputate it. Gung ho shit. But I was okay, and they got the frags out.

Once the NVA shot down a small observation plane, and we were looking for it. We saw these scouts for the NVA. One was a captain. The other was a sergeant. They were sharp. In the blue uniforms. They had the belt with the red star. They were bouncing across the rice fields, and we hidin'. They was walking through there, so we snatched them. Me and Davis.

We radio in, right? They sent the helicopter to pick us up, bring 'em back. Intelligence was shocked. The gooks wasn't in pajamas. They had on uniforms. They were equipped. Intelligence interrogated them, and they got the whole battalion to go out and look for the plane.

In the helicopter one of the gooks spitted in this lieutenant's face.

When we found the plane, it had been stripped. Nothin' but a shell. The pilot was gone.

We told intelligence the prisoners was ours. So finally, they gave them to the company and left.

I was still messing around in the plane when I heard these shots go off. The NVA captain tried to run, and he was shot. Shot about 20 times. They killed him.

So one of our officers looked at the NVA sergeant and just said, "You can have him."

So at that time they had this game called Guts. Guts was where they gave the prisoner to a company and everybody would get in line and do something to him.

We had a lot of new guys in the company that had never seen a dead NVA. And the officer was telling them to get in line. If they didn't do anything, he wanted them to go past and look at him anyway.

That's how you do this game Guts.

So they took the NVA's clothes off and tied him to a tree. Everybody in the unit got in line. At least 200 guys.

The first guy took a bayonet and plucked his eye out. Put the bayonet at the corner of the eye and popped it. And I was amazed how large your eyeball was.

Then he sliced his ear off. And he hit him in the mouth with his .45. Loosened the teeth, pulled them out.

Then they sliced his tongue. They cut him all over. And we put that insect repellent all over him. It would just irritate his body, and his skin would turn white. Then he finally passed out.

Some guys be laughing and playing around. But a lotta guys, maybe 30, would get sick, just vomit and nauseated and passed out.

The officer be yelling, "That could be your best friend on that tree. That could be you. You ever get captured, this could be you."

I don't know when he died. But most of the time he was alive. He was hollering and cursing. They put water on him and shaking him and bringin' him back. Finally they tortured him to death. Then we had to bury him. Bury both him and the lieutenant.

A couple of days later we found three guys from the 101st that was hung up on a tree, that had been tortured. Hands was tied. Feet was tied. Blood was everywhere. All you saw was a big, bloody body. Just butchered up. That's how they left GIs for us to see.

They didn't have name patch. All we knew was two was white, one black. And the airborne patch. We had to bury 'em.

Before the Tet Offensive, all the fighting was in the jungles. We might search and destroy some hamlet. But Tet Offensive, the snipers went in the cities. And we wasn't used to that street fighting.

We was in Tuy Hoa. And funny thing. Louis got in one of these little bunkers that the French had left on the street, like a pillbox. He was hiding. And we said, "Come on. We got to move out."

Louis said, "Hell, no. I ain't moving out. I'm safe. Nobody know where I'm at."

And we kept on saying, "Man, we gon' leave you here if you don't come on and move out."

And we start moving out.

And Louis said, "What the hell. Y'all can't do nothing without me anyway." And laughed.

Soon as he got out of his crouch behind the pillbox and got up, that's when he got hit. Got shot in the chest, in the head. A sniper. And we had to leave him. We had to leave him right there.

They gave us some half-ass story that they sent him home. They sent boxes home. A lot of times we couldn't get a helicopter in, the terrain was terrible. So we had to bury 'em. By the time the maggots ate them up, what they gon' get out the ground? If they find them.

"The night after Louis got killed, Taylor just broke down. I mean just boohoo and cry. Crying is kind of contagious. When one guy start crying, before you know it, you got a whole platoon of guys just sobbing.

And we all knew Louis was suppose to go home in a week.

But Taylor was just messed up. He would keep saying he couldn't take it no more.

He was always singing old hymns. I had him carrying 200 pounds of ammo once, and when I got to the hill to set up for the night, I said, "Taylor, where's my ammo?" He said, "Man, you know that song about loose my shackles and set me free? I had to get free about a mile down the road. I got rid of that stuff in that stream. Them chains of slavery."

This other time we were going through the wood, and this branch hit Taylor across the nose. He passed out, and would not move. Lieutenant told Taylor if he don't get up, I'll shoot you. He said, "You might as well shoot me, 'cause I feel like I'm already dead. I am not moving till I see the Red Cross helicopter come." So they carried Taylor in. The next thing I know, they told me Taylor got caught off limits in the city.

Ferguson was with him. See, they used to do things like getting a tooth pulled. You never tell them you had a toothache and fill it. Say pull it. That's two days in the rear. The doctor told Ferguson there wasn't no cavity. Ferguson said, "I don't care. It hurts. I want it out."

So Ferguson and Taylor suppose to be sick. But Taylor said he fell in love with one of them little dinks, and him and Ferguson was in the hootch with mama san. They fell asleep at night. And that's when the NVA come out, take over the cities. Taylor said a platoon of them was coming down the street. Taylor said, "I was laying there beside my baby. Then I think I couldn't pass for a gook. So I am ready to run at all times. My eyes was like flashlights. I didn't even blink. We stayed at the window all night."

When the sun came up, they took off. They couldn't get back in time. Top sergeant met them at the gate and said, "If y'all well enough to fuck, y'all well enough to fight." They got some suspended rank for being AWOL and was sent back to the field.

Then one night, Taylor was sitting on a hill trying to convince us that he saw the Statue of Liberty. He had been smoking, and there was a tree way out. He kept saying, "Sir Ford. Sir Ford. Ain't that the bitch?" I said, "What?" He said, "The world moves, right?" I said, "Right." He said, "Well, we getting closer to New York, 'cause I can see the bitch. Goddamn, that's the bitch, man."

They had to come give him tranquilizers.

Before I went home, the company commanders in Bravo and Echo got killed. And rumor said their own men did it. Those companies were pressed because the captains do everything by the book. And the book didn't work for Vietnam. They had this West Point thing about you dug a foxhole at night. Put sandbags around it. You couldn't expect a man to cut through that jungle all day, then dig a hole, fill up the sandbags, then in the morning time dump the sandbags out, fill your foxhole back up, and then cut down another mountain. Guys said the hell with some foxhole. And every time you get in a fire fight, you looking for somebody to cover your back, and he looking around to see where the captain is 'cause he gon' fire a couple rounds at him. See, the thing about Vietnam, your own men could shoot you and no one could tell, because we always left weapons around and the Viet Congs could get them.

The war never got worse than this time in April. The whole battalion was out in the jungles. We got attacked. We got hit bad. This was a NVA unit. This wasn't no Viet Cong. They were soldiers.

They would come on waves. The back unit didn't even have weapons. They would pick up the weapons from the units that scarified themselves and keep on coming. It made it look like we had shot this person and he fell and then kept on runnin' instead of somebody comin' behind him. It played a mental thing on you.

That's when we start hollering, "We gon' burn this jungle down. Get Puff out here, and get the mortars and flame throwers. Puff helped. It's a bad warship. It comes in with them rockets and them guns. Puff the Magic Dragon lets you know it's there.

But I was scared of Puff. He wounded about six of our guys. I ain't wanna see Puff. I was scared of Puff.

Then we called in for mortar. And the mortar squad hit about six or seven of us. Rounds dropped too short. Miscalculated or whatever.

Then I saw a guy that just came in country. A little white boy named Irving, came from Kansas City. Real nice fella; used to talk how the cattle comes down the street in Kansas City. He got shot in the head. And I went over and grabbed him. The bullet went through his eye. Real small hole. But I put my hands behind his head, and the whole back of his head came off in my hands. I just froze.

I was scared to drop it. Scared to move. I was just sittin' there. And this is where Davis helped.

Davis screamed, "Nigger, stop half-steppin'. We gotta move."

Then the lieutenant start yelling about hold your position, hold your position. Davis said, "The hell with some position. Move back. Move back."

We were getting hit terribly.

Davis knew it. And Davis was a private. A private.

Davis saved us.

When I got out of the service, I went back to Food and Drug, the lab technician thing. But I was carrying this pistol all the time, so people come up and say, "Why don't you go in the police department?"

I joined in December '69. And because I was a LURP and had these medals, they figured I wasn't scared of anything. So they asked me to work undercover in narcotics. I did it for 19 months. Around 7th and T, 9th and U, all in the area. The worst in D.C. I would try to buy drugs on a small scale, like $25. Heroin and cocaine. Then I gradually go up to where I could buy a spoon, $100. Then I could buy a ounce for a $1,000. I got robbed three times, hit in the head with a gun once. But my investigation was so successful that they didn't lock anybody up until it was all over.

I threw a great big party at the Diplomat Motel. I had 34 arrest warrants. I invited all the guys that I bought dope from. About 20 of them showed up. All dressed up, and everybody had Cadillacs and Mercedes. We had agents everywhere outside. Then I told them, "I am not a dope pusher like y'all scums." They laughed. I said, "Y'all scums of the earth selling dope to your own. Take the dope up in Georgetown if you want to do something with it. Heroin. Cocaine. Get rid of it." All of them laughed and laughed. And I said, "When I call your name, just raise your hand, 'cause you'll be under arrest for selling these heroins." And they laughed. And I call their names, and they raise their hand. Then these uniforms came in, and it wasn't funny anymore.

But they put out a $25,000 contract on me.

I was in Judge Sirica's court when they brought in the big dealer, Yellow Thompson. He had got a lot of confidence in me. Called me son all the time. He took me to New York and Vegas and showed me his connections in the Mafia and introduced me to some stars. He waved at me, and I waved back. Then they introduced everybody to the jury to make sure nobody in the jury knew any of the government witnesses. When they call on Special Agent Richard Ford, I stood up. And Thompson looked at me and started crying. He had a heart attack right there. I went to see him in the hospital though. I told him, "You cheap son-of-a-bitch. What's this twenty-five-thousand-dollar contract? But first of all, I don't have nothin' personal against you. I can't stand heroin dealers. I got children, and a family. I was on my job, and you wasn't on yours. If you was, you wouldn't have sold a newcomer that heroin." We got along terrific after that. But I had to go see this numbers man, White Top. And he and the man behind him took me down to 9th Street in this Lincoln to this club. Everybody sayin', "There go Rick, that no-good police." But White Top and this dude bought me a drink. They didn't drink nothing. Just said, "This is my son. Whatever he did, it's over with. This is my son." They let me go, because I was not touching the numbers, just the drugs.

I got the gold medal from the police department, and they sent me and my wife to Greece. I got the American Legion Award, too, 'cause I was a Vietnam veteran doing all this good police work. But I left the department, because they wanted me to testify against policemen taking bribes. I said if you want me in internal affairs, make me a sergeant. They said if

you want to stay in narcotics, we'll get you in the federal bureau.

I was a federal agent until this thing went down in Jersey. We was working police corruption. This lieutenant was stealing dope out the property office and selling it back on the street. But somethin' told me the investigation just wasn't right. We had a snitch telling us about the lieutenant. But he had all the answers. He knew everything. He knows too much. I think he's playing both ends against the middle. So one night, my partner and me are walking down this street going to meet the lieutenant to buy these heroins. This scout car comes driving down on us, hits us both, and the lieutenant jumps out and shoots me in the head. He knows that even if he didn't sell no dope, we gon' nab him. I didn't have no gun, but I reach like I do from instinct. And the lieutenant took off. He went to jail, and the prisoners tried to rape him, kill him.

I retired on disability, because the wound gives me headaches. I do a little private security work now for lawyers, and I try to keep in touch with Davis and the other guys.

Davis tried to get a job with the New Orleans police, but they said he was too short. When it comes to weapons, Sir Davis is terrific. But he's been in trouble. A drug thing, two assaults. He writes me sometimes. Tells me his light bulb is out. They trained us for one thing. To kill. Where is he gonna get a job? The Mafia don't like blacks.

Hill went home first. Said send him all our grenades. He was on his way to Oakland to join the Panthers. Never heard nothin' about him again.

Fowler got shot through the chest with a BAR. But he got home. He stays in trouble. He's serving 15–45 in Lewisburg for armed robbery.

Holmes got to computer school. He's doing okay in San Diego. I don't know what happened to Ferguson and Taylor.

Sir Drawers came over to see me for the Vietnam Veterans Memorial. He is still out of work. We marched together. When we got to the memorial, I grabbed his hand. Like brothers do. It was all swollen up.

We looked for one name on the memorial. Louis. We found it, and I called his mother. I told her it was nice, and she said she might be able to see it one day.

But I think the memorial is a hole in the ground. It makes me think they ashamed of what we did. You can't see it from the street. A plane flying over it can't see nothing but a hole in the ground.

And it really hurt me to see Westmoreland at the memorial, 'cause he said that we had no intentions of winning the war. What the hell was we over there for then? And the tactical thing was we fought it different from any way we was ever trained to fight in the States. They tell you about flanks, platoons, advance this. It wasn't none of that. It was just jungle warfare. You jumped up and ran where you could run.

We went to church on the Sunday after the memorial thing, I was doing pretty good about Vietnam the last five years, 'cause I was active a whole lot. If I ever sit down and really think about it, it's a different story.

My sister's husband was with me. He got shrapnel in his eye. His vision is messed up. There were 2,000 people in the church. And the pastor gave us space to talk, 'cause we were the only two that went to Vietnam. My brother-in-law is a correction officer at the jail. So we've always been kind of aggressive. Ain't scared that much. But we got up there to talk, and we couldn't do nothing but cry. My wife cried. My children cried. The whole church just cried.

I thought about Louis and all the people that didn't come back. Then people that wasn't even there tell us the war was worthless. That a man lost his life following orders. It was worthless, they be saying.

I really feel used. I feel manipulated. I feel violated.

Colonel
Fred V. Cherry
Suffolk, Virginia

Fighter Pilot
35th Tactical Fighter Squadron
U.S. Air Force
Karot (Thailand) Air Force Base
October 1964—December 1964
Takhli (Thailand) Air Force Base
May 1965—July 1965
October 16, 1965—October 25, 1965
Various Prison Camps, Hanoi
October 25, 1965—February 12, 1973

All day long these aircraft would be flying at very low altitudes. Very slow. You could see the pilot, and we would wave to him.

There was this Navy auxiliary base near where I lived in Suffolk, Virginia. World War II had started, and the Navy was training pilots there.

I could see them do combat maneuvering, and I said that's adventure. I was still in elementary school, but I knew I wanted to fly.

Then I heard about the Tuskegee Airmen, the black pilots being trained for the 99th Pursuit Squadron. They went over to North Africa and Italy. I was keeping real close track in *The Afro-American and the Norfolk Journal & Guide*, the black newspapers. Yeah, they were doing a good job. Matter of fact, when I read that Lucky Lester shot down these three Nazi planes, I thought this was great. I said to myself, I'm going to be a fighter pilot just as soon as I get old enough.

My parents were just rural people. My father was a laborer, plus he farmed truck crops. Beans and peas and potatoes. We always owned our property. He worked places like the fertilizer factory and the railroads, puttin' in the rails and ties. My mother was a housewife that worked in the fields in the farming season. All they had was elementary school.

There were eight of us—four brothers and four sisters. But we were all kind of tough. I guess we picked it up in the family. I never saw a weakness in the family. My parents were always fair in doing things for people. And we went to church, and they taught us what the Bible says: "Do unto others as you would have them do unto you."

My family was really respected by whites in that area—as much respect as a black could hope to get from a white at that time.

We lived in an area where there might be a white home next to a black home. Ain't no problem there. But you go over to the white farmhouse to get some homemade butter, and you had to "Miss" and "Mister" them. You had to give the whites that master-type respect all the time. The man next door would be *Mister* Gregory. If it came out of your mouth any other way, they wouldn't allow you to have whatever you wanted. They would call my mother Leola, and my father John. Whites always called blacks by their first name. It was sort of understood you had your place.

I remember one day when my older brother, James, was riding with another friend on two bicycles. He was maybe fifteen. One of those two-lane country roads. There weren't many cars that drove down the highways back then. Well, this car pulls along, and it's two white teenagers. I saw 'em reach out and hit James in the back of the head. The bicycle and he went end over end. They were laughing, and they probably said, "Knock that nigger over on his bike."

I was angry, but my mother tried to smooth it over for us juniors. She said, "Well, James is all right. He's not hurt, so don't worry about it. You don't know who it was, so you can't mention it to their parents." Nothing came of it, but it stuck in my mind.

Being in a rural area, there weren't segregated swimming pools or recreation centers where you had to face that kind of racism. But the schools were all segregated. The whites had buses. We had no buses. So on the rainy days, the snowy days, the half-full buses would drive past us, and we would just go on walkin' that 3 miles each way.

But East Suffolk High School, where we went, was a very good school, because back in those times, in the all-black schools, the teachers really cared. They really cared. You would learn, or you would get whacked a little bit. And which I think is great.

My father passed away when I was eleven, and I went to live with my sister Beulah and her husband, Melvin Watts, My mother wasn't too particular in that you had to go to school, but my sister was. She pushed me. She thought I should be a doctor. I felt that also for a while. I majored in biology in college at Virginia Union. But I later decided that medicine isn't really what I wanted to do. I couldn't do my best in it. What I really wanted to do was fly airplanes.

In my second year of college I heard that if you qualified in all respects, you only had to have two years of college to go from civilian life straight into aviation cadet training. So I went to see this Navy recruiter in Portsmouth. I didn't know that the Navy didn't have any black aviators. The recruiter told me to fill out this application for enlisted service. I said, "No. I want to be a pilot." He said, "Oh." And he told me that the individual I would have to talk to was not in the office, and I could stop in some other day.

I went back three more times, and I was told this commander was never in. On the fourth time, I saw this door creeping close. I knew he was there and had been there every time before. I just sort of exploded. I kicked the door open. He thought I was coming across the desk. I said a few choice words to him. They were rather obscene. Then I told him I didn't want any part of his Navy.

Two years later, just before I graduated from college, I went to Langley Air Force Base in Norfolk. I took a whole battery of mental and physical tests for flight school. There were 20 of us, and I was the only black. And this white sergeant did something that in that day he certainly didn't have to do. He congratulated me on the highest overall score in the group. In October of 1951 I started flight school.

In Korea I flew 53 missions in the F-89G fighter-bomber, close air support and interdiction, hitting bridges, dams, railroads deep behind enemy lines. We were carrying 1,000-pound bombs, napalm, 5-inch rockets, and .50-caliber machine guns. I never encountered enemy aircraft, but I had to worry about ground fire. I was hit in the tail pipe once while carrying napalm, but I made it home. It was almost totally dark. I say we had a quarter-mile vision. And I was hit at 50 feet. That's low. That's low. But I climbed up, and the air got thin enough to put the fire out.

I had no problems with the orders to go to Vietnam. It was just like the people in South Vietnam wanna be free to make their own decisions, to have a democratic government. And the Commies were trying to take over. And being a serviceman, when the commander in chief says time to go, we head out.

I'm flying a F-105 by now. It was fast. Mach 2.5. Had good range. Dependable. Comfortable. Good weapons. Good navigational systems. But it was primarily a tactical bomber.

We could carry up to 16 750-pound bombs. On a normal flight, we'd have 10, and then 2.5-inch rockets, and a 20-millimeter cannon, which was a real jewel. It was a far cry from what I could load on a F-84 or F-100.

The F-4 Phantom was certainly a better aircraft for air-to-air combat. And sometimes they would give us coverage. But the F-105 could carry a bigger load, faster and farther. I really loved that airplane.

In 1964 we mainly hit the supplies going down the Ho Chi Minh Trail in Laos. But in 1965 it was sort of open bombing against the North. The initial targets were radar installations. Then we went after military barracks, and some bridges and roads. At the time they didn't have the SAMs, just plain old .57-caliber antiaircraft weapons with radar control. But they were pretty accurate.

I was leading the squadron that day, the twenty-fifth of October '65. The weather was bad. But they sent my wingman up and said you got a mission. The Ironhand. That's the code name for the missile installations. So I rushed down and got briefed and picked up my maps. We had snake eyes, 500-pound target bombs. And CUBs. Cluster bomb utility. A pellet bomb. This would be my fiftieth mission in this war.

We refueled over Laos, the 19th Parallel. Then just east of Dien Bien Phu, we cut down to low altitude. I mean low. We call it the deck—50 to 100 feet. Just clearing the trees and sometimes below 'em to get under the radar net. I had to keep the wingman and everybody else higher than me. You gotta watch what's gonna be in the way of the wingman, 'cause he's not watching. He's watchin' the lead, and everybody's watchin' him. You flying for all four other guys.

We were on the deck 34 minutes at 500 knots when we reached the IP, the predetermined point, after which you don't make any deviations and just head for the target. And the maximum release altitude for the reference scan was 100 feet. To get the maximum effect for the bombing. Any higher, half of 'em be blowin' themselves up before they get to the ground.

About three minutes from the target, I could see 'em shootin' at me. Just rifle fire. Everybody carried a rifle down there. They just fired up in the air, and you run into it. Then I heard a thump. And I turned off the electrical stuff and hydraulics. I thought they hit something electrical.

I went right to the target, released my weapons, and started headin' out to the Tonkin Gulf, where the Navy could pick me up. The last thing I said to the flight was, "Let's get the F out of here."

Then smoke started to boil up from behind the instrument panel. Electrical smoke. I reached over to turn off the battery and the two generators. And before my hand got to the panel, the airplane exploded. Just blew up. The smoke was so dense, I couldn't see outside of the cockpit. I got a real jolt. Nothing like that thump. I couldn't see whether I was upright, upside down, or what. I just pulled the nose up a few degrees to give me the best ejection altitude. I ejected instantly. At 400 feet. And I prayed.

My lap belt didn't work automatically, so the parachute didn't open automatically. At the speed I was going, that would have ripped my parachute apart, and I would hit the ground with no chute. The maximum speed to eject at so it won't be fatal is 575 miles an hour. I was doing almost 700. The fact that these gadgets didn't work is why I'm sittin' here now.

I looked around, and I was still in the seat. I reached down and pulled my ripcord. I saw the wingman. I looked down. And boom, boom, boom. I hit the ground.

The wingman radioed back, "Our lead got out. We saw him hit the ground, but I don't think he was conscious."

It looked like I was lying down on the ground, but I was sitting actually. It was 11:44 A.M. I was two minutes from the coast.

I fell right into the arms of a dozen militia. They all had guns. And about a dozen kids with hoes. Now I thought they might chop me up into little pieces with all those farm tools, but they just stood back and giggled. I could hear the bullets zinging past that short time I was coming down, but once I hit the ground, they stopped shooting.

They wanted me to put up both hands. And I could only get up one hand. I didn't realize that my left shoulder was all smashed and my left wrist was broken. It wasn't painful at the time 'cause the nerves were dead initially. Well, I said damn. I can't be moving around. I had my .38 butt showin'. That was what they feared most. So I sort of leaned into my battered arm and shoulder, and from above my head I pointed to my left side. About three times of that, they got the picture. So they move in very slowly, and the first thing they did was relieve me of my piece. Then they took my hunting knife, and they kinda relaxed. Then they took the parachute and my anti-G suit. And they wanted me to get out of my flight suit. It's on very tight. And this Vietnamese wasn't gon' just slide it down, he wanted to cut it someplace. So he brought this knife down. And I scooted back. The knife ended up stickin' in the ground, right between my legs, an inch from my genitals. I was able to calm 'em enough to show 'em how it all works. I took one zipper, and I opened it. They thought that was fun. So they played with the zippers for a minute or so. Up and down. *Zzzzzzzz.* Now the guy with the knife, he's gonna cut my boots off. Well, I didn't want to part with my boots. I started kicking and rolling around on the ground. After a minute, whoever was in charge told him to let me keep my boots.

Now they got me dressed the way they want me, and they are going to walk me 3 miles to this village. I didn't know my ankle was broken, too. I was dusty, hot, sweaty, and naturally, pissed off 'cause I was shot down. Didn't wanna be there. I'm thinkin' about two, three, four months. I'm not thinkin' 'bout years. I'm not even thinkin' six months.

I was the forty-third American captured in the North. The first black. And we are 40 miles east, northeast of Hanoi.

As we got closer and closer to the village, the gongs were gongin'. And that's callin' out the people. So more and more people start to line up along the rice paddies. They were comin' from everywhere. And the militia took me inside this hut in the village. And a medic came in and put something like Mercurochrome on the cuts I got on my face when the instrument panel shattered. And I sat and I sat. After a while, they took all of my paraphernalia, my pens and my pencils, my watch and my Air Force class ring. Then they tied my elbows back behind me again. And they put a black cape over my white T-shirt. My flight suit was still tied around my waist. And they started trekking me down the road again. I didn't have any idea at the time, but I was going to walk 5 more miles to this vehicle.

My shoulder and this ankle beginnin' to pain. And you know how somethin's frightenin' and your heart starts to pound. I never had that. I guess I was too ornery.

Sort of a crowd is followin' me now. And this Vietnamese keeps runnin' up the back of my ankles with this bicycle. I managed to get hold of the handlebars of his bicycle, and I shoved he and bicycle over the hedgerow into the rice paddy. Naturally, he was terribly angry. And he came like he was coming to get me. The honcho sends him back and wouldn't let him go on with us.

Near this time, two jets come over the mountain really low and slow. They're lookin' for me. I'm sure they're honing in on my beeper in my parachute, which is probably back at the village. And the militia shove me in the rice paddy. Luckily the jets didn't see us, 'cause they would've shot us all up. They would think that I'm not there because my parachute is someplace else.

And this guy jumps on me, straddling my back. And he puts his automatic weapon right behind my ear with my nose pretty much in the dirt. And I said to myself, you know, this man might even shoot me.

When we got to the vehicle, they had a cameraman there. And he wanted to take pictures of me walkin' towards him. I wouldn't do it. I'd frown up and fall on my knees and turn my back. Finally, they quit. They never took any pictures. And they got me in the jeep.

And I'm tired and sleepy. My elbows are still tied, so I can't lean back. I kept nudging this guard back there with me, tryin' to tell 'em to loosen the nylon cord. He keep saying, "No. No. No." I was ornery. I tried to push him out of the jeep with my shoulders. He was sort of hangin' off the side when he yells somethin' to the guards up front. They were just constantly talkin' and gigglin'. Then they told him to loosen my arms. The first place they tried to interrogate me appeared to be a secondary school. And they put me in this hut. I did what I was s'posed to do. Name, rank, serial number, date of birth. And I started talking about the Geneva Convention. And they said forget it. "You a criminal."

It was about 500 people out in this schoolyard chattin' Vietnamese. And the interrogator said they said, "Kill the Yankee." I said, "Well, kill me. You are going to kill me sooner or later." So we went round and round, and they got tired of it.

When they were taking me back to the jeep, a Vietnamese reached through a little circle of people around me and rubbed my hand, as if I'm s'posed to rub off on him. Well, all the bolts went forward on the rifles. I don't know if the militia thought he was trying to stab me or what. But he just scooted down and went through the crowd like you see a snake go through the grass, just the top of the grass moving. I think if he'd been in the open, they probably would've shot him.

The next place I end up was Hoa Lo Prison, which we called the Hanoi Hilton. The first place Americans were brought for serious interrogation and torture. They played rough. And they took me to a room with stucco walls. We called it the Knotty Room. It was about ten o'clock, and I still hadn't eaten since I left the base.

They interrogatin' me all night. Asking me military questions. "Who was in your squadron?" They brought in my maps, which they found where the airplane crashed. They didn't have my point of departure. They didn't have my point of return. I knew what the headings were in my head. They said I killed 30 people. I told them I didn't hurt anybody. Then I made up stuff. I told them I was flying a RF-105. A reconnaissance plane for taking pictures. We don't have any such airplane. We had the capability, but they never made it operational. They said, "You no have RF-105s."

I said, "We sure do. I had one."

"How does it work?"

"I have no idea. The pilot push the button. Leave it on to where you s'posed to be. Then turns it off. That's all the pilot knows. Okay?"

Some time later, I saw in one of their magazines a picture of the tail of a F-105, and it was called a RF-105. I thought it had to be mine. I don't think anybody else told them that lie.

They would kick the chair out from under me and bang my head on the table. I thought, Damn, that shit really hurts. Then, I'd just relax and think of something pleasant. I would be still flying air-to-air combat. Anything far away from this. But I was totally exhausted, and my head would go down to sleep. And they would just pull it back up and bang it down.

Just before daybreak they took me to this cell. It had the biggest rats you ever saw in your life. They would gnaw through the bottom of the wooden door. And I was sleeping on a concrete floor. No blanket. Just my flight suit. After a few days, they gave me a mosquito net. And that was God's gift to get that mosquito net.

Every morning they would take me to a place we called Heartbreak. These cells were their torture chambers. Built-in leg irons. And very high security.

At the time, James Stockdale and Duffy Hutton, Navy pilots, and Tom Curtis, an Air Force buddy, were in the camp. They were the first guys I made verbal communication with. They gave me the little bit of information they had acquired and told me to hang in there with the Code of Conduct.

I was taken to Cu Loc Prison—the Zoo—in southwest Hanoi on November 16. A Navy guy, Rodney

Knutson, was in the cell next to me. In the morning and in the night one of us would tap one time and the other would answer with two taps. But I didn't see any Americans until the twenty-seventh, when they brought in Porter Halyburton, a Navy lieutenant jg, who got shot down five days before me. He looked like a scared rabbit, like I did.

Hally was a Southerner, who went to Sewanee Military Academy in Tennessee and Davidson College in North Carolina. The guards knew I was from the South, too. They figured under those pressures we can't possibly get along. A white man and a black man from the American South. And they got a long-term game to run.

At the time, Hally is a very handsome, young gent. Early twenties. Coal-black hair. And just what you expect a Frenchman would look like. I figured any white I saw in Vietnam other than our guys would be French. I thought he was a French spy put in my cell to bleed me of information.

He didn't trust me either.

He had a problem believing that I fly. And a major, too. He hadn't seen any black pilots in the Navy, and he didn't know anything about the Air Force. They had told him in the Navy that one reason blacks couldn't fly was 'cause they had a depth-perception problem.

For days we played games with each other. Feelin' each other out. We would ask each other a question. And we both would lie. He would change the name of the ship he came from. I didn't tell him much more than I told the Vietnamese, like I had flown out of South Vietnam. I figured he went back and told them the same lies I told him.

Finally, we got to the place where we could trust each other. It started when he told me about bathing. "When's the last time you bathed, washed up?"

I said, "Almost a month, I guess."

"Well, you should go at least every three or four days. I'll ask the guard."

Then he taught me the code. The first series of taps was in a line, and the next series in the column. Well, I learned it in reverse.

Hally said, "What in the hell is that?"

And I got vindictive. "That's what you told me."

"You learned it outta phase."

It didn't take long to learn it right. It's amazing how sharp the old mind gets when it doesn't have a lot to do.

Then he slipped out and kinda whispered it to Knutson next door.

Our cell door opened onto a porch. Then it was left down a hallway. We had peepholes. And if you caught the guard just right, you could slip out. But before long, they did something about the peepholes.

In December my ankle had swollen so big they let somebody come put a cast on it. They didn't x-ray it. But luckily it turned out okay. Only thing I haven't had trouble with since. My wrist had healed by itself, but I was in constant pain with my shoulder.

Early in February, when the bombing paused and President Johnson sent his fourteen-point peace plan to President Ho Chi Minh, they decided to schedule those of us still laying around injured for operations in case peace came and we'd be goin' home. On the ninth they operated on my shoulder and put me in a torso cast down to my hipline. But I didn't get a penicillin pill or a shot.

Ho Chi Minh gave President Johnson a very definite negative. The U.S. and its lackeys should withdraw all their troops from South Vietnam and allow the Vietnamese people to settle their own affairs. They said that from day one, and they said it when we left. And they got just that.

When they decided that we weren't going home, you were just left in the state that you were in. No medicine. No treatment. And I was in a bad state with this torso cast.

After a while, the incisions got infected. There are sores all over my body, and the pus is caking up. By early March, I'm just phasin' in and out. I'm totally immobile.

Hally was feeding me. And he always made me welcome to any part of his food. If he thought I'd want the greens out of his soup, he'd give them to me. After I got really bad, they gave me sugar for energy. It was really something desired by all of us. Put it on the bread, and it would taste pretty good. Hally had the opportunity to eat the sugar himself, but he didn't.

I don't know why, but I would dream then about vanilla wafers and canned peaches. I just felt like it would be the best thing to taste in the world.

I couldn't stand up. Hally would take me to the wash area, hold me against the wall while he manipulated his towel, wet it, soap it, and wash my whole body. I was an invalid.

I would tell him when I had to go to the bucket. He'd put me on the edge of the bunk. Lean me back so I wouldn't pass out. And sturdy me over the bucket until I do what I had to do.

He'd take whatever clothes he had to make me a doughnut to sleep on. Naturally it got covered with the drainage he would have to wash out. And the room smelled like hell. Oh, terrible. And Hally had to keep the wounded side of me by the window to try to keep some of the smell out.

I was just lying there dying.

And in the delirium I was having illusions like you can't believe.

I just would leave my body.

I would go right through the wall.

One time, when I was coherent, I told Hally, "We have B-58s in the war now." I had been on a mission in a B-58 the night before. "They gave me an air medal, but I told them to give it to Jerry Hopper, another guy in the squadron. I told 'em I have enough."

Hally says, "That right?"

"Yes. The war'll be over soon."

Another time I left my body and went into town. Before then, when they moved you, it was in blindfolds. And if you could peek, you couldn't tell much 'cause it was at night. But the first time I was able to see anything in daylight in Hanoi, I recognized a stream, bridges, and other things I saw when I left my body.

Then my temperature really got high. I was just burning. I wasn't eating anything. My body was eating itself. And I found myself in this little, sorta greasy-spoon restaurant, we would call it. It was in South Vietnam. I was hungry, and this Vietnamese lady was frying pork chops on this vertical grill. I'm just waiting to get my order to eat. And this little fella comes in and says he's from somewhere just in the middle of North Vietnam. Says he was at a radar site, and he took care of the air conditioning. I told him I'm a prisoner and I have to go back to North Vietnam. And I said I'm having problems with my air conditioning. He said he'd see what he could do for me when he got back to the radar base.

Well, I wake up. Sorta come around. And I think I'm dying. I just can't stand the heat. I open my eyes, and I see right up on my chest two little men, 'bout a foot high. Big eyes and big heads. They are dark, but I can't make out their features. Their hands are almost normal size. And I see them working around my chest. To me, it's my air conditioning. Just every few seconds I say, "Please hurry." Then my temperature would break. And I would think, Thank God they did it in time.

And I'm scared the guards will see them and take them away. I can't raise up to look for them, so I call Hally.

"Did you see anything off the end of the bunk?"

"Like what?"

"Well, do you see anything?"

"No."

"'Bout time for the guard, isn't it? You don't see anything look like little men?"

He looks again. "No. I don't see anything."

Hally didn't say, "Fred, have you gone crazy?" He was really cool. He accepted these little men and pretended they kept my air conditioning going.

Finally, on March 18, they took me to the hospital to take the cast off. I was down from 135 pounds to 80 pounds. When the guys in the camp saw 'em take me on a stretcher, they said, "He's gone. We'll never see Fred alive again."

When they took the cast off, a lot of skin came off with it. Then they washed me down with gasoline out of a beer bottle. That was 'bout the pits. I passed out from the fumes. I think my pulse stopped, because when I came to, they were slapping my arteries. Then they gave me a blood transfusion, fed me intravenously, and sent my butt right back to Hally.

The cast is off, but I'm still opened up. The flesh is draining away. The bed sores are opened up, 6, 7 inches up my back. Hally keeps my shoulder wrapped, but it's still smellin'.

On April 10, they finally operated. I was so weak they kept me there 22 days. They put me in a little damp room at the end of a hallway, away from everybody. The guard would bring me food twice a day, but he didn't particularly wanna feed me. I couldn't move my hands. I'm all hooked up. But these two teenage girls who cleaned the rooms would bring me fruit and candy. One would watch for the guard, while the other would take a whole banana and just stick it down my mouth. And when they gave me hard candy, they would try to tell me, don't let it get stuck in your throat.

After a while, I started to get a bad infection again. I mean really bad. It looks like gangrene is settin' in. So they decide to take me and John Pitchford—I think he got shot in the arm—to the hospital for an operation. It's the night of July 6, when they took everybody else to march down the streets of Hanoi.

This time there was no anesthetic. They just took a scalpel and cut away the dead flesh, scraped at the infection on the bones. I knew about what they should have to do, so I knew they were makin' it more painful than necessary, being very sadistic. I couldn't believe that a human being s'posed to be practicin' medicine was doing this.

Well, I knew they wanted me to cry out. Like a test of wills. We gon' break him.

Balls of perspiration was poppin' off me. Size of your fingertips. I was totally dehydrated. It was the worst straight pain I had yet known.

They had my face covered with a sheet. And they kept raising it to see if I'm going to beg for mercy, going to scream.

And each time they looked down at me, I would look at them and smile.

They kept at it for three hours. And I kept thinkin', I can take it.

When they gave up, I was still smilin'.

Hally got back to the cell first. The public had gotten unruly during the march. They could hardly control them. They were kickin' the guys, throwin' rocks at them. Hally was all black and blue.

When the guard brought me to the door, Hally gasped, "Fred."

Blood was running everywhere, down to my feet. Hally caught me, and put me in my bunk. "Fred, what in the world did they do to you?" He thought I had been where he had been.

I cried, "Oh, Hally."

We both shed a tear or two.

"No, no. I went to the hospital."

Four days later, the guards came to get Hally. They just walk in and say, put on your long-sleeve prison pajamas, gather your stuff, and let's go.

Tears start to roll down my eyes. I'm just hoping nothing happens to him.

We cried.

And he was gone. It took about two minutes.

It was the most depressing evening of my life. I never hated to lose anybody so much in my entire life. We had become very good friends. He was responsible for my life.

Then they moved in John Pitehford and Art Cormier. From August 4 to the end of the year, they would torture us once or twice a day. They wanted everything they could get about your personal life, your family. I would tell them anything, like I didn't have children. And they would make you redo it. You are tellin so many lies, they know you are lying.

They would cup their hands and hit you over the ears. And the guard would come up behind you and kick the stool out. Or make you stand on your knees with your hands in the air. Or stand at attention with your nose to the wall, both hands in the air. In my case, one hand is all I can get up.

There was an officer we called Dum Dum, because he really was kinda stupid. One day in August of 1967, he said, "You have a bad attitude, and you disobey camp regulations. You communicate with other criminals. You must be punished. You must have 'iron discipline.' I said, Oh, shit. The torture is starting again.

I ended up in a place we called the Gatehouse with Larry Guarino and Don Burns. Except when you would eat—twice a day if you're lucky—and go wash, they kept you in manacles and leg irons.

Dum Dum would order the fan-belt treatment, beating with strips of rubber. Or you would be struck with bamboo. And you would fall around the floor because of the irons.

In November they took us to a building called the Barn. Burns was already there. He had lost 30 pounds. He was death warmed over. I was coughing up a big lump of somethin'. it was too dark in the damn cell to see what I was spittin' in the night bucket. We took a little white pot from where we bathed back to the cell, and I coughed into it.

I says, "Damn, it's blood."

Larry says, "We gon' have to tell the officer."

"No. No. I ask them for something, they gon' ask me for something. I ain't giving nothing." Not after three months of having my ass beaten.

"Well, we're going to because there's something wrong." Thank God he did.

Some days later they x-rayed me at the hospital. After they brought me back, this officer came in. I knew something was wrong. This officer got so nice. But he just told me I had a problem. Not until early February do they tell me I have a bone that's in my lung, very close to my heart. I'm thinkin' it came off the rib cage from the beatings. I knew the shoulder area had fused together.

But they didn't open me up until the first of May. They removed my seventh rib to get the chips out. And when they put me back together, they did one thing I'm sure was intentional. They left some nondissolvable stitches in.

The Vietnamese guarding my hospital room would make me get up and mop the floor. But this lady who worked in the kitchen sorta chewed him out when she saw it. He wasn't the worst guard in the world, because he would close the door so nobody else would see her moppin' the floor instead of me. And she would bring me whole loaves of bread and put them in the drawer by the head stand. She knew nobody was gonna look in there, because they didn't want to touch anything I touched as sick as I always was.

They brought me back to the camp on May 27 and kept me in solitary. That stretch would run 53 weeks, the longest of 700 days of solitary that I would have.

Now they want me to make tapes, write statements denouncing the war, denouncing our government, and telling young GIs, especially black ones, they don't have any business in Vietnam fightin' for the American imperialists.

They want it from me more than anybody because I was the senior black officer. They wanted it bad. And by this time, our black guys are doing good work, hurtin' 'em down South.

Until the end of November they interrogated me four or five hours a day. Two of 'em, the good guy and the bad guy. The bad guy never gets to be the good guy. But the vice camp commander, he swings both ways. We called him Lump. He had a tumor on his forehead. The good guy was Stag. That's an acronym for Sharper Than the Average Gook. He was a very good interrogator. He read a lot of novels, and he knew black literature. He had read *Raisin in the Sun* and *Invisible Man*. He knew more about Malcolm X than I did. And we was versed in Stokely Carmichael's philosophy. Absolutely, Stokely was helping them with broadcasts from Hanoi.

In those brainwashing sessions, Stag would say, "Xu, we will change your base, your foundation."

They called each of us by a Vietnamese name. A *xu* is a little brass coin, like a penny. Maybe they gave me the name because of my color. Regardless, they made me feel that I was worth less than a penny.

I said, "You tryin' to brainwash me?"

And he would back off a little. They hated the word brainwash. Scared 'em.

Stag and Lump couldn't understand why I couldn't be on their side, on the side of another colored race. I told them, "I am not Vietnamese. My color doesn't have nothin' to do with it. We have problems in the U.S., but you can't solve them. Like you, I am a uniformed soldier, if I have you in the position you have me, I wouldn't expect you to do what you want me to."

I'm being as tactful as I can."

"A soldier's a soldier. Things go on that we have no control over. I'm still an officer in the United States services. I will respect that, and I would hope that you will respect that of me. I can't do what you ask."

They never got to home plate. Just like when they beat me, I always kept in mind I was representing 24 million black Americans. If they are going to kill me, they are going to have to kill me. I'm just not going to denounce my government or shame my people. All this time the wound don't heal up, because of these stitches. They looked like fishing cord to me. All black. But they're swearing there wasn't anything there. It would heal up.

They say, "No, no. These honorable stitches. Don't have to take out."

When I asked for a Band-Aid to cover the hole, Stag said, "We don't have. Many injured Vietnamese. We must use all medicine for Vietnamese."

I was hemorrhaging daily. And one time I woke up, and the stuff comin' out of the hole looked green. I am having a serious problem.

So when I go to interrogation, I ask for a pill. They said no. So I start quiverin' and shakin' on the stool. Stag starts to get excited, and he has a guard take me to my cell. Then they bring me out into the yard, so all the guys can see them give me medication. And when they pulled the needle of penicillin out of my arm, I was so infected, honest to goodness, that it felt like I was gettin' ready to explode. My body was so poisoned, I was about as sick as any time before.

The next day they took me to the hospital, took the stitches out, and cleaned up the hole. They knew exactly where the stitches were. And from that day, November 28 to the next February, 1969, they stopped puttin' the pressure on.

They put me back with Art Cormier in April. And for several days I was coughin' up blood clots in the mornin'. I think it was because I was tryin' to exercise, primarily runnin' in place. And I had to cut that out.

One morning I spit into a piece of paper, because it felt like somethin' in my throat that wasn't normal.

I said, "Art, you won't believe this."

He said, "What you got?"

"Look at this."

It looked like a piece of regular fishing cord. Almost one year to the day they had operated, I had coughed up a piece of the stitching.

So we showed it to the guard, and he sent for the medic. Then they gave me some antibiotics.

I had been coughing up so much blood and mucus that the stitching was coming out that they hadn't removed.

I stayed With Art until the escape attempt May 10. Ed Atterbury and John Dramesi dyed themselves with a mix made from iodine pills, went through the roof and over the wall, shorting out the electrical shock on the barbed wire. But they were captured before morning. They brought them back blindfolded to the headquarters building in the camp. Then they were taken off to torture. Atterbury was never seen again.

By now we had secret committees for everything. We had the morale committee. We had an entertainment committee. Education committee. And, of course, we had the escape committee. And that was the one they really wanted to know about now.

So for months they really got hard on us. There was a shortage of water and toilet paper. They cut down your bath time to once every two weeks. No more cigarettes. And they nailed boards over the windows, so there was no fresh air. And they separated the senior officers, like me and Art and Bud Day, and worked us over with bamboo and rubber straps in the interrogation room. I don't think anyone got it nearly as bad as Bud and Dramesi.

It was no point in me thinkin' about escape at the Hanoi Hilton with only one good hand and one good leg. And I just forgot about gettin' over the wall. It was too high. I didn't have anything in my room to climb up on. And there was broken glass cemented to the top of the wall. Since they drove me in from forty miles, I knew all the checkpoints. You're not goin' anyplace. And at the Zoo, the senior officer would never approve anybody as injured and crippled as I was trying it. But I always thought about it.

And we always thought about rescue. We had a whole plan for aidin' any outside force that came to rescue us. We were organized into teams to go after the guards. We had plans to take over. We knew who would go to which doors first.

I learned about the Son Tay raid when they took us all to the Hanoi Hilton. The Green Berets got in there but found no Americans. That was in November of 1970. We put the story together from drawings the South Vietnamese prisoners made and left for us to find. They showed something like a C-130 transport, walls, guards, and bodies on the ground.

Not more than a dozen guys ever did anything that was aid to the enemy. Most of them were young troops, Army and Marine, who were captured in the South. But there were two senior officers who refused to take orders from us, made tapes for them to play on Radio Hanoi, and met with the antiwar people, the Jane Fonda and Ramsey Clark types.

Those two got good treatment. Good treatment. Extra food. Different food. Stuff to read. They could stay outside most of the day. They didn't lock 'em up until late in the evening. And they had fish bowls in their cell.

We were furious. And the Vietnamese knew it. They wouldn't let us get close to them. They would have been hurt very badly. Or worse.

I had less respect for those two than I did for our captors. Most of us did. We considered them traitors then. And I feel the same way today.

A few guys went through deep depressions and weren't cooperatin' with us as much as they should. But that is normal when you go through a deep depression. We just wouldn't let them quit. We would just keep bangin' on their walls and tell them if the guard hears, you are just as involved as us, so you might as well bang back. And it worked. They would start answering.

No matter how rough the tortures were, no matter how sick I became, I never once said to myself, I want to take my own life or quit. I would just pray to the Supreme Being each morning for the best mind to get through the interrogations, and then give thanks each night for makin' it through the day. And you would meditate with your cellmate. Or tap the letter C from wall to wall through the camp. Then everyone would stop for silent prayer. C was the call for church.

Man, did we miss the movies. And when we finally got together, we have a movie committee, too. Bradley Smith, a Navy guy, could give you the best movie reviews you could ever hope for in your life. He would hardly miss a detail. Last almost as long as the movie. You could just close your eyes and see it.

John Pitchford was a racin' enthusiast. He knows every horse ever raced. He could do the same thing with a Kentucky Derby race Bradley did with a movie.

But I was fortunate to know one guy who talked sex from the time he got up until the time he was sleepin'. That's every day. And I really tuned it in. For the first several months, I was kind of pushin' it in the background. Then for months and months I was too far gone to think about it. And when you become more relaxed, natural things happen. If you didn't masturbate, you'd have wet dreams.

Man, in solitary, in the darkness, you would see everything you have ever done. You would fantasize anything you wanted. The mind goes like a computer. It picks up from everywhere, compensating for all the deprivations that you're goin' through.

Women? I had fantasy affairs with the ordinary women that I met in my lifetime. I had fantasy affairs with the most beautiful women in the world. Jewels of women. I did movie stars. I never would've been so successful out here.

I always wanted to race cars. I would race cars for hours on a race track. And I've never been on one in my life. And I would do air-to-air combat. And I would calculate and recalculate a bomb release. Lots of that.

And I would re-create the times I'd go picnicking with my children. Play ball with the boys. And come home and give everybody a ride through the area on a motor scooter. And I would imagine what size they are now.

In my dreams I always went somewhere and had to go right back, or go to the airport but the plane had left.

One time I was home. My daughter was walkin' down the country path. She was cryin'. And I never got to ask her why. I had to go back.

When I was shot down, the Air Force got my family out of Japan back to Virginia as soon as possible. Donald was twelve, Fred was ten, Debbie was eight, and Cynthia was six. Beulah sheltered them until they found a house near Langley, and they had all the facilities, Navy and Air Force, they needed within 15 minutes.

My wife got my first letter in December of 1969. My mother got to see it before she died of a stroke a few months later. She died believin' I was comin' home.

I got my first letter from home in May of 1970. From my sister. She had a helluva time gettin' forms from the Air Force to write to me or to send packages. 'Cause she wasn't the next of kin.

My wife was tellin' the kids that I was dead. I wasn't comin' home.

In November '72 I received a letter from my oldest son.

By then we knew the negotiations were going on in Paris. We could hear the B-52s. And we knew that they were going to solve it. When the bombing stopped, we knew they didn't have any more missiles. And that the agreements were going to be signed.

The sick and wounded, the guys who had been there the longest, were the first to fly out. But the Vietnamese sorta squeezed in the guys who had gone along with them. I guess that was more payoff for being traitors.

The first meal I wanted when I got to the Philippines was sausage and eggs.

I told the dietician, "One platter of scrambled eggs. One platter of sausage patties. Laid on two plates." She said, "But, sir. it's five o'clock in the afternoon."

"I don't care."

She thought I had been to sleep and woke up thinking it was morning.

She brought the two plates. And I ate it. I ate it. I ate it.

Then I called Beulah.

She said, "You don't have a very nice situation to come back to."

I didn't ask any questions.

I said, "I guess I understand."

I didn't receive a single letter or package from my wife. And I'm not crazy. She's either dead, or she's taken off. I was really hopin' it was the way it was. I was hopin' it would be that way than she died.

"How are the kids?"

She said, 'They're okay.'"

Then Beulah told me the boys had dropped out of high school and were in the Army.

I thought they would have been in school, but little did I know.

General Chappie James was handling the return of POWs. We were old friends, and he knew about my situation at home. So he sent a friend of ours, Colonel Clark Price, to escort me home.

Clark told me another man was involved. A child was born in October '69. A girl. The money was gone. My allotments. Salary. Everything. And the kids were in the Army.

I didn't even ask him about my coins. I got depressed; the boys weren't in school.

I wanted to be taken to Norfolk Naval Hospital in Portsmouth. That was closest to home. But Clark said Andrews Air Force Base near Washington, D.C., might be better, considering the situation I was returning to. I guess many people were afraid I might have been crazy enough to do somethin' violent. They didn't want to put me where the sparks might fly.

I asked to see Beulah and her husband. My sons made arrangements to get there. My daughters didn't come at first. They were living with my wife. Even after my name appeared in the newspapers that we were being released, she still told them I wasn't coming home. It was mistake.

When she did come to Andrews, I told Clark I didn't want to see her.

Clark said, "I think you should."

"Okay."

I wouldn't see her with the door closed. My attorney told me not to put myself in a position where I could have the opportunity to cohabitate.

I asked her to be reasonable, to agree to an uncontested divorce so the stuff won't come out and embarrass the kids.

She said no, she didn't want a divorce. And she tried to fight it. I understand that, too. You been gettin' a nice fat check all these years, and all of a sudden, you ain't got it. Who's gonna take care of this and that?

There was no waiting period for the divorce. 'Cause I'd been separated seven and a half years.

I sued the Air Force because they were negligent in handling my money while I was away. About $150,000. And the U.S. Court of Claims upheld me. In the services we have volunteers and active-duty people who look after families split apart like mine was. They knew every letter that went one way or the other, so they knew she wasn't writing me. Something's gotta be wrong. They let her take the money out of my account to have the child in a civilian hospital. They didn't question that. The $450 a month allotment that was going to my savings bank? They gave her that, too. A form was signed on October 25, 1965, three days after I was shot down. It had to be forged. But the people handlin' the POW families were so into keepin' these families quiet, they'd do anything.

I hope my case sets a precedent. A serviceman who gets in a position like mine must be better looked after in the future.

They gave me an extensive battery of mental and physical tests at Andrews. They said the best thing they could give me was a little more forward movement in my arm.

I said, "No. What the hell. I've lived with it all these years and got used to it."

The only time it's aggravating is when I'm trying to do something like hang a picture. Or reach over my head. Now I can change a light bulb almost as fast with one hand as you can with two.

Physically, I can never recover totally. I still suffer muscle spasms. My eyes are not as good as they should be at this point in my life. That's because of all the periods of darkness. The years of darkness. And I don't hear too well out of my left ear. That was where the right hook usually got to first. But I still feel extremely fortunate.

They gave me the Air Force Cross, two Bronze Stars, and two Purple Hearts for resisting the enemy. I had already received the Distinguished Flying Cross and the Silver Star before for action in combat.

I had reached the rank of full colonel two months before my release.

In September of '81 I retired. Seventy percent disability. Thirty years.

I never dreamed about Vietnam. Not once since comin' back. But I still think about how we could have won the war. It should have been planned to hit the military targets early. It was only near the end that we started. And there would have been a lot less lives lost. And with proper leadership South Vietnam would've lasted a hell of a lot longer than it did. The war just went the way it did because the military was not allowed to win it. That's all.

I don't harbor no animosities against the Vietnamese people at all. North or South. Except as individuals. Isolated cases.

I guess I would still like to get my hands on Dum Dum. I'd like to have Dum Dum. I would know Dum Dum anyplace.

There were Vietnamese who were compassionate. The ones who fed me with bananas and pieces of candy in the hospital, taking a great risk to do that. And the doctor who acted like a doctor whatever the policy was in treating a prisoner. And the guard who caught me red-handed communicatin'. And he refused to turn me in because of my health being on the low side at the time. All he said was, "No, Xu. No. No."

After the release, I kept in touch with Hally. In 1977 he spent two weeks with me while he was doing research at the Pentagon for his master's degree. I gave him the key to my home in Silver Spring, Maryland. I gave him the key to a car.

We talked about how we looked at each other the first time we met. We talked about what we learned from each other. We remembered certain guys and tried to track down where they were. We rehashed the whole thing.

Naturally, I thanked him again for really, really saving my life. Other guys would've done the same thing, okay? But they didn't have the opportunity.

One daughter—the one who cried in my dream—lives with me now and goes to college. And back home in Suffolk there is a Colonel Fred Victor Cherry Scholarship Fund to help capable kids who run short of money get to College.

And I speak across the country for the Tuskegee Airmen's Association—black fighter pilots of the last three wars—telling young black people to study engineering, science, and technology.

Maybe one of those young black lads that hears me will walk across a field one day, look up at an airplane, like I did so long, long ago, and say, "I'm going to fly. I'm going to be a fighter pilot."

Document 23.6 President Nixon's "Vietnamization" Policy

The Vietnamization policy was a plan for the withdrawal of American forces in Vietnam, and a system to provide aid and advice to the South Vietnamese military, which would also bear the brunt of their country's defense. The following speech delivered by Nixon was televised in November 1969, outlining his proposal.

President Nixon Announces the "Vietnamization" of the War

Richard M. Nixon

Let me briefly explain what has been described as the Nixon doctrine—a policy which not only will help end the war in Vietnam but which is an essential element of our program to prevent future VietNams.

We Americans are a do-it-yourself people. We are an impatient people. Instead of teaching someone else to do a job, we like to do it ourselves. And this trait has been carried over into our foreign policy.

In Korea and again in Vietnam, the United States furnished most of the money, most of the arms, and most of the men to help the people of those countries defend their freedom against Communist aggression.

Before any American troops were committed to Vietnam, a leader of another Asian country expressed this opinion to me when I was traveling in Asia as a private citizen. He said: "When you are trying to assist another nation defend its freedom, U.S. policy should be to help them fight the war, but not to fight the war for them."

Well, in accordance with this wise counsel, I laid down in Guam three principles as guidelines for future American policy toward Asia:

- First, the United States will keep all of its treaty commitments.
- Second, we shall provide a shield if a nuclear power threatens the freedom of a nation allied with us or of a nation whose survival we consider vital to our security.
- Third, in cases involving other types of aggression, we shall furnish military and economic assistance when requested in accordance with our treaty commitments. But we shall look to the nation directly threatened to assume the primary responsibility of providing the manpower for its defense. . . .

The defense of freedom is everybody's business—not just America's business. And it is particularly the responsibility of the people whose freedom is threatened. In the previous administration we Americanized the war in Vietnam. In this administration we are Vietnamizing the search for peace.

The policy of the previous administration not only resulted in our assuming the primary responsibility for fighting the war but, even more significantly, did not adequately stress the goal of strengthening the South Vietnamese so that they could defend themselves when we left.

The Vietnamization plan was launched following Secretary [of Defense] Laird's visit to Vietnam in March. Under the plan, I ordered, first, a substantial increase in the training and equipment of South Vietnamese forces.

In July, on my visit to Vietnam, I changed General Abrams' orders so that they were consistent with the objectives of our new policies. Under the new orders, the primary mission of our troops is to enable the South Vietnamese forces to assume the full responsibility for the security of South VietNam. . . .

We have adopted a plan which we have worked out in cooperation with the South Vietnamese for the complete withdrawal of all U.S. combat ground forces and their replacement by South Vietnamese forces on an orderly scheduled timetable. This withdrawl will be made from strength and not from weakness. As South Vietnamese forces become stronger, the rate of American withdrawal can become greater. . . .

If the level of infiltration or our casualties increase while we are trying to scale down the fighting, it will be the result of a conscious decision by the enemy.

Hanoi could make no greater mistake than to assume that an increase in violence will be to its advantage. If I conclude that increased enemy action jeopardizes our remaining forces in Vietnam, I shall not hesitate to take strong and effective measures to deal with that situation.

This is not a threat. This is a statement of policy which as Commander in Chief of our Armed Forces I am making in meeting my responsibility for the protection of American fighting men wherever they may be.

My fellow Americans, I am sure you can recognize from what I have said that we really only have two choices open to us if we want to end this war:

- I can order an immediate, precipitate withdrawal of all Americans from Vietnam without regard to the effects of that action.

Department of State Bulletin, November 24, 1969.

- Or we can persist in our search for a just peace, through a negotiated settlement if possible or through continued implementation of our plan for Vietnamization if necessary—a plan in which we will withdraw all of our forces from Vietnam on a schedule in accordance with our program, as the South Vietnamese become strong enough to defend their own freedom.

I have chosen this second course. It is not the easy way. It is the right way. It is a plan which will end the war and serve the cause of peace, not just in Vietnam but in the Pacific and in the world.

In speaking of the consequences of a precipitate withdrawal, I mentioned that our allies would lose confidence in America.

Far more dangerous, we would lose confidence in ourselves. Oh, the immediate reaction would be a sense of relief that our men were coming home. But as we saw the consequences of what we had done, inevitable remorse and divisive recrimination would scar our spirit as a people. . . .

If [this plan] does succeed, what the critics say now won't matter. If it does not succeed, anything I say then won't matter.

I know it may not be fashionablea to speak of patriotism or national destiny these days. But I feel it is appropriate to do so on this occasion.

Two hundred years ago this nation was weak and poor. But even then, America was the hope of millions in the world. Today we have become the strongest and richest nation in the world. The wheel of destiny has turned so that any hope the world has for the survival of peace and freedom will be determined by whether the American people have the moral stamina and the courage to meet the challenge of free-world leadership.

Let historians not record that when America was the most powerful nation in the world we passed on the other side of the road and allowed the last hopes for peace and freedom of millions of people to be suffocated by the forces of totalitarianism.

And so tonight—to you, the great silent majority of my fellow Americans—I ask for your support.

I pledged in my campaign for the Presidency to end the war in a way that we could win the peace. I have initiated a plan of action which will enable me to keep that pledge.

The more support I can have from the American people, the sooner that pledge can be redeemed; for the more divided we are at home, the less likely the enemy is to negotiate at Paris.

Let us be united for peace. Let us also be united against defeat. Because let us understand: North Vietnam cannot defeat or humiliate the United States. Only Americans can do that.

Chapter 23 Worksheet and Questions

1. How did U.S. foreign policy evolve from World War II to the end of the Vietnam Conflict?

_____

_____

_____

_____

_____

_____

_____

_____

_____

_____

2. How did the Vietnam Conflict differ from previous American wars?

_____

_____

_____

_____

_____

_____

_____

_____

_____

_____

3. In Lyndon Johnson's address to the Congress regarding the Gulf of Tonkin incident, what reasons were given for U.S. military involvement in Vietnam?

_____

_____

_____

_____

_____

_____

_____

_____

_____

_____

4. Discuss the impact of American protest movements during the Vietnam War.

_____

_____

_____

_____

_____

_____

_____

_____

_____

_____

_____

5. Discuss the experiences of American soldiers in Vietnam—compare/contrast the difference between the experiences of the African-American troops and White troops.

_____

_____

_____

_____

_____

_____

_____

_____

_____

_____

_____

_____

_____

_____

_____

_____

_____

_____

_____

_____

_____

_____

_____

Watergate: Our Long National Nightmare

Car 727 . . . open door at the Watergate Office building . . . possible burglary . . . see the watchman. With that police call in Washington D.C. and the arrest of the burglars in the offices of the Democratic National Chairman, Watergate became part of United States political and historical record. Watergate, the crime, was a failed burglary attempt. Watergate, the cover-up, was about hiding years of illegal actions by the Nixon Administration. Some historians argue that both were inevitable, just waiting for the "right" man to be in the White House to abuse the powers of the government to a breaking point.

Why was Watergate "inevitable"? Some historians point to the Cold War, and the growth of wiretapping and secret operations in conducting national affairs. By the 1960s both the FBI and the CIA were employed illegally to spy on political opponents, or engaged in burglary against radicals and alleged subversives. The Cold War prompted the growth of the Imperial Presidency, with administration powers expanding without restraint, and "emergency powers" allowing the government to engage in undeclared wars or to take any action in the name of "national security."

The trappings of the presidency increased along with the powers. Instead of the representative of the common American, by 1972 the President commanded a fleet of 5 Boeing 707s, 11 Jetstars, 16 helicopters, and 3 yachts. Private retreats at Camp David, San Clemente, and Key Biscayne were maintained at public expense. Were presidents losing touch with the democratic ideal of the nation?

Two other factors fueled Watergate. One was the desire of the Nixon White House for absolute control of information and secrecy, and the other was a desire to win the 1972 presidential election in historic fashion. When Dr. Daniel Ellsberg, an official in the Defense Department, leaked the *Pentagon Papers* to the *New York Times*, the Nixon Administration challenged their publication in the courts, and lost 6-3 in the Supreme Court. Furious at the leaking of a real history of United States involvement in Vietnam, and concerned that the truth might cost support for the war, Nixon created the "Plumbers." Officially designed to stop leaks, this White House Special Investigations Unit spent most of its time attacking designated political enemies and anti-war advocates. As the President himself declared, they were not going to worry about legal niceties, but "we are going to use any means" against his enemies. (At the same time the Plumbers were created, President Nixon advocated a special congressional investigation committee, sure that it would find a circle of Jews in the government and media who were out to get him.) The Plumbers burglarized the office of Ellsberg's psychiatrist in an attempt to find damaging information for use in court or as blackmail. They investigated the private lives, juvenile court records, and mail of Nixon critics, manufactured and planted false information with friendly newspaper columnists, and justified every action as national security operations. President Nixon and Charles Colson advocated burglarizing or fire-bombing the Brookings Institution, a moderate Washington think-tank, to get the copy of the *Pentagon Papers* stored there. The actions of the Plumbers were at the heart of the abuse-of-power charges against the President, and the Watergate cover-up was intended to protect the White House from being linked to their illegal activities. Chief Plumber G. Gordon Liddy reported directly to John Ehrlichman, the president's chief domestic policy advisor.

After winning the presidency in 1968 with a minority of the popular vote, Richard Nixon wanted to win by a historic landslide in 1972. The Federal Election Campaign Act required that all donations and expenses over $100 be reported, in an attempt to rein in influence-buying and runaway election costs. To get around legal requirements and allow the President to appear above politics, the Committee to Re-Elect the President (CREEP) was formed. Day-to-day affairs of the campaign were controlled by Attorney General John Mitchell, who oversaw millions of dollars of illegal contributions entering CREEP safes. To gather "political intelligence" on their enemies, the Plumbers were transferred to CREEP, where they conducted a campaign of dirty tricks to damage the reputations and end the campaigns of many prominent Democrats. In late 1971, Liddy presented an idea to the Attorney General and other leaders for political sabotage of the Democratic Convention, including the use of wiretaps, rigged photographs, and hired call girls to compromise various Democrats. When that plan was rejected, the backup was bugging the offices of Larry O'Brien at Democratic National Headquarters.

Less than a week after the June 17, 1972 burglary, President Nixon was involved in the cover-up. He was concerned that Howard Hunt knew too much about earlier White House operations, discussed hush money to buy silence, asked if Liddy was willing to have everything pinned on himself, suggested using the CIA to stop the FBI investigation, and authorized millions in bribes to keep the burglars quiet. Early plans unraveled when Judge John Sirica ordered the defendants to tell who ordered the burglary, and threatened to sentence them to 40 years in prison for refusing to tell. At this, one of the defendants, James W. McCord, sent a letter to the judge, saying they all committed perjury at the urging of John Dean, Counsel to the President, and John Mitchell, the United States Attorney General. In a classic attempt at damage control, the President had a televised address (see Document 24.1) and announced the resignation of his top aides, all of whom were already named in connections to the cover-up.

In May 1973 the United States Senate established a select committee to investigate Watergate under the leadership of North Carolinian Sam Ervin. Over the next few months the committee and the United States public learned of other burglaries and illegal actions sanctioned by the White House, learned that the highest-ranking law enforcement officer in the country (John Mitchell) personally approved criminal actions to benefit the Nixon re-election, and learned that the White House had an "enemies list" used by the Internal Revenue Service and other agencies to attack them. But the greatest shock came when Alexander Butterfield testified under oath on July 13th that there was a recording system in the Oval Office, and that "everything was taped." This meant that every claim of criminal wrong-doing could be checked against the actual record.

For the next year, special prosecutors, the Senate Watergate Committee, the House Judiciary Committee, and the President struggled over the tapes. President Nixon claimed "executive privilege" for the tapes and refused to hand them over, a claim that would be rejected at every court level. When Special Prosecutor Archibald Cox pressed the President for the tapes, Nixon ordered his new Attorney General, Elliot Richardson, to fire Cox. Richardson refused, and resigned as a matter of principle. Nixon then ordered the Deputy Attorney General William Ruckelshaus to fire Cox, and when he refused Nixon fired him instead. Solicitor General Robert Bork, now acting AG, fired Cox, later declaring that if this is what the President wants it is right. The outrage over these actions, known as the Saturday Night Massacre, forced Nixon on the defensive. Under pressure, he begins to release the tapes, and a new Special Prosecutor, Leon Jaworski, is named.

But even the gradual release of tapes raised questions of White House honesty. First Nixon's lawyers announced that two of the nine tapes no longer existed, and then revealed that eighteen and a half minutes of a crucial June 20, 1972 conversation between Haldeman and the President had been somehow erased. The investigating committees consulted electronics experts, who when asked if the erasure could be an accident, agreed it would have to be an accident repeated at least five times. Alexander Haig, the new White House Chief of Staff, cynically suggested that some "sinister force" erased the tape. In April 1974 the President refused to turn over 64 more subpoenaed tapes, but provided the Judiciary Committee with heavily edited transcripts. These transcripts hurt his image as much as his refusal to obey the courts. The foul language, anti-Semitism, and paranoia in the transcripts offended the President's allies, and gave the nation a picture of a small-minded and vindictive man desperately holding onto power by any means.

With the accumulated evidence, the House Judiciary Committee voted three articles of impeachment on July 27–30, 1974. Five days later the "Smoking Gun" tape is released, showing the President planning the cover-up days after the break-in. Haldeman later declared that Nixon orchestrated the cover-up from the very beginning. Facing certain impeachment in the House of Representatives, and conviction and removal from office in the Senate, Richard Nixon resigned from office on August 9, 1974.

During the course of the scandal, Vice President Spiro Agnew resigned and was jailed for income tax evasion. Forty other administration officials were indicted or jailed for crimes. While Richard Nixon spent the next 20 years rehabilitating his reputation and fighting to keep the rest of the tapes "silent," they became public after his death. The 3,700 hours of Nixon White House tapes released between 1996 and 2000 confirm once and for all his guilt.

Considering the Evidence in the Readings

In the following documents you get a brief insight into the workings of the Nixon White House. Remember to consider his goals and audience in his public speeches, compared with the bluntness of his taped discussions. Use the same reference when examining the Articles of Impeachment. Who is the House Judiciary speaking to when they make the case for impeachment?

Document 24.1 President Nixon's Address to the Nation about the Watergate Investigations, April 30, 1973

Despite White House Press Secretary Ron Ziegler's claim that the Watergate break-in was just "a third-rate burglary attempt," the story would not go away. The trial of the Watergate burglars in January 1973 and the formation of the Senate Select Committee on Presidential Campaign Activities (better known as the Ervin Committee) were followed by James McCord's letter to Judge John Sirica. This bombshell started to unravel the cover-up, directly tied the burglars to senior White House staff, and claimed that the White House applied pressure for the burglars to plead guilty and stay quiet in return for payoffs. Official statements from the White House on April 17, 1973 claimed President Nixon had no prior knowledge of the break-in, and promised that major new developments were pending in the investigation. Attempting to cut the investigation off from the White House, President Nixon made the following major television address on April 30, 1973. What is the focus of this speech? How does he deflect attention from Watergate and appear "presidential?" How does the President appear to accept responsibility while blaming others for campaign crimes and activities?

Richard M. Nixon

Good evening:

I want to talk to you tonight from my heart on a subject of deep concern to every American.

In recent months, members of my Administration and officials of the Committee for the Re-Election of the President—including some of my closest friends and most trusted aides—have been charged with involvement in what has come to be known as the Watergate affair. These include charges of illegal activity during and preceding the 1972 Presidential election and charges that responsible officials participated in efforts to cover up that illegal activity.

The inevitable result of these charges has been to raise serious questions about the integrity of the White House itself. Tonight I wish to address those questions.

Last June 17, while I was in Florida trying to get a few days rest after my visit to Moscow, I first learned from news reports of the Watergate break-in.

I was appalled at this senseless, illegal action, and I was shocked to learn that employees of the Re-Election Committee were apparently among those guilty. I immediately ordered an investigation by appropriate Government authorities. On September 15, as you will recall, indictments were brought against seven defendants in the case.

As the investigations went forward, I repeatedly asked those conducting the investigation whether there was any reason to believe that members of my Administration were in any way involved. I received repeated assurances that there were not. Because of these continuing reassurances, because I believed the reports I was getting, because I had faith in the persons from whom I was getting them, I discounted the stories in the press that appeared to implicate members of my Administration or other officials of the campaign committee.

Until March of this year, I remained convinced that the denials were true and that the charges of involvement by members of the White House Staff were false. The comments I made during this period, and the comments made by my Press Secretary in my behalf, were based on the information provided to us at the time we made those comments. However, new information then came to me which persuaded me that there was a real possibility that some of these charges were true, and suggesting further that there had been an effort to conceal the facts both from the public, from you, and from me.

As a result, on March 21, I personally assumed the responsibility for coordinating intensive new inquiries into the matter, and I personally ordered those conducting the investigations to get all the facts and to report them directly to me, right here in this office.

I again ordered that all persons in the Government or at the Re-Election Committee should cooperate fully with the FBI, the prosecutors, and the grand jury. I also ordered that anyone who refused to cooperate in telling the truth would be asked to resign from Government service. And, with ground rules adopted that would preserve the basic constitutional separation of powers between the Congress and the Presidency, I directed that members of the White House Staff should appear and testify voluntarily under oath before the Senate committee which was investigating Watergate.

I was determined that we should get to the bottom of the matter, and that the truth should be fully brought out—no matter who was involved.

At the same time, I was determined not to take precipitate action and to avoid, if at all possible, any action that would appear to reflect on innocent people. I wanted to be fair. But I knew that in the final analysis, the integrity of this office—public faith in the integrity of this office—would have to take priority over all personal considerations.

Today, in one of the most difficult decisions of my Presidency, I accepted the resignations of two of my closest associates in the White House—Bob Haldeman, John Ehrlichman—two of the finest public servants it has been my privilege to know.

I want to stress that in accepting these resignations, I mean to leave no implication whatever of personal wrongdoing on their part, and I leave no implication tonight of implication on the part of others who have been charged in this matter. But in matters as sensitive as guarding the integrity of our democratic process, it is essential not only that rigorous legal and ethical standards be observed but also that the public, you, have total confidence that they are both being observed and enforced by those in authority and particularly by the President of the United States. They agreed with me that this move was necessary in order to restore that confidence.

Because Attorney General Kleindienst—though a distinguished public servant, my personal friend for 20 years, with no personal involvement whatever in this matter—has been a close personal and professional associate of some of those who are involved in this case, he and I both felt that it was also necessary to name a new Attorney General.

The Counsel to the President, John Dean, has also resigned.

As the new Attorney General, I have today named Elliot Richardson, a man of unimpeachable integrity and rigorously high principle. I have directed him to do everything necessary to ensure that the Department of Justice has the confidence and the trust of every law-abiding person in this country.

I have given him absolute authority to make all decisions bearing upon the prosecution of the Watergate case and related matters. I have instructed him that if he should consider it appropriate, he has the authority to name a special supervising prosecutor for matters arising out of the case.

Whatever may appear to have been the case before, whatever improper activities may yet be discovered in connection with this whole sordid affair, I want the American people, I want you to know beyond the shadow of a doubt that during my term as President, justice will be pursued fairly, fully, and impartially, no matter who is involved. This office is a sacred trust and I am determined to be worthy of that trust.

Looking back at the history of this case, two questions arise:

How could it have happened?

Who is to blame?

Political commentators have correctly observed that during my 27 years in politics I have always previously insisted on running my own campaigns for office.

But 1972 presented a very different situation. In both domestic and foreign policy, 1972 was a year of crucially important decisions, of intense negotiations, of vital new directions, particularly in working toward the goal which has been my overriding concern throughout my political career—the goal of bringing peace to America, peace to the world.

That is why I decided, as the 1972 campaign approached, that the Presidency should come first and politics second. To the maximum extent possible, therefore, I sought to delegate campaign operations, to remove the day-to-day campaign decisions from the President's office and from the White House. I also, as you recall, severely limited the number of my own campaign appearances.

Who, then, is to blame for what happened in this case?

For specific criminal actions by specific individuals, those who committed those actions must, of course, bear the liability and pay the penalty.

For the fact that alleged improper actions took place within the White House or within my campaign organization, the easiest course would be for me to blame those to whom I delegated the responsibility to run the campaign. But that would be a cowardly thing to do.

I will not place the blame on subordinates—on people whose zeal exceeded their judgment and who may have done wrong in a cause they deeply believed to be right.

In any organization, the man at the top must bear the responsibility. That responsibility, therefore, belongs here, in this office. I accept it. And I pledge to you tonight, from this office, that I will do everything in my power to ensure that the guilty are brought to justice and that such abuses are purged from our political processes in the years to come, long after I have left this office.

Some people, quite properly appalled at the abuses that occurred, will say that Watergate demonstrates the bankruptcy of the American political system. I believe precisely the opposite is true. Watergate represented a series of illegal acts and bad judgments by a number of individuals. It was the system that has brought the facts to light and that will bring those guilty to justice—a system that in this case has included a determined grand jury, honest prosecutors, a courageous judge, John Sirica, and a vigorous free press.

It is essential now that we place our faith in that system—and especially in the judicial system. It is essential that we let the judicial process go forward, respecting those safeguards that are established to protect the innocent as well as to convict the guilty. It is essential that in reacting to the excesses of others, we not fall into excesses ourselves.

It is also essential that we not be so distracted by events such as this that we neglect the vital work before us, before this Nation, before America, at a time of critical importance to America and the world.

Since March, when I first learned that the Watergate affair might in fact be far more serious than I had been led to believe, it has claimed far too much of my time and my attention.

Whatever may now transpire in the case, whatever the actions of the grand jury, whatever the outcome of any eventual trials, I must now turn my full attention—and I shall do so—once again to the larger duties of this office. I owe it to this great office that I hold, and I owe it to you—to my country.

I know that as Attorney General, Elliot Richardson will be both fair and he will be fearless in pursuing this case wherever it leads. I am confident that with him in charge, justice will be done.

There is vital work to be done toward our goal of a lasting structure of peace in the world—work that cannot wait, work that I must do.

Tomorrow, for example, Chancellor Brandt of West Germany will visit the White House for talks that are a vital element of "The Year of Europe," as 1973 has been called. We are already preparing for the next Soviet-American summit meeting later this year.

This is also a year in which we are seeking to negotiate a mutual and balanced reduction of armed forces in Europe, which will reduce our defense budget and allow us to have funds for other purposes at home so desperately needed. It is the year when the United States and Soviet negotiators will seek to work out the second and even more important round of our talks on limiting nuclear arms and of reducing the danger of a nuclear war that would destroy civilization as we know it. It is a year in which we confront the difficult tasks of maintaining peace in Southeast Asia and in the potentially explosive Middle East.

There is also vital work to be done right here in America: to ensure prosperity, and that means a good job for everyone who wants to work; to control inflation, that I know worries every housewife, everyone who tries to balance a family budget in America; to set in motion new and better ways of ensuring progress toward a better life for all Americans.

When I think of this office—of what it means—I think of all the things that I want to accomplish for this Nation, of all the things I want to accomplish for you.

On Christmas Eve, during my terrible personal ordeal of the renewed bombing of North Vietnam, which after 12 years of war finally helped to bring America peace with honor, I sat down just before midnight. I wrote out some of my goals for my second term as President.

Let me read them to you.

"To make it possible for our children, and for our children's children, to live in a world of peace.

"To make this country be more than ever a land of opportunity—of equal opportunity, full opportunity for every American.

"To provide jobs for all who can work, and generous help for those who cannot work.

"To establish a climate of decency and civility in which each person respects the feelings and the dignity and the God-given rights of his neighbor.

"To make this a land in which each person can dare to dream, can live his dreams—not in fear, but in hope—proud of his community, proud of his country, proud of what America has meant to himself and to the world."

These are great goals. I believe we can, we must work for them. We can achieve them. But we cannot achieve these goals unless we dedicate ourselves to another goal:

We must maintain the integrity of the White House, and that integrity must be real, not transparent. There can be no whitewash at the White House.

We must reform our political process—ridding it not only of the violations of the law but also of the ugly mob violence and other inexcusable campaign tactics that have been too often practiced and too readily accepted in the past, including those that may have been a response by one side to the excesses or expected excesses of the other side. Two wrongs do not make a right.

I have been in public life for more than a quarter of a century. Like any other calling, politics has good people and bad people. And let me tell you, the great majority in politics—in the Congress, in the Federal Government, in the State government—are good people. I know that it can be very easy, under the intensive pressures of a campaign, for even well-intentioned people to fall into shady tactics—to

rationalize this on the grounds that what is at stake is of such importance to the Nation that the end justifies the means. And both of our great parties have been guilty of such tactics in the past.

In recent years, however, the campaign excesses that have occurred on all sides have provided a sobering demonstration of how far this false doctrine can take us. The lesson is clear: America, in its political campaigns, must not again fall into the trap of letting the end, however great that end is, justify the means.

I urge the leaders of both political parties, I urge citizens, all of you, everywhere, to join in working toward a new set of standards, new rules and procedures to ensure that future elections will be as nearly free of such abuses as they possibly can be made. This is my goal. I ask you to join in making it America's goal.

When I was inaugurated for a second time this past January 20, 1 gave each member of my Cabinet and each member of my senior White House Staff a special 4-year calendar, with each day marked to show the number of days remaining to the Administration. In the inscription on each calendar, I wrote these words: "The Presidential term which begins today consists of 1,461 days—no more, no less. Each can be a day of strengthening and renewal for America; each can add depth and dimension to the American experience. If we strive together, if we make the most of the challenge and the opportunity that these days offer us, they can stand out as great days for America, and great moments in the history of the world."

I looked at my own calendar this morning up at Camp David as I was working on this speech. It showed exactly 1,361 days remaining in my term. I want these to be the best days in America's history, because I love America. I deeply believe that America is the hope of the world. And I know that in the quality and wisdom of the leadership America gives lies the only hope for millions of people all over the world that they can live their lives in peace and freedom. We must be worthy of that hope, in every sense of the word. Tonight, I ask for your prayers to help me in everything that I do throughout the days of my Presidency to be worthy of their hopes and of yours.

God bless America and God bless each and every one of you.

NOTE: The President spoke at 9:01 p.m. from the Oval Office at the White House. His address was broadcast live on nationwide radio and television.

Document 24.2 Articles of Impeachment: President Richard M. Nixon, July 27, 1974

After the "Saturday Night Massacre" of October 23, 1973, twenty-two separate bills were introduced in the House of Representatives calling for the impeachment of President Nixon. But rather than rushing into an emotional, partisan attack on the President, the Democrat-controlled House allowed the legal process to proceed at a normal pace. Not until February 6, 1974 did the House authorize the Judiciary Committee (by a vote of 410-4) to specifically investigate whether "sufficient grounds" existed to impeach the president. This committee, chaired by Peter Rodino, began its deliberations on May 9, 1974, after a Washington grand jury named the president as an "unindicted co-conspirator" and after the president turned over edited manuscripts of tapes. After months of investigation, hearing witnesses and reviewing evidence, the Judiciary Committee voted three articles of impeachment. Faced with overwhelming evidence of Presidential misconduct, many Republicans joined the Democrats in voting for impeachment. What are the basic charges against President Nixon? How well are they detailed and supported in the articles?

House Judiciary Committee

Article I

In his conduct of the office of President of the United States, Richard M. Nixon, in violation of his constitutional oath faithfully to execute the office of President of the United States and, to the best of his ability, preserve, protect, and defend the Constitution of the United States, and in violation of his constitutional duty to take care that the laws be faithfully executed, has prevented, obstructed, and impeded the administration of justice, in that:

On June 17, 1972, and prior thereto, agents of the Committee for the Reelection of the President committed unlawful entry of the headquarters of the Democratic National Committee in Washington, District of Columbia, for the purpose of securing political intelligence. Subsequent thereto, Richard M. Nixon, using the powers of his high office, engaged personally and through his close subordinates and agents, in a course of conduct or plan designed to delay, impede, and obstruct the investigation of such unlawful entry; to cover up, conceal and protect those responsible; and to conceal the existence and scope of other unlawful covert activities.

The means used to implement this course of conduct or plan included one or more of the following:

1. making false or misleading statements to lawfully authorized investigative officers and employees of the United States;

2. withholding relevant and material evidence or information from lawfully authorized investigative officers and employees of the United States;

3. approving, condoning, acquiescing in, and counseling witnesses with respect to the giving of false or misleading statements to lawfully authorized investigative officers and employees of the United States and false or misleading testimony in duly instituted judicial and congressional proceedings;

4. interfering or endeavoring to interfere with the conduct of investigations by the Department of Justice of the United States, the Federal Bureau of Investigation, the Office of Watergate Special Prosecution Force, and Congressional Committees;

5. approving, condoning, and acquiescing in, the surreptitious payment of substantial sums of money for the purpose of obtaining the silence or influencing the testimony of witnesses, potential witnesses or individuals who participated in such unlawful entry and other illegal activities;

6. endeavoring to misuse the Central Intelligence Agency, an agency of the United States;

7. disseminating information received from officers of the Department of Justice of the United States to subjects of investigations conducted by lawfully authorized investigative officers and employees of the United States, for the purpose of aiding and assisting such subjects in their attempts to avoid criminal liability.

8. making or causing to be made false or misleading public statements for the purpose of deceiving the people of the United States into believing that a thorough and complete investigation had been conducted with respect to allegations of misconduct on the part of personnel of the executive branch of the United States and personnel of the Committee for the Re-election of the President, and that there was no involvement of such personnel in such misconduct; or

9. endeavoring to cause prospective defendants, and individuals duly tried and convicted, to expect favored treatment and consideration in return for their silence or false testimony, or rewarding individuals for their silence or false testimony.

In all of this, Richard M. Nixon has acted in a manner contrary to his trust as President and subversive of constitutional government, to the great prejudice of the cause of law and justice and to the manifest injury of the people of the United States.

Wherefore Richard M. Nixon, by such conduct, warrants impeachment and trial, and removal from office.

Article II

Using the powers of the office of President of the United States, Richard M. Nixon, in violation of his constitutional oath faithfully to execute the office of President of the United States and, to the best of his ability, preserve, protect, and defend the Constitution of the United States, and in disregard of his constitutional duty to take care that the laws be faithfully executed, has repeatedly engaged in conduct violating the constitutional rights of citizens, impairing the due and proper administration of justice and the conduct of lawful inquiries, or contravening the laws governing agencies of the executive

This conduct has included one or more of the following:

1. He has, acting personally and through his subordinates and agents, endeavored to obtain from the Internal Revenue Service, in violation of the constitutional rights of citizens, confidential information contained in income tax returns for purposes not authorized by law, and to cause, in violation of the constitutional rights of citizens, income tax audits or other income tax investigations to be initiated or conducted in a discriminatory manner.

2. He misused the Federal Bureau of Investigation, the Secret Service, and other executive personnel, in violation or disregard of the constitutional rights of citizens, by directing or authorizing such agencies or personnel to conduct or continue electronic surveillance or other investigations for purposes unrelated to national security, the enforcement of laws, or any other lawful function of his office; he did direct, authorize, or permit the use of information obtained thereby for purposes unrelated to national security, the enforcement of laws, or any other lawful function of his office; and he did direct the concealment of certain records made by the Federal Bureau of Investigation of electronic surveillance.

3. He has, acting personally and through his subordinates and agents, in violation or disregard of the constitutional rights of citizens, authorized and permitted to be maintained a secret investigative unit within the office of the President, financed in part with money derived from campaign contributions, which unlawfully utilized the resources of the Central Intelligence Agency, engaged in covert and unlawful activities, and attempted to prejudice the constitutional right of an accused to a fair trial.

4. He has failed to take care that the laws were faithfully executed by failing to act when he knew or had reason to know that his close subordinates endeavored to impede and frustrate lawful inquiries by duly constituted executive, judicial, and legislative entities concerning the unlawful entry into the headquarters of the Democratic National Committee, and the cover up thereof, and concerning other unlawful activities including those relating to the confirmation of Richard Kleindienst as Attorney General of the United States, the electronic surveillance of private citizens, the break-in into the offices of Dr. Lewis Fielding and the campaign financing practices of the Committee to Re-elect the President.

5. In disregard of the rule of law, he knowingly misused the executive branch, including the Federal Bureau of Investigation, the Criminal Division, and the Office of Watergate Special Prosecution

Force, of the Department of Justice, and the Central Intelligence Agency, in violation of his duty to take care that the laws be faithfully executed.

In all of this, Richard M. Nixon has acted in a manner contrary to his trust as President and subversive of constitutional government, to the great prejudice of the cause of law and justice and to the manifest injury of the people of the United States.

Wherefore Richard M. Nixon, by such conduct, warrants impeachment and trial, and removal from office.

—Adopted July 29 by a 28–10 vote

Article III

In his conduct of the office of President of the United States, Richard M. Nixon, contrary to his oath faithfully to execute the office of President of the United States and, to the best of his ability, preserve, protect, and defend the Constitution of the United States, and in violation of his constitutional duty to take care that the laws be faithfully executed, has failed without lawful cause or excuse to produce papers and things as directed by duly authorized subpoenas issued by the Committee on the Judiciary of the House of Representatives on April 11, 1974, May 15, 1974, May 30, 1974, and June 24, 1974, and willfully disobeyed such subpoenas. The subpoenaed papers and things were deemed necessary by the Committee in order to resolve by direct evidence fundamental, factual questions relating to Presidential direction, knowledge, or approval of actions demonstrated by other evidence to be substantial grounds for impeachment of the President. In refusing to produce these papers and things Richard M. Nixon, substituting his judgment as to what materials were necessary for the inquiry, interposed the powers of the Presidency against the lawful subpoenas of the House of Representatives, thereby assuming to himself functions and judgments necessary to the exercise of the sole power of impeachment vested by the Constitution in the House of Representatives.

In all of this, Richard M. Nixon has acted in a manner contrary to his trust as President and subversive of constitutional government, to the great prejudice of the cause of law and justice, and to the manifest injury of the people of the United States.

Wherefore, Richard M. Nixon by such conduct, warrants impeachment and trial, and removal from office.

—Adopted July 30 by a 21–17 vote

Document 24.3 The "Smoking Gun" Tape of Conversation in the Oval Office, June 30, 1972

Of the 60 hours of tapes subpoenaed by the Special Prosecutor, none was as damning as the "Smoking Gun" tape of June 23, 1972. The three Oval Office conversations on that tape confirmed the claims in John Dean's testimony, that President Nixon knew about, participated in, and planned the cover-up from the start. This tape was not released until *after* the House Judiciary Committee voted for impeachment. The evidence in this tape is supported by the 3,700 hours of tapes released for public use since the former President died in 1994. As you read the transcripts of this tape, answer Republican Senator Howard Baker's question: What did the President know, and when did he know it?

Hearings before the Committee on the Judiciary, House of Representatives, 93rd Congress, 2nd session.

One of the subjects of the June 30, 1972, discussion among the President, Haldeman and Mitchell was Mitchell's resignation as head of CRP:

"HALDEMAN, Well, there maybe is another facet. The longer you wait the more risk each hour brings. You run the risk of more stuff, valid or invalid, surfacing on the Watergate caper—type of thing—

"MITCHELL. You couldn't possibly do it if you got into a—

"HALDEMAN.—the potential problem and then you are stuck—

"PRESIDENT. Yes, that's the other thing, if something does come out, but we won't—we hope nothing will. It may not. But there is always the risk.

"HALDEMAN. As of now there is no problem there. As, as of any moment in the future there is at least a potential problem.

"PRESIDENT. Well, I'd cut the loss fast. I'd cut it fast. If we're going to do it I'd cut it fast. That's my view, generally speaking. And I wouldn't—and I don't think, though, as a matter of fact, I don't think the story, if we, if you put it in human terms—I think the story is, you're positive rather than negative, because as I said as I was preparing to answer for this press conference, I just wrote it out, as I usually do, one way—terribly sensitive [unintelligible]. A hell of a lot of people will like that answer. They would. And it'd make anybody else who asked any other question on it look like a selfish son-of-a-bitch, which I thoroughly intended them to look like."

* * *

"MITCHELL. [Unintelligible] Westchester Country Club with all the sympathy in the world.

"PRESIDENT. That's great. That's great.

"MITCHELL. (Unintelligible] don't let—

"HALDEMAN. You taking this route—people won't expect you to—be a surprise.

"PRESIDENT. No, if it's a surprise. Otherwise, you're right, it will be tied right to Watergate. [Unintelligible]—tighter if you wait too long, till it simmers down.

"HALDEMAN. You can't if other stuff develops on Watergate. The problem is, it's always potentially the same thing.

"PRESIDENT. Well if it does, don't just hard-line.

"HALDEMAN. [Unintelligible] That's right. In other words, it'd be hard to hard-line Mitchell's departure under—

"PRESIDENT. That's right. You can't do it. I just want it to be handled in a way Martha's not hurt.

"MITCHELL. Yeah, okay." (Book II, 515–516)

"H. Now, on the investigation, you know the Democratic break-in thing, we're back in the problem area because the FBI is not under control, because Gray doesn't exactly know how to control it and they have—their investigation is now leading into some productive areas—because they've been able to trace the money—not through the money itself—but through the bank sources—the banker. And, and it goes in some directions we don't want it to go. Ah, also there have been some things—like an informant came in off the street to the FBI in Miami who was a photographer or has a friend who is a photographer who developed some films through this guy Barker and the films had pictures of Democratic National Committee letterhead documents and things. So it's things like that that are filtering in. Mitchell came up with yesterday, and John Dean analyzed very carefully last night and concludes, concurs now with Mitchell's recommendation that the only way to solve this, and we're set up beautifully to do it, ah, in that and that—the only network that paid any attention to it last night was NBC, they did a massive story on the Cuban thing.

"P. That's right.

"H. That the way to handle this now is for us to have Walters call Pat Gray and just say, 'Stay to hell out of this—this is ah, business here we don't want you to go any further on it.' That's not an unusual development, and ah, that would take care of it.

"P. What about Pat Gray—you mean Pat Gray doesn't want to?

"H. Pat does want to. He doesn't know how to, and he doesn't have . . . any basis for doing it. Given this, he will then have the basis. He'll call Mark Felt in. . . .

"P. Yeah.

"H. He'll call him and say, 'We've got the signal from across the river to put the hold on this.' And that will fit rather well because the FBI agents who are working on the case, at this point, feel that's what it is. . . .

"H. And you seem to think the thing to do is get them to stop?

"P. Right, fine." (WHT, June 23 , 1972, 10.04–11:39 A.M., 2–5)

Document 24.4 President Richard M. Nixon, Resignation Speech, August 8, 1974

After the release of the "Smoking Gun" tape, 11 Republican members of the House Judiciary Committee, who voted against the Articles of Impeachment, announced their intention to switch their votes. Republican Senators informed the president that once the House formally impeached him, his conviction and removal from office by the Senate was assured. By this time, dozens of former members of the Nixon administration were already serving time in jail for various crimes. On August 8, 1974, in a defiant television address, President Nixon announced his intention to resign from office. Note his arguments about why he is resigning. What is he careful not to talk about or admit? How believable are his arguments?

The President Resigns

Richard M. Nixon

Good evening:

This is the 37th time I have spoken to you from this office, where so many decisions have been made that shaped the history of this Nation. Each time I have done so to discuss with you some matter that I believe affected the national interest.

In all the decisions I have made in my public life, I have always tried to do what was best for the Nation. Throughout the long and difficult period of Watergate, I have felt it was my duty to persevere, to make every possible effort to complete the term of office to which you elected me.

In the past few days, however, it has become evident to me that I no longer have a strong enough political base in the Congress to justify continuing that effort. As long as there was such a base, I felt strongly that it was necessary to see the constitutional process through to its conclusion, that to do otherwise would be unfaithful to the spirit of that deliberately difficult process and a dangerously destabilizing precedent for the future.

But with the disappearance of that base, I now believe that the constitutional purpose has been served, and there is no longer a need for the process to be prolonged.

I would have preferred to carry through to the finish, whatever the personal agony it would have involved, and my family unanimously urged me to do so. But the interests of the Nation must always come before any personal considerations.

From the discussions I have had with Congressional and other leaders, I have concluded that because of the Watergate matter, I might not have the support of the Congress that I would consider necessary to back the very difficult decisions and carry out the duties of this office in the way the interests of the Nation will require.

I have never been a quitter. To leave office before my term is completed is abhorrent to every instinct in my body. But as President, I must put the interests of America first. America needs a full-time President and a full-time Congress, particularly at this time with problems we face at home and abroad.

To continue to fight through the months ahead for my personal vindication would almost totally absorb the time and attention of both the President and the Congress in a period when our entire focus should be on the great issues of peace abroad and prosperity without inflation at home.

Therefore, I shall resign the Presidency effective at noon tomorrow. Vice President Ford will be sworn in as President at that hour in this office.

As I recall the high hopes for America with which we began this second term, I feel a great sadness that I will not be here in this office working on your behalf to achieve those hopes in the next 2 1/2 years. But in turning over direction of the Government to Vice President Ford, I know, as I told the Nation when I nominated him for that office 10 months ago, that the leadership of America will be in good hands.

In passing this office to the Vice President, I also do so with the profound sense of the weight of responsibility that will fall on his shoulders tomorrow and, therefore, of the understanding, the patience, the cooperation he will need from all Americans.

Resignation Speech, Richard M. Nixon.

As he assumes that responsibility, he will deserve the help and the support of all of us. As we look to the future, the first essential is to begin healing the wounds of this Nation, to put the bitterness and divisions of the recent past behind us and to rediscover those shared ideals that lie at the heart of our strength and unity as a great and as a free people.

By taking this action, I hope that I will have hastened the start of that process of healing which is so desperately needed in America.

I regret deeply any injuries that may have been done in the course of the events that led to this decision. I would say only that if some of my judgments were wrong—and some were wrong—they were made in what I believed at the time to be the best interest of the Nation.

To those who have stood with me during these past difficult months—to my family, my friends, to many others who joined in supporting my cause because they believed it was right—I will be eternally grateful for your support.

And to those who have not felt able to give me your support, let me say I leave with no bitterness toward those who have opposed me, because all of us, in the final analysis, have been concerned with the good of the country, however our judgments might differ.

So, let us all now join together in affirming that common commitment and in helping our new President succeed for the benefit of all Americans.

I shall leave this office with regret at not completing my term, but with gratitude for the privilege of serving as your President for the past 5 1/2 years. These years have been a momentous time in the history of our Nation and the world. They have been a time of achievement in which we can all be proud, achievements that represent the shared efforts of the Administration, the Congress, and the people.

But the challenges ahead are equally great, and they, too, will require the support and the efforts of the Congress and the people working in cooperation with the new Administration.

We have ended America's longest war, but in the work of securing a lasting peace in the world, the goals ahead are even more far-reaching and more difficult. We must complete a structure of peace so that it will be said of this generation, our generation of Americans, by the people of all nations, not only that we ended one war but that we prevented future wars.

We have unlocked the doors that for a quarter of a century stood between the United States and the People's Republic of China.

We must now ensure that the one quarter of the world's people who live in the People's Republic of China will be and remain not our enemies, but our friends.

In the Middle East, 100 million people in the Arab countries, many of whom have considered us their enemy for nearly 20 years, now look on us as their friends. We must continue to build on that friendship so that peace can settle at last over the Middle East and so that the cradle of civilization will not become its grave.

Together with the Soviet Union, we have made the crucial breakthroughs that have begun the process of limiting nuclear arms. But we must set as our goal not just limiting but reducing and, finally, destroying these terrible weapons so that they cannot destroy civilization and so that the threat of nuclear war will no longer hang over the world and the people.

We have opened the new relation with the Soviet Union. We must continue to develop and expand that new relationship so that the two strongest nations of the world will live together in cooperation rather than confrontation.

Around the world—in Asia, in Africa, in Latin America, in the Middle East—there are millions of people who live in terrible poverty, even starvation. We must keep as our goal turning away from production for war and expanding production for peace so that people everywhere on this Earth can at last look forward in their children's time, if not in our own time, to having the necessities for a decent life.

Here in America, we are fortunate that most of our people have not only the blessings of liberty but also the means to live full and good and, by the world's standards, even abundant lives. We must press on, however, toward a goal, not only of more and better jobs but of full opportunity for every American and of what we are striving so hard right now to achieve, prosperity without inflation.

For more than a quarter of a century in public life, I have shared in the turbulent history of this era. I have fought for what I believed in, I have tried, to the best of my ability, to discharge those duties and meet those responsibilities that were entrusted to me.

Sometimes I have succeeded and sometimes I have failed, but always I have taken heart from what Theodore Roosevelt once said about the man in the arena, "whose face is marred by dust and sweat and blood, who strives valiantly, who errs and comes short again and again because there is not effort without error and shortcoming, but who does actually strive to do the deed, who knows the great enthusiasms, the great devotions, who spends himself in a worthy cause, who at the best knows in the end the triumphs of high achievements and who at the worst, if he fails, at least fails while daring greatly."

I pledge to you tonight that as long as I have a breath of life in my body, I shall continue in that spirit. I shall continue to work for the great causes to which I have been dedicated throughout my years as a Congressman, a Senator, Vice President, and President, the cause of peace, not just for America. but among all nations—prosperity, justice, and opportunity for all of our people.

There is one cause above all to which I have been devoted and to which I shall always be devoted for as long as I live.

When I first took the oath of office as President 5 1/2 years ago, I made this sacred commitment: to "consecrate my office, my energies, and all the wis-dom I can summon to the cause of peace among nations."

I have done my very best in all the days since to be true to that pledge. As a result of these efforts, I am confident that the world is a safer place today not only for the people of America but for the people of all nations, and that all of our children have a better chance than before of living in peace rather than dying in war.

This, more than anything, is what I hoped to achieve when I sought the Presidency. This, more than anything, is what I hope will be my legacy to you, to our country, as I leave the Presidency.

To have served in this office is to have felt a very personal sense of kinship with each and every American. In leaving it, I do so with this prayer: May God's grace be with you in all the days ahead.

Chapter 24 Worksheet and Questions

1. Throughout the entire Watergate scandal, President Nixon could never publicly admit doing anything illegal. He went out of his way to deflect blame from himself, even when he *appeared* to accept responsibility for wrong-doing. What examples of shifting blame for events do you see in the April 30, 1973 and August 8, 1974 speeches?

    _____

    _____

    _____

    _____

    _____

    _____

    _____

    _____

2. One of the tapes President Nixon resisted releasing to the Special Prosecutor was the "Smoking Gun" tape, containing three conversations discussing the break-in and cover-up just days after the arrests at Democratic Headquarters. In these conversations, what are the major concerns of the President and his chief-of-staff H.R. Haldeman? How do they propose solving the potential crises facing the White House? What do these conversations reveal about the character and morality of the Nixon White House, and what crimes are committed in these discussions?

    _____

    _____

    _____

    _____

    _____

    _____

    _____

3. The Articles of Impeachment were passed a week before the "Smoking Gun" tape became public. After its release, 11 Republicans on the Judiciary Committee switched their votes in favor of impeachment. What crimes do the articles accuse the president of committing? Knowing what you do now about the Nixon Administration, could more charges be added?

_____

_____

_____

_____

_____

_____

_____

_____

_____

4. Although it caused his impeachment and resignation, Nixon barely mentioned Watergate in his resignation speech. What topics does he focus on? Why does he claim to be resigning? Why do you think he resigned?

_____

_____

_____

_____

_____

_____

_____

_____

_____

Chapter 25

Culture Wars

At the 1992 Republican National Convention, Pat Buchanan declared, "There is a religious war going on in our country for the soul, of America. It is a cultural war, as critical to the kind of nation we will one day be—as was the Cold War itself." His statement captured the tenor of American politics. For the last two decades or more, Democrats and Republicans have blamed each other for the nastiness of and loss of civility in politics. They have accused each other of creating political gridlock and practicing the politics of personal destruction. Senior statesmen, political pundits, and historians have recounted stories of how, in the past, politicians sat down over "bourbon and branch water" to hammer out their differences. No longer. "Compromise" in 1990 took on the meaning of defeat and a failure to stick to one's principles.

The new politics began with the presidency of Ronald Reagan, who brought philosophically conservative Republicans together with a constellation of new Conservative Christian churches, organizations, media, and voters. For these Conservatives, all political issues—whether taxes, schools, or abortion—had a moral dimension; consequently, political differences became cultural differences. Debates between Republicans and Democrats about taxes were not only questions of policy or the economic reasons for cutting taxes, but of morality, the relationship between a "good" government and a "good" people. How a person voted then expressed both an economic preference and, more significantly, a moral or immoral position. Conservatives projected an image of themselves under siege by the forces of Liberalism: big government, liberal news media, secular humanism, multiculturalism, gays, lesbians, abortionists, elites, and feminists, or (as they characterized them) the supporters of the Democratic Party who controlled the government and shaped culture. Against these enemies, they portrayed themselves as agents of good, restoring patriotism, Christianity, family values, and American greatness. For their part, Democrats struggled to find a response. While Bill Clinton served two terms as president, while he was in office, Republicans gained control of the House of Representatives. In 2000, Republicans elected George W. Bush president and in the 2004 election returned him to office, while Republicans became a majority in the Senate. Throughout this period (and to the present), Republicans and Democrats have practiced politics as warfare, projecting very different images of themselves and their opposition.

The Democratic Party that Reagan defeated in 1982 had been in disarray for a decade. Humorist Will Rogers would have been at home in it. Decades earlier he had observed, "I'm not a member of an organized political party; I'm a Democrat." Since the time of Franklin D. Roosevelt, the Democratic Party operated as a loose coalition of labor unions, minorities, poor people, and academics—groups constituting large majorities in the nation's cities. By the 1960s, Liberals controlled both houses in Congress, and the presidency. They enacted their most important legislation since Roosevelt's New Deal with the Civil Rights Act (1964), the Voting Rights Act (1965), and Lyndon Johnson's Great Society programs. Yet at the same time, the party began fragmenting. Party leaders found it increasingly difficult to accommodate the host of new groups fostered by the Civil Rights Movement and the Vietnam War, while retaining support of the older constituencies.

By 1972, the coalition had grown to include Blacks, Hispanics, Asians, gays, lesbians, feminists, environmentalists, anti-war groups, and student leftists. Party organizers worried about the viability of a party composed of groups whose members identified themselves first with a race, ethnicity, ideology, or cause. This politics of identity seemed to emphasize differences rather than commonalties. The search for a way to unite the Party became a constant refrain at party gatherings. Jesse Jackson spoke of common ground and established the "Rainbow Coalition." Others explored the possibilities of multiculturalism and diversity as concepts to provide a common cause. Complicating these efforts, under President Jimmy Carter the economy suffered from extremely high rates of interest, inflation, and unemployment, while the nation's power seemed enfeebled by the country's inability to resolve the problems of its dependence upon foreign oil or Iran's seizure of hostages from the American embassy in Teheran.

With a fragmented Democratic Party, foundering economy, and questions about national security, Ronald Reagan won large majorities in the 1980 presidential race. The Republican promised to restore the country to greatness. To do so, he offered the traditional conservative prescriptions for economic recovery and military strength. Yet, unlike traditional conservatives, he wedded those initiatives to a moralistic understanding of the American people that emphasized patriotism, a heroic past, belief in God, family values, and individual initiative. From Reagan's and the new Conservative's perspective, applying conservative remedies to economic, social, and military problems would also promote spiritual renewal, or the Puritan City upon a Hill, "morning in America" or America "riding tall" again. At the same time that Republicans promoted their new agenda, they carefully contrasted it to (in their terms) the failed policies of big-government Democrats. In so doing, they strove both to discredit and morally stigmatize Democratic political philosophy or liberalism, and policies like Johnson's Great Society programs.

Reagan and the new Conservatives promoted a philosophy that rested upon the ideas of small government, low taxes, and a strong national defense. They repudiated the Democratic belief in the use of government to solve problems like poverty and unemployment. In fact, from their perspective, the "dead hand of government" created those problems by suffocating businesses and the economy. With Reagan in office, Republicans moved on all three fronts. To bring about smaller government, the Republicans sought to eliminate federal programs. Reagan succeeded in the area of social welfare, ending the Comprehensive Training and Employment Act agencies, but failed to disband the Department of Education and Department of Energy. Reagan reduced the size of other programs: food stamps, Aid to Families with Dependent Children, unemployment compensation, the Environmental Protection Agency, and the Department of Education.

In addition to cutting the size of government, Reagan and the Republicans were committed to reducing governmental regulation of businesses. Placing conservatives in charge of regulatory agencies and reducing the size of their staffs, the administration relaxed the enforcement of regulations in the areas of equal rights, affirmative action, worker health and safety, health care, and especially the environment. As the second linchpin of Reagan conservatism, taxes were reduced in 1981. Congress enacted Reagan's plan for a 25-percent cut on all income taxes. Businesses received tax breaks as well. Conservatives explained that this "Supply-Side Economics" policy would free up funds for investment and consequently stimulate the economy. With respect to his third goal, Reagan increased the Defense budget. He authorized spending of over a billion dollars on the military, and initiated new weapons systems like the Strategic Defense Initiative (popularly known as Star Wars), the B-1 bomber, and the MX missile.

While promoting his agenda and pushing his measures through Congress, Reagan and other members of his administration constantly reinforced his moral message as well. As frequently as Reagan and the Republicans promoted conservative policies, they invoked the theme of moral restoration. Many in the media interpreted this as a sop to Christian conservatives, as Republican leadership made little effort to enact conservative social proposals. Nevertheless, many in the administration and among its supporters, most notably William Bennett, advanced a moral philosophy that complemented the traditional conservative political philosophy. Reagan spoke of a heroic American past that explained American progress and success as the sum total of achievements made by hard-working, patriotic individuals possessed of a faith in God and commitment to family. In this narrative (supported by Lynne Cheney, who chaired the National Endowment for the Humanities, and the historian Gertrude Himmelfarb), Liberals, particularly radicals in the 1960s, rejected this American heritage and instead turned to government to solve human problems.

With a Liberal philosophy came Liberal values, or the rejection of moral absolutes and the acceptance of moral relativism and situational ethics. Government in the hands of Liberals became an instrument of oppression used against conservatives and corrupting other Americans. Welfare was the most egregious example. Democrats may have been well intended in establishing welfare programs to assist the poor, unemployed, and disadvantaged, but instead (again, from the Conservative view) they inflicted incalculable moral damage. Reagan insisted that welfare stripped away the values of self-reliance and hard work. Consequently, welfare engendered unemployment, crime, and unwed mothers.

Similarly, Affirmative Action programs repudiated the idea of shared American values, replacing it with multiculturalism while dispensing special rights to groups based upon ethnicity and race. According to these Republicans, the Democrats' rejection of shared values denied the possibility of absolute values, which led them to endorse homosexuality and abortion. In the schools, Liberals had imposed a secular curriculum that abolished prayer and denied federal funding to religious institutions. Government controlled by Liberals, then, stood opposed to the citizens populating Reagan's America. Conversely, Republicans presented themselves as rooting out discredited government programs and affirming moral standards. By 1992, some, like Pat Buchanan, cast the political conflict between Democrats and Republicans as a cultural war for the soul of America.

Buchanan's pronouncement resonated with conservative Christians, who had reached that conclusion a decade earlier. Fundamentalists, Evangelicals, Pentecostals, and other conservative Protestant denominations grew rapidly during the 1970s and 1980s. Many adapted electronic technology to spread the word; over 220 religious television programs were on the air by the 1980s. Jimmy Swaggart's program from the World Ministry Center, Jimmy and Tammy Bakker's Praise the Lord Club, Pat Robertson's 700 Club, and the Christian Broadcasting Network reached national audiences. Initially the programs focused on worship, conversion, healing, and religious missions. During the 1970s, however, social and political issues assumed greater importance. Jerry Falwell, who broadcast the *Old Time Gospel Hour*, became the first to organize conservative Christians politically. In 1979, he established the Moral Majority, to support the creation of Fundamentalist churches and schools. He also used the organization to organize support against abortion, feminism, pornography, homosexuality, and the decline of family values. In 1979, Ed McAteer added the Religious Roundtable to the Moral Majority's operations, to conduct conservative political discussions. Ronald Reagan attended a conference in 1980. During the election that year, the Moral Majority registered voters, sent mailings, supported Reagan's policies, and got out the vote. With Reagan's victory, Falwell became one of the principal spokespersons and organizers for the new Christian Right.

Conservative Christians differed little from Conservative Republicans in terms of policies and their moral implications. However, where politicians spoke only in general terms of the importance of religious belief, the Christian conservatives claimed a Biblical basis for their positions. Fundamentalists understood Reagan's moralistic history of America in terms of God's special dispensation for Americans. From this perspective, God had guided and taken an active role in American history. Others focused more on the Christian basis of American law, and of the Constitution itself. In either case, American history was the history of Christians, and could only be understood with reference to the Bible. The Conservative Christian narrative, like Reagan's, reached its turning point when Liberals took control of government. Because they adopted secular humanist beliefs, Liberals or Democrats sought solutions to human problems in government rather than in God and the Bible. Lacking divine guidance, their policies were necessarily flawed and sinful. Thus, for the Fundamentalists, Democratic programs for the environment, health care, taxes, trade, or anything else were inherently in error, because they were at odds with the Conservative Christian understanding of government and humans. This also explained the Liberal propensity for other sinful attitudes, beliefs, and behaviors, like support for multiculturalism, homosexuality, feminism, and abortion.

Fundamentalists echoed the Conservative calls for a restoration of good government. However, like Falwell, they saw the solution to the problem of liberal error in a return to Biblical basics. The church played a crucial role in this process. Ministers had to mold, educate, and guide Christian voters and citizens. Voting represented a moral act in which voters sorted out the moral and sinful choices confronting them. Further, like any moral act, how they voted had consequences for their future salvation or damnation. Christians also functioned as citizens. In that role, they engaged sin in American society. What became known as the Culture War had its origin in these activities. Churches and ministers organized the Christian responses to sinful behaviors produced by a Liberal culture. Falwell and the Moral Majority compiled a long list of unacceptable ideas and practices. Subsequently, other Christian organizations added to it. Usually, ending the practice of abortion received the highest priority. Another "unacceptable idea" given particular emphasis was "family values" or threats to two-parent, heterosexual families in which spouses embraced Biblical gender roles. Conservatives viewed feminism as a threat to male authority in the family. They saw gay and lesbian lifestyles, and their demand for equal rights, as a threat both to the family and to the precepts of Biblical morality.

A host of issues involving schools came to the forefront. From the Fundamentalist perspective, public schools stood as bastions of secular humanism, a perspective inimical to Christian thought and practices, embracing the unassisted human capacity to shape the world. Conservatives believed the school system had failed after the abolition of school prayer. Further decline followed from the introduction into the curriculum of sex education, historical revisionism, and evolutionary science. Christians would solve those problems through government funding for private, religious schools or school-choice programs in which the tax dollars budgeted for each student could be transferred to a school of the parents' choice. Conservative Christians ran for and won offices on local and state school boards as well. Christians also took issue with popular culture, particularly pornography, the influence of the liberal press, and ruling elites. Finally, the Christian Right organized millions of voters in every election to support Republican nominees. In so doing, they became an important and influential part of the Republican Party.

Democrats discounted what they saw as simplistic moralism and Sunday School theology. Throughout the 1980s, they continued to search for a platform that would unify the disparate elements of the party while attacking the consequences of Republican policies. They criticized Reagan's tax cuts for dramatically increasing the disparity in income between the richest and poorest Americans. In fact, throughout the decade, wages of working people grew very little, and actually fell in terms of what they could purchase. Further, poverty increased for the first time since the 1960s. Reagonomics had also generated enormous deficits, which rose three quarters of a billion dollars in 1980 to nearly five billion in 1992. If economic arguments, appeals to working-class interests, and promises to different Democratic constituencies had worked in the past, they seemed less and less attractive to voters in the 1980s and 1990s. Given a choice between old Democratic and new Republican platforms, voters sided with Conservatives. In this as well, Republicans drew strong support from the suburbs, which for the first time in 1980 represented a majority of the population. Democrats continued to win elections in the highly urbanized states of the Northeast, West Coast, and Great Lakes. Nevertheless, between 1994 and 2004 they lost their majorities in the House of Representatives and Senate, and among the nation's governors,

Among Democrats, Bill Clinton managed to compete successfully with Conservative Republicans in two presidential races. A chair of the Democratic Leadership Conference (DLC) while Governor of Arkansas, Clinton played an important role in recasting Democratic policies, as well as the Party's image. Clinton and the DLC took a page from the Republicans, to unify the Democrats and attract independent voters; they needed to project a more compelling image than that of the Conservative Republicans. Rather than focusing on values, these Democrats focused on the future. The party needed to prepare America for the challenges of the twenty-first century and the nation's role in global events. The collapse of the Soviet Union and the end of the Cold War left the country without a well defined foreign policy. With economists Lester Thurow and Robert Reich (Clinton's Secretary of Labor), Clinton believed that America's position in the new world order was the key to its future, and would determine its prospects both at home and internationally. They portrayed the United States as one part, albeit a very significant one, of an interdependent global system. As such, what happened in the United States affected other nations; similarly, America could not avoid the effects of events taking place in other parts of the world.

This meant that the United States had to engage other nations, and cooperate with them to manage the global system or contain conflicts, encourage communication, and promote economic growth. Clearly, in an interdependent world, individual countries could no longer control their futures. Economic competition represented the most obvious example. The nation's economy at home was directly tied to the economies of other nations. The country competed globally; its success or failure had consequences for jobs, production, and markets at home. Americans were familiar with the loss of factory jobs to new plants built in other nations by foreign companies as well as by U.S. corporations. Given the low wages that attracted companies to overseas locations, Clinton and the DLC Democrats doubted the United States could do much to preserve manufacturing. Alternatively, they understood that America's role in the global economy would be one in which work required high skills, advanced knowledge, complex technology, and high pay. That is, Americans would work in areas like biotechnology, nanotechnology, aeronautics, computer programming, telecommunications, materials science, and a host of entertainment, legal, insurance, and medical services. Furthermore, the nation possessed the resources needed to assume this position, in the form of first-rate universities, colleges, and community colleges, as well as the infrastructure for exchanging digital information.

For the new Democrats, the government's role was first to insure that Americans possessed the skills and knowledge needed to compete in the global economy. Second, government had to restructure itself and address social problems to promote global competitiveness. In the 1992 election, Clinton contrasted the new Democrats' hopeful and progressive future with a conservative Republican alternative that had failed economically and that seemed determined to divide the American people through endless and rancorous debates over values. After the election, political analysts focused on the lack of what loser George Bush called "the vision thing" as a determining factor in the election.

Assuming office, Clinton worked to translate the DLC perspective into legislation. To coordinate global economic relationships, he gained Senate ratification of the North American Free Trade Association, which would reduce obstacles to trade among Mexico, Canada, and the United States. Clinton also obtained Senate approval for the General Agreement on Tariffs and Trade, which reduced tariffs or taxes on trade among nations. The agreement also provided protection for patents and copyrights. Like Clinton, the DLC Democrats viewed these measures as promoting economic growth at home and abroad. To ensure American competitiveness and economic expansion, they established job training programs to provide unemployed workers with the skills needed in the new economy. They increased funding to community colleges for the same reason.

For the Clinton Democrats, America's role in the new global order also called for restructuring government and addressing social problems. They recognized that old "Great Society" liberalism was no longer viable, either in terms of policy or in attracting voters. Clinton declared, "The era of big government is over," and delegated the project of streamlining the federal government to a commission led by Vice President Al Gore.

Clinton also addressed the huge (almost five trillion dollar) national deficit. The deficit threatened economic growth by raising interest rates and competing for capital that could be used to fund business growth. The Arkansas Democrat called for tax increases on the wealthiest Americans, and agreed to cut domestic spending. Deficits dropped, and by the last two years of his second term, the budget ran at a surplus. Clinton's social legislation contained some surprises. He called for and received Congressional passage of welfare reform, limiting the length of time a person could receive assistance and tying it to job training.

The measure had the advantage of attracting Republican voters, but also conformed to his overarching understanding that the country could not afford to waste one person. All Americans were needed to compete in and prepare for global competition. A second initiative proved less successful. Clinton appointed his wife, Hilary, to chair a commission mandated with designing a national healthcare plan. Every industrialized nation in the world possessed national healthcare systems. At the same time, many Americans no longer received insurance from their employers, and could not afford it. Opposition from Republicans and health industry lobbyists led Clinton to shelve the plan.

Republicans frequently complained that the DLC Democrats had stolen their issues. Historically, Republicans supported smaller government, free trade, deficit reduction, and welfare reform. Clinton recast these issues to conform to his view of an interrelated global system. However, many Democrats viewed the approach as too Republican as well, and many abandoned it. Furthermore, in many respects Bill and Hilary Clinton represented the kind of liberals whom conservative Republicans had attacked since the late 1970s. Hilary Clinton struck conservatives as a feminist role model. After an affair with Monica Lewinsky, Bill Clinton's morals were seen as those that conservatives had long associated with liberalism. In the next two Presidential elections, the alliance between conservative Republicans and the Christian Right prevailed over Democrats who returned to more traditional, old Democratic strategies. The Culture Wars continued, and expanded to include the question of stem cell research as well as the treatment of Christians by foreign governments.

Clearly the conflict between the political parties is a war between cultures. The question remains as to whether or not it is simply a conflict between parties or one that has fundamentally divided the American people. That is, the projection of different images has been important in attracting people to work in the party machinery, getting out the vote, setting the party platforms, and pushing legislation. Furthermore, it has produced hundreds of millions of dollars in political contributions. Nevertheless, voters are put in the position of making a choice between candidates selected by the political parties. It remains unclear whether, in making that choice, they are much affected by the culture wars.

Considering the Evidence of the Readings

The documents in this chapter focus on the contemporary issue of a "culture war." With one exception, the authors are politicians or assume a political role. Three documents present the Conservative case from the perspective of a president, a religious leader, and a media pundit (running for president at the time). The Liberal position is articulated by a president and a religious leader. When examining the readings, look for the reasons Conservatives believe that the current culture is "liberal" and the affects it has upon values and politics. How did Conservatives view the role of religion in society and government? On the other hand, how do the Liberals counter these accounts by focusing upon the importance of diversity and the need to prepare for a global economy? Do they see any role for religion and values in modern culture? Finally, the last article is by a political scientist who questions the idea that we have a culture war. If that is so, how does he explain all of the arguments about it and how do the majority of Americans feel about it?

Document 25.1 President Reagan Inaugurates the New Conservative Approach

This document contains President Ronald Reagan's First Inaugural Address, or the first speech he gave upon becoming President. In it, he explains what issues and beliefs are most important to him, and states that he will use them to guide his presidency. Focus on his comments about the issues, especially economics, that concern him, the effects of big or liberal government, the role of values or morality and religion, and the characteristics of the American people. The speech marks an important change in the direction of American politics. Reagan commits himself to taking the country in a new, conservative direction. See the introduction to the chapter for a more complete discussion.

Senator Hatfield, Mr. Chief Justice, Mr. President, Vice President Bush, Vice President Mondale, Senator Baker, Speaker O'Neill, Reverend Moomaw, and my fellow citizens:

To a few of us here today, this is a solemn and most momentous occasion; and yet, in the history of our Nation, it is a commonplace occurrence. The orderly transfer of authority as called for in the Constitution routinely takes place as it has for almost two centuries and few of us stop to think how unique we really are. In the eyes of many in the world, this every-four-year ceremony we accept as normal is nothing less than a miracle.

Mr. President, I want our fellow citizens to know how much you did to carry on this tradition. By your gracious cooperation in the transition process, you have shown a watching world that we are a united people pledged to maintaining a political system which guarantees individual liberty to a greater degree than any other, and I thank you and your people for all your help in maintaining the continuity which is the bulwark of our Republic.

The business of our nation goes forward. These United States are confronted with an economic affliction of great proportions. We suffer from the longest and one of the worst sustained inflations in our national history. It distorts our economic decisions, penalizes thrift, and crushes the struggling young and the fixed-income elderly alike. It threatens to shatter the lives of millions of our people.

Idle industries have cast workers into unemployment, causing human misery and personal indignity. Those who do work are denied a fair return for their labor by a tax system which penalizes successful achievement and keeps us from maintaining full productivity.

But great as our tax burden is, it has not kept pace with public spending. For decades, we have piled deficit upon deficit, mortgaging our future and our children's future for the temporary convenience of the present. To continue this long trend is to guarantee tremendous social, cultural, political, and economic upheavals.

You and I, as individuals, can, by borrowing, live beyond our means, but for only a limited period of time. Why, then, should we think that collectively, as a nation, we are not bound by that same limitation?

We must act today in order to preserve tomorrow. And let there be no misunderstanding—we are going to begin to act, beginning today.

The economic ills we suffer have come upon us over several decades. They will not go away in days, weeks, or months, but they will go away. They will go away because we, as Americans, have the capacity now, as we have had in the past, to do whatever needs to be done to preserve this last and greatest bastion of freedom.

In this present crisis, government is not the solution to our problem.

From time to time, we have been tempted to believe that society has become too complex to be managed by self-rule, that government by an elite group is superior to government for, by, and of the people. But if no one among us is capable of governing himself, then who among us has the capacity to govern someone else? All of us together, in and out of government, must bear the burden. The solutions we seek must be equitable, with no one group singled out to pay a higher price.

We hear much of special interest groups. Our concern must be for a special interest group that has been too long neglected. It knows no sectional boundaries or ethnic and racial divisions, and it crosses political party lines. It is made up of men and women who raise our food, patrol our streets, man our mines and our factories, teach our children, keep our homes, and heal us when we are sick—professionals, industrialists, shopkeepers, clerks, cabbies, and truckdrivers. They are, in short, "We the people," this breed called Americans.

Well, this administration's objective will be a healthy, vigorous, growing economy that provides equal opportunity for all Americans, with no barriers born of bigotry or discrimination. Putting America back to work means putting all Americans back to work. Ending inflation means freeing all Americans from the terror of runaway living costs. All must share in the productive work of this "new beginning" and all must share in the bounty of a revived economy. With the idealism and fair play which are the core of our system and our strength, we can have a strong and prosperous America at peace with itself and the world.

So, as we begin, let us take inventory. We are a nation that has a government—not the other way around. And this makes us special among the nations of the Earth. Our Government has no power except that granted it by the people. It is time to check and reverse the growth of government which shows signs of having grown beyond the consent of the governed.

It is my intention to curb the size and influence of the Federal establishment and to demand recognition of the distinction between the powers granted to the Federal Government and those reserved to the States or to the people. All of us need to be reminded that the Federal Government did not create the States; the States created the Federal Government.

Now, so there will be no misunderstanding, it is not my intention to do away with government. It is, rather, to make it work—work with us, not over us; to stand by our side, not ride on our back. Government can and must provide opportunity, not smother it; foster productivity, not stifle it.

If we look to the answer as to why, for so many years, we achieved so much, prospered as no other people on Earth, it was because here, in this land, we unleashed the energy and individual genius of man to a greater extent than has ever been done before. Freedom and the dignity of the individual have been more available and assured here than in any other place on Earth. The price for this freedom at times has been high, but we have never been unwilling to pay that price.

It is no coincidence that our present troubles parallel and are proportionate to the intervention and intrusion in our lives that result from unnecessary and excessive growth of government. It is time for us to realize that we are too great a nation to limit ourselves to small dreams. We are not, as some would have us believe, doomed to an inevitable decline. I do not believe in a fate that will fall on us no matter what we do. I do believe in a fate that will fall on us if we do nothing. So, with all the creative energy at our command, let us begin an era of national renewal. Let us renew our determination, our courage, and our strength. And let us renew our faith and our hope.

We have every right to dream heroic dreams. Those who say that we are in a time when there are no heroes just don't know where to look. You can see heroes every day going in and out of factory gates. Others, a handful in number, produce enough food to feed all of us and then the world beyond. You meet heroes across a counter—and they are on both sides of that counter. There are entrepreneurs with faith in themselves and faith in an idea who create new jobs, new wealth and opportunity. They are individuals and families whose taxes support the Government and whose voluntary gifts support church, charity, culture, art, and education. Their patriotism is quiet but deep. Their values sustain our national life.

I have used the words "they" and "their" in speaking of these heroes. I could say "you" and "your" because I am addressing the heroes of whom I speak—you, the citizens of this blessed land. Your dreams, your hopes, your goals are going to be the dreams, the hopes, and the goals of this administration, so help me God.

We shall reflect the compassion that is so much a part of your makeup. How can we love our country and not love our countrymen, and loving them, reach out a hand when they fall, heal them when they are sick, and provide opportunities to make them self-sufficient so they will be equal in fact and not just in theory?

Can we solve the problems confronting us? Well, the answer is an unequivocal and emphatic "yes." To paraphrase Winston Churchill, I did not take the oath I have just taken with the intention of presiding over the dissolution of the world's strongest economy.

In the days ahead I will propose removing the roadblocks that have slowed our economy and reduced productivity. Steps will be taken aimed at restoring the balance between the various levels of government. Progress may be slow—measured in inches and feet, not miles—but we will progress. Is it time to reawaken this industrial giant, to get government back within its means, and to lighten our punitive tax burden. And these will be our first priorities, and on these principles, there will be no compromise.

On the eve of our struggle for independence a man who might have been one of the greatest among the Founding Fathers, Dr. Joseph Warren, President of the Massachusetts Congress, said to his fellow Americans, "Our country is in danger, but not to be despaired of. . . . On you depend the fortunes of America. You are to decide the important questions upon which rests the happiness and the liberty of millions yet unborn. Act worthy of yourselves."

Well, I believe we, the Americans of today, are ready to act worthy of ourselves, ready to do what must be done to ensure happiness and liberty for ourselves, our children and our children's children.

And as we renew ourselves here in our own land, we will be seen as having greater strength throughout the world. We will again be the exemplar of freedom and a beacon of hope for those who do not now have freedom.

To those neighbors and allies who share our freedom, we will strengthen our historic ties and assure them of our support and firm commitment. We will match loyalty with loyalty. We will strive for mutually beneficial relations. We will not use our friendship to impose on their sovereignty, for our own sovereignty is not for sale.

As for the enemies of freedom, those who are potential adversaries, they will be reminded that peace is the highest aspiration of the American people. We will negotiate for it, sacrifice for it; we will not surrender for it—now or ever.

Our forbearance should never be misunderstood. Our reluctance for conflict should not be misjudged as a failure of will. When action is required to preserve our national security, we will act. We will maintain sufficient strength to prevail if need be, knowing that if we do so we have the best chance of never having to use that strength.

Above all, we must realize that no arsenal, or no weapon in the arsenals of the world, is so formidable as the will and moral courage of free men and women. It is a weapon our adversaries in today's world do not have. It is a weapon that we as Americans do have. Let that be understood by those who practice terrorism and prey upon their neighbors.

I am told that tens of thousands of prayer meetings are being held on this day, and for that I am deeply grateful. We are a nation under God, and I believe God intended for us to be free. It would be fitting and good, I think, if on each Inauguration Day in future years it should be declared a day of prayer.

This is the first time in history that this ceremony has been held, as you have been told, on this West Front of the Capitol. Standing here, one faces a magnificent vista, opening up on this city's special beauty and history. At the end of this open mall are those shrines to the giants on whose shoulders we stand.

Directly in front of me, the monument to a monumental man: George Washington, Father of our country. A man of humility who came to greatness reluctantly. He led America out of revolutionary victory into infant nationhood. Off to one side, the stately memorial to Thomas Jefferson. The Declaration of Independence flames with his eloquence.

And then beyond the Reflecting Pool the dignified columns of the Lincoln Memorial. Whoever would understand in his heart the meaning of America will find it in the life of Abraham Lincoln.

Beyond those monuments to heroism is the Potomac River, and on the far shore the sloping hills of Arlington National Cemetery with its row on row of simple white markers bearing crosses or Stars of David. They add up to only a tiny fraction of the price that has been paid for our freedom.

Each one of those markers is a monument to the kinds of hero I spoke of earlier. Their lives ended in places called Belleau Wood, The Argonne, Omaha Beach, Salerno and halfway around the world on Guadalcanal, Tarawa, Pork Chop Hill, the Chosin Reservoir, and in a hundred rice paddies and jungles of a place called Vietnam.

Under one such marker lies a young man—Martin Treptow—who left his job in a small town barber shop in 1917 to go to France with the famed Rainbow Division. There, on the western front, he was killed trying to carry a message between battalions under heavy artillery fire.

We are told that on his body was found a diary. On the flyleaf under the heading, "My Pledge," he had written these words: "America must win this war. Therefore, I will work, I will save, I will sacrifice, I will endure, I will fight cheerfully and do my utmost, as if the issue of the whole struggle depended on me alone."

The crisis we are facing today does not require of us the kind of sacrifice that Martin Treptow and so many thousands of others were called upon to make. It does require, however, our best effort, and our willingness to believe in ourselves and to believe in our capacity to perform great deeds; to believe that together, with God's help, we can and will resolve the problems which now confront us.

And, after all, why shouldn't we believe that? We are Americans. God bless you, and thank you.

Document 25.2 Conservative Christians and the Role of Religion in Government

In this document, the Reverend Jerry Falwell presents the ideas of conservative Christians. Falwell proposes creating a very different relationship between religion and government. Focus on his views about the relationship between religious morality and government, his criticism of big or liberal government and its effects, and what issues people and governments should address. Falwell was one of the first Fundamentalist Christians to address political issues. He proceeded to organize conservative Christians to achieve the goals he sets forth in the document. In 1979 he established the Moral Majority, Inc. as a network for Christian churches to educate voters about the political issues, compile mailing lists of Christians, register voters, and encourage voting. Falwell regularly spoke at the Religious Roundtable, part of Moral Majority, Inc., and brought politicians to speak with conservative Christians. He became very influential in the Republican Party as a spokesperson for issues, and in getting out the vote on Election Day.

We must review our government and see where our leadership has taken us today and where our future leaders must take us tomorrow if we are to remain a free America. It is a sad fact today that Americans have made a god of government. They are looking to government rather than to God, who ordained government. The United States is a republic where laws rule. Although the people of the United States have a vote, America is not a democracy in the sense that the majority rules. Her citizens elect representatives who represent them and govern them by laws. I believe that God promoted America to a greatness no other nation has ever enjoyed because her heritage is one of a republic governed by laws predicated on the Bible.

America is facing a vacuum of leadership not only in regard to her elected officials, but also among her citizens who are not standing for what is right and decent. We need in America today powerful, dynamic, and godly leadership. Male leadership in our families is affecting male leadership in our churches, and it is affecting male leadership in our society. As we look across our nation today we find a tremendous vacuum of godly men who are willing to be the kind of spiritual leaders who are necessary not only to change a nation, but also to change the churches within our nation and the basic units of our entire society, our families.

If a man is not a student of the Word of God and does not know what the Bible says, I question his ability to be an effective leader. Whatever he leads, whether it be his family, his church, or his nation, will not be properly led without this priority. God alone has the wisdom to tell men and women where this world is going, where it needs to go, and how it can be redirected. Only by godly leadership can America be put back on a divine course. God will give national healing if men and women will pray and meet God's conditions, but we must have leadership in America to deliver God's message.

We must reverse the trend America finds herself in today. Young people between the ages of twenty-five and forty have been born and reared in a different world than Americans of years past. The television set has been their primary baby-sitter. From the television set they have learned situation ethics and immorality—they have learned a loss of respect for human life. They have learned to disrespect the family as God has established it. They have been educated in a public-school system that is permeated with secular humanism. They have been taught that the Bible is just another book of literature. They have been taught that there are no absolutes in our world today. They have been introduced to the drug culture. They have been reared by the family and by the public school in a society that is greatly void of discipline and character-building. These same young people have been reared under the influence of a government that has taught them socialism and welfarism. They have been taught to believe that the world owes them a living whether they work or not.

I believe that America was built on integrity, on faith in God, and on hard work. I do not believe that anyone has ever been successful in life without being willing to add that last ingredient—diligence or hard work. We now have second- and third-generation welfare recipients. Welfare is not always wrong. There are those who do need welfare, but we have reared a generation that understands neither the dignity nor the importance of work.

Every American who looks at the facts must share a deep concern and burden for our country. We are not unduly concerned when we say that there are some very dark clouds on America's horizon. I am not a pessimist, but it is indeed a time for truth. If Americans will face the truth, our nation can be turned around and can be saved from the evils and the destruction that have fallen upon every other nation that has turned its back on God.

There is no excuse for what is happening in our country. We must, from the highest office in the land right down to the shoe-shine boy in the airport, have a return to biblical basics. If the Congress of our United States will take its stand on that which is right and wrong, and if our President, our judiciary system, and our state and local leaders will take their stand on holy living, we can turn this country around.

I personally feel that the home and the family are still held in reverence by the vast majority of the American public. I believe there is still a vast number of Americans who love their country, are patriotic, and are willing to sacrifice for her. I remember the time when it was positive to be patriotic, and as far as I am concerned, it still is. I remember as a boy, when the flag was raised, everyone stood proudly and put his hand upon his heart and pledged allegiance with gratitude. I remember when the band struck up "The Stars and Stripes Forever," we stood and goose pimples would run all over me. I remember when I was in elementary school during World War II, when every report from the other shores meant something to us. We were not out demonstrating against our boys who were dying in Europe and Asia. We were praying for them and thanking God for them and buying war bonds to help pay for the materials and artillery they needed to fight and win and come back.

I believe that Americans want to see this country come back to basics, back to values, back to biblical morality, back to sensibility, and back to patriotism. Americans are looking for leadership and guidance. It is fair to ask the question, "If 84 per cent of the American people still believe in morality, why is America having such internal problems?" We must look for the answer to the highest places in every level of government. We have a lack of leadership in America. But Americans have been lax in voting in and out of office the right and the wrong people.

My responsibility as a preacher of the Gospel is one of influence, not of control, and that is the responsibility of each individual citizen. Through the ballot box Americans must provide for strong moral leadership at every level. If our country will get back on the track in sensibility and moral sanity, the crises that I have herein mentioned will work out in the course of time and with God's blessings.

It is now time to take a stand on certain moral issues, and we can only stand if we have leaders. We must stand against the Equal Rights Amendment, the feminist revolution, and the homosexual revolution. We must have a revival in this country. It can come if we will realize the danger and heed the admonition of God found in 2 Chronicles 7:14, "If my people, which are called by my name, shall humble themselves, and pray, and seek my face, and turn from their wicked ways; then will I hear from heaven, and will forgive their sin, and will heal their land."

As a preacher of the Gospel, I not only believe in prayer and preaching, I also believe in good citizenship. If a labor union in America has the right to organize and improve its working conditions, then I believe that the churches and the pastors, the priests, and the rabbis of America have a responsibility, not just the right, to see to it that the moral climate and conscience of Americans is such that this nation can be healed inwardly. If it is healed inwardly, then it will heal itself outwardly.

It is not easy to go against the tide and do what is right. This nation can be brought back to God, but there must first be an awareness of sin. The Bible declares, "Righteousness exalteth a nation: But sin is a reproach to any people." (Pr. 14:34) It is right living that has made America the greatest nation on earth, and with all of her shortcomings and failures, America is without question the greatest nation on the face of God's earth. We as Americans must recommit ourselves to keeping her that way. Our prayers must certainly be behind our President and our Congress. We are commissioned by Scripture (1. Tm. 2:1-3) to pray for those who are in authority, but we would also remind our leaders that the future of this great nation is in their hands. One day they will stand before God accountable with what they have done to ensure our future. God has charged us as Americans with great privileges, but to whom much is given "much is required." We are faced with great responsibilities. Today, more than at any time in history, America needs men and women of God who have an understanding of the times and are not afraid to stand up for what is right.

Americans have been silent much too long. We have stood by and watched as American power and influence have been systematically weakened in every sphere of the world.

We are not a perfect nation, but we are still a free nation because we have the blessing of God upon us. We must continue to follow in a path that will ensure that blessing. We must not forget the words of our national anthem:

"Oh! thus be it ever, when free men shall stand
Between their loved homes and the war's desolation
Blest with victory and peace, may the heav'n rescued land

Praise the Power that hath made and preserved us a nation.
Then conquer we must, when our cause it is just,
And this be our motto: 'In God is our trust.'"

We must not forget that it is God Almighty who has made and preserved us a nation.

Let us never forget that as our Constitution declares, we are endowed by our Creator with certain inalienable rights. It is only as we abide by those laws established by our Creator that He will continue to bless us with these rights. We are endowed our rights to freedom and liberty and the pursuit of happiness by the God who created man to be free and equal.

The hope of reversing the trends of decay in our republic now lies with the Christian public in America. We cannot expect help from the liberals. They certainly are not going to call our nation back to righteousness and neither are the pornographers, the smut peddlers, and those who are corrupting our youth. Moral Americans must be willing to put their reputations, their fortunes, and their very lives on the line for this great nation of ours. Would that we had the courage of our forefathers who knew the great responsibility that freedom carries with it. Patrick Henry said, "It is natural to man to indulge in the illusions of hope. We are apt to shut our eyes against a painful truth. . . . Is this the part of wise men, engaged in a great and arduous struggle for liberty? Are we disposed to be a number of those who, having eyes, see not, and having ears, hear not, the things which so nearly concern their temporal salvation? For my part, whatever anguish of spirit it may cost, I am willing to know the whole truth; to know the worst and to provide for it. . . . Is life so dear or peace so sweet, as to be purchased at the price of chains or slavery? Forbid it, Almighty God! I know not what course others may take, but as for me, give me liberty or give me death!"

More than ever before in the history of humanity, we must have heroes, those men and women who will stand for what is right and stand against what is wrong, no matter what it costs. Today we need men and women of character and integrity who will commit themselves to letting their posterity know the freedom that our Founding Fathers established for this nation. Let us stand by that statement in the Declaration of Independence that cost our forefathers so much: ". . . with a firm Reliance on the Protection of divine Providence, we mutually pledge to each other our lives, our Fortunes, and our sacred Honor."

Our Founding Fathers separated church and state in function, but never intended to establish a government void of God. As is evidenced by our Constitution, good people in America must exert an influence and provide a conscience and climate of morality in which it is difficult to go wrong, not difficult for people to go right in America.

I am positive in my belief regarding the Constitution that God led in the development of that document, and as a result, we here in America have enjoyed 204 years of unparalleled freedom. The most positive people in the world are people who believe the Bible to be the Word of God. The Bible contains a positive message. It is a message written by 40 men over a period of approximately 1,500 years under divine inspiration. It is God's message of love, redemption, and deliverance for a fallen race. What could be more positive than the message of redemption in the Bible? But God will force Himself upon no man. Each individual American must make His choice.

Peter Marshall knew that the choices of individuals determine the destiny of a nation. He immigrated to the United States as a young man and worked his way through seminary by digging ditches and doing newspaper work. His years in the ministry culminated with the pastorate of the historic New York Avenue Presbyterian Church in Washington, D.C. (Abraham Lincoln's church), located two blocks from the White House. Dr. Marshall became chap-

lain of the Senate in January 1947. He died suddenly in January 1949 while still holding office. He was a dynamic Christian and was called by many a reporter the "conscience of the Senate."

Peter Marshall summed it up well when in a sermon to the New York Presbyterian Church he challenged its members with these words: "Today, we are living in a time when enough individuals, choosing to go to hell, will pull the nation down to hell with them. The choices you make in moral and religious questions determine the way America will go. The choice before us is plain, Christ or chaos, conviction or compromise, discipline or disintegration. I am rather tired about hearing about our rights and privileges as American *citizens*. The time has come, it now is, when we ought to hear about the duties and responsibilities of our citizenship. America's future depends upon her accepting and demonstrating God's government. It is just as plain and clear as that."

Americans must no longer linger in ignorance and apathy. We cannot be silent about the sins that are destroying this nation. The choice is ours. We must turn America around or prepare for inevitable destruction. I am listening to the sounds that threaten to take away our liberties in America. And I have listened to God's admonitions and His direction—the only hopes of saving America. Are you listening too?

Document 25.3 Pat Buchanan Describes the Culture Wars

This document contains a speech that Pat Buchanan delivered at the 1992 Republican National Convention. He had run and lost in the primaries against Republican incumbent President George Bush, whom he considered too moderate. In this speech he throws his support behind Bush, but calls for a culture war to preserve conservative Christian morality. Many political analysts argue that the speech did tremendous harm to Bush's campaign. In the address, he contrasts conservative Republicans with Democrats. He suggests that the differences between the two are profound and morally based. There is no room for compromise; one must prevail, and so a war between the two cultures is taking place. Focus on his views about Ronald Reagan's presidency, the relationship between government and religious morality, what moral values separate Republicans and Democrats, and what issues government should address. Buchanan had served as speech writer for President Richard Nixon and was White House Communications Director for President Ronald Reagan. He also pursued a career as a columnist and political commentator on several television shows.

Well, we took the long way home, but we finally got here. And I want to congratulate President Bush, and remove any doubt about where we stand: The primaries are over, the heart is strong again, and the

Buchanan Brigades are enlisted—all the way to a great comeback victory in November.

Like many of you last month, I watched that giant masquerade ball at Madison Square Garden—where 20,000 radicals and liberals came dressed up as moderates and centrists—in the greatest single exhibition of cross-dressing in American political history.

One by one, the prophets of doom appeared at the podium. The Reagan Decade, they moaned, was a terrible time in America; and the only way to prevent even worse times, they said, is to entrust our nation's fate and future to the party that gave us McGovern, Mondale, Carter and Michael Dukakis.

No way, my friends. The American people are not going to buy back into the failed liberalism of the 1960s and '70s—no matter how slick the package in 1992.

The malcontents of Madison Square Garden notwithstanding, the 1980s were not terrible years. They were great years. You know it. I know it. And the only people who don't know it are the carping critics who sat on the sidelines of history, jeering at one of the great statesmen of modern time.

Out of Jimmy Carter's days of malaise, Ronald Reagan crafted the longest peacetime recovery in U.S. history—3 million new businesses created, and 20 million new jobs.

Under the Reagan Doctrine, one by one, the communist dominos began to fall. First, Grenada was liberated, by U.S. troops. Then, the Red Army was run out of Afghanistan, by U.S. weapons. In Nicaragua, the Marxist regime was forced to hold free elections—by Ronald Reagan's contra army—and the Communists were thrown out of power.

Have they forgotten? It was under our party that the Berlin Wall came down, and Europe was reunited. It was under our party that the Soviet Empire collapsed, and the captive nations broke free.

It is said that each president will be recalled by posterity—with but a single sentence. George Washington was the father of our country. Abraham Lincoln preserved the Union. And Ronald Reagan won the Cold War. And it is time my old colleagues, the columnists and commentators, looking down on us tonight, from their anchor booths and sky boxes, gave Ronald Reagan the credit he deserves—for leading America to victory in the Cold War.

Most of all, Ronald Reagan made us proud to be Americans again. We never felt better about our country; and we never stood taller in the eyes of the world.

But, we are here, not only to celebrate, but to nominate. And an American president has many, many roles.

He is our first diplomat, the architect of American foreign policy. And which of these two men is more qualified for that role? George Bush has been U.N. ambassador, CIA director, envoy to China. As vice president, he co-authored the policies that won the Cold War. As president, George Bush presided over the liberation of Eastern Europe and the termination of the Warsaw Pact. And Mr. Clinton? Well, Bill Clinton couldn't find 150 words to discuss foreign policy in an acceptance speech that lasted an hour. As was said of an earlier Democratic candidate, Bill Clinton's foreign policy experience is pretty much confined to having had breakfast once at the International House of Pancakes.

The presidency is also America's bully pulpit, what Mr. Truman called, "pre-eminently a place of moral leadership." George Bush is a defender of right to life, and life-long champion of the Judeo-Christian values and beliefs upon which this nation was built.

Mr. Clinton, however, has a different agenda. At its top is unrestricted abortion on demand. When the Irish-Catholic governor of Pennsylvania, Robert Casey, asked to say a few words, on behalf of the 25 million unborn children destroyed since Roe v. Wade, he was told there was no place for him at the podium of Bill Clinton's convention, no room at the inn.

Yet, a militant leader of the homosexual rights movement could rise at that convention and exult: "Bill Clinton and Al Gore represent the most pro-lesbian and pro-gay ticket in history." And so they do.

Bill Clinton supports school choice—but only for state-run schools. Parents who send their children to Christian schools, or Catholic schools, need not apply. Elect me, and you get two for the price of one, Mr. Clinton says of his lawyer-spouse. And what does Hillary believe? Well, Hillary believes that 12-year-olds should have a right to sue their parents, and she has compared marriage as an institution to slavery—and life on an Indian reservation. Well, speak for yourself, Hillary.

Friends, this is radical feminism. The agenda Clinton & Clinton would impose on America—abortion on demand, a litmus test for the Supreme Court, homosexual rights, discrimination against religious schools, women in combat—that's change all right. But it is not the kind of change America wants. It is not the kind of change America needs. And it is not the kind of change we can tolerate in a nation that we still call God's country.

A president is also commander-in-chief, the man we empower to send sons and brothers, fathers and friends, to war. George Bush was 17 when they bombed Pearl Harbor. He left his high school class, walked down to the recruiting office, and signed up to become the youngest fighter pilot in the Pacific War. And Mr. Clinton? When Bill Clinton's turn came in

Vietnam, he sat up in a dormitory in Oxford, England, and figured out how to dodge the draft.

Which of these two men has won the moral authority to call on Americans to put their lives at risk? I suggest, respectfully, it is the patriot and war hero, Navy Lt.j.g George Herbert Walker Bush.

My friends, this campaign is about philosophy, and it is about character; and George Bush wins on both counts—going away; and it is time all of us came home and stood beside him.

As running mate, Mr. Clinton chose Albert Gore. And just how moderate is Prince Albert? Well, according to the Taxpayers Union, Al Gore beat out Teddy Kennedy, two straight years, for the title of biggest spender in the Senate.

And Teddy Kennedy isn't moderate about anything.

In New York, Mr. Gore made a startling declaration. Henceforth, he said, the "central organizing principle" of all governments must be: the environment.

Wrong, Albert!

The central organizing principle of this republic is freedom. And from the ancient forests of Oregon, to the Inland Empire of California, America's great middle class has got to start standing up to the environmental extremists who put insects, rats and birds—ahead of families, workers and jobs.

One year ago, my friends, I could not have dreamt I would be here. I was then still just one of many panelists on what President Bush calls, "those crazy Sunday talk shows."

But, I disagreed with the president; and so we challenged the president in the Republican primaries, and fought as best we could. From February to June, he won 33 primaries. I can't recall exactly how many we won.

But, tonight, I want to talk to the 3 million Americans who voted for me: I will never forget you, nor the great honor you have done me. But, I do believe, deep in my heart, that the right place for us to be now—in this presidential campaign—is right beside George Bush. This party is our home, this party is where we belong. And, don't let anyone tell you any different.

Yes, we disagreed with President Bush, but we stand with him for freedom-of-choice religious schools, and we stand with him against the amoral idea that gay and lesbian couples should have the same standing in law as married men and women.

We stand with President Bush for right to life, and for voluntary prayer in the public schools—and against putting American women in combat. And we stand with President Bush in favor of the right of small towns and communities to control the raw sewage of pornography that pollutes our popular culture. We stand with President Bush in favor of federal judges who interpret the law as written, and against Supreme Court justices who think they have a mandate to rewrite our Constitution.

My friends, this election is about much more than who gets what. It is about who we are. It is about what we believe, it is about what we stand for as Americans. There is a religious war going on in our country for the soul of America. It is a cultural war, as critical to the kind of nation we will one day be—as was the Cold War itself. And in that struggle for the soul of America, Clinton & Clinton are on the other side, and George Bush is on our side. And, so, we have to come home—and stand beside him.

My friends, in those six months—from Concord to California—I came to know our country better than ever before in my life, and I collected memories that will be with me always.

There was that day-long ride through the great state of Georgia in a bus Vice President Bush himself had used in 1988—a bus they called Asphalt One. The ride ended with a 9 p.m. speech, in front of a magnificent Southern mansion, in a town called Fitzgerald.

There were the workers at the James River Paper Mill, in the frozen North Country of New Hampshire, hard, tough men, one of whom was silent, until I shook his hand. Then, he looked up in my eyes, and said, "Save our jobs!"

There was the legal secretary at the Manchester airport on Christmas Day, who told me she was going to vote for me, then broke down crying, saying, "I've lost my job, I don't have any money; they're going to take away my daughter. What am I going to do?"

My friends, even in tough times, these people are with us. They don't read Adam Smith or Edmund Burke, but they came from the same schoolyards and playgrounds and towns as we did. They share our beliefs and convictions, our hopes and our dreams. They are the conservatives of the heart. They are our people. And, we need to reconnect with them. We need to let them know we know they're hurting. They don't expect miracles, but they need to know we care.

There were the people of Hayfork, the tiny town high up in California's Trinity Alps, a town that is now under a sentence of death, because a federal judge has set aside 9 million acres for the habitat of the spotted owl—forgetting about the habitat of the men and women who live and work in Hayfork. And there where the brave live the family values we treasure, and who still believe deeply in the American dream.

Friends, in those wonderful 25 weeks, the saddest days were the days of the bloody riot in L.A., worst in our history. But even out of that awful tragedy can come a message of hope.

Hours after the violence ended I visited the Army compound in south L.A., where an officer of the 18th Cavalry, that had come to rescue the city, introduced me to two of his troopers. They could not have been 20 years old. He told them to recount their story.

They had come into Los Angeles late on the second day; and they walked up a dark street, where the mob had looted and burned every building but one, a convalescent home for the aged. The mob was head-ing in, to ransack and loot the apartments of the terrified old men and women. When the troopers arrived, M-16s at the ready, the mob threatened and cursed, but the mob retreated. It had met the one thing that could stop it: force, rooted in justice, backed by courage.

Greater love than this hath no man than that he lay down his life for his friend. Here were 19-year-old boys ready to lay down their lives to stop a mob from molesting old people they did not even know. And, as they took back the streets of Los Angeles, block by block, so we must take back our cities, and take back our culture, and take back our country.

God bless you, and God bless America.

Document 25.4 Jesse Jackson Seeks Common Ground in a Divided Party

This document contains Jesse Jackson's address to the 1988 Democratic National Convention. Jackson had sought the party's nomination and attracted a significant amount of support. At the time, the Democrats were struggling to unite as a party. The wide range of groups, with equally wide-ranging demands for the party platform, made that effort extremely difficult. In the speech, Jackson explains the common ground that Democrats share, and urges them to come together in support of the nominee, Michael Dukakis. Focus on Jackson's view of diversity in the party, how he finds common ground among the various groups making up the party, and what issues the Democrats should address. Jackson worked with Martin Luther King, Jr. in the Civil Rights Movement. He twice ran for the Democratic presidential nomination. His commitment to equal rights and opportunity found expression in the Rainbow Coalition, a multicultural organization dedicated to promoting opportunity and equality.

Thank you. Thank you. Thank you.

Tonight, we pause and give praise and honor to God for being good enough to allow us to be at this place at this time. When I look out at this convention, I see the face of America: Red, Yellow, Brown, Black and White. We are all precious in God's sight—the real rainbow coalition.

All of us—all of us who are here think that we are seated. But we're really standing on someone's shoulders. Ladies and gentlemen, Mrs. Rosa Parks—the mother of the civil rights movement.

[*Mrs. Rosa Parks is brought to the podium.*]

I want to express my deep love and appreciation for the support my family has given me over these past months. They have endured pain, anxiety, threat, and fear. But they have been strengthened and made secure by our faith in God, in America, and in you. Your love has protected us and made us strong. To my wife Jackie, the foundation of our family; to our five children whom you met tonight; to my mother, Mrs. Helen Jackson, who is present tonight; and to our grandmother, Mrs. Matilda Burns; to my brother Chuck and his family; to my mother-in-law, Mrs. Gertrude Brown, who just last month at age 61 graduated from *Hampton Institute*—a marvelous achievement.

I offer my appreciation to Mayor Andrew Young who has provided such gracious hospitality to all of us this week.

And a special salute to President Jimmy Carter. President Carter restored honor to the White House after Watergate. He gave many of us a special opportunity to grow. For his kind words, for his unwavering commitment to peace in the world, and for the voters that came from his family, every member of his family, led by Billy and Amy, I offer my special thanks to the Carter family.

My right and my privilege to stand here before you has been won, won in my lifetime, by the blood and the sweat of the innocent.

Twenty-four years ago, the late Fannie Lou Hamer and Aaron Henry—who sits here tonight from Mississippi—were locked out onto the streets in Atlantic City; the head of the Mississippi Freedom Democratic Party.

But tonight, a Black and White delegation from Mississippi is headed by Ed Cole, a Black man from Mississippi; twenty-four years later.

Many were lost in the struggle for the right to vote: Jimmy Lee Jackson, a young student, gave his life; Viola Liuzzo, a White mother from Detroit, called "nigger lover," and brains blown out at point blank range; [Michael] Schwerner, [Andrew] Goodman and [James] Chaney—two Jews and a Black—found in a common grave, bodies riddled with bullets in Mississippi; the four darling little girls in a church in Birmingham, Alabama. They died that we might have a right to live.

Dr. Martin Luther King Jr. lies only a few miles from us tonight. Tonight he must feel good as he looks down upon us. We sit here together, a rainbow, a coalition—the sons and daughters of slavemasters and the sons and daughters of slaves, sitting together around a common table, to decide the direction of our party and our country. His heart would be full tonight.

As a testament to the struggles of those who have gone before; as a legacy for those who will come after; as a tribute to the endurance, the patience, the courage of our forefathers and mothers; as an assurance that their prayers are being answered, that their work has not been in vain, and, that hope is eternal, tomorrow night my name will go into nomination for the Presidency of the United States of America.

We meet tonight at the crossroads, a point of decision. Shall we expand, be inclusive, find unity and power; or suffer division and impotence?

We've come to Atlanta, the cradle of the Old South, the crucible of the New South. Tonight, there is a sense of celebration, because we are moved, fundamentally moved from racial battlegrounds by law, to economic common ground. Tomorrow we'll challenge to move to higher ground.

Common ground. Think of Jerusalem, the intersection where many trails met. A small village that became the birthplace for three great religions—Judaism, Christianity, and Islam. Why was this village so blessed? Because it provided a crossroads where different people met, different cultures, different civilizations could meet and find common ground.

When people come together, flowers always flourish—the air is rich with the aroma of a new spring.

Take New York, the dynamic metropolis. What makes New York so special? It's the invitation at the Statue of Liberty, "Give me your tired, your poor, your huddled masses who yearn to breathe free." Not restricted to English only. Many people, many cultures, many languages with one thing in common: They yearn to breathe free. Common ground.

Tonight in Atlanta, for the first time in this century, we convene in the South; a state where Governors once stood in school house doors; where Julian Bond was denied a seat in the State Legislature because of his conscientious objection to the Vietnam War; a city that, through its five Black Universities, has graduated more black students than any city in the world. Atlanta, now a modern intersection of the New South.

Common ground. That's the challenge of our party tonight—left wing, right wing.

Progress will not come through boundless liberalism nor static conservatism, but at the critical mass of mutual survival—not at boundless liberalism nor static conservatism, but at the critical mass of mutual survival. It takes two wings to fly. Whether you're a hawk or a dove, you're just a bird living in the same environment, in the same world.

The Bible teaches that when lions and lambs lie down together, none will be afraid, and there will be peace in the valley. It sounds impossible. Lions eat lambs. Lambs sensibly flee from lions. Yet even lions and lambs find common ground. Why? Because neither lions nor lambs want the forest to catch on fire. Neither lions nor lambs want acid rain to fall. Neither lions nor lambs can survive nuclear war. If lions and lambs can find common ground, surely we can as well—as civilized people.

The only time that we win is when we come together. In 1960, John Kennedy, the late John Kennedy, beat Richard Nixon by only 112,000 votes—less than one vote per precinct. He won by the margin of our hope. He brought us together. He reached out. He had the courage to defy his advisors and inquire about Dr. King's jailing in Albany, Georgia. We won by the margin of our hope, inspired by courageous leadership. In 1964, Lyndon Johnson brought both wings together—the thesis, the antithesis, and the creative synthesis—and together we won. In 1976, Jimmy Carter unified us again, and we won. When do we not come together, we never win. In 1968, the vision and despair in July led to our defeat in November. In 1980, rancor in the spring and the summer led to Reagan in the fall. When we divide, we cannot win.

We must find common ground as the basis for survival and development and change and growth.

Today when we debated, differed, deliberated, agreed to agree, agreed to disagree, when we had the good judgment to argue a case and then not self-destruct, George Bush was just a little further away from the White House and a little closer to private life.

Tonight, I salute Governor Michael Dukakis. He has run—He has run a well-managed and a dignified campaign. No matter how tired or how tried, he always resisted the temptation to stoop to demagoguery.

I've watched a good mind fast at work, with steel nerves, guiding his campaign out of the crowded field without appeal to the worst in us. I've watched his perspective grow as his environment has expanded. I've seen his toughness and tenacity close up. I know his commitment to public service. Mike Dukakis' parents were a doctor and a teacher; my parents a maid, a beautician, and a janitor. There's a great gap between Brookline, Massachusetts and Haney Street in the Fieldcrest Village housing projects in Greenville, South Carolina.

He studied law; I studied theology. There are differences of religion, region, and race; differences in experiences and perspectives. But the genius of America is that out of the many we become one.

Providence has enabled our paths to intersect. His foreparents came to America on immigrant ships; my foreparents came to America on slave ships. But whatever the original ships, we're in the same boat tonight.

Our ships could pass in the night—if we have a false sense of independence—or they could collide and crash. We would lose our passengers. We can seek a high reality and a greater good. Apart, we can drift on the broken pieces of Reaganomics, satisfy our baser instincts, and exploit the fears of our people. At our highest, we can call upon noble instincts and navigate this vessel to safety. The greater good is the common good.

As Jesus said, "Not My will, but Thine be done." It was his way of saying there's a higher good beyond personal comfort or position.

The good of our Nation is at stake. It's commitment to working men and women, to the poor and the vulnerable, to the many in the world.

With so many guided missiles, and so much misguided leadership, the stakes are exceedingly high. Our choice? Full participation in a democratic government, or more abandonment and neglect. And so this night, we choose not a false sense of independence, not our capacity to survive and endure. Tonight we choose interdependency, and our capacity to act and unite for the greater good.

Common good is finding commitment to new priorities to expansion and inclusion. A commitment to expanded participation in the Democratic Party at every level. A commitment to a shared national campaign strategy and involvement at every level.

A commitment to new priorities that insure that hope will be kept alive. A common ground commitment to a legislative agenda for empowerment, for the John Conyers bill—universal, on-site, same-day registration everywhere. A commitment to D.C. statehood and empowerment—D.C. deserves statehood. A commitment to economic set-asides, commitment to the Dellums bill for comprehensive sanctions against South Africa. A shared commitment to a common direction.

Common ground.

Easier said than done. Where do you find common ground? At the point of challenge. This campaign has shown that politics need not be marketed by politicians, packaged by pollsters and pundits. Politics can be a moral arena where people come together to find common ground.

We find common ground at the plant gate that closes on workers without notice. We find common ground at the farm auction, where a good farmer loses his or her land to bad loans or diminishing markets. Common ground at the school yard where teachers cannot get adequate pay, and students cannot get a scholarship, and can't make a loan. Common ground at the hospital admitting room, where somebody tonight is dying because they cannot afford to go upstairs to a bed that's empty waiting for someone with insurance to get sick. We are a better nation than that. We must do better.

Common ground. What is leadership if not present help in a time of crisis? And so I met you at the point of challenge. In Jay, Maine, where paper workers were striking for fair wages; in Greenville, Iowa, where family farmers struggle for a fair price; in Cleveland, Ohio, where working women seek comparable worth; in McFarland, California, where the children of Hispanic farm workers may be dying from poisoned land, dying in clusters with cancer; in an AIDS hospice in Houston, Texas, where the sick support one another, too often rejected by their own parents and friends.

Common ground. America is not a blanket woven from one thread, one color, one cloth. When I was a child growing up in Greenville, South Carolina and grandmama could not afford a blanket, she didn't complain and we did not freeze. Instead she took pieces of old cloth—patches, wool, silk, gabardine, crockersack—only patches, barely good enough to wipe off your shoes with. But they didn't stay that way very long. With sturdy hands and a strong cord, she sewed them together into a quilt, a thing of beauty and power and culture. Now, Democrats, we must build such a quilt.

Farmers, you seek fair prices and you are right—but you cannot stand alone. Your patch is not big enough.

Workers, you fight for fair wages, you are right—but your patch labor is not big enough.

Women, you seek comparable worth and pay equity, you are right—but your patch is not big enough.

Women, mothers, who seek Head Start, and day care and prenatal care on the front side of life, relevant jail care and welfare on the back side of life, you are right—but your patch is not big enough.

Students, you seek scholarships, you are right—but your patch is not big enough.

Blacks and Hispanics, when we fight for civil rights, we are right—but our patch is not big enough.

Gays and lesbians, when you fight against discrimination and a cure for AIDS, you are right—but your patch is not big enough.

Conservatives and progressives, when you fight for what you believe, right wing, left wing, hawk, dove, you are right from your point of view, but your point of view is not enough.

But don't despair. Be as wise as my grandmama. Pull the patches and the pieces together, bound by a common thread. When we form a great quilt of unity and common ground, we'll have the power to bring about health care and housing and jobs and education and hope to our Nation.

We, the people, can win.

We stand at the end of a long dark night of reaction. We stand tonight united in the commitment to a new direction. For almost eight years we've been led by those who view social good coming from private interest, who view public life as a means to increase private wealth. They have been prepared to sacrifice the common good of the many to satisfy the private interests and the wealth of a few.

We believe in a government that's a tool of our democracy in service to the public, not an instrument of the aristocracy in search of private wealth. We believe in government with the consent of the governed, "of, for and by the people." We must now emerge into a new day with a new direction.

Reaganomics: Based on the belief that the rich had too much money [sic]—too little money and the poor had too much. That's classic Reaganomics. They believe that the poor had too much money and the rich had too little money—so they engaged in reverse Robin Hood—took from the poor, gave to the rich, paid for by the middle class. We cannot stand four more years of Reaganomics in any version, in any disguise.

How do I document that case? Seven years later, the richest 1 percent of our society pays 20 percent less in taxes. The poorest 10 percent pay 20 percent more: Reaganomics.

Reagan gave the rich and the powerful a multibillion-dollar party. Now the party is over. He expects the people to pay for the damage. I take this principal position, convention, let us not raise taxes on the poor and the middle-class, but those who had the party, the rich and the powerful, must pay for the party.

I just want to take common sense to high places. We're spending one hundred and fifty billion dollars a year defending Europe and Japan 43 years after the war is over. We have more troops in Europe tonight than we had seven years ago. Yet the threat of war is ever more remote.

Germany and Japan are now creditor nations; that means they've got a surplus. We are a debtor nation—means we are in debt. Let them share more of the burden of their own defense. Use some of that money to build decent housing. Use some of that money to educate our children. Use some of that money for long-term health care. Use some of that money to wipe out these slums and put America back to work!

I just want to take common sense to high places. If we can bail out Europe and Japan; if we can bail out Continental Bank and Chrysler—and Mr. Iacocca, make [sic] 8,000 dollars an hour—we can bail out the family farmer.

I just want to make common sense. It does not make sense to close down six hundred and fifty thousand family farms in this country while importing food from abroad subsidized by the U.S. Government. Let's make sense.

It does not make sense to be escorting all our tankers up and down the Persian Gulf paying $2.50 for every one dollar worth of oil we bring out, while oil wells are capped in Texas, Oklahoma, and Louisiana. I just want to make sense.

Leadership must meet the moral challenge of its day. What's the moral challenge of our day? We have public accommodations. We have the right to vote. We have open housing. What's the fundamental challenge of our day? It is to end economic violence. Plant closings without notice—economic violence. Even the greedy do not profit long from greed—economic violence.

Most poor people are not lazy. They are not black. They are not brown. They are mostly White and female and young. But whether White, Black or Brown, a hungry baby's belly turned inside out is the same color—color it pain; color it hurt; color it agony.

Most poor people are not on welfare. Some of them are illiterate and can't read the want-ad sections. And when they can, they can't find a job that matches the address. They work hard everyday.

I know. I live amongst them. I'm one of them. I know they work. I'm a witness. They catch the early bus. They work every day.

They raise other people's children. They work everyday.

They clean the streets. They work everyday. They drive dangerous cabs. They work everyday. They change the beds you slept in in these hotels last night and can't get a union contract. They work everyday.

No, no, they are not lazy! Someone must defend them because it's right, and they cannot speak for themselves. They work in hospitals. I know they do. They wipe the bodies of those who are sick with fever and pain. They empty their bedpans. They clean out their commodes. No job is beneath them, and yet when they get sick they cannot lie in the bed they made up every day. America, that is not right. We are a better Nation than that. We are a better Nation than that.

We need a real war on drugs. You can't "just say no." It's deeper than that. You can't just get a palm reader or an astrologer. It's more profound than that.

We are spending a hundred and fifty billion dollars on drugs a year. We've gone from ignoring it to focusing on the children. Children cannot buy a hundred and fifty billion dollars worth of drugs a year; a few high-profile athletes—athletes are not laundering a hundred and fifty billion dollars a year—bankers are.

I met the children in Watts, who, unfortunately, in their despair, their grapes of hope have become raisins of despair, and they're turning on each other and they're self-destructing. But I stayed with them all night long. I wanted to hear their case.

They said, "Jesse Jackson, as you challenge us to say no to drugs, you're right; and to not sell them, you're right; and not use these guns, you're right." (And by the way, the promise of CETA [Comprehensive Employment and Training Act]; they displaced CETA—they did not replace CETA.)

"We have neither jobs nor houses nor services nor training—no way out. Some of us take drugs as anesthesia for our pain. Some take drugs as a way of pleasure, good short-term pleasure and long-term pain. Some sell drugs to make money. It's wrong, we know, but you need to know that we know. We can go and buy the drugs by the boxes at the port. If we can buy the drugs at the port, don't you believe the Federal government can stop it if they want to?"

They say, "We don't have Saturday night specials anymore." They say, "We buy AK47's and Uzi's, the latest make of weapons. We buy them across and along these boulevards."

You cannot fight a war on drugs unless and until you're going to challenge the bankers and the gun sellers and those who grow them. Don't just focus on the children; let's stop drugs at the level of supply and demand. We must end the scourge on the American Culture.

Leadership. What difference will we make? Leadership. Cannot just go along to get along. We must do more than change Presidents. We must change direction.

Leadership must face the moral challenge of our day. The nuclear war build-up is irrational. Strong leadership cannot desire to look tough and let that stand in the way of the pursuit of peace. Leadership must reverse the arms race. At least we should pledge no first use. Why? Because first use begets first retaliation. And that's mutual annihilation. That's not a rational way out.

No use at all. Let's think it out and not fight it our because it's an unwinnable fight. Why hold a card that you can never drop? Let's give peace a chance.

Leadership. We now have this marvelous opportunity to have a breakthrough with the Soviets. Last year 200,000 Americans visited the Soviet Union. There's a chance for joint ventures into space—not Star Wars and war arms escalation but a space defense initiative. Let's build in the space together and demilitarize the heavens. There's a way out.

America, let us expand. When Mr. Reagan and Mr. Gorbachev met there was a big meeting. They represented together one-eighth of the human race. Seven-eighths of the human race was locked out of that room. Most people in the world tonight—half are Asian, one-half of them are Chinese. There are 22 nations in the Middle East. There's Europe; 40 million Latin Americans next door to us; the Caribbean; Africa—a half-billion people.

Most people in the world today are Yellow or Brown or Black, non-Christian, poor, female, young and don't speak English in the real world.

This generation must offer leadership to the real world. We're losing ground in Latin America, Middle East, South Africa because we're not focusing on the real world. That's the real world. We must use basic principles—support international law. We stand the most to gain from it. Support human rights—we believe in that. Support self-determination—we're built on that. Support economic development—you know it's right. Be consistent and gain our moral authority in the world. I challenge you tonight, my friends, let's be bigger and better as a Nation and as a Party.

We have basic challenges—freedom in South Africa. We've already agreed as Democrats to declare South Africa to be a terrorist state. But don't just stop there. Get South Africa out of Angola; free Namibia; support the front line states. We must have a new humane human rights consistent policy in Africa.

I'm often asked, "Jesse, why do you take on these tough issues? They're not very political. We can't win that way."

If an issue is morally right, it will eventually be political. It may be political and never be right. Fannie Lou Hamer didn't have the most votes in Atlantic City, but her principles have outlasted every delegate who voted to lock her out. Rosa Parks did not have the most votes, but she was morally right. Dr. King didn't have the most votes about the Vietnam War, but he was morally right. If we are principled first, our politics will fall in place.

"Jesse, why do you take these big bold initiatives?" A poem by an unknown author went something like this: "We mastered the air, we conquered the sea, annihilated distance and prolonged life, but we're not wise enough to live on this earth without war and without hate."

As for Jesse Jackson: "I'm tired of sailing my little boat, far inside the harbor bar. I want to go out where the big ships float, out on the deep where the great ones are. And should my frail craft prove too slight for waves that sweep those billows o'er, I'd rather go down in the stirring fight than drowse to death at the sheltered shore."

We've got to go out, my friends, where the big boats are.

And then for our children. Young America, hold your head high now. We can win. We must not lose you to drugs and violence, premature pregnancy, suicide, cynicism, pessimism and despair. We can win. Wherever you are tonight, I challenge you to hope and to dream. Don't submerge your dreams. Exercise above all else, even on drugs, dream of the day you are drug free. Even in the gutter, dream of the day that you will be up on your feet again.

You must never stop dreaming. Face reality, yes, but don't stop with the way things are. Dream of things as they ought to be. Dream. Face pain, but love, hope, faith and dreams will help you rise above the pain. Use hope and imagination as weapons of survival and progress, but you keep on dreaming, young America. Dream of peace. Peace is rational and reasonable. War is irrationable [sic] in this age, and unwinnable.

Dream of teachers who teach for life and not for a living. Dream of doctors who are concerned more about public health than private wealth. Dream of lawyers more concerned about justice than a judgeship. Dream of preachers who are concerned more about prophecy than profiteering. Dream on the high road with sound values.

And then America, as we go forth to September, October, November and then beyond, America must never surrender to a high moral challenge.

Do not surrender to drugs. The best drug policy is a "no first use." Don't surrender with needles and cynicism. Let's have "no first use" on the one hand, and clinics on the other. Never surrender, young America. Go forward.

America must never surrender to malnutrition. We can feed the hungry and clothe the naked. We must never surrender. We must go forward.

We must never surrender to illiteracy. Invest in our children. Never surrender; and go forward. We must never surrender to inequality. Women cannot compromise ERA or comparable worth. Women are making 60 cents on the dollar to what a man makes. Women cannot buy meat cheaper. Women cannot buy bread cheaper. Women cannot buy milk cheaper. Women deserve to get paid for the work that you do. It's right! And it's fair.

Don't surrender, my friends. Those who have AIDS tonight, you deserve our compassion. Even with AIDS you must not surrender.

In your wheelchairs. I see you sitting here tonight in those wheelchairs. I've stayed with you. I've reached out to you across our Nation. And don't you give up. I know it's tough sometimes. People look down on you. It took you a little more effort to get here tonight. And no one should look down on you, but sometimes mean people do. The only justification we have for looking down on someone is that we're going to stop and pick them up.

But even in your wheelchairs, don't you give up. We cannot forget 50 years ago when our backs were against the wall, Roosevelt was in a wheelchair. I would rather have Roosevelt in a wheelchair than

Reagan and Bush on a horse. Don't you surrender and don't you give up. Don't surrender and don't give up!

Why I cannot challenge you this way? "Jesse Jackson, you don't understand my situation. You be on television. You don't understand. I see you with the big people. You don't understand my situation."

I understand. You see me on TV, but you don't know the me that makes me, me. They wonder, "Why does Jesse run?" because they see me running for the White House. They don't see the house I'm running from.

I have a story. I wasn't always on television. Writers were not always outside my door. When I was born late one afternoon, October 8th, in Greenville, South Carolina, no writers asked my mother her name. Nobody chose to write down our address. My mama was not supposed to make it, and I was not supposed to make it. You see, I was born of a teenage mother, who was born of a teen-age mother.

I understand. I know abandonment, and people being mean to you, and saying you're nothing and nobody and can never be anything.

I understand. Jesse Jackson is my third name. I'm adopted. When I had no name, my grandmother gave me her name. My name was Jesse Burns 'til I was 12. So I wouldn't have a blank space, she gave me a name to hold me over. I understand when nobody knows your name. I understand when you have no name.

I understand. I wasn't born in the hospital. Mama didn't have insurance. I was born in the bed at [the] house. I really do understand. Born in a three-room house, bathroom in the backyard, slop jar by the bed, no hot and cold running water. I understand. Wallpaper used for decoration? No. For a windbreaker. I understand. I'm a working person's person. That's why I understand you whether you're Black or White. I understand work. I was not born with a silver spoon in my mouth. I had a shovel programmed for my hand.

My mother, a working woman. So many of the days she went to work early, with runs in her stockings. She knew better, but she wore runs in her stockings so that my brother and I could have matching socks and not be laughed at at school. I understand.

At 3 o'clock on Thanksgiving Day, we couldn't eat turkey because momma was preparing somebody else's turkey at 3 o'clock. We had to play football to entertain ourselves. And then around 6 o'clock she would get off the Alta Vista bus and we would bring up the leftovers and eat our turkey—leftovers, the carcass, the cranberries—around 8 o'clock at night. I really do understand.

Every one of these funny labels they put on you, those of you who are watching this broadcast tonight in the projects, on the corners, I understand. Call you outcast, low down, you can't make it, you're nothing, you're from nobody, subclass, underclass; when you see Jesse Jackson, when my name goes in nomination, your name goes in nomination.

I was born in the slum, but the slum was not born in me. And it wasn't born in you, and you can make it.

Wherever you are tonight, you can make it. Hold your head high; stick your chest out. You can make it. It gets dark sometimes, but the morning comes. Don't you surrender!

Suffering breeds character, character breeds faith. In the end faith will not disappoint.

You must not surrender! You may or may not get there but just know that you're qualified! And you hold on, and hold out! We must never surrender!! America will get better and better.

Keep hope alive. Keep hope alive! Keep hope alive! On tomorrow night and beyond, keep hope alive!

I love you very much. I love you very much.

Document 25.5 Clinton Describes the New World Order

This document contains President Bill Clinton's speech to inaugurate the Dole Institute. In it, he provides a candid discussion of his views about the U.S. role in the world. Focus on his views about why political debate has become so nasty (or seems like a culture war), the interrelatedness of the world, what governments and people need to do in a global environment, and the importance of diversity. Clinton defeated Republican Senator Robert Dole in the 1996 presidential race. Nevertheless, Dole respected Clinton's view of the world and invited him to be the keynote speaker at the opening of the Robert J. Dole Institute of Politics. As president, Clinton tried to redefine the Democratic Party and project a new image of it. At the center of his philosophy was his understanding of an interrelated world system. For a more complete discussion, see the introduction to the chapter.

Thank you. Thank you very much. Thank you very much. I was looking at this crowd and listening to the warm welcome, thinking how kind and generous Bob Dole is to arrange for 90% of my total vote in Kansas to come here and listen to me speak today.

[Laughter and Applause]

. . . Maybe I got 95% of my voters here today. But I want to talk about why we work together and when we don't. And I want you to think about it. First, it really is partly a matter of psychology. By temperament and experience, as I've heard Bob say many times, in politics there are talkers and there are doers. Now, I never met a politician that didn't like to talk, and we do. But we always kept score by what we did, not but what we said. And if you look at it that way, you work hard, you get the job done, you spread the credit around, then you go on to the next problem. I think that's very, very important. So how come it doesn't happen more often? Or when it does, you don't see it? Back in 1996, on the PBS program "Frontline" there was a documentary about the Clinton-Dole race, in which a writer for the *New Yorker Magazine*, Rick Hertzberg, said the following thing. (I think he was criticizing us, but I couldn't be sure) He said of Senator Dole and me, he said, "They're both people who would rather settle something. They would rather come to an agreement than have the battle of Armageddon. That makes them alike in certain ways." Now, some people think compromise is bad. In the 1960s when there was so much controversy in America over the Vietnam War, most of the haters in American politics were on the left, and I was often very uncomfortable because I didn't agree with our policy either, but a lot of the people who agreed with me thought there was something wrong with our leaders. I didn't. I don't think there's something wrong with you if you just got a wrong attitude or just make a mistake, and I never liked all that harsh rhetoric. I don't think President Johnson ever wanted one person to die who didn't have to die. I don't think he ever wanted anything but what he thought was right and best for America. Now I saw the other day Mr. Grover Norquist who organizes a lot of the ultraconservative interest groups once a week in Washington said (I hate to tell Governor Sebelius this) he said his main goal was to bring the same bitter partisanship that exists in Washington to every state capitol in America. I think that's a bad idea, and I'm not running for anything, so I can say what I think now.

[Applause]

The good news about not being President is you can say what you think, and the bad news is no one cares anymore. So, but I can do that. Listen to what Senator Dole talked about. And what you applauded for. He worked with Senator Moynahan on social security, with Senator McGovern on food stamps. He supported voting rights and supported its extension, the Voting Rights Act, consistently, for 25 years. He was one of the major movers behind the Americans with Disabilities Act, one of the most important pieces of social legislation since World War II.

[Applause]

When 9/11 happened, we got together and raised $110 million with the first college, as you heard, the first University contributions we got from KU, but we raised $110 million to pay for a college scholarship for the children and family members of every person killed or disabled, and when we talked about it, one of the things that we told the people who talked to us about helping was that we would only do it if these scholarships were available not simply to the American families who were victims, but for those from 70 other countries who were killed in the United States because they came here looking for the American dream.

[Applause]

And one of the reasons that I asked Senator Dole to head the International Commission on Missing Persons in the former Yugoslavia is that in an age when there is so much divisiveness and so much ethnic and religious and animosity, he believes that people in Kansas and people in Kosovo have more in common than what separates them, and I think that is very important.

[Applause]

So here's what I want to say, whether you're a Republican or a Democrat, whether you consider yourself a liberal or a conservative, whether you're still trying to make up your mind, I want to start with an outline of where I think the world is and why I think there's so much partisanship today. And what I want to challenge you to do is not to agree with me, but to decide, to think. The most important thing you can get out of a University education is not any particular set of information or skills. It is the ability to think, to reason. And then—

[Applause]

Then you can spend the rest of your life doing what Bob and I did and being frustrated by it, because once you get to where you can think, you realize you're not smart enough to understand everything, and you spend your whole life searching for some way to make sure that your mind and your heart and your spirit are all in the same place at the same time, going in the same direction. But first, you have to understand. Now, here's my take on where we are. I don't ask you to agree with me, but if you don't, ask yourself what you think. When our country was founded, the founding fathers said they pledged their lives, their fortunes, their sacred honor to an eternal mission. What was it? To form a more perfect union. Now, there are two or three ideas that are important there. I'll just mention two of them. One is the idea of union. The only reason you unite is because you need somebody else, right? The only purpose for having a union is that you can do more with somebody else than you can do all by yourself or with just your crowd. The second and equally important thing, which accounts for a lot of the fights I've had in my political life is our framers were essentially both deeply religious and deeply influenced by the scientific revolution, and the rationalism of the 18th century. They did not say form a perfect union. They said form a more perfect union. What does that mean? That means we will never be perfect, because there will always be problems as long as humans occupy the earth and because nobody is smart enough to have the whole truth. Now, you may not agree with that. You may believe some people do have the whole truth and therefore they have a right to impose that truth on everybody else. But that's not what the framers believed. They didn't say we're going to form a perfect union. They said our kids will be able to have a union more perfect than ours, and our grandchildren more perfect again and their grandchildren more perfect again and we will never achieve perfection. And so we set up this government that had both enough power to do what people needed to do to have a union and enough protection from power to guarantee that the government could never become the primary force in our lives, that people could pursue their private lives, their personal lives, build their families, say what was on their mind, worship God as they please or if they didn't please. That's the way it was set up. Now —

[Applause]

When we have understood what our mission was, we have enjoyed a fairly high level of bipartisanship, even though there have been great fights and great disagreements. At the end of World War II, with the bitter memory of our withdrawal from the world after World War I and what happened afterward, the Depression and the second World War, and with the looming threat of the Soviet Union and the beginning of the Cold War, and with the fresh evidence of the sacrifice of people like Bob Dole and over 400,000 Americans who never came home, the United States for the first time decided that we must be permanently involved in the world on the side of freedom.

In 1989, over 40 years afterward, when the Berlin Wall fell, and we saw all that joyous celebration, it fell in no small measure because every President from Harry Truman to George Bush believed that the United States had a mission of freedom in the world, and that was part of our more perfect union. And we could not be safe at home unless we tried to be a force for good around the world. Did we make mistakes from time to time? I think we did. But as I said when I went to Vietnam with our ambassador, Pete Peterson, who was a POW there for six and a half years, I told the leaders, I said, "You know, Pete was in prison here for six and a half years and I was on the other side, but we had one thing in common. We both thought we were doing what was right for freedom." Don't you ever think the Americans who came here wanted to colonize Vietnam, just like we don't want to colonize Iraq. We don't go places to control them. We go places to try to help people become free.

[Applause]

Now, I say that to try to drive this point home. You may agree or disagree with our policy in Iraq. You may think, for example, we should have put more emphasis in Afghanistan, where the Al Qaida are, because they're the ones that caused 9/11. But—

[Applause]

Wait, wait, wait. This is thinking time, not cheering time. You can cheer later if you like it. But think. The point I wish to make is this. You should have disagreements with your leaders and your colleagues, but if it becomes immediately a question of questioning people's motives, and if immediately you decide that somebody who sees a whole new situation differently than you must be a bad person and somehow twisted inside, we are not going to get very far in forming a more perfect union. Now, why does it happen? Here's why. Because at the end of the Cold War, the paradigm, the way we looked at the world evaporated and we had to create a new one. It was my great good fortune, but also challenge to become the first president to serve my entire term in the Post-Cold War era, to be the first president of the 21st century, as well as the last president of the 20th century. America is in one of those periods where we are trying to come to grips with fundamental questions. How are we going to relate to globalization, how are we going to relate to the global threat on terror? What is the role of government in our lives now? What are we to make of all this new diversity? Is it going to—the religious and racial and ethnic diversity—is it going to make us more fractured or will it make us more interesting and more unified? These are big, big questions. When the Cold War was over and the industrial age began to be replaced by an information age, ever more globalized, we changed the way we work, the way we live, the way we relate to each other and certainly the way we relate to the rest of the world in ways that are marvelous and ways that are frightening. The intense political conflict that has marked the last 10 years or so is in large measure a result of that. The Democratic Party had to reform itself because we were used to being in power at a time when we wanted to preserve and extend the benefits of social justice, civil rights, social security, health care. We weren't used to the conditions I found in 1992: a decrepit economy, high crime, big questions to face about how we were going to relate to the rest of the world. The Republican party thought government was supposed to protect us in the Cold War and old-fashioned conservatives, including most of the governors that I served with in my long tenure, define conservatism thus, they were fiscally conservative, they thought other things being equal, the private sector should be given a chance to solve problems before the government did, and that if the government had to be brought in, other things being equal, we should try to solve these problems at the state and local government before the federal government came in. That was the definition of a conservative, for almost all my life. Now, slowly, over the last 20 years, a bitter anti-government, anti-tax feeling, combined with the religious right has essentially defined government differently. And so now you wind up with—I mean I sound like Calvin Coolidge compared to these guys running things in Washington now, and the question of deficits and things like that. But it's important for you to understand that both parties are trying to build one slightly right-of-center, one slightly left-of-center, a new consensus that actually responds to the challenges of the 21st century world. And as long as we don't have that, extremists will have more influence than they ought to, and politics will be more bitter than it should be. Now, that's my explanation. There is another explanation for the Washington I found, which is the story of the guy that was walking along the Grand Canyon. You know this story? Nice man is walking along the side of the Grand Canyon, slips off and is falling to certain death. And he sees this twig sticking out of the canyon and grabs it and it breaks his fall and then he sees the roots start to come out of the side and he knows he's done for and he says, "God, why me? I'm a good man, I worked hard, paid taxes all my life, I'm a really good man, why me?" This thunderous voice comes out of heaven and says, "Son, there's just something about you I don't like."

[Laughter]

Now, if you don't believe in explanations like that, then you have to ask yourself "Why is this happening?" I'll give you some evidence. Arguably the most partisan time in American history in terms of personal attacks, before the last 10 years, was in the early republic. Go back and read what Thomas Jefferson and John Adams and their supporters said about each other. Those guys started this country off and quit talking for 20 years because they were so mean. Why? Because after George Washington left the scene, who knew what America meant? We didn't have a national economy. Were we going to build one? We didn't have a national legal system. Were we going to have one? And why the matter was in doubt, the partisanship raged. So instead of moaning about this or throwing up your hands about this, let's get about the business at hand. How should we look at the 21st century world? How can we develop a consensus that we can then have a Republican and a Democratic response to that would be civilized and lead to positive, constructive, honorable compromise? This is the best I can do. I believe we live in an age normally referred to as globalization, sometimes referred to as the global information society. I prefer the term "interdependence." Because it goes far beyond economics. There's good and bad in it. I have a cousin that lives in the hills of Northwest Arkansas that plays chess over the internet with a guy in Australia twice a week. They take turns figuring out who's got to stay up late. On the other hand, 9/11 was a testimony to the power of inter-dependence. Don't you agree? The Al Qaida, what did they do? They used open borders, easy travel, easy access to information and technology to turn an airplane into a weapon of mass destruction, to murder 3,100 people nearly, in Washington, Pennsylvania and New York from 70 countries. It's a story of global inter-dependence. The dark side of global inter-dependence. When I was President, 30% of the economic growth that we had came from trade. When I was President, Senator Dole was always pushing me until we got it right—to end the ethnic slaughter in Bosnia. A hundred years ago, we wouldn't have known how to find Bosnia on a map. But it offended us because we had to watch those people being killed just because they were Muslims being slaughtered, and because we wanted Europe to be united and peaceful and democratic for the first time in history, to make the Cold War all worthwhile. So then we would be united, we'd be working together, we'd be fighting the problems of the rest of the world together. That, too, is inter-dependence. So if it can be positive or negative, it's obvious what we ought to be doing. If you agree with me. We need a strategy that builds up the positive and beats down the negative. We need to recognize that inter-dependence is inherently an unstable condition. And we need to move the world toward a more integrated, global community defined by three things, shared benefits, shared responsibilities and shared values. That's what I believe. Now —

[Applause]

Here's the point I want to make. This may seem simple to you, but if everybody thought that way, then in every area, there would be a slightly liberal or a slightly conservative way to do that, and then we would have all these debates, and in all probability, as free discussion usually does, it would lead to the best possible outcome. I'll just give you an example.

In my view, there are five big issues here, for whatever it's worth.

Number one, we have to have a strategy to fight the new security threats of terror and weapons of mass destruction that is both offensive and defensive. What's the best way to have homeland defense? If you have limited amount of money, if you think about it like this, then you can say, well, I think what we should do is triple or quadruple the number of containers we're checking at the ports and airports for biological or chemical weapons or somebody else can say, no, I think we should be reinforcing the bridges or putting guards outside the electrical plants that have nuclear power or whatever you think. But the point is, if you're focused on it that way, you can focus on homeland defense. What's the best way to pursue an offensive strategy? Is it to go to Iraq and establish a beach head of freedom in the Middle East or is it to stay in Afghanistan and root out the Al Qaida, and then turn your attention to the rest of the world? But once you're focused on it, you can have a civilized debate, and if you both agree on the issue, then just because somebody has got a different idea than you do about how to handle it, you don't think there's something wrong with them.

So that's the first thing. Second thing we have to do is to have a strategy to make a world with more partners and fewer terrorists. Now, why do I say that? Besides the fact that I'm a Democrat. Why would I say that? Why should every American think that? Even people that don't believe in social programs? Because if you believe the world is inter-dependent and you cannot kill, occupy, or imprison all your actual or potential adversaries, sooner or later you have to make a deal. That's what politics is. If there's a factual matter, that's what I talked until I was blue in the face in the Middle East about, they walked

away from that peace deal in 2000. It was the dumbest thing I've ever seen in my life. All we've got now is the Middle East is not a bit less inter-dependent today than it was when we made seven years of progress toward peace. We got 3,000 dead Palestinians, about 9200 dead—I mean 920 dead Israelis. They're no less inter-dependent. Nothing has changed except more people are dead and now more people are mad and there's less trust and it's harder to deal with it, but they are not a bit less inter-dependent. So you remember that. If you're in any environment in life that you don't have total control over, you have to make a deal. That's what politics is. And that's why compromise is honorable, not dishonorable.

[Applause]

So, anyway, so how would you go about making a world with more friends than fewer enemies? Well, first of all, you gotta realize that half the people that live on earth aren't part of this globalized economy that works. On earth, half the people live on less than $2 a day, of the 6 billion people on earth, 1 billion live on less than $1 a day, a billion and a half people never get a clean glass of water, a billion people go to bed hungry every night, 10 million kids die of preventable childhood diseases, and one in four deaths every year on earth now come from AIDS, TB, Malaria and infections related to diarrhea. Most of them are little children who never got a single clean glass of water in their lives. So for a tiny fraction of what we spend on defense and homeland defense, and I do mean tiny, we could double what we spend to help put all the children in the world who aren't in school in school, to pay our fair share of the fight against the world's diseases—

[Applause]

—and to do these other things. And to give you an example, after 9/11, I think we increased—I believe this is right. I think we increased defense and homeland defense 60 something billion dollars in one year. We could double our assistance programs in these other areas, double them, for about 10 or 12. In a budget that must now be nearly $2 trillion, I don't know what it is. I haven't looked at it. I don't have to look at it anymore, so I don't, but I think that's about what it is. So you got to have a strategy for terror, a strategy for more friends. The third thing I think is to find more ways to cooperate institutionally. This is a big challenge for America because we're going through a period in history when we have unrivalled military economic, and political power. So every time we make a deal with anybody to do anything, we're giving up some of our freedom of action. Maybe a good deal for them, not a good deal for us because most of the time we can do whatever we please. The problem is, we will not be the only military, economic, and political superpower forever. If present growth rates continue, China, India, and the European Union will equal or surpass the United States sometime in the 21st century, just because of their size. They may not ever have to reach the per capita income we do to have greater output. So I think we should do that, but if you believe that, then it puts a whole different cast on the debates you hear today over putting up missile defense, getting rid of the antiballistic missile treaty, should we be part of the comprehensive treaty, should we be part of the criminal court, should we be part of the Kyoto Climate Change Accord, and I say that, I didn't join—there's one I didn't join. I didn't join the land mine treaty because they wrote it in a way that was absolutely hostile to the United States, and we have the finest record of any country in the world in promoting demining in the last 15 years, and it had enormous bipartisan support. Bob supported it. And so I'm not saying we can join every treaty, but I'm saying we should have a preference for being part of every conceivable network that will bring people together, because I can tell you something. It's just like any club you belong to, any organization you belong to, it builds the habit of working with other people. And the more you're in the habit of believing that if you stay on the team, good things will happen, as compared to if you get off the team, the more likely we are to find peace and resolution to the problems of the 21st century. So I think that's very, very important and now I want to make just two more points. So terror, more friends, more cooperation. Fourth thing is, we have to keep making America better. A lot of our influence in the world comes not from the size of our military or our arsenal of weapons, but from the power of our example. One of the schools that was destroyed in New York City on September 11th, 2001, the children had to leave and go meet in a temporary facility. So Hillary and I went to this school to see these kids, elementary school kids. 600 kids from over 80 different national racial and ethnic groups. One school. If we can prove that freedom brings mutual respect and that people can be proud of their heritage and proud of their religion, and proud of everything that's special and still bound together in a more perfect union, that will do as much to undermine the long-term appeal of terror as anything else we can do. Just continuing to prove America works.

[Applause]

Now, last thing I want to say is this. I don't want you to think I'm flaky here, but I believe this. Like I said, no consequences, I don't really care what you think. But anyway, none of this will happen until we move the American people's way of thinking about other people forward. And let me explain what I mean by that. You guys love your basketball team. I like the Arkansas Razorbacks. We're all pulling for different people in the NBA playoffs. We have wars you know who you're for—you got over 600 people from Kansas in Iraq today putting their lives on the line. We think in categories that are oppositional. And we have to organize ourselves in little boxes. I see a man, I see a woman, I see somebody that's white, I see somebody that's black, I see somebody that's brown, all right. I see a Baptist, a Catholic, a Jew, a Muslim, a Buddhist, a Sikh. I mean, if we couldn't put ourselves in boxes, nobody could function. You think about how many University courses are designed to giving people more boxes to think with. You got this amorphous reality out there and the person with a largest number of boxes who can keep them all straight is called a genius. Right? That's all true, but at some point it has to become irrelevant. The whole story of humanity is a story of forming a more perfect union. Ever since our fore bearers stood up on the African savanna, something over 100,000 years ago, they learned to relate to other people, first they were in clans. Then larger tribes, then villages, and they would come into contact with wider and wider circles of people that had different views and felt threatened, and there would be fighting and killing, but sooner or later, before they destroyed the human race, they'd find a way to get along. In the 20th century, our weapons were so powerful, we nearly got it wrong.

But we escaped. We gave in to neither the tyranny of Hitler or the tyranny of communism or the power of our weapons to destroy. We threaded a big needle there. And everybody that made a contribution deserves our gratitude. But the point I want to make is that if you believe to go back to the founders that our job is to form a more perfect union and nobody has got the whole truth, then everybody's got a contribution to make. And I think America, if we're ever going to truly defeat terror without changing the character of our own country or compromising the future of our children, has got to not only say, "Okay, I want to shoulder my responsibilities, I want to create my share of opportunities" but we have to find a way to define the future in terms of a humanity that goes beyond our country, that goes beyond any particular race, that goes beyond any particular religion.